Essentials of Criminal Justice

Second Edition

Joseph J. Senna

Northeastern University

Larry J. Siegel

University of Massachusetts–Lowell

West/Wadsworth Publishing Company
I(T)P® An International Thomson Publishing Company

Belmont, CA • Albany, NY • Bonn • Boston • Cincinnati • Detroit • Johannesburg • London • Madrid
Melbourne • Mexico City • New York • Paris • San Francisco • Singapore • Tokyo • Toronto • Washington

Criminal Justice Editor: Sabra Horne
Development Editor: Dan Alpert
Assistant Editor: Claire Masson
Editorial Assistant: Jeff Kellner
Marketing Manager: Mike Dew
Senior Project Coordinator: Debby Kramer
Production: Nancy Sjoberg/Del Mar Associates
Print Buyer: Karen Hunt
Permissions Editor: Veronica Oliva
Designer: David Farr/Imagesmythe
Illustrator: Gail Williams
Photo Research: Linda L. Rill
Cover Designer: Stephen Rapley/Nea Hanscomb
Compositor: Digital Output
Printer: R. R. Donnelley & Sons/Roanoke
Cover Printer: Phoenix Color Corp.

Printed in the United States of America
1 2 3 4 5 6 7 8 9 10

For more information, contact Wadsworth Publishing Company, 10 Davis Drive, Belmont, CA 94002, or electronically at
http://www.thomson.com/wadsworth.html

International Thomson Publishing Europe
Berkshire House 168-173
High Holborn
London, WC1V 7AA, England

International Thomson Editores
Campos Eliseos 385, Piso 7
Col. Polanco
11560 México D.F. México

Thomas Nelson Australia
102 Dodds Street
South Melbourne 3205
Victoria, Australia

International Thomson Publishing Asia
221 Henderson Road
#05-10 Henderson Building
Singapore 0315

Nelson Canada
1120 Birchmount Road
Scarborough, Ontario
Canada M1K 5G4

International Thomson Publishing Japan
Hirakawacho Kyowa Building, 3F
2-2-1 Hirakawacho
Chiyoda-ku, Tokyo 102, Japan

International Thomson Publishing GmbH
Königswinterer Strasse 418
53227 Bonn, Germany

International Thomson Publishing Southern Africa
Building 18, Constantia Park
240 Old Pretoria Road
Halfway House, 1685 South Africa

Library of Congress Cataloging-in-Publication Data
Senna, Joseph J.
     Essentials of criminal justice / Joseph J. Senna, Larry J. Siegel.
  —2nd ed.
      p.   cm.
    Includes bibliographical references and index.
    ISBN 0-534-53514-3
    1. Criminal justice, Administration of—United States. 2. Police—United States. 3. Criminal procedure—United States. 4. Criminal law—United States. 5. Corrections—United States. I. Siegel, Larry J. II. Title.
HV9950.S46 1997
                                                  97-26783
364.973—dc21
                                                  CIP

About the Authors

Joseph J. Senna was born in Brooklyn, New York. He graduated from Brooklyn College, Fordham University Graduate School of Social Service, and Suffolk University Law School. Mr. Senna has spent over fifteen years teaching law and justice courses at Northeastern University. In addition, he has served as an Assistant District Attorney, Director of Harvard Law School Prosecutorial Program, and consultant to numerous criminal justice organizations. His academic specialties include the areas of Criminal Law, Constitutional Due Process, Criminal Justice, and Juvenile Law.

Mr. Senna lives with his family in Winchester, Massachusetts. He is currently completing work on a criminal law textbook and serves as an adjunct professor of criminal justice at colleges in the Boston area. Both Mr. Senna and Dr. Siegal have begun writing a juvenile justice text—their fifth collaborative effort.

Larry J. Siegel was born in the Bronx in 1947. While attending City College of New York in the 1960s he was introduced to the study of crime and justice in courses taught by sociologist Charles Winick. After graduation he attended the newly opened program in criminal justice at the State University of New York at Albany, where he earned both his MA and Ph.D. and studied with famed scholars such as Michael Hindelang, Gilbert Geis, and Donald Newman. After completing his graduate work, Dr. Siegel began his teaching career at Northeastern University, where he worked closely with colleague Joseph Senna on a number of texts and research projects. After leaving Northeastern, he held teaching positions at the University of Nebraska–Omaha and Saint Anselm College in New Hampshire. He is currently a professor at the University of Massachusetts–Lowell.

Dr. Siegel has written extensively in the area of crime and justice, including books on juvenile law, delinquency, criminology and criminal procedure. He is a court certified expert on police conduct and currently heads the graduate program in criminal justice at the University of Massachusetts–Lowell. He resides in Bedford, New Hampshire with his wife Therese J. Libby, Esq. and their children.

Contents

Part 1
The Nature of
Crime, Law, and
Criminal Justice

Part 2
The Police and
Law Enforcement

CHAPTER 5
Police in Society: History and Organization   140

CHAPTER 6
The Police: Role and Function   164

Part 3
Courts and
Adjudication

Preface

Crime seems everywhere today, from the bizarre (cases featured on the evening news) to the humdrum (incidents of urban violence, vandalism, and theft that are so common that the general public takes little notice). The government tells us that Americans commit almost 40 million criminal acts each year, that a large portion of the teenage population drinks and takes drugs, and that almost all of us will one day become a crime victim. The public imagination has been captivated by a number of highly publicized criminal cases, ranging from that of Timothy McVeigh, convicted for killing 150 people in the bombing of the Murrah Federal Building in Oklahoma City, to that of O. J. Simpson, the famed football star acquitted of murder after the "trial of the century." These high-profile cases have become media events that promote intense public interest in crime and justice.

Considering the immediacy of the crime problem, the attention it gets in the media, and its focus as a political issue, it is not surprising that interest in criminal justice is at an all-time high. People are demanding greater police protection, more efficient court processes, and more effective correctional treatment facilities. To meet this demand, colleges and universities are today graduating an increasing number of criminal justice majors who seek employment in the justice system and who are being educated to improve its operations and increase its effectiveness.

As professors of criminal justice for the past two decades, we have tried to share our interest in and knowledge of the field in our textbook *Introduction to Criminal Justice,* first published in 1978 and now in its seventh edition. However, not all criminal justice courses require such a lengthy and elaborate book. Some instructors use supplementary reading material in their courses, while others use more discussion, films, and visual aids. Some schools operate on the semester level while other use trimester or quarterly systems and may find a more abbreviated book easier to cover during an 11- or 12-week schedule. We developed *Essentials of Criminal Justice* as a more concise version of our introductory text. It contains all the elements of our more comprehensive book and has been updated to reflect the structural and procedural changes that have occurred during the past few years.

This new edition of *Essentials of Criminal Justice* provides a concise and accurate statement of the vital goals, aims, and practices of the criminal justice system and its most critical institutions. It includes the most critical legal cases, research studies, and policy initiatives that have appeared in the past few years. It provides a groundwork for the study of criminal justice by analyzing and describing the agencies of justice and the procedures they use to identify and treat criminal offenders. It covers what most experts believe are the critical issues in criminal justice and analyzes their impact on the justice system. It focuses on critical policy issues in the criminal justice system, including preventive detention, shock incarceration, community policing, alternative sentencing, gun control, the war on drugs, and the death penalty. So while this book is more condensed than our introductory text, it retains all of the most important issues in the criminal justice system.

Our primary goals in writing this edition include (1) to provide students with a solid basis of knowledge about the criminal justice system, (2) to be as up to date as possible, (3) to be objective and unbiased, and (4) to be concise in presentation and format while still retaining an interesting and engaging style. We have tried to provide a text that is highly informative but not as detailed as *Introduction to Criminal Justice,* seventh edition.

Organization
of This Edition

Part 1 gives the student a basic introduction to crime, law, and justice. The first chapter covers the problem of crime in America, agencies of justice, the juvenile justice system, and the formal justice process, and it introduces students to the concept of the informal justice system that involves discretion, deal making, and plea bargains. The chapter also provides material on career opportunities in criminal justice to give students some idea of the career choices available. Chapter 2 discusses the nature, extent, and cause of crime and victimization: How is crime measured? Where and when does it occur? Who commits crime? Who are its victims? What social factors influence the crime rate? Why do people commit crime? Chapter 3 provides a discussion of the criminal law and its relationship to criminal justice. It covers the legal definition of crime, the defenses to crime, including the insanity defense, and issues in procedural law. Finally, Chapter 4 discusses the major perspectives on justice and how they impact on efforts to control drugs and violence.

Part 2 provides an overview of the law enforcement field. Four chapters cover the history and development of criminal justice organizations, the functions of police in modern society, issues in policing, and the police and the rule of law. This section emphasizes community policing and community crime prevention, private security, and other current issues.

Part 3 is devoted to the adjudication process, from pretrial indictment to the sentencing of criminal offenders. Chapter 9 focuses on the organization of the court system, including the role of judge, prosecuting attorney, and defense counsel. Chapter 10 deals with pretrial procedures, including bail and plea bargaining, while Chapter 11 covers the criminal trial, and 12 covers criminal sentencing. Topics included within Part 3 involve bail reform, court organization, sentencing policy, capital punishment, indigent defense systems, attorney competence, preventive detention, the jury trial, courtroom work groups, and extralegal factors in sentencing.

Part 4 focuses on the correctional system, including probation and the intermediate sanctions of house arrest, intensive supervision, and electronic monitoring. The traditional correctional system of jails, prisons, community-based corrections, and parole are also discussed at length. Such issues as the prison and jail overcrowding and parole effectiveness are discussed.

Great care has been taken to organize the text to reflect the structure and process of justice. Each chapter attempts to be comprehensive, self-contained, and orderly.

Learning Tools

The text contains the following features designed to help students learn and comprehend the material:

- **Analyzing Criminal Justice Issues** Every chapter contains boxed inserts on intriguing issues concerning criminal justice policy or processes. Within the boxed inserts are critical thinking sections that help students conceptualize problems of concern to the criminal justice system. For example, in Chapter 14, super maximum-security prisons are discussed, while in Chapter 13, "Can Alternative Sanctions Work?" is the topic.

- **Law in Review** Major Supreme Court cases that influence and control the justice system are evaluated in some detail in these boxed inserts. For example, there is discussion of *United States v. Salerno* on preventive detention and of *United States v. Ross* on automobile searches.

- **Criminal Justice and the Media** Each chapter also contains boxes that focus on a popular movie or TV show—such as *Lonestar, Dead Man Walk-*

ing, or *Seven*—to show how the media represent the criminal justice system. How accurate is the media's depiction of the system?

- **Art** The book contains more than 150 photos, tables, and charts that dramatize the events that occur in the criminal justice system and help students visualize its processes. The text is in full color so that the many photos and graphics can be as effective as possible.

Acknowledgments

The preparation of this text would not have been possible without the aid of our colleagues who reviewed the text and give us material to use in its preparation. These colleagues include Joe W. Becraft, Portland Community College; Bruce Bikle, Portland State University; Kathleen A. Cameron, Arizona State University; Janet Foster Goodwill, Yakima Valley Community College; Kathrine A. Johnson, Kentucky State University; and Margaret Vandiver, University of Memphis.

In addition, important information was provided by Eve Buzawa, Frank Cullen, Lee Ellis, James A. Fox, John Goldkamp, Jack Greene, Bob Langworthy, John Laub, Jack McDevitt, Marty Schwartz, Larry Sherman, and Sam Walker; Marv Zalman and the staff at the Institute for Social Research at the University of Michigan; the National Center for State Courts; the Police Foundation; the Sentencing Project; Kathleen Maguire and the staff of the Hindelang Research Center at SUNY–Albany; James Byrne of the Criminal Justice Research Center at the University of Massachusetts–Lowell; and Kristina Rose and Janet Rosenbaum of the National Criminal Justice Reference Service.

And, of course, our colleagues at Wadsworth Publishing did their usual outstanding job of aiding us in the preparation of this new edition. The form and content of this new edition were directed by our new editor, Sabra Horne. It has been a pleasure working with Sabra and our other new colleagues at Wadsworth/West: editorial assistant Kate Barrett, project coordinator Debby Kramer, production manager Nancy Sjoberg, copy editor Jackie Estrada, photo editor Linda L. Rill, and marketing manager Mike Dew. This is the first book we have written with our new Wadsworth team, and these folks made us feel right at home. They must be given a lot of credit for putting together a beautiful design and going out of their way to be patient, kind, and sensitive.

Essentials of Criminal Justice

Second Edition

CHAPTER 1

The Criminal Justice System: History, Organization, and Process

O n November 12, 1996 Amy Grossberg, an 18-year-old freshman at the University of Delaware, was picked up by her boyfriend, Brian Peterson, also 18 and a student at Gettysburg College, who took her to a nearby Comfort Inn Motel in Pennsylvania. There, without any medical assistance, Amy gave birth to a child.[1] The young couple had kept Amy's pregnancy secret from family and friends back home. When the couple returned to Delaware, things began to go awry. Rushed to a hospital after she began suffering postpartum distress, Amy told doctors that soon after its birth the baby had been placed in a plastic bag and disposed of in a dumpster. After finding the child's remains, police made a preliminary determination that the newborn's death had been caused by violent shaking and blunt-force head trauma. Grossberg was arrested; a few days later Peterson emerged from hiding and turned himself into police.

At first report, Delaware prosecutors announced that they would seek the death penalty in the case because the victim was younger than 14 years old. At their arraignment on December 17, 1996, the couple grasped each other's fingertips; their lawyers told reporters that "they feel a great deal of compassion toward each other." Defense lawyers also claimed that the baby had "congenital brain damage" before it was born and that the couple had not intended to harm the deceased child.[2]

How can the behavior of high school sweethearts Peterson and Grossberg ever be adequately explained? They came from affluent families and were considered an ideal match in their wealthy hometown of Franklin Lakes, New Jersey. How can such impulsive, destructive behavior from such an unlikely source ever be predicted or prevented? Is it fair to splash these young people's names across newspaper headlines before they have even been tried? How does such

Amy Grossberg and her boyfriend, Brian Peterson, are accused of killing and disposing of their newborn child in a motel dumpster. How can we explain such seemingly irrational behavior by two kids who had never before been in trouble? Does their alleged behavior deserve to be punished in the same way as a murder of an adult committed by two drug addicts desperate for cash?

negative publicity ultimately affect their chances of getting a fair trial? And, in the event that such a high-profile case is dropped for lack of evidence, what chance do these youngsters have of ever resuming a "normal life"? Ask Richard Jewell, the man "convicted in the press" of the Olympic Park bombing in Atlanta, only to be exonerated and the case dropped.

Tragic stories such as this one give the general public the impression that crime is everywhere and can affect anyone. The media are filled with stories of gang-related drive-by shootings in which innocent bystanders are killed, incidents in which a disgruntled employee brings a gun to work and starts shooting, and convenience-store robberies in which clerks and customers are shot. Many Americans have learned to fear predatory criminals while growing skeptical of the ability of the government to do something about crime. It is not surprising, then, that many people routinely arm themselves with handguns to protect themselves and their property.

Forming a buffer between the public and the lawbreakers it fears is the **criminal justice system.** This loosely organized collection of agencies is charged with, among other matters, protecting the public, maintaining order, enforcing the law, identifying transgressors, bringing the guilty to justice, and treating criminal behavior. The public depends on this vast system, which employs close to 2 million people and costs taxpayers about *$100 billion a year,* to protect them from evil doers and restore justice to their lives.[3]

This textbook serves as an introduction to the study of criminal justice. This first chapter introduces some basic issues. It begins with an overview of the crime problem, then turns to a definition of the concept and the study of criminal justice. The chapter introduces the major components and processes of the criminal justice system so that students can develop an overview of how the system functions. Finally, it discusses careers in criminal justice to connect the study of criminal justice to future professional employment choices.

We live in a country in which crime is commonplace. Crime touches on all segments of society. Both the poor and the affluent engage in criminal activity. Crime cuts across racial, class, and gender lines. It involves some acts that shock the conscience and others that may seem to be relatively harmless human foibles.

Criminal acts may be the work of strangers, so-called **predatory criminals** who care little for the lives of their victims. In addition to more typical crimes, news accounts have focused on "thrill killings"—impulsive acts of violence in which a stranger is killed as an act of daring or recklessness, as when adolescents throw a boulder from a highway overpass onto an oncoming car. Another media favorite is cult killings, especially if they involve devil-worshipping groups who conduct the black mass and kill "nonbelievers" on orders from leaders. In contrast, many crimes are committed by friends and family members, including date rape, spouse abuse, child abuse, elderly abuse, and sexual abuse; as a group, these acts are referred to as **intimate violence.**

Regardless of whether crime is the work of strangers or trusted associates, most people view it as a major social problem. Public opinion polls indicate that a majority of citizens (77%) believe that we are losing ground in the war against crime.[4] More than 80% do not have a great deal of confidence in the criminal justice system; more than 40% say they are afraid to walk alone at night in their own neighborhood.[5]

While we often hear older people say "Crime is getting worse every day" and "I can remember when it was safe to walk the streets at night," their memories may be colored by wishful thinking: Crime and violence have existed in this country for more than 200 years.

Crime and violence were not unknown when the nation was first formed.[6] Guerrilla activity was common before, during, and after the Revolutionary War. Bands supporting the British (Tories) and the American revolutionaries engaged in savage attacks on each other using hit-and-run tactics, burning, and looting.

Early settlers were disproportionately young and male, typically laborers who paid for their passage with a work contract. Because young men far outnumbered eligible women, many could not marry, and their aggressive natures remained unrestrained by any calming influence of family life and parental responsibility. In an important new book called *Violent Land,* historian David Courtwright describes how 18th- and 19th-century cultural factors worsened the already high crime rates among the settlers and immigrants.[7] For instance, on the Western frontier, the population was predominately young bachelors, sensitive about honor, hostile to members of other racial or ethnic groups, heavy drinkers, morally indifferent, heavily armed, and unchecked by adequate law enforcement. It is not surprising, considering this explosive mix, that 20% of the 89,000 miners who arrived in California during the gold rush of 1849 were dead within six months. While many died from disease, others succumbed to drink and violence. Smoking, gambling, and heavy drinking became a cultural imperative, and those who were disinclined to indulge were considered social outcasts.

Is Crime a Recent Development?

The struggle over slavery during the mid-19th century begat decades of conflict, crime, and violence, including a civil war. After the war, night riders and Ku Klux Klan members were active in the South, using vigilante methods to maintain the status quo and terrorize former slaves. The violence also spilled over into bloody local feuds in the hill country of southern Appalachia. Factional hatreds, magnified by the lack of formal law enforcement and grinding poverty, gave rise to violent attacks and family feuding. Some former Union and Confederate soldiers, heading west with the dream of finding gold or starting a cattle ranch, resorted to theft and robbery. Train robbery was popularized by the Reno Brothers of Indiana and bank robbery by the James-Younger gang of Missouri.

While the postwar era generated criminal gangs, it also produced widespread business crime. The great "robber barons" bribed government officials and plotted

Post–Civil War Developments

*Bonnie Parker vamps for the camera, circa 1930. She and her partner, Clyde Barrow, have been romanticized in song and film (*Bonnie and Clyde *with Warren Beatty and Faye Dunaway playing the leads). They are, however, believed to have killed 13 people, making them serial killers. Violence rates were higher in the 1930s than they are today. What does that suggest about such suspected causes of violence as violent TV shows and rock music?*

to corner markets and obtain concessions for railroads, favorable land deals, and mining and mineral rights on government land. The administration of President Ulysses Grant was tainted by numerous corruption scandals.

Crime at the Turn of the Century

From 1900 to 1935, the nation experienced a sustained increase in criminal activity. This period was dominated by Depression-era outlaws who became mythic figures. Charles "Pretty Boy" Floyd was a folk hero among the sharecroppers of Eastern Oklahoma, while the nation eagerly followed the exploits of its premier bank robber, John Dillinger, until he was killed in front of a Chicago movie house. The infamous "Ma" Barker and her sons—Lloyd, Herman, Fred, and Arthur—are credited with killing more than 10 people, while Bonnie Parker and Clyde Barrow killed more than 13 before they were slain in a shootout with federal agents.

While these relatively small and mobile outlaw gangs were operating in the Midwest, more organized gangs flourished in the nation's largest cities. The first criminal gangs had formed back before the Civil War in urban slums such as the Five Points and Bowery neighborhoods in New York City. Though they sported colorful names, such as the Plug Uglies, the Hudson Dusters, and the Dead Rabbits, these gangs engaged in mayhem, murder, and extortion. They were the forerunners of the organized crime families that developed in New York and later spread to Philadelphia, Chicago, New Orleans, and other major urban areas.

The crime problem in the United States has been evolving along with the nation itself. Crime has provided a mechanism for the frustrated to vent their anger, for business leaders to maintain their positions of wealth and power, and for those outside the economic mainstream to take a shortcut to the American Dream. To protect itself from this ongoing assault, the public has supported development of a great array of government agencies whose stated purpose is to control and prevent crime; to identify, apprehend, and bring to trial those who choose to violate the law; and to devise effective methods of criminal correction. These agencies make up what is commonly referred to today as the criminal justice system, and it is to their nature and development we now turn our attention.

Since concern about crime is not a recent phenomenon, it comes as no surprise that considerable thought has been given to the goal of effective crime control. A sustained effort has been made to create agencies of government whose mission is identifying criminal suspects, providing them with a fair hearing on the charges against them, and, in the event they are found guilty as charged, furnishing them with fair and effective correctional treatment.

The debate over the proper course for effective crime control can be traced back to the publication in 1764 of Italian social thinker Cesare Beccaria's famous treatise *On Crimes and Punishments.* Beccaria, an Italian social philosopher, made a convincing argument against the use of torture and capital punishment, common practices in the eighteenth century. He persuasively argued that only the minimum amount of punishment was needed to control crime if criminals could be convinced that their law violations were certain to be discovered and swiftly punished.[8]

Ever since Beccaria's momentous work was brought to the public's attention, experts have sought the formula for a social policy that would effectively control crime, treat criminals, protect victims, and benefit society as a whole. Within fifty years of the book's publication, the first police agency, the London Metropolitan Police, was developed to keep the peace and identify criminal suspects, and the first prisons were created to provide nonphysical correctional treatment. Nonetheless, there was little recognition that these fledgling agencies of justice worked together in any systematic fashion. In fact, it was not until 1919 that the concept of a criminal justice system began to be recognized. It was in that year that the Chicago Crime Commission, a professional association funded by private contributions, was created.[9] This organization acted as a citizen's advocate group and kept track of the activities of local justice agencies. The commission still carries out its work today.

The pioneering work of the Chicago group was soon copied in a number of other jurisdictions. The Cleveland Crime Commission was formed in 1922, and similar projects were conducted by the Missouri Crime Survey (1926) and the Illinois Crime Survey (1929).[10]

In 1931 President Herbert Hoover appointed the National Commission of Law Observance and Enforcement, which is commonly known today as the Wickersham Commission. This national study group made a detailed analysis of the U.S. justice system and helped usher in the era of treatment and rehabilitation. It showed in great detail the variety of rules and regulations that governed the system and exposed how difficult it was for justice personnel to keep track of the system's legal and administrative complexity.[11]

The modern era of criminal justice began when the American Bar Association funded a series of studies in the 1950s and 1960s that examined the hidden workings of the criminal justice system.[12] These research efforts resulted in volumes that examined the workings of police arrest procedures, the pretrial process, and punishment. Then, in 1967, the President's Commission on Law Enforcement and the Administration of Justice (the "Crime Commission"), which had been appointed by President Lyndon Johnson, published its final report, *The Challenge of Crime in a Free Society.*[13] This group of practitioners, educators, and attorneys was charged with creating a comprehensive view of the criminal justice process and recommending reforms. Concomitantly, in 1968 Congress passed what is referred to as the Safe Streets Act, providing for the expenditure of federal funds for state and local crime control efforts.[14] This act helped launch a massive campaign to restructure the justice system by funding the **Law Enforcement Assistance Administration (LEAA),** which provided hundreds of millions of dollars in aid to local and state justice agencies.

Throughout its 14-year history, the LEAA was the agency that provided the majority of federal funds to states for criminal justice activities. It required states to establish a state criminal justice planning agency responsible for developing an annual comprehensive criminal justice plan; it then funneled development and operating funds to the states for law enforcement purposes. From 1969 to 1980, the LEAA gave over $7.7 billion to state and local criminal justice agencies. On April 15, 1982 the program came to an end when Congress ceased funding it.

During its lifetime, the LEAA received widespread and valid criticism for providing insufficient funds to have a substantial impact on rising crime rates and for allowing political pressure from the White House and Congress to influence its policies. High staff turnover, lack of leadership, and shifting priorities also contributed to negative public opinion about the LEAA.

The Effect of LEAA

Despite its well-documented failures, the LEAA helped "invent" the field of criminal justice. Federal funds inspired institutions of higher education to develop academic programs in criminal justice. The LEAA provided millions of dollars in scholarship money for the education of police officers and other criminal justice personnel. Without federal money, the most important graduate programs in criminal justice would probably not have been implemented, and many of the professors teaching this course today might have gone into other fields of study. In addition, federal money helped fund some of the most important research and demonstration projects of the 1960s and 1970s, which are mentioned throughout the text. Even though the LEAA is gone, the federal government continues to fund the National Institute of Justice (NIJ) and the Bureau of Justice Statistics (BJS), which carry out a more limited role in supporting criminal justice research and development and publishing extremely valuable data and research findings. In 1994 Congress approved a new crime bill that provides billions for improving the justice system and expanding its personnel.

The criminal justice system has become a fixture of American life. Numerous public and private groups have attempted to influence its direction by formulating standards for its operations and objectives.[15] Academic programs have been devised to educate students on the intricacies of the legal process. Major research efforts have been aimed at developing a better understanding of criminal justice processes. These efforts have generated widespread interest in the study and understanding of criminal justice.

The Study of Criminal Justice

The term **criminal justice** refers to an area of knowledge devoted to controlling crime through the scientific administration of police, court, and correctional agencies. It is an interdisciplinary field making use of the knowledge bases of sociology, psychology, law, public policy, and other related fields.

Criminal justice is essentially an agency of **social control:** society considers some behaviors so dangerous and destructive that it chooses to either strictly control their occurrence or outlaw them outright. It is the job of the agencies of justice to prevent these behaviors by apprehending and punishing transgressors or deterring their future occurrence. Although society does maintain other forms of social control, such as parental and school-based discipline, these mechanisms are designed to deal with moral and not legal misbehavior. Only the criminal justice system maintains the power to control crime and punish criminals.

As a result of these efforts, an interdisciplinary field of criminal justice has come into being. Nearly every federal, state, and local crime control program now uses the term *criminal justice system* in one way or another. Rather than treating police, court, and correctional agencies as thousands of independent institutions, it has become common to view them as components in a large, integrated "people-processing system" that manages law violators from the time of their arrest through trial, punishment, and release.

To study criminal justice and train students for management roles in justice-related agencies, more than 600 departments or colleges of criminal justice have been developed in institutions of higher education. Academic institutions have become a major resource for those trying to find solutions to the crime problem; university involvement in problems of criminal justice has provided needed resources and authenticity to a relatively new field.

Criminal justice is truly an interdisciplinary field. A number of academic disciplines have been drawn upon to develop insights into the causes and prevention of criminal behavior. Sociologists have long studied the social and environmental factors associated with crime and delinquency. Psychologists have sought to determine whether the typical offender's criminal behavior is symptomatic of some emotional or mental health problem. Legal scholars have focused on such issues as the effect of legal rule changes on the justice process and the relationship between social control and civil liberties, considering such questions as what effect a Supreme Court decision prohibiting the police from shooting unarmed suspects who are fleeing arrest will have on police behavior.[16]

The field of criminal justice is also aided by a variety of other disciplines. Historians have developed an understanding of the historical context of the law and the development of early justice agencies. Political scientists explore the roles of federal and state governments, political parties, and pressure groups in relation to urban problems, examine legislation, and study how government influences the justice system. Some economists have applied economic theory to crime, suggesting that people commit crime after conducting a cost-benefit analysis of the gains they may make from a criminal act compared to the losses they may suffer if apprehended.

Even members of the physical sciences have become active in criminal justice. For example, forensic chemists work closely with police agencies in developing scientific techniques for analyzing evidence. Biologists and medical doctors have conducted studies on the biochemical and physical bases of criminal behavior and the effect of diet and medication on the treatment of known offenders, finding indications that improving diets can affect behavior positively.[17]

An Interdisciplinary Field

What exists, then, is a great deal of information taken from various disciplines and consolidated as the knowledge base for a new area of study. Understanding what knowledge is represented in this field helps us reach a working definition of criminal justice study:

> The study of criminal justice may be defined as the use of the scientific method to understand the administration, procedures, and policies of those agencies of government charged with enforcing the law, adjudicating crime, and correcting criminal conduct. The study of criminal justice involves analyzing how these institutions influence human behavior and how they are in turn influenced by law and society.

Defining Criminal Justice Study

Note how this definition recognizes that criminal justice is essentially a social institution. Its study involves analyzing how the justice system relates to social values, norms, and trends: The justice system responds to social values and behavior, and, conversely, social values and behavior are influenced by the justice system.

As social scientists, criminal justice experts try to bring carefully controlled scientific methods, such as surveys and experiments, to bear on their subject matter whenever possible. Using these methods, they focus their attention on the inner processes of the agencies of justice: police and law enforcement organizations; courts and related institutions, such as the district attorney's office; and correctional agencies, such as jails, prisons, and parole authorities. Criminal justice, then, is a field of study that deals with the nature of crime in society and that analyzes the formal processes and social agencies that have been established for crime control.

The Criminal Justice System

The contemporary criminal justice system in the United States is monumental, costing taxpayers about $100 billion per year, including more than $40 billion for police, $20 billion for the court and legal system, and $30 billion for corrections. These costs are on the rise, having increased more than 160% in the past 15 years.[18]

One reason the justice system is so expensive to run is that it employs more than 1.8 million people, including over 850,000 in law enforcement and 370,000 in corrections. It consists of over 55,000 public agencies, including approximately 17,000 police agencies, nearly 17,000 courts, over 8,000 prosecutorial agencies, about 6,000 correctional institutions, and over 3,500 probation and parole departments. There are also capital costs. State jurisdictions are now conducting a massive correctional building campaign, adding tens of thousands of prison cells. It costs about $70,000 to build a prison cell, and about $25,000 per year to keep an inmate in prison; juvenile institutions cost about $30,000 per year per resident. And beyond the direct costs of funding police, courts, and corrections, many more crime-related expenses are incurred by federal, state and local governments. For example, federal drug control efforts now cost an additional $14 billion per year.[19]

The system is so big because it must process, treat, and care for millions of people each year. While the crime rate has stabilized in the 1990s, about 15 million people are still being arrested each year, including almost 3 million for serious felony offenses.[20] In addition, about 1.5 million juveniles are handled annually by the juvenile courts.[21] Each year about 168,000 adults are convicted of a violent felony; convictions for property, drug, and other felonies add 1.1 million people to the system each year.[22]

Considering the enormous number of people processed each year, it comes as no surprise that the correctional system population is at an all-time high; more than 5 million people are under the control of the correctional system. There are now about 1.6 million men and women in the nation's jails and prisons,[23] while an additional 3.8 million adult men and women are on probation or parole—a number that has been increasing by more than 3% each year since 1990[24] (see Figure 1.1).

What are the major components of this immense system, and what are their duties? What are the major stages in the "formal" criminal justice process, and how are decisions made at each of these critical junctures? What is the "informal" justice process, and how does it operate? These important questions are addressed in the following sections.

Components of Criminal Justice

The control and prevention of criminal activity and the treatment and reform of criminal offenders are carried out by the police, the courts, and the correctional system.

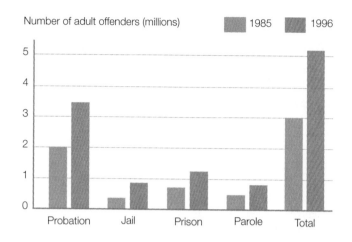

Number of adult offenders (millions)   1985   1996

Figure 1.1
**Correctional populations
in the United States,
1985–1996.** The correctional
system contains more than
5 million people.
SOURCE: Darrell Gilliard and Allen
Beck, *Prisoners, 1995* (Washington,
D.C.: Bureau of Justice Statistics,
1996), p. 1, updated.

The Police

Police departments are those public agencies created to maintain order, enforce the criminal law, provide emergency services, keep traffic on streets and highways moving freely, and create a sense of community safety. The system and process of criminal justice depends on effective and efficient police work, particularly when it comes to preventing and detecting crime and apprehending and arresting criminal offenders. As our society becomes more complex, new functions are required of the police officer. Today, police officers work actively with the community to prevent criminal behavior; they help divert members of special needs populations, such as juveniles, alcoholics, and drug addicts, from the criminal justice system; they participate in specialized units such as juvenile and drug prevention squads; they cooperate with public prosecutors to initiate investigations into organized crime and drug trafficking; they resolve neighborhood and family conflicts; and they provide emergency services, such as preserving civil order during strikes and political demonstrations.

Because of these expanded responsibilities, the role of the police officer has become more professional. The officer must not only be technically competent to investigate crimes but also be aware of the rules and procedures associated with investigation of criminal activity, apprehension, and arrest. The police officer must be aware of the factors involved in the causes of crime in order to screen and divert offenders who might be better handled by other, more appropriate agencies. They must also be part community organizer, social worker, family counselor, dispute resolver, and emergency medical technician.

Police officers today are required to exercise a great deal of individual discretion in deciding whether to arrest, refer, or simply investigate a situation further; their actions represent the exercise of discretionary justice.

The Courts

The criminal court is considered by many to be the core element in the administration of criminal justice:

> It is [the] part of the system that is the most venerable, the most formally organized, and the most elaborately circumscribed by law and tradition. It is the institution around which the rest of the system has developed and to which the rest of the system is in large measure responsible. It regulates the flow of the criminal process under governance of the law. . . . It is expected to articulate the community's most deeply held, most cherished views about the relationship of individual and society.[25]

The criminal court houses the process by which the criminal responsibility of defendants accused of violating the law is determined. Ideally, the court is expected to convict and sentence those found guilty of crimes while ensuring that the innocent are freed without any consequence or burden. The court system is formally required to seek the truth, to obtain justice for the individual brought

The role of the police officer has become more professional. The officer must be aware of the rules and procedures associated with arrest, apprehension, and investigation of criminal activity. A police officer must also be part community organizer, social worker, family counselor, dispute resolver, and emergency medical technician.

before its tribunals, and to maintain the integrity of the government's rule of law. However, overburdened courts are often the scenes of informal bargain justice, which is designed to get the case over with as quickly as possible and at the least possible cost. While the criminal court ideally should hand out fair and evenhanded justice in a forum of strict impartiality and fairness, this standard of justice has not been maintained in millions of cases heard each year in the nation's criminal court system. Instead, a system of "bargain justice" has developed that encourages defendants to plead guilty. This means that most criminal defendants do not go to trial but instead work out a deal with the prosecutor in which they agree to plead guilty as charged in return for a more lenient sentence, the dropping of charges, or some other considerations. Critics have tried to limit plea bargaining in recent years, but so far it remains a difficult practice to control.

At the conclusion of the adjudication and in the event that the defendant is found guilty, either by his or her own admission of guilt or a decision made by a judge or jury, the criminal court judge is responsible for sentencing the offender. Whatever sentence is ordered by the court may serve not only to rehabilitate the offender but also to deter others from crime. Once sentencing is accomplished, the corrections component of the criminal justice system begins to function.

The entire criminal court process is undertaken with the recognition that the rights of the individual should be protected at all times. These rights—determined by federal and state constitutional mandates, statutes, and case law— form the foundation for individual protection of the accused. They include such basic concepts as the right to an attorney, the right to a jury trial, and the right to a speedy trial. A defendant also has the right to be given due process, or to be treated with fundamental fairness. This includes the right to be present at trial, to be notified of the charge(s), to have an opportunity to confront hostile witnesses, and to have favorable witnesses appear. Such practices are an integral part of a system and process that seeks to balance the interests of both the individual and the state.

The Court System. The court system administering the criminal process includes lower criminal courts, superior courts, and appellate courts. Each state and the federal government has its own independent court structure unique to that particular jurisdiction. Where a crime is a violation of state law, it is ordinarily prosecuted in the state court, while offenses against federal laws are generally handled by the federal court system.

The lower criminal courts of any state, variously called police courts, district courts, or recorder's courts, deal with the largest number of criminal offenses. Referred to as the people's courts, they are scattered throughout the state by county, town, or geographic district. They daily handle a large volume of criminal offenses, including such crimes as assault and battery, disorderly conduct, breaking and entering, possession of drugs, petty larceny, traffic violations, and juvenile offenses. Many cases are disposed of without trial, either because the defendant pleads guilty or because the circumstances of the offense do not warrant further court action. In the event that a trial is required in the lower courts, it often occurs before a judge, rather than a jury, because the defendant often waives the constitutional right to a jury trial. Lower criminal courts, although primarily responsible for misdemeanor offenses, also process the first stage of felony offenses by holding preliminary hearings, making bail decisions, and conducting trials of certain felonies where they have jurisdiction as defined by statute.

In sum, the lower criminal courts often dispense routine and repetitious justice and are burdened with a heavy responsibility they are not generally equipped to fulfill. Characterized by cramped courtrooms, limited personnel, and a tendency to rely on bargain justice (plea bargains), they remain a critical problem area in criminal justice administration.

The superior courts, or major trial courts, have general jurisdiction over all criminal offenses but ordinarily concentrate on felony offenses. They conduct jury trials with much formality and with strict adherence to the defendant's constitutional rights. In addition to conducting trials, these courts accept guilty pleas, generally give offenders longer sentences because of the more serious nature of their crimes, and, in certain instances, review sentences originally imposed by lower courts.

The highest state court is a supreme, or appeals, court, whose functions are similar to those of the U.S. Supreme Court in the federal judicial system. State supreme courts are primarily appellate courts that do not conduct criminal trials. Appellate courts deal with procedural errors arising in the lower courts that are considered violations of rights guaranteed by state constitutions or the U.S. Constitution, such as the use of illegal evidence. Questions of fact decided in the original trial are not ordinarily reviewed in the appellate process. The appellate court has the authority to affirm, modify, or reverse decisions of the lower criminal court.

The Prosecution and the Defense. The prosecutor and the defense attorney are the opponents in what is known as the **adversary system.** These two parties oppose each other in a hotly disputed contest—the criminal trial—in accordance with rules of law and procedure. In every criminal case, the state acts against and the defense attorney for the defendant before an impartial judge or jury, with each side trying to bring evidence and arguments forward to advance its case. Theoretically, the ultimate objective of the adversary system is to seek the truth, in this way determining the guilt or innocence of the defendant from the formal evidence presented at the trial. The adversary system ensures that the defendant is given a fair trial, that the relevant facts of a given case emerge, and that an impartial decision is reached.

The *prosecutor* is the public official who represents the government and presents its case against the defendant, who is charged with a violation of the criminal law. Traditionally, the prosecutor is a local attorney whose area of jurisdictional responsibility is limited to a particular county or city. The prosecutor is known variously as a district attorney or a prosecuting attorney and is either an elected or an appointed official. On a state level, the prosecutor may be referred to as the attorney general, while in the federal jurisdiction, the title is United States attorney.

The prosecutor is responsible not only for charging the defendant with the crime but also for bringing the case to trial and to a final conclusion. The prosecutor's authority ranges from determining the nature of the charge to reducing the charge by negotiation or recommending that the complaint be dismissed. The prosecutor also participates in bail hearings, presents cases before a grand jury, and appears for the state at arraignments. In sum, the prosecutor is responsible for presenting the state's case from the time of the defendant's arrest through conviction and sentencing in the criminal court.

The prosecutor, like the police officer, exercises a great deal of discretion; he or she can decide initially whether or not to file a criminal charge, determine what charge to bring, or explore the availability of noncriminal dispositions. Prosecutorial discretion would not be as important as it is were it desirable to prosecute all violations of the law. However, full enforcement of every law is not practical, since most police officers and prosecutors ordinarily lack sufficient resources, staff, and support services to carry out that goal. Therefore, it makes sense to screen out cases where the accused is obviously innocent, where the evidence is negligible, or where criminal sanctions may seem inappropriate. Instead of total or automatic law enforcement, a process of selective or discretionary enforcement exists; as a result, the prosecutor must make many decisions that significantly influence police operations and control the actual number of cases processed through the court and correctional systems.

The *defense attorney,* on the other hand, is responsible for providing legal defense representation to the defendant. This role involves two major functions: protecting the constitutional rights of the accused, and presenting the best possible legal defense for the defendant.

The defense attorney represents a client from initial arrest through the trial stage, during the sentencing hearing, and, if needed, through the process of appeal. The defense attorney is also expected to enter into plea negotiations and obtain for the defendant the most suitable bargain regarding type and length of sentence.

Any person accused of a crime can obtain the services of a private attorney if he or she can afford to do so. One of the most critical questions in the criminal justice system has been whether an indigent (poor) defendant has the right to counsel. The federal court system has long provided counsel to the indigent on the basis of the Sixth Amendment of the U.S. Constitution, which gives the accused the right to have the assistance of defense counsel. Through a series of landmark U.S. Supreme Court decisions, beginning with *Powell v. Alabama* in 1932 and continuing with *Gideon v. Wainwright* in 1963 and *Argersinger v. Hamlin* in 1972, the right of a criminal defendant to have counsel has become fundamental to our system of criminal justice.[26] Today, state courts must provide counsel to indigent defendants who are charged with criminal offenses where the possibility of incarceration exists. Consequently, more than a thousand public defender agencies have been set up around the United States that provide free legal counsel to indigent defendants.

Corrections

Following a criminal trial resulting in conviction and sentencing, the offender enters the correctional system. After many years of indifference, public interest in corrections has grown as a result of well-publicized prison riots, such as the one that occurred in New York's Attica facility in 1971, and the alleged inability of the system to rehabilitate offenders.

In the broadest sense, corrections involve community supervision or probation, various types of incarceration (including jails, houses of correction, and state prisons), and parole programs for both juvenile and adult offenders. Corrections ordinarily represent the postadjudicatory care given to offenders when a sentence is imposed by the court and the offender is placed in the hands of the correctional agency.

Complicating this system is the expected dramatic explosion in the correctional population. The prison population has more than doubled since 1985, and more than 30 states are under court order to reduce prison crowding.[27]

Despite its tremendous size and cost, the correctional system suffers from an extremely poor performance record. It has not been able to offer public protection, nor does it effectively rehabilitate criminal offenders. It is plagued with high **recidivism** rates (many offenders return to crime shortly after incarceration), which are believed to result from the lack of effective treatment and training programs within incarceration facilities, poor physical environments and health conditions, and the fact that offender populations in many institutions are subjected to violence from other inmates and guards.

Despite these problems, corrections play a critical role in the criminal justice system. By exercising control over those sentenced by the courts to incarceration or community supervision, the system acts as the major sanctioning force of the criminal law. As a result, the system of corrections has many responsibilities, among them protecting society, deterring crime, and—equally important—rehabilitating offenders. Achieving both proper restraint and effective reform of the offender is the system's most frustrating, yet awesome, goal. The major components of correction include probation, confinement, and parole.

Probation. Probation is a judicial action or legal disposition that allows the offender to remain in the community, subject to conditions imposed by court order, under the supervision of a probation officer. It enables the offender to continue working while avoiding the pains of imprisonment.

At the same time, social services are provided to help the offender adjust in the community. Counseling, assistance from social workers, and group treatment, as well as the use of community resources to obtain employment, welfare, and housing, are offered to the offender while on probation.

In recent years, the concept of probation has been enhanced with a variety of **intermediate sanctions** that serve as alternatives to incarceration. These typically involve probation plus such additional penalties as house arrest, fines, forfeiture of property, intensive supervision, victim restitution, and even monitoring by computer. Some jurisdictions have instituted nonsecure community-based correctional centers for first-time offenders where they live while holding a job or obtaining an education. Another innovation is the **boot camp,** a type of correctional institution in which inmates undergo a relatively short period of intensive physical training believed to instill in them both pride and discipline. Intermediate sanctions hold the promise of being less costly and less intrusive than traditional methods of incarceration and may become the method of choice in offender rehabilitation.

Confinement. The state reserves the right through the criminal law to incarcerate convicted criminals in secure institutions of correction and reform. In the narrow sense, the system of corrections represents the institutional care of offenders brought into the criminal justice system. A person given a sentence involving incarceration ordinarily is confined to a correctional institution for a specified period of time. Different types of institutions are used to hold offenders:

- **Jails** hold offenders convicted of minor offenses or misdemeanors and "detainees"—people awaiting trial or those involved in other proceedings, such as grand jury deliberations, arraignments, or preliminary hearings. The jail is ordinarily operated by local government and is often under the jurisdiction of the county sheriff. Many jails have poor physical conditions, lack adequate staff, and maintain a custodial philosophy. Little is done in the way of inmate treatment, principally because the personnel and institutions lack the qualifications, services, and resources.

- **Prisons** or penitentiaries are state-operated facilities that house felony offenders sentenced by the criminal courts.

Most new inmates are first sent to a reception and classification center, where they are given a diagnostic evaluation and assigned to an institution that meets their individual needs as much as possible within the system's resources.

The diagnostic process in the reception center may range from a physical examination and a single interview to an extensive series of psychiatric tests, orientation sessions, and personal interviews. Classification is a way of evaluating inmates and assigning them to appropriate placements and activities within the state institutional system.

After classification, and depending on their need for treatment and the level of risk they present, inmates are assigned to either minimum-, medium-, or maximum-security institutions. Maximum-security institutions have high walls, barred cells, and careful security measures and house the most dangerous inmate population. Medium-security institutions may physically resemble more guarded institutions, but their inmate population requires less control and therefore can receive more intensive treatment. Minimum-security institutions may have private dormlike rooms and offer inmates much freedom and good correctional programs.

Parole. Few offenders released from correctional institutions serve their entire sentence behind prison walls. Most receive early release because they have accumulated time off for good behavior, referred to as "good time." About 40% reenter the community via the discretionary parole system. Under this approach, inmates are reviewed by a parole board after they have served the portion of their sentence required by law (the minimum sentence).

Some states now use mandatory release in which parole eligibility is determined upon entry into the institution. Mandatory release dates are based on sentence length and available "good time." It is also possible to be released on completion of the entire sentence without good time credit or parole, but relatively few inmates serve their entire sentence; typically inmates serve about one-third of their sentence. It is also possible to be released via pardon—a form of executive clemency.

After their release, offenders are supervised by parole authorities who help them find employment, deal with family and social difficulties, and gain treatment for emotional or substance abuse problems. If the offender violates conditions of community supervision, parole may be revoked. In that event, the parolee may be sent back to the correctional institution.

While these institutions and organization make up the heart of the criminal justice system, they are duplicated in part in a parallel system designed to care for and correct juvenile offenders. This juvenile justice system is discussed next.

The Juvenile Justice System

Independent of but interrelated with the adult criminal justice system, the juvenile justice system is primarily responsible for dealing with juveniles who commit crimes (delinquents) and those who are incorrigible, truants, runaways, or unmanageable (status offenders).

The policy of treating juveniles who commit criminal acts separately from adults is a relatively new one. Until the late 19th century, youthful criminals were tried in adult courts and punished in adult institutions. However, 19th-century reformers, today known as "child savers," lobbied to separate young offenders from serious adult criminals. Their efforts were rewarded when the first separate juvenile court was set up in Chicago in 1899. Over the next 20 years, most other states created separate juvenile court and correctional systems.

At first, the juvenile system was based on the philosophy of *parens patriae.* This meant that the state was acting in the best interests of children in trouble who could not care for themselves. Under the *parens patriae* doctrine, delinquents and status offenders (sometimes called "wayward minors" or "children in need of supervision," these youths were truant, runaways, or simply beyond control of parental authority) were tried in an informal juvenile court hearing without the benefit of counsel or other procedural rights. The juvenile correctional system, designed for treatment rather than punishment, was usually located in small institutions referred to as schools or camps. (The first juvenile

Table 1.1
Shifting Philosophies of Juvenile Justice

Time Frame	Activity
Prior to 1900s	Juveniles treated similar to adult offenders. No distinction by age or capacity to commit criminal acts.
From 1899 to 1950s	Children treated differently, beginning with Illinois Juvenile Court Act of 1899. By 1925, juvenile court acts established in virtually every state.
1950s to 1960s	Widespread use of incarceration for relatively minor crimes. Lack of procedural due process. Abuse of power in institutions.
1960s to 1970s	Introduction of constitutional due process into the juvenile justice system. Punishing children or protecting them under *parens patriae* requires due process of law.
1970s to 1980s	Failure of rehabilitation and due process protections to control delinquency leads to shift to crime control and punishment philosophy similar to adult criminal justice system.
1990s	Mixed constitutional protections with some treatment. Uncertain goals and programs; juvenile justice system relies on punishment and deterrence.

reform school was opened in 1847 in Massachusetts.) After the separate juvenile justice system was developed, almost all incarcerated youths were maintained in separate juvenile institutions that stressed individualized treatment, education, and counseling.

Critics charged that the juvenile justice system's reliance on informal procedure often violated a child's constitutional rights to due process of law. It seemed unfair to place a minor child, tried without benefit of an attorney or other legal safeguards granted to adult defendants, in a remote incarceration facility. In the 1960s the Supreme Court revolutionized the juvenile justice system when, in a series of cases—the most important being *In re Gault*—it granted procedural and due process rights, such as the right to legal counsel, to juveniles at trial. The Court recognized that many youths were receiving long sentences without the benefit of counsel and other Fifth and Sixth Amendment rights and that many institutions did not carry out their treatment role. Consequently, the juvenile justice process became similar to the adult process.

In the 1970s, recognizing the stigma placed on a youth by the "delinquency" label, every effort was made to remove or divert youths from the official justice process and place them in alternative, community-based treatment programs. One state, Massachusetts, went so far as to close its secure correctional facilities and place all youths, no matter how serious their crimes, in community programs. The various philosophical stages in the historical development of the juvenile justice system are summarized in Table 1.1.

Today, concern over juvenile violence has caused some critics to question the juvenile justice system's treatment philosophy. Some states, such as New York, have liberalized their procedures for trying serious juvenile offenders in the adult system, consequently making them eligible for incarceration in adult prisons. The general trend has been to remove as many nonviolent and status offenders as possible from secure placements in juvenile institutions and at the same time to lengthen the sentences of serious offenders or to move such offenders to the adult system. Kids who are waived to the adult system today face long prison sentences and even the death penalty.

Some of the similarities and differences between the adult and juvenile justice systems are listed in Table 1.2. Although there are many similarities between rights and privileges in both systems, there are some important differences.

Similarities Between Juvenile and Adult Justice Systems	Differences Between Juvenile and Adult Justice Systems
Police officers, judges, and correctional personnel use discretion in decision making in both the adult and the juvenile systems.	The primary purpose of juvenile procedures is protection and treatment. With adults, the aim is to punish the guilty.
The right to receive *Miranda* warnings applies to juveniles as well as to adults.	Age determines the jurisdiction of the juvenile court. The nature of the offense determines jurisdiction in the adult system.
Juveniles and adults are protected from prejudicial lineups or other identification procedures.	Juveniles can be apprehended for acts that would not be criminal if they were committed by an adult (status offenses).
Similar procedural safeguards protect juveniles and adults when they make an admission of guilt.	Juvenile proceedings are not considered criminal; adult proceedings are.
Prosecutors and defense attorneys play equally critical roles in juvenile and adult advocacy.	Juvenile court procedures are generally informal and private. Those of adult courts are more formal and are open to the public.
Juveniles and adults have the right to counsel at most key stages of the court process.	Courts cannot release identifying information about a juvenile to the press, but they must release information about an adult.
Pretrial motions are available in juvenile and criminal court proceedings.	Parents are highly involved in the juvenile process but not in the adult process.
Negotiations and plea bargaining exist for juvenile and adult offenders.	The standard of arrest is more stringent for adults than for juveniles.
Juveniles and adults have a right to a hearing and an appeal.	Juveniles are released into parental custody. Adults are generally given the opportunity for bail.
The standard of evidence in juvenile delinquency adjudications, as in adult criminal trials, is proof beyond a reasonable doubt.	Juveniles have no constitutional right to a jury trial. Adults have this right. Some state statutes provide juveniles with a jury trial.
Juveniles and adults can be placed on probation by the court.	Juveniles can be searched in school without probable cause or a warrant.
Both juveniles and adults can be placed in pretrial detention facilities.	A juvenile's record is generally sealed when the age of majority is reached. The record of an adult is permanent.
Juveniles and adults can be kept in detention without bail if they are considered dangerous.	A juvenile court cannot sentence juveniles to county jails or state prisons; these are reserved for adults.
After trial, both can be placed in community treatment programs.	The U.S. Supreme Court has declared that the Eighth Amendment does not prohibit the death penalty for crimes committed by juveniles ages 16 and 17, but this is not a sentence given to children under 16.

Juveniles can be taken into custody and placed in an institution for acts (status offenses) made illegal because of their age, such as being truant from school or running away from home. They do not have the right to a jury trial, and juvenile hearings are still closed to the public. However, juveniles who are waived to the adult court can be incarcerated in prisons and even subject to the death penalty. The different terminologies used in the juvenile and adult justice systems are compared in Table 1.3. These differences reflect the effort to protect adolescents

	Juvenile Terms	Adult Terms
The person and the act	Delinquent child	Criminal
	Delinquent act	Crime
Preadjudicatory stage	Take into custody	Arrest
	Petition	Indictment
	Agree to a finding	Plead guilty
	Deny the petition	Plead not guilty
	Adjustment	Plea bargain
	Detention facility; child-care shelter	Jail
Adjudicatory stage	Substitution	Reduction of charges
	Adjudicatory or fact-finding hearing	Trial
	Adjudication	Conviction
Postadjudicatory stage	Dispositional hearing	Sentencing hearing
	Disposition	Sentence
	Commitment	Incarceration
	Youth development center; treatment center, training school	Prison
	Residential child-care facility	Halfway house
	Aftercare	Parole

from the stigma of a criminal label. Note how juveniles are never arrested or convicted; they are taken into custody and adjudicated.

The juvenile justice system is a vast enterprise today. Juvenile courts process more than 1.5 million delinquents each year, an increase of more than 40% since 1985. About 320,000 youths are placed in juvenile detention centers awaiting trial. Each year about 265,000 delinquent youths are placed on probation, and another 150,000 are placed in some form of secure treatment center. An additional 125,000 status offenders are handled by the court, 11,000 of whom are placed out of their homes. The number of children waived to the adult court, about 12,000 annually, is on the rise, having increased 71% since 1985.[28]

The Formal Criminal Justice Process

Another way of understanding criminal justice is to view it as a process that takes an offender through a series of steps, beginning with arrest and concluding with reentry into society. The emphasis throughout the process is on the offender and the various sequential stages, or decision points, through which he or she passes. At each of these points, a determination is made to assign the case to the next stage of the system or to discharge the suspect without further action. This decision making is often a matter of individual discretion, based on a variety of factors and perceptions. Legal factors, including the seriousness of the charges, available evidence, and the suspect's prior record, are usually considered legitimate influences on decision making. Troubling is the fact that such extralegal factors as the suspect's race, gender, class, and age may influence decision outcomes. There is a significant and ongoing debate over the impact of extralegal factors in the decision to arrest, convict, and sentence suspects: Critics believe a suspect's race, class, and gender can often determine the direction a case will take, while supporters argue that the system is relatively fair and unbiased.[29]

The concept of the formal justice process is important because it implies every criminal defendant charged with a serious crime is entitled to the full range of rights under law. Knowing that every individual is entitled to his or her day in court, to be represented by competent counsel in a fair trial before an impartial jury, with trial procedures subject to review by a higher authority, is central to the American concept of liberty. The kangaroo court and summary punishment are elements of political systems that most Americans fear and despise. The fact that all criminal defendants are entitled to a full range of legal

An investigation can take but a few minutes, as when a police officer sees a crime in progress and is able to apprehend the suspect within minutes. Here police officers respond to a bank robbery in progress in North Hollywood, California on February 28, 1997. This robbery made national headlines because the robbers were heavily armed, wore body armor, and chose to shoot it out with officers rather than surrender. The suspects died after a fierce gunfight captured on videotape by helicopter news crews.

rights and constitutional protections is one of the basic guarantees of American democracy.

The 15-Step Process

A comprehensive view of the formal criminal process would normally include 15 steps.

1. *Initial contact.* The initial contact stage involves an act or incident that makes a person the subject of interest to the agencies of justice. In most instances, initial contact is a result of a police action: While they are on patrol, police officers observe a person acting suspiciously and conclude the suspect is under the influence of drugs; police officers are contacted by a victim who reports a robbery, and they respond by going to the scene of the crime; an informer tells police about some ongoing criminal activity in order to receive favorable treatment. In some cases, the initial contact is a result of the police department's responding to a request by the mayor or other political figures to control an ongoing social problem, such as gambling, prostitution, or teenage loitering. Further efforts may be terminated if the police believe that the case is trivial, unimportant, unfounded, or a personal matter.

2. *Investigation.* The purpose of the investigatory stage of the justice process is to gather enough evidence to identify, arrest, and bring the offender to trial. During the investigation, police are allowed to search the crime scene, interview witnesses, and question suspects about their whereabouts and activities. An investigation can take but a few minutes, as in the case of a police officer seeing a crime in progress and apprehending the suspect at the scene. Or it can take many months and involve hundreds of police officers. However, the investigation will be terminated and no further action taken if police conclude that the perpetrator cannot be identified or that the case is not important enough to warrant further allocation of resources.

3. *Arrest.* An arrest occurs when the police take a person in custody and the suspect believes that he or she has *lost his or her liberty*. An arrest is considered legal when all the following conditions exist: (a) the police officer believes there

is sufficient evidence, referred to as **probable cause,** that a crime is being or has been committed and the suspect is the person who committed it; (b) the officer deprives the individual of freedom; and (c) the suspect believes that he or she is now in the custody of the police. The police officer is not required to use the word *arrest* or any similar term to initiate an arrest, nor does the officer have to bring the suspect to the police station.

To make an arrest in a misdemeanor, the officer must have witnessed the crime personally, known as the **in-presence requirement,** while a felony arrest can be made based on the statement of a witness or victim. An arrest can also be made upon the issuance of an arrest warrant by a local magistrate or judge.

It is possible for suspects to be released after arrest if further information indicates that a mistake has been made, if the victim does not wish the case to proceed, or if a suitable alternative to official processing can be reached, as when the arrestee agrees to some condition such as breaking off all contact with the victim. The decision to release a suspect is an important aspect of police discretion.

Because the police may wish to restrain a suspect briefly while they check his or her story and activities, the courts have allowed police to briefly detain suspects with less than probable cause. A detention, by definition only a few minutes in duration, falls between arrest and freedom.

4. *Custody.* The moment after an arrest is made, the detained suspect is considered in police custody. At this juncture the police will record his or her name and address and the nature of the complaint filed (commonly called "booking," after the practice of logging information in a record book; of course, it is more likely today to record information in a computer than a book). The police may also search the suspect for weapons or contraband, interrogate him or her to gain more information, such as whether the person had any accomplices, or even encourage the suspect to confess to the crime. The police may want to enter the suspect's home, car, or office to look for further evidence. Similarly, the police may want to bring witnesses to view the suspect in a **lineup** or in a one-to-one confrontation. And during custody, the police are allowed to obtain a suspect's fingerprints and photo and to draw blood. Because these procedures are so crucial and can have a great bearing at a later trial, the U.S. Supreme Court has granted suspects in police custody protection from the unconstitutional abuse of police power, such as illegal searches and intimidating interrogations.

5. *Charging.* If sufficient evidence exists to charge a person with a crime, the case is turned over to the prosecutor's office for additional processing. If the case involves a misdemeanor, the prosecutor will file a charges document generally called a *complaint* before the court that will try the case. If the case involves a felony, the prosecutor must decide whether to bring the case forward, depending on the procedures used in the jurisdiction and the nature of the crime, to either a grand jury or a preliminary hearing (see below). In either event, the decision to charge the suspect with a specific criminal act involves many factors, including evidence sufficiency, crime seriousness, case pressure, and political issues. Prosecutors may decide to take no further action, referred to as a **nolle prosequi,** and the case is terminated. "Nolle pros" may be motivated by evidence insufficiency, reluctant witnesses, or office policy; for example, obscenity cases are usually dropped in certain jurisdictions.

6. *Preliminary hearing/grand jury.* Because a person faces great financial and personal costs when he or she is forced to stand trial for a felony, the U.S. Constitution mandates that the government must first prove that there is probable cause that the accused committed the crime he or she is charged with and that a trial is warranted under the circumstances. In about half the states and the federal system, this decision is rendered by a group of citizens brought together to form a **grand jury.** The grand jury considers the case in a closed hearing in which only the prosecutor presents evidence. If the evidence is sufficient, the jury will

issue a **bill of indictment,** which specifies that the accused must stand trial for a specific crime.

In the remaining states, the grand jury has been replaced with a **preliminary hearing.** In these jurisdictions, a charging document called an **information** is filed before a lower trial court, which then conducts an open hearing on the merits of the case. This procedure is sometimes referred to as a *probable cause hearing.* The defendant and his or her attorney may appear at this hearing and dispute the prosecutor's charges. If the prosecutor's evidence is accepted as factual and sufficient, the suspect will be called to stand trial for the crime. The charges will be dropped if the grand jury (or magistrate in a preliminary hearing) believe there is an insufficient factual basis to charge the suspect.

7. *Arraignment.* Before the trial begins, the defendant is **arraigned,** or brought before the court that will hear the case. At the arraignment, the formal charges are read, the defendant is informed of his or her constitutional rights (for example, the right to be represented by legal counsel), an initial plea may be entered in the case (not guilty or guilty), a trial date set, and bail issues considered. A guilty plea at this juncture is usually part of a deal in which the defendant agrees to some consideration, such as making restitution, or to a treatment plan, such as entering an alcohol treatment program in exchange for the guilty plea. If a guilty plea is registered, formal processing is terminated.

8. *Bail or detention.* Bail is a money bond, the amount of which is set by judicial authority. The purpose of bail is to ensure the return of a criminal defendant for trial while allowing the person pretrial freedom to prepare his or her defense. Defendants who do not show up for trial forfeit their bail. Those people who cannot afford to put up bail or who cannot borrow sufficient funds for it remain in state custody prior to trial. In most instances, this means an extended stay in a county jail or house of correction. Most jurisdictions allow defendants awaiting trial to be released on their own recognizance (promise to the court), without bail, if they are stable members of the community and have committed nonviolent crimes.

9. *Plea bargaining.* Soon after an arraignment, if not before, defense counsel will meet with the prosecution to see whether the case can be brought to a conclusion without a trial. This might mean filing the case while the defendant participates in a community-based treatment program for substance abuse or psychiatric care, for example. Most commonly, the defense and prosecution discuss a possible guilty plea in exchange for reducing or dropping some of the charges or agreeing to a request for a more lenient sentence. It is generally accepted that almost 90% of all cases end in a plea bargain, rather than a criminal trial.

10. *Trial/adjudication.* If an agreement cannot be reached or if the prosecution does not wish to arrange a negotiated settlement of the case, a full-scale inquiry into the facts of the case commences. The criminal trial is held before a judge ("bench trial") or jury who will decide whether the evidence against the defendant is sufficient beyond a reasonable doubt. The defendant may be found guilty or not guilty as charged. Sometimes in a jury trial, a decision cannot be reached, resulting in a deadlocked or hung jury and leaving the case unresolved and open for a possible retrial. Upon a verdict of "not guilty," the formal criminal process is terminated and the double jeopardy clause of the Constitution's Fifth Amendment protects the defendant from retrial on the same charges.

11. *Disposition/sentencing.* If after a criminal trial the accused has been found guilty as charged, he or she will be returned to court for sentencing. Possible dispositions may include a fine, probation, a period of incarceration in a penal institution, or some combination of these. In cases involving first-degree murder, about 35 states and the federal government allow the death penalty.

Dispositions are usually made after the probation department conducts a presentence investigation that evaluates the defendant and determines his or her potential for successful rehabilitation if given a period of community supervision or whether he or she needs secure confinement. Sentencing is a key decision point in the criminal justice system because in many jurisdictions, judicial discretion can result in people receiving vastly different sentences despite having committed the same crime.

12. *Postconviction remedies.* After conviction and if the defendant believes he or she was not treated fairly by the justice system, the defendant may **appeal** the conviction before an appellate court. An appeals court reviews the procedures used during the processing of the case to determine whether an error was made in the conduct of the trial. It considers such questions as whether evidence was used properly, whether the judge conducted the trial in an approved fashion, whether the jury was representative, and whether the attorneys in the case acted appropriately. If the court rules that the appeal has merit, it can hold that the defendant be given a new trial or, in some instances, order his or her outright release. Outright release can be ordered when the state prosecuted the case in violation of the double jeopardy clause of the U.S. Constitution or when it violated the defendant's right to a speedy trial.

13. *Correctional treatment.* After sentencing, the offender is placed within the jurisdiction of state or federal correctional authorities. He or she may serve a probationary term, be placed in a community correctional facility, serve a term in a county jail, or be housed in a prison. During this stage of the criminal justice process, the offender may be asked to participate in rehabilitation programs designed to help him or her make a successful readjustment to society. He or she may be forced to radically adjust his or her personality and lifestyle.

14. *Release.* On completion of his or her sentence and period of correction, the offender will be free to return to society. Release may be earned by serving the maximum sentence given by the court or through an early-release mechanism, such as parole or pardon. Most inmates do not serve the full term of their sentence. Offenders sentenced to community supervision simply finish their term and resume their lives in the community.

15. *Postrelease.* After termination of correctional treatment, the offender will have to make a successful return to the community. This adjustment is usually aided by corrections department staff members who attempt to counsel the offender through the period of reentry into society. The offender may be asked to spend some time in a community correctional center, which acts as a bridge between a secure treatment facility and absolute freedom. Offenders may find that their conviction has cost them some personal privileges, such as the right to hold certain kinds of employment. These privileges may be returned by court order once the offenders have proven their trustworthiness and willingness to adjust to society's rules.

> The image that comes to mind is an assembly line conveyor belt down which moves an endless stream of cases, never stopping, carrying them to workers who stand at fixed stations and who perform on each case as it comes by the same small but essential operation that brings it one step closer to being a finished product, or to exchange the metaphor for the reality, a closed file. The criminal process is seen as a screening process in which each successive stage—prearrest investigation, arrest, postarrest investigation, preparation for trial, trial or entry of plea, conviction, disposition—involves a series of routinized operations whose success is gauged primarily by their tendency to pass the case along to a successful conclusion.[30]

The Criminal Justice Assembly Line

So Herbert Packer describes the criminal justice process. According to this view, each of the fifteen stages we've described is actually a decision point through which cases flow (see Figure 1.2). For example, at the investigatory stage, police must decide whether to pursue the case or terminate involvement because there is insufficient evidence to identify a suspect, the case is considered trivial, the victim decides not to press charges, and so on. Or at the bail stage, a decision must be made whether to set so high a bail that the defendant remains

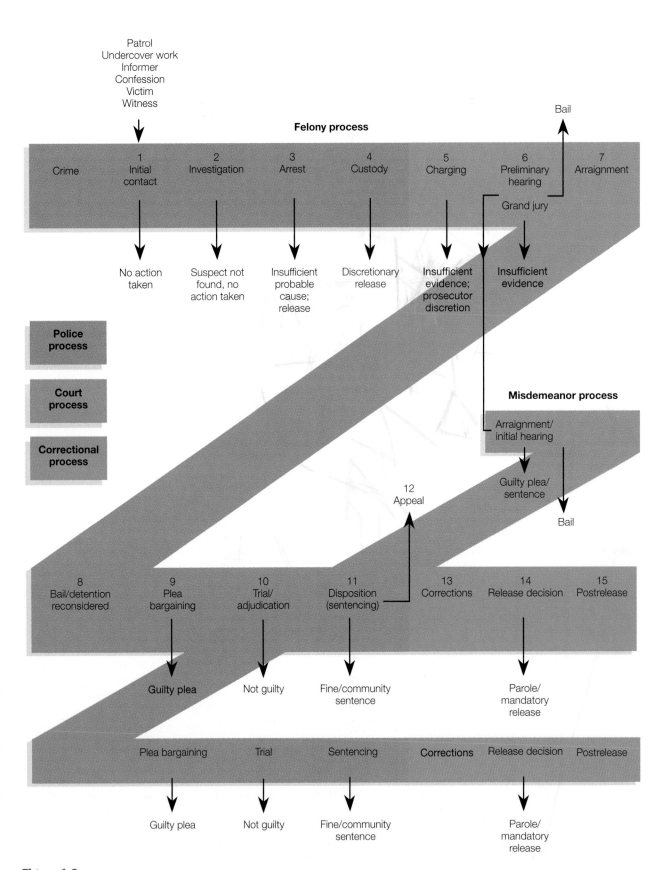

Patrol
Undercover work
Informer
Confession
Victim
Witness

Felony process

Bail

	1	2	3	4	5	6	7
Crime	Initial contact	Investigation	Arrest	Custody	Charging	Preliminary hearing	Arraignment

Grand jury

No action taken

Suspect not found, no action taken

Insufficient probable cause; release

Discretionary release

Insufficient evidence; prosecutor discretion

Insufficient evidence

Police process

Court process

Correctional process

Misdemeanor process

Arraignment/ initial hearing

Guilty plea/ sentence

Bail

12
Appeal

8	9	10	11	13	14	15
Bail/detention reconsidered	Plea bargaining	Trial/ adjudication	Disposition (sentencing)	Corrections	Release decision	Postrelease

Guilty plea

Not guilty

Fine/community sentence

Parole/ mandatory release

Plea bargaining	Trial	Sentencing	Corrections	Release decision	Postrelease

Guilty plea

Not guilty

Fine/community sentence

Parole/ mandatory release

Figure 1.2
The critical stages in the justice process follow an assembly line.

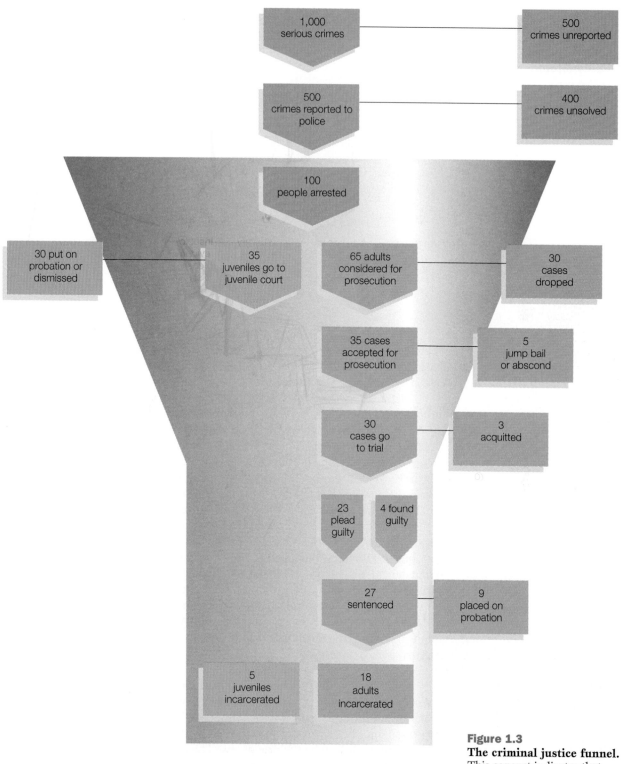

Figure 1.3
The criminal justice funnel. This concept indicates that only a small percentage of serious crimes result in convictions and incarceration.

SOURCE: Patrick Langan and Richard Solari, *National Judicial Reporting Program, 1990* (Washington, D.C.: Bureau of Justice Statistics, 1993); Edward Lisefski and Donald Manson, *Tracking Offenders, 1984* (Washington, D.C.: Bureau of Justice Statistics, 1988).

in custody, set a reasonable bail, or release the defendant on his or her own recognizance without requiring any bail at all. Each of these decisions can have a critical effect on the defendant, the justice system, and society. If an error is made, an innocent person may suffer or a dangerous individual may be released to continue to prey upon society.

Figure 1.3 illustrates the approximate number of offenders removed from the criminal justice system at each stage of the process. As the figure shows, relatively few arrestees are bound over for trial, convicted, and eventually sentenced

Table 1.4
The Interrelationship
of the Criminal Justice
System and the Criminal
Justice Process

The System: Agencies of Crime Control	The Process
1. Police	1. Contact 2. Investigation 3. Arrest 4. Custody
2. Prosecution and defense	5. Complaint/charging 6. Grand jury/preliminary hearing 7. Arraignment 8. Bail/detention 9. Plea negotiations
3. Court	10. Adjudication 11. Disposition 12. Appeal/postconviction remedies
4. Corrections	13. Correction 14. Release 15. Postrelease

to prison. One study of more than half a million felony arrests made in eight states found that while 59% of arrestees were convicted, only about 10% of the cases resulted in a prison sentence.[31]

In actual practice, many suspects are released before trial because of a procedural error, evidence problems, or other reasons that result in a nolle prosequi, the decision of a prosecutor to drop the case. Though most cases that go to trial wind up in a conviction (because almost all defendants accept guilty pleas), others are dismissed by the presiding judge because of the defendant's failure to appear or because of procedural irregularities. So, the justice process can be viewed as a funnel that holds a lot of cases at its mouth and relatively few at its end.

Theoretically, nearly every part of the process requires that individual cases be disposed of as quickly as possible. However, the criminal justice process is slower and more tedious than desired because of congestion, inadequate facilities, limited resources, inefficiency, and the nature of governmental bureaucracy. When defendants are not processed smoothly, often because of the large caseloads and inadequate facilities that exist in many urban jurisdictions, the procedure breaks down, the process within the system fails, and the ultimate goal of a fair and efficient justice system cannot be achieved. Table 1.4 shows the interrelationship of the component agencies of the criminal justice system and the criminal justice process.

The Informal Justice System

The "traditional" model of the criminal justice system sees the procedure as a series of decision points that convey offenders from initial contact to final release. Each stage of the system, beginning with investigation and arrest and ending after a sentence has been served, is defined by time-honored administrative procedures and controlled by the rule of law. The public's perception of the system, fueled by the media, is that it is composed of daredevil, crime-fighting police officers who never ask for overtime or sick leave, crusading district attorneys who stop at nothing to send the mob boss up the river, wily defense attorneys who neither ask clients for upfront cash nor cut office visits to play golf, no-nonsense judges who are never inept political appointees, and tough wardens who rule the yard with an iron hand.

Though this "ideal" model of justice still merits concern and attention, it would be overly simplistic to assume that the system works this way for every case. While there is little question that a few cases receive a full measure of rights and procedures, many are settled in an informal pattern of cooperation between the major actors in the justice process. For example, police may be willing to make a deal with a suspect in order to gain his or her cooperation, and the prosecutor bargains with the defense attorney to gain a plea of guilty as charged in return for a promise of leniency. Law enforcement agents and court officers are allowed tremendous discretion in their decisions to make an arrest, bring formal charges, handle a case informally, substitute charges, and so on. Crowded courts operate in a spirit of getting the matter settled quickly and cleanly, rather than engage in long, drawn-out criminal proceedings with an uncertain outcome.

While the traditional model regards the justice process as an adversary proceeding in which the prosecution and defense are combatants, the majority of criminal cases are actually cooperative ventures in which all parties get together to work out a deal; this is often referred to as the **courtroom work group**.[32] This group, made up of the prosecutor, defense attorney, judge, and other court personnel, functions to streamline the process of justice through the extensive use of plea bargaining and other alternatives. Rather than looking to provide a spirited defense or prosecution, these legal agents, who have often attended the same schools and know each other and worked together for many years, try to work out a case to their advantage through an informal legal process that sometimes disregards the interests of the defendant and the public. In most criminal cases, cooperation rather than conflict between prosecution and defense appears to be the norm. It is only in a few widely publicized criminal cases involving rape or murder that the adversarial process is called into play. Consequently, upward of 80% of all felony cases and over 90% of misdemeanors are settled without trial.

What has developed is a system in which criminal court experiences can be viewed as a training ground for young defense attorneys looking for seasoning and practice, a means for newly established lawyers to receive government compensation for cases taken to get their practice going, or an arena in which established firms can place their new associates for experience before they are assigned to paying clients. Similarly, successful prosecutors can look forward to a political career or a highly paid partnership in a private firm. To further their career aspirations, prosecutors must develop and maintain a winning track record in criminal cases. No district attorney wants to become a Hamilton Burger, the fictional prosecutor who lost every case to the legendary Perry Mason. While the courtroom work group limits the constitutional rights of defendants, it may be essential for keeping

Figure 1.4
Chance of Punishment.
With the justice system overcrowded and overburdened, relatively few offenders go through the process from its beginning to its end. For example, out of an estimated 5.5 million burglaries committed each year, only 114,000 burglars are eventually imprisoned.
SOURCE: Kathleen Maguire and Ann Pastore, eds., *Sourcebook of Criminal Justice Statistics* (Washington, D.C.: U.S. Government Printing Office, 1996).

Prison

| Total acts | Reported to police | Arrests | Convictions |
| 5.5 million | 2.5 million | 390,000 | 114,000 |

60,000

The "Wedding Cake" Model of Justice

Samuel Walker, a justice historian, has come up with a rather dramatic way of describing the informal justice process: He compares it to a four-layer cake, as depicted in Figure 1.A.

Level I

The first layer of Walker's model is made up of celebrated cases involving the wealthy and famous—such as athlete O. J. Simpson, heavyweight boxing champion Mike Tyson, socialite William Kennedy Smith, and financier Michael Milken—or the not-so-powerful who victimize a famous person, such as John Hinckley, Jr., who shot President Ronald Reagan, or Sirhan Sirhan, who assassinated Senator Robert Kennedy.

Other cases fall into the first layer because they are widely reported in the media and become the subject of a TV miniseries. The Peterson-Grossberg case is an example of such a high-profile case. The murder trial of Eric and Lyle Menendez for killing their wealthy parents was a first-layer case because of the sensational nature of the crime and the consequent media coverage. The media usually focus on hideous or unusual cases, such as Jeffrey Dahmer's killing and mutilation of 15 men in Milwaukee.

Also included within Level I are relatively unknown cases that become celebrated when they serve as vehicles for important Supreme Court decisions. *Miranda v. Arizona* and *Gideon v. Wainwright* reached legal prominence when they defined the defendant's right to legal counsel at arrest and trial.

Cases in the first layer of the criminal justice wedding cake usually receive the full array of criminal justice procedures, including competent defense attorneys, expert witnesses, jury trials, and elaborate appeals. Prosecutors are more than willing to bring these cases to trial because the media attention helps them launch political careers—but only when they win, of course. Because the public hears so much about these cases, it believes them to be a norm, but in reality they are quite rare.

Level II

In the second layer are the serious felonies—rapes, robberies, and burglaries—that have become all too routine in U.S. society. They are in the second layer because they are serious crimes committed by experienced offenders. Burglaries are included if the amount stolen is quite high and the techniques used indicate the suspect is a real pro. Violent crimes, such as rape and assault, are vicious incidents against an innocent victim and may involve a weapon and extreme violence. Robberies involve large amounts of money and suspects who brandish handguns or other weapons and are considered career criminals. Police, prosecutors, and judges all agree that these are serious cases, worthy of the full attention of the justice system. Offenders in such cases receive a full jury trial and, if convicted, can look forward to a prison sentence.

Level III

Though they can also be felonies, crimes that fall in the third layer of the wedding cake are either less serious offenses, committed by young or first-time offenders, or offenses involving people who knew each other or were otherwise related: an inebriated teenager committed a burglary and netted $50; the rape victim had gone on a few dates with her assailant before he attacked her; the robbery involved members of a rival gang and no weapons; the assault was the result of a personal dispute and where there is some question as to who hit whom first. Agents of the criminal justice system relegate these cases to the third level because

our overburdened justice system afloat. Moreover, while informal justice exists, it is not absolutely certain that it is inherently unfair to both the victim and the offender. The research evidence shows that the defendants who benefit the most from informal court procedures commit the least serious crimes, while the more chronic offender gains relatively little[33] (see Figure 1.4 on page 27).

The "wedding cake" model of informal justice described in the box above is an intriguing alternative to the traditional criminal justice flowchart. Criminal justice officials do handle individual cases quite differently. Yet there is a high degree of consistency with which particular types or classes of cases are dealt in

they see them as less important and deserving of attention. Level III crimes may be dealt with by an outright dismissal, a plea bargain, a reduction in charges, or, most typically, a probationary sentence or intermediate sanction, such as victim restitution.

Level IV
The fourth layer of the cake is made up of the millions of misdemeanors, including disorderly conduct, shoplifting, public drunkenness, and minor assault. These are handled by the lower criminal courts in assembly-line fashion. Few defendants insist on exercising their constitutional rights, because the delay would cost them valuable time and money. Since the typical penalty is a small fine, everyone wants to get the case over with. In a sense, the experience of going to court is the real punishment in a misdemeanor case. Few petty cases actually involve any jail time.[34]

The wedding cake model depicts the justice system in political terms. Cases that are "important" because they involve famous people or generate media interest go to the top of the pile. In contrast, cases in which the poor victimize one another get little formal interest from the justice system. The typical criminal case is handled as if it were a civil complaint or lawsuit: A settlement agreeable to all parties involved—defendant, victim, defense attorney, prosecutor, and police—seems the best course of action.

Critical Thinking Questions
1. Is it fair to base the level of care and concern in the criminal justice process on the notoriety of a case? Might this not encourage attorneys to defend clients on the basis of the media potential of the case? Can you identify people who have been prosecuted and disproportionately punished because they may have been famous? For example, would Mike Tyson have been tried and sent to prison if he were an unknown? Or do you think that the famous are often able to "get away with murder"?

2. Is it fair to ignore a defendant's personal circumstances and those of his victim? For example, if you were a judge, would you punish a 15-year-old who punched another 15-year-old boy after an argument the same way you would if he had punched a 25-year-old married woman who was pregnant at the time? If not, what factors would influence your decision?

Source: Samuel Walker, *Sense and Nonsense About Crime and Drugs*, 3rd ed. (Belmont, Calif.: Wadsworth, 1994), 29–38.

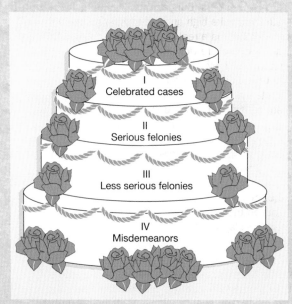

Figure 1.A

The criminal justice "wedding cake." The criminal justice system has been compared to a wedding cake by Samuel Walker.

Source: Based on Samuel Walker, *Sense and Nonsense About Crime* (Monterey, Calif.: Brooks/Cole, 1985).

every legal jurisdiction. Police and prosecutors in Los Angeles and Boston, New York and San Antonio will each handle the murder of a prominent citizen in a similar fashion. They will also deal with the death of an unemployed street person killed in a brawl similarly. Yet, in each jurisdiction, the two cases will be handled very differently from each other. The bigwig's killer will receive a full-blown jury trial (with details on the 6:00 news); the drifter's killer will get a quick plea bargain. The model is useful because it helps us realize that all too often, public opinion about criminal justice is formed on the basis of what happened in a celebrated case that is actually quite atypical. In fact, as the Criminal Justice and the

Chapter 1

The Criminal Justice System: History, Organization, and Process

Ransom

Agents of the criminal justice system routinely confront calculating, well-armed criminals who use loads of high-tech gear to carry out their fiendish plots. Crime victims are wealthy, attractive, and glamorous and, if the cops can't solve the crime, they think nothing of single-handedly foiling the criminals. *Sure* they do—if the victim is played by Mel Gibson, one of Hollywood's most prominent leading men.

In the hit 1996 film *Ransom,* Gibson plays Tom Mullen, a self-made millionaire who owns an airline. He, his wife Kate (Renee Russo), and son Sean (Brawley Nolte) live the good life in a New York City penthouse. Tom has clawed his way to the top of the executive ladder, taking risks, and even having an innocent man jailed in order to keep control of the airline.

Then one day a well-coordinated band of kidnappers snatch young Sean in broad daylight in Central Park. Tom contacts the FBI, which sends a crack team led by agent Lonnie Hawkins (Delroy Lindo), who tries to find and trap the kidnappers. However, the "bad guys" are led by shrewd New York City detective Jimmy Shaker (Gary Sinise). They use their inside information and advanced communications gear to stay one step ahead of the "Feds."

When Tom goes to make delivery of the $2 million ransom, the nighttime drop goes awry when helicopters filled with FBI sharpshooters kill Cubby (Donnie Wahlberg), one of the kidnappers.

Convinced that the criminals will never release his son alive, Tom makes a surprising television announcement; he will not pay the ransom money but instead will turn it into a bounty on the head of the crime's mastermind: "Two million dollars for the first person to turn in the leader, dead or alive." In a surprising twist, Detective Shaker turns on his accomplices, killing them and leading authorities to believe that he solved the crime and is entitled to the reward. However, when he goes to collect from Tom, the young Sean recognizes the kidnapper's voice and his plan unravels. Tom offers to take Shaker to a bank to get the cash, but when stopped by police, Shaker panics and tries to escape. Tom pursues him through the streets of New York and in a dramatic ending tosses Shaker through a store window, where he is impaled by glass and then shot dead by police.

Ransom is typical of the media's "vision" of the criminal justice system, which is that most cases fall in the top layer of the criminal justice "wedding cake." They involve attractive victims and cunning, well-prepared criminals. The stakes are high, the law enforcement agents are dedicated, street battles and shootouts are common, lots of people die, and in the end the case is always solved. Because either the criminal or the victim is attractive, articulate, and well educated, the two often form a close bond or friendship, or one of them becomes romantically involved with a law enforcement agent. Other films of this type are *The Jagged Edge* (Glenn Close and Jeff Bridges), *Basic Instinct* (Sharon Stone and Michael Douglas), and *The Fugitive* (Harrison Ford and Tommy Lee Jones).

Films such as *Ransom* give the public a distorted view of the criminal justice system. While it is true that some cases do involve the wealthy and glamorous, they are actually rare and far between. The great majority of victims and criminals come from the lower end of the socioeconomic scale, living in slum housing and not penthouses. Few crimes involve millions of dollars; most criminals "earn" far less than minimum wage for their efforts.

Like other criminals portrayed in the media, the kidnappers in *Ransom* have advanced communications and surveillance gear, vehicles, and other high-tech equipment at their disposal. They are always one step ahead of the FBI. One wonders why such brilliant and resourceful tacticians have to resort to crime to get ahead!

It is also rare to have victims track down offenders on their own, risking life and limb to bring them to justice. When was the last time you saw a shootout in the street or heard about a multibillionaire airline owner duking it out with a criminal? Probably never, unless you bought a ticket to see *Ransom*!

Media box on page 30 shows, first-layer cases are what Hollywood films like to make the public believe the criminal justice system is all about.

In sum, the justice system is large, complex, and multifaceted. It offers an intriguing challenge for those who desire to work within its structure, as well as many career opportunities for motivated individuals who seek to understand and improve its operations.

Criminal Justice as a Career

The criminal justice system provides numerous career opportunities. The preceding sections identified some of the many roles in the justice process. Some who choose to go into the field are motivated by the desire to help people and get into social service work. Others are more interested in law enforcement and policing. Another choice is teaching and research, while others want to supplement their criminal justice education with legal studies in order to take on the role of defense counsel, prosecutor, or magistrate. Of course, some enterprising people are able to take on a number of these endeavors at some time during their criminal justice career: A police officer might earn a doctorate and go into teaching, a probation officer may go to law school and become a prosecutor, a professor might be appointed head of a state corrections department, and so on. Let us now examine some of the specialties within the field of criminal justice to get an idea of some of these career alternatives.[35]

Law Enforcement

Over half a million people are employed in policing and law enforcement in the United States. The following are but a few areas in which a person's criminal justice career can involve enforcement of the criminal law.

Municipal Police Officer. The majority of people in law enforcement work for city police departments. The work of the patrol officer, traffic cop, and detective is familiar to anyone who watches TV or goes to movies (although the accuracy of the portrayal by those entertainment vehicles is highly suspect). Beyond these familiar roles, however, police work also includes a great many administrative and service jobs, such as officer training, communications, records management, purchasing, and so on. A student interested in a police career but not necessarily excited by the idea of roaming the streets chasing after bad guys will find that police work has a great deal of other opportunities to offer.

The salary range for police officers is quite wide. Nationally, the average entry salary is about $27,000, and the maximum salary for a patrol officer reached after about six years is $36,356. However, salaries are often affected by region and jurisdiction size. For example, the starting pay for officers on the Pacific Coast is about $35,000, with an average of $44,000 after four years.[36] Similarly, police chiefs average about $49,397. However, chiefs average slightly more than $101,000 in cities of over 1 million population.[37]

While police salaries are not high in some regions, officers can supplement their income with extra duty and overtime. Police officers in some cities in Massachusetts start at about $30,000 a year. If they earn an undergraduate degree, they get an extra 20% on their base pay; a master's or law degree increases their starting pay by 25%. Overtime and special detail pay can add to this sum. It is not uncommon for uniformed police officers to double their salaries with extra work details to top $100,000 in a single year.[38]

Civilian Employees. In addition to sworn personnel, many police agencies hire civilian employees who bring special skills to the department. For example, it is common in the computer age for departments to employ information resource managers who are charged with improving data processing, integrating the

Chapter 1

The Criminal Justice System: History, Organization, and Process department's computer information database with others in the state, operating computer-based fingerprint identification systems and other high-tech investigation devices, and linking with national computer systems such as the FBI's National Crime Information system, which holds the records of millions of criminal offenders.

State and County Law Enforcement. In addition to city police agencies, state and county governments also provide career opportunities in law enforcement. The state police and county sheriff's department do much the same work as city police agencies—traffic, patrol, and investigation—depending on their area of jurisdiction. These agencies commonly take on a greater law enforcement role in more rural areas and provide ancillary services, such as running the local jail or controlling traffic, in urban centers. Similar to the situation for police officers, state and county law enforcement pay is influenced by size and region. For example, the average pay for the senior county law enforcement agent is about $43,000; in western counties of over 1 million population, the chief averages about $97,000.

State agencies also hire investigators as part of their enforcement mandate. For example, the California Department of Insurance employs fraud investigators to conduct felony investigations of insurance fraud and related statutes. They also employ property controllers to handle property seized in investigations of insurance fraud.[39] Similarly, the California Division of Consumer Affairs employs investigators to enforce rules and regulations relating to consumer protection.[40] State investigators carry out many of the tasks of other law enforcement officers, including serving warrants, making arrests, and conducting undercover investigations.

Federal Law Enforcement. The federal government also employs thousands of law enforcement personnel in such agencies as the Federal Bureau of Investigation, the Drug Enforcement Agency, the Secret Service, and so on. These agencies are often considered the elite of the law enforcement profession, and standards for entry are quite high. The duties of these federal agencies include upholding federal laws controlling counterfeiting, terrorism, espionage, bank robbery, and importation and distribution of controlled substances, among others.

Private Security. The field of private security also offers many career opportunities. Some positions are in large security companies, such as Pinkerton's or Wackenhut. Others are in company security forces, such as those maintained by large retail chains, manufacturing companies, and railroads. Public institutions such as hospitals, airports, and port facilities also have security teams. For example, large retail chains typically employ loss prevention agents who are responsible for the protection of company assets.

Other private companies maintain their own enforcement branches. Insurance firms hire field investigators to determine the origin and cause of accidents, fires, and other events for which the company is liable. Insurance investigators also handle claims in which client fraud is suspected.

These are but a few of the many careers in law enforcement. Table 1.5 provides a more complete list of opportunities.

Correctional Service Work

A significant number of people who work in the field of criminal justice become involved in its social service side. Many opportunities are available to provide direct service to people both before they actually get involved with the law and after they have come to the attention of criminal justice agencies.

Table 1.5
Careers in Law Enforcement
SOURCE: Harr and Hess, *Seeking Employment in Law Enforcement, Private Security, and Related Fields* (St. Paul: West Publishing, 1992), pp. 16–17.

Careers in Law Enforcement	
Arson investigator	Jailer
Attache	Juvenile specialist
Ballistics expert	K-9 handler
Booking officer	Narcotics agent
Border Patrol officer	Operations specialist
Chaplain	Patrol officer
Chief of police	Personnel specialist
Chief of staff	Photographer
Commander of field operations	Pilot
Commissioner	Police attorney/legal adviser
Communications officer	Police psychologist
Community safety coordinator	Police/school liaison officer
Community service officer	Police surgeon
Conservation officer	Polygraph operator
Crime lab technician	Professor
Crime prevention specialist	Psychiatric adviser
Customs officer	Public relations officer
Data processing specialist	Public safety director
Deputy	Radio communications specialist
Deputy chief	Records management director
Detective	Scientist
Detention officer	Security specialist
Director of research and development	Secret Service agent
Director of scientific services	Serology specialist
Director of standards and training	Sheriff
Document specialist	Street crimes specialist
Emergency management coordinator	Superintendent of police
Evidence technician	SWAT team member
FBI special agent	Traffic officer
Fingerprint expert	Training director
Firearms instructor	Treasury agent
Forensic scientist	Trooper
Gaming enforcement agent	Undercover operative
Gang investigator	Undersheriff
Inspector	U.S. marshal
Instructor	Water patrol
Intelligence officer	Witness protection agent
Investigator	

Probation Officer. Probation officers supervise offenders who have been placed under community supervision by the criminal court. Their duties include counseling clients to help them adjust to society. This may be done through family counseling, individual counseling, or group sessions. Probation officers are trained to use the resources of the community to help their clients. Their work involves them in the personal, family, and work problems of their clients.

Starting pay in probation may range from the mid-twenties per year to about $40,000 in some states. Chief probation officers do quite better. A recent opening for a chief probation officer in Fresno, California that required a bachelor's degree and five years' administrative experience was advertised at $85,000 to $103,000; a similar announcement for San Francisco's chief juvenile probation officer offered $94,000 to $114,000.

Community Correctional Counselor. There are thousands of community-based correctional facilities around the country. These house nonviolent criminals serving out their prison sentences and inmates transferred from high-security institutions near the completion of their prison terms; separate facilities are maintained for juvenile offenders. These settings also provide ample opportunity for direct service work, since the overwhelming majority of programs emphasize the value of rehabilitation and treatment. Community-based corrections provide the setting for some of the most innovative treatment techniques used in the criminal justice system.

Secure Correctional Work. Numerous opportunities exist for working in secure correctional settings. While some may view correctional work as a matter of guarding incarcerated inmates, that narrow perspective is far from accurate. Correctional workers are charged with overseeing a great variety of activities that may involve them in budgeting, management, training, counseling, classification, planning, and human services.

Correctional treatment staff engage in such tasks as vocational and educational training, counseling, recreational work, and so on. Almost every correctional institution has a social service staff that helps inmates adjust to the institution and prepare for successful reentry into the outside world. In addition, correctional settings require security staff, maintenance workers, medical staff, clergy, and other types of personnel.

Salaries in the correctional field vary widely based on skill level, experience, responsibilities, and the size of the institution. Correctional guards may start at about $20,000 a year, while administrators make considerably more. For example, Broward County, Florida recently listed a position for assistant director of its Detention Division, which oversees the county jail, for a salary of up to $77,582. A director of a juvenile facility may be hired in the $60,000–$70,000 range, depending on its geographical location.

Parole and After Care. Parole and after-care workers supervise offenders upon their release from correctional treatment. This work involves helping individuals find jobs, achieve their educational objectives, sort out their family problems, and so on. Parole officers employ various counseling techniques to help clients clarify their goals and find ways of surmounting obstacles so that they can make a successful readjustment to the community.

Law and the Courts

The criminal justice system provides many opportunities for people interested in working in the legal system and the courts. Of course, in most instances, these careers require postgraduate education, such as law school or a course in court management.

Prosecutor. Prosecutors represent the state in criminal matters. They bring charges against offenders, engage in plea bargaining, conduct trials, and help determine sentences. Prosecutors work at the local, county, state, and federal levels of government. For example, an assistant U.S. attorney general would prosecute violations of federal law in one of the 91 U.S. district courts.

Defense Counsel. All criminal defendants are entitled to legal counsel. Therefore, agencies such as the public defender's office have been created to provide free legal services to indigent offenders. In addition, private attorneys often take on criminal cases without compensation as a gesture of community service or are assigned cases by the court for modest compensation (referred to as a **pro bono** case). Defense attorneys help clients gather evidence to support their innocence; represent them at pretrial, trial, and sentencing hearings; and serve as their advocate if an appeal is filed upon conviction. A legal career is, of course, quite desirable and lucrative, with starting salaries in major big-city firms approaching $75,000. Law school admissions are highly competitive, and students interested in attending are cautioned to maintain the highest levels of academic achievement.

Judge. Judges carry out many functions during the trial stage of justice. They help in jury selection, oversee the admission of evidence, and control the flow of the trial. Most important, they are entrusted with the duty of ensuring that the trial is conducted within the boundaries of legal fairness. Although many criminal defense attorneys and prosecutors aspire to become judges, few are actually chosen for this honor. As might be expected, senior judges are paid quite well, and six-figure salaries are not uncommon.

Staff Counsel. A number of public agencies will hire a staff counsel to give legal advice, prepare legal memoranda and reports, respond to inquiries, draft proposed legislation, and advise administrators on the legal ramifications of policy changes. Staff counsel typically are paid in the $50,000 range to start, depending on their experience and specialized knowledge; more senior staff counsel might be hired at $60,000 plus.

Court Administrator. Most court jurisdictions maintain an office of court administration. These individuals help in case management and ensure that the court's resources are used in the most efficient manner. Court administrators are usually required to receive advanced education in programs that specialize in court management, such as those at the University of Southern California and American University in Washington, D.C. Chief court administrators are involved in financial management, human resources, case flow management, and statistical analysis, among other duties. Pay is quite high. A recent opening in New Jersey's Mercer County was advertised at $72,719 to $101,188 for someone with a bachelor's degree and seven years' experience.

In addition to work within the agencies of justice themselves, it is also possible to make a career in criminal justice that involves teaching, research, or administration.

Research, Administration, and Teaching

Private Sector Research. A number of private sector institutes and research firms—such as the Rand Corporation in Santa Monica, California, Abt Associates in Cambridge, Massachusetts, and the Battelle Institute in Seattle—employ research scientists who conduct criminal justice–related research. In addition, a number of private nonprofit organizations are devoted to the study of criminal justice issues, including the Police Executive Research Forum, the Police Foundation, and the International Association of Chiefs of Police, all located in the Washington, D.C. area; the National Council on Crime and Delinquency in San Francisco; and the VERA Foundation in New York.

Many universities also maintain research centers that for many years have conducted ongoing efforts in criminal justice, often with funding from the government and private foundations. For example, the Institute for Social Research at the University of Michigan has conducted an annual survey of teenage substance abuse; the Hindelang Research Center at the State University of New York at Albany produces the *Sourcebook of Criminal Justice Statistics,* an invaluable research tool; the National Neighborhood Foot Patrol Center at Michigan

State University conducts research on community policing; and the Criminal Justice Research Center at the University of Massachusetts–Lowell is involved in measuring the effectiveness of probation supervision.

Most people who work for these research centers hold advanced degrees in criminal justice or other applied social sciences. Some of the projects carried out by these centers, such as the study of career criminals conducted by Rand Corporation scientists and the Police Foundation's study of the deterrent effect of police patrol, have had a profound effect on policymaking within the criminal justice system.

Public Sector Research. Most large local, state, and federal government agencies contain research arms that oversee the evaluation of ongoing criminal justice programs and plan for the development of innovative efforts designed to create positive change in the system. For example, most state corrections departments have planning and research units that monitor the flow of inmates in and out of the prison system and help evaluate the effectiveness of prison programs, such as work furloughs. On a local level, larger police departments commonly employ civilian research coordinators who analyze police data in order to improve the effectiveness and efficiency of police services.

The most significant contribution to criminal justice research made by the public sector is probably that of the federal government's Bureau of Justice Statistics and National Institute of Justice (NIJ), which are the research arms of the U.S. Justice Department. In recent years, these agencies have supported some of the most impressive and important of all research studies on criminal justice issues, such as sentencing, plea bargaining, and victimization.

Research salaries are generally high. For example, the Washington State Court Administrator's Office recently advertised for a research manager with a Ph.D. and five years' experience at a starting salary of up to $64,668.

System Administration. It is also common for the federal and state governments to maintain central criminal justice planning offices that are responsible for setting and implementing criminal justice policy or for distributing funds for policy implementation. For example, the NIJ sets priorities for criminal justice research and policy on an annual basis, then distributes funds to local and state applicants willing to set up and evaluate demonstration projects. The NIJ has targeted the following areas: apprehension, prosecution, and adjudication of criminal offenders; public safety and security; punishment and control of offenders; victims of crime; white-collar and organized crime; criminal careers; drugs and alcohol and crime; forensic science; offender classification; and violent criminal behavior.[41]

A number of states also have criminal justice administrative agencies that set policy agendas and coordinate state efforts to improve the quality of the system. Planners and analysts working for these agencies are expected to hold a master's degree and are typically hired in the $40,000–$50,000 range.

College Teaching. There are more than 600 criminal justice education programs in the United States. These include specialized criminal justice programs, programs in which criminal justice is combined with another department (such as sociology or political science), and programs that offer a concentration in criminal justice as part of another major.

Criminal justice educators have a career track similar to that of most other teaching specialties. Regardless of the level they teach at—associate, baccalaureate, or graduate—their course will reflect the core subject matter of criminal justice, including courses on policing, the courts, and the correctional system.

Criminal Justice on the Net

"Anatomy of a Murder: A Trip Through Our Nation's Legal Justice System" is a unique web site that puts you right in the middle of the action in a criminal murder trial. By logging on to this site, you will be able to follow the story of a defendant as he faces one of the most serious charges that the legal justice system of the United States can levy against an individual. This is more than an exciting fictional story, however. Every aspect of the tale is researched and legally accurate. As the story unfolds, you will see the events of a criminal prosecution as they would actually unfold; nothing is made up or embellished. Legal terms, where they are used, can be looked up in the glossary provided. The site also contains discussion of relevant Supreme Court cases and other information about the justice system.

http://tqd.advanced.org/2760/ homep.html

Summary

The term *criminal justice* became prominent around 1967, when the President's Commission on Law Enforcement and the Administration of Justice began a nationwide study of the nation's crime problem. Since then, a field of study has emerged that uses knowledge from various disciplines in an attempt to understand what causes people to commit crimes and how to deal with the crime problem. Criminal justice, then, consists of the study of crime and of the agencies concerned with its prevention and control.

Criminal justice is both a system and a process. As a system, it ideally functions as a cooperative effort among the primary agencies—police, courts, and corrections. The process, on the other hand, consists of the actual steps the offender takes from the initial investigation through trial, sentencing, and appeal.

In many instances, the criminal justice system works informally in order to expedite the disposal of cases. Criminal acts that are very serious or notorious may receive the full complement of criminal justice processes, from arrest to trial. However, less serious cases are often settled when a bargain is reached between the prosecution and the defense.

Many careers are open to people interested in working within the criminal justice system. Among the options are police work, social service, research, administration, and teaching.

Key Terms

criminal justice system
predatory criminals
intimate violence
Law Enforcement Assistance
    Administration (LEAA)
criminal justice
social control
adversary system
recidivism

intermediate sanctions
boot camp
jails
prisons
probable cause
in-presence requirement
lineup
nolle prosequi
grand jury

bill of indictment
preliminary hearing
information
arraigned
appeal
courtroom work group
pro bono

Questions

1. Which criminal behavior patterns pose the greatest threat to the public? Should the justice system devote greater resources to combating these crimes? If so, which crime patterns should be deemphasized?

2. What factors contributed to the high crime rates among settler and immigrant groups? Do conditions exist in some areas of the country that produce high crime rates for similar reasons?

3. Some people believe that violent movies and TV shows are the cause of the high violent crime rate in the United States. Might their suspicions be considered invalid in light of the fact that crime rates were actually higher in the 19th century than they are today?

4. Describe the differences between the formal and informal justice systems. Is it inherently unfair for prosecutors and defense attorneys to work out a "deal"?

5. What are the layers of the criminal justice "wedding cake"? Give an example of a crime for each layer. Is it fair to treat some offenders differently because they or their victims are celebrities?

Notes

1. Elizabeth Gleick, "Three Kids, One Death," *Time,* 2 December 1996, p. 69.

2. Theresa Humphery, "Teens Linked to Son's Death Say He Had Brain Damage," *Boston Globe,* 18 December 1996, p. A3.

3. Kathleen Maguire and Ann Pastore, eds., *Sourcebook of Criminal Justice Statistics, 1995* (Washington, D.C.: U.S. Government Printing Office, 1996), p. 27.

4. Data taken from a Times Mirror survey reported in Maguire and Pastore, *Sourcebook of Criminal Justice Statistics, 1995,* p. 129.

5. Gallup poll data reported in Maguire and Pastore, *Sourcebook of Criminal Justice Statistics, 1995,* p. 151.

6. This section leans heavily on Ted Robert Gurr, "Historical Trends in Violent Crime: A Critical Review of the Evidence," in Michael Tonry and Norval Morris, eds., *Crime and Justice: An Annual Review of Research,* vol. 3 (Chicago: University of Chicago Press, 1981); Richard Maxwell Brown, "Historical Patterns of American Violence," in Hugh Davis Graham and Ted Robert Gurr, eds., *Violence in America: Historical and Comparative Perspectives* (Beverly Hills, Calif.: Sage Publications, 1979).

7. David Courtwright, "Violence in America," *American Heritage* 47 (1996): 36–52, quote p. 36; *Violent Land: Single Men and Social Disorder from the Frontier to the Inner City* (Cambridge, Mass.: Harvard University Press, 1996).

8. Cesare Beccaria, *On Crimes and Punishments* (1764, reprint ed., Indianapolis: Bobbs-Merrill, 1963).

9. Samuel Walker, *Popular Justice* (New York: Oxford University Press, 1980).

10. Ibid.

11. Ibid.

12. Samuel Walker, "Origins of the Contemporary Criminal Justice Paradigm: The American Bar Foundation Survey, 1953–1969," *Justice Quarterly* 9 (1992): 47–76.

13. President's Commission on Law Enforcement and the Administration of Justice, *The Challenge of Crime in a Free Society* (Washington, D.C.: U.S. Government Printing Office, 1967).

14. See Public Law 90-351, Title I—Omnibus Crime Control Safe Streets Act of 1968, 90th Congress, 19 June 1968.

15. American Bar Association, *Project on Standards for Criminal Justice* (New York: Institute of Judicial Administration, 1968–1973); National Advisory Commission on Criminal Justice, *Standards and Goals, A National Strategy to Reduce Crime* (Washington, D.C.: U.S. Government Printing Office, 1973).

16. Frank Zarb, "Police Liability for Creating the Need to Use Deadly Force in Self-Defense," *Michigan Law Review* 86 (1988): 1982–2009.

17. See, for example, Stephen Schoenthaler and Walter Doraz, "Types of Offenses Which Can Be Reduced in an Institutional Setting Using Nutritional Intervention," *International Journal of Biosocial Research* 4 (1983): 74–84.

18. Maguire and Pastore, *Sourcebook of Criminal Justice Statistics, 1995,* p. 3.

19. Ibid., p. 16.

20. Federal Bureau of Investigation, *Crime in the United States, 1995* (Washington, D.C.: U.S. Government Printing Office, 1996), p. 208.

21. Jeffrey Butts, *Offenders in Juvenile Court, 1994* (Washington, D.C.: Office of Juvenile Justice and Delinquency Prevention, 1996).

22. *Felony Sentences in State Courts, 1992* (Washington, D.C.: Bureau of Justice Statistics, 1995).

23. Darrell K. Gilliard and Allen J. Beck, *Prison and Jail Inmates, 1995* (Washington, D.C.: Bureau of Justice Statistics, 1996).

24. These data were collected and analyzed by Allen J. Beck, Jodi M. Brown, and Darrell K. Gilliard of the Bureau of Justice Statistics, 1996.

25. President's Commission on Law Enforcement and the Administration of Justice, *Challenge of Crime,* p. 125.

26. *Powell v. Alabama,* 287 U.S. 45, 53 S.Ct. 55, 77 L.Ed. 158 (1932); *Gideon v. Wainwright,* 372 U.S. 335, 83 S.Ct. 792, 9 L.Ed. 2d 799 (1963); *Argersinger v. Hamlin,* 407 U.S. 25, 92 S.Ct. 2006, 32 L.Ed. 2d 530 (1972).

27. See Robyn Cohen, *Prisoners in 1990* (Washington, D.C.: Bureau of Justice Statistics, 1991).

28. Jeffrey Butts, *Offenders in Juvenile Court, 1994* (Washington, D.C.: Office of Juvenile Justice and Delinquency Prevention, 1996).

29. For an analysis of this issue, see William Wilbanks, *The Myth of a Racist Criminal Justice System* (Monterey, Calif.: Brooks/Cole, 1987); Stephen Klein, Joan Petersilia, and Susan Turner, "Race and Imprisonment Decisions in California," *Science* 247 (1990): 812–816; Alfred Blumstein, "On the Racial Disproportionality of the United States Prison Population," *Journal of Criminal Law and Criminology* 73 (1982): 1259–1281; Darnell Hawkins, "Race, Crime Type and Imprisonment," *Justice Quarterly* 3 (1986): 251–269.

30. Herbert L. Packer, *The Limits of the Criminal Sanction* (Stanford, Calif.: Stanford University Press, 1975), p. 21.

31. Jacob Perez, *Tracking Offenders, 1988* (Washington, D.C.: Bureau of Justice Statistics, 1991), p. 2.

32. James Eisenstein and Herbert Jacob, *Felony Justice* (Boston: Little, Brown, 1977); Peter Nardulli, *The Courtroom Elite* (Cambridge, Mass.: Ballinger, 1978); Paul Wice, *Chaos in the Courthouse* (New York: Praeger, 1985); Marcia Lipetz, *Routine Justice: Processing Cases in Women's Court* (New Brunswick, N.J.: Transaction Books, 1983).

33. Douglas Smith, "The Plea Bargaining Controversy," *Journal of Criminal Law and Criminology* 77 (1986): 949–967.

34. Malcolm Feeley, *The Process Is the Punishment* (New York: Russell Sage Foundation, 1979).

35. Salaries and positions mentioned in the following sections were from job announcements listed in the *Criminal Justice Newsletter* between 1995 and 1997.

36. Tari Renner and Anne Peterson, *Police and Fire Department Personnel and Expenditures, 1995* (Washington, D.C.: International City/County Management Association, 1996), p. 110.

37. Gwen Hall, *Salaries of Municipal Officials, 1995;* Tari Renner and Anne Peterson, *Police and Fire Department Personnel and Expenditures, 1995* (Washington, D.C.: International City/County Management Association, 1996), pp. 76–94.

38. Brian Mooney, "Salaries of Seven Boston Officers Topped $100,000," *Boston Globe,* 2 February 1989, p. 21.

39. California Department of Insurance, 100 Van Ness Avenue, San Francisco, Calif.

40. Department of Consumer Affairs, 444 North Third Street, Sacramento, Calif.

41. National Institute of Justice, *Research Program Plan, Fiscal Year 1989* (Washington, D.C.: National Institute of Justice, 1988).

The Nature of Crime and Victimization

I f the criminal justice system is to become an effective instrument to reduce or control criminal behavior, administrators and policymakers must have up-to-date, accurate information about the nature and extent of crime. The policies and procedures of the justice system cannot exist in an informational vacuum. Unless we have accurate information about crime, we cannot be sure whether a particular policy, process, or procedure has the effect its creators envisioned. For example, a state may enact a new law requiring that anyone who uses a firearm to commit a crime serve a mandatory prison term. The new statute is aimed directly at reducing the incidence of violent crimes, such as murder, armed robbery, and assault. The effectiveness of this statutory change cannot be demonstrated without hard evidence that the use of firearms actually declined after the law was instituted and that the use of knives or other weapons did not increase. Without being able to measure crime accurately, it would be impossible to either understand its cause or plan its elimination.

Another of the goals of criminal justice study is to develop an understanding of the nature and cause of crime and victimization. Without knowing why crime occurs or the factors that influence the crime rate, it would be difficult to create effective crime reduction programs. We would never be sure whether efforts were being aimed at the proper audience or, if they were, whether they were the efforts most likely to produce positive change. For example, a crime-prevention program based on providing jobs for unemployed teenagers would only be effective if, in fact, crime is linked to unemployment. Similarly, a plan to reduce prison riots by eliminating the sugar intake of inmates is feasible only if research shows a link between diet and violence.

In addition to understanding the nature and cause of criminal behavior, it is important for criminal justice policymakers to study and understand the role of victims in the crime process. Such knowledge is essential for developing strategies to reduce the probability of predatory crime while providing information

Chapter 2
—
The Nature of Crime and Victimization

that people can use to decrease their likelihood of becoming a target of predatory criminals.

This chapter discusses some of the basic questions in the study of crime and justice: How is crime defined? How is crime measured? How much crime is there, and what are its trends and patterns? Why do people commit crime? How many people become victims of crime, and under what circumstances does victimization take place?

The Concept of Crime

How can we understand the concept of crime? Actually, there are two competing models of what the term *crime* truly means. According to the *consensus view,* crimes are behaviors that (1) are essentially harmful to a majority of citizens living in society and (2) have been controlled or prohibited by the existing criminal law. The **criminal law** is a set of rules that express the norms, goals, and values of a majority of society. Consequently, the criminal law has a **social control** function—restraining those who would take advantage of others' weakness for their own personal gain and thereby endanger the social framework. While differences in behavior can be tolerated within a properly functioning social system, behaviors that are considered inherently destructive and dangerous are outlawed to maintain the social fabric and ensure the peaceful functioning of society. The consensus view is so named because it infers that the great majority of citizens agree that certain behaviors must be outlawed or controlled and that the criminal law is designed to protect citizens from harm.

A second and opposing view is that the law and therefore the concept of crime is influenced by people who hold social power and use it to mold the law to reflect their way of thinking. Crime and law are not objective concepts; there is no absolute "right and wrong." Instead, crimes are subjective concepts that take on a spin reflecting the attitudes, morals, values, and needs of those in power. For example, various groups have tried to influence laws regulating the possession of handguns, the use of drugs and alcohol, and the availability of abortions and to exert social, economic, and political influence to impose their definition of right and wrong on the rest of the population.[1]

According to this *critical view,* the criminal law is a flexible instrument that may change according to the whim of powerful individuals and groups who use it to reflect their views of right and wrong. Groups able to assert their political and economic power use the law and the criminal justice system to advance their own causes and control the behavior of those who oppose their ideas and values.[2] For example, property crimes are punished heavily in order to protect the wealth of the affluent; drug laws ensure that workers will be productive, clear headed, and sober.

Despite these differences, there is general agreement that the criminal law defines crime, that this definition is constantly changing and evolving, that social forces mold the definition of crimes, and that the criminal law has a social control function. Therefore, as used here, the term **crime** is defined as

> a violation of social rules of conduct, interpreted and expressed by a written criminal code, created by people holding social and political power. Its content may be influenced by prevailing public sentiments, historically developed moral beliefs, and the need to protect public safety. Individuals who violate these rules may be subject to sanctions administered by state authority, which include social stigma and loss of status, freedom, and, on occasion, their life.

Sources of Crime Data

Criminal justice scholars use a variety of techniques to study crime and its consequences. Some of the major sources of crime data are discussed in this section.

Survey Data

You may have read that teenage drug use has been on the rise. How can the daily substance abuse of American teenagers possibly be calculated? The answer is by having them participate in an anonymous survey asking questions about their substance abuse. A drug use survey can provide information on the percentage of students who use drugs and the type of adolescent who becomes a drug user. Conducted annually, surveys can provide information on long-term trends in alcohol and drug usage.[3]

Most survey data come from samples in which a limited number of subjects are randomly selected from a larger population. If the sample is carefully drawn, every individual in the population has an equal chance of being selected for the study. Consequently, complex statistical analysis can be used to make inferences from the small sample to the larger population. For example, a sample of 10,000 high school seniors can be selected at random and asked about the frequency of their use of alcohol and drugs. From this relatively small sample, estimates can then be made of drug use among the millions of high school seniors in the United States.

As a source of crime information, survey data consist of information obtained from interviews and questionnaires focusing on people's behaviors, attitudes, beliefs, and abilities. Criminological surveys provide a valuable source of information on particular crime problems, such as drug use, that are rarely reported to police and may therefore go undetected. Because they typically include a variety of questions, surveys provide information on the background and personal characteristics of offenders.

Surveys are also an invaluable source of information on the nature and extent of criminal victimization. The **National Crime Victimization Survey (NCVS),** conducted by the U.S. Department of Justice, uses a large, carefully drawn sample of citizens who are queried about their experiences with criminal activity during the past year. The NCVS enables crime experts to estimate the total number of criminal incidents that occur each year, including those that are never reported to police; it is one of the most important sources of crime data.[4]

A significant proportion of criminal justice data come from the compilation and evaluation of official records. The records may be acquired from a variety of sources, including schools, courts, police departments, social service centers, and correctional agencies.

Aggregate Record Data

Records can be used for a number of purposes. Prisoners' files can be analyzed in an effort to determine what types of inmates adjust to prison and what types tend to be disciplinary problems or suicidal. Educational records are important indicators of intelligence, academic achievement, school behavior, and other information that can be related to criminal behavior patterns. However, the most important source of crime data is records compiled by police departments and annually collected and analyzed by the Federal Bureau of Investigation; these are referred to as the **official crime statistics.**

The FBI compiles the official crime data in a yearly publication referred to as the **Uniform Crime Reports (UCR),** which is a compendium of data on where, when, and how much crime occurred during the prior year.[5]

A variety of other sources of crime information exist in addition to survey and record data.

Other Sources of Crime Data

Observation. The systematic observation, recording, and deciphering of types of behavior within a sample or population is a common method of criminal justice data collection. Some observation studies are conducted in the field, where the researcher observes subjects in their natural environments; other observations take place in a contrived, artificial setting or a laboratory. For example, kids will watch a violent TV show in a university psychology lab and researchers will record their behavior to determine whether it undergoes a discernible change.

Still another type of observation study is called **participant observation.** In this type of research, the criminologist joins the group being studied and behaves as a member of the group. It is believed that participation enables the scientist to better understand the motives subjects may have for their behavior and attitudes. Participation also enables the researcher to develop a frame of reference similar to that of the subjects and to better understand how the subjects interact with the rest of the world. Participant observation studies allow the researcher to gain insights into behavior that might never be available otherwise.

Interviews. Some criminal justice researchers conduct in-depth interviews with a small sample of offenders in order to gain insight into their lives. For example, a recent study by Claire Sterck-Elifson focused on the lives of middle-class female drug abusers.[6] The 34 interviews she conducted provide insight into a group whose behavior might not be captured in a large-scale survey. Sterck-Elifson found that these women were introduced to cocaine at first "just for fun." "I do drugs," one 34-year-old lawyer told her, "because I like the feeling. I would never let drugs take over my life."[7] Unfortunately, a number later lost control of their habit and suffered both emotional and financial stress.

Life History. Another technique of criminal justice data collection is the **life history.** This method uses personal accounts of individuals who have had experience in crime, deviance, and other related areas. Diaries or autobiographies can be used; sometimes an account is given to an interested second party to record "as told to."[8] Life histories provide insights into the human condition that other, less personal research methods cannot hope to duplicate.

Each of the sources of crime data collection helps criminal justice experts understand the nature and extent of criminal behavior in the United States. Usually, three separate measures are used: official record data, self-report crime survey data, and victim survey data. Each of these sources can be used independently, but taken together, they provide a detailed picture of the crime problem. While the data provided by these three sources of crime data diverge in many key areas, they have enough similarities to enable crime experts to draw some conclusions about crime in the United States. Each method is discussed in detail in the following sections.

Official Crime Data

The national crime rate is usually equated with the aggregate criminal incidence record data collected by the FBI from police departments around the United States.

Prepared by the FBI, the Uniform Crime Reports are the best known and most widely cited source of crime statistics.[9] The FBI receives and compiles reports from over 16,000 police departments serving a majority of the population of the United States. Its major unit of analysis is the **Part I,** or **index, crimes:** murder and nonnegligent manslaughter, forcible rape, robbery, aggravated assault, burglary, larceny/theft, arson, and motor vehicle theft (see Table 2.1). **Part II,** or **nonindex, offenses** include all other crimes other than traffic violations, such as drug offenses, liquor law violations, sex offenses, juvenile offenses such as running away, and weapons offenses.

The FBI tallies and annually publishes the number of Part I crimes reported by city, county, standard metropolitan statistical area, and geographical division of the United States. In addition to these statistics, the UCR provides information on the number and characteristics of individuals, including the age, sex, and race, who have been arrested for both Part I and Part II offenses. For the eight index (Part I) crimes, every incident reported to police is counted and reported by the FBI. Information on the number of arrestees and their personal characteristics is reported for both Part I and Part II crimes.

The UCR also includes other information, such as the value of stolen merchandise, the number of law enforcement officers assaulted or killed, and the total number of full-time sworn officers and other personnel.

Table 2.1
FBI Index Crimes
SOURCE: Federal Bureau of Investigation, *Crime in the United States, 1995* (Washington, D.C.: U.S. Government Printing Office, 1996), p. 320.

Part I Crimes	Description
Criminal homicide	a. *Murder and nonnegligent manslaughter:* the willful (nonnegligent) killing of one human being by another. Deaths caused by negligence, attempts to kill, assaults to kill, suicides, accidental deaths, and justifiable homicides are excluded. Justifiable homicides are limited to: (1) the killing of a felon by a law enforcement officer in the line of duty; and (2) the killing of a felon by a private citizen. b. *Manslaughter by negligence:* the killing of another person through gross negligence. Traffic fatalities are excluded. While manslaughter by negligence is a Part I crime, it is not included in the crime index.
Forcible rape	The carnal knowledge of a female forcibly and against her will. Included are rapes by force and attempts or assaults to rape. Statutory offenses (no force used—victim under age of consent) are excluded.
Robbery	The taking or attempting to take anything of value from the care, custody, or control of a person or persons by force or threat of force or violence and/or by putting the victim in fear.
Aggravated assault	An unlawful attack by one person on another for the purpose of inflicting severe or aggravated bodily injury. This type of assault is usually accompanied by the use of a weapon or by means likely to produce death or great bodily harm. Simple assaults are excluded.
Burglary	Breaking or entering. The unlawful entry of a structure to commit a felony or a theft. Attempted forcible entry is included.
Larceny/theft (except motor vehicle theft)	The unlawful taking, carrying, leading, or riding away of property from the possession or constructive possession of another. Examples are thefts of bicycles or automobile accessories, shoplifting, pocket picking, or the stealing of any property or article which is not taken by force and violence or by fraud. Attempted larcenies are included. Embezzlement, "con" games, forgery, worthless checks, etc., are excluded.
Motor vehicle theft	The theft or attempted theft of a motor vehicle. A motor vehicle is self-propelled and runs on the surface and not on rails. Specifically excluded from this category are motorboats, construction equipment, airplanes, and farming equipment.
Arson	Any willful or malicious burning or attempt to burn, with or without intent to defraud, a dwelling, house, public building, motor vehicle or aircraft, personal property of another, etc.

The UCR uses three methods to express crime data. First, the number of crimes reported to the police and the number of arrests made are expressed as raw figures (for example, about 21,000 murders occurred in 1996). Second, percent changes in the amount of crime between years is computed (for example, murder decreased about 11% between 1995 and 1996). Third, the crime rate per 100,000 people is computed. That is, when the UCR indicates that the murder rate was 8 in 1996, it means that about 8 people in every 100,000 were murdered between January 1 and December 31 of 1996. The equation used is:

Expressing Crime Data

$$\frac{\text{Number of reported crimes}}{\text{Total U.S. population}} \times 100{,}000 = \text{Rate per } 100{,}000$$

Rate per 1,000 population

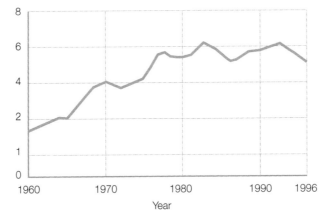

Official Crime Trends

Crime is not new to this century.[10] Studies have indicated that a gradual increase in the crime rate, especially in violent crime, occurred from 1830 to 1860. Following the Civil War, this rate increased significantly for about 15 years. From 1880 up to the Depression (about 1930), crime rates generally decreased. Then another general increase, or **crime wave,** was recorded, corresponding to Prohibition, the rise of gangsterism, and the Depression. Crime rates increased gradually following the 1930s until the 1960s, when the growth rate became much greater (see Figure 2.1). The homicide rate, which had declined from the 1930s to the 1960s, also began a period of sharp increase that continued through the 1970s and into the 1980s.

The number of crimes reported to the police peaked at about 14 million in 1991 and then began to decrease. Both the number of crimes and rate of crime have been in decline ever since. In 1996 about 13.4 million crimes were reported to the FBI, a decrease of about 3% from the year before. The overall crime rate declined more than 7% between 1992 and 1996, and violence rates fell by more than 14%. It remains to be seen whether crime rates will continue to stabilize or turn course and continue their increase.

Violent Crime Trends. The violent crimes reported by the FBI include murder, rape, assault, and robbery. In 1996 about 1.5 million violent crimes were reported to police, a rate of around 680 per 100,000 Americans. According to the UCR, violence in the United States has decreased during the 1990s, reversing a long trend of skyrocketing increases.

Particularly encouraging has been the decrease in the number and rate of murders. The murder statistics are generally regarded as the most accurate aspect of the UCR. Figure 2.2 illustrates homicide rate trends since 1900. Note how the rate peaked around 1930, then fell, rose dramatically around 1960, and peaked once again in 1991 when the number of murders topped 24,000 for the first time in the nation's history. In 1996 the murder rate declined 11% from the prior year, and about 20,000 murders were committed, down almost 4,000 from the peak; there was also an 8% decline in armed robbery. The decline in the violence rate was both unexpected and welcome; some major cities such as New York report a significant decline of over 50% in their murder rates through the 1990s.

Although violence has tapered off in the 1990s, the number and rate of violent crime remain higher today than a decade ago. And while the number of murders has declined in the 1990s, it is also higher today than it was in 1983–1986, when fewer than 20,000 per year were being committed.

Property Crime Trends. The property crimes reported in the UCR include robbery, larceny, motor vehicle theft, and arson. In 1996 about 12 million property crimes were reported, a rate of about 4,500 per 100,000 population.

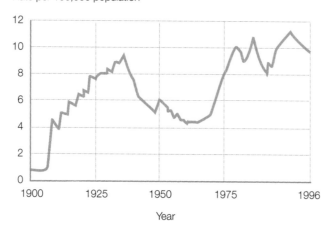

Rate per 100,000 population

Figure 2.2
**Homicide rate trends,
1900–1996.**
Source: UCR 1995, updated, 1996.

Like violent crime, property crime has declined since 1991. However, unlike the violent crime rate, property crimes did not undergo a rapid increase in the 1980s: Between 1981 and 1993, the number of property crimes increased less than 5%, compared to a more than 30% increase in violent crime. Of all property crimes, only motor vehicle theft showed appreciable gains during the past decade, increasing more than 20% in number. In contrast, the number of burglaries declined almost 20%. Because property crimes make up the bulk of reported crimes, the decline in the property crime rate over the past few years has resulted in stability in the overall crime rate.

While property crime rates have generally stabilized or declined, millions of offenses are still committed each year, far more than in other industrialized nations. A comparison of crime rates in the United States and other nations is made in the Analyzing Criminal Justice Issues box, "International Crime Trends."

Arrest Trends. The FBI also records the number of people arrested each year for both index and nonindex crimes. In 1995 about 15 million arrests were recorded, including almost 3 million for index crimes, a rate of about 5,800 per 100,000. These data do not necessarily mean that 5,800 Americans in every 100,000 are arrested each year, because an individual may have multiple arrests during a calendar year.

In the past five years, the number of arrests has increased 5%, and during the past ten years, the annual number of arrests has risen almost 17%. One reason for the decade-long increase in the arrest rate has been the crackdown on crime involving drugs. During the decade, drug abuse arrests rose more than 65%.

How successful are police agencies in solving reported crimes? To provide an answer, the FBI tallies crimes cleared by arrest (reported crimes in which at least one person is arrested and turned over for prosecution). The UCR indicates that police typically clear slightly more than 20% of all reported crimes, a rate that has remained stable over time.

Solving Crime

As Figure 2.3 shows (on page 50), police are able to "solve" (that is, arrest someone for) about three times as many violent crimes as property crimes (45% versus 18%). Victims of violent crime are usually able to describe or identify their assailant, most often because the perpetrator of a violent crime is likely to be a friend, acquaintance, or relative of the victim. Police departments generally devote more resources to solving violent crimes than property offenses.

UCR data consistently show that police are able to "solve" only one in five reported crimes. The inability of law enforcement agencies to improve arrest ratios has been one of the factors persuading police administrators to rethink the role of police as crime fighters and reorient their departments toward community service and neighborhood problem solving.[11]

International Crime Trends

How do crime rates in the United States compare with those in other nations? According to the Senate Judiciary Committee on Violence, the United States is "the most violent and self-destructive nation on earth." The Committee reports that the United States led the world with its murder, rape, and robbery rates, noting that the U.S. murder rate is 4 times as great as Italy's, 9 times England's, and twice that of war-torn Northern Ireland. The robbery rate in the United States was 47 times higher than that in Ireland and over 100 times greater than that in Greece! If the United States had the same murder rate as England's, it would have experienced 2,500 homicides, instead of about 20,000. Violence against women is a particularly serious problem. The rape rate in the United States is 8 times higher than in France, 15 times higher than in England, 20 times than in Portugal, 23 times than in Italy, and 46 times than in Greece.

Is the World Catching Up?

While the United States is still the "world leader" in violence, there is evidence of a disturbing upswing in violent crime abroad. For example, there has been a sharp increase in the murder rate in England, Germany, and Sweden. Racial assaults and hate crime have increased dramatically in Germany and England. Russia and the former Soviet republics have seen the rise of large-scale organized crime gangs that commonly use violence and intimidation.

Fueling the rise in European violence has been a dramatic growth in the number of illegal guns smuggled in from the former Soviet republics. Unrestrictive immigration has brought newcomers who face cultural differences, lack of job prospects, and racism. Social and economic pressures, including unemployment and cutbacks in the social welfare system.

Japanese citizens stand below a poster describing wanted suspects. Although crime rates in Europe and Asia are lower than those in the United States, they seem to be rapidly increasing. Does that mean that as nations modernize, industrialize, and become more affluent their crime rates will likewise increase?

Patterns of Crime

Part I and Part II arrest data can both be used to tell us a lot about the patterns of crime in our nation.[12] Some of the most important patterns are discussed here.

Ecological and Seasonal Differences. A distinct relationship exists between crime rates and urbanization. Areas with rural and suburban populations are more likely to have much lower crime rates than large urban areas. This finding, consistent over many years, suggests that the crime problem is linked to the social forces operating in the nation's largest cities—overcrowding, poverty, social inequality, narcotics use, and racial conflict. This pattern is illustrated by the fact

There have also been reports of increased criminal activity in Asia. For example, juvenile delinquency in the island nation of Singapore is on the rise—the number of arrests of young people more than doubled between 1991 and 1995. The delinquency increase is ironic considering that Singapore's draconian justice policies became notorious in 1993 when American teen Michael Fay was flogged after being convicted for vandalism.

Singapore is not alone among Asian nations experiencing an upsurge in crime. Authorities in Vietnam report a troubling increase in street crimes such as burglary and theft. Many crimes are drug related: There are an estimated 200,000 opium addicts in the country, and almost 50,000 acres of land are now being cultivated for growing the poppy from which heroin is produced. Although it is difficult to obtain accurate crime data from China, the world's largest nation seems to be going through a crackdown on criminal offending. In the first few months of 1996, Chinese courts sentenced more than 100,000 street criminals, including 1,000 given death sentences and many thousands more life in prison. During a single month (June 1996), 250 people were executed. The current wave of punishments is a response to a significant increase in street crimes, including robberies and drug trafficking.

Rising world crime rates may be tied in part to a rapid increase in the female crime rate. Countries such as Germany, France, Brazil, and India all report an increase in robberies and drug trafficking involving female offenders. In Italy, the 23-year-old daughter of a slain Mafia chieftain took over her father's criminal activities, a development that would be unheard of only a few years ago. While some nations (Poland, the Philippines, Argentina) have not experienced rising female crime rates, the trend is global, linked to the growing emancipation of women in developing countries. Thus, although crime rates are still comparably low overseas, these trends indicate that international crime rates may yet converge.

Critical Thinking Questions

1. What policies can be developed to bring the crime rate down in the United States? Is it feasible to tackle the social sources of crime by making families more cohesive, ending poverty, or reducing drug use?

2. Regardless of why crime rates are so high, might it not be possible to reduce them through aggressive law enforcement policies and the incapacitation of known criminals?

Sources: "With Women's Liberation Comes a Growing Involvement in Crime," *CJ International* 12 (1996): 19; "Crime Crackdown Continues as Statistics Increase," *CJ International* 12 (1996): 8; Sean Malinowski, "Battling and Emerging Crime Problem," *CJ International* 12 (1996): 3–4; "Singapore Says Delinquency Up," *Boston Globe,* 17 February 1996, p. 4; James Lynch, "A Serious Cross-National Comparison of the Length of Custodial Sentences for Crimes," *Justice Quarterly* 10 (1993); Gunther Kaiser, "Juvenile Delinquency in the Federal Republic of Germany," *International Journal of Comparative and Applied Criminal Justice* 16 (1992): 185–197; Marc Mauer, *Americans Behind Bars: The International Use of Incarceration* (Washington, D.C.: Sentencing Project, 1994); Elizabeth Neuffer, "Violent Crime Rise Fueling Fears in a Changing Europe," *Boston Globe,* 10 April 1994, p. 1; Committee on the Judiciary of the U.S. Senate, *Fighting Crime in America: An Agenda for the 1990s,* 12 March 1991.

that typically about 25% of all homicides occur in just seven cities: New York, Los Angeles, Chicago, Detroit, Houston, Philadelphia, and Washington, D.C. (although New York had a dramatic decrease in murders in 1995–1996).

UCR data also show that crime rates are highest in the summer months, most likely because people spend so much time outdoors and are less likely to secure their homes, and schools are closed and young people have greater opportunity for criminal activity. Crime rates are also related to the region of the country. The West and South usually have significantly higher rates than the Midwest and New England (see Figure 2.4).

Figure 2.3
Percentage of crimes cleared by arrest.
SOURCE: UCR, 1995.

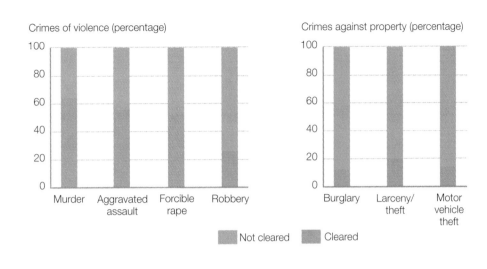

Crimes of violence (percentage)

Crimes against property (percentage)

Not cleared   Cleared

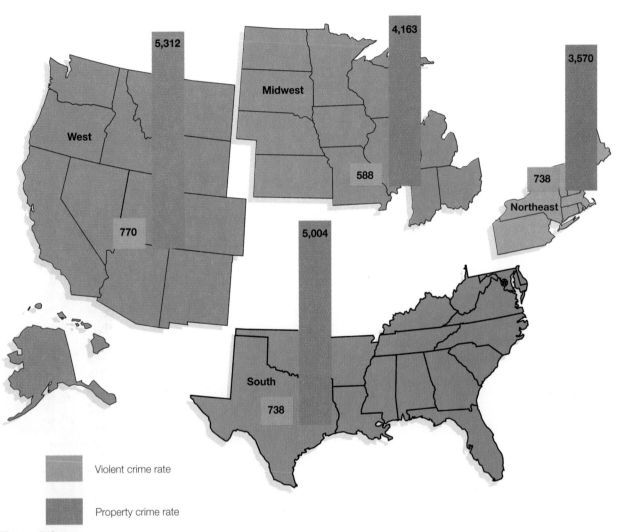

Violent crime rate

Property crime rate

Figure 2.4
Regional violent and property crime rates (per 100,000 inhabitants).
SOURCE: UCR, 1995.

Gender and Crime. UCR arrest data consistently show that males have a much higher crime rate than females. The overall arrest ratio is about three to one and approaches seven to one for violent crimes.

In the past decade, the female serious crime rate has risen almost three times as fast as that of males. While males arrests increased 12%, females arrests increased 38%, including an increase of 86% in violent crimes.

Some experts attribute this to the emergence of a "new female criminal" whose criminal activity mirrors the changing role of women in modern society.[13] As women's roles in the workplace have become more similar to men's, it is not surprising that their crime rates are converging. Others disagree and find that female emancipation has had relatively little influence on criminality. Criminologist Darrell Steffensmeier has found that gender-based crime rate differences remain significant and argues that the emancipation of women has had relatively little influence on female crime rates.[14] He disputes the fact that increases in the female arrest rate reflect economic or social change brought about by the women's movement. For one thing, many female criminals come from the socioeconomic class least affected by the women's movement; their crimes seem more a function of economic inequality than women's rights. It is possible, then, that women are being arrested more often today not because of changes in their crime rate but because police are more willing to arrest and formally process female offenders, a result of the feminist movement's call for equal treatment for men and women; this is referred to as the "chivalry hypothesis."[15]

Race and Crime. UCR arrest statistics also reveal distinct racial patterns in the crime rate. Overall, about 31% of all people arrested are African American, 67% are Anglo, and the remainder are split among Native Americans and Alaskans, Asians, and Pacific Islanders.

African Americans are arrested for murder, rape, and robbery at a rate higher than their relative representation in the population; an absolute majority of people arrested for murder and robbery are African Americans.

These data have proven to be controversial. Some criminologists argue that racial differences in the crime rate are caused by law enforcement practices that discriminate against African Americans.[16] In contrast, other experts view the official crime statistics as being an accurate reflection of the African American crime rate. Their view is that racism, differential opportunity, powerlessness, and other social problems in the United States have resulted in a higher African American crime rate as an expression of anger and frustration.[17] African Americans also have a significantly greater chance of being the target of violence. Nonwhites at birth are more than five times as likely to become murder victims as whites. These data indicate why the crime problem is of special significance for the black community.

Social Class and Crime. Researchers have used UCR data in conjunction with census data to determine whether crime is associated with poverty, unemployment, and lower-class status.[18] Official data seem to indicate that crime rates are highest in deprived, inner-city slum areas and that the level of poverty in an area can predict its crime rate.[19]

A number of explanations have been offered for the association between social class and official crime rates. One view is that the social forces in a high-risk, socially disorganized neighborhood—poverty, dilapidated housing, poor schools, broken families, drugs, and street gangs—significantly increase the likelihood that residents will engage in criminality.[20] As the social system in decayed urban areas breaks down and the rule of law becomes a distant threat, slum neighborhoods attract criminals and deviants who find the decayed environment suitable for their law-violating behavior. The moral vacuum of the slum acts as a magnet for deviants and undesirables who help conditions grow steadily worse.[21]

Another view is that crime rates are high in deteriorated areas where the disadvantaged and the affluent live side by side. In these neighborhoods, social differences are magnified, and less affluent residents perceive a feeling of relative deprivation. This perception of social inequality results in a higher crime rate.[22]

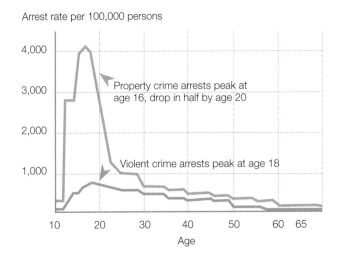

Arrest rate per 100,000 persons

Property crime arrests peak at age 16, drop in half by age 20

Violent crime arrests peak at age 18

Some criminologists still question whether a class-crime relationship really exists. It is possible that the poor are arrested more often than the affluent because police are more likely to patrol in underclass areas and apprehend lower-class criminals. While the class-crime relationship has been the subject of almost constant research, the true association between these variables is far from determined.[23] However, the consensus of opinion is that a significant relationship exists between class position and crime and that the indigent are more likely to violate the law than the affluent.

Age and Crime. UCR arrest data consistently show a significant relationship between age and crime: Young people between the ages of 15 and 25 are responsible for an overwhelming number of all arrests; in contrast, people aged 60 and over are relatively crime-free. Figure 2.5 compares age and arrest data. The peak age for property crime is about 16, and for violence, it is 18. Almost half of all serious crime arrests involve people ages 24 and under; in contrast, people over 45 accounted for only about 7.3% of all arrests.

How can the age-crime relationship be explained? One factor is lifestyle; many young people are part of a youth culture that favors risk taking, short-run hedonism, and other behaviors that may involve them in law violation. Youths have limited financial resources and may resort to theft and drug dealing for income. The high-risk lifestyle of most youths ends as they mature and become involved in forming a family and a career.[24] Some adolescents may desist from crime when they begin to understand that the chances of winning friends, happiness, and wealth via crime are limited. A more simple explanation is biological: Young people have the energy, strength, and physical skill needed to commit crime, all of which erode with age.[25]

While there is little disagreement that young people are more crime-prone than the middle-aged, the association between age and crime has proven to be one of enduring controversy. One view is that all people commit less crime as they age. That is, regardless of race, gender, class, or any other personal characteristic, younger persons commit more crime than older ones.[26] Even high-risk offenders and drug addicts eventually slow down. They may continue to commit crime in their maturity, but the frequency of their law violations is lower than in their youth.[27]

Another view is that while it is true that most offenders reduce their criminal activity as they age, there is a group who enter into a life of crime early in their adolescence and maintain a high rate of criminal violations throughout their life span.[28] These **chronic offenders** are immune to both the ravages of age and the punishments of the justice system. More important, this small group may be responsible for a significant portion of all serious criminal behavior.[29]

Are the Uniform Crime Reports Accurate?

There is no question that the FBI and many of its contributing law enforcement agencies have made a serious attempt to measure the incidence and amount of crime and delinquency in the United States. Nonetheless, a great deal of criticism has been directed at the actual validity of the national crime statistics and official statistics in general. Two issues most disturb critics: (1) the failure or refusal of many citizens to report criminal acts to police and (2) the problems caused by variations in law enforcement practices.

Crime victims are believed to report fewer than half of all criminal acts to police. Their reasons are varied. Many individuals in lower-class areas neglect to carry property insurance and therefore believe it is useless to report theft-related offenses to police since "nothing can be done." In other cases, victims may fail to notify police because they fear reprisals from friends or family members of the offenders.[30] Rape victims may not report the crime if they fear negative reactions from family and friends. Assaults also go unreported if victims feel they are a private matter. People do not report such crimes as robbery, burglary, and larceny if they believe that nothing could be done and that the victimization is "not important enough" to interest the police.

The UCR may also suffer because police departments make errors when they record and report criminal activity. The manner in which police interpret the definitions of index crimes may affect reporting practices.[31] For example, it is possible that local police departments make systematic errors in UCR reporting.[32] Some may overlook crimes, while others count acts as crimes when in fact no crime actually occurred; for example, a lost wallet may be reported stolen. There are also regional differences in the way crimes are defined; what may be a burglary in one state is considered a breaking and entering in another. The frequency of one index crime—arson—may be seriously underreported because many fire departments do not report suspicious fires to the UCR and those that do exclude many fires that are probably set by arsonists.[33]

Other reasons used to question the accuracy of the UCR include the fact that no federal crimes are reported, reports are voluntary and vary in accuracy and completeness, and not all police departments submit reports. Each act is listed as a single offense for some crimes but not others. For example, if a man robbed six people in a bar, the offense is listed as one robbery; but if he assaulted or murdered them, it would be listed as six assaults or six murders. And if multiple crimes are committed by an offender, only the most serious is recorded. If an addict rapes, robs, and murders a victim, only the murder is recorded as a crime. And, in some crime categories, uncompleted acts are lumped together with completed ones.[34]

Because of these and other problems, justice experts often question the validity of the UCR as a source for criminal justice research. However, the UCR is still a useful source of crime data.[35] While it is true that many crimes are not reported to the police, the unreported crimes tend to be the less serious ones that may not even satisfy the legal requirements of criminality. Research shows that the police are in general agreement about what a "serious" crime entails: it involves bodily injury; it involves a significant amount of lost property; it is committed by a stranger; it involves breaking and entering. When the criminal act meets one or more of these criteria, it has a good chance of being reported to the FBI.[36]

Even if the number of reported crimes is less than the total number of crimes committed, the overall reliability of the UCR makes it a valuable source of crime data. Because measurement errors are most likely constant over time, the UCR's ability to identify trends and patterns in the crime rate is probably more accurate than its ability to count the exact number of crimes committed annually. Because crime is counted in a consistent fashion, if the UCR says crime increased 20% between 1985 and 1997, we might not be sure how many crimes were committed in those years but we would be confident that more crimes were committed in 1997 than in 1985 and that the increase was about 20%.

Revising the UCR

To help improve the quality of UCR statistics, the FBI is revising the report form and content to provide more detailed information on individual criminal incidents. It is planned that instead of submitting statements of reported crimes and summary statements of resulting arrests, local police agencies will provide at least a brief account of each incident within the existing Part I crime categories. Police agencies will provide detailed reports on 23 crime patterns, including incident, victim, and offender information. Crime categories in which expanded information will be provided include such new areas as blackmail and bribery. These additional data will allow development of a national database on the nature of crime, victims, and criminals. More stringent auditing techniques will be imposed to ensure the accuracy and completeness of the material being submitted by the police.[37]

When implemented, the new UCR program may bring about greater uniformity in cross-jurisdictional reporting and improve the accuracy of official crime data. While three jurisdictions are already participating in the revised program, full national data are not available at the time of this writing.

Self-Report Data

While the UCR is the most significant method of measuring crime rates and trends, it does not measure important criminal behaviors, such as drug use, nor does it tell us much about individual criminals. Consequently, another method of collecting crime data, called **self-report surveys,** has been developed. Self-report surveys ask respondents to tell about their criminal and deviant activities. Typically, these surveys are distributed to large groups of people to guarantee the anonymity of respondents. Self-report surveys have often been used in schools to measure the delinquent activity of youths, but they may also be used with adults, such as prison inmates, to measure their criminal behaviors.

A typical self-report instrument provides a list of criminal acts and asks the subjects to indicate how often in the past year (or in their lifetime) they have participated in each act (see Table 2.2). Sometimes for a single study self-report

Table 2.2
Self-Report Survey Questions

Please indicate how often in the past 12 months you did each act. (Check the best answer.)	Never did act	One time	2–5 times	6–9 times	10+ times
Stole something worth less than $50	——	——	——	——	——
Stole something worth more than $50	——	——	——	——	——
Used cocaine	——	——	——	——	——
Been in a fistfight	——	——	——	——	——
Carried a weapon such as a gun or knife	——	——	——	——	——
Fought someone using a weapon	——	——	——	——	——
Stole a car	——	——	——	——	——
Used force to steal					
(For boys) Forced a girl to have sexual relations against her will	——	——	——	——	——

surveys will be distributed to thousands of people chosen randomly in various sites around the United States.

Self-report studies have two main advantages: (1) they measure the so-called "dark figures" of crime—such acts as drug use, gambling, and alcohol abuse, which often are not reported in official data sources and victimization surveys—and (2) they can be used to collect personal information from offenders, such as intelligence level, attitudes, values, and family relationships, that is unavailable from other crime data sources.

What do self-report studies tell us? Overall, they reinforce the fact that crime is much more common than the UCR indicates.[38] Adolescents report significant and widespread involvement in delinquent activity and drug abuse. Self-report studies indicate that youth crime is spread throughout society: lower-, middle-, and upper-class kids all use drugs, engage in theft, and damage property.[39] When truancy, alcohol consumption, petty theft, and recreational drug use are included in self-report scales, almost everyone tested is found to have violated some law. Furthermore, self-report surveys dispute the notion that criminals and delinquents specialize in one type of crime or another; offenders seem to engage in a "mixed bag" of crime and deviance.[40]

It has been estimated that almost 90% of all youths commit delinquent and criminal acts. It is not unusual for self-report surveys to find combined substance abuse, theft, violence, and damage rates of more than 50% among suburban, rural, and urban high school youths. What is surprising is the consistency of these findings in samples taken from southern, eastern, midwestern, and western states.

When the results of recent self-report surveys are compared with various studies conducted over a 20-year period, a uniform pattern emerges. The use of drugs and alcohol increased markedly in the 1970s and then leveled off in the 1980s and began to increase in the 1990s; the rates of theft, violence, and damage-related crimes seem more stable. Although a self-reported crime wave has not occurred, neither has there been any visible reduction in self-reported criminality.

One of the most important sources of self-report data is the annual national survey of over 2,500 high school seniors conducted by the Institute for Social Research (ISR) at the University of Michigan.[41] The data from a recent ISR survey presented in Figure 2.6 show that young people commit a great deal of crime: About one-third of high school seniors reported stealing something in the last 12 months, 10% stole something worth more than $50, 29% admitted shoplifting, and 24% engaged in breaking and entering. High school kids also engaged in violent acts: 15% got into serious fights, and 13% said they had injured someone badly. ISR surveys conducted during the past decade indicate that the extent of self-reported delinquency has been quite stable over time. The fact that at least one-third of all U.S. high school students engaged in theft and 20% committed a violent act during the past year shows that criminal activity is widespread and not restricted to a few "bad apples."

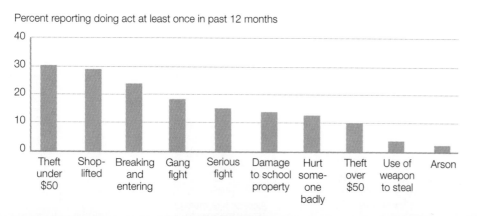

Percent reporting doing act at least once in past 12 months

Figure 2.6
Self-reported delinquent acts.

SOURCE: Institute for Social Research, *Monitoring the Future, 1995* (Ann Arbor: University of Michigan, 1996).

Self-Reported Drug Use

Probably the most important use of self-report surveys has been to monitor adolescent drug abuse. ISR researchers have conducted a survey of about 17,000 high school seniors each year since 1975, asking them about their lifetime and current drug usage.[42] In recent years, the survey has expanded and now includes kids in the 8th and 10th grades (this expansion means that the national survey now contains kids who might drop out before the 12th grade).

The data indicate that since 1980, U.S. students have significantly decreased the extent and frequency of their drug use. Far fewer kids today use drugs than in 1980. Reductions have been observed in the use of the most common drug types, including cocaine, marijuana, and stimulants (such as amphetamines). Similar trends have been recorded in daily and monthly drug usage.

Although the lifetime use of all drugs has declined from a high point in the late 1970s and early '80s, when more than half of all students had tried drugs, it has once again begun to increase in the 1990s. What is most disturbing is that the proportion of 8th-graders having used any illicit drug in the 12 months prior to the survey doubled between 1991 and 1996. Since 1992 the proportion of students in 10th grade taking drugs rose more than two-thirds, and by half among 12th graders. As Figure 2.7 indicates drug use is still a significant problem among adolescents.

Figure 2.7
Lifetime use of selected drugs by grade, 1996.

SOURCE: Institute for Social Research, *Monitoring the Future, 1995* (Ann Arbor: University of Michigan, 1996).

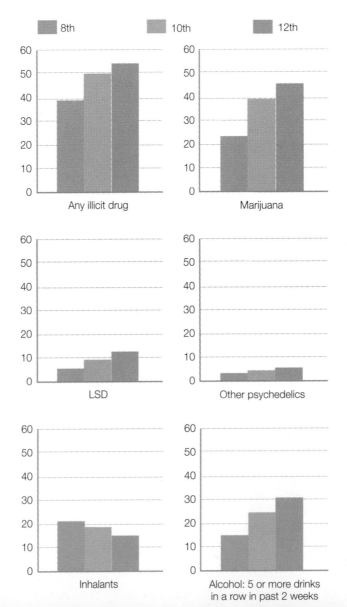

Drug use remains a major social problem. Even if the overall rate of drug abuse has declined, there is still reason for great concern. Here an antidrug rally takes place in Exposition Park in Los Angeles. Can public opinion sway drug users? Or are such rallies directed at influencing government agencies to put more resources into controlling drugs?

While the ISR survey indicates that drug use is increasing, the results must be interpreted with caution. Drug users may boastfully overinflate the extent of their substance abuse, underreport out of fear, or simply be unaware or forgetful. Another problem is that the survey misses kids who are institutionalized and may be heavy drug users; it is also possible that the heaviest drug users simply refuse or are unable to answer surveys.

While these lapses are troubling, because the ISR survey is administered yearly, in a consistent fashion, any sources of inaccuracy are consistent over time. That is, overreporting and underreporting and missing subjects should have a consistent effect in every survey year. Consequently, the ISR survey is probably a reliable indicator of drug use trends in the general population.

Drug use remains a major social problem. Even if the overall rate of drug abuse has declined since the 1970s, there is still reason for great concern. First, even assuming that substance abuse has dropped, millions of young Americans still use illicit drugs every month, and, if anything, this number is most likely underreported. That so many high school students regularly drink, smoke, and take drugs and that usage is increasing indicates that continued efforts are required in the fight against substance abuse.

The ISR's research on drug use illustrates how self-report surveys can be used to collect important information that is otherwise unobtainable and that may diverge sharply from the impression promoted in the media and accepted by the general public.

On the receiving end of crime are its victims. For many years, victims and victimization were not considered important topics for criminal justice study. Victims were viewed as the passive receptors of a criminal's anger, greed, or frustration; they were simply in the wrong place at the wrong time. In the late 1960s, a number of pioneering studies found that victims actually could tell us a lot about the crime problem and that, contrary to popular belief, the victim's role is an important one in the crime process.[43] This early research encouraged development of the most widely used and most extensive victim survey to date, the National Crime Victimization Survey.[44]

The NCVS is conducted by the Bureau of Justice Statistics of the U.S. Department of Justice in cooperation with the U.S. Bureau of the Census. This national survey uses a complex, multistage sampling technique to choose a sample

Are Drug Surveys Valid?

Victimization Data: The NCVS

of about 60,000 households, containing about 120,000 individuals over 12 years of age. Respondents are asked about their experiences as victims of crimes, including personal and household larcenies, burglary, motor vehicle theft, assault, robbery, and rape. This large sample can then be used to create estimates of crime and victimization occurring in the United States as a whole. The interview completion rate in the national sample is about 95% or more of those selected to be interviewed in any given period. Because the response rate is so high, the population estimates are expected to be relatively accurate.

In 1992 the NCVS was redesigned to improve its validity. One important change is that victims are now asked directly if they had been raped or sexually assaulted. In the past, rape was indirectly surveyed with the question "Did anything else happen to you?" The redesign significantly altered the number of reported incidents because it changed the format in which questions were asked, prompted respondents to remember details of victim incidents, and created some heretofore unknown categories such as nonrape sexual assaults. Because of the redesign, the total number of victimizations reported jumped by more than 10 million over previous years, making long-term comparisons difficult.

Victimization in the United States

According to the most recently available NCVS data (1995), about 40 million personal crimes occur each year. A stable but steady decrease has occurred in the total number of victimizations in the 1990s, a finding that reflects the official crime (UCR) data. For example, between 1993 and 1995 the number of victimizations declined by about 4 million, or almost 10%. The decline in violent crimes measured by the NCVS has been even greater than that recorded by the UCR. Especially encouraging was the significant decline of 18% in reported rapes in a single year (1994–1995).

While its decline mirrors recent UCR trends, it is quite apparent that the number of crimes accounted for by the NCVS is considerably larger than the number of crimes reported to the FBI. For example, while the UCR recorded about 540,000 robberies in 1995, the NCVS estimates that about 1.1 million actually occurred. The reason for such discrepancies is that fewer than half of the violent crimes, less than one-third the personal theft crimes (such as pocket picking), and fewer than half of the household thefts are reported to police. The reasons most often given by victims for not reporting crime include believing that "nothing can be done about it," that it was a "private matter," or that they did not want to "get involved." Victims seem to report to the police only crimes that involve considerable loss or injury. If we are to believe NCVS findings, the official statistics do not provide an accurate picture of the crime problem, as many crimes go unreported to the police.

Victim Characteristics

Several social and demographic characteristics distinguish victims from nonvictims. The most important of these involve gender, age, income, marital status, and race.

Gender. The NCVS provides information on the background characteristics of the victims of crime. Gender affects victimization risk. Men are much more likely than women to be victims of robbery and aggravated assault; they are also more likely to experience theft, but the differences are less pronounced. While women are far more likely to be the victim of sexual assault (3.7 per 1,000), the NCVS estimates that 0.2 males are assaulted per 1,000 population; assuming a male population of 125 million, that means more than 20,000 males are raped or sexually assaulted each year.

When men are the victim of violent crime, the perpetrator is described as a stranger. Women are much more likely to be attacked by a relative than men; about two-thirds of all attacks against women were committed by a husband or boyfriend, family member, or acquaintance. In two-thirds of sexual assaults, the victim knew the attacker.

Age. Young people face a much greater victimization risk than older persons do. Victim risk diminishes rapidly after age 25. The elderly, who are thought of as being the helpless targets of predatory criminals, are actually much safer than their grandchildren. People over 65, who make up 14% of the population, account for 1% of violent victimizations; teens 12–19, who also make up 14% of the population, account for 32% of crime victims.

The association between age and victimization may be bound up in the lifestyle shared by young people. Adolescents often stay out late at night, go to public places, and hang out with other kids who have a high risk of criminal involvement. Most adolescents ages 12 to 19 are attacked by offenders in the same age category, while a great majority of adults are victimized by adult criminals. Teens face a high victimization risk because they spend a great deal of time in the most dangerous building in the community: the local schoolhouse!

A recent survey of state correctional inmates underscores the risks faced by young people. About 19% of all state inmates surveyed had committed a crime against a person under 18 years of age; 20% of violent criminals had committed a crime against children. About 7 of 10 offenders with child victims reported that they had been imprisoned for a rape or sexual assault.

Income. The poorest Americans might be expected to be the most likely victims of crime, since they live in areas that are crime-prone: inner-city, urban neighborhoods. The NCVS does in fact show that the least affluent (annual incomes of less than $7,500) are by far the most likely to be victims of violent crimes, and this association occurs across all gender, racial, and age groups. While the poor are almost twice as likely to be the victims of burglary, the wealthy are more likely to be the target of theft crimes, such as pocket picking and purse snatching. Perhaps the affluent, who sport more expensive attire and drive better-make cars, earn the attention of thieves looking for attractive targets.

Victim data suggest that thieves choose their targets carefully, selecting those who seem best able to provide them with a substantial haul. In contrast, the targets of violence are among the nation's poorest people. And while the wealthy face a higher rate of personal theft, the poorest are the most likely to be the victim of burglaries, most likely because they live in close proximity to their attackers.

Marital Status. Marital status also influences victimization risk. The unmarried or never married are victimized more often than married people or widows and widowers. These relationships are probably influenced by age, gender, and lifestyle. Many of the young people who have the highest victim risk are actually too young to have been married. Younger, unmarried people also go out in public more often and interact with high-risk peers, increasing their exposure to victimization. In contrast, widows, who are more likely to be older females, suffer much lower victimization rates because they interact with older people, are more likely to stay home at night, and avoid public places. These data are further evidence of the relationship between lifestyle and victimization risk.

Race. One of the most important distinctions found in the NCVS data is the racial differences in the victim rate. African Americans experience violent crimes at a higher rate than other groups. NCVS data show that African American citizens have strikingly higher rates of violent personal crimes than whites. While the race-specific risk of theft victimization is more similar, African Americans are still more likely to be victimized than whites.

Crimes committed against African Americans tend to be more serious than those committed against whites. For example, African Americans experience higher rates of aggravated assault, while whites were more often the victims of simple assault. The most striking difference recorded by the NCVS is in the incidence of robberies: African Americans are about three times as likely to become robbery victims as whites.

Young African American males are also at great risk for homicide victimization. They face a murder risk 4 or 5 times greater than that of young African American females, 5 to 8 times higher than that of young white males, and 16 to 22 times higher than that of young white females. A longitudinal analysis conducted by the Centers for Disease Control indicates that the murder victimization rate of African American males is increasing at a much faster pace than for these other groups.[45]

Why do these discrepancies exist? Young black males tend to live in the nation's largest cities in areas beset by alcohol and drug abuse, poverty, racial discrimination, and violence. Forced to live in the nation's most dangerous areas, their lifestyle places them in the highest at-risk population group.

The Ecology of Victimization

The NCVS data parallel the crime patterns found in the UCR. Most victimizations occur in large urban areas; rural and suburban victim rates are far lower. Most incidents occur during the evening hours (6 P.M. to 6 A.M.). Generally, more serious crimes take place after 6 P.M.; less serious, before 6 P.M. For example, aggravated assaults occur at night, while simple assaults are more likely to take place during the daytime.

The most likely site for a victimization, especially a violent crime such as rape, robbery, and aggravated assault, is an open, public area, such as a street, park, or field. Sadly, one of the most dangerous public places is a public school building. About 10% of all U.S. youth ages 12 to 19 (approximately 2 million kids) are crime victims while on schoolgrounds each year.[46] It seems that the best way to avoid victimization is to stay home at night with the doors and windows locked!

An overwhelming number of victimizations involve a single person. Most victims report that their assailant was not armed (except for the crime of robbery, where about half the offenders carry weapons). In the robberies and assaults involving injury, however, a majority of the assailants are reported as armed. The use of guns and knives is about equal, and there does not seem to be a pattern of a particular weapon being used for a particular crime.

Victims and Their Criminal

The NCVS data can tell us something about the characteristics of people who commit crime. Of course, this information is available only on criminals who actually came in contact with the victim through such crimes as rape, assault, or robbery.

Most offenders and victims did not know each other; about 50% of all violent crimes are committed by strangers. However, women seem much more likely than men to be victimized by acquaintances. In fact, a majority of female assault victims know their assailants. In all, about 50% of all violent crimes are committed by people who were known to their victim, including family members, spouses, parents, children, and siblings.

A majority of victims report that the crime was committed by a single offender over the age of 20. About one-fourth of victims indicate that their assailant was a young person 12 to 20 years of age. This may reflect the criminal activities of youth gangs and groups in the United States.

Whites are the offenders in a majority of single-offender rapes and assaults, while there is no racial pattern in single-offender robberies. However, multiple-offender robberies are more likely committed by African Americans.

The NCVS has recently begun to ask victims if their assailants were under the influence of drugs or alcohol. In response, victims report that substance use was involved in 30% of the violent crime incidents, including 40% of the rapes and 30% of the assaults.[47]

The NCVS data suggest that the risk of becoming a crime victim over one's lifetime is a function of personal characteristics and lifestyle. Victimization risk can be increased by being in public places in urban areas late at night. Victimization can be reduced by moving to a suburb and avoiding public places in the evening. The NCVS, then, seems to be indicating that the likelihood of a crime occurring depends, to some extent, on victim behavior.

Repeat Victimization

Does prior victimization enhance or reduce the chances of future victimization? It is possible that there are stable patterns of behavior that encourage victimization and that a few people who maintain them become "chronic victims," constantly the target of predatory crimes. It is also possible that "once burnt, twice shy": People who have been victimized take precautions to limit their risk.

Most research efforts do in fact show that prior victimization is a strong predictor of future victimization: Individuals who have had prior victimization experiences have a significantly higher chance of repeat victimization than people who have been nonvictims.[48] Research shows that households that have experienced victimization in the past are the ones most likely to experience it again.[49] Repeat victimizations are most likely to occur in areas with high crime rates, and they account for a significant portion of all criminal acts. One study found that during a four-year period 40% of all trauma patients in an urban medical center in Ohio were repeat victims.[50]

What factors predict chronic victimizations? It is possible that some combination of personal and social factors encourages victimization risk. Most revictimizations happen soon after a previous crime, suggesting that repeat victims share some personal characteristic that makes them a magnet for predators.[51] For example, kids who are shy, physically weak, or socially isolated may be prone to being bullied in the schoolyard.[52]

Repeat victimization may also be a function of rational choice and offender decision making: Offenders "learn" the weaknesses of victims and use them over and over again. For example, the abusive husband finds out that his battered wife will not call police and repeatedly victimizes her; when police do not respond to reported hate crimes the perpetrators learn they have little to fear from the law.[53]

Critique of the NCVS

Like the UCR, the NCVS and all other victim surveys suffer from some methodological problems, so their findings must be interpreted with caution. Among the problems are

1. Overreporting due to victims' misinterpretation of events. For example, a lost wallet is reported as stolen, or an open door is viewed as a burglary attempt.

2. Underreporting due to embarrassment in reporting crime to interviewers, fear of getting into trouble, or simply forgetting an incident.

3. Inability to record the personal criminal activity of those interviewed, such as drug use or gambling.[54]

Are the Data Sources Compatible?

Are the various sources of criminal statistics compatible? Each has its own strengths and weaknesses. The UCR is carefully tallied and contains data on the number of murders and people arrested that the other sources lack, yet it omits the many crimes that victims choose not to report to the police. The NCVS contains important information on the personal characteristics of victims and unreported crimes, but the data consist of population estimates made from relatively limited samples (about 100,000) so that even narrow fluctuations in the reporting rates of some crimes can have a major impact on findings; the NCVS is also subject to inaccurate reporting by victims. Self-report surveys can provide important information on the personal characteristics of offenders, unavailable from any other source. Yet at their core, self-report surveys rely on the honesty of criminal offenders, a population not normally known for accuracy and integrity.

Despite these differences, a number of prominent criminologists have found that the various sources of crime data are more compatible than was first believed.

For example, while the absolute numbers of crimes recorded by the three data sources do not coincide, the crime patterns, changes, and fluctuations they record are often quite similar.[55] For example, all three sources are in general agreement about the personal characteristics of serious criminals, where and when crime occurs, and general crime patterns.

Despite similarities, comparing the data sources can sometimes result in confusing and contradictory findings. Because each source of crime data uses a different method to obtain results, differences inevitably occur between them. These differences must be carefully considered when interpreting the data on the nature of and trends in crime.

Explaining Crime Trends

What factors produce increases or decreases in the crime rate? How can the recent decline in the violence rate be explained? Why did crime increase in the 1980s and decline in the 1990s? A number of critical factors have been used to explain crime rate trends; a few of the most important are discussed here.

Younger Criminals

Criminologists view change in the age distribution of the population as having the greatest influence on recent violent crime trends: As a general rule, the crime rate follows the proportion of young males in the population. The postwar baby-boom generation reached their teenage years in the 1960s, just as the crime rate began a sharp increase. Since both the victims and perpetrators of crime tend to fall in the 18–25 age category, the rise in crime reflected the age structure of society. With the "graying" of society in the 1980s and a decline in the birth rate, it was not surprising that the overall crime rate declined between 1990 and 1996. The number of juveniles should be increasing over the next decade, and some criminologists fear a return to escalating crime rates.

Despite the recent dip in juvenile violence rates, this generation of teens seem more violent than earlier cohorts. Between 1970 and 1996, the rate of adolescents arrested for homicide *more than doubled,* while homicide arrest rates for adults actually *declined.*[56] It remains to be seen whether teenage crime rates will continue their upward progression; stabilization would substantially lower crime rates, as teens make up a significant proportion of offenders.

Economic Problems

There is still debate over the effects of the economy on crime rates. Some experts believe that a poor economy actually helps to lower crime rates! Unemployed parents are at home to supervise children and guard their homes. Because there is less money to spend, a poor economy means that there are actually fewer valuables around worth stealing. And it seems unlikely that law-abiding, middle-aged workers will suddenly turn to a life of crime if they are laid off during an economic downturn.

If economic weakness and unemployment is sustained for a long period, it may eventually influence crime rates. A long-term economic recession, such as the one that occurred in the late 1980s, may have produced the climate of hopelessness in the nation's largest cities that increased violence rates between 1985 and 1990. Teenage unemployment rates were especially high. The improving national economy in the 1990s coincides with a decrease in crime.

Social Problems

As the level of social problems increases, so, too, do crime rates. Increases in the number of single-parent families, in divorce and dropout rates, in nonrecreational drug use, and in teen pregnancies may also influence crime rates. Cross-national research indicates that child homicide rates are greatest in those nations, including the United States, that have the highest rates of illegitimacy and teenage mothers.[57] As illegitimacy rates rise and social spending is cut, the rate of violent crime might trend upward. Social malaise may explain why some cities and regions have higher crime rates than others.

Firearms

The availability of firearms may influence the crime rate. There is evidence that more guns than ever before are finding their way into the hands of young people. The number of juveniles arrested on weapons charges rose 75% between 1986 and 1995.[58] Joseph Sheley and James Wright conducted a comprehensive analysis of data acquired from 835 male inmates in six correctional facilities and 758 male students in ten inner-city high schools. More than half of the high school students had friends who owned guns, and 42% routinely carried them around outside the home! Sheley and Wright also found a disturbing trend of gun ownership and use among both inmates (86%) and students (30%).[59]

Gangs

Another factor may be the explosive growth in teenage gangs. Surveys indicate that there are more than 500,000 gang members in the United States. There has been an upswing in gang violence. For example, Chicago, which had never experienced more than 88 gang homicides prior to 1990, had 240 in 1994 and almost as many in 1995.[60] One reason is that there is a clear connection between gang membership and firearm use. Gang boys engage in a far higher level of firearm possession than other boys, and gang members participate in firearm-related activity much more often than nonmembers.

Drugs

Increasing drug use may affect crime rates. According to Alfred Blumstein, groups and gangs involved in the urban drug trade recruit juveniles because they work cheaply, are immune from heavy criminal penalties, and are "daring and willing to take risks."[61] Arming themselves for protection, these drug-dealing kids present a menace that persuades neighborhood adolescents to arm themselves for protection. The result is an "arms race" that produces an increasing spiral of violence.

Some experts tie increases in the violent crime rate between 1980 and 1990 to the "crack cocaine" epidemic that swept the nation's largest cities at that time and the drug-trafficking gangs that fought over "drug turf." These well-armed gangs did not hesitate to use violence to control territories, intimidate rivals, and increase "market share." With the waning of the crack epidemic (users are now switching to heroin), violence seems to have subsided in New York City and other metropolitan areas where the crack epidemic was rampant.[62]

Some law enforcement experts have suggested that reduction in crime rates may be attributed to aggressive police practices that target "quality of life" crimes such as panhandling, graffiti, petty drug dealing, and loitering. By showing that even the smallest infractions will be dealt with seriously, aggressive police departments may be able to discourage potential criminals from committing even more serious crimes.

It is also possible that tough laws targeting drug dealing and repeat offenders with lengthy prison terms can have an effect on crime rates. The fear of punishment may inhibit some would-be criminals. Lengthy sentences also help boost the nation's prison population. It is possible that placing a significant number of potentially high-rate offenders behind bars helps stabilize crime rates.

What the Future Holds

It is always risky to speculate about the future of crime trends, since current conditions can change rapidly. But some criminologists have gone out on a limb to predict future patterns. Darrell Steffensmeier and Miles Harer suggest that violent crime will drop during the remainder of the 1990s as the baby boomers pass into middle and old age; they speculate that the property crime rate will at first decline, then level off and begin rising toward the end of the decade as the baby-boomlet kids born in the early 1980s begin to hit their "peak" crime years. After the year 2000, they predict both property and violent crimes will increase.[63] Steffensmeier and Harer believe that the age structure of society is the single most powerful influence on the crime rate.

In a similar vein, criminologist James A. Fox predicts a significant increase in teen violence if current trends persist. As of 1996, there were 39 million children in the country under age 10, more than we have had for decades. Many of them lacking stable families and adequate supervision, these kids will soon be entering their "prime crime" years. As a result, Fox predicts a wave of youth violence that will be even worse than that of the past ten years. If current trends persist, the number of juvenile homicides should grow from less than 4,000 today to about 9,000 in 2004.[64] Of course, such predictions are based on population trends and can be thrown off by changes in the economy, justice policy, drug use, gun availability, gang membership trends, and other sociocultural forces. Fox suggests that if social conditions worsen, teen homicide might increase even more. It is also possible that current national outrage over violent crime will help make violence so unpalatable that local residents will be willing to take drastic actions to reduce crime, including cooperating with the police and pressuring neighborhood families to control their adolescent children.

Why Do People Commit Crime?

While the various sources of criminal statistics can tell us about the *nature* of crime patterns and trends, it is also important to know *why* an individual commits crime in the first place. Such knowledge is critical if programs are to be devised to deter or prevent crime. If, for example, people commit crime because they are poor and desperate, the key to crime prevention might be a job program and government economic aid. If, however, the root cause of crime is a poor family life marked by conflict and abuse, then providing jobs will not help bring down the crime rate; family counseling and parenting skills courses would prove to be more effective.

There is still a great deal of uncertainty about the "real" cause of crime. Some of the more popular explanations are discussed in the following sections.

Because They Want To: Choice Theory

One prominent view of criminality is that people choose to commit crime after weighing the potential benefits and consequences of their criminal acts. According to this **choice theory,** people commit crime if they believe it will provide immediate benefits without the threat of long-term risks. For example, before concluding a drug sale, experienced traffickers will mentally balance the chances of making a large profit with the consequences of being apprehended and punished for drug dealing. They know that most drug deals are not detected and that the potential for enormous, untaxed profits is great. They evaluate their lifestyle and determine how much cash they need to maintain their standard of living, which is usually extravagant. They may have borrowed to finance the drug deal, and their creditors are not usually reasonable if loans cannot be repaid promptly. They also realize that they could be the target of a "sting" operation by undercover agents and, if caught, will get a long mandatory sentence in a forbidding federal penitentiary. If they conclude that the potential for profits is great enough, their need for cash urgent, and the chances of apprehension minimal, they will carry out the deal. If, however, they believe that the transaction will bring them only a small profit and a large risk of apprehension and punishment, they may forgo the deal as too risky. Crime, then, is a matter of personal choice.

According to this view, crimes are events that occur when offenders decide to risk crime after considering personal needs (a desire for money, excitement, experience, or revenge), situational factors (how well a target is protected, the risk of apprehension, the chance for hurting bystanders), and legal factors (the efficiency of police, the threat of legal punishment, the effect of a prior criminal record on future punishment). The decision to commit a specific crime is thus a matter of personal decision making based on a weighing of available information.[65]

The main principles of choice theory are

1. All people of their own free will can choose between conventional or criminal behaviors.

2. For some people, criminal solutions are more attractive because they require less effort for greater gain.

3. People will refrain from antisocial acts if they believe that the punishment or pain they will receive for their actions will be greater than any potential gain.

4. The punishments threatened by the existing criminal law are the primary deterrent to crime.

In recent years, there has been interest in finding a biological basis of crime. **Biological theories** can be divided into three broad areas of focus: biochemical factors, neurological problems, and genetic influence.

Biochemical Factors. It is possible that crime and violence are functions of biochemical abnormality. Such biochemical factors as vitamin and mineral deficiencies, improper diet, environmental contaminants, and allergies have been linked to antisocial behavior.[66] Research focusing on the behavior of jailed inmates has shown that subjects who maintain high levels of sugar and caffeine in their diet are more likely to engage in antisocial behavior than control-group subjects with diets low in those substances.[67] While these results are impressive, a number of biologists have questioned this association, and some recent research efforts have failed to find a link between sugar consumption and violence.[68] Studies of school-age children have failed to show that kids who use sugar in their diet are any more aggressive than those who are given aspartame (Nutrasweet) or saccharin for a sweetener; if anything, sugar seems to have a calming effect on the children.[69]

A great deal of research has linked hormonal activity to aggressive behavior. Some criminologists argue that gender differences in the crime rate can be linked to the male hormone testosterone and its assumed effect on behavior.[70]

In sum, biochemical studies suggest that criminal offenders have abnormal levels of organic or inorganic substances that influence their behavior and in some way make them prone to antisocial behavior.

Neurological Problems. Another area of interest to biocriminologists is the relationship of brain activity to behavior. Biocriminologists have used the electroencephalogram to record the electrical impulses given off by the brain. Preliminary

Because They're Different: Biological Theories

studies indicate that 50%–60% of those with behavior disorders display abnormal recordings.[71]

People with an abnormal cerebral structure referred to as minimal brain dysfunction (MBD) may experience periods of explosive rage.[72] Brain dysfunction is sometimes manifested as an attention deficit disorder (ADD), another suspected cause of antisocial behavior. About 3% of all U.S. children, primarily boys, are believed to suffer from this disorder, and it is the most common reason children are referred to mental health clinics. The condition usually results in poor school performance, bullying, stubbornness, and a lack of response to discipline.[73]

Genetic Abnormalities. It is possible that violent behavior is inherited and a function of a person's genetic makeup. One approach has been to evaluate the behavior of adopted children. If an adopted child's behavior patterns run parallel to those of his or her biological parents, it would be strong evidence to support a genetic basis for crime. Preliminary studies conducted in Europe have indicated that the criminality of the biological father is a strong predictor of a child's antisocial behavior.[74] The probability that a youth will engage in crime is significantly enhanced when both biological and adoptive parents exhibit criminal tendencies.

Genetic influences on crime have been tested by measuring the behavior of twins. If inherited traits are related to criminality, it should be expected that twins would be more similar in their antisocial activities than other sibling pairs. Since most twins are brought up together, however, determining whether behavior similarities are a function of environmental influences or genetics is difficult. To overcome this problem, biocriminologists usually compare identical, or monozygotic (MZ), twins with fraternal, or dizygotic (DZ), twins of the same sex. Since MZ twins are genetically identical, their behavior would be expected to be more similar than that of DZ twins. A recent symposium on the genetics of criminal behavior concluded that the behavior of some twin pairs displayed similarities that could be explained only by their genetic makeup.[75]

Is it possible that criminal traits are inherited? While some may scoff at the notion, one of the leading experts in this field, David Rowe, recently reviewed the available research and concluded that individuals who share genes are alike in personality regardless of how they are reared; in contrast, environment induces little or no personality resemblance in twin pairs.[76]

It's in Their Heads: Psychological Theories

Sometimes when we hear of a particularly gruesome crime, we say of the criminal, "That guy must be crazy." It comes as no surprise, then, that some experts believe that the onset of criminality is caused by psychological factors.

Psychoses. There are actually a number of views on this subject. According to the **psychoanalytic view,** some people encounter problems during their early development that cause an imbalance in their personality. Some may become psychotics who cannot restrain their impulsive behavior. One type of psychosis is schizophrenia, a condition marked by incoherent thought processes, a lack of insight, hallucinations, feelings of persecution, and so on. Schizophrenics may suffer delusions and feel persecuted, worthless, and alienated.[77] David Berkowitz, known as the "Son of Sam," John Hinckley, Jr., who attempted to assassinate President Ronald Reagan, and Milwaukee cannibal Jeffrey Dahmer are examples of people suffering from severe psychological disorders.

Social Learning. Another psychological view is that criminal behavior is learned through interactions with others. According to **social learning** theorists, people act aggressively because, as children, they modeled their behavior after the violent acts of adults.[78]

One area of particular interest to social learning theorists is whether the media can influence violence. Studies have shown that youths exposed to aggressive, antisocial behavior on television and in movies are likely to copy that violent behavior. Laboratory studies generally conclude that violence on television can lead to aggressive behavior by children and teenagers who watch such programs.[79] Whether the evidence obtained in controlled laboratory studies can be applied to the "real world" is still being debated.[80] Considering that the average child watches more than 20 hours of TV a week, any link between TV violence and criminal behavior is quite important.

The Psychopath. Psychologists have explored the link between personality and crime. Evidence exists that aggressive youth have unstable personality structures often marked by hyperactivity, impulsiveness, and instability. One area of particular interest to criminology is the identification of the psychopathic (sometimes referred to as the antisocial or sociopathic) personality.

Psychopaths are believed to be dangerous, aggressive, antisocial individuals who act in a callous manner. They neither learn from their mistakes nor are deterred by punishments.[81] Although they may appear charming and have at least average intelligence, psychopaths lack emotional depth, are incapable of caring for others, and maintain an abnormally low level of anxiety. They are likely to be persistent alcohol and drug abusers.[82]

The concept of the psychopathic personality is important for criminology, because it has been estimated that somewhere between 10% and 30% of all prison inmates can be classified as psychopaths or sociopaths or as having similar character disorders.[83] Psychopathy has also been linked to the phenomenon of serial murder.[84] The accompanying Criminal Justice and the Media box is an illustration of this theme.

Although psychologists are still not certain of its cause, a number of factors are believed to contribute to the development of a psychopathic personality. They include having a psychopathic parent, parental rejection and a lack of love during childhood, and inconsistent discipline.[85] Some psychologists suspect that psychopathy is a function of physical abnormality, especially the activity of the autonomic nervous system. Studies measuring the physical makeup of clinically diagnosed psychopaths indicate that such persons react differently to pain and have lower arousal levels to noise and environmental stimuli than control subjects do.[86] Another view is that the psychopathic personality is imprinted at birth and is relatively unaffected by socialization.[87] These people are among the most disturbed offenders who may be at risk for chronic offending. The chronic offender is discussed in the accompanying Analyzing Criminal Justice Issues box on page 70.

There seems to be an economic bias in the crime rate: Prisons are filled with the poor and hopeless, not the rich and famous. Because crime patterns have a decidedly social orientation, sociological explanations of crime have predominated in criminology.

According to **social structure theory,** the United States is a stratified society. The contrast between the lifestyles of the wealthiest members of the upper class and the poorest segment of the lower class is striking. The gap between the richest and the poorest Americans seems to be growing wider; the number of families living in poverty doubled in the past decade. About 20 million high school dropouts face dead-end jobs, unemployment, and social failure. Because of their meager economic resources, lower-class citizens are often forced to live in slum areas marked by substandard housing, inadequate health care, poor educational opportunities, underemployment, and despair. Many families are fatherless and husbandless, headed by a female who is the sole breadwinner and who is often forced to go on welfare.

Because They're Poor: Social Structure Theory

Seven

The box office hit *Seven* is one of a long line of films that have portrayed a psychotic serial killer locking horns with police officers.

In *Seven* police officers David Mills (Brad Pitt) and William Somerset (Morgan Freeman) are called to the scene of a particularly gruesome crime: A man had literally been forced to eat until he burst. The killer left the message "glutton" on the wall. Soon after, other mutilated and tortured bodies turn up, with the inscriptions "greed," "pride," "sloth," and "lust"; each victim is killed in a bizarre and horrible fashion.

Somerset, the older detective approaching retirement, and his brash young partner quickly link the killings to the "seven deadly sins" and search the library for clues. As they close in, the killer, identified only as "John Doe" (played chillingly by Kevin Spacey), surprises everyone and gives himself up. He says he will make a full confession after he shows Mills and Somerset where he has hidden the last two bodies. As they stand on a remote highway, a delivery truck shows up; the driver claims he was paid $500 to deliver a mysterious box. Somerset reluctantly opens the package and finds the head of Detective Mills's beautiful wife, Tracy (Gwyneth Paltrow), who has been tortured and slain by John Doe. Doe taunts detective Mills, who in a fit of rage kills the handcuffed Doe. The film ends with a shattered Mills being taken away in a patrol car.

Directed by David Fincher, *Seven* follows in the footsteps of such film depictions of serial killers as *The Stepfather* and *The Silence of the Lambs* (which won an Oscar for best picture). The killer is portrayed as a sophisticated and intelligent person who plans extremely complex crimes.

While the theme of the crazed serial killer is exciting and scary to a movie audience, relatively few murders are carried out by serial killers. In fact, experts on serial killers estimate that fewer than 50 are active at any one time. Even if each kills 10 people per year, that is 500 out of 24,000 murders. So while the threat of serial killing should not be discounted, you are much more likely to be killed by a drunk driver than a maniacal murderer.

The film takes great liberty with its depiction of how the police department handles the case. Only these two officers are assigned to the investigation, even though the bodies keep piling up at a rapid pace. They make no effort to contact state police or federal authorities for assistance. Also lost in the gruesome carnage is the fact that the Pitt character plays an officer who has recently moved to the big city from a rural area. Yet he is immediately assigned to the detective branch and asked to head up a major homicide investigation, a turn of events that would not occur on any police force except one located in a Hollywood studio.

The problems of lower-class culture are particularly acute for racial and ethnic minorities who have an income level significantly lower than that of whites and an unemployment rate almost twice as high. They now face the deterioration of the manufacturing economy in the urban United States. Hundreds of thousands of jobs have been lost, further weakening the economic future of young minority men and women.

The crushing burden of urban poverty results in the development of a culture of poverty.[88] This subculture is marked by apathy, cynicism, helplessness, and distrust. The culture is passed from one generation to another so that slum dwellers become part of a permanent underclass, "the truly disadvantaged."[89] Considering the social disability suffered by lower-class slum dwellers, it is not surprising that they turn to crime as a means of support and survival.

Living in deteriorated inner-city, socially disorganized neighborhoods, forced to endure substandard housing and schools, and cut off from conventional society, lower-class slum dwellers are faced with a constant assault on their self-image and sense of worth. In these areas, the forces of social control have broken down. Criminal acts and drug dealing provide a means of survival in an otherwise bleak existence. This is referred to as social disorganization theory.

Another by-product of life in lower-class slum areas is the frustration and anger people experience because they lack the ability to achieve legitimate social and financial success. This is referred to as **strain.** In lower-class slum areas, strain occurs because legitimate avenues for success are all but closed. With no acceptable means for obtaining success openly, people may either use deviant methods for obtaining their goals, such as theft or violence, or reject socially acceptable goals and seek others that are more easily satisfied, such as being a gang leader. When individuals cannot hope to fulfill their ambitions and dreams because they come from a poor background, they turn to crime and violence.[90]

Not all criminologists agree that the cause of crime can be found solely within the culture of poverty.[91] Some argue that people commit crime as a result of the experiences they have while they are being socialized by the various organizations, institutions, and processes of society. People are most strongly influenced toward criminal behavior by poor family relationships, destructive peer-group relations, educational failure, and labeling by agents of the justice system. Although lower-class citizens have the added burdens of poverty and strain, even

Socialized to Crime: Social Process Theories

People are most strongly influenced toward criminal behavior by poor family relationships, destructive peer-group relations, educational failure, and labeling by agents of the justice system. Although lower-class citizens have the added burdens of poverty and strain, even middle-class or upper-class citizens may turn to crime if their socialization is poor or destructive. Kids may be influenced to commit crime and take drugs because of peer group pressure. Crime becomes "seductive" when it can impress peer group members.

Chapter 2

The Nature of Crime and Victimization

The Chronic Offender

One of the most dramatic developments in the study of crime and delinquency has been the "discovery" of the chronic offender. Researchers increasingly recognize that a relatively few offenders commit a significant percentage of all serious crimes in the community and that such offenders who are juveniles grow up to become chronic adult criminals who contribute notably to the total adult crime rate.

Chronic offenders can be distinguished from conventional criminals. The latter category contains law violators who may commit and be apprehended for a single instance of criminal behavior, usually of relatively minor seriousness—shoplifting, simple assault, petty larceny, and so on. The chronic offender is one who has serious and persistent brushes with the law, who is building a career in crime, and whose behavior may be excessively violent and destructive.

The concept of the chronic career offender is most closely associated with the research efforts of Marvin Wolfgang and his associates at the University of Pennsylvania. In 1972, Wolfgang, Robert Figlio, and Thorsten Sellin published a landmark study, *Delinquency in a Birth Cohort,* that has had a profound influence on the very concept of the criminal offender. Wolfgang, Figlio, and Sellin used official records to follow the criminal careers of a cohort of 9,945 boys born in Philadelphia in 1945 until they reached 18 years of age in 1963. About two-thirds of the cohort (6,470) never had contact with police authorities, while the remaining 3,475 had at least one contact with the police during their minority. Of these, a relatively small group of 627 boys were arrested five times or more. These "chronic offenders" were responsible for 5,305 arrests, 51.9% of the total. Even more striking was the involvement of chronic offenders in serious criminal acts. Of the entire sample, they committed 71% of the homicides, 73% of the rapes, 82% of the robberies, and 69% of the aggravated assaults. Arrest and punishment did little to deter the chronic offenders. In fact, punishment was inversely related to chronicity—the stricter the sanctions they received, the more likely they were to engage in repeated criminal behavior.

Since the Philadelphia survey was carried out, a number of other independent studies, including one of a larger Philadelphia cohort of children born in 1958, have also confirmed the existence of a chronic, repeat offender.

The Stability of Crime

The chronic offender research indicates that young persistent offenders grow up to become repeat adult offenders. The stability of criminal careers was detected by Paul Tracy and Kimberly Kempf-Leonard in their important follow-up study of all subjects in the second (1958) Philadelphia cohort. By age 26, those delinquents with high rates of juvenile offending, who had started their delinquent career early, who had committed a violent crime, and who continued offending throughout adolescence were the ones most likely to persist as adults. Tracy and Kempf-Leonard found that delinquents who had begun their offending career with serious violent offenses were the ones most likely to

middle-class or upper-class citizens may turn to crime if their socialization is poor or destructive.

Social process theory points to research efforts linking family problems to crime as evidence that **socialization,** not social structure, is the key to understanding the onset of criminality. The quality of family life is considered to be a significant determining factor in adolescent development.[92] Among the most important research efforts are those showing that inconsistent discipline, poor supervision, and a lack of warm parent-child relationships are closely related to a child's deviant behavior.[93] Educational experience has also been found to have a significant impact on behavioral choices. Kids who fail at school and eventually drop out are the ones most likely to engage in criminal behavior. A recent analysis of the findings of 118 studies of educational achievement found that academic performance was a significant predictor of crime and delinquency. Although white children and males seem more deeply influenced by school failure, all children who fail in school offend more frequently, commit more serious and violent offenses, and persist in their offending into adulthood.[94]

persist. The severity of offending, not the frequency, had the greatest impact on later adult criminality.

The Cause of Chronic Offending

The existence of a chronic offender presents a dilemma for those who believe that the criminal offender can be successfully treated with some combination of educational, vocational, and psychological counseling and support. If, in fact, only a small group of offenders are responsible for almost all serious crimes, it follows that there must be some personal characteristic that sets chronic offenders apart from both noncriminals and nonchronic offenders. Environmental and socialization factors alone cannot explain why one young offender desists from crime, while another, living in the same area and experiencing similar environmental conditions, becomes a chronic offender who escalates the frequency and seriousness of his or her criminal activity.

A number of criminologists have suggested that chronic offending is caused by some individual trait, genetic condition, or physical characteristic. These conditions may exist before birth or may be a function of birth complications—factors that for all practical purposes are uncontrollable. Some preliminary research efforts indicate that such factors as limited intelligence (as measured by IQ tests) and impulsive personality predict chronic offending.

Early onset of offending has been associated with chronic offending. Kids who are found to be disruptive and antisocial as early as age five or six are the ones most likely to exhibit stable, long-term patterns of disruptive behavior through adolescence. They have measurable behavior problems in such areas as learning and motor skills, cognitive abilities, family relations, and other areas of social, psychological, and physical functioning. Youthful offenders who persist are more likely to abuse alcohol, get into trouble while in military service, become economically dependent, have lower aspirations, get divorced or separated, and have a weak employment record.

Critical Thinking Questions

1. The record number of inmates currently in prison and jail reflects the justice system's efforts to curb career offenders and the "lock 'em up and throw away the key" philosophy. This solution is troubling to civil libertarians since it involves possible errors in the prediction of a person's future behavior. Might not some people be unfairly punished because their background characteristics mistakenly indicate they are chronic offenders? Conversely, might not some serious offenders be overlooked because they have a more conventional background? No prediction method is totally accurate, and error can involve a significant infringement on a person's civil rights. Should people be punished because their past deeds indicate a risk of future criminality? Or should criminal punishment be based on the current criminal act?

SOURCES: Paul Tracy and Kimberly Kempf-Leonard, *Continuity and Discontinuity in Criminal Careers* (New York: Plenum Press, 1996); Elizabeth Kandel and Sarnoff Mednick, "Perinatal Complications Predict Violent Offending," *Criminology* 29 (1991): 519–29; Marvin Wolfgang, Robert Figlio, and Thorsten Sellin, *Delinquency in a Birth Cohort* (Chicago: University of Chicago Press, 1972); Marvin Wolfgang, "Delinquency in Two Birth Cohorts," in *Perspective Studies of Crime and Delinquency*, ed. Katherine Teilmann Van Dusen and Sarnoff Mednick (Boston: Kluwer-Nijhoff, 1983), pp. 7–17.

Learning to Be Bad. There is disagreement over the relationship between social processes and crime. Some crime experts maintain that all people are "born innocent" but some are then exposed to and learn criminal techniques and attitudes from peers and family members.[95] Individuals learn both the techniques of committing crime, such as how to hot-wire a car or break into a home, and the attitudes that support crime. For example, delinquents learn how to "neutralize" the guilt they might have felt because they broke the law by blaming the victim ("He had it coming") or excusing their guilt ("I had to stick up for my friends"). Learning the attitudes and techniques of crime is an essential ingredient of a criminal career.

Learning to Be Good. Another view is that all people are born "bad" and must be socialized to become "good." All people have the potential to engage in antisocial behavior and must be socialized to conform. Kids who become criminals are the ones whose bond to critical individuals and institutions is strained or broken. For example, they have weak attachments to parents and peers and little commitment

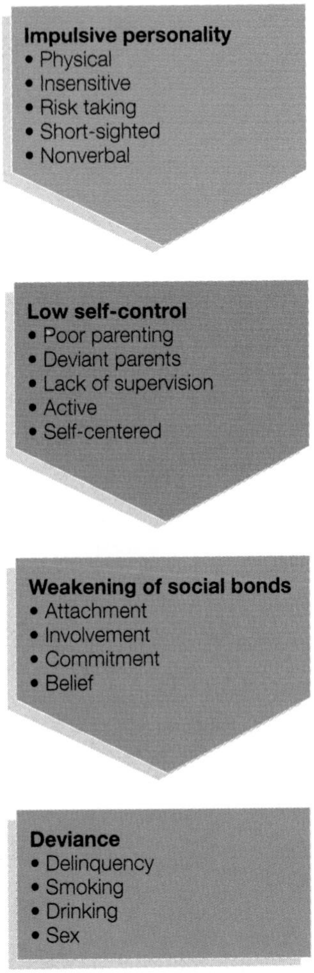

Impulsive personality
- Physical
- Insensitive
- Risk taking
- Short-sighted
- Nonverbal

Low self-control
- Poor parenting
- Deviant parents
- Lack of supervision
- Active
- Self-centered

Weakening of social bonds
- Attachment
- Involvement
- Commitment
- Belief

Deviance
- Delinquency
- Smoking
- Drinking
- Sex

Figure 2.8
Self-control and crime.

to school or their future. Without such attachments, they are free to engage in antisocial behavior; they are out of control.

In his **social control theory,** sociologist Travis Hirschi suggests that the bond to society is formed from a number of elements:

- *Attachment.* Involves caring for and valuing relationships with others, including parents, friends, and teachers. A person with a strong sense of attachment will seek out the advice of teachers, associate with friends, and maintain strong ties with family members; these activities are believed to shield a person from criminal temptations.

- *Commitment.* The time, energy, and effort expended in the pursuit of conventional lines of action. Commitments may embrace such activities as spending time in school or working to save money for the future. The more committed one is, the less risk one has of engaging in criminal activity.

- *Involvement.* Participation in conventional activities, such as school, recreation, church, family, or hobbies. The youth who is always active will not have time for delinquent acts.

- *Belief.* Adhering to commonly held moral values, such as sharing, sensitivity to others, obeying the law, and refraining from hurting others. Kids who hold conventional beliefs will be able to avoid crime.[96]

According to Hirschi, people whose bond to society is secure are unlikely to engage in criminal misconduct because they have a strong stake in society. Those who find their social bond weakened are much more likely to succumb to the temptations of criminal activity.

In an important work, *A General Theory of Crime,* Travis Hirschi, with Michael Gottfredson, argues that the bond to society may be weakened because some people have limited **self-control.**[97] They tend to be impulsive, insensitive, physical, risk taking, short-sighted, and nonverbal. They have a "here and now" orientation and refuse to work for distant goals; they lack diligence, tenacity, and persistence in a course of action. People lacking self-control tend to be adventuresome, active, physical, and self-centered. As they mature, they have unstable marriages, jobs, and friendships (see Figure 2.8). Criminal acts are attractive to them because they provide easy and immediate gratification, or as Gottfredson and Hirschi put it, "money without work, sex without courtship, revenge without court delays."

It's a "Dog Eat Dog World": Conflict Theory

Conflict theory views the economic and political forces operating in society as the fundamental causes of criminality. The criminal law and criminal justice system are viewed as vehicles for controlling the poor members of society. The criminal justice system is believed to help the powerful and rich impose their particular morality and standards of good behavior on the entire society, while it protects their property and physical safety from the have-nots, even though the cost may be the legal rights of the lower class. Those in power control the content and direction of the law and legal system. Crimes are defined in a way that meets with the needs of the ruling classes. The theft of property worth $5 by a poor person can be punished much more severely than the misappropriation of millions by a large corporation. Those in the middle class are drawn into this pattern of control because they are led to believe they, too, have a stake in maintaining the status quo and should support the views of the upper-class owners of production.[98]

One branch of conflict theory—called critical, radical, or Marxist criminology—focuses on the crime-producing forces contained within the capitalist system. These theorists devote their research efforts to exposing discrimination and class bias in the application of laws and justice. They trace the history of criminal sanctions to show how those sanctions have corresponded to the needs of the wealthy. They attempt to show how police, courts, and correctional agencies have served as tools of the powerful members of society.

There are other branches of conflict theory. **Radical feminists** have tried to explain how capitalism places particular stress on women and to explicate the role of male dominance in female criminality.[99] Radical feminists view female crime as originating with the onset of male supremacy (patriarchy), the subsequent subordination of women, male aggression, and efforts of men to control females sexually.[100] They focus on the social forces that shape women's lives and experiences to explain female criminality. For example, they attempt to show how the sexual victimization of girls is a function of male socialization, because so many young males learn to be aggressive and exploitive of women. Exploited at home, female victims try to cope by running away and by engaging in premarital sex and substance abuse. The double standard means that female adolescents still have a much narrower range of acceptable behavior than male adolescents. Any sign of misbehavior is viewed as a substantial challenge to authority that requires immediate control. Feminist scholars view the female criminal as a victim of gender inequality.

Left realists attempt to reconcile critical views with the social realities of crime and its impact on the lower class. They recognize that predatory crimes are not "revolutionary" acts and that crime is an overwhelming problem for the poor. Regardless of its origins, according to left realists, crime must be dealt with by the police and courts.[101] **Peacemaking criminology** views crime as just another form of violence, along with war and genocide. Peacemakers call for universal social justice as a means of eliminating antisocial acts.[102] Peacemakers advocate restoring criminals back into society, referred to as **restorative justice.**

Theories of Victimization

For many years, criminological theory focused on the actions of the criminal offender; the role of the victim was virtually ignored. Then a number of scholars found that the victim is not a passive target in crime but someone whose behavior can influence his or her own fate.[103] The criminal might have been a predator, but the victim may have helped encourage or initiate the criminal action.

These early works helped focus attention on the role of the victim in the crime problem and led to further research efforts that have sharpened the image of the crime victim. There are a number of theories of why people become victims of crime.

Victim Precipitation

Victim precipitation refers to the fact that victims may have actually initiated the confrontation that led to their injury or death. The victim may have provoked or threatened the attacker, used "fighting words," or even attacked first.[104] The concept of victim precipitation implies that in some but not all crimes, the victim provoked or instigated the crime: The crime could not have taken place unless the victim actually cooperated with the criminal.

Lifestyle

The cause of victimization has also been linked to lifestyle and activity. NCVS data show that most victimizations occur in public places, in urban areas, during the evening. Victimization is rare among married people who stay home at night in their rural home and avoid public places. People who engage in high-risk behaviors, such as consuming large amounts of alcohol or spending weekend nights away from home, put themselves at risk of being crime targets.[105]

People who live in high-crime areas, spend time in public places, go out late at night, and so on are the ones most likely to interact with lawbreakers who have similar lifestyles. In other words, crime is an inevitable consequence of potential victims and criminals sharing a similar lifestyle.

Routine Activities

The **routine activities** approach holds that the incidence of criminal activity and victimization is related to the nature of normal, everyday patterns of human behavior. According to originators Lawrence Cohen and Marcus Felson, predatory

Figure 2.9
Routine activities theory.

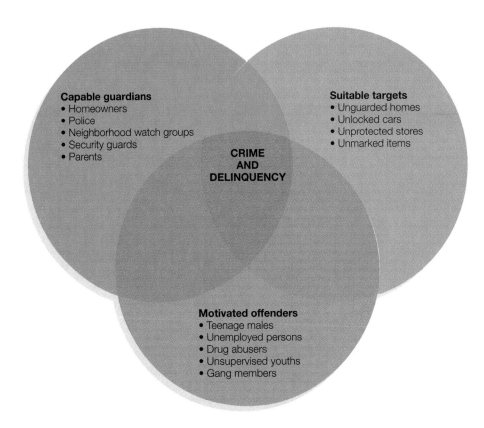

crime rates can be explained by three factors: the supply of motivated offenders (such as large numbers of unemployed teenagers); suitable targets (goods that have value and can be easily transported, such as VCRs); and the absence of effective guardians for protection (such as police and security forces or home security devices) (see Figure 2.9).[106]

The routine activities view of victimization suggests that people's daily activities may put them at risk of being the target of criminal behavior. If people leave unguarded valuables in their home, they increase the likelihood of becoming burglary victims; if they walk at night in public places, they increase the risk of becoming the target of violence.[107]

According to this approach, the likelihood of victimization is a function of both the behavior of potential victims and criminal opportunity. For example, if family income increases because of the number of women employed in the workforce and because of this, the average family is able to afford more luxury goods, such as TVs and VCRs, we might expect a comparable increase in the crime rate because the number of "suitable targets" has expanded while the number of "capable guardians" left to protect the home has been reduced.[108] In contrast, crime rates may go down during times of high unemployment simply because there is less to steal and there are more people at home to guard their possessions. The routine activities approach seems a promising way of understanding crime and victimization patterns and predicting the probability of victim risk.

Crime Theory in Review

There are probably so many views of crime causation because there are so many types of crimes. It is possible that all explanations are partially correct: Some people commit crime because they are poorly socialized; some succumb to the obstacles placed in their path by lower-class life; others have psychological or biological problems; some are victims of class conflict. The various forms of crime theory are summarized in Table 2.3.

Theory	Major Premise
Choice theory	
	People commit crime when they perceive that the benefits of law violation outweigh the threat and pain of punishment.
Biosocial theories	
Biochemical	Crime, especially violence, is a function of diet, vitamin intake, hormonal imbalance, or food allergies.
Neurological	Criminals and delinquents often suffer brain impairment. Attention deficit disorder and minimum brain dysfunction are related to antisocial behavior.
Genetic	Delinquent traits and predispositions are inherited. The criminality of parents can predict the delinquency of children.
Psychological theories	
Psychoanalytic	The development of personality early in childhood influences behavior for the rest of a person's life. Criminals have weak egos and damaged personalities.
Social learning	People commit crime when they model their behavior after others they see being rewarded for the same acts. Behavior is enforced by rewards and extinguished by punishment.
Social structure theories	
Social disorganization	The conflicts and problems of urban social life and communities control the crime rate. Crime is a product of transitional neighborhoods that manifest social disorganization and value conflict.
Strain	People who adopt the goals of society but lack the means to attain them seek alternatives, such as crime.
Social process theories	
Learning theory	People learn to commit crime from exposure to antisocial behaviors. Criminal behavior depends on the person's experiences with rewards for conventional behaviors and punishments for deviant ones. Being rewarded for deviance leads to crime.
Social control theory	A person's bond to society prevents him or her from violating social rules. If the bond weakens, the person is free to commit crime.
Self-control theory	Crime and criminality are separate concepts. People choose to commit crime when they lack self-control. People lacking self-control will seize criminal opportunities.
Conflict theories	
Conflict theory	People commit crime when the law, controlled by the rich and powerful, defines their behavior as illegal. The immoral actions of the powerful go unpunished.
Radical feminist theory	The capital system creates patriarchy, which oppresses women. Male dominance explains gender bias, violence against women, and repression.
Left realism	Crime is a function of relative deprivation; criminals prey on the poor. The theory represents a compromise between conflict and traditional criminology.
Peacemaking	Peace and humanism can reduce crime; conflict resolution strategies can work. Peacemaking offers a new approach to crime control through mediation.
Victimization theories	
Routine activities theory	Crime is a function of the availability of the victim, the presence of an offender, and the absence of an effective guardian.

Table 2.3
Concepts and Theories of Criminology: A Review

Criminal Justice on the Net

The Internet has many sources for finding out more about criminal justice research, data, and crime patterns. For example, large-scale projects are often conducted by private agencies that provide resources and expertise. The Vera Institute of Justice is a private, nonprofit organization dedicated to making government politics and practices more humane, fair, and efficient. Vera works with government and local communities to expand the practice of justice:

http://broadway.vera.org/index.html

What causes crime? If you are interested about why kids join gangs, you might want to visit the National Youth Gang Center. This site provides critical information about youth gangs and effective responses to them:

http://www.iir.com/nygc/nygc.html

Although crime rates may be higher in the United States than in most other Western cultures, criminal behavior is certainly an international phenomenon. To learn more about international crime rates and trends, log onto the United Nations Crime and Justice Information Network, or UNCJIN. This electronic clearinghouse acts as a coordinator for the international exchange and dissemination of information on crime prevention and criminal justice issues:

http://www.ifs.univie.ac.at/~uncjin/uncjin.html

Imagine if you will, an organization that networks together communications among police chiefs, police officers, crime analysts, detectives, security personnel, and other people around the world interested in tracking and analyzing international crime data in a scholarly manner. To learn more about the International Association of Crime Analysts, log on to their web site at

http://web2.airmail.net/iaca/join.htm

It is even possible to learn more about criminological theory on the web. Want to learn just about everything there is to know about Marxist theory? The Marxism-Leninism Project sets out the theories of Marxism in the words of the founders of Marxism and of the greatest of their followers:

http://www.idbsu.edu/surveyrc/Staff/jaynes/marxism/intro.html

Social process theories link improper socialization to crime. One important aspect of socialization is parenting—poor parenting has been linked to the onset of delinquency. There are many groups and individuals who attempt to teach positive parenting skills. Learn more about some of these techniques at the following site:

http://www.empoweringpeople.com/

Summary

Today, we get our information on crime from a number of sources. One of the most important is the Uniform Crime Reports compiled by the FBI. This national survey of serious criminal acts reported to local police departments indicates that more than 13 million index crimes (murder, rape, burglary, robbery, assault, larceny/theft, and motor vehicle theft) occurred in 1996. Critics have questioned the validity of the UCR. They point out that many people fail to report crime to police because of fear, apathy, or lack of respect for law enforcement. In addition, questions have been raised about the accuracy of police records and reporting practices. To remedy this situation, the federal government has sponsored a massive victim survey designed to uncover the true amount of annual crime. The National Crime Victimization Survey (NCVS) reveals that more than 30 million serious personal crimes are committed every year and that the great majority are not reported to police. A third form of information is self-report surveys, which ask offenders themselves to tell about their criminal behaviors.

Except for a recent upsurge in teen drug use, all three data sources indicate that crime rates have declined in the 1990s.

The various sources of criminal statistics tell us a lot about the nature and patterns of crime. Rate increases have been attributed to the influence of drugs, the economy, the age structure, social decay, and other factors.

Many crime victims do not report criminal incidents to the police because they believe that nothing can be done or that they should not get involved. However, recent evidence indicates that the crimes not reported to the police are less serious than reported crimes. Consequently, the crime patterns found in all three data sources may be more similar than some critics believe.

There are distinct patterns to crime. It occurs more often in large cities during the summer and at night. Some geographic areas (the South and the Far West) have higher crime rates than others (the Midwest and New England).

Arrest and victim data indicate that males, minorities, the poor, and the young have relatively high rates of criminality. Victims of crime have many of the same demographic characteristics as criminals. They tend to be poor, young, male, and members of a minority group. However, households that experience crime tend to have a higher relative income than those that avoid victimization.

For the most part, criminals tend to victimize people who share their personal characteristics. For example, crime is intraracial. People can increase the risk of victimization by choosing a lifestyle that includes acts associated with high degrees of victimization, such as frequenting public places at night.

The police cannot do much about crime. About 20% of all reported crimes are solved by police. However, there is a positive relationship between crime seriousness and the probability of a successful clearance. That is, murders and rapes are much more often solved than car thefts or larcenies.

There is more than one approach to understanding the cause of crime and its consequences. A number of diverse schools of criminological theory exist. Some focus on the individual, while others view social factors as the most important element in producing crime.

Key Terms

criminal law
social control
crime
National Crime Victimization
 Survey (NCVS)
official crime statistics
Uniform Crime Reports (UCR)
participant observation
life history
Part I (index) crimes
Part II (nonindex) offenses

crime wave
chronic offenders
self-report surveys
choice theory
biological theories
psychoanalytic view
social learning
social structure theory
strain
social process theory
socialization

social control theory
self-control
conflict theory
radical feminists
left realists
peacemaking criminology
restorative justice
victim precipitation
routine activities

Questions

1. Why are crime rates higher in the summer than during other seasons?
2. What factors account for crime rate trends?
3. What factors are present in poverty-stricken urban areas that produce high crime rates?
4. It seems logical that biological and psychological factors might explain why some people commit crime. How would a biologist or a psychologist explain the fact that crime rates are higher in the West than in the Midwest? That there is more crime in the summer than in the winter?
5. If crime is a routine activity, what steps should you take to avoid becoming a crime victim?

77

Notes

1. Howard Becker, *Outsiders,* 2nd ed. (New York: Macmillan, 1972).

2. For a general discussion of Marxist thought on the criminal law, see Michael Lynch and W. Byron Groves, *A Primer in Radical Criminology,* 2nd ed. (New York: Harrow and Heston, 1990), pp. 6–26.

3. See, for example, Lloyd Bachman, Patrick O'Malley, and Jerald Bachman, *Monitoring the Future,* 1995 (Ann Arbor: University of Michigan, Institute for Social Research, 1994).

4. Craig Perkins and Patsy Klaus, *Criminal Victimization, 1994* (Washington, D.C.: Bureau of Justice Statistics, 1996). Herein cited as NCVS, 1994.

5. The arrest data used in this chapter, updated with preliminary 1995 data, come from FBI, *Crime in the United States, 1995* (Washington, D.C.: U.S. Government Printing Office, 1996). Herein cited as UCR, 1995.

6. Claire Sterck-Elifson, "Just for Fun?: Cocaine Use Among Middle-Class Women," *Journal of Drug Issues* 26 (1996): 63–76.

7. Ibid., p. 63.

8. Carl Klockars, *The Professional Fence* (New York: Free Press, 1976); Darrell Steffensmeier, *The Fence: In the Shadow of Two Worlds* (Totowa, N.J.: Rowman and Littlefield, 1986).

9. At the time of this writing, the latest volume of the UCR was the Federal Bureau of Investigation's *Crime in the United States, 1995.* Wherever possible, statistics in this volume will be supplemented by estimates based on data from the 1996 crime survey, made public in FBI, *Crime in the United States, 1996, Preliminary Annual Report* (Washington, D.C.: U.S. Government Printing Office, May 1997).

10. Clarence Schrag, *Crime and Justice: American Style* (Washington, D.C.: U.S. Government Printing Office, 1971), p. 17.

11. Malcolm Sparrow, Mark Moore, and David Kennedy, *Beyond 911: A New Era for Policing* (New York: Basic Books, 1990).

12. The findings in this section are based on 1992 UCR statistics, updated with 1993 data.

13. Freda Adler, *Sisters in Crime* (New York: McGraw-Hill, 1975); Rita James Simon, *The Contemporary Woman and Crime* (Washington, D.C.: U.S. Government Printing Office, 1975).

14. Darrel Steffensmeier and Renee Hoffman Steffensmeier, "Trends in Female Delinquency," *Criminology* 18 (1980): 62–85; see also idem, "Crime and the Contemporary Woman: An Analysis of Changing Levels of Female Property Crime, 1960–1975," *Social Forces* 57 (1978): 566–584; Joseph Weis, "Liberation and Crime: The Invention of the New Female Criminal," *Crime and Social Justice* 1 (1976): 17–27; Carol Smart, "The New Female Offender: Reality or Myth," *British Journal of Criminology* 19 (1979): 50–59; Steven Box and Chris Hale, "Liberation/Emancipation, Economic Marginalization or Less Chivalry," *Criminology* 22 (1984): 473–478.

15. Joseph Weis, "Liberation and Crime: The Invention of the New Female Criminal," *Crime and Social Justice* 1 (1976): 17–27; Steven Box and Chris Hale, "Liberation/Emancipation, Economic Marginalization or Less Chivalry," *Criminology* 22 (1984): 473–478.

16. Daniel Georges-Abeyie, "Race, Ethnicity, and the Spatial Dynamic: Toward a Realistic Study of Black Crime, Crime Victimization, and the Criminal Justice Processing of Blacks," *Social Justice* 16 (1989): 35–54.

17. Ibid.

18. Emilie Andersen Allan and Darrell Steffensmeier, "Youth, Underemployment and Property Crime: Differential Effects of Job Availability and Job Quality on Juvenile and Young Adult Arrest Rates," *American Sociological Review* 54 (1989): 107–123.

19. For a general view, see James Byrne and Robert Sampson, *The Social Ecology of Crime* (New York: Springer-Verlag, 1985).

20. Douglas Smith and G. Roger Jarjoura, "Social Structure and Criminal Victimization," *Journal of Research in Crime and Delinquency* 25 (1988): 27–52; Janet Heitgerd and Robert Bursik, Jr., "Extracommunity Dynamics and the Ecology of Delinquency," *American Journal of Sociology* 92 (1987): 775–787; Ora Simcha-Fagan and Joseph Schwartz, "Neighborhood and Delinquency: An Assessment of Contextual Effects," *Criminology* 24 (1986): 667–703.

21. Rodney Stark, "Deviant Places: A Theory of the Ecology of Crime," *Criminology* 25 (1987): 893–910.

22. Judith Blau and Peter Blau, "The Cost of Inequality: Metropolitan Structure and Violent Crime," *American Sociological Review* 47 (1982): 114–129.

23. Charles Tittle and Robert Meier, "Specifying the SES/Delinquency Relationship," *Criminology* 28 (1990): 271–295.

24. Herman Schwendinger and Julia Schwendinger, "The Paradigmatic Crisis in Delinquency Theory," *Crime and Social Justice* 18 (1982): 70–78.

25. Michael Gottfredson and Travis Hirschi, "The True Value of Lambda Would Appear to Be Zero: An Essay on Career Criminals, Criminal Careers, Selective Incapacitation, Cohort Studies and Related Topics," *Criminology* 24 (1986): 213–234; further support for their position can be found in Lawrence Cohen and Kenneth Land, "Age Structure and Crime," *American Sociological Review* 52 (1987): 170–183.

26. Travis Hirschi and Michael Gottfredson, "Age and the Explanation of Crime," *American Journal of Sociology* 89 (1983): 552–584.

27. Ibid.

28. Alfred Blumstein, Jacqueline Cohen, and David Farrington, "Criminal Career Research: Its Value for Criminology," *Criminology* 26 (1988): 1–35.

29. Arnold Barnett, Alfred Blumstein, and David Farrington, "Probabilistic Models of Youthful Criminal Careers," *Criminology* 25 (1987): 83–107; David Greenberg, "Age, Crime, and Social Explanation," *American Journal of Sociology* 91 (1985): 1–21.

30. NCVS, 1992.

31. Duncan Chappell, Gilbert Geis, Robert Hardt, and Larry Siegel, "Forcible Rape: A Comparative Study of Offenses Known to the Police in Boston and Los Angeles," in *Studies in Sociology of Sex,* ed. James Henslin (New York: Appleton-Century-Crofts, 1971), pp. 169–193.

32. Lawrence Sherman and Barry Glick, "The Quality of Arrest Statistics," *Police Foundation Reports* 2 (1984): 1–8.

33. Patrick Jackson, "Assessing the Validity of Official Data on Arson," *Criminology* 6 (1988): 181–195.

34. Leonard Savitz, "Official Statistics," in *Contemporary Criminology,* ed. L. Savitz and N. Johnston (New York: Wiley, 1982), pp. 3–15.

35. Michael Hindelang, Travis Hirschi, and Joseph Weis, *Measuring Delinquency* (Beverly Hills, Calif.: Sage, 1981).

36. Walter Gove, Michael Hughes, and Michael Geerken, "Are Uniform Crime Reports a Valid Indicator of the Index Crimes? An Affirmative Answer with Minor Qualifications," *Criminology* 23 (1985): 451–501.

37. U.S. Department of Justice, *The Redesigned UCR Program* (Washington, D.C.: U.S. Department of Justice, n.d.).

38. The following classic studies were among the first to have noted the great discrepancy between official statistics and self-report studies: Maynard Erickson and LaMar Empey, "Court Records, Undetected Delinquency and Decision-Making," *Journal of Criminal Law, Criminology, and Police Science* 54 (1963): 456–469; Martin Gold, "Undetected Delinquent Behavior," *Journal of Research in Crime and Delinquency* 3 (1966): 27–46; James Short and F. Ivan Nye, "Extent of Unrecorded Delinquency, Tentative Conclusions," *Journal of Criminal Law, Criminology, and Police Science* 49 (1958): 296–302.

39. Charles Tittle, Wayne Villemez, and Douglas Smith, "The Myth of Social Class and Criminality: An Empirical Assessment of the Empirical Evidence," *American Sociological Review* 43 (1978): 643–646.

40. D. Wayne Osgood, Lloyd Johnston, Patrick O'Malley, and Jerald Bachman, "The Generality of Deviance in Late Adolescence and Early Adulthood," *American Sociological Review* 53 (1988): 81–93.

41. Jerald Bachman, Lloyd Johnston, and Patrick O'Malley, *Monitoring the Future, 1995* (Ann Arbor: University of Michigan, Institute for Social Research, 1996).

42. Lloyd Johnston, Patrick O'Malley, and Jerald Bachman, *National Survey Results on Drug Use,* press release, 28 January 1996.

43. Philip Ennis, *Criminal Victimization in the United States, Field Survey 2* (Washington, D.C.: President's Commission on Law Enforcement and Criminal Justice, 1967).

44. Data in these sections come from NCVS, 1992.

45. U.S. Center for Disease Control, "Homicide Among Young Black Males—United States, 1978–1987," *Morbidity and Mortality Weekly Report* 39 (1990): 869–873.

46. Lisa Bastian and Bruce Taylor, *School Crime* (Washington, D.C.: Bureau of Justice Statistics, 1991), p. 1.

47. NCVS, 1992, p. 58.

48. Janet Lauritsen and Kenna Davis Quinet, "Repeat Victimizations Among Adolescents and Young Adults," *Journal of Quantitative Criminology* 11 (1995): 143–163.

49. Denise Osborn, Dan Ellingworth, Tim Hope, and Alan Trickett, "Are Repeatedly Victimized Households Different?" *Journal of Quantitative Criminology* 12 (1996): 223–245.

50. Terry Buss and Rashid Abdu, "Repeat Victims of Violence in an Urban Trauma Center," *Violence and Victims* 10 (1995): 183–187.

51. Graham Farrell, "Predicting and Preventing Revictimization," in *Crime and Justice: An Annual Review of Research,* vol. 20, ed. Michael Tonry and David Farrington (Chicago: University of Chicago Press, 1995), pp. 61–126.

52. Ibid., p. 121.

53. Graham Farrell, Coretta Phillips, and Ken Pease, "Like Taking Candy, Why Does Repeat Victimization Occur?" *British Journal of Criminology* 35 (1995): 384–399.

54. Helen Eigenberg, "The National Crime Survey and Rape: The Case of the Missing Question," *Justice Quarterly* 7 (1990): 655–671.

55. Alfred Blumstein, Jacqueline Cohen, and Richard Rosenfeld, "Trend and Deviation in Crime Rates: A Comparison of UCR and NCS Data for Burglary and Robbery," *Criminology* 29 (1991): 237–263.

56. Glenn Pierce and James Alan Fox, *Recent Trends in Violent Crime: A Closer Look* (Boston: National Crime Analysis Program, Northeastern University, 1992).

57. Rosemary Gartner, "Family Structure, Welfare Spending, and Child Homicide in Developed Democracies," *Journal of Marriage and the Family* 53 (1991): 231–240.

58. UCR, 1995, p. 212.

59. Joseph Sheley and James Wright, *In the Line of Fire: Youth, Guns, and Violence in Urban America* (New York: Aldine de Gruyter, 1995).

60. Carolyn Block, Michael Biritz, Ayad Paul Jacob, Irving Spergel, and Susan Grossman, "The Early Warning System for Street Gang Violence: A Community Approach to Gang Violence Reduction," paper presented at the annual meeting of the American Society of Criminology, Chicago, November 1996.

61. Alfred Blumstein, "Violence by Young People: Why the Deadly Nexus," *National Institute of Justice Journal* 229 (1995): 2–9.

62. Bruce Johnson, Andrew Golub, and Jeffrey Fagan, "Careers in Crack, Drug Use, Drug Distribution, and Nondrug Criminality," *Crime and Delinquency* 41 (1995): 275–295.

63. Darrell Steffensmeier and Miles Harer, "Did Crime Rise or Fall During the Reagan Presidency? The Effects of an 'Aging' U.S. Population on the Nation's Crime Rate," *Journal of Research in Crime and Delinquency* 28 (1991): 330–339.

64. James A. Fox, *Trends in Juvenile Violence: A Report to the United States Attorney General on Current and Future Rates of Juvenile Offending* (Boston, Mass.: Northeastern University, 1996).

65. Lawrence Cohen and Richard Machalek, "A General Theory of Expropriative Crime: An Evolutionary Ecological Approach," *American Journal of Sociology* 94 (1988): 465–501.

66. Leonard Hippchen, "Some Possible Biochemical Aspects of Criminal Behavior," *Journal of Behavioral Ecology* 2 (1981): 1–6.

67. B. D'Asaro, C. Grossback, and C. Nigro, "Polyamine Levels in Jail Inmates," *Journal of Orthomolecular Psychiatry* 4 (1975): 149–152.

68. H. Bruce Ferguson, Clare Stoddart, and Jovan Simeon, "Double-Blind Challenge Studies of Behavioral and Cognitive Effects of Sucrose-Aspartame Ingestion in Normal Children," *Nutrition Reviews Supplement* 44 (1986): 144–158; Gregory Gray, "Diet, Crime and Delinquency: A Critique," *Nutrition Reviews Supplement* 44 (1986): 89–94.

69. Mark Wolraich, Scott Lindgren, Phyllis Stumbo, Lewis Steginik, Mark Appelbaum, and Mary Kiritsy, "Effects of Diets High in Sucrose or Aspartame on the Behavior and Cognitive Performance of Children," *The New England Journal of Medicine* 330 (1994): 303–306.

70. Alan Booth and D. Wayne Osgood, "The Influence of Testosterone on Deviance in Adulthood: Assessing and Explaining the Relationship," *Criminology* 31 (1993): 93–118.

71. D. Williams, "Neural Factors Related to Habitual Aggression—Consideration of Differences Between Habitual Aggressives and Others Who Have Committed Crimes of Violence," *Brain* 92 (1969): 503–520.

72. R. R. Monroe, *Brain Dysfunction in Aggressive Criminals* (Lexington, Mass.: D.C. Heath, 1978); L. T. Yeudall, *Childhood Experiences as Causes of Criminal Behavior*, Senate of Canada, issue no. 1, Thirteenth Parliament, Ottawa, Canada, 1977.

73. Terrie Moffitt and Phil Silva, "Self-Reported Delinquency, Neuropsychological Deficit, and History of Attention Deficit Disorder," *Journal of Abnormal Child Psychology* 16 (1988): 553–569.

74. B. Hutchings and S. A. Mednick, "Criminality in Adoptees and Their Adoptive and Biological Parents: A Pilot Study," in *Biosocial Bases of Criminal Behavior*, ed. S. A. Mednick and Karl O. Christiansen (New York: Gardner Press, 1977).

75. Michael Lyons, "A Twin Study of Self-Reported Criminal Behavior," and Judy Silberg, Joanne Meyer, Andrew Pickles, Emily Simonoff, Lindon Eaves, John Hewitt, Hermine Maes, and Michael Rutter, "Heterogeneity Among Juvenile Antisocial Behaviors: Findings from The Virginia Twin Study of Adolescent Behavioral Development," in The Ciba Foundation Symposium, *Genetics of Criminal and Antisocial Behavior* (Chichester, England: Wiley, 1995).

76. David Rowe, *The Limits of Family Influence: Genes, Experiences and Behavior* (New York: Guilford Press, 1995), p. 64.

77. August Aichorn, *Wayward Youth* (New York: Viking, 1965).

78. This discussion is based on three works by Albert Bandura: *Aggression: A Social Learning Analysis* (Englewood Cliffs, N.J.: Prentice-Hall, 1973); *Social Learning Theory* (Englewood Cliffs, N.J.: Prentice-Hall, 1977); and "The Social Learning Perspective: Mechanisms of Aggression," in *The Psychology of Crime and Criminal Justice*, ed. H. Toch (New York: Holt, Rinehart and Winston, 1979), pp. 198–326.

79. U.S. Department of Health and Human Services, *Television and Behavior* (Washington, D.C.: U.S. Government Printing Office, 1982).

80. Richard Kania, "T.V. Crime and Real Crime: Questioning the Link," paper presented at the annual meeting of the American Society of Criminology, Chicago, November 1988.

81. David Lykken, "Psychopathy, Sociopathy, and Crime," *Society* 34 (1996): 30–38.

82. Steven Smith and Joseph Newman, "Alcohol and Drug Abuse–Dependence Disorders in Psychopathic and Nonpsychopathic Criminal Offenders," *Journal of Abnormal Psychology* 99 (1990): 430–439.

83. Ibid.

84. Jack Levin and James Alan Fox, *Mass Murder* (New York: Plenum Books, 1985).

85. Spencer Rathus and Jeffrey Nevid, *Abnormal Psychology* (Englewood Cliffs, N.J.: Prentice-Hall, 1991), pp. 310–316.

86. Ibid.

87. Samuel Yochelson and Stanton Samenow, *The Criminal Personality* (New York: Jason Aronson, 1977).

88. Oscar Lewis, "The Culture of Poverty," *Scientific American* 215 (1966): 19–25.

89. William Julius Wilson, *The Truly Disadvantaged* (Chicago: University of Chicago Press, 1987).

90. Robert Merton, "Social Structure and Anomie," in *Social Theory and Social Structure*, ed. Robert Merton (Glencoe, Ill.: Free Press, 1975).

91. Charles Tittle, Wayne Villemez, and Douglas Smith, "The Myth of Social Class and Criminality: An Empirical Assessment of the Evidence," *American Sociological Review* 43 (1978): 643–656.

92. Rolf Loeber and Magda Stouthamer-Loeber, "Family Factors as Correlates and Predictors of Juvenile Conduct Problems and Delinquency," in *Crime and Justice*, vol. 7, eds. Michael Tonry and Norval Morris (Chicago: University of Chicago Press, 1986), pp. 29–151.

93. Ibid.

94. Eugene Maguin and Rolf Loeber, "Academic Performance and Delinquency," in *Crime and Justice: An Annual Review of Research*, vol. 20, ed. Michael Tonry and David Farrington (Chicago: University of Chicago Press, 1996), pp. 145–264.

95. For examples of learning theories, see Edwin Sutherland and Donald Cressey, *Criminology*, 8th ed. (Philadelphia: Lippincott, 1970); Ronald Akers, *Deviant Behavior: A Social Learning Approach*, 2nd ed. (Belmont, Mass.: Wadsworth, 1977); Gresham Sykes and David Matza, "Techniques of Neutralization: A Theory of Delinquency," *American Sociological Review* 22 (1957): 664–670; David Matza, *Delinquency and Drift* (New York: Wiley, 1964).

96. Travis Hirschi, *Causes of Delinquency* (Berkeley: University of California Press, 1969).

97. Michael Gottfredson and Travis Hirschi, *A General Theory of Crime* (Stanford, Calif.: Stanford University Press, 1990).

98. W. Byron Groves and Robert Sampson, "Critical Theory and Criminology," *Social Problems* 33 (1986): 58–80.

99. Kathleen Daly and Meda Chesney-Lind, "Feminism and Criminology," *Justice Quarterly* 5 (1988): 438–497.

100. For a general review of this issue, see Sally Simpson, "Feminist Theory, Crime and Justice," *Criminology* 27 (1989): 605–632; Daly and Chesney-Lind, "Feminism and Criminology"; James Messerschmidt, *Capitalism, Patriarchy and Crime* (Totowa, N.J.: Rowman and Littlefield, 1986).

101. See, generally, Jock Young, *Realist Criminology* (London: Sage, 1989).

102. Harold Pepinsky, "Violence as Unresponsiveness: Toward a New Conception of Crime," *Justice Quarterly* 5 (1988): 539–587.

103. Hans Von Hentig, *The Criminal and His Victim: Studies in the Sociobiology of Crime* (New Haven, Conn.: Yale University Press, 1948), p. 384.

104. Marvin Wolfgang, *Patterns of Criminal Homicide* (Philadelphia: University of Pennsylvania Press, 1958).

105. James Lasley and Jill Leslie Rosenbaum, "Routine Activities and Multiple Personal Victimization," *Sociology and Social Research* 73 (1988): 47–48.

106. Lawrence Cohen and Marcus Felson, "Social Change and Crime Rate Trends: A Routine Activities Approach," *American Sociological Review* 44 (1979): 588–608; Lawrence Cohen, Marcus Felson, and Kenneth Land, "Property Crime Rates in the United States: A Macrodynamic Analysis, 1947–1977, with Ex-Ante Forecasts for the Mid-1980s," *American Journal of Sociology* 86 (1980): 90–118; for a review, see James LeBeau and Thomas Castellano, "The Routine Activities Approach: An Inventory and Critique" (Carbondale, Ill.: Center for the Studies of Crime, Delinquency and Corrections, Southern Illinois University, unpublished, 1987).

107. Steven Messner and Kenneth Tardiff, "The Social Ecology of Urban Homicide: An Application of the 'Routine Activities' Approach," *Criminology* 23 (1985): 241–267; Philip Cook, "The Demand and Supply of Criminal Opportunities," in *Crime and Justice*, vol. 7, ed. Michael Tonry and Norval Morris (Chicago: University of Chicago Press, 1986), pp. 1–28; Ronald Clarke and Derek Cornish, "Modeling Offender's Decisions: A Framework for Research and Policy," in *Crime and Justice*, vol. 6, ed. Michael Tonry and Norval Morris (Chicago: University of Chicago Press, 1985), pp. 147–187.

108. Cohen, Felson, and Land, "Property Crime Rates in the United States."

Criminal Law: Substance and Procedure

T his chapter focuses on the basic principles of the substantive criminal law, which regulates conduct in our society. In addition, the chapter discusses constitutional criminal procedure, showing how the rules of procedure, laid out in the U.S. Constitution and interpreted over time by the Supreme Court, control the operations of the justice system.

The **substantive criminal law** defines crime in U.S. society. Each state government and the federal government has its own criminal code, developed over many generations and incorporating moral beliefs, social values, and political, economic, and other societal concerns. The criminal law is a living document, constantly evolving to keep pace with society and its needs. The rules designed to implement the substantive law are known as *procedural law*. It is concerned with the criminal process—the legal steps through which an offender passes—commencing with the initial criminal investigation and concluding with release

of the offender. Some elements of the law of **criminal procedure** are the rules of evidence, the law of arrest, the law of search and seizure, questions of appeal, and the right to counsel. Many of the rights that have been extended to offenders over the past two decades lie within procedural law.

A working knowledge of the law is critical for the criminal justice practitioner. In our modern society, the rule of law governs almost all phases of human enterprise, including commerce, family life, property transfer, and the regulation of interpersonal conflict. It contains elements that control personal relationships between individuals and public relationships between individuals and the government. The former is known as **civil law,** while the latter is criminal law; both concepts are distinguished later in this chapter. Because the law defines crime, punishment, and procedure, which are the basic concerns of the criminal justice system, it is essential for students to know something of the nature, purpose, and content of the substantive and procedural criminal law.

Chapter 3
—
Criminal Law: Substance and Procedure

The roots of the criminal codes used in the United States can be traced back to such early legal charters as the Babylonian Code of Hammurabi (2000 B.C.), the Mosiac Code of the Israelites (1200 B.C.), and the Roman Twelve Tables. During the 6th century, under the leadership of Byzantine emperor Justinian, the first great codification of law in the Western World was prepared. Justinian's *Corpus Juris Civilis,* or body of civil law, summarized the system of Roman law that had developed over a thousand years. Rules and regulations to ensure the safety of the state and the individual were organized into a code and served as the basis for future civil and criminal legal classifications. Centuries later, French emperor Napoleon I created the French civil code, using Justinian's code as a model. France and the other countries that have modeled their legal systems on French and Roman law have what are known as civil law systems. Thus, the concept of law and crime has evolved over thousands of years.[1]

Before the Norman Conquest in 1066, the legal system among the early Anglo-Saxons was decentralized. The law often varied from county to county, and very little was written, except for laws covering crimes. Before A.D. 1000 crimes were viewed as personal wrongs, and compensation was often paid to the victim. Major violations of custom and law included violent acts, theft, and disloyalty to the lord. For certain actions, such as treason, the penalty was often death. For other crimes, such as theft, compensation could be paid to the victim. Thus, to some degree, the early criminal law sought to produce an equitable solution to both private and public disputes.[2]

The Common Law

A more immediate source for much U.S. law is the English system of jurisprudence that developed after the Norman Conquest. Prior to the ratification of the U.S. Constitution in 1788 and the development of the first state legal codes, formal law in the original colonies was adopted from existing English law, which is known today as the **common law.** Common law first came into being during the reign of King Henry II (1154–1189), when royal judges were appointed to travel to specific jurisdictions to hold court and represent the Crown. Known as circuit judges, they followed a specific route (circuit) and heard cases that had been under the jurisdiction of local courts.[3] The royal judges began to replace local custom with a national law that was followed in courts throughout the country; thus, the law was "common" to the entire nation. The common law developed when English judges actually created many crimes by ruling that certain actions were subject to state control and sanction. The most serious offenses, such as murder, rape, treason, arson, and burglary, which had been viewed largely as personal wrongs (torts for which the victim received monetary compensation from the offender), were redefined by the judges as offenses against the state, or crimes. Thus, common law crimes are actions defined by judges as crimes (judge-made crimes).

The English common law evolved constantly to fit specific incidents that the judges encountered. In fact, legal scholars have identified specific cases in which judges created new crimes, some of which exist today. For example, in the **Carriers case** (1473), an English court ruled that a merchant who had been hired to transport merchandise was guilty of larceny (theft) if he kept the goods for his own purposes.[4] Before the *Carriers* case, the common law had not recognized a crime when people kept something that was voluntarily placed in their possession, even if the rightful owner had only given them temporary custody of the merchandise. Breaking with legal tradition, the court recognized that the commercial system could not be maintained unless the law of theft were changed. Thus, larcenies defined by separate and unique criminal laws—such as embezzlement, extortion, and false pretenses—came into existence.

Over time, such common law decisions made by judges in England produced a body of rules and legal principles about crime and punishment that formed the basis of our early American legal system.

Prior to the American Revolution, this common law was the law of the land in the colonies. The original colonists abided by the various common law rulings and adopted them to fit their needs, making extensive changes in them when necessary. After the War of Independence, most state legislatures incorporated the common law into standardized legal codes. Over the years, some of the original common law crimes have changed considerably due to revisions. For example, the common law crime of rape originally applied only to female victims. This has been replaced in a number of jurisdictions by general sexual assault statutes that condemn sexual attacks against any person, male or female. Similarly, statutes prohibiting such offenses as the sale and possession of narcotics or the pirating of videotapes have been passed to control human behavior unknown at the time the common law was formulated. Today, criminal behavior is defined primarily by statute. With few exceptions, crimes are removed, added, or modified by the legislature of a particular jurisdiction.

The Principle of **Stare Decisis**

One of the principal components of the common law was its recognition of the **law of precedent.** Once a decision had been made by a court, that judicial decision was generally binding on other courts in subsequent cases. This principle is based on judge-made law, or case law created by judicial decisions. For example, if a homeowner who killed an unarmed intruder was found not guilty of murder on the ground that he had a right to defend his property, that rule would be applied in subsequent cases involving the same set of facts. In other words, a decision on the issue of self-defense in that case would be followed in that jurisdiction by the same court or a lesser court in future cases presenting the same legal problem. Since the common law represented decisions handed down by judges, as distinguished from law that is determined by statutes, it was essential that the rule of precedent be followed. This legal principle, known as **stare decisis,** originated in England and is still used as the basis for deciding future cases.[5] *Stare decisis* is firmly rooted in the U.S. system of jurisprudence and serves to furnish the courts with a clear guide for the adjudication of similar issues. The courts are generally bound by the principle of *stare decisis* to follow criminal law as it has been judicially determined in prior cases. This rule helps promote fairness and reliability in judicial decision making. The Latin *stare decisis* means "let the decision stand, or precedent."

Criminal Law and Civil Law

In modern U.S. society, law can be divided into two broad categories: criminal law and civil law. All law other than criminal law is known as civil law; it includes tort law (personal wrongs and damages), property law (the law governing the transfer and ownership of property), and contract law (the law of personal agreements).

The differences between criminal law and civil law are significant because, in the U.S. legal system, criminal proceedings are completely separate from civil actions.

The major objective of the criminal law is to protect the public against harm by preventing criminal offenses. The primary concern of the civil law—in the area of private wrongs, or **torts,** for example—is that the injured party be compensated for any harm done. The aggrieved person usually initiates proceedings to recover monetary damages. In contrast, when a crime is committed, the state initiates the legal process and imposes a punishment in the form of a criminal sanction. Furthermore, in criminal law, the emphasis is on the **intent** of the individual committing the crime; a civil proceeding gives primary attention to affixing the blame each party deserves for producing the damage or conflict.

Despite these major differences, criminal and civil law share certain features. Both seek to control people's behavior by preventing them from acting in an undesirable manner, and both impose sanctions on those who commit violations of the law. The payment of damages to the victim in a tort case, for example, serves some of the same purposes as the payment of a fine in a criminal case. The criminal law sentences offenders to prison, while the civil law also imposes confinement on such individuals as the mentally ill, alcoholic, and mentally defective. In addition, many actions, such as assault and battery, various forms of larceny, and negligence, are the basis for criminal as well as civil actions.

Table 3.1 summarizes the major similarities and differences between the criminal law and tort law. The widely publicized case of O. J. Simpson provides a good example, as the same case went through both criminal and civil proceedings. In the so-called Trial of the Century—Part I, the famous athlete was tried by the State of California and acquitted of the murder of his wife, Nicole, and her friend, Ron Goldman, in a criminal prosecution. As a defendant, Simpson

Table 3.1
A Comparison of Criminal
and Tort Law

Similarities
Both criminal and tort law seek to control behavior. Both laws impose sanctions. Similar areas of legal action exist, such as personal assault and control of white-collar offenses (for instance, environmental pollution).

Differences	
Criminal Law	**Tort Law**
Crime is a public offense.	Tort is a civil or private wrong.
The sanction associated with criminal law is incarceration or death.	The sanction associated with a tort is monetary damages.
The right of enforcement belongs to the state.	The individual brings the action.
The government ordinarily does not appeal.	Both parties can appeal.
Fines go to the state.	The individual receives damages as compensation for harm done.

was required to be in court but did not have to testify during the trial. The standard of proof "beyond a reasonable doubt" was used to assess the evidence, and the verdict had to be unanimous. A conviction would have brought a sentence of life in prison.

In the Trial of the Century—Part II, the Estate of Nicole Simpson and the family of Ron Goldman sued O. J. Simpson for the wrongful deaths of his estranged wife and her friend in a civil trial. This was a lawsuit brought by the family of the deceased against the person believed to have caused the death. Simpson was not required to be in court, but when called by either side he had to provide testimony. No television cameras were allowed in the courtroom, whereas the criminal trial was televised on a Court TV network. The burden of proof in the civil case was "preponderance of the evidence," or which side had the most convincing case before the jury. In addition, only nine of twelve jurors had to agree on a general verdict, and any judgment involved money and not imprisonment.

The five major sources of the criminal law are (1) common law, (2) statutes, (3) case decisions, (4) administrative rules and regulations, and (5) constitutional laws.[6]

Sources of the Criminal Law

Common Law and Statutes

The common law crimes adopted into state codes form one major source of the substantive criminal law today. At common law, crimes had a general meaning, and everyone basically understood the definition of such actions as murder, larceny, and rape. Today, statutes enacted by state and federal legislative bodies have built on these common law meanings and often contain more detailed and specific definitions of the crimes. Statutes are thus a way in which the criminal law is created, modified, or expunged. They reflect existing social conditions and deal with issues of morality, such as gambling and sexual activity, as well as traditional common law crimes, such as murder, burglary, and arson.

Case Decisions

Case law and judicial decision making also change and influence laws. For example, a statute may define murder as the "unlawful killing of one human being by another with malice." Court decisions might help explain the meaning of the term *malice* or clarify whether *human being* includes a fetus. A judge may rule that a statute is vague, deals with an act no longer of interest to the public, or is an unfair exercise of state control over an individual. Conversely, some judges may interpret the law so that behaviors that were previously acceptable become outlawed. For example, judges in a particular jurisdiction might find all people who sell magazines depicting nude men and women guilty of the crime of selling obscene material, whereas in the past obscenity was interpreted much more narrowly. Or some courts might consider drunken driving a petty crime, while others might interpret the statute on driving under the influence more severely.

Administrative Rule Making

Administrative agencies with rule-making authority also develop measures to control conduct in our society.[7] Some agencies regulate taxation, health, environment, and other public functions; others control drugs, illegal gambling, or pornographic material. The listing of prohibited drugs by various state health boards, for example, is an important administrative control function. Parole boards are administrative agencies that implement the thousands of regulations governing the conduct of criminal offenders after their release from prison. Such rules are called *administrative rules with criminal sanctions,* and agency decisions about these rules have the force and authority of law.

Constitutional Law and Its Limits

Regardless of its source, all criminal law in the United States must conform to the rules and dictates of the U.S. Constitution.[8] In other words, any criminal law that conflicts with the various provisions and articles of the Constitution will eventually be challenged in the appellate courts and stricken from the legal code by judicial order (or modified to adhere to constitutional principles). As Chief Justice John Marshall's opinion in *Marbury v. Madison* indicated, "If the courts are to regard the Constitution and the Constitution is superior to any ordinary act of the legislature, the Constitution and not such ordinary act must govern the case to which they apply."[9] This landmark case of 1803 established the concept of judicial review. All laws, including criminal statutes, must therefore meet constitutional standards or be declared invalid.

Among the general limitations set by the Constitution are those that forbid the government to pass *ex post facto* laws. Such laws make an action a crime that was not a crime at the time it was done; they create crimes (or penalties) that could be enforced retroactively (though civil penalties, such as those set in tax laws, can be retroactive). The Constitution also forbids *bills of attainder:* legislative acts that inflict punishment without a judicial trial. In addition, criminal laws have been interpreted as violating constitutional principles if they are too vague or overbroad to give clear meaning of their intent. For example, a law forbidding adults to engage in "immoral behavior" could not be enforced, because it does not use clear and precise language or give adequate notice as to which conduct is forbidden.[10] The Constitution also forbids laws that make a person's status a crime. For example, addiction to narcotics cannot be made a crime, though laws can forbid the sale, possession, and manufacture of dangerous drugs.

In general, the Constitution has been interpreted to forbid any criminal law that violates a person's right to be treated fairly and equally; this principle is referred to as *substantive due process.* Usually, this means that before a new law can be created, the state must show that there is a compelling need to protect public safety or morals.

Crimes and Classifications

The decision of how a crime should be classified rests with the individual jurisdiction. Each state has developed its own body of criminal law and consequently determines its own penalties for the various crimes. Thus, the criminal law of a given state defines and grades offenses, sets levels of punishment, and classifies crimes into categories. Over the years, crimes have been generally grouped into (1) felonies, misdemeanors, and violations; and (2) other statutory classifications, such as juvenile delinquency, sex offender categories, and multiple- or first-offender classifications. In general terms, felonies are considered serious crimes, misdemeanors are seen as less serious crimes, and violations may be noncriminal offenses, such as traffic offenses and public drunkenness. Some states consider violations civil matters, while others classify them as crimes.

The most common classification in the United States is the division between felonies and misdemeanors.[11] This distinction is based primarily on the degree of seriousness of the crime. Distinguishing between a felony and a misdemeanor is sometimes difficult. Simply put, a **felony** is a serious offense, while a **misdemeanor** is a less serious one.

Black's Law Dictionary defines the two terms as follows:

> A felony is a crime of a graver or more atrocious nature than those designated as misdemeanors. Generally it is an offense punishable by death or imprisonment in a penitentiary. A misdemeanor is lower than a felony and is generally punishable by fine or imprisonment otherwise than in a penitentiary.[12]

Each jurisdiction in the United States determines by statute what types of conduct constitute felonies or misdemeanors. The most common definition of a felony is that it is a crime punishable in the statute by death or by imprisonment in a state or federal prison. In Massachusetts, for example, any crime that a statute punishes by imprisonment in the state prison system is considered a felony, and all other crimes are misdemeanors.[13] Another way of determining what category an offense falls into is by providing in the statute that a felony is any crime punishable by imprisonment for more than one year. In the former method, the place of imprisonment is critical; in the latter, the length of the prison sentence distinguishes a felony from a misdemeanor.

In the United States today, felonies include serious crimes against the person, such as criminal homicide, robbery, and rape, as well as such crimes against property as burglary and larceny. Misdemeanors include petit (or petty) larceny, assault and battery, and the unlawful possession of marijuana. The least serious, or petty, offenses, which often involve criminal traffic violations, are called infractions or violations.

The felony-misdemeanor classification has a direct effect on the offender charged with the crime. A person convicted of a felony may be barred from certain fields of employment or some professions, such as law and medicine. A felony offender's status as an alien in the United States might also be affected, or the offender might be denied the right to hold public office, vote, or serve on a jury.[14] These and other civil liabilities exist only when a person is convicted of a felony offense, not a misdemeanor.

Whether the offender is charged with a felony or a misdemeanor also makes a difference at the time of arrest. Normally, the law of arrest requires that if the crime is a misdemeanor and has not been committed in the presence of a police officer, the officer cannot make an arrest. This is known as the in-presence requirement. However, the police officer does have the legal authority to arrest a suspect for a misdemeanor at a subsequent time by the use of a validly obtained arrest warrant. In contrast, an arrest for a felony may be made regardless of whether the crime was committed in the officer's presence, as long as the officer has reasonable grounds to believe that the person has committed the felony.

In addition to the felony-misdemeanor classifications, crimes may be classified according to the characteristics of the offender. All states, for example, have juvenile delinquency statutes that classify children under a certain age as juvenile delinquents if they commit acts that would constitute crimes if committed by adults. Some states have special statutory classifications for sex offenders, multiple offenders, youthful offenders, and first offenders. Generally, no special statutory classification exists for white-collar crimes, such as embezzlement, fraud, and income tax violation, which usually involve nonviolent conduct.

Felonies and Misdemeanors

Other Statutory Classifications

There is no single universally accepted legal definition of a crime. Because the determination of what constitutes a crime rests with the individual jurisdiction, the federal government and each of the states have their own body of criminal law. Most general legal definitions of a crime are basically similar, however. A crime can be defined as follows:

> A **crime** is (1) a legal wrong (2) prohibited by the criminal law (3) prosecuted by the state (4) in a formal court proceeding (5) in which a criminal sanction or sentence may be imposed.

As determined by most legal systems, crime can result from the commission of an act in violation of the law or from the omission of a required legal act. For example, a crime can be an intentional act of striking another person or of stealing someone else's property. But it can also involve the failure of a person to act, such as the failure to file an income tax return, parental failure to care for a child, or failure to report a crime or an automobile accident.

The legal definition of a crime involves the elements of the criminal acts that must be proven in a court of law if the defendant is to be found guilty. For the most part, common criminal acts have both mental and physical elements, both of which must be present if the act is to be considered a legal crime. The following definition of the crime of burglary in the nighttime, as stated in the Massachusetts General Laws, is an example of the mental and physical elements of the substantive criminal law:

> Whoever breaks and enters a dwelling house in the nighttime, with intent to commit a felony, or whoever, after having entered with such intent, breaks such dwelling house in the nighttime, any person being lawfully therein, and the offender being armed with a dangerous weapon at the time of such breaking or entry, or so arming himself in such house or making an actual assault on a person lawfully therein, [commits the crime of burglary].[15]

Certain basic elements are required for an act to be considered a crime. For the crime of burglary, the state must prove that the defendant actually entered a home by force and was not invited in, that the defendant carried an identifiable weapon, that the crime occurred after sundown, and that the act was intentional. These elements form what is known as the ***corpus delicti,*** or "body of the crime." The term *corpus delicti* is often misunderstood. Some people, for in-

A crime is (1) a legal wrong (2) prohibited by the criminal law (3) prosecuted by the state (4) in a formal court proceeding (5) in which a criminal sanction or sentence may be imposed. Crime can result from the commission of an act in violation of the law or from the omission of a required legal act, as when a person fails to file an income tax return. For the most part, the definition of a crime requires both mental and physical elements: the act itself and the intent to commit the act.

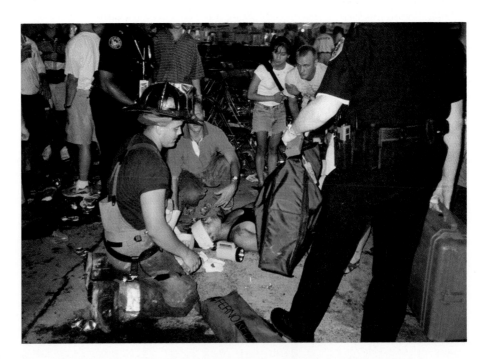

stance, wrongly believe that it refers to the body of the deceased in a homicide. *Corpus delicti* describes all the elements that together constitute a crime; it includes (1) the *actus reus,* (2) the *mens rea,* and (3) the combination of *actus reus* and *mens rea.*

The term **actus reus,** which translates as "guilty act," refers to the forbidden act itself. The criminal law uses it to describe the physical crime and the commission of the criminal act (or omission of the lawful act). In *Criminal Law,* Wayne LaFave and Austin Scott state:

> Bad thought alone cannot constitute a crime, there must be an act, or an omission to act where there is a legal duty to act. Thus, the common-law crimes are defined in terms of act or omission to act and statutory crimes are unconstitutional unless so defined. A bodily movement, to qualify as an act forming the basis of criminal liability, must be voluntary.[16]

The physical act in violation of the criminal statute is usually clearly defined within each offense. For example, in the crime of manslaughter, the unlawful killing of a human being is the physical act prohibited by a statute; in burglary, it is the actual breaking and entering into a dwelling house or other structure for the purpose of committing a felony.

Regarding an omission to act, many jurisdictions hold a person accountable if a legal duty exists and the offender avoids it. In most instances, the duty to act is based on a defined relationship, such as parent-child, or on a contractual duty, such as lifeguard-swimmer. The law, for example, recognizes that a parent has a legal duty to protect a child. When a parent refuses to obtain medical attention for the child and the child dies, the parent's actions constitute an omission to act, and that omission is a crime.

The second element basic to the commission of any crime is the establishment of the **mens rea,** translated as "guilty mind." *Mens rea* is the element of the crime that deals with the defendant's intent to commit a criminal act and includes such states of mind as concealing criminal knowledge (scienter), recklessness, negligence, and criminal purpose.[17] A person ordinarily cannot be convicted of a crime unless it is proven that he or she intentionally, knowingly, or willingly committed the criminal act.

The following case illustrates the absence of *mens rea.* A student at a university took home some books, believing them to be her own, and subsequently found that the books belonged to her classmate. When she realized that the books did not belong to her, she returned them to their proper owner. The student could not be prosecuted for theft because she did not intend to steal the books in the first place; she did not knowingly take the books and therefore lacked sufficient knowledge that her act was unlawful.

The third element needed to prove the *corpus delicti* of a crime is the relationship of the act to the criminal intent or result. The law requires that the offender's conduct must be the approximate cause of any injury resulting from the criminal act. If, for example, a man chases a victim into the street intending to assault him and the victim is struck and killed by a car, the accused could be convicted of murder if the court felt that his actions made him responsible for the victim's death. If, however, a victim dies from a completely unrelated illness after being assaulted, the court must determine whether the death was a probable consequence of the defendant's illegal conduct or whether it would have resulted even if the assault had not occurred.

Existence of a criminal intent and a wrongful act must both be proved before an individual can be found guilty of committing a crime. However, certain statutory

Actus Reus

Mens Rea

Relationship of Mens Rea *and* Actus Reus

Strict Liability

offenses exist in which *mens rea* is not essential. These offenses fall within a category known as public welfare, or **strict liability,** crimes. A person can be held responsible for such a violation independent of the existence of intent to commit the offense. Strict liability criminal statutes generally include narcotics control laws, traffic laws, health and safety regulations, sanitation laws, and other regulatory statutes. For example, a driver could not defend himself against a speeding ticket by claiming that he was unaware of how fast he was going and did not intend to speed, nor could a bartender claim that a juvenile to whom she sold liquor looked quite a bit older. No state of mind is generally required where a strict liability statute is violated.[18] These laws are generally an exception to the requirement that all crimes include a *mens rea* or guilty mind. Ordinarily, only a wrongful act is needed for a conviction under a strict liability statute.

Criminal Responsibility

The idea of criminal responsibility is also essential to any discussion of criminal law. The law recognizes that certain conditions of a person's mental state might excuse him or her from acts that otherwise would be considered criminal. These factors have been used in legal defenses to negate the intent required for the commission of a crime. For example, a person who kills another while insane may argue in court that he or she was not responsible for criminal conduct. Similarly, a child who violates the law may not be treated as an adult offender. These types of "excuses" are defenses in which the defendant is not considered responsible or blameworthy for having engaged in criminal conduct. Three major types of criminal defense are detailed in this section: insanity, intoxication, and age.

Legal Definition of Insanity

Over the years, the legal system has struggled to define the rules relating to the use of **insanity** as a defense in a criminal trial. The tests for criminal responsibility involving insanity followed by U.S. courts are (1) the M'Naghten rule, (2) the irresistible impulse test, (3) the Durham rule, and (4) the substantial capacity test.

The **M'Naghten rule,** or the right-wrong test, is based on the decision in the *M'Naghten* case. In 1843 Daniel M'Naghten shot and killed Edward Drummond, believing Drummond to be Sir Robert Peel, the British prime minister. M'Naghten was prosecuted for murder. At his trial, he claimed that he was not criminally responsible for his actions because he suffered from delusions at the time of the killing. M'Naghten was found not guilty by reason of insanity. Because of the importance of the case and the unpopularity of the decision, the House of Lords reviewed the decision and asked the court to define the law with respect to crimes committed by persons suffering from insane delusions. The court's answer became known as the M'Naghten rule and has subsequently become the primary test for criminal responsibility in the United States. The M'Naghten rule can be stated as follows:

> A defendant may be excused from criminal responsibility if at the time of the committing of the act the party accused was labouring under such a defect of reason, from a disease of the mind, as not to know the nature and quality of the act he was doing, or if he did know it, that he did not know that he was doing what was wrong.[19]

Thus, according to the M'Naghten rule, a person is basically insane if he or she is unable to distinguish between right and wrong as a result of some mental disability.

Over the years, the courts have become critical of the M'Naghten rule. Many insane individuals are able to distinguish between right and wrong. Also, clear determinations by the courts of such terms as "disease of the mind," "know," and "the nature and quality of the act" have never been made. As a result, many jurisdictions that follow the M'Naghten rule have supplemented it with the **irresistible impulse test.** This rule excuses from criminal responsibility a person whose mental disease makes it impossible to control personal conduct. The criminal may be able to distinguish between right and wrong but may be unable to exercise self-control because of a disabling mental condition. Almost half of the states use a combined M'Naghten rule–irresistible impulse test.

Another rule for determining criminal insanity is the **Durham rule.** Originally created in New Hampshire in 1871, the Durham rule was reviewed and subsequently adopted by the Court of Appeals for the District of Columbia in 1954, in the case of *Durham v. United States.*[20] In that opinion, Judge David Bazelon rejected the M'Naghten formula and stated that an accused is not criminally responsible if the unlawful act was the product of mental disease or defect. This rule, also known as the *products test,* is based on the contention that insanity represents many personality factors, not all of which may be present in every case. It leaves the question of deciding whether a defendant is insane in the hands of jurors.

The Durham rule has been viewed with considerable skepticism, primarily because the problem of defining "mental disease," "defect," and "product" does not give the jury a reliable standard by which to make its judgment. Consequently, it has been dropped in the jurisdictions that experimented with it.

Another test for criminal insanity, which has become increasingly popular in many courts, is the **substantial capacity test.** In summary, as presented in Section 4.01 of the American Law Institute's Model Penal Code, this test states:

> A person is not responsible for criminal conduct if at the time of such conduct as a result of mental disease or defect he lacks substantial capacity whether to appreciate his criminality (wrongfulness) of his conduct or to conform his conduct to the requirements of law.[21]

This rule is basically a broader restatement of the M'Naghten rule–irresistible impulse test. It rejects the Durham rule because of its lack of standards and its inability to define the term "product." The most significant feature of this test is that it requires only a lack of "substantial capacity" rather than complete impairment of the defendant's ability to know and understand the difference between right and wrong. Twenty-four states use the substantial capacity test as defined by the American Law Institute.[22]

Table 3.2 summarizes various rules for determining criminal insanity. In reality, only a small number of offenders actually use the insanity defense, because

Test	Legal Standard Because of Mental Illness	Final Burden of Proof	Who Bears Burden of Proof
M'Naghten	"Didn't know what he was doing or didn't know it was wrong"	Varies from proof by a balance of probabilities on the defense to proof beyond a reasonable doubt on the prosecutor	
Irresistible impulse	"Could not control his conduct"	Beyond reasonable doubt	Prosecutor
Durham rule	"The criminal act was caused by his mental illness"	Beyond reasonable doubt	Prosecutor
Substantial capacity	"Lacks substantial capacity to appreciate the wrongfulness of his conduct or to control it"	Beyond reasonable doubt	Prosecutor
Current federal law	"Lacks capacity to appreciate the wrongfulness of his conduct"	Clear and convincing evidence	Defense

Table 3.2
Insanity Defense Standards
SOURCE: National Institute of Justice, *Crime Study Guide: Insanity Defense,* by Norval Morris (Washington, D.C.: U.S. Department of Justice, 1986), p. 3.

many cases involving insane offenders are processed through civil commitment proceedings.

The insanity defense has been controversial for many years. In the early 1980s, the debate intensified when John Hinckley, Jr., was acquitted on insanity grounds in the assassination attempt on President Ronald Reagan. Congress responded with the Insanity Defense Reform Act of 1984, which weakened the defense.

Today, the insanity defense is on trial again. John DuPont, the wealthy industrial heir, failed in using the tough Pennsylvania insanity law to defend himself in connection with the shooting death of Olympic wrestler David Schultz in 1996. This defense also failed in the recent trial of John Salvi, charged with the 1994 murder of two abortion clinic workers in Massachusetts.

Because many states have rewritten their insanity laws to severely limit the availability of the defense, and some have abolished it outright, defendants are finding that insanity pleas are failing as the public grows impatient with violent crime. Studies show that, nationwide, the insanity defense is raised in only about 1% of all felony crimes and succeeds in only a small fraction of these cases.[23]

Intoxication

As a general rule, intoxication, which may include drunkenness or being under the influence of drugs, is not considered a defense. However, a defendant who becomes involuntarily intoxicated under duress or by mistake may be excused for crimes committed. Voluntary intoxication may also lessen the degree of a crime. For example, a judgment may be decreased from first- to second-degree murder because the defendant uses intoxication to prove the lack of the critical element of *mens rea,* or mental intent. Thus, the effect of intoxication on criminal liability depends on whether the defendant uses the alcohol or drugs voluntarily. For example, a defendant who enters a bar for a few drinks, becomes intoxicated, and strikes someone can be convicted of assault and battery. On the other hand, if the defendant ordered a nonalcoholic drink that was spiked by someone else, the defendant may have a legitimate legal defense.

Because of the frequency of crime-related offenses involving drugs and alcohol, the impact of intoxication on criminal liability is a persistent issue in the criminal justice system. The connection between drug use, alcoholism, and violent street crime has been well documented. Although those in law enforcement and the judiciary tend to emphasize the use of the penal process in dealing with problems of chronic alcoholism and drug use, others in corrections and crime prevention favor approaches that depend more on behavioral theories and the social sciences. For example, in the case of *Robinson v. California,* the U.S. Supreme Court struck down a California statute making addiction to narcotics a crime, on the ground that it violated the defendant's rights under the Eighth and Fourteenth Amendments to the U.S. Constitution.[24] On the other hand, the landmark decision in *Powell v. Texas* placed severe limitations on the behavioral science approach in *Robinson* when it rejected the defense of chronic alcoholism of a defendant charged with the crime of public drunkenness.[25]

Age

The law holds that a child is not criminally responsible for actions committed at an age that precludes a full realization of the gravity of certain types of behavior. Under common law, there is generally a conclusive presumption of incapacity for a child under age 7, a reliable presumption for a child between the ages of 7 and 14, and no presumption for a child over the age of 14. This generally means that a child under age 7 who commits a crime will not be held criminally responsible for these actions and that a child between 7 and 14 may be held responsible. These common law rules have been changed by statute in most jurisdictions. Today, the maximum age of criminal responsibility for children ranges from 14 to 17 or 18, while the minimum age may be set by statute at 7 or under 14.[26] In addition, every jurisdiction has established a juvenile court system to deal with juvenile offenders and children in need of court and societal supervision. Thus, the mandate of the juvenile justice system is to provide for the care and protection of children under a given age established by state statute. In certain situations, a juvenile court may transfer a more serious chronic youthful offender to the adult criminal court.

Criminal defenses may also be based on the concept of justification or excuse. In other words, certain defenses allow for the commission of a crime to be justified or excused on grounds of fairness and public policy. In these instances, defendants normally acknowledge that they committed the act but claim that they cannot be prosecuted because they were justified in doing so. The following major types of criminal defenses involving justification or excuse are explained in this section: (1) consent, (2) self-defense, (3) entrapment, (4) double jeopardy, and (5) mistake, compulsion, and necessity.

As a general rule, the victim's consent to a crime does not justify or excuse the defendant who commits the action. The type of crime involved generally determines the validity of consent as an appropriate legal defense. Such crimes as common law rape and larceny require lack of consent on the part of the victim. In other words, a rape does not occur if the victim consents to sexual relations. In the same way, a larceny cannot occur if the owner voluntarily consents to the taking of the property. Consequently, in such crimes consent is an essential element of the crime, and it is a valid defense where it can be proven or shown that it existed at the time the crime was committed. In statutory rape, however, consent is not an element of the crime and is considered irrelevant, because the state presumes that young people are not capable of providing consent.

In certain instances, the defendant who admits to the acts that constitute a crime may claim to be not guilty because of an affirmative **self-defense.** To establish the necessary elements to constitute self-defense, the defendant must have acted under a reasonable belief that he or she was in danger of death or great harm and had no means of escape from the assailant.

As a general legal rule, however, a person defending himself or herself may use only such force as is reasonably necessary to prevent personal harm. A person who is assaulted by another with no weapon is ordinarily not justified in hitting the assailant with a baseball bat. A person verbally threatened by another is not justified in striking the other party. If a woman hits a larger man, generally speaking the man would not be justified in striking the woman and causing her physical harm. In other words, to exercise the self-defense privilege, the danger to the defendant must be immediate. In addition, the defendant is obligated to look for alternative means of avoiding the danger, such as escape, retreat, or assistance from others.

The famous 1984 case of Bernhard Goetz, the celebrated "subway shooter," is a well-known example of legal self-defense versus unlawful vigilantism in an urban setting.[27] Goetz, a 37-year-old businessman, shot four black teenagers on a New York City subway train after being asked for $5. Three of the teens were carrying sharpened screwdrivers and had prior arrest records; they had allegedly threatened Goetz. New York state law allows a victim to shoot in self-defense only if there is reasonable belief that the assailant will use deadly force and if the victim cannot escape.

After a much publicized refusal by a first grand jury to indict Goetz for attempted murder, Goetz was subsequently indicted, tried, and acquitted in 1987 of attempted murder and assault but was convicted of illegal possession of an unlicensed concealed handgun. Goetz claimed he shot the four youths in self-defense because he feared he was about to be robbed. This bitter and controversial case finally came to an end in January 1989, when Goetz was given a one-year jail

Consent

Self-Defense

sentence for the illegal handgun charge. According to the prosecution, Goetz had taken the law into his own hands. Goetz maintained that society needs to be protected from criminals. Today, there is a good deal of debate over the application of self-defense to a woman who is battered by her husband and then kills him. This is known as the "battered-wife syndrome" (or in cases involving child abuse, the battered-child syndrome). Self-defense here often requires the presence of imminent danger and the inability to escape from the assailant.

Entrapment

The term **entrapment** refers to an affirmative defense in the criminal law that excuses a defendant from criminal liability when law enforcement agents use traps, decoys, and deception to induce criminal action. It is generally legitimate for law enforcement officers to set traps for criminals by getting information about crimes from informers, undercover agents, and codefendants. Police officers are allowed to use ordinary opportunities for defendants to commit crime and to create these opportunities without excessive inducement and solicitation to commit and involve a defendant in a crime. However, when the police instigate the crime, implant criminal ideas, and coerce individuals into bringing about a crime, defendants have the defense of entrapment available to them. Entrapment is not a constitutional defense but has been created by court decision and statute in most jurisdictions.

The degree of government involvement in a criminal act leading to the entrapment defense has been defined in a number of U.S. Supreme Court decisions beginning in 1932. The majority view of what constitutes entrapment can be seen in the 1932 case of *Sorrells v. United States*.[28] During Prohibition, a federal officer passed himself off as a tourist while gaining the defendant's confidence. The federal agent eventually enticed the defendant to buy illegal liquor for him. The defendant was then arrested and prosecuted for violating the National Prohibition Act. The Supreme Court held that the officer used improper inducements that amounted to entrapment. In deciding this case, the Court settled on the "subjective" view of entrapment, which means that the predisposition of the defendant to commit the offense is the determining factor in entrapment. Following the *Sorrells* case, the Supreme Court stated in *Sherman v. United States* that the function of law enforcement is to prevent crime and to apprehend criminals, not to implant a criminal design, originating with officials of the government, in the mind of an innocent person.[29]

In the latest entrapment case, in which a defendant ordered magazines depicting nude boys and was pursued by the government for over two and a half years for violating a new law relating to minors, the Court held that the defendant was entrapped. Any predisposition to break the law was held to be the result of government coaxing (see *Jacobson v. United States*).

Consequently, the major legal rule today considers entrapment primarily in light of the defendant's predisposition to commit a crime. A defendant with a criminal record would have a tougher time using this defense successfully than one who had never been in trouble before.

Double Jeopardy

By virtue of the Fifth Amendment, "No person shall be subject for the same offense to be twice put in jeopardy of life or limb."[30] The objective of this constitutional protection is to prohibit the reprosecution of a defendant for the same offense by the same jurisdiction. Thus, a person who has been tried for armed robbery by a judge or jury may not be tried again in that state for the same incident.

A review of the **double jeopardy** question involves a number of issues: (1) Does prosecution for the same or similar offenses by the state and federal governments constitute double jeopardy? (2) When does double jeopardy attach in a criminal prosecution? (3) What effect does the double jeopardy clause have on sentencing provisions?

The issue of federal versus state prosecutions arises with offenses that are crimes against the state as well as against the federal government. The U.S. Supreme Court has held, in the case of *Bartkus v. Illinois* (1959) and in numerous other cases, that both state and federal prosecutions against a defendant for the same crime are not in violation of the Fifth Amendment.[31] The Court reasoned that every citizen is a citizen of the United States and of a state. Consequently, either or both jurisdictions can try to punish an offender. On the other hand, a state can try an accused only once. The state has the responsibility either to convict the defendant legally or to acquit the defendant on all charges. The Fifth Amendment prohibits a second prosecution, unless there has been an appeal by the defendant. The state may obtain a second trial in cases involving a mistrial, a hung jury, or some other trial defect.

With regard to when double jeopardy attaches, the general rule is that the Fifth Amendment applies when a criminal trial begins before a judge or jury. In the case of *Benton v. Maryland* (1969), the U.S. Supreme Court held that the double jeopardy provisions of the Fifth Amendment were applicable to the states.[32] The accused has the right to be tried until a final determination of the case is made.

As a general matter, the double jeopardy clause prohibits successive prosecutions and punishments for the same offense. In addition, ending the debate that has gone on for over a decade, the Supreme Court decided in 1996 (*United States v. Ursery*) that civil forfeiture proceedings for a defendant's property associated with a parallel criminal prosecution do not trigger the double jeopardy provisions. This decision means that a defendant can lose both liberty and property. Also, it now is easier for the government to take virtually all property used to perpetrate criminal activity.[33]

Mistake or ignorance of the law is generally no defense to a crime. According to the great legal scholar William Blackstone, "Ignorance of the law, which everyone is bound to know, excuses no man."[34] Consequently, a defendant cannot present a legitimate defense by saying he or she was unaware of a criminal law, had misinterpreted the law, or believed the law to be unconstitutional.

On the other hand, mistakes of fact, such as taking someone else's coat that is similar to your own, may be a valid defense. If the jury or judge as trier of fact determines that criminal intent was absent, such an honest mistake may remove the defendant's criminal responsibility.

Compulsion or coercion may also be a criminal defense under certain conditions. In these cases, the defendant has been forced into committing a crime. For this defense to be upheld, a defendant must show that the actions were the only means of preventing death or serious harm to self or others. For example, a bank employee might be excused from taking bank funds if she can prove that her family was being threatened and that consequently she was acting under duress. But there is widespread general agreement that duress is no defense to an intentional killing.

Closely connected to the defense of compulsion is that of necessity. According to the Model Penal Code (a substantive model of the criminal code used as a guide by states), "Necessity may be an acceptable defense, provided the harm to be avoided is greater than the offense charged."[35] In other words, the defense of necessity is justified when the crime was committed because the circumstances could not be avoided. For example, a husband steals a car to bring his pregnant wife to the hospital for an emergency delivery, or a hunter shoots an animal of an endangered species that was about to attack his child. The defense has been found inapplicable, however, in cases where defendants sought to shut down nuclear power plants or abortion clinics or to destroy missile components under the belief that the action was necessary to save lives or prevent a nuclear war. Even those who use a controlled substance such as marijuana for medicinal

Mistake, Compulsion, and Necessity

A Time to Kill

A Time to Kill, the first novel by highly popular author John Grisham, was also made into a successful 1996 film. The story concerns the brutal rape and beating of Tonya, the ten-year-old daughter of Carl Lee Hailey (played by Samuel L. Jackson), a Mississippi factory worker, by two drunken racist thugs. Shocked by his daughter's injuries and the fact that the rape left her incapable of ever bearing children, Carl Lee decides to take the law into his own hands. He waits in the courthouse and guns the culprits down, accidentally shooting a local law enforcement officer in the process. The local cop, Carl Lee's friend, loses his leg.

Carl Lee hires a young lawyer, Jake Brigance (Matthew McConaughey), to defend him in court. Jake's defense is that Carl Lee could not form the intent to commit the crime because the rage he felt had caused a form of temporary insanity. He is aided in the case by a volunteer, Ellen Roark (Sandra Bullock), an energetic, Boston-born law student at the University of Mississippi. Jake is also guided by veteran attorney Lucien Wilbanks (Donald Sutherland), his mentor who has fallen from prominence and become an alcoholic. Wilbanks is prompted to help because Jake must face a ruthless and seasoned prosecutor, Rufus Buckley (Kevin Spacey), who views the trial as a political springboard.

As the trial progresses, Freddie Cobb (Kiefer Sutherland), brother of one of the slain men, joins the Ku Klux Klan and gets them involved in the trial. They threaten Jake and his wife, burn their home, and as-

sault Ellen Roark. The trial, held before tough Judge Omar Noose (Patrick McGoohan) and an all-white jury, goes badly, and Jake's witnesses are discredited. However, in a stirring closing statement, Jake asks the jury to imagine that the girl who has been assaulted and brutalized is white, and when they do, the jury tearfully finds Carl Lee not guilty.

A Time to Kill is good drama, but is it good law? It is unlikely that Carl Lee would simply be found "not guilty" after he had armed himself, lay in wait, and killed two men for revenge. Although slimy and reprehensible, the culprits had not been charged with a capital crime, and their crime did not warrant death. Given the circumstances, Carl Lee would most likely be convicted of at least manslaughter rather than being found not guilty. Rage and anger are not recognized as a defense to crime. If the relatives of victims were allowed to kill criminals they felt had not been punished sufficiently by the law, the entire criminal justice system would be compromised. Could Ron Goldman's father kill O. J. Simpson with impunity simply because he believes Simpson has not been sufficiently punished? Ironically, Carl Lee did not wait to find out how the rapists were going to be dealt with before taking the law into his own hands. What would have happened if they had gotten a 50-year sentence? Would that have been sufficient? Carl Lee also shot and seriously wounded a police officer, but he was not tried on charges for this crime. The case does show that juries do in fact have a lot of discretion in making their judgments and that on occasion they let their emotions dictate the law.

purposes often cannot claim vindication based on medical necessity, although some courts have viewed this as a legitimate defense.[36]

In recent years, mental distress seems to be a favorite maneuver in high-profile criminal cases. Lorena Bobbitt was acquitted by convincing a jury that physical and sexual abuse removed responsibility for her mutilation of her husband by cutting off his penis. The first trial of the Menendez brothers for killing their parents resulted in a hung jury with a childhood abuse defense, but they were subsequently convicted in a second trial and given a life sentence.

Rage and anger are not proof of mental illness, and jealousy is no defense or excuse for murder. Such defenses are often known as "abuse excuses" or soft defenses. They might also include such excuses as premenstrual syndrome, post-traumatic stress, black rage, cocaine-induced psychosis, XYY chromosome pattern, and many others. All of these conditions boil down to one issue: an effort by the defense attorney to limit individual responsibility.

In recent years, many states and the federal government have been examining and revising their substantive and procedural criminal codes. An ongoing effort has been made to update legal codes so that they provide an accurate reflection of public opinion, social change, technological innovation, and other important social issues. What kinds of criminal statutes do we need today? Should it be a crime to aid and abet a suicide? Michigan is one of the first places in the world to consider legalizing physician-assisted suicide as a result of the recent trial of Dr. Jack Kevorkian. Yet in 1997, the U.S. Supreme Court rejected a constitutional "right to die." What about a "stalking" statute that would make it a crime to harass or follow someone? In many jurisdictions, it is still a crime to have sexual relations with any person other than your spouse.

In 1995, 1996, and 1997 the most popular criminal law statutes passed by state legislatures included:

1. *Domestic or family violence laws.* Experts believe these statutes are essential to support individuals and families at risk from domestic violence and abuse.[37]

2. *Tough recidivist and "truth in sentencing" laws.* These statutes are aimed at keeping violent and repeat offenders in prison longer. "Three strikes and you're out" continues to be the call in states seeking to impose long, often life sentences without parole for two-time or three-time repeat offenders.[38]

Substantive Criminal Law Reform

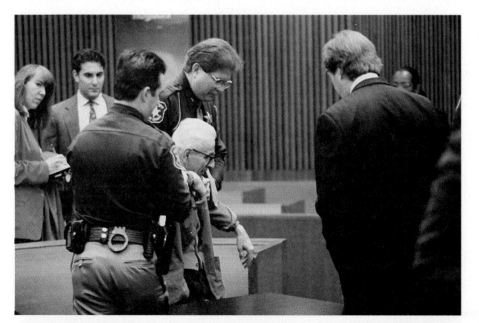

Many states and the federal government have been examining and revising their substantive and procedural criminal codes so that they reflect current public opinion, social change, technological innovation, and other important social issues. Dr. Jack Kevorkian, shown here going limp in a Michigan courtroom, has been at the heart of efforts to formulate laws allowing (or prohibiting) physician-assisted suicide. The issue will be considered by the United States Supreme Court.

Chapter 3

Criminal Law: Substance and Procedure

3. *Community notification laws.* One such law, known as "Megan's law," was passed in New Jersey after the killing of a child by a convicted sex offender who, unknown to the community, had moved in across the street from the victim. Virtually all the states have enacted "Megan"–type laws implementing sex offender registration and notification requirements. Can these statutes stop sexual predators? Do they violate an individual's constitutional rights?[39]

4. *Laws transferring juveniles to adult courts.* Prosecuting and handling serious, violent juvenile offenders in the adult criminal justice system has been an integral part of new juvenile crime legislation in many jurisdictions. Some new laws change the age criteria for discretionary transfer to adult court, while others provide that certain serious crimes by juveniles must be handled in the adult system.[40]

What was a crime thirty years ago—such as performing an abortion—may no longer be a crime today. In this instance, clouds of protest continue to surround the issue as pro- and anti-abortion groups argue the merits of such decisions by the government. Conversely, what was unregulated behavior in the past, such as using children to pose for adult sex publications, may be outlawed because of public concern and outrage.[41]

One aspect of criminal law reform involves weeding out laws that seem archaic in light of what is now known about human behavior. For example, alcoholism is now considered a disease that should be treated, not an offense that should be punished. Many experts believe that such offenses as drunkenness, disorderly conduct, vagrancy, gambling, and minor sexual violations are essentially social problems and should not be dealt with by the criminal justice system.

Other criminal law revisions reflect increasing awareness about problems that confront American society. As mentioned previously, a number of states have eliminated traditional rape laws and replaced them with sexually neutral assault statutes that recognize that men as well as women can be the victims of rape. Most jurisdictions have adopted laws that require people in certain occupations, such as teachers and doctors, to report suspected cases of child abuse to the proper authorities.

The RICO Statute

In an effort to control organized crime, Congress passed the **Racketeer Influenced and Corrupt Organization (RICO) Act.** This law prevents people from acquiring or maintaining an interest in an ongoing enterprise, such as a union or legitimate business, with funds derived from illegal enterprises and racketeering activities.[42]

RICO did not create new categories of crime, but it did create new categories of offenses in racketeering activity, which it defined as involvement in two or more acts prohibited by 24 existing federal statutes and 8 state statutes. The offenses listed in RICO include such state-defined crimes as murder, kidnapping, gambling, arson, robbery, bribery, extortion, and narcotic violations and such federally defined crimes as bribery, counterfeiting, transmission of gambling information, prostitution, and mail fraud.

Individuals convicted under RICO are subject to long prison terms and huge fines. Additionally, the accused must forfeit to the U.S. government any interest in a business in violation of RICO. These penalties are much more potent than simple conviction and imprisonment. In addition, a separate civil provision of the law permits private parties to sue for racketeering and obtain treble damages.

Using RICO, the U.S. attorneys for New York, Boston, and Chicago have attacked the leadership of major organized crime families and obtained convictions of high-ranking mafiosi during the late 1980s and early 1990s. In a trailblazing case, the U.S. attorney for New York used RICO and language in the Securities and Exchange Act of 1934 to successfully prosecute Ivan Boesky and others for insider-trading crimes.[43] Although it has been slow to respond to such criminal violations over the years, the federal government now maintains that insider-trading violations will receive full attention in the future. The major purpose of the RICO statute, however, was to address the infiltration of legitimate business by organized crime.

One of the most significant criminal law revisions in the last decade was the 1984 Federal Crime Control Act.[44] This legislation reformed a code that was criticized for its complexity and inconsistency. Among the most important changes was the treatment of the insanity defense. In the past, federal prosecutors had the burden of proving that a defendant was sane. Now the burden of proof for insanity has shifted to the defendant. In addition, the 1984 federal code eliminated parole and required that criminal punishments be imposed more fairly and evenhandedly. Another important provision allowed judges to detain offenders in jail before their trials if they were considered a danger to the community and themselves. Preventive detention was a significant change in the nation's bail system. Despite these changes, in comparison with the revisions that have taken place in many states, the federal criminal law has not been extensively overhauled.

In addition, amid much national concern about drugs, Congress passed the Omnibus Drug Law of 1988.[45] Earmarking over $2 billion for antidrug activities, the law called for increased drug education and treatment programs and broader federal drug interdiction efforts. This legislation is the basis for U.S. drug enforcement policy today.

Under the Bush administration, the 101st Congress passed the Crime Control Act of 1990. Some significant changes were part of this legislation, including improvements in public defender services; the implementation of "shock incarceration" programs in federal and state correctional systems; reforms for the investigation of child abuse cases; efforts to aid crime victims through the Victims

Federal Crime Legislation

Overseeing the administration of justice at the federal level for most of the 1990s, Attorney General Janet Reno has enforced such important legislation as the Brady Handgun Control Law of 1993, which requires a five-business-day waiting period before an individual can buy a handgun, and the Crime Control Act of 1994, which expanded the scope of the death penalty and authorized billions of dollars for more police officers, prisons, and crime prevention programs.

Rights and Restitution Act of 1990; authorization for a study of mandatory sentencing by the U.S. Sentencing Commission; provisions dealing with drugs; and the development of new offenses and penalties relating to the savings and loan scandals.[46]

The desire to be tough on crime is often one of the top priorities for politicians. Recent federal crime legislation under the Clinton administration has included the Brady Handgun Control Law of 1993, requiring a five-business-day waiting period before an individual can buy a handgun, and the Violent Crime Control and Law Enforcement Act of 1994, expanding the scope of the death penalty and authorizing billions of dollars for more police officers, prisons, and crime prevention programs.[47] The Crime Control Act of 1994 is the largest crime bill in U.S. history. President Clinton considered this legislation one of the crowning achievements of his first term and touted the law in his campaign to beat Senator Robert Dole in the 1996 presidential election.

One of the most significant recent pieces of crime legislation is the Antiterrorism and Effective Death Penalty Act of 1996. The "Terrorism Law" was passed as a direct result of the 1995 bombing of the federal building in Oklahoma City. Many of the new law's provisions relate to terrorist activity as well as revisions to federal habeas corpus proceedings. Known as the great writ, this is a procedure for obtaining judicial determination of the legality of an individual's custody. The emphasis is on reducing the delay often attributable to habeus corpus proceedings in capital cases.[48]

Constitutional Criminal Procedure

Whereas substantive criminal law primarily defines crimes, the law of criminal procedure consists of the rules and procedures that govern the pretrial processing of criminal suspects and the conduct of criminal trials. The principles that govern criminal procedure flow from the relationship between the individual and the state and include (1) a belief in the presumption of innocence, (2) the right to a defense against criminal charges, and (3) the requirement that the government should act in a lawful manner. In general, these policies are mandated by the provisions of state constitutions. A sound understanding of criminal procedure requires an awareness of constitutional law.

The U.S. Constitution

The U.S. Constitution has played and continues to play a critical role in the development of the criminal law used in the criminal justice system. The forerunner of the Constitution was the Articles of Confederation, adopted by the Continental Congress in 1781. This document was found to be generally inadequate as the foundation for effective government, because it did not create a proper balance of power between the states and the central government. As a result, in 1787 the Congress of the Confederation adopted a resolution calling for a convention of delegates from the original states. Meeting in Philadelphia, the delegates' express purpose was to revise the Articles of Confederation. The work of that convention culminated in the drafting of the Constitution; it was ratified by the states in 1788 and put into effect in 1789. In its original form, the Constitution consisted of a preamble and seven articles. The Constitution divided the powers of government into three independent but equal parts: the executive, the legislative, and the judicial branches. The purpose of the separation of powers was to ensure that no single branch of the government could usurp power for itself and institute a dictatorship. The measures and procedures initiated by the framers of the Constitution have developed over time into our present form of government.

How does the Constitution, with its formal set of rights and privileges, affect the operations of the criminal justice system? One way is to guarantee that no one branch of government can in and of itself determine the fate of those accused of crimes. The workings of the criminal justice process illustrate this principle. A police officer, who represents the executive branch of government, makes an arrest on the basis of laws passed by the legislative branch, and the accused is subsequently tried by the judiciary. In this way, citizens are protected from the arbitrary abuse of power by any single element of the law.

In addition to providing protection by ensuring a separation of powers within the government, the Constitution controls the operations of the criminal justice system. It does so by guaranteeing individual freedoms in the ten amendments added to it on December 15, 1791, collectively known as the **Bill of Rights.**[49]

The Bill of Rights

The Bill of Rights was added to the Constitution to prevent government from usurping the personal freedoms of citizens. In its original form, the Constitution contained few specific guarantees of individual rights. The Founding Fathers, aware of the past abuses perpetrated by the British government, wanted to ensure that the rights of citizens of the United States would be safe. The Bill of Rights was adopted only to protect individual liberties from being abused by the national government, however, and did not apply to the actions of state or local officials. This oversight resulted in abuses that have been rectified only with great difficulty and even today remain the subject of court action.

Over the last four decades, the U.S. Supreme Court's interpretation of the Constitution has served as the basis for the creation of legal rights of the accused. The principles that govern criminal procedure are required by the U.S. Constitution and Bill of Rights. Of primary concern are the Fourth, Fifth, Sixth, and Eighth Amendments, which limit and control the manner in which the federal government operates the justice system. In addition, the due process clause of the Fourteenth Amendment has helped define the nature and limits of governmental action against the accused on a state level.

The Fourth Amendment is especially important for the criminal justice system because it means that police officers cannot indiscriminately use their authority to investigate a possible crime or arrest a suspect unless either or both actions are justified by the law and the facts of the case. Stopping, questioning, or searching an individual without legal justification represents a serious violation of the Fourth Amendment right to personal privacy.

Limiting the admissibility of confessions that have been obtained unfairly is another method of controlling police behavior. The right against **self-incrimination** is frequently asserted by a defendant in an effort to exclude confessions or admissions that might be vital to the government's case. In such instances, the application of the Fifth Amendment to the U.S. Constitution is critical to the criminal justice system.

The Fifth Amendment has in fact had a tremendous impact on the U.S. criminal justice system. In 1966, in the landmark case of *Miranda v. Arizona,* the U.S. Supreme Court held that a person accused of a crime has the right to refuse to answer questions when placed in police custody.[50]

The Sixth Amendment guarantees the defendant the right to a speedy and public trial by an impartial jury, the right to be informed of the nature of the charges, and the right to confront any prosecution witnesses. This amendment has had a profound effect on the treatment of persons accused of crimes and has been the basis for numerous significant Supreme Court decisions that have increased the rights of criminal defendants.

Many Supreme Court decisions regarding the Sixth Amendment have also concerned the individual's right to counsel. The right of a defendant to be represented by an attorney has been extended to numerous stages of the criminal justice process, including pretrial custody, identification and lineup procedures, preliminary hearing, submission of a guilty plea, trial, sentencing, and postconviction appeal.

According to the Eighth Amendment, "Excessive bail shall not be required, nor excessive fines imposed, nor cruel and unusual punishments inflicted." Bail is a money bond put up by the accused to attain freedom between arrest and trial. Bail is meant to ensure a trial appearance, since the bail money is forfeited if the defendant misses the trial date. The Eighth Amendment does not guarantee a constitutional right to bail but rather prohibits the exactment of excessive bail. Nevertheless, since many state statutes place no precise limit on the amount of bail a judge may impose, many defendants who cannot make bail are often placed in detention while awaiting trial.

Another goal of the framers of the Constitution was to curtail the use of torture and excessive physical punishment. Consequently, the prohibition against cruel and unusual punishment was added to the Eighth Amendment. This prohibition has affected the imposition of the death penalty and other criminal dispositions and has become a guarantee that serves to protect both the accused and convicted offenders from actions regarded as unacceptable by a civilized society.

These key amendments furnish the basis for our system of criminal procedure.

The State Criminal Justice System Under the Constitution

The Fourteenth Amendment has been the vehicle most often used to apply the protection of the Bill of Rights to the states. The most important aspect of this amendment is the clause that says no state shall "deprive any person of life, liberty, or property, without due process of law." This meant that the same general constitutional restrictions previously applicable to the federal government were to be imposed on the states. It is essential to keep the following constitutional principles in mind:

1. The first ten amendments (Bill of Rights) originally applied only to the federal government. They were designed to protect citizens against injustices inflicted by federal authorities. The Bill of Rights restricts the actions of the federal government and does not apply to the states.

2. The Fourteenth Amendment's due process clause applies to state governments. It has been used to provide individuals in all states with the basic liberties guaranteed by the Bill of Rights.

3. The U.S. Supreme Court has expanded the rights of defendants in the criminal justice system by interpreting the due process clause to mean that the states must be held to standards similar to those applicable to the federal government by the Bill of Rights.

Through a long series of court decisions, the Supreme Court has held that the guarantees of the First, Fourth, Fifth, Sixth, and Eighth Amendments apply to the states as well as to the federal government. It is based on the theory of selective incorporation, which states that the Bill of Rights does apply to the states through the due process clause of the Fourteenth Amendment but only on a case-by-case basis. Advocates of this theory believe that some of the provisions of the Bill of Rights may be binding on the states—such as the right to a jury trial or the right to be free from self-incrimination—but that these should apply only after a careful consideration of the facts, or merits, of each case.

Using this formula, the incorporation of the provisions of the Bill of Rights into the Fourteenth Amendment moved forward slowly on a case-by-case basis, accelerating in 1953 when Earl Warren became chief justice of the Supreme Court. Under his leadership, the due process movement reached its peak. The Court decided numerous landmark cases focusing on the rights of the accused and brought about a revolution in the area of constitutional criminal procedure. The Warren Court of the 1960s granted many new rights to those accused of crimes and went so far as to impose specific guidelines on the policies of police, courts, and correctional services that ensured that due process of law would be maintained.

Today, the Fourteenth Amendment's due process clause has been interpreted by the U.S. Supreme Court to mean that an accused in a state criminal case is virtually entitled to the same protections available under the federal Bill of Rights.

The concept of **due process** has been used as a basis for incorporating the Bill of Rights into the Fourteenth Amendment. Due process has also been used to evaluate the constitutionality of legal statutes and to set standards and guidelines for fair procedures in the criminal justice system.

In seeking to define the meaning of the term, most legal experts believe that it refers to the essential elements of fairness under law.[51] *Black's Law Dictionary* presents an elaborate and complex definition of due process:

> Due process of law in each particular case means such an exercise of the powers of government as the settled maxims of law permit and sanction, and under such safeguards for the protection of individual rights as those maxims prescribe for the class of cases to which the one in question belongs.[52]

This definition basically refers to the legal system's need for rules and regulations that protect individual rights. Due process seeks to ensure that no person will be deprived of life, liberty, or property without notice of charges, assistance from legal counsel, a hearing, and an opportunity to confront those making the accusations. Basically, due process is intended to guarantee that fundamental fairness exists in each individual case. This doctrine of fairness as expressed in due process of law is guaranteed under both the Fifth and Fourteenth Amendments.[53] Abstract definitions are only one aspect of due process. Much more significant are the procedures that give meaning to due process in the everyday practices of the criminal justice system. In this regard, due process provides numerous procedural safeguards for the offender, including the following:

1. Notices of charges

2. A formal hearing

3. The right to counsel or some other representation

4. The opportunity to respond to charges

5. The opportunity to confront and cross-examine witnesses and accusers

6. The privilege to be free from self-incrimination

7. The opportunity to present one's own witnesses

8. A decision made on the basis of substantial evidence and facts produced at the hearing

9. A written statement of the reasons for the decision

10. An appellate review procedure

Exactly what constitutes due process in a specific case depends on the facts of the case, the federal and state constitutional and statutory provisions, previous court decisions, and the ideas and principles that society considers important at a given time and in a given place.[54] Justice Felix Frankfurter emphasized this point in *Rochin v. California* (1952):

> Due process of law requires an evaluation based on a disinterested inquiry pursued in the spirit of science on a balanced order of facts, exactly and clearly stated, on the detached consideration of conflicting claims . . . on a judgment not ad hoc and episodic but duly mindful of reconciling the needs both of continuity and of change in a progressive society.[55]

The interpretations of due process of law are not fixed but rather reflect what society deems fair and just at a particular time and place. The degree of loss suffered by the individual (victim or offender) balanced against the state's interests

In re Gault (1967)— Procedural Due Process

Facts

Gerald Gault, 15 years of age, was taken into custody by the sheriff of Gila County, Arizona. His arrest was based on the complaint of a woman who said that he and another boy had made an obscene telephone call to her. Gerald was then under a six-month probation for stealing a wallet. Because of the verbal complaint, Gerald was taken to the children's home. His parents were not informed that he was being taken into custody. His mother appeared in the evening and was told by the superintendent of detention that a hearing would be held in the juvenile court the following day. On the day in question, the police officer who had taken Gerald into custody filed a petition alleging his delinquency. Gerald, his mother, and the police officer appeared before the judge in his chambers. The complainant was not at the hearing. Gerald was questioned about the telephone calls and was sent back to the detention home and then subsequently released a few days later.

On the day of Gerald's release, his mother received a letter indicating that a hearing would be held on Gerald's delinquency a few days later. A hearing was held, and the complainant was not present. No transcript or recording was made of the proceedings, and the juvenile officer stated that Gerald had admitted making the lewd telephone calls. Neither the boy nor his parents were advised of any right to remain silent or to be represented by counsel or of any other constitutional rights. At the conclusion of the hearing, the juvenile court committed Gerald as a juvenile delinquent to the state industrial school in Arizona for the period of his minority.

This meant that Gerald at the age of 15 was being sent for a period of incarceration in the state school until age 21, or unless discharged sooner, whereas an adult charged with the same crime would have received a maximum punishment of no more than a $50 fine or two months in prison.

Decision

Gerald's attorneys filed a habeas corpus writ, which was denied by the superior court of the state of Arizona; that decision was subsequently affirmed by the Arizona Supreme Court. On appeal to the U.S. Supreme Court, Gerald's counsel argued that the juvenile code of Arizona under which Gerald was found delinquent was invalid because it was contrary to the due process clause of the Fourteenth Amendment. In addition, the attorney argued Gerald had been denied the following basic due process rights: (1) notice of charges with regard to the timeliness and specificity of the charges, (2) right to counsel, (3) right to confrontation and cross-examination, (4) privilege against self-incrimination, (5) right to a transcript of the trial record, and (6) right to appellate review. In deciding the case, the Supreme Court had to decide whether procedural due process of law within the context of fundamental fairness under the Fourteenth Amendment applied to juvenile delinquency proceedings in which a child is committed to a state industrial school.

The Court, in a far-reaching opinion written by Justice Abe Fortas, agreed that Gerald's constitutional rights had been violated. Notice of charges is an essential ingredient of due process of law, as is the right to counsel, the right to cross-examine and to confront witnesses, and the privilege against self-incrimination. The questions of whether a juvenile has a right to appellate review and a right to a transcript were not answered by the Court in this decision.

Significance of the Case

The *Gault* case established that a child has procedural due process constitutional rights as listed above in delinquency adjudication proceedings based on alleged misconduct where the consequences are that the child may be committed to a state institution. The case was confined to rulings at the adjudication stage of the juvenile process.

This decision was significant not only because of the procedural reforms, such as the right to counsel, but also because of its far-reaching impact throughout the entire juvenile justice process. *Gault* led to the development of due process standards at the pretrial, trial, and posttrial stages of the juvenile process. While recognizing the history and the development of the juvenile court, it sought to accommodate the motives of rehabilitation and treatment with children's rights. It recognized the principles of fundamental fairness of the law, for children as well as for adults. Judged in the context of today's juvenile justice system, *Gault* redefined the relationship between the juvenile, the parents, and the state. It remains the single most significant constitutional case in the area of juvenile justice.

Source: *In Re Gault* 387, U.S. (1967).

also determines which and how many due process requirements are ordinarily applied. The issue of due process is analyzed in the Supreme Court case **In re Gault** (see Law in Review box), which deals with a juvenile's rights in court.

Future Directions in Criminal Law

Despite current problems with the criminal justice system, much progress has been made in the field of criminal law and constitutional procedure over the past 30 years. The future direction of the criminal law in the United States remains unclear. Yet there seems to be less tolerance for government corruption, more public interest in fixed sentences and capital punishment, and more conservative decision making by judicial bodies. Attention will probably be paid to the substantive nature of criminal law in the future, particularly where it is important in the preservation of U.S. society. For example, special prosecutors, using criminal statutes involving conspiracy, perjury, and fraud, were able to uncover the illegal operations in the Nixon administration of the 1970s and to examine the Reagan administration's activities in the 1980s. In the Bush and Clinton administrations of the 1990s, efforts have been made to prosecute such diverse crimes as those in the scandals involving savings and loan associations and the alleged infiltration of legitimate businesses by organized crime. The criminal law system has demonstrated amazing resilience in its ability to prosecute public officials and private citizens whose behavior has damaged the government.

Both an expansion and a contraction of the criminal law itself can also be anticipated. Areas of expansion will probably include a greater emphasis on controlling career criminals. Laws making it easier for states to punish serious juvenile offenders and incarcerate them in secure adult institutions will probably be passed. More attention will be given to white-collar crimes, as well as to drug-related crimes and terrorism. Corporations are almost certainly going to be held accountable for their illegal acts, especially those that result in physical as well as economic harm. Stock market and computer activities will receive close scrutiny by law enforcement agencies, as will child abuse and family violence.

Software piracy in particular will receive greater emphasis as computers and technology play an ever-increasing role in our society. This will lead to the development of criminal statutes allowing for the prosecution of software theft by computer, as well as Internet violations on a global basis.

Finally, the legal system will continue to be faced with difficult challenges involving AIDS (acquired immune deficiency syndrome). Some criminal laws specifically attempt to control the activities of prisoners, prostitutes, drug users, and criminal defendants who are HIV-positive to protect others from contracting the disease.

Regardless of what changes occur in the future, the criminal law system will continue to deal with four fundamental problems: (1) defining and classifying antisocial behavior; (2) establishing appropriate criminal sanctions or punishments; (3) applying the proper degree of criminal responsibility; and (4) determining what departures from due process of law safeguards may require the reversal of a conviction.

The Role of the Supreme Court

More than any other factor, the role of the Supreme Court will dominate the future direction of criminal law and procedure in the United States. The Supreme Court has been the setting for some of the important recent events in the administration of criminal justice. For example, the Court took a decidedly liberal turn in granting individual rights for the accused during the Earl Warren era of the 1960s. In the 1970s and 1980s, Nixon's conservatives—Justices Warren Burger and William Rehnquist—curbed the growth of criminal procedure rights. With the replacement of liberal Justice William Brennan by conservative David Souter of New Hampshire in 1990, the Court continued to hand down legally conservative opinions favoring state law enforcement over criminal defendants. For instance, the justices made it easier for police with no warrants to search buses for drugs or to open and examine suitcases found in car trunks.[56] The Court also allowed prosecutors to use coerced confessions as evidence against defendants and even authorized the jailing of individuals for up to 48 hours without a hearing.[57] In addition, the Court's decision to permit the use of evidence about a victim's character and the impact on the victim's family at the sentencing phase of death penalty cases overturned an earlier ban against the use of such information.[58] These decisions illustrate the conservative trend in the Supreme Court on criminal law issues in the early 1990s.

This trend became more pronounced with the controversial appointment of conservative U.S. Court of Appeals Judge Clarence Thomas to the high court in 1991, replacing retiring liberal Justice Thurgood Marshall.

On the other hand, many experts believed that President Bill Clinton's appointment of Judge Ruth Bader Ginsburg in 1993 to succeed Justice Byron White could forestall the Court's conservatism. Despite her background in women's advocacy, Ginsburg was widely viewed as a jurist with moderate views, particularly on criminal law. Her emphasis, however, continues to be on gender issues.

In 1994, President Clinton appointed Stephen Breyer, a Boston federal appellate court judge, to replace retiring Justice Harry Blackmun. Because Breyer does not have a distinct ideology and is the most junior justice, his appointment does not appear to affect the moderate to conservative bent of the Court significantly.

In the 1995–1996 term, for instance, the Supreme Court continued its tough treatment of criminal defendants. The Court decided that parallel civil forfeiture proceedings for property associated with a drug prosecution do not trigger the double jeopardy provisions of the Fifth Amendment.[59] Overturning federal appellate decisions involving prisoners' rights, the Court clearly established that inmates do not have an abstract free-standing right to a law library or legal assistance, but rather only a right of access to the courts.[60] Finally, in the important case of *Felker v. Turpin,* the Court upheld provisions of the recent Antiterrorism and Effective Death Penalty Act of 1996 by making it much more difficult for a state prisoner filing successive federal habeas corpus petitions to obtain relief and gain his or her release.[61] The Court's conservative bloc also asserted itself in the 1996–1997 term by striking down a key provision of the Brady gun law, allowing states to continue to confine sexual offenders once their sentences were complete, and limiting death row appeals.

But the overall philosophical direction of the Court may be veering toward a more middle road, particularly with the election of President Clinton to a second term. If one or more of the three most senior justices retire shortly (Rehnquist, age 72; Stevens, age 76; and O'Connor, age 67), Clinton will have the opportunity to shape the direction of the Court well into the next century.[62]

Criminal Justice on the Net

Many historical sources of the law are available on the Internet. For example, some of the antecedents of American law can be found in the British Bill of Rights (1689), located at:

http://www.unicorn.com//lib/ ukbor.html

Another important source of the law is the Magna Carta, the great charter of English liberty decreed by King John at Runnymede on June 15, 1215. The charter and all its provisions can be accessed at:

http://www.ecst.csuchico.edu/ ~rodmur/docs/Magna.html

The Magna Carta had a significant effect on American law. Before penning the Declaration of Independence—the first of the American Charters of Freedom—in 1776, the Founding Fathers searched for a historical precedent for asserting their rightful liberties from King George III and the English Parliament. They used the Magna Carta as a guide. For an analysis of this issue see:

**http://www.nara.gov/exhall/
charters/magnacarta/magintrp.html**

Summary

The criminal justice system is basically a legal system. Its foundation is the criminal law, which is concerned with people's conduct. The purpose of criminal law is to regulate behavior and maintain order in society. What constitutes a crime is defined primarily by the state and federal legislatures and reviewed by the courts.

What is considered criminal conduct changes from one period to another. Social norms, values, and community beliefs play major roles in determining what conduct is antisocial. Crimes are generally classified as felonies or misdemeanors, depending on their seriousness. Since a crime is a public wrong against the state, the criminal law imposes sanctions in the form of fines, probation, or imprisonment on a guilty defendant.

Under the criminal law, all adults are presumed to be aware of the consequences of their actions, but the law does not hold an individual blameworthy unless that person is capable of intending to commit the crime of which he or she is accused. Such factors as insanity, a mental defect, or age mitigate a person's criminal responsibility.

States periodically revise and update the substantive criminal law and the procedural laws in their penal codes; the latter deal with the rules for processing the offender from arrest through trial, sentencing, and release. An accused must be provided with the guarantees of due process under the Fifth and Fourteenth Amendments to the U.S. Constitution.

Key Terms

substantive criminal law
criminal procedure
civil law
common law
Carriers case
law of precedent
stare decisis
torts
intent
felony

misdemeanor
crime
corpus delicti
actus reus
mens rea
strict liability
insanity
M'Naghten rule
irresistible impulse test
Durham rule

substantial capacity test
self-defense
entrapment
double jeopardy
Racketeer Influenced and Corrupt
    Organization (RICO) Act
Bill of Rights
self-incrimination
due process
In re Gault

Questions

1. What are the specific aims and purposes of the criminal law? To what extent does the criminal law control behavior?

2. What kinds of activities should be labeled criminal in contemporary society? Why?

3. What is a criminal act? What is a criminal state of mind? When are individuals liable for their actions?

4. Discuss the various kinds of crime classifications. To what extent or degree are they distinguishable?

5. In recent years, numerous states have revised their penal codes. What are some of the major categories of substantive crimes you think should be revised?

6. Entrapment is a defense when the defendant was entrapped into committing the crime. To what extent should law enforcement personnel induce the commission of an offense?

7. What legal principles can be used to justify self-defense? Considering that the law seeks to prevent crime, not promote it, are such principles sound?

8. What are the minimum standards of criminal procedure required in the criminal justice system?

9. Discuss the current philosophical position of the U.S. Supreme Court regarding the issue of constitutional criminal procedure.

Notes

1. Some of the historical criminal law concepts discussed here are a synthesis of those contained in Fred Inbua, James Thompson, and James Zagel, *Criminal Law and Its Administration* (Mineola, N.Y.: Foundation Press, 1974); Jerome Hall, *General Principles of Criminal Law* (Charlottesville, Va.: Michie, 1961); Richard Singer and Martin Gardner, *Crimes and Punishment: Cases, Materials and Readings in Criminal Law* (New York: Matthew Bender, 1989).

2. See, generally, Sanford Kadish and Monrad Paulsen, *Criminal Law and Its Processes* (Boston: Little, Brown, 1975); see also J. Dressler, *Understanding Criminal Law* (New York: Matthew Bender, 1987).

3. See T. F. Pluckett, *A Concise History of the Common Law* (Boston: Little, Brown, 1956); see also E. Allan Farnworth, *An Introduction to the Legal System of the United States* (New York: Oceana Publications, 1963).

4. *Carriers Case Yearbook,* 13 Edward IV 9.pL.5 (1473).

5. 372 U.S. 335, 83 S.Ct. 792, 9 L.Ed.2d 799 (1963).

6. See, generally, Wayne R. LaFave and Austin W. Scott, *Criminal Law* (St. Paul: West Publishing Horn Book Series, 1986).

7. E. Gellhorn, *Administrative Law and Process* (St. Paul: West Publishing Nutshell Series, 1981).

8. See John Weaver, *Warren—The Man, the Court, the Era* (Boston: Little, Brown, 1967); see also "We the People," *Time,* 6 July 1987, p. 6.

9. *Marbury v. Madison,* 5 U.S. (1 Cranch) 137, 2 L.Ed. 60 (1803).

10. Thomas Gardner, *Criminal Law* (St. Paul: West Publishing, 1985), pp. 15–18.

11. See American Law Institute, Model Penal Code, Sec. 104.

12. Henry Black, *Black's Law Dictionary,* rev. 5th ed. (St. Paul: West Publishing, 1979), pp. 744, 1150.

13. Mass. Gen. Laws, Chap. 274, Sec. 1.

14. Sheldon Krantz, *Law of Corrections and Prisoners' Rights, Cases and Materials,* 3rd ed. (St. Paul: West Publishing, 1986), p. 702; Barbara Knight and Stephen Early, Jr., *Prisoners' Rights in America* (Chicago: Nelson-Hall, 1986), Chapter 1; see also Fred Cohen, "The Law of Prisoners' Rights—An Overview," *Criminal Law Bulletin* 24 (188):321–349.

15. See Mass. Gen. Laws Ann. Chap. 266, Sec. 14.

16. LaFave and Scott, *Criminal Law,* p. 177; see, generally, Frank Miller, Robert Dawson, George Dix, and Raymond Parnas, *Cases and Materials on Criminal Justice Administration,* 3rd ed. (New York: Foundation Press, 1988).

17. See American Law Institute, Model Penal Code, Sec. 2.02; see also *United States v. Bailey,* 444 U.S. 394, 100 S.Ct. 624, 62 L.Ed.2d 575 (1980).

18. See *United States v. Balint,* 258 U.S. 250, 42 S.Ct. 301, 66 L.Ed. 604 (1922); see also *Morissette v. United States,* 342 U.S. 246, 72 S.Ct. 240, 96 L.Ed. 288 (1952).

19. 8 English Reporter 718 (1943).

20. 94 U.S. App. D.C. 228, 214 F.2d 862 (1954).

21. American Law Institute, Model Penal Code, Sec. 4.01.

22. Bureau of Justice Statistics, *Report to the Nation on Crime and Justice,* 2nd ed. (Washington, D.C.: Bureau of Justice Statistics, 1988), p. 87.

23. Richard Schmitt, "Defenses Down—Insanity Pleas Fail a Lot of Defendants," *The Wall Street Journal,* 29 February 1996, p. A1.

24. 370 U.S. 660, 82 S.Ct. 1417, 8 L.Ed.2d 758 (1962).

25. 392 U.S. 514, 88 S.Ct. 2145, 20 L.Ed.2d 1254 (1968).

26. Samuel M. Davis, *Rights of Juveniles: The Juvenile Justice System* (New York: Boardman, 1974—update 1993); Chapter 2; Larry Siegel and Joseph Senna, *Juvenile Delinquency: Theory, Practice and Law* (St. Paul: West Publishing, 1996).

27. *People v. Goetz,* 68 N.Y.2d 96, 497 N.E.2d 41, 506 N.Y.S.2d 18 (1986); see also "New York Court Upholds Goetz Gun Conviction," *Boston Globe,* 23 November 1988, p. 5.

28. 287 U.S. 435, 53 S.Ct. 210, 77 L.Ed. 413 (1932).

29. 356 U.S. 369, 78 S.Ct. 819, 2 L.Ed.2d 848 (1958); see also *Jacobson v. United States,* 503 U.S. 540, 112 S.Ct. 1535, 118 L.Ed.2d 174 (1992).

30. U.S. Constitution, Fifth Amendment.

31. 359 U.S. 121, 72 S.Ct. 676, 3 L.Ed.2d 684 (1959).

32. 395 U.S. 784, 89 S.Ct. 2056, 23 L.Ed.2d 707 (1969).

33. *United States v. Ursery,* 116 S.Ct. 2135 (1996).

34. William Blackstone, *Commentaries on the Law of England,* vol. 1, ed. Thomas Cooley (Chicago: Callaghan, 1899), pp. 4, 26. Blackstone was an English barrister who lectured on the English common law at Oxford University in 1753.

35. American Law Institute, Model Penal Code, Sec. 2.04.

36. *Commonwealth v. Berrigan,* 509 Pa. 118, 501 A.2d 226 (1985); see also *State v. Tate,* 102 N.J. 64, 505 A.2d 941 (1986).

37. See in general "Violence Against Women Act" in *The State of America's Children—Year-book* (Washington, D.C.: Children's Defense Fund, 1995), p. 73.

38. Donna Hunzeker, "Significant State Anti-Crime Legislation," *National Conference of State Legislatures* 19 (1994); see also Hunzeker, "State Sentencing Systems and Truth in Sentencing," *National Conference of State Legislatures,* 20 (1995).

39. Daniel Armagh, "Registration and Community Notification Laws," *The Prosecutor* 30 (1996): 10–11; Joel Rudin, "Megan's Law—Can It Stop Sexual Predators—And at What Cost Constitutional Rights?" *ABA Journal on Criminal Justice* 11 (1996):2–11.

40. See Melissa Sickmund, "How to Get Juveniles to Criminal Court," *Office of Juvenile Justice and Delinquency Prevention Update* (Washington, D.C.: Bureau of Justice Statistics, 1994).

41. In *New York v. Ferber,* 458 U.S. 747, 102 S.Ct. 3348, 73 L.Ed.2d 1113 (1982), the Supreme Court upheld state laws that ban the use of children in sexually explicit publications even if they are not legally obscene.

42. 18 U.S.C.A. Sec. 1961–1968 (Amended in 1978, 1984, and 1986). "Enterprise" includes both legitimate and illegitimate associations.

43. See John Brooks, *The Takeover Game* (New York: E. P. Dutton, 1987), p. 319. See also James Stewart, *Den of Thieves* (New York: Simon & Schuster, 1991), a complete analysis of the insider-trading scandal.

44. Comprehensive Crime Control Act of 1984, Title 18, U.S.C.; see also Albert P. Melone, "The Politics of Criminal Code Revision," *Capital U.S. Review* 15 (1986):191.

45. Omnibus Drug Law, H5210, *Congressional Quarterly,* 29 October 1988, p. 3145.

46. Tom Smith, "Legislative and Legal Developments in Criminal Justice," *Journal on Criminal Justice* 5 (1991):36–37; see also Gary Weiss, "The Mob on Wall Street," *Business Week,* 16 December 1996, pp. 92–93.

47. For an intensive summary of the Violent Crime Control and Law Enforcement Act of 1994, see *Criminal Law Reporter,* Bureau of National Affairs, 55:2305–2430 (1994); see also Tom Smith, "Legislative and Legal Developments," *A.B.A. Journal on Criminal Justice* 11 (1996):50–52.

48. Antiterrorism and Effective Death Penalty Act of 1996. Public Law No. 104-132 (1996).

49. For a real-world application and the impact of the Bill of Rights on criminal justice in particular, see Ellen Alderman and Caroline Kennedy, *In Our Defense—The Bill of Rights in Action* (New York: William Morrow, 1991).

50. 384 U.S. 436, 86 S.Ct. 1602, 16 L.Ed.2d 694 (1966).

51. See Essay, *Time,* 26 February 1973, p. 95; also, for a tribute to the Bill of Rights and due process, see James MacGregor Burns and Steward Burns, *The Pursuit of Rights in America* (New York: Knopf, 1991).

52. Black, *Black's Law Dictionary,* p. 449.

53. See, generally, Joseph J. Senna, "Changes in Due Process of Law," *Social Work* 19 (1974):319; see also the interesting student rights case *Goss v. Lopez,* 419 U.S. 565, 95 S.Ct. 729, 42 L.Ed.2d 725 (1975).

54. 342 U.S. 165, 72 S.Ct. 205, 95 L.Ed. 183 (1952).

55. Ibid., at 172, 72 S.Ct. at 209.

56. *Florida v. Bostick,* 501 U.S. 429, 111 S.Ct. 2382, 115 L.Ed.2d 389 (1991); *California v. Acevedo,* 500 U.S. 565, 111 S.Ct. 1982, 114 L.Ed.2d 619 (1991).

57. *Arizona v. Fulminante,* 499 U.S. 279, 111 S.Ct. 1246, 113 L.Ed.2d 302 (1991); *Riverside v. McLaughlin,* 500 U.S. 44, 111 S.Ct. 1661, 114 L.Ed.2d 49 (1991).

58. *Payne v. Tennessee,* 501 U.S. 128, 111 S.Ct. 2597, 115 L.Ed.2d 720 (1991).

59. *United States v. Ursery,* 116 S.Ct. 2135 (1996).

60. *Lewis v. Casey,* 116 S.Ct. 2320 (1996).

61. *Felker v. Turpin,* 116 S.Ct. 2333 (1996).

62. David J. Garrow, "The Rehnquist Reins," *The New York Times Magazine,* 6 October 1996.

Confronting Crime

N ow that we have developed some understanding of the agencies and processes of justice, the nature and cause of crime, and the functions of the criminal law, it is time to focus on the criminal justice system and its efforts to confront and control crime in the United States. Although it has been more than 25 years since the field of criminal justice began to be the subject of both serious academic study and attempts at unified policy formation, significant debate continues over the general direction the system should take, how the problem of crime control should be approached, and the most effective method of dealing with known criminal offenders. After decades of effort in research and policy analysis, it is clear that criminal justice is far from a unified field. Practitioners, academics, and commentators alike have expressed irreconcilable differences concerning its goals, purpose, and direction. This lack of consensus is particularly vexing when the multitude of problems facing the justice system are considered. The agencies of justice must attempt to

eradicate such seemingly diverse social problems as substance abuse, gang violence, and environmental contamination while at the same time respecting individual liberties and civil rights. It is also assumed that the agencies of the justice system can efficiently carry out a variety of diverse tasks and that their representatives possess a wide range of knowledge of law, psychology, and social welfare.

This chapter reviews the major perspectives on justice and some of the critical issues facing the field. First, the focus is on the various perspectives on justice: What should be the goals and objectives of the criminal justice system? Then the chapter turns to a discussion of how the system is confronting some of the major forms of crime in the United States: How can drug abuse and violence be controlled or eliminated?

Considering the complexity of criminal justice, it should not be surprising that no single view of the concept dominates the field. Those who work within the profession or study its processes often hold competing views on how the justice system works and how it should operate. In fact, people who hold opposing views sometimes share the same job responsibilities or duties, resulting in intra-agency conflict. In academic departments, opposing views on the nature of justice can heat up faculty politics.

What are the dominant views of the criminal justice system today? What is the role of the justice system, and how should it approach its tasks? The different perspectives on criminal justice are discussed in this section.

Crime Control
Perspective

Advocates of the **crime control perspective** believe that the proper role of the justice system is to prevent crime through the judicious use of criminal sanctions. If the justice system operated effectively, potential criminals would be deterred from committing law violations, while those who did commit crime would be apprehended, tried, and punished. The justice system should be capable of convincing would-be criminals that "crime does not pay."

According to the crime control perspective, the focus of justice should be on the victim of crime, not the criminal. The ultimate goal of the criminal justice system is to protect innocent people from the ravages of crime. This objective can be achieved through more effective police protection, tough sentences (including liberal use of the death penalty), and the construction of prisons designed to safely incapacitate hardened criminals.

Sure and Swift Justice. Crime control enthusiasts believe in swift and sure justice. They do not want legal technicalities to help the guilty go free and tie the hands of justice. They lobby for the abolition of legal restrictions that control a police officer's ability to search for evidence and interrogate suspects with a free hand. They are angry at judges who let obviously guilty people go free because a law enforcement officer made an unintentional procedural error. They point to evidence showing that as many as 30,000 violent criminals, 62,000 drunk drivers, 46,000 drug dealers, and several hundred thousand other criminals alone go free *every year* in cases dropped because police believe they had violated the suspects' *Miranda* rights.[1] It is not surprising when they lobby for the abolition of the exclusionary rule and the *Miranda* decision and applaud when the Supreme Court hands down rulings that increase police power in a case such as *Ohio v. Robinette* (1996), which held that police do not have to tell motorists stopped for a traffic violation that they are actually free to go before asking permission to search the car.[2] Overzealous, publicity-seeking defense lawyers who specialize in freeing notorious killers and rapists on legal technicalities or the insanity defense are the subject of unrestrained scorn.

Advocates of the crime control perspective are also skeptical of the criminal justice system's ability to rehabilitate offenders. Most treatment programs are ineffective because the justice system is simply not equipped to treat people who have a long history of antisocial behavior. From both a moral and a practical standpoint, the role of criminal justice should be the control of antisocial people. If not to the justice system, then to whom can the average citizen turn for protection from society's criminal elements?

Crime Control in Action. The crime control perspective was one of the first views of criminal justice and is still a dominant force today. Its roots can be traced to the 18th century, when legal philosophers first began to argue that punishment should be designed to deter crime without resorting to sadism and brutality. It fell out of favor in the mid-20th century, when a more liberal view of criminal justice, favoring offender treatment and rehabilitation, dominated. However, during the conservative resurgence in the 1970s and 1980s, the crime control perspective emerged once again as an important factor in justice policy. The appointment of conservatives to the Supreme Court and other federal courts, the toughening of federal and state sentencing codes, and the resumption of the use of capital punishment all reflected the crime control perspective.

Today, the crime control perspective exerts a powerful influence on criminal justice policy. A great deal of recent state and federal legislation has created "law and order"–oriented programs, such as mandatory minimum prison sentences for those convicted of violent crimes. The Supreme Court has generally eased restrictions on police operations, allowing police more freedom to detain and search suspects and make arrests.

There is also the widespread belief that criminal tendencies are inherited and that criminals are wicked or damaged people who cannot be rehabilitated and therefore should be set apart from society. The crime control perspective seems a logical approach for those people concerned with law and order and the control of street crime.

The crime control model has spurred creation of mandatory sentencing statutes, which require convicted offenders to do prison time for drug and violent crimes, and of habitual offender ("three strikes and you're out") laws, which significantly increase penalties for chronic offenders. Such conservative crime control policies have resulted in a prison population that now tops 1 million and costs in excess of $30 billion to operate. Yet the general public continues to favor a "get tough" stance against crime. Surveys suggest that most Americans favor strict law enforcement measures. State governments have responded to voter demands and are ready and willing to spend money on correctional construction while cutting back on welfare and education.

Nowhere can the influence of the crime control perspective be more clearly seen than in the adoption of capital punishment by a majority of states and the federal government. To a crime control advocate, the use of the death penalty is morally justified because the state has a duty to protect the lives of its citizens. Capital punishment also is a reflection of the public will, since most U.S. citizens favor the death penalty for convicted murderers. Crime control advocates also favor the death penalty because they are concerned about research showing that convicted killers who are sent to prison often serve only a small percentage of their sentence in confinement and that more than 240 people on death row had prior convictions for murder.[3] It is not surprising, considering the influence of the crime control model, that 56 people were executed in 1996, the most since 1960.[4]

Those who favor crime control point to the declining crime rate in the 1990s as evidence that "get tough" policies are working. Crime rates have fallen because hard-core predatory criminals are now being imprisoned for long periods of time while novice and would-be offenders have been deterred by the threat of tough prison sentences and the death penalty.

Those who advocate the **rehabilitation perspective** see the justice system as a means of caring for and treating people who cannot manage themselves. They view crime as an expression of frustration and anger created by social inequality. Crime can therefore be controlled by giving people the means to improve their lifestyle through conventional endeavors.

The rehabilitation concept assumes that people are at the mercy of social, economic, and interpersonal conditions and interactions. Criminals themselves are the victims of racism, poverty, strain, blocked opportunities, alienation, family disruption, and other social problems. They live in disorganized neighborhoods that are incapable of providing proper education, health care, or civil services. Society must help them compensate for their social problems.

Crime can be controlled by helping people find legitimate ways of obtaining wealth, power, and prestige and coping with their life situations. Methods to achieve these goals include job training, family counseling, educational services, and crisis intervention. It is far less expensive and more efficient and humane to

Rehabilitation Perspective

Figure 4.1
How many prisoners have had prior offenses?
SOURCE: Lawrence Greenfeld and Allen Beck, *Survey of State Prison Inmates 1991* (Washington, D.C.: Bureau of Justice Statistics, 1994), p. 13.

Inmate surveys indicate that
• Over 60% of inmates had been incarcerated in the past.
• Some 94% of inmates had been convicted of a violent crime or had a previous sentence to probation or incarceration.
• About 45% of inmates had 3 or more prior sentences to probation or incarceration.
• About 5% had 11 or more priors.

treat potential young offenders and help them become established in the community than to wait until they violate the law and then punish them with a prison sentence and lock them into a life of crime.

Focus on the Offender. In contrast to the crime control perspective, the rehabilitation perspective places its emphasis on the criminal offender. It disputes the crime control perspective's emphasis on punishment and control. Even if every criminal were apprehended and incarcerated, destructive social conditions would create a new generation of law violators in the nation's ghettos and poverty areas. Most people are not deterred by a prison experience, and many inmates are repeat offenders (see Figure 4.1).

Punishment seems to have little effect on the average offender. The only solution is to provide help. Society has a choice: "pay now," by funding treatment and educational programs, or "pay later," when disenfranchised youth enter costly correctional facilities. Far from proving the success of crime control policies, the current decline in the crime rate is a momentary respite before the "storm." As the teenage population of at-risk kids begins to expand, so, too, will crime rates.

Punishment Is Harmful. A rehabilitation advocate rejects punishment as a means of crime control. Particularly troubling is the use of capital punishment because of its inherent brutality and futility. Its use signifies that society has given up on offenders and precludes any hope they can be turned into law-abiding citizens. Advocates of the death penalty feed the public images of maniacal killers who must be executed to protect innocent children; in truth, the typical person sentenced to death is a young man who kills someone during an armed robbery. The mass murderer is actually rarely sentenced to death. Has society not progressed beyond the cruel punishments used in ancient civilizations?

Rehabilitation in Action. The rehabilitation view was extremely influential in the 1960s and early 1970s, when the government's ability to devise programs to counteract crime was viewed with optimism. The Kennedy and Johnson administrations invited well-known liberal academics and social policy experts to Washington to help shape government programs. The federal government lent support to direct service programs at the grassroots level. Large-scale anticrime and delinquency prevention programs were implemented that emphasized community development, job training, educational enrichment, and political organizing. In addition, a multitude of programs were created at every level of government to offer social services to known offenders who desired to "go straight." Among the best known was the detached street worker program, in which social workers were matched and worked closely with street gangs.[5] Other programs attempted to revitalize entire city neighborhoods with a variety of work and education programs.[6]

In the 1980s, the rehabilitation view fell into disfavor with many members of the general public and the professional community. Despite costly government interventions, treatment efforts had apparently failed to reduce the crime rate. A series of research studies found that most programs designed to rehabilitate known offenders did not really work as well as expected.[7] The failure of rehabilitation programs to receive unqualified support eroded confidence in the ability of the justice system to improve the lives of known criminals and offer alternatives to potential offenders. The cost of funding effective rehabilitation efforts, coupled with the public's fear of violent crime, helped erode the dominance of the rehabilitation philosophy in the criminal justice system.

The justice system has by no means terminated its efforts to treat offenders, however. While some research evaluations question the effectiveness of rehabilitation, others show that many programs do produce desired effects.[8] Numerous treatment programs continue to exist in the various criminal justice agencies around the United States. Most long-term correctional facilities maintain counseling programs, educational efforts, and job training courses. Probation departments operate a full range of community-based programs for offenders who do not need secure confinement. Agencies of the juvenile justice system generally remain committed to a rehabilitation orientation. The public still favors attempting to rehabilitate offenders and are willing to vote funds for treatment. For example, in 1996 Arizona voters approved a bill requiring probation and participation in drug treatment programs for all offenders convicted of possession.[9]

While it is wrong to say that everything works, it may be premature to say that nothing works.[10] As the Analyzing Criminal Justice Issues box suggests, the rehabilitation perspective may have a resurgence.

In his classic work *The Limits of the Criminal Sanction,* Herbert Packer contrasted the crime control perspective with a view that he referred to as the due process model.[11] According to Packer, due process combines elements of the liberals' concern for the individual with the concept of legal fairness guaranteed by the U.S. Constitution.

Advocates of the **due process perspective** argue that the greatest concern of the justice system should be providing fair and equitable treatment to those accused of crime. This means providing impartial hearings, competent legal counsel, equitable treatment, and reasonable sanctions. It follows that the use of discretion within the justice system should be strictly monitored to ensure that no one suffers from racial, religious, or ethnic discrimination.

Due Process Perspective

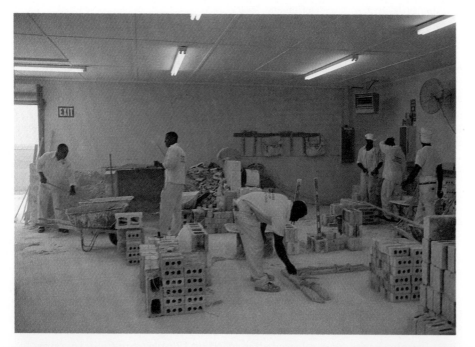

Numerous treatment programs continue to exist in the various criminal justice agencies around the United States. Most long-term correctional facilities maintain counseling programs, educational efforts, and job training courses. Correctional institutions attempt to provide inmates with job skills that may help them gain meaningful employment upon their release.

What to Do About Crime

Elliott Currie and James Q. Wilson are two scholars with opposing views on how best to deal with the crime problem. Currie the liberal and Wilson the conservative have both been influential in shaping crime policy.

Currie's View

In 1985 Elliott Currie published his well-received book *Confronting Crime,* in which he set out a liberal agenda for reducing the crime problem. Currie's book helped clarify the goals of the rehabilitation perspective and provided a blueprint for change in the justice system. He argued that conservative crime control policies are highly confused and ineffectual. The crime rate could be reduced if efforts focused instead on young offenders before they actually became enmeshed in the justice system. The crime problem, he forcefully argued, can be traced directly to social inequality, great extremes of poverty and hopelessness, ineffective national policies to deal with unemployment and underemployment, the destruction of community and family ties because of social mobility, and the pressure placed on the family by our technical society.

To combat crime, the justice system must ease social problems with such efforts as more formal police responses to domestic violence disputes and the strengthening of community ties through using foot patrols and hiring teens to be auxiliary police officers. Intensive probation and restitution should be used as alternatives to incarceration. Every effort should be made to expand intensive rehabilitation services for youthful offenders at the local community level. Aid must be provided to the victims of family violence. Neighborhood dispute resolution teams and community-based family support programs, especially those that respect cultural diversity, can be directed at improving family services, helping teenage parents, and providing educational enrichment for youths.

In more recent writings, including *Reckoning,* an analysis of American culture and drug use, Currie confirms his view that crime can be controlled by "human-ecological" means. These include: (1) an emphasis on high-quality early education, such as the Head Start program; (2) expanded health and mental health services for high-risk children and adults, including prenatal and postnatal care; (3) greater commitment to family support programs; (4) providing education and training for productive work opportunities; and (5) providing adequate shelter and housing for all Americans. "In the long run," he writes, "dealing with America's drug crisis means attacking the conditions which breed it—a principle we have come to accept in most other realms of life" (p. 280). The funding for this social engineering would come from a progressive tax that would shift the burden to the wealthiest Americans.

Wilson's View

In contrast to Currie's liberal vision, Wilson links high American violent crime rates to the erosion of "those ancient bonds of custom, family and village that once held in check some of our better and many of our worst impulses"(p. 26). With growing personal freedom and a lack of informal social control, there has been an overreliance on the criminal justice system and the threat of punishment to control antisocial behavior. This task becomes formidable as the family's influence withers, drugs and guns become more accessible, and the "glorification of violence becomes more commonplace." The result is that those most vulnerable to crime increase the frequency and intensity of their offending. Instead of the at-risk adolescents getting drunk on weekends and committing a single theft with a friend, they get high on crack every day, join a gang, obtain an automatic weapon, and engage in chronic offending.

Wilson's strategy for combating these high-rate offenders rests on a more aggressive response by the criminal justice system. Police should actively seek out known troublemakers, confront them, and conduct frequent frisks for weapons. Police should also be aware of the probationers and parolees living in their area of jurisdiction, and these known offenders should be subject to random testing by antidrug officers. Police patrol should be directed at the "hot spots" of crime where

Chances of Error. Those who advocate the due process orientation are quick to point out that the justice system remains an adversary process that pits the forces of an all-powerful state against those of a solitary individual accused of a crime. If concern for justice and fairness did not exist, the defendant who lacked resources could easily be overwhelmed. They point to miscarriages of justice, such as the case of Clarence Chance and Benny Powell who, wrongfully convicted of murdering a county sheriff, were released after spending 17½ years in California pris-

drug users hang out; these directed patrols can be more effective than random ones. Still another promising tactic is to have police strictly enforce truancy and curfew laws. Idle boys may find the opportunity to impress their friends irresistible; removing the opportunity for crime will reduce their chances of risky behavior.

Wilson also suggests that incarcerating large numbers of high-risk offenders can help contain the crime rate, but only to a limited extent. Incarcerating some criminals, such as robbers, can reduce the robbery rate. But a strict incarceration policy may have little effect on drug dealing, for example, because incarcerated dealers will be replaced by newcomers eager to enter the drug trade. A strict incarceration policy may also be ineffective in controlling the violent behavior of disaffected alienated urban youth. Building more prison cells will help, Wilson claims, but the costs of construction and administration may not pay off in dramatically reduced crime rates.

According to Wilson, social engineering may be an answer. Wilson notes that there is a close link between the number of single-parent children born in poverty and crime rates. Young girls must be discouraged from having children they cannot care for; as he puts it, "Wrongful behavior—neglectful, immature, or incompetent parenting; the production of out-of-wedlock babies—ought to be stigmatized" (p. 34).

In order to get government assistance, unwed mothers should be required to live at home with their parents or, if that is not possible, should be forced to enter group homes where they can be taught parenting skills and their babies can get proper medical care. It is essential that at-risk children be identified at an early stage and taught self-control if they are to break from the cycle of poverty and despair that breeds crime and drug abuse.

Common Ground?

Currie and Wilson are often viewed as having opposing visions on solving the crime problem. Yet they share some common ground. Both believe that government intervention, including law enforcement and correctional programs, can restrict crime rates. Both agree that family functioning is a key factor and that at-risk children can be helped through government interven-

tion. Where they differ is on the type of intervention and the direction it should take. While Wilson considers young criminals to be "risk takers," lacking in self-control, whose behavior can be curtailed and controlled by effective law enforcement, Currie calls for more rehabilitation-oriented programs. And while Currie opts for government job and welfare programs to reduce the number of at-risk youth in the environment, Wilson believes that government programs should be designed to reduce the number of out-of-wedlock children.

Critical Thinking Skills

1. According to Currie, crime rates could be slashed if income inequality were reduced and the underemployed given better work opportunities. Is the socioeconomic class system in the United States so rigid that the lower class is actually prevented from entering mainstream society? Aren't there programs in almost every community that already provide educational opportunities for the "deserving poor"? And considering the success of the free market system, would increased government control and regulation of the marketplace threaten our economic structure?

2. Wilson finds that the family is key to reducing crime rates. Is it not naive to suppose that family relations can be improved by outside social action? Can placing teen mothers in group homes reduce the number of out-of-wedlock kids? Might the general public resist paying for this type of service? Would kids growing up in these shelters be spared the problems of the street, or would they be stigmatized and labeled, reducing their life chances? If the quality of family life cannot be changed, are crime control efforts inherently futile?

3. Suppose for a moment that research shows that for every 10% increase in the prison population, the crime rate is reduced 5%. Would this finding justify a massive effort to build and fill prisons with the hope of eradicating crime? How many millions of people can we incarcerate? Is there a limit?

SOURCES: James Q. Wilson, "What to Do About Crime," *Commentary* 98 (1994): 25–35; Elliott Currie, *Confronting Crime: An American Challenge* (New York: Pantheon, 1985); idem, *Reckoning: Drugs, The Cities, and The American Future* (New York: Hill and Wang, 1993); idem, "Confronting Crime: Looking Toward the Twenty-Fifth Century," *Justice Quarterly* 6 (1989): 6–25.

ons.[12] Their wrongful conviction would have been even more tragic if they had been executed for their crimes. In 1996 the Institute for Law and Justice, a Virginia-based research firm, issued a report showing that at least 28 cases of sexual assault have been overturned because DNA evidence proved the men could have not committed the crime; the inmates averaged 7 years in prison before their release.[13] Because such mistakes can happen, even the most apparently guilty offender deserves all the protection the justice system can offer.

Due Process in Action. In the 1960s the Supreme Court, under the leadership of Chief Justice Earl Warren, began gradually expanding the due process rights of offenders. Criminal defendants were granted the right to an attorney at almost all stages of the justice process; the exclusionary rule was applied to the states; for the first time juvenile offenders were eligible for due process rights; and efforts were made to grant prison inmates fundamental legal entitlements. Since 1980 this due process revolution has waned. A more conservative Supreme Court, filled with Reagan and Bush appointees, has handed down decisions expanding the police officer's ability to search for and seize evidence and to question suspects and has curtailed the rights of juvenile offenders and prison inmates.

While the most important legal rights won by criminal defendants in the 1960s and 1970s remain untouched (for example, the right to have a fair and impartial jury of one's peers), there is little urgency today to increase the scope of their civil rights. While the "due process" revolution may have cooled, recent developments in the justice system may encourage a new set of concerns for due process advocates. For example, the overcrowding crisis in the nation's correctional system has prompted questions about what constitutes proper conditions for inmates and whether overcrowded facilities are in themselves a violation of due process.[14]

Nonintervention Perspective

The fourth approach to criminal justice is known as the **nonintervention perspective.** Those who espouse this viewpoint hold that justice agencies should limit their involvement with criminal defendants when at all possible. Regardless of whether intervention is designed to punish or treat people, its ultimate effect is often harmful. Whatever their goals or design, programs that involve people with a social control agency, such as the police, a mental health department, the correctional system, or a criminal court, will have long-term negative effects. Once involved with such an agency, criminal defendants may be watched, may be considered dangerous and untrustworthy by others, and may acquire a lasting record or label that has negative connotations. Eventually, they may even come to believe what their official record suggests: that they are bad, evil, outcasts, troublemakers, or crazy. Noninterventionists are concerned about the effect of stigma and are influenced by labeling theory.

More than 20 years ago, when distrust of government was running high because of the Watergate and other political scandals, noninterventionists called for limiting government's ability to take control of the lives of people, especially minors, who ran afoul of the law. States moved to **decriminalize** (reduce criminal penalties) or legalize nonserious **victimless crimes,** such as the possession of small amounts of marijuana, public drunkenness, and vagrancy. Noninterventionists demanded the removal of nonviolent offenders from the nation's correctional system, a policy referred to as **deinstitutionalization.** First offenders who committed minor crimes were to be removed from the formal trial process and placed in informal, community-based treatment programs, a process known as **pretrial diversion.** Each of these initiatives was designed to help people avoid the stigma associated with contact with the criminal justice system.

Nonintervention in Action. The noninterventionist movement came under heavy criticism because little evidence could be developed to show that efforts to restrict intervention work any better than programs based on crime control or rehabilitation. *Beyond Probation,* an important study by Charles Murray and Louis Cox, found that the deterrent effect of punitive programs may actually reduce recidivism far more effectively than innovative, community-based efforts founded on the principles of nonintervention.[15] There is more evidence that the impact of punishment is a crime deterrent than there is that the stigma of formal criminal justice processing actually harms offenders.[16]

States have attempted to decriminalize (reduce criminal penalties for) or legalize nonserious victimless crimes, such as the possession of small amounts of marijuana, public drunkenness, and vagrancy. While these measures keep nondangerous offenders out of jail, it does not help them with their problems. Many of these troubled people live on the streets of the nation's largest cities.

Widening the Net. There has also been suspicion that efforts designed to avoid intervention actually work to enmesh those accused of crime more firmly in the grasp of the agencies of justice, a process called **widening the net.** This refers to the phenomenon in which nonintervention programs actually create more contact with the justice system than crime control–oriented programs do. Some treatment-oriented diversion programs actually increase intervention because they require clients to participate in long-term counseling programs rather than simply pay a fine or be placed on probation. One type of deviant label is substituted for another because clients are considered "emotionally unstable" rather than "criminal."

Despite such criticism, the nonintervention philosophy still flourishes. Pretrial, trial, and posttrial programs developed to reduce intervention are quite active today. Efforts continue to be made to keep as many young offenders as possible out of secure detention facilities (by making bail more readily available) and out of prisons and jails (through the use of alternative sanctions, such as house arrest and electronic monitoring).[17] There have been efforts to decriminalize some acts and legalize others. On January 16, 1997 marijuana was sold legally for the first time since the 1930s in the United States when a store in San Francisco, the Cannabis Cultivators Club, began selling "pot" to those who need it for medical reasons. Prices ranged from $5 to $65 per ⅛-ounce bag.[18]

The **justice perspective** combines both liberal and conservative views of justice. Advocates believe that while the purpose of the justice system is to control crime and punish those who violate the law, there must also be fairness, equality, and strict control of discretion when the law is applied.

Justice Perspective

Chapter 4

—

Confronting Crime

119

Just Desert. The justice perspective holds that rehabilitating criminals through correctional treatment efforts is futile. Correctional institutions are places of punishment and confinement and therefore cannot serve as treatment centers. Any effort to individualize treatment and distinguish between criminal offenders will create a sense of unfairness that can interfere with readjustment to society. If two people commit the same crime but receive different sentences due to treatment considerations, the injustice will increase frustration and anger among the inmate population. The criminal justice system must increase fairness by reducing discretion and unequal treatment. Law violators should be evaluated on the basis of their current behavior and not on how their treatment will influence others. The justice model holds that the deterrent effects of a criminal sentence should not be considered, because it is unfair to punish someone solely to prevent others from committing crimes. Nor should criminals be incapacitated because they are believed to be dangerous; it is unfair to incarcerate people based on often-misguided predictions of their future behavior. The core principle of the justice model is that the treatment of criminal offenders must be based solely on current behavior: Punishment must be equitably administered and based on "just desert."

Justice in Action. The justice model plays an extremely influential role in the criminal justice system today. One effort has been the creation of **determinate sentencing** models that authorize similar sentences for every offender convicted of a particular crime. Just desert–based sentences make use of guidelines to control judicial authority in sentencing and to ensure that people convicted for the same crime get similar sentences. The federal criminal code mandates that judges use sentencing guidelines to control their decision making and reduce discretion. The justice perspective influence has also caused some states to abolish parole (early release from prison) in an effort to ensure that each inmate serves the full sentence he or she received at trial. In sum, efforts are being made to take the discretion out of the justice system and reduce the disparity with which people are treated.

Conflict Perspective

The **conflict perspective** holds that the justice system is a state-supported institution designed to control the have-not members of society and keep power in the hands of the affluent. The justice system has become a tool of oppression because society is dominated by intergroup and intragroup conflict. The criminal process serves as an instrument of control, preventing the socially deprived from exercising their civil rights and allowing members of the privileged classes to accumulate an unequal distribution of the nation's wealth. Police are used to interfere with strikes and union activities. Law enforcement agencies infiltrate and compromise dissident political groups. The courts have one standard for the poor and another for the wealthy. Only the affluent can afford private attorneys, pay investigators and expert witnesses, and employ the legal tools needed to win acquittal. And in the rare instance when a member of the upper class is found guilty of serious crime, he or she is either granted probation or allowed to serve time in a minimum-security, "country club" facility rather than in a dangerous state institution. The lenient treatment given **white-collar criminals** in the nation's courts can be contrasted with the harsh punishments meted out to lower-class property offenders.

Sentencing Disparity. Conflict scholars have tried to promote change in the system of justice by pointing up such problems as discrimination and inequality in the way the law is enforced. There seems to be one standard for whites and another for minorities. And efforts to make the system fair and equal have not been successful. For example, the federal government efforts to control sentencing disparity by creating guidelines (as called for by the justice model) has been criticized on the grounds that under existing standards African Americans are punished more harshly than whites. Critics charge that the penalty for possession of crack cocaine is much harsher than the penalty for powdered cocaine. Because African Americans are much more likely to be prosecuted for crack and whites for powder, the guidelines are essentially unfair. In 1996 the U.S. Supreme Court declined to change the law, despite evidence that almost all those sentenced for crack possession were African American.[19] In the view of conflict advocates, it is thus not surprising that minorities are overrepresented in the nation's prison system.

Conflict in Action. There is little question that policymakers are more sensitive than ever to issues of considerable importance to conflict thinkers: the misuse of power, discrimination by government officials, unfair application of the law, and the disadvantages suffered by the poor. This heightened sensitivity has been translated into efforts to correct some major abuses: Indigent defendants are now entitled to free legal counsel; police officers are strictly scrutinized when they use their weapons; and the government has pledged to prosecute business-people who commit corporate or white-collar crimes. In our post-Watergate, post-Iran-Contra society, where suspicion of the government is common, some major conflict propositions seem to be receiving increasingly greater public interest. Incidents such as the Rodney King beating in Los Angeles fuel speculation that the justice system is inherently unfair and biased.

Restorative Justice. Growing out of the conflict perspective has been the peace-making or **restorative justice** movement, which has at its theme mutual aid rather than coercive punishment. Members of the peacemaking movement are now trying to find humanist solutions to delinquency, drug abuse, and other social problems.[20] Rather than punishment and prison, they advocate such policies as mediation and conflict resolution. Peacemakers embrace the idea of having offenders meet with their victims in order to understand their problems and perhaps repay them for their loss and suffering. Rather than harsh treatment and punishment, peacemakers advocate reconciliation and restitution.[21]

The influence of each perspective can be seen in the justice system today (see Figure 4.2). During the past decade, the crime control and justice models have dominated. Laws have been toughened and the rights of the accused curtailed, the prison population has grown, and the death penalty has been used against convicted murderers. In the mid-1980s, when the crime rate was dropping, these policies seemed to be effective. They may be questioned now that crime has become a major national issue.

While the general public still favors punitive policies, efforts are still made to rehabilitate offenders, to provide them with elements of due process, and to give them the least intrusive treatment possible. Police, courts, and correctional agencies supply a wide range of treatment and rehabilitation programs to offenders in all stages of the criminal justice system. Whenever possible, those accused of crime are treated informally in nonrestrictive, community-based programs, and the effects of stigma are guarded against. While the legal rights of offenders are being closely scrutinized by the courts, the basic constitutional rights of the accused remain inviolate. Guardians of due process have made sure that defendants are allowed the maximum protection possible under the law. For example, criminal defendants have been awarded the right to competent legal counsel at trial; merely having a lawyer to defend them is not considered sufficient legal protection.[22]

In sum, understanding the justice system today requires analyzing a variety of occupational roles, institutional processes, legal rules, and administrative doctrines. Each of the predominant views of criminal justice provides a vantage point for understanding and interpreting these rather complex issues. No single view is the right or correct one. Each individual must choose the perspective that best fits his or her own ideas and judgment—or they can all be discarded and the individual's own view substituted.

Perspectives in Perspective

Figure 4.2
Perspectives on justice: key concerns and concepts.

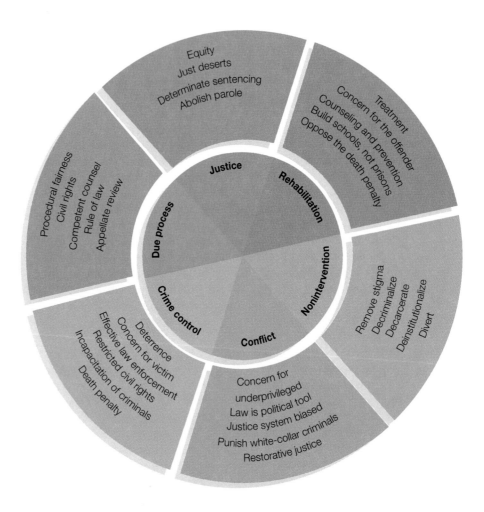

Considering the multiplicity of perspectives and goals in the criminal justice system, it should come as no surprise that there are many unresolved issues that present an important challenge to scholars and practitioners alike. Debate continues over the direction of criminal justice policy and the role the system should play in controlling the behavior of criminals, victims, and the general public. How far should the justice system go in confronting crime? What should be sacrificed when the legal rights of individuals interfere with effective crime control? What is the most efficient approach to controlling the crime patterns of greatest concern to the U.S. public? The following sections examine the efforts being made to control two of the most significant forms of illegal behavior: drug abuse and violence. Following this discussion is an analysis of how current efforts to control crime may interfere with personal rights and liberties.

Controlling the Drug Trade

For both political and social reasons, a massive and concerted effort has been made to control the flow of illegal drugs into the United States. The most important reason is the mounting evidence of a significant association between substance abuse and criminality. Research indicates that about 75% of all arrestees test positively for some drug use.[23] It is still uncertain whether drug abuse actually causes criminal behavior, as most users began committing crime before they began taking drugs, and few users report committing crimes solely to obtain drug money.[24] However, there seems to be evidence that both drugs and crime are part of a deviant lifestyle, characterized by substance abuse, criminality, illegal sexual activity, and other antisocial behaviors.[25] Adolescent drug users show a disturbing tendency to engage in sex for profit to finance their drug habits. Sex

with multiple partners and drug use have been intimately linked to the spread of the HIV virus and AIDS.[26]

One reason it has proven so difficult to control drug sales is the enormous profits involved: 500 kilos of coca leaves worth $4,000 to a grower yields about 8 kilos of street cocaine valued at a quarter of a million dollars. A drug dealer who can move 100 kilos of coke into the United States can make $2.5 million in one shipment. An estimated 1,000 tons of cocaine is produced in Latin America each year, and law enforcement officials are able to seize about one-third. Government crackdowns simply serve to drive up the price of drugs and encourage more illegal entrepreneurs to enter the market. Today, youth gangs have become a prime source of cocaine and crack sales in urban areas, and the Hell's Angels motorcycle club is thought to be a primary distributor of amphetamines.

Agencies of the criminal justice system have used a number of strategies to reduce drug trafficking and the use of drugs. Some have relied on a strict crime control orientation, while others emphasize rehabilitation strategies.

Source Control

One crime control approach to the drug problem is to deter the sale and importation of drugs through the systematic apprehension of large-volume drug dealers, coupled with the enforcement of strict drug laws that carry heavy penalties. This approach is designed to punish known drug dealers and users and deter those who are considering entering the drug trade.

A major effort has been made to cut off supplies of drugs by destroying crops and arresting members of drug cartels in drug-producing countries; this approach is known as **source control** (see Figure 4.3). The federal Drug Enforcement Administration (DEA) has been in the vanguard of encouraging exporting nations to step up efforts to destroy drug crops and prosecute dealers. Hundreds of U.S. soldiers are stationed in Central and South America to help train local narcotics forces and aid their intelligence gathering. Three South American nations, Peru, Bolivia, and Colombia, have agreed to coordinate control efforts with the United States. In 1989 the United States invaded Panama with 20,000 troops to stop its leader, General Manuel Noriega, from assisting drug traffickers.

Translating words into deeds is a formidable task. Drug lords are willing and able to fight back through intimidation, violence, and corruption. The Cali and Medellin drug cartels in Colombia have not hesitated to use violence and

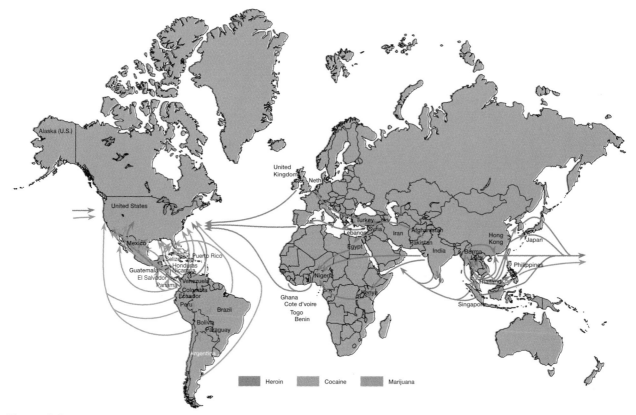

Figure 4.3
How drugs get to the United States.

Source: Marianne Zawitz, *Drugs, Crime, and the Justice System* (Washington, D.C.: Bureau of Justice Statistics, 1994), pp. 47–51.

assassination to protect their interests. Drug trafficking to the United States increased even after government crackdowns in Colombia had resulted in the death of Carlos Lehder, the leader of the Medellin cartel. After his death, the Medellin cartel's business was taken over and expanded by rivals waiting for its fall. The locus of drug exporting soon shifted to Mexico.

Adding to control problems is the fact that the drug trade is an important source of revenue for the exporting countries, and destroying the drug trade undermines their economy. For example, about 60% of the raw coca leaves used to make cocaine for the United States is grown in Peru. The drug trade supports 250,000 Peruvians and brings in over $3 billion annually. Bolivia, which supplies 30% of the raw cocaine for the U.S. market, supports 350,000 people with profits from the drug trade; coca is its single leading export. About 20% of Colombia's overseas exports are made by drug cartels that refine the coca leaves into cocaine, which is then shipped to the United States.[27] It would take billions in annual U.S. economic aid to convince farmers in these countries to give up cultivating drug crops. And even if the government of one nation would be willing to cooperate in vigorous drug suppression efforts, suppliers in other nations, eager to cash in on the seller's market, would be encouraged to turn more acreage over to coca, poppy, or marijuana production.

Interdiction Strategies

Another crime control approach to the drug problem has been to interdict drug supplies as they enter the country. Border patrols and military personnel using sophisticated hardware have been involved in massive interdiction efforts; many multimillion-dollar seizures have been made. Yet the United States' borders are so vast and unprotected that meaningful interdiction is quite difficult. To aid law enforcement agencies, the U.S. military has become involved in stemming the flow of drugs across the border. The cost of staffing listening posts and patrolling borders is growing rapidly and today is over $1 billion per year.[28]

Border control may be an inherently limited drug control strategy. Even if all importation were eliminated, homegrown marijuana and lab-made drugs, such as LSD and PCP, could become drugs of choice. Even now, their easy availability and relatively low cost are increasing their popularity.

Local, state, and federal law enforcement agents have also been actively fighting against drugs. One approach is to direct efforts at large-scale drug rings. Federal and local narcotics agencies routinely announce the seizure of large quantities of drugs.[29] Even if efforts directed at large-scale dealers were always effective, which they are not, little evidence exists that law enforcement efforts alone could end drug distribution. A largely successful effort by the FBI to smash traditional organized crime families has helped decentralize drug dealing. Filling the void have been Asian, Latin American, and Jamaican groups, motorcycle clubs, and local gangs, such as Los Angeles's Crips and Bloods.[30] Ironically, it has proven easier for federal agents to infiltrate and prosecute traditional organized crime groups than to take on drug-dealing gangs.

Law Enforcement Strategies

Police can also target, intimidate, and arrest street-level dealers and users in an effort to make drug use so much of a hassle that consumption is cut back and the crime rate reduced. Among the approaches tried are "reverse stings," in which undercover agents pose as dealers to arrest users who approach them for a buy. Police have attacked fortified crack houses with heavy equipment to breach their defenses. They have used federal racketeering laws to seize the assets of known dealers. Special task forces of local and state police have used undercover operations and drug sweeps to discourage both dealers and users.[31]

While some street-level enforcement efforts have been successful, others are considered failures. Drug sweeps have clogged courts and correctional facilities with petty offenders while proving a costly drain on police resources. A displacement effect is also suspected: Stepped-up efforts to curb drug dealing in one area or city simply encourage dealers to seek out friendlier territory.[32]

Another crime control approach is intensifying criminal punishments for drug dealing. If the benefits of drug dealing can be offset by the pains of punishment and imprisonment, the "rational" drug trafficker will look for a new line of employment.

Punishment Strategies

A number of initiatives have been undertaken to make the prosecution and punishment of drug offenders a top priority. The Federal Anti-Drug Abuse Act of 1988 provides minimum mandatory prison sentences for serious drug crimes, with especially punitive sentences for anyone caught distributing drugs within 1,000 feet of a school playground, youth center, or other areas where minors congregate.[33] The federal government has made the arrest and conviction of drug traffickers a top priority, increasing the number of drug-related convictions in federal courts. In 1984 there were about 9,000 defendants in federal court charged with violating drug laws; by 1995, 18,500 drug cases were heard.[34] State prosecutors have expanded their investigations into drug importation and distribution and created special prosecutors to expedite drug cases. The effort may be working in some jurisdictions. One study of court processing in New York found that cases involving crack had a higher probability of pretrial detention, felony indictment, and incarceration sentences than other criminal cases.[35] Once convicted, drug dealers are subject to very long sentences. Research by the federal government shows that the average sentence for drug offenders sent to federal prison is now about 8 years.[36]

Punishment strategies can have their downside. Defense attorneys consider delay tactics as sound legal maneuvering in drug-related cases. Courts are so backlogged that prosecutors are anxious to plea-bargain. Despite the uniformly "get tough" rhetoric of politicians, many narcotics dealers are treated leniently. Even so, the huge increase in prosecutions and the development of tough laws mandating that convicted dealers serve time means that many of the inmates who are jamming the prisons were involved in drug-related crimes. To relieve overcrowded conditions, many drug offenders sent to prison do not serve their entire sentence. The average prison stay is slightly less than one year. In fact, of all criminal types, drug offenders spend the least amount of their sentence behind bars.[37]

Prevention Strategies

Advocates of the rehabilitation model have suggested strategies aimed at reducing the desire to use drugs and increasing incentives for users to eliminate substance abuse. One approach relies on drug prevention—convincing nonusers to not start using drugs. The most well known program is Drug Abuse Resistance Education, or DARE. This is an elementary-school course designed to give students the skills for resisting peer pressure to experiment with tobacco, drugs, and alcohol. It is unique because it employs uniformed police officers to carry the antidrug message to the students before they enter junior high school. The program focuses on five major areas:

1. Providing accurate information about tobacco, alcohol, and drugs

2. Teaching students techniques to resist peer pressure

3. Teaching students respect for the law and law enforcers

4. Giving students alternatives to drug use

5. Building the self-esteem of students

DARE is based on the concept that young students need specific analytical and social skills to resist peer pressure and say no to drugs. Instructors work with children to raise their self-esteem, provide them with decision-making tools, and help them identify positive alternatives to substance use. So far, police in more than 800 jurisdictions have received DARE training and given the program to millions of students.[38]

Despite its popularity, DARE's evaluations have not shown that it is effective at reducing student drug use.[39] While there are indications that DARE may be effective with some subsets of the population, such as female and Hispanic students, overall success appears problematic at best.[40] One problem may be that typically little distinction is made when enrolling students in the program, so that classrooms may contain some youths who are receptive to the DARE message and others who are openly hostile.[41] A number of prominent locations, including Seattle and Spokane, Washington, have recently dropped the DARE program because community and law enforcement officials were skeptical about its drug-reducing capability.[42]

Treatment Strategies

The rehabilitation model suggests that it is possible to treat known users, get them clean of drugs and alcohol, and help them to reenter conventional society. A number of drug offender treatment strategies have been implemented. One approach rests on the assumption that users have low self-esteem and holds that treatment efforts must focus on building a sense of self. In this approach, users participate in outdoor activities and wilderness training to create self-reliance and a sense of accomplishment.[43]

More intensive efforts use group therapy approaches relying on group leaders who once were substance abusers. Group sessions try to give users the skills and support that can help them reject the social pressure to use drugs. These programs are based on the Alcoholics Anonymous approach, which holds that users must find within themselves the strength to stay clean and that peer support from those who understand the users' experiences can help them achieve a drug-free life.

Residential programs have been established for the more heavily involved users, and a large network of drug treatment centers has been developed. Some are detoxification units that use medical procedures to wean patients from the more addicting drugs onto others, such as **methadone,** the use of which can be more easily regulated. Methadone, a drug similar to heroin, is given to addicts at clinics under controlled conditions. Methadone programs have been undermined because some users sell their methadone on the black market, while others supplement their dosages with illegally obtained heroin.

Correctional administrators have attempted to develop therapeutic communities (TC) within their institutions in an attempt to deal with the psychological causes of drug use. Hypnosis, aversion therapy (getting users to associate drugs with unpleasant sensations, such as nausea), counseling, biofeedback, and other techniques are often used. Within the prison setting, TC procedures include encounter groups, seminars, and similar group activities. These groups focus on self-discipline, self-worth, self-confidence, self-awareness, respect for authority, and acceptance of guidance for problem areas.[44] Residents are also assigned prison industry jobs and are given responsibility for maintenance of the community in order to build their confidence. It is common to have more experienced residents share their insights by teaching the newer members of the community and by assisting in the day-to-day operation of the facility.

Despite their good intentions, little evidence exists that these treatment programs can efficiently end substance abuse. A stay in a treatment program can help stigmatize residents as "addicts," even though they never used hard drugs; while in treatment they may be introduced to hard-core users with whom they may associate upon release. Users often do not enter these programs voluntarily and have little motivation to change.[45]

Even those who could be helped soon learn that there are simply more users who need treatment than there are beds in treatment facilities. Although the number of addicts who are being treated under the auspices of the criminal justice system has been growing, the majority of offenders with substance abuse problems still do not receive treatment. According to one recent estimate, the number of drug-using arrestees who are probably in need of treatment exceeds 2 million each year (980,000 need treatment for cocaine use, 280,000 for opiates, 27,000 for amphetamines, and 780,000 for injection drug use).[46] These numbers overwhelm existing treatment capability.

Legalization

Despite the massive effort to control drug usage through both crime control and rehabilitation strategies, the fight has not been successful. Getting people out of the drug trade is difficult, because drug trafficking offers enormous profits and dealers and users both lack meaningful economic alternatives. Controlling drugs by convincing known users to quit is equally hard; few treatment efforts have proven successful.

If drugs were legalized, the argument goes, distribution could be controlled by the government. Both price and the distribution method could be regulated, reducing addicts' cash requirements. Some people want to see drugs legalized so they can be used for medical purposes. Here Ken Estes, a paraplegic working at Oakland's Cannabis Buyers Club (an underground facility), prepares packets of marijuana for people who use it for medical reasons.

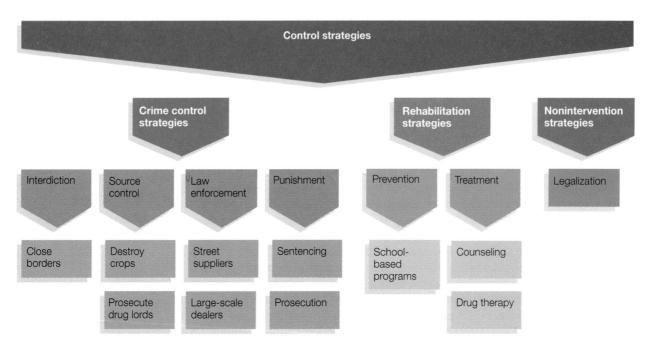

Figure 4.4
Strategies for controlling drugs.

Considering these problems, some commentators, relying on a noninterventionist strategy, have called for the **legalization** of drugs. If drugs were legalized, the argument goes, distribution could be controlled by the government. Price and the distribution method could be regulated, reducing addicts' cash requirements. Crime rates would be cut because drug users would no longer need the same cash flow to support their habit. Drug-related deaths would decrease since government control would reduce the sharing of needles and thus the spread of AIDS. Legalization would also destroy the drug-importing cartels and gangs. Since drugs would be bought and sold openly, the government would reap a windfall from taxes both on the sale of drugs and the income of drug dealers, which now is untaxed as part of the hidden economy. Drug distribution would be regulated, keeping narcotics out of the hands of adolescents. Those who favor legalization point to the Netherlands as a country that has legalized drugs and remains relatively crime-free.[47]

While this approach might reduce the association between drug use and crime in the short run, it may also have grave social consequences. In the long term, drug use might increase, creating an overflow of nonproductive drug-dependent people who must be cared for by the rest of society. The problems of alcoholism should serve as a warning of what can happen when controlled substances are made readily available. The number of drug-dependent babies could begin to match or exceed the number who are delivered with fetal alcohol syndrome.[48] Drunk-driving fatalities, which today number about 25,000 per year, could be matched by deaths caused by driving under the influence of pot or crack. And while distribution would be regulated, adolescents might possibly have the same opportunity to obtain potent drugs as they now have with beer and liquor.

Are Drug Control Strategies Working?

Are any of these drug control strategies working? (See Figure 4.4.) The answer depends on whom you ask. National surveys sponsored by the federal government indicate that drug use today is far lower than in the past. This dramatic evidence is used as an indicator that the war on drugs is being won with a combination of interdiction, source control, and strict law enforcement. Critics question whether the war on drugs is really successful. Some are troubled by the fact that so many criminal offenders are involved with drugs; about three-quarters of all arrestees test positively for drugs. It is also disturbing that so many young people are still experimenting with addicting drugs. Each year, millions of kids try dangerous drugs for the first time, increasing the population exposed to drug use.[49] Drug use surveys indicate that students have increased their drug use in the 1990s.

If drug use is to be controlled, greater efforts must be devoted to target the hard-core user rather than the recreational user. Pressure must also be placed on producing nations to reduce drug production; economic aid should be given to farmers who have depended on drug crops for their living. These efforts, coupled with increased treatment and education programs, may be the key to reducing the use of drugs in the United States.[50]

Another of the criminal justice system's most formidable tasks is to control the incidence of violent crime. The most common strategy relies on the crime control model: deter violent crime through fear of legal punishments. Most legal jurisdictions emphasize apprehending violent criminals, bringing them to trial, and giving them long prison sentences. In some places, the death penalty has been enacted as a deterrent to violent crimes.

Controlling Violence

Historically, the effort to control violent crimes through deterrence strategies alone has not met with long-term success. One reason for this failure is the nature of violent crime itself. Many violent episodes are the result of emotion-laden, interpersonal conflicts that are quite difficult to deter. As you may recall, many murderers knew their victims; the target of violence is commonly a family member, sweetheart, or friend. Many violent criminals were under the influence of drugs or alcohol at the time they committed their crime. Some have a disturbed personality or are psychopathic, which by definition makes them immune to the threat of punishment. Crime control strategies cannot do much to deter this kind of violence. See the accompanying Criminal Justice and the Media box for Hollywood's take on violent criminals.

What alternatives have been suggested, then, to reduce violence? Certainly one approach is to reduce the root causes of crime—poverty, social inequality, racism, family conflict, and drug abuse. Yet to be effective, such measures must be carried out on a scale that has seemed unachievable.

A more realistic approach has been to encourage community cooperation with police, improve police effectiveness, discourage plea bargaining, and increase prison sentences for the chronic violent offender. Controlling violence through legal action has had the unfortunate side effect of creating an overcrowded prison population that is growing at a far faster pace than the crime rate. Research studies give little support to such policies because former inmates have a significant chance of returning to prison.

The physical environment has also been the focus of violence control efforts.[51] People are installing private security systems and other control mechanisms in their homes and businesses.[52] There are indications that environments can be altered to reduce the threat of violence. For example, neighborhood watch programs have been hailed for their crime-reducing potential.[53] The most often debated violence control program is efforts to restrict or ban the sale and possession of the major instruments of violence: handguns.

Banning Guns

The use of handguns in political crimes, such as the assassination of Robert Kennedy and the shooting of President Ronald Reagan and his press secretary James Brady, has spurred advocacy for controls on the sale of handguns and a ban on cheap "Saturday night specials." Ongoing gang and street violence has spurred calls for laws limiting gun availability. UCR data tell us that about half of all murders and a third of all robberies involve a firearm, including many crimes on schoolgrounds. Handguns are the cause of death for two-thirds of all

Cliffhanger

While the general public may fear random street violence, the media like to focus on devilishly clever "rational" criminals who concoct elaborate plots to steal millions. In the many James Bond films arch criminals hatch schemes ranging from looting Fort Knox (*Goldfinger*) to using an orbiting space station to wipe out humanity and then repopulating the planet with a few chosen perfect specimens (*Moonraker*). Luckily for us, 007 is usually on hand to foil the plot and save the world without mussing his hair.

A recent example of this genre is the hugely successful film *Cliffhanger*. A group of master criminals led by Qualen (John Lithgow) carries out an elaborate scheme to commandeer a federal jet and transport $300 million to their own plane—while in flight! First the crew and guards are killed by Taylor, a rogue agent. Then he arranges for the money cases to be sent across to Qualen's aircraft on wires. When a wounded agent fires his gun, the plan goes awry and the money cases fall into the mountains. After crash-landing, Qualen and his crew capture mountain rangers Hal Tucker and Gabe Walker and force them to be guides through the rugged terrain. Walker, played by Sylvester Stallone, manages to escape and, using all his considerable mountaineering skills, foils the plot. After burning or destroying the money, he kills Qualen in a dramatic finale.

As John Lithgow plays him, Qualen seems more like a former English professor who is upset that he didn't get tenure than a criminal from a troubled background. The gang has all sorts of elaborate electronic communications and location gear, not the least of which is their own jet plane. They are an articulate, educated, highly skilled band who seem more suited to forming a high tech start-up company in Silicon Valley than stealing government funds and killing innocent people. With all their resources and training one wonders why they have to resort to crime.

Equally amazing is the Stallone character, Ranger Gabe Walker. He is continually beaten bloody, shot at, and thrown from cliffs and into freezing rivers. He recuperates instantly without even the need for a Band-Aid. While the average person would be in intensive care for

six months, Stallone shrugs off his injuries and rejoins the fray, keeping one step ahead of the criminal band.

Although films such as *Cliffhanger* encourage people to fight back against criminals, research tells us that they are more likely to run the risk of being seriously injured than those who are willing to submit. Perhaps those people who do fight back are used to seeing films in which the hero emerges unscathed from a battle with a heavily armed criminal group.

Cliffhanger also enforces the media's presumption that bad guys never go to the movies. If they did, they would know that heroes like Sean Connery and Sylvester Stallone always win in the end.

police killed in the line of duty. The presence of firearms in the home has been found to significantly increase the risk of suicide among adolescents, regardless of how carefully the guns are secured or stored.[54]

Congress has attempted to alleviate this problem by passing the Brady Bill, which requires a five-business-day waiting period before a handgun can be purchased; during this period, the purchaser's background can be checked. Also in

1994, Congress banned the sale of automatic weapons. In 1996 the federal government approved the Gun Free School Zone Act, which bars possession of firearms within 1,000 feet of a school (with a few exceptions).[55]

While it seems logical that strict controls or even a ban on the sale and ownership of handguns might help reduce the violence rate, controlling guns is not only a formidable job but a policy that would be resisted by many citizens.[56] Millions of handguns are manufactured each year in the United States.[57] About one-third of these are cheaply made Saturday night specials. Such guns as the Raven Arms MP-25, Davis Industries Davis .38, and Jennings/Bryco Arms J-22 semiautomatic can be made for about $15 each, because zinc alloy is injected into molds in their manufacture. Expensive guns, such as Smith and Wessons or Lugers, use precision-crafted stainless steel. A Colt .45 takes about three hours to make; a Raven is assembled in three minutes. These mass-produced weapons are favored by young street toughs because they are easily concealed and can be bought for as little as $50 on the street; about 30,000 are made and sold each month. Since 1990, more than 40% of all firearms used in felonies have been cheap, mass-produced handguns.[58]

The growth in the number of firearms in the United States has not been limited to handguns. The Bureau of Alcohol, Tobacco, and Firearms estimates that Americans own 2 million to 3 million automatic weapons. In 1989 the U.S. government moved to reduce the use of guns for both criminal and self-protection purposes by banning the importation and sale of 43 types of assault rifles, a ban voluntarily followed by U.S. manufacturers; in 1994 Congress banned all sales of automatic rifles.

Why Do People Own Guns?

Despite its logic, banning handguns and automatic weapons has proven to be difficult. Gun advocacy groups, led by the National Rifle Association, argue that the right to bear arms is guaranteed by the Second Amendment to the U.S. Constitution and that an armed citizenry is a free one.

Gun advocacy is supported by the fact that many gun owners purchase weapons to protect themselves from armed intruders and criminals. Research indicates that people who carry guns are often motivated by self-protection and are not violence-prone personalities.[59] A survey of New York City subway riders found that passengers are likely to carry self-protective devices such as handguns if they believe that local crime is on the increase, that they themselves are likely to become crime victims, and that they are unlikely to be helped if they are attacked; many had prior experience as victims.[60] Store owners in Los Angeles reported that gun purchases increased significantly after the 1992 rioting.

Gun advocates believe that fear of crime is a legitimate reason to bear arms and that people have a right to protect themselves and their family from armed intruders. They point to statistics showing that each year 1,500 to 2,800 predatory criminals are killed by gun-wielding crime victims and that between 8,700 and 16,000 are wounded.[61] Armed victims who fight back are often successful in warding off attackers.

Gun advocates also challenge the role of handguns in crime. While FBI data show that handguns are used in a great many violent crimes, the NCVS indicates that guns are used in only 10% of all violent acts (about 27% of those in which the assailant was armed with a weapon).[62] These facts are all too often ignored or misrepresented by the media, which have an "antigun" bias.[63]

Rather than legal controls, gun advocates call for strict punishment being meted out to anyone who uses a handgun during the commission of a crime.

Does Gun Control Work?

Efforts to control gun ownership have many sources. Each state and many local jurisdictions have laws banning or restricting the sale or possession of guns. Other laws regulate dealers who sell guns. For example, the Federal Gun Control Act prohibits dealers from selling guns to minors, ex-felons, and known drug users. A new provision, referred to as the the *Brady Bill,* requires a waiting

Table 4.1
Federal Laws that
Control Firearms

SOURCE: Federal Gun Control Act, 18
U.S.C. sec. 922 (g) and (n) as
amended; Brady Handgun Violence
Prevention Act (P.L. 103-159)(1993);
Don Manson, *Presale Firearm Checks*
(Washington, D.C.: Bureau of Justice
Statistics, 1997).

The Federal Gun Control Act

Prohibits the sale of firearms to an individual who—
- Is under indictment for, or has been convicted of, a crime punishable by imprisonment for more than 1 year
- Is a fugitive from justice
- Is an unlawful user of a controlled substance
- Has been adjudicated as a mental defective or committed to a mental institution
- Is an alien unlawfully in the United States
- Was discharged from the armed forces under dishonorable conditions
- Has renounced U.S. citizenship
- Is subject to a court order restraining him or her from harassing, stalking, or threatening an intimate partner or child
- Is a person convicted of domestic violence

The Brady Act

"Interim provisions," in force until 1998, require that licensed firearm dealers request a presale check on all potential handgun purchasers from the chief law enforcement officer (CLEO) in the jurisdiction where the prospective purchaser resides.

The CLEO must make a reasonable effort to determine whether the purchaser is prohibited from receiving or possessing a handgun. (This provision was overturned by the Supreme Court in 1997.) The federal firearms licensee must wait 5 business days before transferring the handgun to the buyer unless earlier approval is received from the CLEO. These interim procedures will terminate no later than November 30, 1998.

The interim provision also permits states to follow a variety of alternatives to the 5-day waiting period. These alternatives include states that issue firearm permits, perform "instant checks," or conduct "point-of-sale" checks. To qualify under these alternatives, state law must require that before any licensee completes the transfer of a handgun to a nonlicensee, a government official must verify that possession of a handgun by the transferee would not be a violation of law. Examples of Brady-alternative states include California (point-of-sale check), Virginia (instant check), and Missouri (permit).

After November 1998 instant background checks will be required for purchasers of all firearms. The background check will determine, based on available records, whether an individual is prohibited under the Federal Gun Control Act or state law from receiving or possessing firearms.

Under the "permanent provisions" of the Brady Act, presale inquiries will be made through the National Instant Criminal Background Check System (NICS). The act requires the NICS, which will be operated by the FBI, to be established no later than November 1998. At that time the procedures related to the waiting period of the interim system will be eliminated.

Under the FBI's proposed NICS configuration, state criminal history records will be provided through each state's central repository and the Interstate Identification Index. The index, maintained by the FBI, points instantly to criminal records that states hold. In addition, the FBI will provide records of federal offenses, federally maintained state data, and federal data on nonfelony disqualifications. States responding to NICS inquiries for nonfelony prohibitions will provide their records directly.

period (to do a background check) before a gun can be sold to an applicant (see Table 4.1). The bill was named after former Press Secretary James Brady, who was severely wounded in the attempted assassination of President Ronald Reagan by John Hinckley, Jr. An evaluation of the Brady Bill shows that between March 1994 and June 1996, for all states combined, there were almost 9 million applications to purchase firearms and an estimated 186,000 rejections. On average, each month an estimated 6,600 firearm purchases were prevented by background checks of potential gun buyers during the 28 months after the effective date of the Brady Handgun Violence Prevention Act. The checks revealed purchasers' ineligibility under federal or state laws to buy a handgun or other firearm. Over 70% of the rejected purchasers were convicted or indicted criminals. The data do not indicate whether rejected purchasers later obtained a firearm through other means.[64] (See Chapter 9 for more on the Brady law and its legal challenges.)

Can laws penalizing the use of handguns to commit crime make a difference in the violent crime rate?[65] Some jurisdictions have set mandatory sentences for any crime involving a handgun. Two well-known examples are Michigan's Felony Firearm Statute, which requires that persons convicted of a crime in which a handgun was used receive an additional two years tacked onto their sentence. Massachusetts's Bartley-Fox Law provides a mandatory one-year prison term for possession of a handgun (outside the home) without a permit. Analysis of these statutes' effectiveness find that they had (1) little effect on the sentence given to convicted offenders and (2) little effect on violent crime rates.[66]

More-positive findings have been derived from a long-term evaluation of the District of Columbia's Firearms Control Regulations Act of 1976. This act restricts possession of firearms to persons who already owned and reregistered guns at the time the law was passed.[67] After the initial reregistration, handguns could not be registered and therefore became illegal (it is still possible to buy shotguns and rifles). The law also requires that registered gun owners keep firearms unloaded and disassembled or locked up, except when they are being used for lawful recreational purposes. One study of the program found that while gun-related homicides and suicides remained rather stable in surrounding areas, they significantly declined in the District of Columbia after the gun control law went into effect. Especially significant was the fact that the nongun homicide and suicide rate remained stable in the District, a finding that confirms that the reduction in handgun violence was not part of a general decline in the crime rate. The evaluation of the D.C. law is one of the strongest statements in support of the effectiveness of handgun control laws.[68]

Gun Control Problems

Controlling guns through legislation alone may be difficult to achieve.[69] There are so many guns in the United States today—a conservative estimate is 100 million illegal handguns—that banning their sale would have a relatively small effect for years to come.[70] And if guns are made more valuable by banning their manufacture or sale, illegal importation of guns might increase, as it has for another controlled product, narcotics.

Increasing penalties for gun-related crimes may also be a limited approach because judges are usually reluctant to alter their sentencing policies to accommodate legislators. Regulating dealers is difficult and encourages private sales and bartering. Little evidence exists that if criminals were prevented from easily purchasing cheap, low-caliber Saturday night specials, they would terminate their criminal careers. They might instead turn to using larger-caliber weapons with deadlier effects.[71] Even if purchased by a legitimate gun enthusiast, these weapons can fall into the wrong hands as a result of burglaries and break-ins.[72]

Despite the difficulty of effective control, some combination of oversight and penalty seems imperative, and efforts should be made to discover, if at all possible, whether handgun control could indeed reduce violent crime rates.

The Scope of Social Control

While the agencies of justice are charged with using all appropriate means to control drugs, violence, and white-collar and other crimes, they are also expected to be considerate of the civil rights and privacy of both the general public and criminal suspects. Those who champion the due process perspective are constantly wary of intrusions by the justice system, made in the name of "efficient crime control," into the personal life of "suspects" who maintain a lifestyle or political beliefs that are perceived as threatening.

Similarly, there are questions about the scope of **social control.** Which behaviors should society control with a firm hand, and which should remain beyond the grasp of the law? For example, is the distribution of sexually oriented material a public menace or a protected incidence of free speech? Should sexual relations between consenting adults be subject to government regulation? Should marijuana be legalized? Should abortions be outlawed?

While efforts have been made to increase society's control over some behaviors that are considered a danger to the general public, in other instances efforts by noninterventionists have limited the power of the justice system to regulate human interaction. A number of recent efforts stand out to illustrate the extension of social control by the justice system. For example, the federal government's most recent drug control legislation significantly extends the government's ability to control drug importers and distributors through the use of mandatory prison sentences.[73] A number of states have passed legislation toughening penalties for drunk drivers, to curb the flood of alcohol-related highway fatalities. The federal government has attempted to crack down on the distribution of pornography by significantly increasing its obscenity prosecutions.[74] In synch with this federal effort, local prosecutors brought highly publicized obscenity charges against the curators of Cincinnati's Contemporary Art Center for mounting an exhibit of homoerotic photographs by Robert Mapplethorpe, and prosecutors in Florida filed charges against the rap group 2 Live Crew for producing an allegedly obscene record album.[75] Although neither case resulted in a conviction, they illustrate efforts to control behavior considered by some to be private and nonthreatening.

Reducing Social Control

While the scope of social control has increased in some areas of the law, many experts in criminal justice, law, and the social sciences have suggested that certain offenses should be removed from the criminal statutes. These include public drunkenness, pornography, vagrancy, gambling, marijuana use, prostitution, and sexual acts between consenting adults in private. As noted earlier in this chapter, the reduction or elimination of legal penalties for such acts is referred to as decriminalization.[76] Advocates of the decriminalization approach suggest that the criminal law is overextended when it invokes criminal sanctions in regard to social and moral problems; they believe that the primary purpose of criminal law should be to control serious crimes affecting persons and property. As a result, it is argued that these "victimless" crimes should be the responsibility not of the criminal justice system but of mental health or other social service agencies.

Decriminalization efforts aim to make the criminal law reflective of current social values and attitudes while allowing the overburdened criminal justice system to concentrate on more serious criminal offenses. The decriminalization process has been aided by legal change. For example, the movement to decriminalize the behavior of chronic alcoholics was originally influenced by federal court decisions declaring that a chronic alcoholic could not be found guilty of the crime of public intoxication.[77] In 1968 the U.S. Supreme Court decision of *Powell v. Texas* recognized the criminal justice system's inability to provide rehabilitation for the alcoholic and, in so doing, removed alcoholics from the control of the justice system.[78]

The move to decriminalize victimless crimes received a setback in 1986, when in the case of *Bowers v. Hardwick* the Supreme Court upheld a Georgia statute holding that sexual relations between consenting adults of the same sex are a crime (sodomy). The majority found that homosexuality has long been condemned in Western society and that it is therefore within the state's interest to limit homosexual activity.[79]

The *Bowers* case was a major setback for civil liberties groups that had hoped the Court would decriminalize homosexual behavior in the same manner it had dealt with other sexual matters, such as the use of contraceptives and abortion. However, sexually related behavior has always presented a dilemma for lawmakers, even when there is little conclusive evidence that it is harmful to society. For example, all states continue to ban obscene magazines and films, even though sexually related material has not been clearly linked to crime or violence.[80] And when Hawaii passed legislation to uphold same-sex marriages, the law was struck down by an appellate court judge.

The scope of social control has become a critical issue because government agents now have so many new tools, including computerized databases, aerial surveillance cameras, DNA testing, and highly sensitive listening devices, at their disposal. Civil libertarians and advocates of due process are troubled that the government can use this new technology to monitor suspected and convicted criminals. How far should the government go in an effort to control crime? Are we in danger of becoming dominated by an all-seeing, all-knowing "big brother"?

The new surveillance techniques operate on a number of levels. Computers are used in extensive data retrieval systems to cross-reference people and activities. Information available in national and local databases includes credit ratings, bank accounts, stock transfers, medical information, and outstanding loans.

Computer networks also contain criminal justice system information. The most extensive network is the National Crime Information Center, operated by the Justice Department, which contains an extensive collection of arrest records, allowing local police departments to instantly determine whether a suspect has a record.

Technology has also been improved in the area of visual and audio surveillance. The FBI has made national headlines filming and taping drug deals and organized crime activities. Hundreds of high-tech devices make listening and watching more extensive and virtually self-sufficient. For example, listening devices now use lasers that permit eavesdropping without having to enter a home or secure a warrant. Airborne cameras can monitor human movement from 30,000 feet and help spot fields of marijuana and other illegal drugs.

Electronic equipment is also used to monitor offenders in the community. Instead of a prison or jail sentence, convicted offenders are placed under house arrest and kept under surveillance by a central computer. A government agency, most typically the probation department, keeps track of offenders by requiring them to wear an ankle or neck device that signals a computer if they leave their home without permission.

The dangers represented by the new electronic surveillance are the subject of an important book by sociologist Gary Marx.[81] He lists the following characteristics of these surveillance techniques that set them apart from traditional methods of social control:

1. The new surveillance transcends distance, darkness, and physical barriers.

2. It transcends time; its records can be stored, retrieved, combined, analyzed, and communicated.

3. It has low visibility or is invisible.

4. It is often involuntary.

5. Prevention of future crimes is a major concern.

6. It is capital- rather than labor-intensive.

7. It involves decentralized self-policing.

8. It triggers a shift from targeting a specific suspect to categorical suspicion of everyone.

9. It is more intensive.

10. It is more extensive.[82]

According to Marx, the use of electronic eavesdropping and other modern surveillance methods has changed the relationship between police and the public. New techniques have overcome the physical limitations that existed when surveillance was a function of human labor. Today's electronic devices never rest, are virtually undetectable, and can store information forever. People may now be required to aid in their own monitoring by wearing devices that keep them under scrutiny; electronic devices can follow suspects everywhere, gather extensive information on them, and include thousands in the information net. As Marx puts it, "Between the camera, the tape recorder, the identity card, the metal detector, the tax form, and the computer, everyone becomes a reasonable target."[83]

The dangers of the new surveillance can include a redefinition of the concept of invasion of privacy in which almost any personal information is open to scrutiny, "fishing expeditions" in which the government can do a general check on a citizen without a court order, and the chance that machine error will destroy the lives of innocent people. Society must guard against this intrusion now that computers and other elements of technology have become so sophisticated, as they are often subtle, indirect, invisible, and deceptive.[84]

Criminal Justice on the Net

The Internet can help us learn more about models of justice as well as obtain information on drug and gun control.

According to the crime control model, the victims of crime should be protected from harm. The Office for Victims of Crime (OVC) serves as the federal focal point for addressing the needs and improving the treatment of crime victims. This task includes carrying out the activities mandated by the Victims of Crime Act of 1984 (VOCA), as amended (42 U.S.C. 10601 note) and monitoring compliance with the provisions regarding assistance for federal crime victims of the Victim and Witness Protection Act of 1982. You can reach them at

http://gopher.usdoj.gov/ojp/ovc.html

The rehabilitation model assumes that poverty is the cause of crime and that helping the poor can reduce the crime rate. A number of groups are dedicated to helping the poor. The Coalition for the Homeless is the nation's oldest and most progressive organization helping homeless men, women, and children. Since 1981 the coalition has used litigation, lobbying, grassroots organizing, public education, and direct services in the battle against this crisis. Visit their homepage at

http://www.homeless.24x7.com/ who.html

One approach to reducing the incidence of substance abuse is to educate the public and to provide victim services to those who need help. The mission of Mothers Against Drunk Driving is to stop drunk driving and support victims of this violent crime. They have a Victim Hotline at 1-800-927-6080. The M.A.D.D. homepage describes the organization's goals and programs:

http://www.olympic.net/MADD

There are also groups on the net who seek to control or abolish handgun ownership. The Coalition to Stop Gun Violence was founded in 1974 to combat the growing gun violence problem in the United States. CSGV is a coalition of more than 40 religious, professional, labor, medical, educational, and citizen civic organizations. Visit their web site at

http://www.gunfree.inter.net/

Summary

The role of criminal justice can be interpreted in many ways. People who study the field or work within its agencies bring their own ideas and feelings to bear when they try to decide the right course of action to take or recommend. There are a number of different perspectives on criminal justice today. The crime control perspective is oriented toward deterring criminal behavior and incapacitating serious criminal offenders. In contrast, the rehabilitation model views the justice system as a treatment agency focused on helping offenders. Counseling programs are stressed over punishment and deterrence strategies. Those who hold the due process perspective see the justice system as a legal process. Their concern is that every defendant receive his or her full share of legal rights granted under law.

In addition to these views, the nonintervention model is concerned about stigma and helping defendants avoid a widening net of justice; advocates call for using the least intrusive methods possible. Those who advocate the justice model are concerned with making the system equitable. The arrest, sentencing, and correctional process should be structured so that every person is treated equally. Finally, the conflict view focuses on exposing the political and economic forces that shape justice policy and promote bias and discrimination.

The justice system is now confronting some major crime problems. One important area is the so-called war on drugs. A number of strategies have been attempted, including some based on crime control strategies, such as source control and interdiction at the border. Some efforts are based on the rehabilitation model, such as treatment and education programs. One approach that may be tried is a noninterventionist strategy of legalizing drugs. So far, the war on drugs has had mixed results: drug use is down in the general population but has been increasing in the 1990s. Hard-core users still commit a lot of crime.

Another concern is violent crime. One response to violent crime is to control handguns. Efforts to regulate guns by law or punishment strategies have not worked, because there are so many guns, they can be bought on the black market, and many people feel that citizens have the right to own guns for self-protection.

While the justice system is confronting crime, a danger exists that these efforts will intrude on privacy. New methods of surveillance and data collection make the privacy issue critical.

Key Terms

crime control perspective
rehabilitation perspective
due process perspective
nonintervention perspective
decriminalization
victimless crimes

deinstitutionalization
pretrial diversion
widening the net
justice perspective
determinate sentencing
conflict perspective

white-collar criminals
restorative justice
source control
methadone
legalization
social control

Questions

1. What are the basic elements of each model or perspective on justice? Which best represents your own point of view?
2. How would each perspective on criminal justice consider the use of the death penalty as a sanction for first-degree murder?
3. What are the primary strategies being used to fight the war on drugs? Why are they failing to control hard-core drug use? Which strategy is the most effective?
4. Should possession of all handguns be banned? What about assault rifles? Before you answer, remember how successful efforts to ban narcotics have been.

1. Paul Cassell, "How Many Criminals Has *Miranda* Set Free?" *Wall Street Journal,* 1 March 1995, p. A15.

2. *Ohio v. Robinette,* 95-891 (1996).

3. James Stephan and Tracy Snell, *Capital Punishment, 1994* (Washington, D.C.: Bureau of Justice Statistics, 1996).

4. "56 Executions Last Year, The Most Since 1960, BJS says," *Criminal Justice Newsletter,* 16 December 1996, p. 3.

5. Malcolm Klein, *Street Gangs and Street Workers* (Englewood Cliffs, N.J.: Prentice-Hall, 1971); New York City Youth Board, *Reaching the Fighting Gang* (New York: New York City Youth Board, 1960).

6. Walter Miller, "The Impact of a 'Total Community' Delinquency Control Project," *Social Problems* 10 (1962): 168–191.

7. See, for example, Robert Martinson, "What Works? Questions and Answers About Prison Reform," *Public Interest* 35 (1974): 22–54; Charles Murray and Louis Cox, *Beyond Probation* (Beverly Hills, Calif.: Sage, 1979); for further analysis, see John Whitehead and Steven Lab, "A Meta-Analysis of Juvenile Correctional Treatment," *Journal of Research in Crime and Delinquency* 26 (1989): 223–236.

8. D. A. Andrews, Ivan Zinger, Robert Hoge, James Bonta, Paul Gendreau, and Francis Cullen, "Does Correctional Treatment Work? A Clinically Relevant and Psychologically Informed Meta-Analysis," *Criminology* 28 (1990): 369–404.

9. "Arizona Approves New Drug Plan: Treatment, Not Incarceration," *Criminal Justice Newsletter,* 16 November 1996, p. 4.

10. Paul Gendreau and Robert Ross, "Revivification of Rehabilitation: Evidence from the 1980s," *Justice Quarterly* 4 (1987): 349–407; see also Carol Garrett, "Effects of Residential Treatment on Adjudicated Delinquents: A Meta-Analysis," *Journal of Research in Crime and Delinquency* 22 (1985): 287–308.

11. Herbert Packer, *The Limits of the Criminal Sanction* (Stanford, Calif.: Stanford University Press, 1968), p. 175.

12. "Capital Punishment's Injustice," *Boston Globe,* 30 March 1992, p. 10.

13. "DNA Testing Has Exonerated 28 Prison Inmates, Study Finds," *Criminal Justice Newsletter,* 17 June 1996, p. 2.

14. Henry Pontell and Wayne Welsh, "Incarceration as a Deviant Form of Social Control: Jail Overcrowding in California," *Crime and Delinquency* 40 (1994): 18–36.

15. Charles Murray and Louis Cox, *Beyond Probation: Juvenile Corrections and the Chronic Offender* (Beverly Hills, Calif.: Sage, 1979).

16. Douglas Smith and Patrick Gartin, "Specifying Specific Deterrence: The Influence of Arrest on Future Criminal Activity," *American Sociological Review* 54 (1989): 94–105.

17. Joan Petersilia, *Expanding Options for Criminal Sentencing* (Santa Monica, Calif.: Rand Corporation, 1987).

18. Associated Press, "Club Reopens to Sell Marijuana Legally," *Boston Globe,* 16 January 1997, p. A18.

19. *United States v. Armstrong* (1996).

20. Harold Pepinsky and Richard Quinney, eds., *Criminology as Peacemaking* (Bloomington: University of Indiana Press, 1991).

21. Martin Schwartz and David Friedrichs, "Postmodern Thought and Criminological Discontent: New Metaphors for Understanding Violence," *Criminology* 32 (1994): 221–246.

22. *Strickland v. Washington,* 466 U.S. 668, 104 S.Ct. 2052, 80 L.Ed.2d 674 (1984).

23. *Drug Use Forecasting, 95* (Washington, D.C.: National Institute of Justice, 1996).

24. David Altschuler and Paul Brounstein, "Patterns of Drug Use, Drug Trafficking, and Other Delinquency Among Inner-City Adolescent Males in Washington, D.C.," *Criminology* 29 (1991): 589–621.

25. George Speckart and M. Douglas Anglin, "Narcotics Use and Crime: An Overview of Recent Research Advances," *Contemporary Drug Problems* 13 (1986): 741–769; Charles Faupel and Carl Klockars, "Drugs-Crime Connections: Elaborations from the Life Histories of Hard-Core Heroin Addicts," *Social Problems* 34 (1987): 54–68.

26. James Inciardi, Anne Pottieger, Mary Ann Forney, Dale Chitwood, and Duane McBride, "Prostitution, IV Drug Use, and Sex-for-Crack Exchanges Among Serious Delinquents: Risks for HIV Infection," *Criminology* 29 (1991): 221–235.

27. Brook Larmer, "A Booming Grassroots Business," *Newsweek,* 6 January 1992, p. 23; Drug Enforcement Administration, *National Drug Control Strategy* (Washington, D.C.: U.S. Government Printing Office, 1989).

28. Lane, "The Newest War," *Newsweek,* 6 January 1992, p. 18.

29. "Cocaine Hidden in Concrete Seized," *Boston Globe,* 3 December 1991, p. 3.

30. Rick Graves and Ed Allen, *Narcotics and Black Gangs* (Los Angeles: Los Angeles County Sheriff's Department, n.d.); Scott Armstrong, "Los Angeles Gangs Go National," *Christian Science Monitor,* 19 July 1988, p. 3; Walter Shapiro, "Going After the Hell's Angels," *Newsweek,* 13 May 1985, p. 41.

31. David Hayeslip, "Local-Level Drug Enforcement: New Strategies," *NIJ Reports* (March-April 1989).

32. Mark Moore, *Drug Trafficking* (Washington, D.C.: National Institute of Justice, 1988).

33. Anti-Drug Abuse Act of 1988, Public Law 100-6901 21 U.S.C. 1501; Subtitle A-Death Penalty, Sec. 001, Amending the Controlled Substances Abuse Act, 21 U.S.C. 848.

34. Kathleen Maguire and Ann Pastore, *Sourcebook of Criminal Justice Statistics, 1995* (Washington, D.C.: U.S. Government Printing Office, 1996), p. 490.

35. Steven Belenko, Jeffrey Fagan, and Ko-Lin Chin, "Criminal Justice Responses to Crack," *Journal of Research in Crime and Delinquency* 28 (1991): 55–74.

36. U.S. Sentencing Commission, *Annual Report 1995* (Washington, D.C.: U.S. Sentencing Commission, 1996), p. 62.

37. Ibid., p. 4.

38. Dennis Rosenbaum, Robert Flewelling, Susan Bailey, Chris Ringwalt, and Deanna Wilkinson, "Cops in the Classroom: A Longitudinal Evaluation of Drug Abuse Resistance Education (DARE)," *Journal of Research in Crime and Delinquency* 31 (1994): 3–31.

39. Lloyd Johnston, Jerald Bachman, and Patrick O'Malley, "Annual Survey of Drug Abuse, 1993," news release, University of Michigan, February 1994.

40. Rosenbaum, Flewelling, Bailey, Ringwalt, and Wilkinson, "Cops in the Classroom."

41. Ibid.

42. Los Angeles Times, "Seattle Rethinks Drug Education," *Boston Globe,* 1 December 1996, p. A9.

43. See, generally, Peter Greenwood and Franklin Zimring, *One More Chance* (Santa Monica, Calif.: Rand Corporation, 1985).

44. Douglas S. Lipton, *The Effectiveness of Treatment for Drug Abusers Under Criminal Justice Supervision* (Washington, D.C.: National Institute of Justice, 1995).

45. Eli Ginzberg, Howard Berliner, and Miriam Ostrow, *Young People at Risk: Is Prevention Possible?* (Boulder, Colo.: Westview Press, 1988), p. 99.

46. Cited in Lipton, *The Effectiveness of Treatment for Drug Abusers Under Criminal Justice Supervision.*

47. See, generally, Ralph Weisheit, *Drugs, Crime and the Criminal Justice System* (Cincinnati: Anderson, 1990).

48. James Inciardi and Duane McBride, "Legalizing Drugs: A Gormless, Naive Idea," *Criminologist* 15 (1990): 1–4.

49. Majority Staff, Senate Judiciary Committee, *Fighting Drug Abuse: Tough Decisions for Our National Strategy* (Washington, D.C.: U.S. Senate, 1992).

50. Ibid.

51. Charles Murray, "The Physical Environment and Community Control of Crime," in *Crime and Public Policy,* ed. James Q. Wilson (San Francisco: ICS Press, 1983), pp. 107–125.

52. Oscar Newman, *Defensible Space: Crime Prevention Through Urban Design* (New York: Macmillan, 1972).

53. Peter Finn, *Block Watches Help Crime Victims in Philadelphia* (Washington, D.C.: National Institute of Justice, 1986).

54. David Brent, Joshua Perper, Christopher Allman, Grace Moritz, Mary Wartella, and Janice Zelenak, "The Presence and Accessibility of Firearms in the Home and Adolescent Suicides," *Journal of the American Medical Association* 266 (1991): 2989–2995.

55. "Congress OKs New Version of Gun-Free School Act," *Criminal Justice Newsletter,* 1 November 1996, p. 3.

56. See generally, Gary Kleck, *Point Blank: Guns and Violence in America* (New York: Aldine de Gruyter, 1991).

57. Estimates supplied by the Bureau of Alcohol, Tobacco, and Firearms, 1992.

58. Alix Freedman, "A Single Family Makes Many of Cheap Pistols That Saturate Cities," *Wall Street Journal,* 28 February 1992, p. A1.

59. John Whitehead and Robert Langworthy, "Gun Ownership and Willingness to Shoot: A Clarification of Current Controversies," *Justice Quarterly* 6 (1989): 262–282.

60. Eduard Ziegenhagen and Dolores Brosnan, "Citizen Recourse to Self-Protection: Structural, Attitudinal, and Experiential Factors," *Criminal Justice Policy Review* 4 (1990): 91–104.

61. Gary Kleck, "Crime Control Through the Private Use of Armed Force," *Social Force* 35 (1988): 1–21.

62. Michael Rand, *Handgun Crime Victims* (Washington, D.C.: Bureau of Justice Statistics, 1990), p. 1.

63. Paul Blackman, "The Bigotry of the Anti-Gun Press: A Year in the Lies of the *Washington Post*," paper presented at the annual meeting of the American Society of Criminology, San Francisco, November 1991.

64. Don Manson, *Presale Firearm Checks* (Washington, D.C.: Bureau of Justice Statistics, 1997).

65. Franklin Zimring, "Firearms and Federal Law: The Gun Control Act of 1968," *Journal of Legal Studies* 4 (1975): 133–198.

66. Colin Loftin, Milton Heumann, and David McDowall, "Mandatory Sentencing and Firearms Violence: Evaluating an Alternative to Gun Control," *Law and Society Review* 17 (1983): 287–319.

67. Adapted from Colin Loftin, David McDowall, Brian Wiersema, and Talbert Cottey, "Effects of Restrictive Licensing of Handguns on Homicide and Suicide in the District of Columbia," *New England Journal of Medicine* 325 (1991): 1615–1620.

68. Ibid.

69. See, generally, James Wright, Peter Rossi, and Kathleen Daly, *Under the Gun: Weapons, Crime and Violence in America* (New York: Aldine, 1983).

70. Samuel Walker, *Sense and Nonsense About Crime* (Belmont, Calif.: Wadsworth Publishers, 1985), p. 152.

71. James Wright, "Second Thoughts About Gun Control," *Public Interest* 91 (1988): 23–39.

72. Gary Kleck, "Guns and Violence: An Interpretive Review of the Field," *Social Pathology* 1 (1995): 12–45.

73. Anti-Drug Abuse Act of 1988.

74. Bob Cohn, "The Trials of Adam and Eve," *Newsweek,* 7 January 1991, p. 48.

75. Richard Lacayo, "The Rap Against a Rap Group," *Time,* 25 June 1990, p. 18.

76. See Norval Morris and Gordon Hawkins, *The Honest Politician's Guide to Crime Control* (Chicago: University of Chicago Press, 1970).

77. *Driver v. Hinant,* 356 F.2d 761 (4th Cir. 1966); *Easter v. District of Columbia,* 361 F.2d 50 (D.C. Cir. 1966).

78. *Powell v. Texas,* 392 U.S. 514, 88 S.Ct. 2145, 20 L.Ed.2d 1254 (1968).

79. *Bowers v. Hardwick,* 478 U.S. 186, 106 S.Ct. 2841, 92 L.Ed.2d 140 (1986), *rehearing denied* 478 U.S. 1039, 107 S.Ct. 29, 92 L.Ed.2d 779 (1986).

80. *The Report of the Commission on Obscenity and Pornography* (Washington, D.C.: U.S. Government Printing Office, 1970); *Attorney General's Commission Report on Pornography, Final Report* (Washington, D.C.: U.S. Government Printing Office, 1986), pp. 837–902; Berl Kutchinsky, "The Effect of Easy Availability of Pornography on the Incidence of Sex Crimes," *Journal of Social Issues* 29 (1973): 95–112; Michael Goldstein, "Exposure to Erotic Stimuli and Sexual Deviance," *Journal of Social Issues* 29 (1973): 197–219; John Court, "Sex and Violence: A Ripple Effect," in *Pornography and Aggression,* ed. Neal Malamuth and Edward Donnerstein (Orlando, Fla.: Academic Press, 1984); see also Edward Donnerstein, Daniel Linz, and Steven Penrod, *The Question of Pornography* (New York: Free Press, 1987).

81. Gary Marx, *Undercover: Police Surveillance in America* (Berkeley: University of California Press, 1988).

82. Ibid., pp. 217–219.

83. Ibid., p. 219.

84. Ibid., p. 233.

CHAPTER 5

Police in Society: History and Organization

O n March 3, 1991 the nation was shaken by media coverage of a home video showing a large group of Los Angeles cops brutally beating, kicking, clubbing, and shocking a handcuffed African American, later identified as Rodney King. Stopped for a traffic violation, King suffered nine skull fractures and a shattered eye socket, among other injuries. The officers involved were charged with assault. When they were acquitted after their first trial, Los Angeles broke out in rioting in which more than 50 people died. Two of the officers were later convicted in federal court of violating King's civil rights and were sentenced to prison. On April 19 1994 a Los Angeles jury awarded King $3.8 million in damages stemming from his arrest and beating.[1] In 1995 when O. J. Simpson was found not guilty in the murder trial of his wife Nicole and her friend Ron Goldman, his lawyers based their defense in part on the public's suspicion of the Los Angeles police and the racist attitudes of some L.A. detectives (particularly Mark Fuhrman).

The King and Simpson cases are graphic reminders of the critical and controversial role that police play in the justice system and the need for developing a professional, competent police force. The police are the **gatekeepers** of the criminal justice process. They initiate contact with law violators and decide whether to formally arrest them and start their journey through the criminal justice system, to settle the issue in an informal way (such as by issuing a warning), or to simply take no action at all. The strategic position of law enforcement officers, their visibility and contact with the public, and their use of weapons and arrest power have kept them in the forefront of public thought for most of the 20th century.

Despite these concerns, the majority of citizens give their police force high marks. In fact, recent research by Liqun Cao and his colleagues found that there is actually little difference in the confidence levels African American and white citizens have in the police.[2] Interest in police work continues to expand. Metropolitan police departments are swamped with applications by job seekers who value an exciting, well-paid job that also holds the opportunity to provide valuable community service. So while police agencies are still trying to define their role and effectively marshal their resources, they continue to be held in high esteem by the public they serve.

In this and the following three chapters, we will evaluate the history, role, organizational issues, and procedures of police agents and agencies and discuss the legal rules that control police behavior.

The History of Police

The origin of U.S. police agencies, like that of the criminal law, can be traced to early English society.[3] Before the Norman Conquest, there was no regular English police force. Every person living in the villages scattered throughout the countryside was responsible for aiding neighbors and protecting the settlement from thieves and marauders. This was known as the pledge system. People were grouped in collectives of ten families, called **tithings,** and were entrusted with policing their own minor problems. When trouble occurred, the citizen was expected to make a **hue and cry.** Ten tithings were grouped into a **hundred,** whose affairs were supervised by a constable appointed by the local nobleman. The **constable,** who might be considered the first real police officer, dealt with more serious breaches of the law.[4]

Shires, which resembled the counties of today, were controlled by the **shire reeve** appointed by the Crown or local landowner to supervise the territory and ensure that order would be kept. The shire reeve, a forerunner of today's sheriff, soon began to pursue and apprehend law violators as part of his duties.

In the 13th century, the **watch system** was created to help protect property in England's larger cities and towns. Watchmen patrolled at night and helped protect against robberies, fires, and disturbances. They reported to the area constable, who became the primary metropolitan law enforcement agent. In larger cities, such as London, the watchmen were organized within church parishes and were usually members of the parish they protected.

In 1326 the office of **justice of the peace** was created to assist the shire reeve in controlling the county. Eventually, these justices took on judicial functions in addition to their primary role as peacekeeper. The local constable became the operational assistant to the justice of the peace, supervising the night watchmen, investigating offenses, serving summonses, executing warrants, and securing prisoners. This system helped delineate the relationship between police and the judiciary that has continued for 500 years.

Eighteenth-Century Developments

By the end of the 18th century, the Industrial Revolution had lured thousands from the English countryside to work in the factory towns. The swelling population of urban poor, whose minuscule wages could hardly sustain them, heightened the need for police protection. Henry Fielding, the famed author of *Tom Jones,* organized the Bow Street Runners of London, one of the first local police agencies, to investigate crimes and attempt to bring offenders to justice.

In 1829 Sir Robert Peel, England's home secretary, guided through Parliament an "Act for Improving the Police in and near the Metropolis." The Metropolitan Police Act established the first organized police force in London. Composed of over 1,000 men, the London police force was structured along military lines; its members would be known from then on as *bobbies,* after their creator. They wore a distinctive uniform and were led by two magistrates, who were later given the title of commissioner. However, the ultimate responsibility for the police fell to the home secretary and consequently the Parliament.

The early bobbies suffered many of the same problems that have befallen their heirs. Many were corrupt, they were unsuccessful at stopping crime, and they were influenced by the wealthy. Owners of houses of ill repute who in the past had guaranteed their undisturbed operations by bribing watchmen now turned their attention to the bobbies. Metropolitan police administrators fought constantly to terminate cowardly, corrupt, and alcoholic officers, dismissing in the beginning about one-third of the bobbies each year.

Despite its recognized shortcomings, the London experiment proved a vast improvement over what had come before. It was considered so successful that the metropolitan police soon began providing law enforcement assistance to outlying areas that requested it. Another act of Parliament allowed justices of the peace to establish local police forces, and by 1856 every borough and county in England was required to form its own police force.

Law enforcement in colonial America paralleled the British model. In the colonies, the county **sheriff** became the most important law enforcement agent. In addition to keeping the peace and fighting crime, sheriffs collected taxes, supervised elections, and handled a great deal of other legal business.

Law Enforcement in Colonial America

The colonial sheriff did not patrol or seek out crime. Instead, he reacted to citizens' complaints and investigated crimes that had occurred. His salary was related to his effectiveness and was paid on a fee system. Sheriffs received a fixed amount for every arrest made. Unfortunately, their tax-collecting chores were more lucrative than fighting crime, so law enforcement was not one of their primary concerns.

In the cities, law enforcement was the province of the town marshal, who was aided, often unwillingly, by a variety of constables, night watchmen, police justices, and city council members. However, local governments had little power of administration, and enforcement of the criminal law was largely an individual or community responsibility.

In rural areas in the South, "slave patrols" charged with recapturing escaped slaves were an early if loathsome form of law enforcement.[5] In the western territories, individual initiative was encouraged by the practice of offering rewards for the capture of felons. If trouble arose, the town "vigilance committee" might form a posse to chase offenders. These **vigilantes** were called on to eradicate social problems, such as theft of livestock, through force or intimidation; the San Francisco Vigilance Committee actively pursued criminals in the mid-19th century.

As cities grew, it became exceedingly difficult for local leaders to organize ad hoc citizen vigilante groups. Moreover, the early 19th century was an era of widespread urban unrest and mob violence. Local leaders began to realize that a more structured police function was needed to control demonstrators and keep the peace.

The modern police department was born out of urban mob violence that wracked the nation's cities in the 19th century. Boston created the first formal U.S. police department in 1838. New York formed its police department in 1844; Philadelphia, in 1854. The new police departments replaced the night-watch system and relegated constables and sheriffs to serving court orders and running jails.

Early Police Agencies

At first, the urban police departments inherited the functions of the institutions they replaced. For example, Boston police were charged with maintaining public health until 1853, and in New York, the police were responsible for street sweeping until 1881. Politics dominated the departments and determined the recruitment of new officers and promotion of supervisors. An individual with the right connections could be hired despite a lack of qualifications. Early police agencies were corrupt, brutal, and inefficient.[6]

In the late 19th century, police work was highly desirable because it paid more than most other blue-collar jobs. By 1880 the average factory worker earned $450 a year, while police made $900 annually in large cities. For immigrant groups, having enough political clout to be appointed to the police department was an important step up the social ladder.[7] However, job security was uncertain, because it depended on the local political machine's staying in power.

Police work itself was primitive. There were few of even the simplest technological innovations common today, such as call boxes or centralized record keeping. Most officers patrolled on foot, without backup or the ability to call for help. Officers were commonly taunted by local toughs and responded with force and brutality. The longstanding conflict between police and the public was born in the difficulty that untrained, unprofessional officers had in patrolling the streets of 19th-century U.S. cities and in breaking up and controlling labor disputes. Police were not crime fighters as we know them today. Their major role was maintaining order, and their power was almost unchecked. The average officer had little training, no education in the law, and a minimum of supervision, yet the police became virtual judges of law and fact with the ability to exercise unlimited discretion.[8]

At mid-19th century, the detective bureau was set up as part of the Boston police. Until then, "thief-taking" had been the province of amateur bounty hunters, who hired themselves out to victims for a price. When professional police departments replaced bounty hunters, the close working relationships that developed between police detectives and their underworld informants produced many scandals and, consequently, high personnel turnover.

Police during the 19th century were regarded as incompetent and corrupt and were disliked by the people they served. The police role was only minimally directed at law enforcement. Its primary function was serving as the enforcement arm of the reigning political power, protecting private property, and keeping control of the ever-rising numbers of foreign immigrants.

Twentieth-Century Reform

Police agencies evolved slowly through the second half of the 19th century. Uniforms were introduced in 1853 in New York. The first technological breakthroughs in police operations came in the area of communications. The linking of precincts to central headquarters by telegraph began in the 1850s. In 1867 the first telegraph police boxes were installed; an officer could turn a key in a box, and his location and number would automatically register at headquarters. Additional technological advances were made in transportation. The Detroit police department outfitted some of its patrol officers with bicycles in 1897. By 1913 the motorcycle was being used by departments in the eastern part of the nation. The first police car was used in Akron, Ohio, in 1910, and the police wagon became popular in Cincinnati in 1912.[9] Nonpolice functions, such as care of the streets, began to be abandoned after the Civil War.

Big-city police were still unrespected by the public, unsuccessful in their role as crime stoppers, and uninvolved in progressive activities. The control of police departments by local politicians impeded effective law enforcement and fostered an atmosphere of graft and corruption.

In an effort to reduce police corruption, civic leaders in a number of jurisdictions created police administrative boards to reduce local officials' control over the police. These tribunals were responsible for appointing police administrators and controlling police affairs. In many instances, these measures failed because the private citizens appointed to the review boards lacked expertise in the intricacies of police work.

Another reform movement was the takeover of some big-city police agencies by state legislators. Although police budgets were financed through local taxes, control of police was usurped by rural politicians in the state capitals. New York City temporarily lost authority over its police force in 1857. It was not until the first decades of the 20th century that cities regained control of their police forces.

The Boston police strike of 1919 heightened interest in police reform. The strike came about basically because police officers were dissatisfied with their status in society. Other professions were unionizing and increasing their standards of living, but police salaries lagged behind. The Boston police officers' organization, the Boston Social Club, voted to become a union affiliated with the

American Federation of Labor. The officers struck on September 9, 1919. Rioting and looting broke out, resulting in Governor Calvin Coolidge's mobilization of the state militia to take over the city. Public support turned against the police, and the strike was broken. Eventually, all the striking officers were fired and replaced by new recruits. The Boston police strike ended police unionism for decades and solidified power in the hands of reactionary, autocratic police administrators. In the aftermath of the strike, various local, state, and federal crime commissions began to investigate the extent of crime and the ability of the justice system to deal with it effectively and made recommendations to improve police effectiveness.[10] However, with the onset of the Depression, justice reform became a less important issue than economic revival, and for many years, little changed in the nature of policing.

Around the turn of the century, a number of nationally recognized leaders called for measures to help improve and professionalize the police. In 1893 a professional society, the **International Association of Chiefs of Police (IACP),** was formed. Under the direction of its first president (District of Columbia Chief of Police Richard Sylvester), the IACP became the leading voice for police reform during the first two decades of the twentieth century. The IACP called for creating a civil service police force and for removing political influence and control. It also advocated centralized organizational structure and record keeping to curb the power of politically aligned precinct captains. Still another professional reform the IACP fostered was the creation of specialized units, such as delinquency control squads.

The Emergence of Professionalism

The most famous police reformer of the time was August Vollmer. While serving as police chief of Berkeley, California, Vollmer instituted university training for young officers. He also helped develop the School of Criminology at the University of California at Berkeley, which became the model for justice-related programs around the United States. Vollmer's disciples included O. W. Wilson, who pioneered the use of advanced training for officers when he took over and reformed the Wichita, Kansas, police department in 1928. Wilson was also instrumental in applying modern management and administrative techniques to policing. His text, *Police Administration,* became the single most influential work on the subject.

During this period, police professionalism was equated with an incorruptible, tough, highly trained, rule-oriented department organized along militaristic lines. The most respected department was that in Los Angeles, which emphasized police as incorruptible crime fighters who would not question the authority of the central command.

The Modern Era of Policing: 1960 to 1990

Turmoil and crisis were the hallmarks of policing during the 1960s. Throughout the 1960s, the Supreme Court handed down a number of decisions designed to control police operations and procedures. Police officers were now required to obey strict legal guidelines when questioning suspects, conducting searches and wiretapping, and so on. As the civil rights of suspects were significantly expanded, police complained they were being "handcuffed by the courts."

Policing in the 1960s

Also during the 1960s, civil unrest produced a growing tension between police and the public. African Americans, who were battling for increased rights and freedoms in the civil rights movement, found themselves confronting police lines. When riots broke out in New York, Detroit, Los Angeles, and other cities between 1964 and 1968, the spark that ignited conflict often involved the police. The Criminal Justice and the Media box on *Lone Star* addresses the issue of police and racial conflict. And when students across the nation began marching in anti–Vietnam war demonstrations, local police departments were called on to keep order. Police forces were ill-equipped and poorly trained to deal with these social problems; it is not surprising that the 1960s were marked by a number of bloody confrontations between the police and the public.

Confounding these problems was a rapidly growing crime rate. The number of violent and property crimes increased dramatically during the 1960s. Drug addiction and abuse grew to be national concerns, common in all social classes. Urban police departments were unable to control the crime rate, and police officers resented the demands placed on them by dissatisfied citizens.

Policing in the 1970s

The 1970s witnessed many structural changes in police agencies themselves. The end of the war in Vietnam significantly reduced tensions between students and police. However, the relationship between police and minorities was still

When students across the nation began marching in anti–Vietnam war demonstrations, local police departments were called on to keep order. Police forces were ill-equipped and poorly trained to deal with these social problems. It took a decade for police to overcome their image of agents of repression. The police-student conflict prompted creation of criminal justice programs designed to both educate and "humanize" police officers.

Lone Star

Lone Star weaves an intricate tale about a small Texas town called Frontera. Sam Deeds (Chris Cooper) is a second-generation sheriff recently returned to town. Sam is the son of a legendary lawman named Buddy Deeds (Matthew McConaughey in flashback) who has recently passed on. "Sheriff Deeds is dead," a townsman informs him. "You just Sheriff Junior."

When bones are discovered in the desert at a nearby rifle range, Sheriff Deeds begins to investigate. When the site turns up a Masonic ring, a badge, and human skull, he quickly surmises that the body was that of long missing Sheriff Charley Wade. Buddy Deeds, then a deputy, had faced down his boss, Sheriff Wade (Kris Kristofferson), in a barroom altercation brought about by Wade's corruption and racism. Wade left town with a large sum of money after that confrontation with Buddy and was never heard from again. Buddy was soon elected sheriff with the support of the minority community.

Although Sam Deeds fears that the investigation will prove that his hero father was a killer, he plods on carefully, investigating every lead. Through this device, Lone Star's writer/director John Sayles explores the relationship between law enforcement and the minority community at mid-century. Sheriff Wade was a bully and a sadist who terrorized the Latino and African American communities. He resorted to violence when citizens refused to give in to his demands for graft and bribes. He murdered Mexicans bringing illegal immigrants over the border who did not cut him in on the deal. In contrast, Sheriff Deeds, while a power broker and a schemer, never resorted to the use of violence and was a hero in the minority community. His only blot was forcing his son, Sam, to break off his high school romance with a young Mexican American woman. Now divorced, Sam discovers that his old sweetheart, Pilar (Elizabeth Peña), is a widow and considers taking up with her again despite the strong resistance of her mother, Mercedes (Miriam Colon). As the film winds to a close, Sam finds out that Pilar is his half-sister, the illegitimate child of Buddy and Mercedes, which is why their parents could never let their relationship develop. Sam also finds that this father was not actually responsible for Charley Wade's death.

Lone Star is a wonderful film that captures the rich tapestry of multicultural life in a Texas border town. It depicts in Charley Wade the racism and graft that all too often infected local police agents at that time. However, in its main character, Sam Deeds, it also shows another side of law enforcement, one that emphasizes honesty, caring, and sensitivity to cultural differences. The obvious moral is that some people who are evil may wind up in positions of power, but in the end they get their just deserts.

rocky. Local fears and distrust, combined with conservative federal policies, encouraged police departments to control what was perceived as an emerging minority "threat."[11]

As the decade wore on, police departments began to reexamine their relations with the minority community. Public service officers, sensitivity training, and community advisory boards became standard features in most large police departments. Special police services for juveniles, rape victims, crime prevention, and community relations were created.

Chapter 5

Police in Society:
History and Organization

Increased federal government support for criminal justice greatly influenced police operations. During the 1970s, the Law Enforcement Assistance Administration devoted a significant portion of its funds to police agencies. Although a number of police departments used this money to purchase little-used hardware, such as antiriot gear, most of it went to supporting innovative research on police work and advanced training for police officers. Perhaps most significant, LEAA's Law Enforcement Education Program helped thousands of officers further their college education. Hundreds of criminal justice programs were developed on college campuses around the country, providing a pool of highly educated police recruits. LEAA funds were also used to import or transfer technology originally developed in other fields into law enforcement. Technological innovations involving computers transformed the way police kept records, investigated crimes, and communicated with one another. State training academies improved the way police learn to deal with such issues as job stress, community conflict, and interpersonal relations.

The 1970s also saw more women and minorities recruited to police work. Affirmative action programs helped, albeit slowly, alter the ethnic, racial, and gender composition of U.S. policing.

Policing in the 1980s

As the 1980s began, the police role seemed to be changing significantly. A number of experts acknowledged that the police were not simply crime fighters and called for police to develop a greater awareness of community issues, which resulted in the emergence of the community policing concept.[12]

Police unions, which began to grow in the late 1960s, continued to have a great impact on departmental administration in the 1980s. Unions fought for and won increased salaries and benefits for their members; starting salaries of more than $30,000 are not uncommon in metropolitan police agencies. In many instances, unions eroded the power of the police chief to make unquestioned policy and personnel decisions. During the 1980s, chiefs of police commonly consulted with union leaders before making major decisions concerning departmental operations.

While police operations improved markedly in the 1980s, police departments were also beset by problems that impeded their effectiveness. State and local budgets were cut back during the Reagan administration, while federal support for innovative police programs was severely curtailed with the demise of the LEAA.

In the 1980s, police-community relations continued to be a major problem. Riots and incidents of urban conflict occurred in some of the nation's largest cities.[13] They triggered continual concern about what the police role should be, especially in inner-city neighborhoods. Toward the end of the decade, several police experts decreed that the nation's police forces should be evaluated not on their crime-fighting ability, but on their courteousness, deportment, and helpfulness. Interest renewed in reviving an earlier style of police work featuring foot patrols and increased citizen contact.

Law Enforcement Today

There are approximately 17,000 law enforcement agencies in the United States today, including

- 3,084 sheriff's departments

- 12,361 municipal police agencies

- 1,626 special police forces (those with limited jurisdictions, such as parks, transit systems, airports, colleges, and schools)

- 49 state police (all states except Hawaii)

- 50 federal law enforcement agencies[14]

In total, these agencies employ about 830,000 people, including more than 620,000 sworn officers and about 250,000 civilians. The following sections review the operations and functions of these agencies in greater detail.

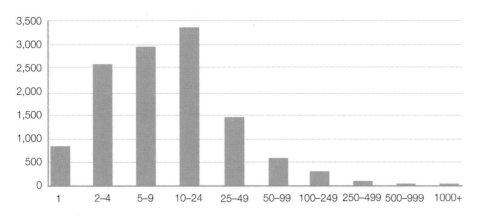

Figure 5.1
Number and size of police departments. Most police departments have fewer than 100 officers; more than 900 have no full-time police officers. In contrast, only 38 have more than 1,000 officers.
SOURCE: Brian Reaves, *Local Police Departments, 1993* (Washington, D.C.: Bureau of Justice Statistics, 1996), pp. 3–4.

Metropolitan Police

City police comprise the majority of the nation's authorized law enforcement personnel.[15] Metropolitan police departments range in size from the New York City Police Department, with its approximately 28,000 sworn officers and 7,000 civilian employees, to police departments in Murdo, South Dakota, and Schoharie, New York, which have a single officer. While most TV police shows feature the activities of big-city police officers, the overwhelming number of departments actually have fewer than 50 officers and serve a population of under 25,000. As Figure 5.1 shows, 38 departments have 1,000 or more officers, while about 850 have a single employee; the modal department has between ten and twenty-four officers. The differences between large metropolitan police departments and smaller, rural departments is discussed in the accompanying Analyzing Criminal Justice Issues box.

The cost of maintaining these police forces is high. The average police officer costs taxpayers about $62,000 per year, including salary, benefits, and other costs; this amounts to an annual cost of over $130 for every resident in the jurisdiction. Residents in larger jurisdictions who want and receive greater police protection pay more than 40% more each year for police services than those living in small towns.

Regardless of their size, most individual metropolitan police departments perform a standard set of functions and tasks and provide similar services to the community. These include

traffic enforcement	emergency medical care
accident investigation	court security
patrol and peacekeeping	civil defense
property and violent crime investigation	civil process service
death investigation	fire services
narcotics and vice control	jail operation
radio communications	ballistics testing
crime prevention	providing tourist information
fingerprint processing	crowd control at public events
search and rescue	license and permit issuance

The police role is expanding, so procedures must be developed to aid special-needs populations, including AIDS-infected suspects, the homeless, and victims of domestic and child abuse.[16]

These are only a few examples of the multiplicity of roles and duties assumed today in some of the larger urban police agencies around the nation. Smaller

Analyzing Criminal Justice Issues

Rural Versus Metropolitan Police

At one time it was assumed that rural police agencies were naturally inefficient because hundreds of small departments in each state were forced to provide duplicate services. Whether unifying smaller police agencies into "superagencies" would improve services was a topic commonly debated among police experts. Although consolidation may provide greater efficiency in some areas, smaller departments can dispense important specialized services that might have to be relinquished if they were combined and incorporated into larger departments.

Recent studies of rural policing have confirmed that there are significant differences between police efforts in metropolitan and small town policing and that consolidation may not be the cure-all it was previously considered. Residents in rural areas hold police in higher esteem than those in urban areas and depend on them to perform a great variety of civic functions because other social service providers are either remote or unavailable.

The daily routine of rural officers is also distinct. Rules and procedures in rural departments are, not surprisingly, less formal than those used in large metropolitan police agencies. With fewer organizational opportunities for advancement, rural officers are more closely tied to the community they serve than the department in which they are employed.

Close community relationships can be a two-edged sword. Since rural areas tend to be close knit, police behavior becomes a topic of close scrutiny. Unlike urban officers who enjoy anonymity and "low visibility," the actions of the rural officer are well known to most of the population. Those who deviate from community and departmental norms are quickly identified. Rural officers may find it hard to separate their personal and professional life; they also have fewer colleagues with whom to socialize and to turn to for support.

So while smaller departments provide closer relationships with the community, consolidation can provide the greater structure and career opportunities, not to mention a sense of personal privacy, that so many officers crave.

Critical Thinking Questions

1. Suppose you were the chief of police in a small town. How could you convince competent officers to relocate to your town? What dangers would you face in keeping officers on the job, and what would you do to maximize long-term commitments?

2. It is often argued that the police role is highly stressful. What stressors exist in rural areas? How are these different from urban police problems? Should police training academies be geared toward the challenges of suburban-rural policing?

SOURCE: Ralph Weisheit, David Falcone, and L. Edward Wells, *Rural Crime and Rural Policing* (Washington, D.C.: National Institute of Justice, 1994).

agencies can have trouble effectively carrying out these tasks; the hundreds of small police agencies in each state often provide duplicative services. Whether unifying smaller police agencies into "superagencies" would improve services is often debated among police experts (see the accompanying box). Smaller municipal agencies can provide important specialized services that might have to be relinquished if they were combined and incorporated into larger departments. Another approach has been to maintain smaller departments but to link them via computerized information sharing and resource management networks.[17]

County Law Enforcement

Most of the nation's county police departments, with their 200,000 employees, are independent agencies whose senior officer, the sheriff, is usually an elected political official (in all states except Rhode Island and Hawaii). The county sheriff's role has evolved from that of the early English shire reeve, whose primary duty was to assist the royal judges in trying prisoners and enforcing sentences. From the time of the westward expansion in the United States until municipal departments were developed, the sheriff was often the sole legal authority over vast territories.

Chapter 5

—

Police in Society: History and Organization

150

The duties of a county sheriff's department vary according to the size and degree of development of the county. The standard tasks of a typical sheriff's department are serving civil process (summons and court orders), providing court security, operating the county jail, and investigating crimes. Less commonly, sheriff's departments may serve as coroners, tax collectors, overseers of highways and bridges, custodians of the county treasury, and providers of fire, animal control, and emergency medical services; in years past, sheriff's offices also conducted executions. Typically, a sheriff's department's law enforcement functions are restricted to unincorporated areas within a county, unless a city or town police department requests its help.

Some sheriff's departments are exclusively law enforcement–oriented; some carry out court-related duties only; some are involved solely in correctional and judicial matters and not in law enforcement. However, a majority are full-service programs that carry out judicial, correctional, and law enforcement activities. As a rule, agencies serving large population areas (over 1 million) are devoted to maintaining county correctional facilities, while those in smaller population areas are focused on law enforcement.

In the past, sheriffs' salaries were almost always based on the fees they received for the performance of official acts. They received fees for every summons, warrant, subpoena, writ, or other process they served; they were also compensated for summoning juries or locking prisoners in cells. Today, sheriffs are salaried to avoid conflict of interest.

Unlike municipal police departments, **state police** were legislatively created to deal with the growing incidence of crime in nonurban areas, a consequence of the increase in population mobility and the advent of personalized mass transportation in the form of the automobile. County sheriffs—elected officials with occasionally corrupt or questionable motives—had proven to be ineffective in dealing with the wide-ranging criminal activities that developed during the latter half of the 19th century. In addition, most local police agencies were unable to effectively protect against highly mobile lawbreakers who randomly struck at cities and towns throughout a state. In response to citizens' demands for effective and efficient law enforcement, state governors began to develop plans for police agencies that would be responsible to the state, instead of being tied to local politics and possible corruption.

State Police

The Texas Rangers, created in 1835, was one of the first state police agencies formed. Essentially a military outfit that patrolled the Mexican border, it was followed by the Massachusetts state constables in 1865 and the Arizona Rangers in 1901. Pennsylvania formed the first truly modern state police in 1905.[18]

Today, about 23 state police agencies have the same general police powers as municipal police and are territorially limited in their exercise of law enforcement regulations only by the state's boundaries. In some jurisdictions, state police are also given special police powers; for example, Maryland employs its state police to serve civil process, while Arizona's Department of Public Safety provides emergency medical services. The remaining state police agencies are primarily responsible for highway patrol and traffic law enforcement. Some state police, such as those in California, direct most of their attention to the enforcement of traffic laws, while those in Georgia, Arkansas, and South Dakota are not responsible for traffic control.

Most state police organizations are restricted by legislation from becoming involved in the enforcement of certain areas of the law. For example, in some jurisdictions, state police are prohibited from becoming involved in strikes or other labor disputes, unless violence erupts.

The nation's 77,000 state police employees (52,000 officers and 25,000 civilians) are not only involved in law enforcement and highway safety but also carry out a variety of functions, including maintaining a training academy and providing emergency medical services. State police crime laboratories aid local departments in investigating crime scenes and analyzing evidence. State police also provide special services and technical expertise in such areas as bomb-site analysis and homicide investigation. Other state police departments, such as California's, are involved in highly sophisticated traffic and highway safety programs, including the use of helicopters for patrol and rescue, the testing of safety devices for cars, and the conducting of postmortem examinations to determine the causes of fatal accidents.

Federal Law Enforcement Agencies

The federal government has a number of law enforcement agencies designed to protect the rights and privileges of U.S. citizens; no single agency has unlimited jurisdiction, and each has been created to enforce specific laws and cope with particular situations. Federal police agencies have no particular rank order or hierarchy of command or responsibility, and each reports to a specific department or bureau.

The Justice Department/Federal Bureau of Investigation (FBI). The **U.S. Department of Justice** is the legal arm of the U.S. government. Headed by the attorney general, it is empowered to (1) enforce all federal laws, (2) represent the United States when it is party to court action, and (3) conduct independent investigations through its law enforcement services.

The Department of Justice maintains several separate divisions that are responsible for enforcing federal laws and protecting U.S. citizens. The Civil Rights Division proceeds legally against violations of federal civil rights laws that protect citizens from discrimination on the basis of their race, creed, ethnic background, age, or sex. Areas of greatest concern include discrimination in education, housing, and employment, including affirmative action cases. The Tax Division brings legal actions against tax violators. The Criminal Division prosecutes violations of the Federal Criminal Code. Its responsibility includes enforcing statutes relating to bank robbery (since bank deposits are federally insured), kidnapping, mail fraud, interstate transportation of stolen vehicles, and narcotics and drug trafficking.

The Justice Department first became involved in law enforcement when the attorney general hired investigators to enforce the Mann Act (forbidding the transportation of women between states for immoral purposes). These investigators were formalized in 1908 into a distinct branch of the government, the Bureau of Investigation; the agency was later reorganized into the **Federal Bureau of Investigation,** under the direction of J. Edgar Hoover (1924–1972).

Today's FBI is not a police agency but an investigative agency with jurisdiction over all matters in which the United States is, or may be, an interested party. It limits its jurisdiction, however, to federal laws, including all federal statutes not specifically assigned to other agencies. Areas covered by these laws include espionage, sabotage, treason, civil rights violations, murder and assault of federal officers, mail fraud, robbery and burglary of federally insured banks, kidnapping, and interstate transportation of stolen vehicles and property.

The FBI has been the most glamorous and widely publicized law enforcement agency. In the 1920s and 1930s, its agents pursued such gangsters as John Dillinger, "Mad Dog" Coll, Bonnie and Clyde, "Machine Gun" Kelly, and "Pretty Boy" Floyd. During World War II, they hunted Nazi agents and prevented any major sabotage on U.S. military bases. After the war, they conducted a crusade against Soviet intelligence agents and investigated organized-crime figures. They have been instrumental in cracking tough criminal cases, which has brought the FBI enormous public respect.

Today, the FBI offers a number of important services to local law enforcement agencies. Its identification division, established in 1924, collects and maintains a vast fingerprint file that can be used by local police agencies. Its sophisticated crime laboratory, established in 1932, aids local police in testing and identifying evidence, such as hairs, fibers, blood, tire tracks, and drugs. The Uniform Crime Report (UCR) is another service of the FBI. The UCR is an annual compilation of crimes reported to local police agencies, arrests, police killed or wounded in action, and other information. Finally, the FBI's National Crime Information Center is a computerized network linked to local police departments that provides ready information on stolen vehicles, wanted persons, stolen guns, and so on.

The FBI mission has been evolving to keep pace with world events. With the end of the Cold War and the reduction of East-West tensions, the FBI's counterintelligence mission has diminished. In some offices, agents have been reassigned to antigang and drug control efforts.[19]

Drug Enforcement Administration. Government interest in drug trafficking can be traced back to 1914, when the Harrison Act established federal jurisdiction over the supply and use of narcotics. A number of drug enforcement units, including the Bureau of Narcotics and Dangerous Drugs, were charged with enforcing drug laws. In 1973, these agencies were combined to form the **Drug Enforcement Administration (DEA).**

Agents of the DEA assist local and state authorities in investigating illegal drug use and carrying out independent surveillance and enforcement activities to control the importation of narcotics. For example, DEA agents work with foreign governments in cooperative efforts aimed at destroying opium and marijuana crops at their source, hard-to-find fields tucked away in the interiors of Latin America, Asia, Europe, and Africa. Undercover DEA agents infiltrate drug rings and simulate buying narcotics to arrest drug dealers.

Other Justice Department Agencies. Other federal law enforcement agencies under the direction of the Justice Department include the U.S. Marshals, the Immigration and Naturalization Service, and the Organized Crime and Racketeering Unit. The U.S. Marshals are court officers who help implement federal court rulings, transport prisoners, and enforce court orders. The Immigration and Naturalization Service is responsible for the administration of immigration laws governing the exclusion and deportation of illegal aliens and the naturalization of aliens lawfully present in the United States. This service also maintains border patrols to prevent illegal aliens from entering the United States. The Organized Crime and Racketeering Unit, under the direction of the U.S. attorney general, coordinates federal efforts to curtail organized crime primarily through the use of federal racketeering laws.

Treasury Department. The U.S. Treasury Department maintains the following enforcement branches:

1. *Bureau of Alcohol, Tobacco, and Firearms.* The BATF helps control sales of untaxed liquor and cigarettes and, through the Gun Control Act of 1968 and the Organized Crime Control Act of 1970, has jurisdiction over the illegal sales, importation, and criminal misuse of firearms and explosives.

2. *Internal Revenue Service.* The IRS, established in 1862, enforces violations of income, excise, stamp, and other tax laws. Its Intelligence Division actively pursues gamblers, narcotics dealers, and other violators who do not report their illegal financial gains as taxable income. For example, the career of Al Capone, the famous 1920s gangster, was brought to an end by the efforts of IRS agents.

3. *Customs Service.* The Customs Service guards points of entry into the United States and prevents smuggling of contraband into (or out of) the country. It ensures that taxes and tariffs are paid on imported goods and helps control the flow of narcotics into the country.

The Bureau of Alcohol, Tobacco, and Firearms helps control sales of untaxed liquor and cigarettes, and, through the Gun Control Act of 1968 and the Organized Crime Control Act of 1970, it has jurisdiction over the illegal sales, importation, and criminal misuse of firearms and explosives. Here ATF officers undergo rigorous training as part of a special response team.

4. *Secret Service.* The Secret Service was originally charged with enforcing laws against counterfeiting. Today, it is also accountable for the protection of the president and the vice-president and their families, presidential candidates, and former presidents. The Secret Service maintains the White House Police Force, which is responsible for protecting the executive mansion, and the Treasury Guard, which protects the mint.

The Future of Law Enforcement

What changes can we expect in U.S. police agencies during the next decade? What are the trends in policing? Where is police work heading?

One view is that police departments will be reshaping their role, deemphasizing crime fighting and stressing community organization and revitalization.[20] Around the country, citizens are demanding that police departments reconsider their image as disinterested outsiders. Community leaders are asking that, instead of riding around anonymously in patrol cars, police officers become actively involved in neighborhood affairs. Programs that do this include neighborhood-based ministations and foot patrols. Departments are also increasing their use of civilian employees, thereby freeing sworn officers for law enforcement tasks.

Police departments are evolving because leaders recognize that traditional models have not been effective: The streets are still not safe; the fear of crime is not declining; respect for the justice system has not been increasing. In the future, the police role may shift farther away from a legalistic style that isolates officers from the public to a service orientation that holds officers accountable to the community and encourages them to learn from the people they serve. This means that the police must actively create a sense of community where none has existed and recruit neighborhood cooperation for crime control and prevention activities.

Decentralization

Another change that police agencies will continue to emphasize is the decentralization of command through the creation of specialized units, substations, and direct response teams. While decentralization does not automatically ensure greater citizen cooperation, it is believed to increase sensitivity to citizen needs, create special knowledge of and commitment to the area served, and foster heightened community trust in the police.

Another innovation that will probably mushroom in the future is the employment of civilians for tasks that are now carried out by sworn officers. As police salaries and benefits increase, civilian employees will become an economic necessity. In addition, employing citizens from the community can help police departments become sensitive to the cultural environment they serve.[21]

Civilian Employees

Police departments will become increasingly more proactive and focus their attention on solving particular community problems. These problems will include domestic abuse, drug dealing, and drunk driving, because police administrators believe that arrests for these crimes may help reduce recidivism and because vocal community groups demand action against violators. There will be new categories of "high-tech" crimes that police agencies will have to deal with, ranging from theft of information and data to electronic counterfeiting. Police officers now trained to prevent burglaries may someday have to learn to create high-tech forensic labs that can identify suspects who are involved in theft of genetically engineered cultures from biomedical labs.[22]

New Crime Categories

Criminal investigation will be enhanced by the application of sophisticated electronic gadgetry: computers, cellular phones, and digital communication devices.[23] It is now recognized that there are geographic "hot spots" where a majority of predatory crimes are concentrated. Computer mapping programs that can translate addresses into map coordinates can now allow departments to identify problem areas for particular crimes, such as drug dealing. Computer maps will allow police to identify the location, time of day, and linkage among criminal events and concentrate their forces accordingly.[24]

One of the biggest problems police will face is shrinking municipal budgets and taxpayer revolts. Being forced to do more with less, police may shift from being labor-intensive, with the stress on random patrols to deter crime, to a more focused approach. This change will be enabled, in part, through relying on technology to improve effectiveness, to shorten response time, and to allow fewer police officers to accomplish more tasks efficiently. Police administrators must also be aware of the potential hazards of placing too much emphasis on constantly increasing performance.

Efficiency

The demographic structure of policing will also evolve. The numbers of minority and female police officers should continue to grow. In the past, white males followed their fathers into a police career. A new generation of minorities and females will now be able to follow their parents into police work.

Diversity

Another trend in police work will be to rely more on technology to improve the effectiveness of police resources.[25] Budget realities demand that police leaders make the most effective use of their forces, and technology seems to be an important method of increasing productivity at a relative low cost. The introduction of technology has already been explosive. In 1964, for example, only one city, St. Louis, had a police computer system; by 1968, 10 states and 50 cities had state-level criminal justice information systems; today, almost every city of more than 50,000 has some sort of computer support services.[26] Table 5.1 lists some of the services that have been computerized in the nation's police departments.

An Era of Technological Change

One of the most important computer-aided tasks is the identification of criminal suspects. Computers now link neighboring agencies so that they can share information on cases, suspects, and warrants. One such system is the Police Information Network, which electronically links the 93 independent law

Table 5.1
Percent of Police Departments Using Computers
SOURCE: Brian Reaves, *Local Police Departments, 1993* (Washington, D.C.: Bureau of Justice Statistics, 1996).

Function	Percent That Use
Record keeping	53%
Criminal investigation	41
Budgeting	31
Crime analysis	29
Dispatch	29
Fleet management	17
Manpower allocation	16
Research/statistics	14
Jail management	4
Inventory	27
Evidence	26
Payroll	20
Drivers' licenses	19
Summonses	18
Vehicle registration	18
UCR incidents	18
Fingerprints	6
Criminal histories	34
Stolen vehicles	34
Calls for service	45
Traffic accidents	42
Stolen property	39
Warrants	36

enforcement agencies in the San Francisco area to allow them to share information. In addition, local departments now use computerized databases to record not only crime-related information but also motor vehicle and business data, workers' compensation files, and other public records that can be used to locate and track wanted felons.[27] On a broader jurisdictional level, the FBI implemented the National Crime Information Center in 1967. This system provides rapid collection and retrieval of data about persons wanted for crimes anywhere in the 50 states.

Identifying Suspects

Computers are also being used to expedite the analysis of evidence. Los Angeles police can instantly cross-reference computer databases (for example, compare files on suspects who own brown Chevrolets with those who have facial scars).[28]

Some police departments are using computerized imaging systems to replace mug books. Photos or sketches are stored in computer memory and easily retrieved for viewing. As Figure 5.2 illustrates, several software companies have developed identification programs that help witnesses create a composite picture of the perpetrator. A vast library of photographed or drawn facial features can be stored in computer files and accessed on a terminal screen. Witnesses can scan through thousands of noses, eyes, and lips until they find those that match the suspect's. Eyeglasses, mustaches, and beards can be added; skin tones can be altered. When the composite is created, an attached camera makes a hard copy for distribution.[29]

Computer systems now used in the booking process can also help in the suspect identification process. During booking, a visual image of the suspect is stored in a computer's memory along with other relevant information. Police can then easily create a "photo lineup" by calling up color photos on the computer monitor of all suspects having a particular characteristic described by a witness.

New techniques are constantly being developed. Soon, through the use of genetic algorithms (mathematical models), a computerized composite image of a

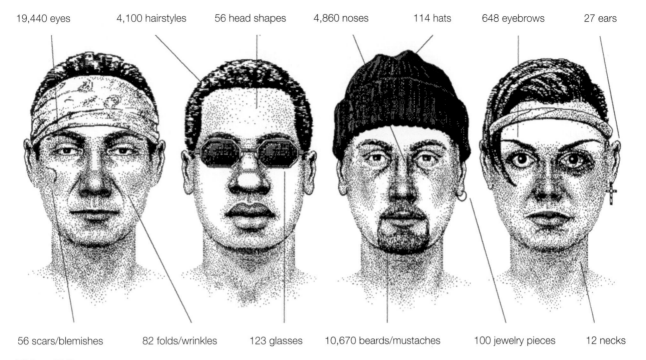

19,440 eyes   4,100 hairstyles   56 head shapes   4,860 noses   114 hats   648 eyebrows   27 ears

56 scars/blemishes   82 folds/wrinkles   123 glasses   10,670 beards/mustaches   100 jewelry pieces   12 necks

Figure 5.2
Computer-generated composites for identifying suspects.
Computer-generated composites can be used to help a witness create a precise sketch of
criminal suspects. The Compusketch© program developed by the Visatex Corporation of
Campbell, California, contains thousands of facial features and details.

suspect's face will be constructed from relatively little information.[30] Digitiza-
tion of photographs will enable the reconstruction of blurred images. Videotapes
of bank robbers or blurred photos of license plates, even bite marks, can be digi-
tized using highly advanced mathematical models.

The use of computerized fingerprint systems is growing around the United
States. Using mathematical models, automated fingerprint identification systems
(AFIS) can classify fingerprints and identify up to 250 characteristics (minutiae)
of the print.[31] These automated systems use high-speed silicon chips to plot each
point of minutiae and count the number of ridge lines between that point and its
four nearest neighbors, which substantially improves its speed and accuracy over
earlier systems. Some police departments, such as the District of Columbia's, report that computerized print systems are allowing them to make over 100 identifications a month from fingerprints taken at a crime scene. AFIS files have been
regionalized. For example, the Western Identification Network serves Alaska,
California, Idaho, Nevada, Oregon, Utah, Washington, and Wyoming.[32]

Fingerprint Analysis

If these computerized fingerprint files become standardized and a national
database is formed, it will be possible to check records in all 50 states to determine whether the suspect's fingerprints match those taken at the crime scene
of previously unsolved cases. A national fingerprint identification system should
become an even more effective tool by the year 2000, because laser technology
should vastly improve fingerprint analysis. Investigators will soon be able to recover prints that in the past were too damaged to be used as evidence. New
breeds of fingerprint analysis will soon be available. The FBI plans to create an
Integrated Automated Fingerprint Identification System that will allow local departments to scan fingerprints, send them electronically to a national depository,
and receive back identification and criminal history of suspects.[33]

DNA profiling allows suspects to be identified on the basis of the genetic material found in hair, blood, and other bodily tissues and fluids. Here a witness holding DNA evidence testifies in a murder case. Most courts now allow DNA evidence to be admitted during trial proceedings.

DNA Profiling

Advanced technology is also spurring new forensic methods of identification and analysis. The most prominent technique is **DNA profiling,** a procedure that has gained national attention because of the O. J. Simpson case. This technique allows suspects to be identified on the basis of the genetic material found in hair, blood, and other bodily tissues and fluids. When DNA is used as evidence in a rape trial, DNA segments are taken from the victim, the suspect, and blood and semen found on the victim. A DNA match indicates a 4 billion-to-one chance that the suspect is the offender.

Two methods of DNA matching are used. The most popular technique, known as RFLP (restriction fragment length polymorphism), uses radioactive material to produce a DNA image on an X-ray film. The second method, PCR (polymerase chain reaction), amplifies DNA samples through molecular photocopying.[34]

In the future, genetic samples may be taken from every infant at birth and each child's unique patterns kept on computer files for instant identification.[35] DNA fingerprinting is now used as evidence in criminal trials in more than 20 states.[36] The use of DNA evidence to gain convictions has also been upheld on appeal.[37] Although some scientists have questioned the accuracy of DNA testing and dispute the infallibility of a DNA match, the use of genetic evidence in criminal trials is likely to continue. One recent national evaluation of the technique by Noreen Purcell and her associates found that prosecutors use DNA when the offender seems "trustworthy"— for example an older, employed person—and this type of physical evidence is believed necessary to undercut the defendant's testimony; conviction rates are increased if prosecutors are able to back up physical evidence with having DNA experts testify at the trial.[38]

Leading the way in the development of the most advanced forensic techniques is the Forensic Science Research and Training Center operated by the FBI in Washington, D.C., and Quantico, Virginia. The lab provides information and services to over 300 crime labs throughout the United States.[39] The National Institute of Justice is also sponsoring research to identify a wider variety of DNA segments for testing and is involved in developing a PCR-based DNA profiling examination, using fluorescent detection, that will reduce the time required for DNA profiling. The FBI is also planning a Combined DNA Index System

(CODIS), a computerized database that will allow DNA taken at a crime scene to be searched electronically to find matches against (a) samples taken from convicted offenders and (b) samples taken from other crime scenes. The first database will allow suspects to be identified, while the second will allow investigators to establish links between crimes, such as those involving serial killers or rapists. A missing persons database is also being planned.[40]

Could a person be arrested, tried, convicted, and put to death based on the fact that his or her DNA matched evidence taken at the scene of a crime? When Timothy Spencer, known as the "South Side Strangler," was executed in Virginia on April 27, 1994, he was the first person convicted and executed almost entirely on the basis of DNA evidence.[41]

Computers will certainly be used in training officers, in the areas of learning, performance evaluation, and field testing.[42] Departments are already using computer simulations to train officers in the use of deadly force.[43]

Administration and Communication

Some programs appear to be highly successful. For example, the St. Petersburg, Florida, police department has equipped all its officers with portable computers, which has significantly cut down on the time needed to write and duplicate reports.[44] Police can now use terminals to draw accident diagrams, communicate with city traffic engineers, and merge their incident reports into other databases. Pen computing, in which officers write directly on a computer screen, eliminates paperwork and increases the accuracy of reports.[45] And, to make this material more accessible to the officer on patrol, head-up display (HUD) units now project information onto screens located on patrol car windshields; police officers can now access computer readouts without taking their eyes off the road![46]

Future police technology will involve more efficient communications systems. Some departments are using cellular phones in their cars to facilitate communications with victims and witnesses.[47] Departments that cover wide geographical areas and maintain independent precincts and substations are experimenting with **teleconferencing** systems that provide both audio and video linkages. Police agencies may use advanced communications gear to track stolen vehicles. Car owners will be able to buy transmitters that give off a signal to a satellite or other listening device that can then be monitored and tracked by the specially equipped patrol cars; this system is being tested.[48] Finally, some departments are linking advanced communications systems with computers, making use of electronic bulletin boards that link officers in an active on-line system, enabling them to communicate faster and more easily.[49]

Because police forces alone can have only a limited influence on controlling crime and protecting victims, alternative methods of policing have been developed. In the next decade, private security forces should significantly affect law enforcement.

Private Policing and Security

The emergence of the private security industry has been dramatic, increasing at a much greater pace than public policing.[50] In fact, as Figure 5.3 shows, it is estimated that more money is spent on private protection than on state-sponsored law enforcement agencies; by the year 2000, over $100 billion will be spent on private security.[51] Today, more than 1.5 million people work in private security—far more than the total number of sworn police officers.

Much of what is known about the national trends in private policing comes from the **Hallcrest Report,** a government-financed survey of the industry that found that the use of private security falls into two major areas.[52] **Proprietary security** is undertaken by an organization's own employees and includes both plainclothes and uniformed agents directed by the organization's head of security. The second type of private security is **contractual services,** such as guards, investigators, and armored cars, provided by private companies, such as Wackenhut and

Figure 5.3

Figure 5.3
Private security versus law enforcement and spending.

SOURCE: William Cunningham, John Strauchs, and Clifford Van Meter, *Private Security: Patterns and Trends* (Washington, D.C.: National Institute of Justice, 1991), p. 3.

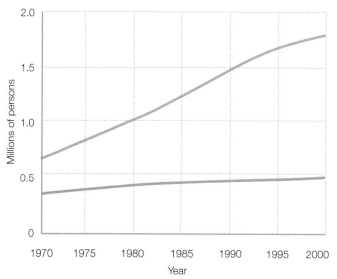

Private security and law enforcement employment

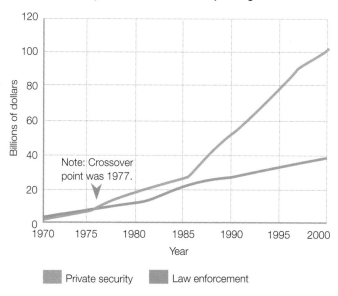

Private security and law enforcement spending

Note: Crossover point was 1977.

Private security   Law enforcement

Pinkerton's. Also included within the category of contractual security is the wide variety of security products, such as safes, electronic access-control devices, and closed-circuit television.

Public-Private Cooperation

Private security forces take on responsibilities that are also within the domain of local police agencies. These include responding to burglar alarms, investigating misdemeanors, enforcing parking restrictions, and providing court security. Despite this overlap, little contact or cooperation used to occur between private and public policing agents. In the 1980s, the International Association of Chiefs of Police, the National Sheriffs' Association, and the American Society for Industrial Security began joint meetings to improve relations between the public and private sectors. In 1986 the Joint Council on Law Enforcement and Private Security Associations was formed.

One reason public-private cooperation is essential is the rise of a movement to privatize services that have been within the jurisdiction of public police agencies. Candidates for privatization include public building security, parking enforcement, park patrol, animal control, special event security (such as rock concerts), funeral escorts, prisoner escorts, and public housing security. About 18 states have already privatized some police functions. In some small towns, private police may even replace the town police force. Reminderville, Ohio experimented with an all-private police force and found that it produced great savings without any drop in service.

One area that may be ideal for privatization is responding to private security systems. The number of private security systems has grown rapidly, along with a corresponding increase in the number of false alarms. In some jurisdictions, 30% of all calls for police service are false alarms. This problem will intensify, because the number of residences with alarm systems should double by the year 2000 (to about 20% of all homes). One approach has been to fine or charge homeowners for repeat false alarm calls. Private firms may be contracted to handle alarm calls and screen out false alarms before notifying police.

The Future of Private Security

The Hallcrest Report estimates that by the year 2000 there will be 750,000 contract guards and 410,000 proprietary security forces. The technology that supports the field will grow rapidly, with more sophisticated alarm systems, access control, and closed-circuit television.

The expanded role of private security is not without its perils. Many law enforcement executives are critical of the quality of private security and believe it has little value as a crime control mechanism. One complaint heard by the Hallcrest researchers was the lack of training and standards in the profession. Still another source of contention between private security and local police agencies is the increasing number of police calls that are a function of private security measures.

The Hallcrest Report recommends a number of strategies to improve the quality of private security: upgrade employee quality; create statewide regulatory bodies and statutes for controlling security firms; require mandatory training; increase police knowledge of private security; expand the interaction between police and private security providers, such as the sharing of information; and transfer some police functions, such as burglar alarm checking, to the private sector. The report recommends that the industry create its own standards similar to those adopted by the British Security Industry Association to professionalize the trade.

National and local police agencies maintain web sites so that you can learn more about what they are doing and access important information. For example, the FBI's Office of Public and Congressional Affairs has assembled a broad selection of information regarding the Bureau's investigations, programs, law enforcement services, accomplishments, and history. All information in this homepage is unclassified and is provided for educational purposes; you can use it as you wish, such as quoting from it in articles and reports. Included in the information provided are recent press releases, FBI history, data on major investigations, the FBI's "Most Wanted List," and information on the FBI Academy and FBI programs and services.

http://www.fbi.gov

If you want to learn more about sheriffs' departments around the United States, the National Sheriffs' Association has its own homepage with links to on-line sheriffs across the United States, training schedules, and information on missing children efforts.

http://www.sheriffs.org

Summary

Present-day police departments have evolved out of early European and colonial American crime control forces.

Many types of organizations are involved in law enforcement activities on the local, state, and federal levels of government. The most visible law enforcement agencies are local police departments, which carry out patrol, investigative, and traffic functions, as well as many support activities.

By the year 2000, police departments will begin to rely on advanced computer-based technology to identify suspects and collate evidence. Automated fingerprint systems and computerized identification systems will become widespread. There is danger that technology may make police overly intrusive and interfere with civil liberties.

In addition to public law enforcement agencies, a large variety of private policing enterprises have developed. These include a multibillion-dollar private security industry and the private employment of public police.

Key Terms

gatekeepers
tithings
hue and cry
hundred
constable
shires
shire reeve
watch system
justice of the peace
sheriff

vigilantes
International Association of Chiefs of Police (IACP)
state police
U.S. Department of Justice
Federal Bureau of Investigation (FBI)
Drug Enforcement Administration (DEA)
DNA profiling

teleconferencing
Hallcrest Report
proprietary security
contractual services

Questions

1. List the problems faced by police departments today that were also present during the early days of policing.

2. Distinguish between the duties of the state police, sheriffs' departments, and local police departments.

3. Why has the private security industry blossomed? What factors will influence the role of private policing during the coming decade?

4. What are some of the technological advances that should help the police solve more crimes? What are the dangers of these advances?

5. Discuss the trends that will influence policing during the coming decade. What other social factors may affect police?

Notes

1. Associated Press, "Jury Awards Rodney King $3.8 Million in Damages," *Boston Globe,* 20 April 1994, p. 1.

2. Liqun Cao, James Frank, and Francis Cullen, "Race, Community Context and Confidence in the Police," *American Journal of Police* 15 (1996): 3–15.

3. This section relies heavily on such sources as Malcolm Sparrow, Mark Moore, and David Kennedy, *Beyond 911, A New Era for Policing* (New York: Basic Books, 1990); Daniel Devlin,

Police Procedure, Administration, and Organization (London: Butterworth, 1966); Robert Fogelson, *Big City Police* (Cambridge: Harvard University Press, 1977); Roger Lane, *Policing the City, Boston 1822–1885* (Cambridge: Harvard University Press, 1967); Roger Lane, "Urban Police and Crime in Nineteenth-Century America," in *Crime and Justice*, vol. 2, ed. Norval Morris and Michael Tonry (Chicago: University of Chicago Press, 1980), pp. 1–45; J. J. Tobias, *Crime and Industrial Society in the Nineteenth Century* (New York: Schocken Books, 1967); Samuel Walker, *A Critical History of Police Reform: The Emergence of Professionalism* (Lexington, Mass.: Lexington Books, 1977); Samuel Walker, *Popular Justice* (New York: Oxford University Press, 1980); President's Commission on Law Enforcement and the Administration of Justice, *Task Force Report: The Police* (Washington, D.C.: U.S. Government Printing Office, 1967), pp. 1–9.

4. Devlin, *Police Procedure, Administration, and Organization*, p. 3.

5. Phillip Reichel, "Southern Slave Patrols as a Transitional Type," *American Journal of Police* 7 (1988): 51–78.

6. Walker, *Popular Justice*, p. 61.

7. Ibid., p. 8.

8. Dennis Rousey, "Cops and Guns: Police Use of Deadly Force in Nineteenth-Century New Orleans," *American Journal of Legal History* 28 (1984): 41–66.

9. Law Enforcement Assistance Administration, *Two Hundred Years of American Criminal Justice* (Washington, D.C.: U.S. Government Printing Office, 1976).

10. National Commission on Law Observance and Enforcement, *Report on the Police* (Washington, D.C.: U.S. Government Printing Office, 1931), pp. 5–7.

11. Pamela Irving Jackson, *Minority Group Threat, Crime, and Policing* (New York: Praeger, 1989).

12. James Q. Wilson and George Kelling, "Broken Windows," *Atlantic Monthly* 249 (March 1982): 29–38.

13. Frank Tippett, "It Looks Just Like a War Zone," *Time,* 27 May 1985, pp. 16–22; "San Francisco, New York Police Troubled by Series of Scandals," *Criminal Justice Newsletter* 16 (1985): 2–4; Karen Polk, "New York Police: Caught in the Middle and Losing Faith," *Boston Globe,* 28 December 1988, p. 3.

14. Data in these sections are from Brian Reaves, *Local Police Departments, 1993* (Washington, D.C.: Bureau of Justice Statistics, 1996).

15. This section relies heavily on data from Reaves, *Local Police Departments, 1993;* see also Federal Bureau of Investigation, *Crime in the United States, 1995* (Washington, D.C.: U.S. Government Printing Office, 1996).

16. See, for example, Susan Martin and Edwin Hamilton, "Police Handling of Child Abuse Cases: Policies, Procedures and Issues," *American Journal of Police* 9 (1990): 1–16.

17. See, for example, Robert Keppel and Joseph Weis, *Improving the Investigation of Violent Crime: The Homicide Investigation and Tracking System* (Washington, D.C.: National Institute of Justice, 1993).

18. Bruce Smith, *Police Systems in the United States* (New York: Harper & Row, 1960), p. 72.

19. Kathleen Grubb, "Cold War to Gang War," *Boston Globe,* 22 January 1992, p. 1.

20. This section leans heavily on Jerome Skolnick and David Bayley, *The New Blue Line* (New York: Free Press, 1986), pp. 210–230.

21. See Stephen Matrofski, "The Prospects of Change in Police Patrol: A Decade in Review," *American Journal of Police* 9 (1990): 1–69.

22. Larry Coutorie, "The Future of High-Technology Crime: A Parallel Delphi Study," *Journal of Criminal Justice* 23 (1995): 13–27.

23. Bill Clede, "Cellular Digital Packet Data: CDPD," *Law and Order* 43 (1995): 36–37.

24. J. Thomas McEwen and Faye Taxman, *Applications of Computerized Mapping to Police Operations* (Alexandria, Va.: Institute for Law and Justice, 1994).

25. Lois Pliant, "Information Management," *Police Chief* 61 (1994): 31–35.

26. Mark Birchler, "Computers in a Small Police Agency," *FBI Law Enforcement Bulletin,* January 1989, pp. 7–9.

27. John Schmitz, "Criminals Versus Computers," *Law and Order* 42 (1994): 80–84.

28. Kristen Olson, "LAPD's Newest Investigative Tool," *Police Chief* 55 (1988): 30.

29. See Judith Blair Schmitt, "Computerized ID Systems," *Police Chief* 59 (1992): 33–45.

30. Richard Rau, "Forensic Science and Criminal Justice Technology: High-Tech Tools for the 90s," *NIJ Reports* 224 (June 1991): 6–10.

31. William Stover, "Automated Fingerprint Identification—Regional Application of Technology," *FBI Law Enforcement Bulletin* 53 (1984): 1–4.

32. Schmitt, "Computerized ID Systems," p. 35.

33. Lois Pliant, "Exploiting Fingerprint Technology," *Police Chief* 61 (1994): 29–34.

34. Rau, "Forensic Science and Criminal Justice Technology."

35. Matt Rodriguez, "The Acquisition of High Technology Systems by Law Enforcement," *FBI Law Enforcement Bulletin* 57 (1988): 10–15.

36. "California Attorney General Endorses DNA Fingerprinting," *Criminal Justice Newsletter,* 1 March 1989, p. 1.

37. *State v. Ford,* 301 S.C. 485, 392 S.E.2d 781 (1990).

38. Noreen Purcell, L. Thomas Winfree, and G. Larry Mays, "DNA (Deoxyribonucleic Acid) Evidence and Criminal Trials: An Exploratory Survey of Factors Associated with the Use of 'Genetic Fingerprinting' in Felony Prosecutions," *Journal of Criminal Justice* 22 (1994): 145–173.

39. Colleen Wade, "Forensic Science Information Resource System," *FBI Law Enforcement Bulletin* 57 (1988): 14–15.

40. John Brown, "DNA Analysis: A Significant Tool for Law Enforcement," *Police Chief* 62 (1994): 51–52.

41. " 'South Side Strangler' Execution Cited as DNA Evidence Landmark," *Criminal Justice Newsletter,* 2 May 1994, p. 3.

42. Paul Smith, "In-Service Training for Law Enforcement Personnel," *FBI Law Enforcement Bulletin* 57 (1988): 20–21.

43. John LeDoux and Henry McCaslin, "Computer-Based Training for the Law Enforcement Community," *FBI Law Enforcement Bulletin* 57 (1988): 8–10.

44. Brewer Stone, "The High-Tech Beat in St. Pete," *Police Chief* 55 (1988): 23–28.

45. "Pen Computing: The Natural 'Next Step' for Field Personnel," *Law and Order* 43 (1995): 37.

46. Miller McMillan, "High Tech Enters the Field of View," *Police Chief* 62 (1994): 29.

47. Ibid., p. 24.

48. Mark Thompson, "Police Seeking Radio Channel for Stolen Auto Tracking System," *Criminal Justice Newsletter,* 15 March 1989, p. 1.

49. John Davis, "Information at Your Fingertips," *Law and Order* 43 (1995): 54–56.

50. Material in this section leans heavily on two sources: William Cunningham, John Strauchs, and Clifford Van Meter, *The Hallcrest Report I: Private Security and Police in America* (Stoneham, Mass.: Butterworth-Heineman, 1985); idem, *The Hallcrest Report II: Private Security Trends, 1970–2000* (Stoneham, Mass.: Butterworth-Heineman, 1990). Both reports are summarized in William Cunningham and Todd Taylor, *The Growing Role of Private Security* (Washington, D.C.: National Institute of Justice, 1984) and William Cunningham, John Strauchs, and Clifford Van Meter, *Private Security: Patterns and Trends* (Washington, D.C.: National Institute of Justice, 1991).

51. National Institute of Justice, *Research Program Plan, Fiscal Year 1989* (Washington, D.C.: National Institute of Justice, 1990), p. 3.

52. Cunningham and Taylor, *The Growing Role of Private Security.*

The Police: Role and Function

This chapter describes the organization of police departments and their various operating branches: patrol, investigation, service, and administration. It discusses the realities and ambiguities of the police role and how the concept of the police mission has been changing radically. The chapter concludes with a brief overview of some of the most important administrative issues confronting U.S. law enforcement agencies.

Police Organization

Most municipal police departments in the United States are independent agencies within the executive branch of government and operating without specific administrative control from any higher governmental authority. On occasion, police agencies will cooperate and participate in mutually beneficial enterprises, such as sharing information on known criminals, or they may help federal agencies investigate interstate criminal cases. Aside from such cooperative efforts, police departments tend to be functionally independent organizations with unique

sets of rules, policies, procedures, norms, budgets, and so on. The unique structure of police agencies greatly influences their function and effectiveness.

Although many police agenices are in the process of rethinking their organization and goals, the majority are still organized in a militaristic, hierarchical manner, as illustrated in Figure 6.1. Within this organizational model, each element of the department normally has its own chain of command. For example, in a large municipal department, the **detective bureau** might have a captain as the director of a particular division (such as homicide), while a lieutenant oversees individual cases and acts as liaison with other police agencies, and sergeants and inspectors carry out the actual field work. Smaller departments may have a captain as head of all detectives, while lieutenants supervise individual subsystems (such as robbery or homicide). At the head of the organization is the **police chief,** who sets policy and has general administrative control over all of the department's various operating branches.

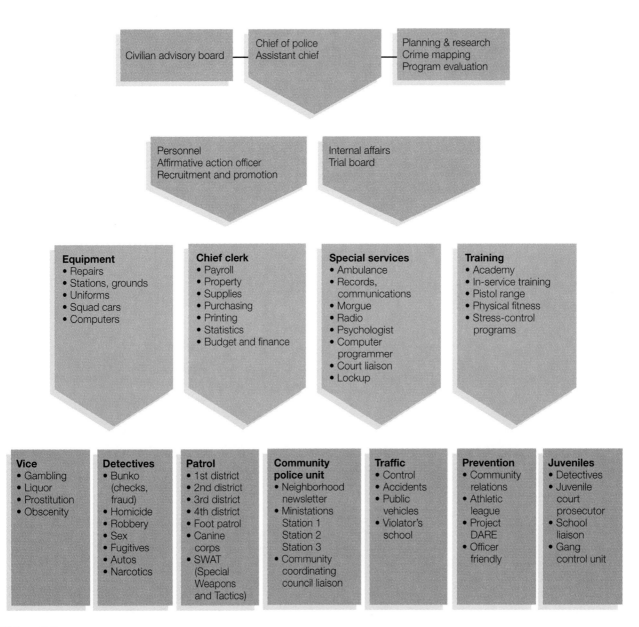

Figure 6.1
Organization of a metropolitan police department.

The typical police department's organizational structure has several problems. It is often difficult for citizens to determine who is actually responsible for the department's policies and operations. Second, the large number of operating divisions and the lack of any clear relationship among them almost guarantee that the decision-making practices of one branch will be unknown to another; two divisions may unknowingly compete with each other over jurisdiction on a particular case.[1]

Most departments also follow a militarylike system in promoting personnel within the ranks; at an appropriate time, a promotion test may be given and, based on his or her scores and recommendations, an officer may be advanced in rank. This organizational style frustrates some police officers from furthering their education, since a college or advanced degree may have little direct impact on their promotion potential or responsibilities. Furthermore, some otherwise competent police officers are unable to increase their rank because of their inability to take tests well.

Most police departments employ a **time-in-rank system** for determining promotion eligibility. This means that before moving up the administrative ladder, an officer must spend a certain amount of time in the next lowest rank; a sergeant cannot become a captain without serving an appropriate amount of time as a lieutenant. While this system is designed to promote fairness and limit favoritism, it also restricts administrative flexibility. Unlike the private sector, where talented people can be pushed ahead in the best interests of the company, the time-in-rank system prohibits rapid advancement. A police agency would probably not be able to hire a computer systems expert with a Ph.D. and give her a command position in charge of its data analysis section. The department would be forced to hire the expert as a civilian employee under the command of a ranking senior officer who may not be as technically proficient.

Under this rank system, a title can rarely be taken away or changed once it is earned. Police administrators become frustrated when qualified junior officers cannot be promoted or reassigned to appropriate positions because they lack time in rank or because less qualified officers have more seniority. Inability to advance through the ranks convinces numerous educated and ambitious officers to seek private employment. The rank system also means that talented police officers cannot transfer to other departments or sell their services to the highest bidder. Time in rank ensures the stability—for better or worse—of police agencies.

In countless books, movies, and TV shows, the public has been presented with a view of policing that romanticizes police officers as fearless crime fighters who think little of their own safety as they engage in daily shoot-outs with Uzi-toting drug runners, psychopathic serial killers, and organized-crime hit men. Occasionally, but not often, fictional patrol officers and detectives seem aware of departmental rules, legal decisions, citizen groups, civil suits, or physical danger. They are rarely faced with the economic necessity of moonlighting as security guards, caring about an annual pay raise, or griping when someone less deserving gets promoted ahead of them for political reasons (see the media box on the *Die Hard* series).

How close is this portrayal of a selfless crime fighter to "real life"? Not very, according to most research efforts. Police officers are asked to deal with hundreds of incidents each year. For example, the Los Angeles Police Department's force of more than 8,000 officers receives about 5 million calls for assistance each year; Houston's 4,000 police officers respond to 2.4 million service calls annually. This translates into 14,000 calls each day in Los Angeles and almost 7,000 in Houston.[2]

Most research efforts show that a police officer's crime-fighting efforts are only a small part of his or her overall activities. Studies of police work indicate that a significant portion of an officer's time is spent handling minor disturbances, service calls, and administrative duties. Studies conducted over the past two decades have found that social-service and administrative tasks consume more than half a police officer's time and account for more than half of his or her calls. Police work, then, involves much more than "catching criminals."[3]

These results are not surprising when UCR arrest data are considered. Each year, about 600,000 local, county, and state police officers make about 14 million arrests, or about 23 each.[4] Of these, about 3 million are for serious index crimes (Part I), or about 5 yearly per officer. Given an even distribution of arrests, it is evident that the average police officer makes 2 arrests per month, and less than 1 felony arrest every two months (Figure 6.2).

The Police Role

Figure 6.2
Annual violent crime and property crime arrests per sworn officer in the nation's six largest departments.
SOURCE: Anthony Pate and Edwin Hamilton, *The Big Six Policing America's Largest Cities* (Washington, D.C.: Police Foundation, 1990), pp. 129–130.

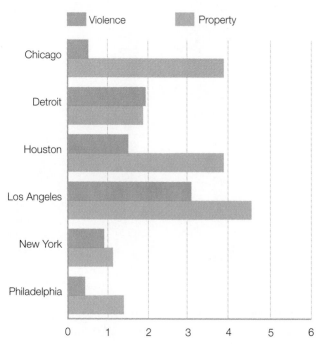

Die Hard

Police get involved in shoot-outs every day and they never have to worry about the consequences. In a typical day, detectives may be forced to blow up buildings, shoot down aircraft, kill scores of people, suffer serious personal injuries, and then calmly shrug it off and go back to work. At least they do if they are like Detective John McClane, hero of the *Die Hard* movies starring Bruce Willis.

We first meet New York City detective McClane when he goes to L.A. to reconcile with his wife (played by Bonnie Bedelia). He arrives at her place of work just as it is being taken over by arch-criminal Hans Gruber (Alan Rickman) and his gang of high-tech criminals. Using all his resources and skill, McClane is able to take out Gruber's gang one by one, despite their being heavily armed and having sophisticated communications gear. In a titanic struggle, McClane defeats Gruber, who falls to his death.

In a sequel, McClane defeats rogue military officers, led by William Sadler and John Amos, who terrorize a Washington airport, and reprises his role once again in *Die Harder* to defeat a contingent of ex–East German army officers led by none other than Gruber's younger brother (played by Jeremy Irons)!

While exciting and entertaining, the *Die Hard* films bear little resemblance to real police work. Any officer who suffered one-tenth the injuries that McClane regularly suffers would be placed on disability leave as soon as he got out of intensive care. Yet although we see McClane being beaten and shot, falling through windows, and running around barefoot on glass, we never feel that he ever misses a day of work, let alone applies for worker's comp.

Even more dubious is the unrestrained use of violence by McClane. The typical police officer would have to be on the job for more than 1,000 years before he or she shot and killed a criminal (given that only about 300 offenders are killed by police each year). We also know that in real life the typical tour of duty results in 0 serious arrests. However, hardly a day goes by without McClane making numerous felony arrests, fighting off terrorists, and shooting multiple perpetrators who get in his way. In the "real world" anytime officers pull and use their weapons they are required to fill out extensive shooting incidence reports, which are reviewed by senior officers. McClane blows up a 747 and never writes a report.

McClane also gets to work for different departments without losing rank. In the first *Die Hard* episode he is a New York cop, in the second he has transferred to L.A., and he is back in New York for the third installment. Such job mobility would be nice, but it only occurs in films.

While it seems likely that urban police make significantly more arrests than suburban or rural officers, few officers in any jurisdiction spend their days catching criminals and engaging in shoot-outs, as Hollywood would like us to believe. One national study conducted by researchers at the Washington D.C.–based Police Foundation, a nonprofit organization that conducts research on law enforcement issues, found that even in the largest cities there are only 3 to 7 property and violent crime arrests per sworn officer each year.

These figures should be interpreted with caution, because not all police officers are engaged in activities that allow them to make arrests, such as patrol or detective work. About one-third of all sworn officers in the nation's largest police departments are in such units as communications, antiterrorism, administration, and personnel and are therefore unlikely to make arrests. Even if the number of arrests per officer were adjusted by one-third, it would still amount to only 9 or 10 serious crime arrests per officer per year. So while police handle thousands of calls each year, relatively few result in an arrest for a serious crime, such as a robbery and burglary, and in suburban and rural areas, years may go by before a police officer arrests someone for a serious crime.

The evidence, then, shows that the police role involves a preponderance of noncrime-related activities and is similar in both large and small departments. Although officers in large urban departments may be called on to handle more felony cases than those in small towns, they, too, will probably find that the bulk of their daily activities are not crime related. In the future, police officers will probably spend even more of their time learning to deal with the social problems exploding across the United States, ranging from women who have been battered in domestic disputes to runaway children.[5] More attention will be paid to **special-needs populations:** substance abusers, the homeless, the mentally ill, and the disabled.[6] Unlike their fictional counterparts who arrest 10 people per hour, most police officers rarely spend their days directly fighting crime.

The activities of most police departments were listed in Figure 6.1. As this figure shows, large metropolitan police departments carry out a wide variety of tasks and maintain a number of highly specialized roles. The most important of these, the patrol and investigation functions, are described in the next sections.

Regardless of style of policing, uniformed patrol officers are the backbone of the police department, usually accounting for about two-thirds of a department's personnel.[7] Patrol officers are the most highly visible components of the entire criminal justice system. They are charged with supervising specific areas of their jurisdiction, called **beats,** whether on foot, in a patrol car, or by motorcycle, horse, helicopter, or even boat.[8] Each beat or patrol area is covered 24 hours a day by different shifts. The major purpose of patrol is to

Patrol Function

1. Deter crime by maintaining a visible police presence

2. Maintain public order (peacekeeping) within the patrol area

3. Enable the police department to respond quickly to law violations or other emergencies

4. Identify and apprehend law violators

5. Aid individuals and care for those who cannot help themselves

6. Facilitate the movement of traffic and people

7. Create a feeling of security in the community.[9]

Patrol officers' responsibilities are immense; they may suddenly be faced with an angry mob, an armed felon, or a suicidal teenager and be forced to make split-second decisions on what action to take. At the same time, they must be sensitive to the needs of citizens who are often of diverse racial and ethnic backgrounds.

Patrol Activities

Most experts agree that the great bulk of police patrol efforts is devoted to what has been described as **order maintenance** or **peacekeeping:** maintaining order and civility within their assigned jurisdiction.[10] Order-maintenance functions fall on the border between criminal and noncriminal behavior. The patrol officer's discretion often determines whether a noisy neighborhood dispute involves the crime of disturbing the peace or whether it can be controlled with street-corner diplomacy and the combatants sent on their way. Similarly, teenagers milling around in the shopping center parking lot can be brought in and turned over to the juvenile authorities or handled in a less formal and often more efficient manner.

So the major role of police seems to be "handling the situation." Police encounter many troubling incidents that need some sort of "fixing up."[11] Enforcing the law might be one tool a patrol officer uses; threat, coercion, sympathy, understanding, and apathy might be others. Most important is keeping things under control so that there are no complaints that the officer is doing nothing or doing too much. The "real" police role, then, may be as a "community problem solver."

Police officers actually practice a policy of selective enforcement, concentrating on some crimes but handling the majority in an informal manner. A police officer is supposed to know when to take action and when not to, whom to arrest and whom to deal with by issuing a warning or some other informal action. If a mistake is made, the officer can come under fire from his or her peers and superiors, as well as the general public. Consequently, the patrol officer's job is extremely demanding and often unrewarding and unappreciated. It is not surprising that the attitudes of police officers toward the public are sometimes characterized as being ambivalent and cynical.[12]

Does Patrol Work?

For many years, preventive police patrol has been considered one of the greatest deterrents to criminal behavior. The visible presence of patrol cars on the street and the rapid deployment of police officers to the scene of a crime were viewed as particularly effective law enforcement techniques. However, research efforts have questioned the basic assumptions of patrol. The most widely heralded attempt at measuring patrol effectiveness was undertaken during the early 1970s in Kansas City, Missouri, under sponsorship of the Police Foundation, a private institute that studies police behavior.[13]

To evaluate the effectiveness of patrol, the researchers divided 15 separate police districts into three groups: One group retained normal police patrol; the second ("proactive") set of districts were supplied with two to three times the normal amount of patrol forces; and the third ("reactive") group had its preventive patrol eliminated, and police officers responded only when summoned by citizens to the scene of a particular crime.

Data from the Kansas City study indicated that these variations in patrol techniques had little effect on the crime patterns in the 15 districts. The presence or absence of patrol did not seem to affect residential or business burglaries, motor vehicle thefts, larcenies involving auto accessories, robberies, vandalism, or other criminal behavior.[14] Moreover, variations in police patrol techniques appeared to have little influence on citizens' attitudes toward the police, their satisfaction with police, or their fear of future criminal behavior.[15]

While the Kansas City study found little evidence that police patrol could deter crime, police in a number of jurisdictions have attempted to test the effectiveness of patrol by targeting areas for increased police presence. The results of these programs suggest that even when the presence of additional police reduces the crime rate, the effect is temporary; when the crackdown is terminated, criminals begin to drift back into the area. In addition, there is the problem of **displacement.** Criminals move from an area targeted for increased police presence to another that is less well protected. When the police leave, they return to "business as usual."

The Kansas City study, although subject to criticism because of its research design, greatly influenced the way police experts viewed the effectiveness of patrol. Its rather lukewarm findings set the stage for community and problem-oriented policing models, which stress social service over crime deterrence (discussed later in this chapter).

However, it may be too soon to dismiss police patrol as a crime-fighting technique. While the mere presence of police may not be sufficient to deter crime, the manner in which they approach their task may make a difference. Police departments that use a **proactive,** aggressive law enforcement style may help reduce crime rates. Jurisdictions that encourage patrol officers to stop motor vehicles to issue citations and to aggressively arrest and detain suspicious persons also experience lower crime rates than jurisdictions that do not follow such proactive policies.[16] Departments that more actively enforce minor regulations, such as disorderly conduct and traffic laws, are also more likely to experience lower felony rates.[17] The downturn in the New York City violent crime rate during the 1990s has been attributed by some to aggressive police work aimed at "lifestyle" crimes: vandalism, panhandling, and graffiti. It is possible that aggressive policing efforts for one type of crime may help reduce the incidence of another, more serious one.[18] And, as the accompanying box shows, aggressively targeting particular crime problems may help reduce crime rates.

Should Patrol Become More Aggressive? Pinpointing why proactive policing works so effectively is difficult. It may have a **deterrent effect:** Aggressive policing increases community perception that police arrest a lot of criminals and that most violators get caught; criminals are scared to commit crimes in a town that has such an active police force! Proactive policing may also help control crime

Proactive policing increases community perception that police arrest a lot of criminals and that most violators get caught. Because aggressive police arrest more suspects, there are fewer left on the street to commit crime; fewer criminals produce lower crime rates. Proactive police strategies may breed resentment in lower-class areas where citizens believe they are targets of police suspicion and suffer from their consequent overreaction.

Chapter 6
▬
The Police: Role and Function

Can Aggressive Policing Work?

Can aggressive patrol programs substantially reduce crime rates? There is growing evidence that directed patrol, narrowly aimed at a particular problem area, may have long-term crime reduction benefits. One such program, known as the Kansas City gun experiment, was directed at restricting the carrying of guns in high-risk places at high-risk times.

Working with academics from the University of Maryland, the Kansas City Police Department focused extra patrol attention to a "hot spot" high-crime area identified by computer analysis of all gun crimes. A pair of two-officer patrol cars focused exclusively on gun detection from 7 P.M. to 1 A.M. seven days a week; the cars did not respond to service calls. During the course of the experiment, the officers worked a total of 200 nights involving 4,512 officer-hours and 2,256 patrol car hours. Of the total, 1,218 officer-hours were spent on gun patrols, while the remaining hours (70%) were spent processing arrests and performing other patrol-related duties.

Over a 29-week period, the gun patrol officers made thousands of car and pedestrian checks and traffic stops and made over 600 arrests. Using frisks and searches, they found 29 guns; an additional 47 weapons were seized by other officers in the experimental area. These seizures increased the total guns found in the area by 65% over the previous six months. The ratio of guns seized per direct patrol time was 1 gun per 84 hours.

How did the gun patrol effort affect crime rates? There were 169 gun crimes in the target beat in the 29 weeks prior to the gun patrol but only 86 while the experiment was underway, a decrease of 49%. Drive-by shootings dropped significantly, as did homicides. Crimes not targeted by the experiment showed little overall change. Importantly, none of the seven contiguous beats showed a significant increase in gun crimes, indicating that there was little crime displacement effect. Community surveys conducted before and after the program was initiated indicated that citizens in the target area were less fearful of crime and more satisfied with their neighborhood than residents in companion areas. After the extra patrols were ended, crime rates went back to their previous levels.

Considering the thousands of guns available in the area, it seems odd that the seizure of 29 additional weapons could have such a dramatic influence on the crime rate. There are three likely explanations for the significant reduction in gun-related crimes. First, it is possible that the weapons seized were taken from high-rate offenders who were among the most likely perpetrators of gun-related crimes. Their "lost opportunity" to commit violent crimes may have resulted in an overall rate decrease. Second, because the gun patrol made more arrests in the area than the norm, it is possible that some of the most violent criminals were incapacitated long enough to account for a crime rate reduction. Finally, as word of the patrol got out, there may have been a general deterrent effect: People contemplating violent crime may have been convinced that apprehension risks were unacceptably high.

Critical Thinking Questions

1. The Kansas City gun patrol experiment suggests that a modest police patrol effort targeting guns can produce dramatic effects on the crime rate. Whether such efforts could become general police policy remains to be seen. They could produce risks to officer safety, provoke hostile reactions from citizens, and make people subject to police searches hostile and angry. Would these risks be acceptable if aggressive police action could significantly reduce the threat of gun violence?

2. Might the concentration of police in some communities with orders to frisk suspected gun carriers provoke angry reactions from citizens who feel they are being targeted unfairly and without respect for their privacy?

SOURCE: Lawrence Sherman, James Shaw, and Dennis Rogan, *The Kansas City Gun Experiment* (Washington, D.C.: National Institute of Justice, 1994).

because it results in conviction of more criminals. Because aggressive police arrest more suspects, there are fewer left on the street to commit crime; fewer criminals produce lower crime rates.

Before a general policy of vigorous police work can be adopted, more research is needed on proactive policing. Not all evaluations have found that aggressive patrol efforts actually bring the crime rate down.[19] The downside of aggressive tactics must also be considered. Proactive police strategies may breed resentment in lower-class areas where citizens believe they are targets of police suspicion and reaction.[20] Evidence exists that such aggressive police tactics as stopping and frisking and rousting teenagers who congregate on street corners plant the seeds from which urban conflict grows.[21] Despite such reservations, many large police jurisdictions have insisted that patrol officers become more aggressive and concentrate on investigating and deterring crimes.

In sum, it is possible that aggressive police patrol may be a more effective, albeit socially costly, crime suppression mechanism than previously thought.

Making Arrests. Is it possible that more formal police action, such as an arrest, can reduce crime? A number of experts have expressed doubt that formal police action can have any general deterrent effect or, if it does, that it would be anything but short-lived and temporary.[22] However, research studies do show that contact with the police may cause some offenders to forgo repeat criminal behavior; formal police action, such as arrest, may in fact deter future criminality. For example, an arrest for drunk driving reduces the likelihood of further driving while intoxicated. An arrest apparently increases people's belief that they will be rearrested if they drink and drive and heightens their perception of the unpleasantness associated with an arrest.[23] There is also evidence that many first offenders will forgo criminal activity after arrest.[24]

Even if formal action does deter crime, police chiefs may find it difficult to convince patrol officers to make more arrests. Despite a departmental policy requiring officers to be more active, police officers may be reluctant to change their style and tactics.[25] Research efforts indicate that departmental directives to make more arrests may have relatively little effect on police behavior.[26] So influencing actual police activities in the field may prove a difficult task.

Controlling Domestic Violence. The most significant tests of the deterrent effect of police arrest power have focused on the ability to reduce repeated domestic violence. These cases are particularly vexing for police administrators because they typically involve repeat incidents and situations in which it is difficult for the officer on the scene to respond effectively.

To test the most appropriate response, police officers who participated in a study conducted in Minneapolis randomly assigned treatments to the domestic assault cases they encountered on their beat. One approach was to give some sort of advice and mediation; another was to send the assailant from the home for eight hours; the third was to arrest the assailant.

The data indicated that when police took formal action (arrest), the chance of repeat offending or **recidivism** was substantially less than when they took less punitive measures, such as warning offenders or ordering them out of the house for a cooling-off period. A six-month follow-up found that only 10% of those who were arrested repeated their violent behavior, while 19% of those advised and 24% of those sent away repeated their offenses.

To supplement the official police data, 205 of the victims were personally interviewed. The victims also reported that an arrest had the greatest benefit in controlling domestic assaults. While 19% of the women whose men had been arrested reported their mates had assaulted them again, 37% of those whose mates had been advised and 33% of those whose mates had been sent away reported additional assaults. In sum, the Minnesota experiment indicated that a formal arrest was the most effective means of controlling domestic violence, regardless of what happened to the offender in court.[27]

The Minneapolis experiment has deeply affected police operations. The findings suggested that actual contact with police and their use of formal actions may have a deterrent effect on a serious crime problem. Not surprisingly, Atlanta, Chicago, Dallas, Denver, Detroit, New York, Miami, San Francisco, and Seattle, among other large cities, have adopted policies encouraging arrests in domestic violence cases.

Although the results of the Minneapolis experiment received quick acceptance, government-funded research replicating the experimental design in other locales, including Omaha, Nebraska, and Charlotte, North Carolina, has failed to duplicate them; in these locales, formal arrest was no greater a deterrent to domestic abuse than warning or advising the assailant.[28]

While this failure to duplicate the deterrent results found in Minneapolis is troubling, there are indications that police actions may, under some conditions, deter domestic abuse.[29] A short-term arrest (custody lasting about 3 hours) may actually be more effective than an arrest followed by a longer period of detention (about 12 hours). However, research shows that even when arrest deters domestic violence in the short run, violence eventually reoccurs.

Explaining why the initial deterrent effect of arrest decays over time is difficult. It is possible that offenders who suffer arrest are initially fearful of punishment but eventually replace fear with anger and violent intent toward their mate when their case does not result in severe punishment. Another possibility is that the true recidivism rate is hidden from researchers. Victims of domestic abuse, realizing that an initial call to the police produced an arrest but not much else, may be reluctant to make subsequent calls or even discuss their predicament with evaluators.[30] Arrests also do little to redress the underlying cause of domestic abuse.

The domestic violence research illustrates the difficulty proving that any sort of police action can deter crime. The original experiment found that the most punitive police action, arrest, can deter crime. Later efforts could not repeat this finding. And even when arrest deterred crime in the short run, crime later reappeared. Can police actions prevent future crime? If even the most vigorous law enforcement efforts cannot deter crime, then police must reconsider their role to improve their effectiveness.

Does Increasing Resources Help?

One reason patrol activity may be less effective than desired is the lack of adequate resources. Does adding more police help bring the crime rate down? Comparisons of police expenditures in U.S. cities indicates that cities with the highest crime rates also spend the most on police services.[31] The actual number of law enforcement officers in a jurisdiction seems to have little effect on area crimes, nor does adding officers lower the crime rate.[32]

Adding resources may not bring the crime rate down, but it may improve the overall effectiveness of the justice system. Communities with relatively high crime rates that devote fewer financial resources to police work find that many cases that result in arrest are dropped before they ever get to trial.[33] It is possible that overworked police in high-crime areas may be processing cases with little hope of prosecution to give the public the message that they are trying to "do something." Inadequate resources make it difficult to gather sufficient evidence to ensure a conviction, and prosecutors are likely to drop these cases. Adding resources, in this instance, could possibly improve the quality of police arrests.

Investigation Function

Since the first independent detective bureau was established by the London Metropolitan Police in 1841,[34] criminal investigators have been romantic figures vividly portrayed in novels, movies such as Eddie Murphy's *Beverly Hills Cop* and Clint Eastwood's *Dirty Harry* series, and television shows such as *Columbo, NYPD Blue,* and *Law and Order.* The fictional police detective is usually depicted as a loner, willing to break departmental rules, perhaps even violate the law, to capture the suspect. The average fictional detective views departmental policies and U.S. Supreme Court decisions as unfortunate roadblocks to police efficiency. Civil rights are either ignored or actively scorned.[35]

Although every police department probably has a few "hell-bent for leather" detectives who take matters into their own hands at the expense of citizens' rights, the modern criminal investigator is most likely an experienced civil servant, trained in investigatory techniques, knowledgeable about legal rules of evidence and procedure, and at least somewhat cautious about the legal and administrative consequences of his or her actions.[36] Although detectives are often handicapped by limited time, money, and resources, they are certainly aware of how their actions will one day be interpreted in a court of law. In fact, police investigators are sometimes accused of being more concerned with the most recent court cases regarding search and seizure and custody interrogation than with engaging in shoot-outs with suspected felons.

Detectives are probably the elite of the police force: They are usually paid more than patrol officers, engage in more interesting tasks, wear civilian clothes, and are subject to a less stringent departmental control than patrol officers.[37]

Detectives investigate the causes of crime and attempt to identify the individuals or groups responsible for committing particular offenses. They may enter a case after patrol officers have made the initial contact, such as when a patrol car interrupts a crime in progress and the offenders flee before they can be apprehended. They can investigate a case entirely on their own, sometimes by following up on leads provided by informants.

Detective divisions are typically organized into sections or bureaus, such as homicide, robbery, or rape. Some jurisdictions maintain morals or **vice squads,** which are usually staffed by plainclothes officers or detectives specializing in victimless crimes, such as prostitution or gambling. Vice squad officers may set themselves up as customers for illicit activities to make arrests. For example, male undercover detectives may frequent public men's rooms and make advances toward entering men; those who respond are arrested for homosexual soliciting. In other instances, female police officers may pose as prostitutes. These covert police activities have often been criticized as violating the personal rights of citizens, and their appropriateness and fairness have been questioned.

Detective work can be viewed as falling into four types of action:

1. A suspect has been apprehended or a subject placed under control, and there is adequate information about the person's behavior.

2. There is reliable information that a crime has been committed, but the suspect has not been identified or, if identified, has not been apprehended. This is the classic problem of **detection:** to discover reliable information that will permit the identification and arrest of a perpetrator.

3. A suspect or subject may be known or even under continuous observation or control, but there is no reliable or adequate information about this person's past behavior, present connections, or future intentions. The investigators are not sure that a crime has been committed but are hoping to discover a crime that can implicate a targeted individual or his or her confederates.

4. The detectives have neither an identified subject nor adequate information. However, they have reason to believe, ranging from a hunch and the tips of untested informants to the implications of other investigative reports, that something may be up or something bears watching.[38] On some occasions detectives may assume a false identity to gain more information. "Going undercover" is the topic of the accompanying Analyzing Criminal Justice Issues box.

Stings

Another approach to detective work, commonly referred to as **sting operations,** involves organized groups of detectives who deceive criminals into openly committing illegal acts or conspiring to engage in criminal activity. Numerous sting operations have been aimed at capturing professional thieves and seizing stolen merchandise. Undercover detectives pose as fences, set up ongoing fencing operations, and encourage thieves interested in selling stolen merchandise. Transactions are videotaped to provide prosecutors with strong cases. Sting operations have netted millions of dollars in recovered property and resulted in the arrests of many criminals.

Going Undercover

The 1997 film *Donnie Brasco* depicts the ordeal of Joe Pistone, alias Donnie Brasco, an undercover FBI agent who successfully infiltrated an organized crime family in New York City. In the deepest and most intense mob infiltration in FBI history, Pistone became torn between his commitment to his job and family and his involvement with his new identity as a mobster. After testifying against organized crime figures, Pistone today is in the witness protection program.

Undercover work can take a number of forms. A lone agent can infiltrate a criminal group or organization to gather information on future criminal activity. For example, a DEA agent may go undercover to gather intelligence on drug smugglers. Undercover officers can also pose as victims to capture predatory criminals who have been conducting street robberies and muggings.

The Dangers of Undercover Work

Undercover work is considered a necessary element of police work, although it can prove quite dangerous for the agent. Police officers may be forced to engage in illegal or immoral behavior to maintain their cover. They also face significant physical danger in playing the role of a criminal and dealing with mobsters, terrorists, and drug dealers. In far too many cases, undercover officers are mistaken for real criminals and are injured by other law enforcement officers or private citizens trying to stop a crime. Arrest situations involving undercover officers may also provoke violence when suspects do not realize they are in the presence of police and therefore violently resist arrest.

Undercover officers may also experience psychological problems. Being away from home, keeping late hours, and always worrying that their identity will be uncovered all create enormous stress. Officers have experienced postundercover stress resulting in trouble at

work and, in many instances, ruined marriages and botched prosecutions. Some have even turned to crime themselves because they are presented with so much temptation. One undercover officer claims, "It's unlike anything else in law enforcement. . . . [A] great deal of hours . . . are spent alone. There is a great deal of pressure. . . . There are a great many temptations out there involving money, narcotics, alcohol . . . [and] women."

Hanging around with criminals for a long period of time, making friends, and earning their trust can also have a damaging psychological impact. As one officer states:

I can remember very distinctly going out and arresting these same people that had become my friends. I can't even talk about it now without getting emotional. They had trusted me, and all of a sudden I was the police and I'm testifying in court against them. It took a long time to get over that.

Law enforcement agencies, including the FBI, are taking this problem quite seriously and now monitor undercover work very closely. Veteran FBI agents interview former undercover agents four to six months after they have left the field to monitor for such stress-related trouble. The bureau also has retained a team of psychologists to deal with the problem.

Examples of undercover officers who succumbed to the stress of their work are legion. FBI agent Dan Mitrione got so caught up in his undercover drug dealing that he took $850,000 in drug profits for himself. Robert Delaney, a New Jersey state police officer, got so involved in his role as "Robert Alan Covert," a fence, that he could not shake his underground identity. His private life suffered as he reverted to the mobster lifestyle that he had successfully adopted for two years. And Patrick Livingstone, who participated in the

While these results seem impressive, sting operations do have drawbacks.[39] By its very nature, a sting involves deceit by police agents that often comes close to entrapment. Sting operations may encourage criminals to commit new crimes because they have a new source for fencing stolen goods. Innocent people may hurt their reputations by buying merchandise from a sting operation when they had no idea the items had been stolen.

In 1992 the Supreme Court recognized the dangers of overzealous sting operations in the case of *Jacobson v. United States.* Jacobson's name was on a list of subscribers to pornographic material because he had legally ordered sexually explicit magazines. After obtaining the list, two federal government agencies sent

pornography business for nearly three years under the alias "Pat Salamone," continued to visit his old bars, bookmakers, and criminal associates after the investigation he had conducted was over. He maintained a bank account and a driver's license in his alias's name and was happy to be known as Pat Salamone. When he was arrested for shoplifting, defense attorneys working for the pornographers he had helped identify used his tainted character to get some charges against their clients dismissed.

Despite its glamour, undercover work has many drawbacks. Sting operations have been criticized for encouraging people to commit crime. By putting the government in the fencing business, such operations blur the line between law enforcement and criminal activity. Undercover work also places serious and potentially fatal stress on detectives. Nonetheless, the FBI reports that as many as 600 agents are on a waiting list to be placed undercover.

Uncovering Undercover Work

Because undercover agents have become so prevalent and sophisticated, aspiring criminals have been forced to adopt their own defensive tactics to root out their opponents. Bruce Jacobs has conducted a series of interviews with heroin user/dealers in order to determine how these "pros" spot "undercover narcs."

Jacobs found that there are two types of "clues" that allow dealers to sniff out police agents. The first he labels *trend discontinuity,* which occurs when a dealer notices a dramatic change of behavior in a friend or associate's behavior. For example, a "regular" suddenly introduces a stranger who wants to buy drugs. Trend discontinuity also occurs when someone who usually buys small quantities of drugs suddenly tries to buy much larger amounts. Why would a known customer "turn"? Most likely to get the charges dropped ("work off the beef") after having been arrested.

The second category of danger signs, labeled *interpersonal illegitimacy,* refers to situations in which unfamiliar buyers broadcast certain verbal or physical

signals that alert dealers to the presence of undercover agents. Physical clues are leaked by inappropriate appearance, body language, and suspicious props. Verbal clues include conversational style, such as being overanxious to buy drugs and not demanding to negotiate price. No matter how scruffy agents try to look, they have trouble duplicating the appearance of real users, who seem more emaciated and have the needle marks to prove their status. Because agents have learned to simulate needle tracks, some dealers require them to "shoot up" in their presence before doing business.

The Jacobs research puts a different spin on the problems of undercover work. His narcotics dealers show why it is so difficult to control crime through law enforcement activities alone: Every technique triggers development of countermeasures to protect criminal enterprise.

Critical Thinking Questions

1. Undercover work involves police officers on the fringe of criminal activity. Even if sting operations result in arrests, do their social costs outweigh the law enforcement benefits? Would a sting operation setting up a fence encourage local people to get involved in crimes they might have avoided because they now have a convenient place to fence stolen goods? Might not the presence of an undercover agent encourage crime because a new, enthusiastic criminal agent is on the scene?

SOURCES: Bruce Jacobs, "Undercover Deception Clues: A Case of Restrictive Deterrence," *Criminology* 31 (1993): 281–299; Mark Porgebin and Eric Poole, "Vice Isn't Nice: A Look at the Effects of Working Undercover," *Journal of Criminal Justice* 21 (1993): 385–396; Gary Marx, *Undercover: Police Surveillance in America* (Berkeley: University of California Press, 1988); Anthony DeStefano, "Undercover Jobs Carry Big Psychological Risk After the Assignment," *Wall Street Journal,* 4 November 1985, p. 1.

mail to him through a fictitious organization that promoted sexual freedom and claimed to be against censorship. After two and a half years of mailings, Jacobson was sent a letter that described censorship as nonsense. When he responded, he received a catalog from which he ordered a magazine depicting young boys engaged in sexual activities. He was arrested and convicted on charges that he had violated the Child Protection Act of 1984, which made the receipt through the mails of sexually explicit depictions of children illegal.

In its ruling, the Court held that the government's two-and-a-half-year campaign to interest Jacobson in pornography amounted to illegal entrapment against a person who was not originally disposed to commit a criminal act. The

Chapter 6
—
The Police: Role and Function

Police detectives do make a valuable contribution to police work because their skilled interrogation and case-processing techniques are essential to eventual criminal conviction. Some detectives make extraordinary efforts to solve crimes. Here an undercover detective in Miami demonstrates his use of a rather unusual camouflage in order to nab some robbers in a restaurant.

fact that Jacobson had previously ordered child pornography merely showed that he was inclined toward certain acts within a broad range of behavior but was not sufficient to indicate specific criminal tendencies. By their long-term campaign, government investigators had pressured him to obtain and read illegal material to fight censorship and maintain individual rights.[40] The Jacobson case is important because it mandates that sting operations cannot entrap otherwise law-abiding citizens to commit crimes they might not have perpetrated had not law enforcement agents applied pressure to interest them in criminal behavior.

Effectiveness of Investigation

Serious criticism has been leveled at the nation's detective forces for being bogged down in paperwork and relatively inefficient in clearing cases. One famous study of 153 detective bureaus found that a great deal of a detective's time was spent in nonproductive work and that investigative expertise did little to solve cases; half of all detectives could be replaced without negatively influencing crime clearance rates.[41]

While some question remains about the effectiveness of investigations, police detectives do make a valuable contribution to police work because their skilled interrogation and case-processing techniques are essential to eventual criminal conviction.[42] Nonetheless, a majority of cases that are solved are done so when the perpetrator is identified at the scene of the crime by patrol officers. Research shows that if a crime is reported while in progress, the police have about a 33% chance of making an arrest; the arrest probability declines to about 10% if the crime is reported 1 minute later, and to 5% if more than 15 minutes has elapsed. As the time between the crime and the arrest grows, the chances of a conviction are also reduced, probably because the ability to recover evidence is lost. Put another way, once a crime has been completed and the investigation is put in the hands of detectives, the chances of identifying and arresting the perpetrator diminish rapidly.[43]

Improving Investigation Effectiveness

A number of efforts have been made to revamp and improve investigation procedures. One practice has been to give patrol officers greater responsibility for conducting preliminary investigations at the scene of the crime. In addition, the old-fashioned precinct detective has been replaced by specialized units, such as homicide or burglary squads, that operate over larger areas and can bring specific expertise to bear. Technological advances in DNA and fingerprint identification have also aided investigation effectiveness.

One reason for the ineffectiveness of investigation is that detectives often lack sufficient resources to carry out a lengthy ongoing probe of any but the most serious cases. Research shows the following:

1. *Unsolved cases.* Almost 50% of burglary cases are screened out by supervisors before assignment to a detective for a follow-up investigation. Of those assigned, 75% are dropped after the first day of the follow-up investigation. While robbery cases are more likely to be assigned to detectives, 75% of them are also dropped after one day of investigation.

2. *Length of investigation.* The vast majority of cases are investigated for no more than 4 hours stretching over 3 days. An average of 11 days elapses between the initial report of a crime and the suspension of the investigation.

3. *Sources of information.* Early in an investigation, the focus is on the victim; as the investigation is pursued, emphasis shifts to the suspect. The most critical information for determining case outcome is the name and description of the suspect and related crime information. Victims are most often the source of information; unfortunately, witnesses, informants, and members of the police department are consulted far less often. However, when these sources are tapped, they are likely to produce useful information.

4. *Effectiveness.* Preliminary investigations by patrol officers are critical. In situations where the suspect's identity is not known immediately after the crime is committed, detectives are able to make an arrest in less than 10% of all cases.[44]

Considering these findings, detective work may be improved if greater emphasis is placed on collecting physical evidence at the scene of the crime, identifying witnesses, checking departmental records, and using informants. The probability of successfully settling a case is improved if patrol officers carefully gather evidence at the scene of a crime and effectively communicate it to detectives working the case. Police managers should pay more attention to screening cases, monitoring case flow and activity, and creating productivity measures to make sure individual detectives and detective units are meeting their goals. Also recommended is the use of targeted investigations that direct attention at a few individuals, such as career criminals, who are known to have engaged in the behavior under investigation.

Many police officers feel unappreciated by the public they serve, which may be due to the underlying conflicts inherent in the police role. Police may want to be proactive crime fighters who initiate actions against law violators; yet most remain reactive, responding when a citizen calls for service. The desire for direct action is often blunted because police are expected to perform many civic duties that in earlier times were the responsibility of every citizen: keeping the peace, performing emergency medical care, dealing with family problems, helping during civil emergencies.

While most of us agree that a neighborhood brawl must be stopped, that shelter must be found for the homeless, and that the inebriate must be taken safely home, few of us want to personally jump into the fray; we would rather "call the cops." The police officer has become a "social handyman" called in to fix up problems that the average citizen wishes would simply go away. Police officers are viewed as the "fire it takes to fight fire."[45] The public needs the police to perform those duties that the average citizen finds distasteful or dangerous,

such as breaking up a domestic quarrel. At the same time, the public resents the power the police have to use force, to arrest people, and to deny people their vices. Put another way, the average citizen wants the police to crack down on undesirable members of society while excluding his or her own behavior from legal scrutiny.

Because of these natural role conflicts, the relationship between the police and the public has been the subject of a great deal of concern. As you may recall, the respect Americans have for police effectiveness, courtesy, honesty, and conduct seems to be dwindling. Citizens may be less likely to go to police for help, to report crimes, to step forward as witnesses, or to cooperate with and aid police. Victim surveys indicate that many citizens have so little faith in the police that they will not report even serious crimes, such as rape or burglary. In some communities, citizen self-help groups have sprung up to supplement police protection.[46] In return, police officers often feel ambivalent and uncertain about the public they are sworn to protect.

Because of this ambivalence and role conflict, more communities are adapting new models of policing that reflect the changing role of the police. Some administrators now recognize that police officers are better equipped to be civic problem solvers than effective crime fighters. Rather than ignore, deny, or fight this reality, police departments are being reorganized to maximize their strengths and minimize their weaknesses. What has emerged is the community policing movement, a new concept of policing designed to bridge the gulf between police agencies and the communities they serve.

Community Policing

A quiet revolution is reshaping American policing.—George Kelling[47]

Police agencies have been trying to gain the cooperation and respect of the communities they serve for more than 30 years. At first, efforts at improving the relationships between police departments and the public involved programs with the general title of **police-community relations (PCR).** These initial PCR programs were developed at the stationhouse and departmental levels and designed to make citizens more aware of police activities, alert them to methods of self-protection, and improve general attitudes toward policing. In the socially turbulent 1960s, many larger departments instituted specialized PCR units, while others pursued improving relations through specialized programs, such as neighborhood watch groups, that instructed citizens in home security measures and enlisted their assistance in watching neighbors' homes. Operation ID, first implemented in Monterey Park, California in 1963, had police officers passing out engraving tools so that citizens could mark their valuables for easy identification if they were stolen and tags to be placed on the front of a home alerting potential thieves that the valuables inside had been marked. Other early PCR programs were crime prevention clinics, citizens' police alert programs, and similar efforts to help people identify suspicious characters in their neighborhoods.

Broken Windows

The community policing model in use today can be traced to a critical 1982 paper by two justice policy experts, George Kelling and James Q. Wilson, who articulated a new approach to improving police relations in the community that has come to be known as the **broken windows model.**[48] Kelling and Wilson made three points:

1. *Neighborhood disorder creates fear.* Urban areas filled with street people, youth gangs, prostitutes, and the mentally disturbed are the ones most likely to maintain a high degree of crime.

2. *Neighborhoods give out crime-promoting signals.* A neighborhood filled with deteriorated housing, unrepaired broken windows, and untended disorderly behavior gives out crime-promoting signals. Honest citizens live in fear in these areas, and predatory criminals are attracted to them.

3. *Police need citizens' cooperation.* If police are to reduce fear and successfully combat crime in these urban areas, they must have the cooperation, support, and assistance of the citizens.

According to the broken windows approach, community relations and crime control effectiveness cannot be the province of a few specialized units housed within a traditional police department. Instead, the core police role must be altered if community involvement is to be won and maintained. To accomplish this goal, urban police departments should return to the earlier style of policing in which officers on the beat had intimate contact with the people they served.

Police departments must totally alter their crime control strategy. Modern police departments generally rely on motorized patrol to cover wide areas, to maintain a visible police presence, and to ensure rapid response time. While effective and economical, the patrol car removes officers from the mainstream of the community, alienating people who might otherwise be potential sources of information and help to the police.

The broken windows approach holds that police administrators would be well served by deploying their forces where they can encourage public confidence, strengthen feelings of safety, and elicit cooperation from citizens. Community preservation, public safety, and order maintenance—not crime fighting—should become the primary focus of patrol. Put another way, just as physicians and dentists practice preventive medicine and dentistry, police should help maintain an intact community structure rather than simply fight crime.

Community Policing in Action

The community policing concept was originally implemented through a number of innovative demonstration projects.[49] Among the most publicized were experiments in **foot patrol,** which took officers out of cars and set them to walking beats in the neighborhood. Foot patrol efforts were aimed at forming a bond with community residents by acquainting them with the individual officers who patrolled their neighborhood, letting them know that police were caring and available. The first foot patrol experiments were conducted in cities in Michigan and New Jersey. An evaluation of foot patrol indicated that while it did not bring the crime rate down, residents in areas where foot patrol was added perceived greater safety and were less afraid of crime.[50]

Since the advent of these programs, hundreds of communities have adopted innovative forms of nonmotorized patrol (including bicycle patrols) that show early signs of success.[51] Decentralized, neighborhood-based precincts have been created to serve as storefront ministations.[52] Officers are chosen for this duty based on their community relations and crime prevention skills; ministation programs have garnered significant community acceptance.[53] Similar programs assign officers to neighborhoods, organize training programs for community leaders, and feature a "bottom-up" approach to dealing with community problems: Decision making involves the officer on the scene, not a directive from central headquarters.[54]

Reducing Community Fear

One of the more important goals of community policing is to reduce the level of fear in the community.[55] Fear reduction is viewed as both an important element of police services to the community and a means of increasing citizen cooperation with police officers.[56] Some of the techniques of fear reduction include

- A police-community newsletter designed to give accurate information to citizens

- A community-organizing response team designed to build a community organization in an area where none has existed

- A citizen contact program that keeps individual officers in the same area of the city, enabling them to make individual contacts with community residents

- A program in which officers recontact victims soon after their victimization to reassure them of police action in the case

- A police community contact center staffed by patrol officers, civilian coordinators, and police aides[57]

The most successful programs give officers the time to meet with local residents to talk about crime in the neighborhood and to use personal initiative to solve problems. Some police departments have set up activity programs for juveniles who might ordinarily have little to do but get involved in gangs.[58] While not all programs work (police-community newsletters and clean-up campaigns do not seem to do much good), the overall impression has been that patrol officers can actually reduce the level of fear in the community.

Philosophy of Community Policing

Community policing means more than implementing direct-action programs.[59] It also refers to a philosophy of policing that requires departments to reconsider their recruitment, organization, and operating procedures.[60] What are some of the most important community policing concepts? First, community policing emphasizes results, not bureaucratic process. Rather than react to problems in the community, police departments take the initiative in identifying issues and actively treating their cause. Problem-solving and analysis techniques replace emphasis on bureaucratic detail. There is less concern with "playing it by the book" and more with getting the job done.

To achieve this, the police must decentralize, an approach sometimes referred to as **innovative neighborhood-oriented policing (INOP)**.[61] Problem solving is best done at the neighborhood level where issues originate, not at a far-off central headquarters. Because each neighborhood has its own particular needs, police decision making must be flexible and adaptive.[62] Decentralization is essential if police agencies are going to understand community problems. Some important INOP programs are discussed in Table 6.1.

Community policing also stresses sharing power with local groups and individuals. A key element of the community policing philosophy is that citizens must actively participate with police to fight crime.[63] This participation might involve providing information in area-wide crime investigations or helping police reach out to troubled youths.

Community policing also means the eventual redesign of police departments. Management's role must be reordered to focus on the problems of the community, not the needs of the police department. The traditional vertical police organizational chart must be altered so that "top-down management" gives way to bottom-up decision making. The patrol officer becomes the manager of his or her beat and a key decision maker. Figure 6.3 shows how one police department is organized for community policing.

Community policing requires that police departments alter their recruitment and training requirements. Future officers must develop community-organizing and problem-solving skills, along with traditional police skills. Their training must prepare them to succeed less on their ability to make arrests or issue citations and more on their ability to solve problems effectively.

Not only is the community policing concept catching on in the United States, it has also captured the interest of police departments around the

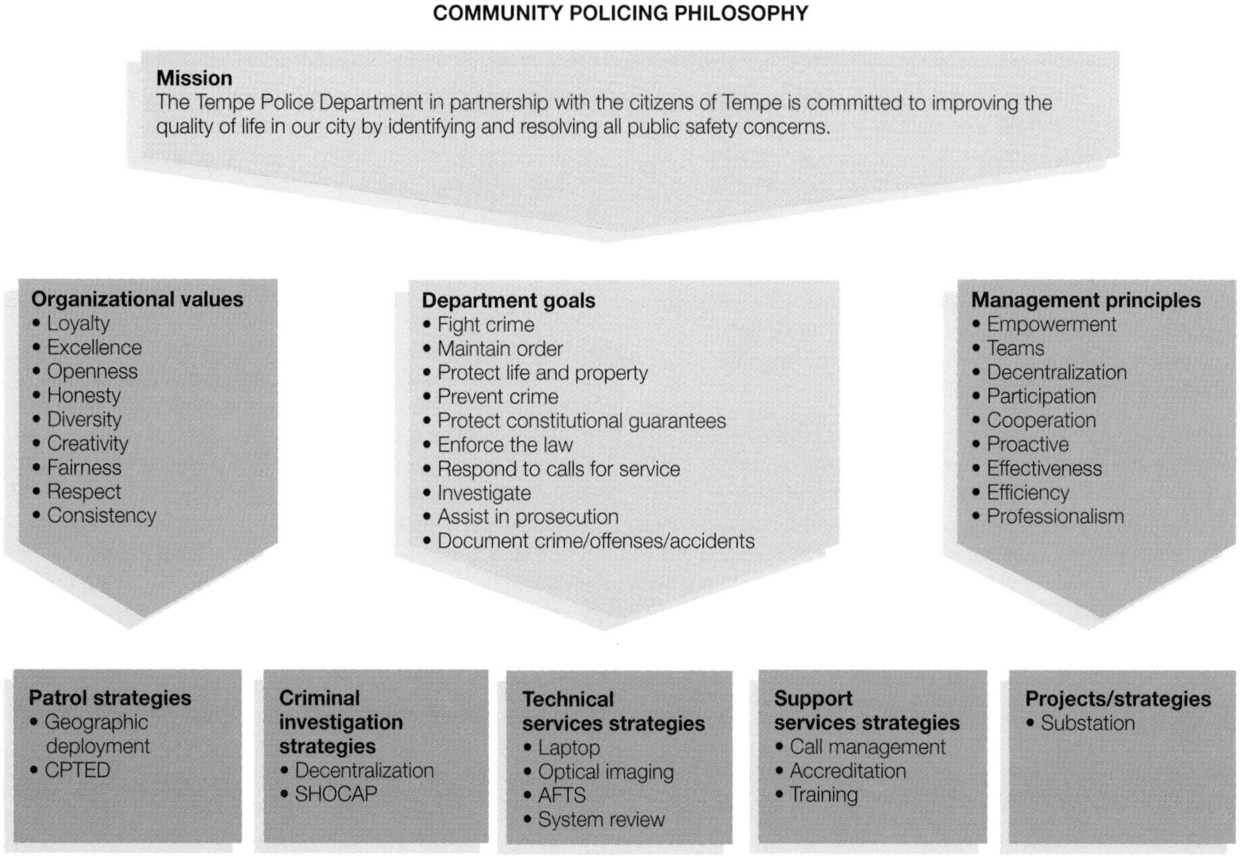

Mission
The Tempe Police Department in partnership with the citizens of Tempe is committed to improving the quality of life in our city by identifying and resolving all public safety concerns.

Organizational values
- Loyalty
- Excellence
- Openness
- Honesty
- Diversity
- Creativity
- Fairness
- Respect
- Consistency

Department goals
- Fight crime
- Maintain order
- Protect life and property
- Prevent crime
- Protect constitutional guarantees
- Enforce the law
- Respond to calls for service
- Investigate
- Assist in prosecution
- Document crime/offenses/accidents

Management principles
- Empowerment
- Teams
- Decentralization
- Participation
- Cooperation
- Proactive
- Effectiveness
- Efficiency
- Professionalism

Patrol strategies
- Geographic deployment
- CPTED

Criminal investigation strategies
- Decentralization
- SHOCAP

Technical services strategies
- Laptop
- Optical imaging
- AFTS
- System review

Support services strategies
- Call management
- Accreditation
- Training

Projects/strategies
- Substation

Figure 6.3
Tempe (Arizona) Police Department planning model.
SOURCE: Tempe, Arizona, Police Department.

world.[64] Community policing is being used in numerous countries, including Denmark, Finland, and Great Britain.

Problem-Oriented Policing

Closely associated with, yet independent from, the community policing concept are **problem-oriented policing** strategies. Traditional police models focus on responding to calls for help in the fastest possible time, dealing with the situation, and then getting on the street again as soon as possible.[65] In contrast, the core of problem-oriented policing is a proactive orientation.

Problem-oriented police strategies require police agencies to identify particular long-term community problems—street-level drug dealers, prostitution rings, gang hangouts—and develop strategies to eliminate them.[66] As with community policing, being problem solvers requires that police departments rely on local residents and private resources. This means that police managers must learn how to develop community resources, design cost-efficient and effective solutions to problems, and become advocates as well as agents of reform.[67]

Problem-oriented policing models are supported by the fact that a great deal of urban crime is concentrated in a few "hot spots."[68] A significant portion of all police calls in metropolitan areas typically radiate from a relatively few locations: bars, malls, the bus depot, hotels, certain apartment buildings.[69] By implication, concentrating police resources on these **hot spots of crime** could appreciably reduce crime.[70]

The new community police models are essentially problem oriented, and both efforts can be combined. For example, in Vancouver, Canada, community police officers assigned to reduce and control street prostitution actually included prostitutes in their planning activities and were able to reduce neighborhood conflict by mediating between residents and prostitutes. They included both groups to help control collateral problems such as drug dealing and pornography.[71]

Problem-oriented strategies can also be developed within traditional police organizations.[72] A well-known example was Operation Pressure Point, a massive police initiative in which an additional 240 officers were dispatched to a high-drug-use area on the Lower East Side of New York. The program combined aggressive law enforcement tactics, including the arrest and detention of all suspects, and undercover surveillance work. Enforcement strategies were used along with community organization programs designed to strengthen neighborhood structure and increase resident support for police operations. Operation Pressure Point successfully reduced drug trafficking in the area while reviving community spirit.[73]

While programs like Operation Pressure Point seem successful, the effectiveness of any street-level problem-solving efforts must be interpreted with caution.[74] It is possible that the criminals will be displaced to other, "safer" areas of the city and will return shortly after the program is called a success and the additional police forces have been pulled from the area.[75]

The core concepts of police work are changing as administrators recognize the limitations and realities of police work in modern society. The oft-repeated charge that police catch relatively few criminals and have little deterrent effect has had a tremendous influence on police policy. On the one hand, many departments are experimenting with programs designed to bring police officers into closer contact with the community to increase citizen cooperation in the fight against crime. Major cities, such as New York, have made implementing community policing models a priority.

If they are to be successful, community policing strategies must be able to react effectively to some significant administrative problems. Police administrators must be able to define the concept of community in terms of an ecological area defined by common norms, shared values, and interpersonal bonds.[76] After all, the main focus of community policing is to activate the community norms that make neighborhoods more crime-resistant. To do so requires a greater identification with ecological areas: if community policing projects cross the boundaries of many different neighborhoods, any hope of learning and accessing community norms, strengths, and standards will be lost.[77]

In addition to the need to understand and identify actual community areas, police departments must also establish the exact role of community police agents. How should they integrate their activities with those of regular patrol forces? For example, should foot patrols have primary responsibility for policing in an area, or should they coordinate their activities with officers assigned to patrol cars? Should community police officers be solely problem identifiers and neighborhood organizers, or should they also be expected to be law enforcement agents who get to the crime scene rapidly and later do investigative work? Can community police teams and regular patrols work together, or must a department abandon traditional police roles and become purely community policing oriented?

It may also be difficult to retrain and reorient police from their traditional roles into a more social service orientation. Most police officers do not have the social service skills required of effective community agents. Surveys report that while police officers are generally favorable to community policing, they also suffer ridicule from their peers because of the "cushy" assignment that is not "real" police work, that they are often unsure of what to do, and that their program has little effect on the crime rate.[78]

Because the community policing model calls for a revision of the police role from law enforcer to community organizer, police training must be revised to reflect this new mandate. Mid-level managers must be recruited and trained who are receptive to and can implement community-change strategies.[79] If community policing is to be adopted on a wide scale, a whole new type of police officer must be recruited and trained in a whole new way. Although these are formidable obstacles to overcome, there is growing evidence that community and problem-oriented policing can work and fit well with traditional forms of policing.[80] Many police experts and administrators have embraced the community and problem-oriented policing concepts as revolutionary revisions of the basic police role. Community policing efforts have been credited with helping reduce crime rates in large cities such as New York and Boston. The most professional and highly motivated officers are the ones most likely to support community policing efforts.[81]

Support Functions

As the model of a typical police department in Figure 6.1 (see page 166) indicates, not all members of a department engage in what the general public regards as "real police work"—patrol, detection, and traffic control. Even in departments that are embracing community and problem-oriented policing, a great deal of police resources are actually devoted to support and administrative functions. While there are too many tasks to mention all in detail, the most important include those discussed here.

Personnel

Many police departments maintain their own personnel service, which carries out such functions as recruiting new police officers, creating exams to determine the most qualified applicants, and handling promotions and transfers.

Internal Affairs

Larger police departments often maintain an **internal affairs** branch, which is charged with policing the police. Internal affairs officers process citizen complaints of police corruption, investigate what may be the unnecessary use of force by police officers, and even probe police participation in actual criminal activity, such as burglaries or narcotics violations. In addition, internal affairs divisions may assist police managers when disciplinary action is brought against individual officers.

Internal affairs is a controversial function since investigators are feared and distrusted by fellow police officers. Nonetheless, rigorous self-scrutiny is the only way police departments can earn the respect of citizens.

Budget and Finance

Most police departments are responsible for the administration and control of their own budgets. This task includes administering payroll, purchasing equipment and services, planning budgets for future expenditures, and auditing departmental financial records.

Records and Communication

Police departments maintain separate units that are charged with maintaining and disseminating information on wanted offenders, stolen merchandise, traffic violators, and so on. Modern data management systems enable police to use their records in a highly sophisticated fashion. For example, officers in a patrol car who spot a suspicious-looking vehicle can instantly receive a computerized rundown on whether it has been stolen. Or, if property is recovered during an arrest, police using this sort of system can determine who reported the loss of the merchandise and arrange for its return.

Another important function of police communication is the effective and efficient dispatching of patrol cars. Again, modern computer technologies have been used to make the most of available resources.[82]

Training

In many departments, training is continuous throughout an officer's career. Training usually begins at a police academy, which may be run exclusively for larger departments or be part of a regional training center servicing smaller and varied governmental units. More than 90% of all police departments require pre-service training, including almost all departments in larger cities (population

Police departments provide emergency aid to the ill, counseling for youngsters, speakers for school and community agencies on safety and drug abuse, and countless other services designed to improve citizen-police interactions. Here a community service officer establishes a bond with youngsters on a local playground.

over 100,000). The average officer receives more than 500 hours of preservice training, including 400 hours in the classroom and the rest in field training. Police in large cities receive over 1,000 hours of instruction divided almost evenly between classroom and field instruction.[83] Among the topics usually covered are law and civil rights, firearms handling, emergency medical care, and restraint techniques.[84]

After assuming their police duties, new recruits are assigned to field-training officers who break them in on the job. However, training does not stop here. On-the-job training is a continuous process in the modern police department and covers such areas as weapons skills, first aid, crowd control, and community relations. Some departments use **roll call training,** in which superior officers or outside experts address police officers at the beginning of the workday. Other departments allow police officers time off to attend annual training sessions to sharpen their skills and learn new policing techniques.

Community Relations

Police departments provide emergency aid to the ill, counsel youngsters, speak to school and community agencies on safety and drug abuse, and provide countless other services designed to improve citizen-police interactions.

Crime Prevention

Larger police departments maintain specialized units that help citizens protect themselves from criminal activity. For example, they advise citizens on effective home security techniques or conduct Project ID campaigns—engraving valuables with an identifying number so that they can be returned if recovered after a burglary; police also work in schools teaching kids how to avoid drug abuse.[85]

Laboratory

Police agencies maintain (or have access to) forensic laboratories that enable them to identify substances to be used as evidence and classify fingerprints.

Planning and Research

Planning and research functions include designing programs to increase police efficiency and strategies to test program effectiveness. Police planners monitor recent technological developments and institute programs to adapt them to police services.

Government spending cutbacks forced by inflation and legislative tax-cutting measures have prompted belt-tightening in many areas of public service. Police departments have not been spared the budgetary pinch caused by decreased government spending. To combat the probable damage that would result from police service cutbacks, police administrators have sought to increase the productivity of their line, support, and administrative staff.

As used today, the term **police productivity** refers to the amount of actual order, maintenance, crime control, and other law enforcement activities provided by individual police officers and concomitantly by police departments as a whole. By improving police productivity, a department can keep the peace, deter crime, apprehend criminals, and provide useful public services without necessarily increasing its costs. This goal is accomplished by having each police officer operate with greater efficiency, thus using fewer resources to achieve greater effectiveness.

Despite the emphasis on increasing police effectiveness, serious questions have been raised about how the police accomplish their assigned tasks.[86] One basic complaint has been that the average patrol officer spends relatively little time on what is considered real police work. More often than not, highly skilled police officers can be found writing reports, waiting in court corridors, getting involved in domestic disputes, and handling what are generally characterized as "miscellaneous noncriminal matters." Police departments are now experimenting with cost-saving reforms that maximize effectiveness while saving taxpayer dollars. For example, J. David Hirschel and Charles Dean describe how a program to summon offenders to court via a "field citation" is considerably cheaper than a formal arrest. Factoring in the cost of rearresting offenders who fail to appear in court, a citation program would save about $72 per case. Considering the millions of arrests made each year, the adoption of a citation policy could produce considerable savings, not to mention the cost-saving effect on the overcrowded jail system.[87] Other cost-saving productivity measures include consolidation, informal arrangements, sharing, pooling, contracting, police service districts, use of civilian employees, multiple tasking, special assignment programs, budget supplementation, and differential police responses.[88]

Consolidation

One way to increase police efficiency is to consolidate police services. This means combining small departments (usually with under ten employees) in ad-

Multiple law enforcement agencies cooperated at the site of the Oklahoma City bombing. It is common for a variety of police agencies to pool resources and cooperate, especially during a major disaster such as the 1995 bombing of the Murrah Federal Building.

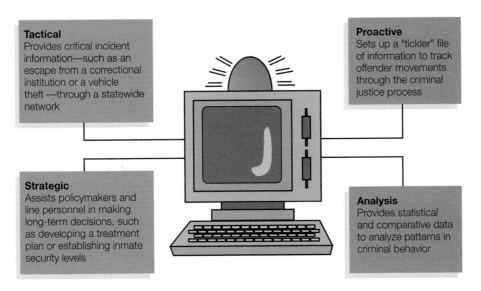

Tactical
Provides critical incident information—such as an escape from a correctional institution or a vehicle theft —through a statewide network

Proactive
Sets up a "tickler" file of information to track offender movements through the criminal justice process

Strategic
Assists policymakers and line personnel in making long-term decisions, such as developing a treatment plan or establishing inmate security levels

Analysis
Provides statistical and comparative data to analyze patterns in criminal behavior

Figure 6.4
Use of a statewide information network to provide information and services to law enforcement agencies.
Maryland's Data Service Division provides data to 174 agencies and 10,000 individual users.
SOURCE: Leonard Sipes, "Maryland's High-Tech Approach to Crime Fighting," *Police Chief* 61 (1994): 18.

joining areas into a superagency that services the previously fragmented jurisdictions. Consolidation has the benefit of creating departments large enough to use expanded services, such as crime labs, training centers, communications centers, and emergency units, that are not cost-effective in smaller departments. This procedure is controversial, since it demands that existing lines of political and administrative authority be drastically changed. Nonetheless, consolidation of departments or special services (such as a regional computer center) has been attempted in California (the Los Angeles Sheriff's Department), Massachusetts, New York, and Illinois.[89]

Informal Arrangements

Unwritten cooperative agreements may be made between localities to perform a task collectively that would be mutually beneficial (such as monitoring neighboring radio frequencies so that needed backup can be provided). An example is the Metro Task Force program implemented in New Jersey that commits state troopers to help local police officers in urban areas for limited times and assignments.[90]

Sharing

Sharing is the provision or reception of services that aid in the execution of a law enforcement function (such as the sharing of a communications system by several local agencies). Some agencies form *mutual aid pacts* so that they can share infrequently used emergency services such as SWAT and Emergency Response Teams.[91] Some states have gone as far as setting up centralized data services that connect most local police agencies into a statewide information net. Maryland's Data Services Division provides the services illustrated in Figure 6.4.[92]

Pooling

Some police agencies combine resources by two or more agencies to perform a specified function under a predetermined, often formalized arrangement with direct involvement by all parties. An example is the use of a city-county law enforcement building or training academy or the establishment of a crime task force.

Contracting

Another productivity measure is a limited and voluntary approach in which one government enters into a formal binding agreement to provide all or certain specified law enforcement services (such as communications or patrol service) to another government for an established fee. Many communities that contract for full law enforcement service do so at the time they incorporate to avoid the costs of establishing their own police capability. For example, five small towns in Florida (Pembroke Park, Lauderdale Lakes, Tamarac, Dania, and Deerfield Beach) contract with the Broward County Sheriff's Department to provide law enforcement for their communities; contracting saves each town millions of dollars.[93]

Police Service Districts

Some jurisdictions have set aside areas, usually within an individual county, where a special level of service is provided and financed through a special tax or assessment. In California, residents of an unincorporated portion of a county may petition to form such a district to provide more intensive patrol coverage than is available through existing systems. Such service may be provided by a sheriff, another police department, or a private person or agency. This system is used in Contra Costa and San Mateo counties in California and Suffolk and Nassau counties in New York.

Civilian Employees

One common cost-saving method is to use civilians in administrative support or even in some line activities. Civilians' duties have included operating communications gear; performing clerical work, planning, and research; and staffing traffic control (meter monitors). Using civilian employees can be a considerable savings to taxpayers, since their salaries are considerably lower than those of regular police officers. In addition, it allows trained, experienced officers to spend more time on direct crime control and enforcement activities.

Another form of civilian help comes in the form of COP programs that use civilian volunteers to supplement police services. For example, the "code blue" program in Fort Worth, Texas is designed to organize neighborhood watch groups that supplement police patrol while providing the delivery of on-site services unavailable before the program was instituted.[94]

Multiple Tasks

Some police officers are trained to carry out other functions of municipal government. For example, in a number of smaller departments, the roles of fire fighters and police officers have been merged into a job called a public safety officer. The idea is to increase the number of people trained in both areas to have the potential for putting more police at the scene of a crime or more fire fighters at a blaze than was possible when the two tasks were separated. The system provides greater coverage at far less cost.[95]

Special Assignments

Some departments train officers for special assignments that are required only occasionally. For example, the Special Enforcement Team in Lakewood, Colorado is trained in a variety of police tasks, such as radar operation, surveillance, traffic investigation, and criminal investigations, but specializes in tactical operations, such as crowd control and security.[96]

Budget Supplementation

It is now common for municipal agencies to seek out innovative sources of income to supplement the department's limited budget. For example, Chicago police instituted a private fund drive that raised over $1.5 million to purchase protective clothing, and other departments have created private foundations to raise funds to support police-related activities. Additional budget supplementing activities include conducting fund-raising events, using traffic fines for police services, enacting special taxes that go directly for police services, and auctioning goods forfeited by crime-involved individuals.

Differential Police Response (DPR)

Differential police response (DPR) strategies maximize resources by differentiating among police requests for services in terms of the form the police response takes. Some calls will result in the dispatch of a sworn officer, others in the dispatching of a less highly trained civilian; calls considered low priority are handled by asking citizens to walk in or to mail in their requests.[97]

In sum, police departments are now implementing a variety of administrative models designed to stretch resources while still providing effective police services.

Criminal Justice on the Net

One of the best sources of information about the police profession is the International Association of Chiefs of Police (IACP). The IACP is the world's senior law enforcement executive association. Founded in 1893, IACP comprises over 14,000 members representing 80 nations. It is headquartered in Alexandria, Virginia, with a permanent staff of approximately 50. Over 150 working professionals serve on the faculty. IACP is guided by an advisory board of 52 police executives representing international, federal, state, and local law enforcement agencies. This group provides policy direction to the professional staff and the association's diverse working groups, divisions, committees, and sections made up of the heads of law enforcement agencies from throughout the world. The groups address contemporary issues facing law enforcement. Learn more about IACP at

http://www.amdahl.com/ext/iacp/

The National Institute of Justice, Office of Science and Technology maintains the Justice Technology Information Network (JUSTNET). This is a service of the National Law Enforcement and Corrections Technology Center (NLECTC), a program of the National Institute of Justice. JUSTNET serves as an information gateway for law enforcement, corrections, and criminal justice technology information, including

- News and information
- National Institute of Justice's Office of Science and Technology
- Regional technology centers services
- News and hot topics from NLECTC
- Manufacturers' worldwide web sites
- Other law enforcement information resources:
  Interactive services
  Data and publications
  Database reports
  Information services and publications
  Standards and testing

Find all this and more at

http://www.nlectc.org

Summary

Today's police departments operate in a military-like fashion; policy generally emanates from the top of the hierarchy. Most police officers, therefore, use a great deal of discretion when making on-the-job decisions.

The most common law enforcement agencies are local police departments, which carry out patrol and investigative functions, as well as many support activities. Many questions have been raised about the effectiveness of police work, and some research efforts seem to indicate that police are not effective crime fighters. However, indications exist that aggressive police work, the threat of formal action, and cooperation between departments can have a measurable impact on crime. To improve effectiveness, police departments have developed new methods of policing that stress community involvement and problem solving. They have also been concerned with developing more effective and productive methods for using their resources.

Key Terms

detective bureau
police chief
time-in-rank system
special-needs population
beats

order maintenance
peacekeeping
displacement
proactive
deterrent effect

recidivism
vice squads
detection
sting operations
police-community relations (PCR)

191

broken windows model
foot patrol
innovative neighborhood-oriented
    policing (INOP)

problem-oriented policing
hot spots of crime
internal affairs

roll call training
police productivity

Questions

1. Should the primary police role be law enforcement or community services?

2. Should a police chief be permitted to promote an officer with special skills to a supervisory position, or should all officers be forced to spend "time in rank"?

3. Do the advantages of proactive policing outweigh the disadvantages?

4. Should all police recruits take the same physical tests, or are different requirements permissible for male and female applicants?

5. Can the police and the community ever form a partnership to fight crime? Does the community policing model remind you of early forms of policing?

Notes

1. Clarence Schrag, *Crime and Justice: American Style* (Washington, D.C.: U.S. Government Printing Office, 1971), pp. 142–150.

2. Anthony Pate and Edwin Hamilton, *The Big Six: Policing America's Largest Cities* (Washington, D.C.: Police Foundation, 1990), pp. 129–130.

3. Velmer Burton, James Frank, Robert Langworthy, and Troy Barker, "The Prescribed Roles of Police in a Free Society: Analyzing State Legal Codes," *Justice Quarterly* 10 (1993): 683–695.

4. Federal Bureau of Investigation, *Crime in the United States, 1995* (Washington, D.C.: U.S. Government Printing Office, 1996), p. 174.

5. Cheryl Maxson, Margaret Little, and Malcolm Klein, "Police Response to Runaway and Missing Children: A Conceptual Framework for Research and Police," *Crime and Delinquency* 34 (1988): 84–102.

6. David Carter and Allen Sapp, "Police Experiences and Responses Related to the Homeless," *Journal of Criminal Justice* 16 (1993): 87–96; Peter Finn and Monique Sullivan, *Police Response to Special Populations* (Washington, D.C.: National Institute of Justice, 1988).

7. Brian Reaves and Pheny Smith, *Law Enforcement Management and Administrative Statistics, 1993: Data for Individual State and Local Agencies with 100 or More Officers* (Washington, D.C.: Bureau of Justice Statistics, 1995).

8. Edward Ammann and Jim Hey, "The Discretionary Patrol Unit," *FBI Law Enforcement Bulletin* 58 (1989): 19–22.

9. American Bar Association, *Standards Relating to Urban Police Function* (New York: Institute of Judicial Administration, 1974), standard 2.2.

10. Albert J. Reiss, *The Police and the Public* (New Haven, Conn.: Yale University Press, 1971), p. 19.

11. James Q. Wilson, *Varieties of Police Behavior: The Management of Law and Order in Eight Communities* (Cambridge, Mass.: Harvard University Press, 1968).

12. See Harlan Hahn, "A Profile of Urban Police," in *The Ambivalent Force,* ed. A. Niederhoffer and A. Blumberg (Hinsdale, Ill.: Dryden Press, 1976), p. 59.

13. George Kelling, Tony Pate, Duane Dieckman, and Charles Brown, *The Kansas City Preventive Patrol Experiment: A Summary Report* (Washington, D.C.: Police Foundation, 1974).

14. Ibid., pp. 3–4.

15. Ibid.

16. James Q. Wilson and Barbara Boland, "The Effect of Police on Crime," *Law and Society Review* 12 (1978): 367–384.

17. Robert Sampson, "Deterrent Effects of the Police on Crime: A Replication and Theoretical Extension," *Law and Society Review* 22 (1988): 163–191.

18. For a thorough review of this issue, see Andrew Karmen, "Why Is New York City's Murder Rate Dropping So Sharply?" (New York: John Jay College, 1996).

19. Alexander Weiss and Sally Freels, "The Effects of Aggressive Policing: The Dayton Traffic Enforcement Experiment," *American Journal of Police* 15 (1996): 45–63.

20. Lawrence Sherman, "Policing Communities: What Works," in *Crime and Justice,* vol. 8, ed. A. J. Reiss and Michael Tonry (Chicago: University of Chicago Press, 1986), pp. 366–379.

21. Ibid., p. 368.

22. H. Lawrence Ross, *Deterring the Drunk Driver: Legal Policy and Social Control* (Lexington, Mass.: D. C. Heath, 1982); Samuel Walker, *Sense and Nonsense About Crime* (Belmont, Calif.: Wadsworth, 1985), pp. 82–85.

23. Perry Shapiro and Harold Votey, "Deterrence and Subjective Probabilities of Arrest: Modeling Individual Decisions to Drink and Drive in Sweden," *Law and Society Review* 18 (1984): 111–149.

24. Mitchell Chamlin, "Crime and Arrests: An Autoregressive Integrated Moving Average (ARIMA) Approach," *Journal of Quantitative Criminology* 4 (1988): 247–255.

25. Frances Lawrenz, James Lembo, and Thomas Schade, "Time Series Analysis of the Effect of a Domestic Violence Directive on the Number of Arrests per Day," *Journal of Criminal Justice* 17 (1989): 493–499.

26. Kathleen Ferraro, "Policing Woman Battering," *Social Problems* 36 (1989): 61–74.

27. See Richard Berk, Gordon Smyth, and Lawrence Sherman, "When Random Assignment Fails: Some Lessons from the Minneapolis Spouse Abuse Experiment," *Journal of Quantitative Criminology* 4 (1989): 209–223.

28. J. David Hirschel, Ira Hutchison, and Charles Dean, "The Failure of Arrest to Deter Spouse Abuse," *Journal of Research in Crime and Delinquency* 29 (1992): 7–33; Franklyn Dunford, David Huizinga, and Delbert Elliott, "The Role of Arrest in Domestic Assault: The Omaha Experiment," *Criminology* 28 (1990): 183–206; David Hirschel, Ira Hutchinson, Charles Dean, Joseph Kelley, and Carolyn Pesackis, *Charlotte Spouse Abuse Replication Project: Final Report* (Washington, D.C.: National Institute of Justice, 1990).

29. Lawrence Sherman, Janell Schmidt, Dennis Rogan, Patrick Gartin, Ellen Cohn, Dean Collins, and Anthony Bacich, "From Initial Deterrence to Long-Term Escalation: Short-Custody Arrest for Poverty Ghetto Domestic Violence," *Criminology* 29 (1991): 821–850.

30. Simon Singer, "The Fear of Reprisal and the Failure of Victims to Report a Personal Crime," *Journal of Quantitative Criminology* 4 (1988): 289–302.

31. Craig Uchida and Robert Goldberg, *Police Employment and Expenditure Trends* (Washington, D.C.: Bureau of Justice Statistics, 1986).

32. Colin Loftin and David McDowall, "The Police, Crime, and Economic Theory: An Assessment," *American Sociological Review* 47 (1982): 393–401.

33. Joan Petersilia, Allan Abrahamse, and James Q. Wilson, "A Summary of RAND's Research on Police Performance, Community Characteristics and Case Attrition," *Journal of Police Science and Administration* 17 (1990): 219–229.

34. See Belton Cobb, *The First Detectives* (London: Faber & Faber, 1957).

35. See, for example, James Q. Wilson, "Movie Cops—Romantic vs. Real," *New York Magazine,* 19 August 1968, pp. 38–41.

36. For a view of the modern detective, see William Sanders, *Detective Work: A Study of Criminal Investigations* (New York: Free Press, 1977).

37. James Ahern, *Police in Trouble* (New York: Hawthorn Books, 1972), pp. 83–85.

38. James Q. Wilson, *The Investigators: Managing FBI and Narcotics Agents* (New York: Basic Books, 1978), pp. 21–23.

39. Robert Langworthy, "Do Stings Control Crime? An Evaluation of a Police Fencing Operation," *Justice Quarterly* 6 (1989): 27–45.

40. *Jacobson v. United States,* 60 U.S.L.W. 4307 (1992).

41. Peter Greenwood and Joan Petersilia, *Summary and Policy Implications,* vol. 1 of *The Criminal Investigation Process* (Santa Monica, Calif.: Rand Corporation, 1975).

42. Mark Willman and John Snortum, "Detective Work: The Criminal Investigation Process in a Medium-Size Police Department," *Criminal Justice Review* 9 (1984): 33–39.

43. Police Executive Research Forum, *Calling the Police: Citizen Reporting of Serious Crime* (Washington, D.C., 1981).

44. John Eck, *Solving Crimes: The Investigation of Burglary and Robbery* (Washington, D.C.: Police Executive Research Forum, 1984).

45. Egon Bittner, *The Functions of Police in Modern Society* (Cambridge, Mass.: Oelgeschlager, Gunn & Hain, 1980), p. 8; see also James Q. Wilson, "The Police in the Ghetto," in *The Police and the Community,* ed. Robert F. Steadman (Baltimore: Johns Hopkins University Press, 1974), p. 68.

46. George Kelling, *Police and Communities: The Quiet Revolution* (Washington, D.C.: National Institute of Justice, 1988).

47. Ibid.

48. George Kelling and James Q. Wilson, "Broken Windows: The Police and Neighborhood Safety," *Atlantic Monthly* 249 (1982): 29–38.

49. For a general review, see Robert Trojanowicz and Bonnie Bucqueroux, *Community Policing: A Contemporary Perspective* (Cincinnati: Anderson Publishing, 1990).

50. Police Foundation, *The Newark Foot Patrol Experiment* (Washington, D.C., 1981).

51. Ray Leal and Armando Abney, "The Effectiveness of Police Bicycle Patrol in a High Urban Crime Area," paper presented at the annual meeting of the American Society of Criminology, San Francisco, November 1991.

52. Lawrence Holland, "Police and the Community—the Detroit Experience," *FBI Law Enforcement Bulletin* 54 (1985): 1–6.

53. Ibid.

54. Trojanowicz and Bucqueroux, *Community Policing: A Contemporary Perspective,* p. 189.

55. Mark Moore and Robert Trojanowicz, *Policing and the Fear of Crime* (Washington, D.C.: National Institute of Justice, 1988), p. 5.

56. George Kelling, *What Works—Research and the Police* (Washington, D.C.: National Institute of Justice, 1988), p. 3.

57. Police Foundation, *The Effects of Police Fear Reduction Strategies: A Summary of Findings from Houston and Newark* (Washington, D.C., 1986).

58. Quint Thurman, Andrew Giacomazzi, and Phil Bogen, "Research Note: Cops, Kids, and Community Policing—An Assessment of a Community Policing Demonstration Project," *Crime and Delinquency* 39 (1993): 554–564.

59. For an analysis, see Lisa Riechers and Roy Roberg, "Community Policing: A Critical Review of Underlying Assumptions," *Journal of Police Science and Administration* 17 (1990): 105–113.

60. See, generally, Lee Brown, "Community Policing: A Practical Guide for Police Executives," in *Perspectives in Policing* (Washington, D.C.: U.S. Government Printing Office, 1989), pp. 1–11.

61. Susan Sadd and Randolph Grinc, *Implementation Challenges in Community Policing* (Washington, D.C.: National Institute of Justice, 1996).

62. Lee Brown, "Neighborhood-Oriented Policing," *American Journal of Police* 9 (1990): 197–207.

63. Walter Baranyk, "Making a Difference in a Public Housing Project," *Police Chief* 61 (1994): 31–35.

64. Jerome Skolnick and David Bayley, *Community Policing: Issues and Practices Around the World* (Washington, D.C.: National Institute of Justice, 1988).

65. Ibid., p. 17.

66. Herman Goldstein, "Improving Policing: A Problem-Oriented Approach," *Crime and Delinquency* 25 (1979): 236–258.

67. Skolnick and Bayley, *Community Policing,* p. 12.

68. Lawrence Sherman, Patrick Gartin, and Michael Buerger, "Hot Spots of Predatory Crime: Routine Activities and the Criminology of Place," *Criminology* 27 (1989): 27–55.

69. Ibid., p. 45.

70. Dennis Roncek and Pamela Maier, "Bars, Blocks, and Crimes Revisited: Linking the Theory of Routine Activities to the Empiricism of 'Hot Spots,'" *Criminology* 29 (1991): 725–753.

71. E. Nick Larsen, "Community Policing and the Control of Street Prostitution," paper presented at the annual meeting of the American Society of Criminology, Chicago, November 1996.

72. Herman Goldstein, "Toward Community-Oriented Policing: Potential, Basic Requirements, and Threshold Questions," *Crime and Delinquency* 33 (1987): 6–30.

73. Lynn Zimmer, "Proactive Policing Against Street-Level Drug Trafficking," *American Journal of Police* 9 (1990): 43–65.

74. Bureau of Justice Assistance, *Problem-Oriented Drug Enforcement: A Community-Based Approach for Effective Policing* (Washington, D.C.: National Institute of Justice, 1993).

75. Ibid., pp. 64–65.

76. Jack R. Greene, "The Effects of Community Policing on American Law Enforcement: A Look at the Evidence," paper presented at the International Congress on Criminology, Hamburg, Germany, September 1988, p. 19.

77. Roger Dunham and Geoffrey Alpert, "Neighborhood Differences in Attitudes Toward Policing: Evidence for a Mixed-Strategy Model of Policing in a Multi-Ethnic Setting," *Journal of Criminal Law and Criminology* 79 (1988): 504–522.

78. "Community Policing Officers See Benefits in Citizen Relations," *Criminal Justice Newsletter* 27 15 February 1986, pp. 4–5.

79. Riechers and Roberg, "Community Policing: A Critical Review of Underlying Assumptions," pp. 112–113.

80. David Kessler, "Integrating Calls for Service with Community- and Problem-Oriented Policing: A Case Study," *Crime and Delinquency* 39 (1993): 485–508.

81. L. Thomas Winfree, Gregory Bartku, and George Seibel, "Support for Community Policing Versus Traditional Policing Among Nonmetropolitan Police Officers: A Survey of Four New Mexico Police Departments," *American Journal of Police* 15 (1996): 23–47.

82. See, for example, Richard Larson, *Urban Police Patrol Analysis* (Cambridge, Mass.: MIT Press, 1972).

83. Brian Reaves, *State and Local Police Departments, 1990* (Washington, D.C.: Bureau of Justice Statistics, 1992), p. 6.

84. Philip Ash, Karen Slora, and Cynthia Britton, "Police Agency Officer Selection Practices," *Journal of Police Science and Administration* 17 (1990): 258–269.

85. Dennis Rosenbaum, Robert Flewelling, Susan Bailey, Chris Ringwalt, and Deanna Wilkinson, "Cops in the Classroom: A Longitudinal Evaluation of Drug Abuse Resistance Education (DARE)," *Journal of Research in Crime and Delinquency* 31 (1994): 3–31.

86. Greenwood and Petersilia, *Summary and Policy Implications;* Peter Greenwood et al., *Observations and Analysis,* vol. 3 of *The Criminal Investigation Process* (Santa Monica, Calif.: Rand Corporation, 1975).

87. J. David Hirschel and Charles Dean, "The Relative Cost-Effectiveness of Citation and Arrest," *Journal of Criminal Justice* 23 (1995): 1–12.

88. Adapted from Terry Koepsell and Charles Gerard, *Small Police Agency Consolidation: Suggested Approaches* (Washington, D.C.: U.S. Government Printing Office, 1979).

89. Thomas McAninch and Jeff Sanders, "Police Attitudes Toward Consolidation in Bloomington/Normal, Illinois: A Case Study," *Journal of Police Science and Administration* 16 (1988): 95–105.

90. James Garofalo and Dave Hanson, *The Metro Task Force: A Program of Intergovernmental Cooperation in Law Enforcement* (Washington, D.C.: National Institute of Justice, 1984).

91. Mike D'Alessandro and Charles Hoffman, "Mutual Aid Pacts," *Law and Order* 43 (1995): 90–93.

92. Leonard Sipes, Jr., "Maryland's High-Tech Approach to Crime Fighting," *Police Chief* 61 (1994): 18–20.

93. Nick Navarro, "Six Broward County Cities Turn to the Green and Gold," *Police Chief* 59 (1992): 60.

94. Greg Givens, "A Concept to Involve Citizens in the Provision of Police Services," *American Journal of Police* 12 (1993): 1–9; for a review, see, Stephen Mastrofski, "Varieties of Community Policing," *American Journal of Police* 12 (1993): 65–75.

95. For a detailed review of this issue, see John Crank, "Patterns of Consolidation Among Public Safety Departments, 1978–1988," *Journal of Police Science and Administration* 17 (1990): 277–288.

96. Kenneth Perry, "Tactical Units Reduce Overtime Costs," *Police Chief* 52 (1985): 57–58.

97. Robert Worden, "Toward Equity and Efficiency in Law Enforcement: Differential Police Response," *American Journal of Police* 12 (1993): 1–24.

Chapter 6

The Police: Role and Function

CHAPTER 7

Issues in Policing

S *ociety's trashy behavior winds up in cops' hands.*—William Bennett[1]

For the past three decades, much public interest has focused on the function of police. The U.S. public seems genuinely concerned today about the quality and effectiveness of local police. Most citizens seem to approve of their local law enforcement agents; 60% say they have a "great deal of confidence" in the police.[2] While this is encouraging, approval is skewed along racial lines: Whites are almost twice as likely to have confidence in the police (65%) than African American citizens (31%).

The general public is not the only group concerned about police attitudes and behavior. Police administrators and other law enforcement experts have focused their attention on issues that may influence the effectiveness and efficiency of police performance in the field. Some of their concerns are outgrowths of the development of policing as a profession: Does an independent police culture exist, and what are its characteristics? Do police officers develop a unique "working personality," and if so, does it influence their job performance? Are there police officer "styles" that make some police officers too aggressive and others inert and passive? Is policing too stressful an occupation?

Another area of concern is the social composition of police departments: Who should be recruited as police officers? Are minorities and women being attracted to police work, and what have their experiences been on the force? Should police officers have a college education?

Important questions are also being raised about the problems police departments face interacting with the society they are entrusted with supervising: Are police officers too forceful and brutal, and do they discriminate in their use of deadly force? Are police officers corrupt, and how can police deviance be controlled?

All professions have unique characteristics that distinguish them from other occupations and institutions. Policing is no exception. Police experts have long sought to understand the unique nature of the police experience and determine how the challenges of police work shape the field and its employees. In this section, some of the factors that make policing unique are discussed in detail. The accompanying box on Criminal Justice and the Media discusses *NYPD Blue,* which has as a theme the police profession.

NYPD Blue

The gritty police drama *NYPD Blue* presents the on-going saga of a group of streetwise New York detectives assigned to the One-Five precinct. Detective Andy Sipowicz (Dennis Franz) is a recovering alcoholic who lost both his family and his self-respect after battling the bottle for decades. Although now sober and happily married to assistant district attorney Sylvia Costas (Sharon Lawrence), Sipowicz is easily enraged by the deadbeats he meets on the job. He exhibits multiple personality traits, at times a coarse racist and at other times a kind, good-hearted man with high morals. Sipowicz is tortured by the death of his older son, Andy Jr., who was killed while trying to prevent a robbery.

Paired with Sipowicz is his alter ego, Detective Bobby Simone (Jimmy Smits). Simone is smooth, articulate, and attractive. Although bearing his own pain from a tough childhood and the death of his wife from breast cancer, he is able to contain his emotions behind a cool facade. While he and Sipowicz don't always see eye to eye on cases, they are both dogged investigators who have mastered the technique of getting suspects to confess and implicate others.

Among other detectives in the precinct is Diane Russell, also a recovering alcoholic, who is romantically involved with Bobby Simone. Russell's traumatic childhood with a sexually abusive father has left her emotionally scarred. Lieutenant Arthur Fancy (James McDaniel), an African American who leads the squad, is acutely aware of the scrutiny he's placed under by his superiors. Fancy commands everyone's respect because he is a stand-up guy willing to give detectives like Sipowicz some slack when they err in judgment. Rounding out the cast is a Detective James Martinez (Nicholas Turturro), a young, idealistic Latino officer, and Detective Greg Medavoy (Gordon Clapp) who, despite being a walking bundle of neuroses and insecurity, is a good investigator who has managed to earn the respect of his co-workers. Over the years of the show's production, a number of other characters have drifted in and out of the cast, the most important of which was Detective John Kelly (David Caruso), Sipowicz's longtime partner.

NYPD Blue aims for authenticity by using New York street scenes and characters. Unlike so many other cop shows and movies, few criminals are affluent, highly educated society folk. The detectives rarely use their weapons, engage in high-speed chases, or pursue criminals by jumping from one rooftop to another. They

rarely sustain injury or get beaten to a pulp by criminals only to be on the job an hour later (that's for Bruce Willis in *Die Hard* and Mel Gibson in *Lethal Weapon*). In fact, the thought of Sipowicz jumping from one rooftop to another or pursuing a criminal down the street is ludicrous: It is doubtful whether he can lace up his own shoes.

Like their real-life counterparts, the detectives have a myriad social and personal problems, including obesity and alcoholism, conditions that rarely afflict superheros (Medavoy and Sipowicz are always dieting; Sipowicz and Russell are members of Alcoholics Anonymous). However, like other fictional detectives, the squad always solve their cases, get the bad guys to talk, and are able to concentrate on a single case for days on end till it is solved. The most glaring inconsistency, though, is Bobby Simone's wardrobe. Any detective who dressed as well as Simone would come under the scrutiny of the Internal Affairs Division, wanting him to explain how he affords his Calvin Klein suits and Armani jackets on a detective's pay!

Police experts have found that the experience of becoming a police officer and the nature of the job itself cause most officers to band together in a police subculture, characterized by cynicism, clannishness, secrecy, and insulation from others in society—the so-called **blue curtain.** Police officers tend to socialize together and believe that their occupation cuts them off from relationships with civilians. Joining the police subculture means always having to stick up for fellow officers against outsiders, maintaining a tough, macho exterior personality, and distrusting the motives and behavior of outsiders.[3]

Six core beliefs are viewed as being the heart of the police culture today:

1. Police are the only real crime fighters. The public wants the police officer to fight crime; other agencies, both public and private, only play at crime fighting.

2. No one else understands the real nature of police work. Lawyers, academics, politicians, and the public in general have little concept of what it means to be a police officer.

3. Loyalty to colleagues counts above everything else. Police officers have to stick together because everyone is out to get the police and make the job more difficult.

4. It is impossible to win the war against crime without bending the rules. Courts have awarded criminal defendants too many civil rights.

5. Members of the public are basically unsupportive and unreasonably demanding. People are quick to criticize police unless they need police help themselves.

6. Patrol work is the pits. Detective work is glamorous and exciting.[4]

These cultural beliefs make it difficult for police to accept new ideas and embrace innovative concepts, such as community policing.

The forces that support a police culture generally are believed to develop out of on-the-job experiences. Most officers, both male and female, originally join police forces because they want to help people, fight crime, and have an interesting, exciting, prestigious career with a high degree of job security.[5] Recruits often find that the social reality of police work does not mesh with their original career goals. They are unprepared for the emotional turmoil and conflict that accompany police work today.

Membership in the police culture helps recruits adjust to the rigors of police work and provides the emotional support needed for survival.[6] The culture encourages decisiveness in the face of uncertainty and the ability to make split-second judgments that may later be subject to extreme criticism. Hard-core officers who view themselves as crime fighters are the ones most likely to value solidarity and depend on the support and camaraderie of their fellow officers.[7]

In sum, the police culture has developed in response to the insulated, dangerous lifestyle of police officers. Policing is a dangerous occupation, and the availability of unquestioned support and loyalty of their peers is not something officers could readily do without.[8]

Police officers develop a unique set of personality traits that distinguish them from the average citizen. The typical police personality has been described as dogmatic, authoritarian, suspicious, racist, hostile, insecure, conservative, and cynical.[9] **Cynicism** has been found on all levels of policing, including among chiefs of police, and throughout all stages of a police career.[10] Maintenance of these negative values and attitudes is believed to cause police officers to be secretive and isolated from the rest of society, producing the blue curtain.[11]

The police officer's "working personality" is shaped by constant exposure to danger and the need to use force and authority to reduce and control threatening situations.[12] Police feel suspicious of the public they serve and defensive about the actions of their fellow officers.

There are two opposing viewpoints on the cause of this phenomenon. One position holds that police departments attract recruits who are by nature cynical, authoritarian, secretive, and so on.[13] Other experts maintain that socialization and experience on the police force itself cause these character traits to develop in police officers.

Since the first research measuring police personality was published, numerous efforts have been made to determine whether the typical police recruit does indeed possess a unique personality that sets him or her apart from the average citizen. The results have been mixed.[14] While some research concludes that police values are different from those of the general adult population, other efforts reach an opposing conclusion; some have found that police officers are actually more psychologically healthy than the general population, less depressed and anxious, and more social and assertive.[15] Recent research on police personality found that police officers highly value such personality traits as warmth, flexibility, and emotion; these traits are far removed from rigidity and cynicism.[16]

Since research has found evidence supportive of both viewpoints, no one position dominates on the issue of how the police personality develops, or even if one actually exists.

In what is probably the most well-known study of police personality, *Behind the Shield* (1967), Arthur Niederhoffer examined the assumption that most police officers develop into cynics as a function of their daily duties.[17] Among his most important findings were that police cynicism did increase with length of service, that patrol officers with college educations become quite cynical if they are denied promotion, and that military-like police academy training caused new recruits to quickly become cynical about themselves. For example, Niederhoffer found that nearly 80% of first-day recruits believed that the police department was an "efficient, smoothly operating organization"; two months later, less than a third professed that belief. Similarly, half the new recruits believed that a police superior was "very interested in the welfare of his subordinates"; two months later, that number had declined to 13%.[18]

The development of negative attitudes by police officers may have an extremely damaging effect on their job performance. A police officer's feelings of cynicism seem to intensify the need to maintain respect and exert authority over others.[19] As police escalate their use of authority, citizens learn to distrust and fear them. These feelings of hostility and anger in turn create feelings of potential danger among police officers, resulting in "police paranoia."[20] Cynical attitudes make police very conservative and resistant to change, factors that interfere with the efficiency of police work.[21]

Policing Style

Policing encompasses a multitude of diverse tasks, including peacekeeping, criminal investigation, traffic control, and providing emergency medical service. Part of the socialization as a police officer is developing a working attitude, or **style,** through which he or she approaches policing. For example, some police officers may view their job as a well-paid civil service position that stresses careful compliance with written departmental rules and procedures. Other officers may see themselves as part of the "thin blue line" that protects the public from wrongdoers. They will use any means to get the culprit, even if it involves such cheating as planting evidence on an obviously guilty person who so far has escaped arrest. Should the police bend the rules to protect the public? This has been referred to as the "Dirty Harry problem," after the popular Clint Eastwood movie character who routinely (and successfully) violated all known standards of police work.[22]

Several studies have attempted to define and classify police styles into behavioral clusters. These classifications, called *typologies,* attempt to categorize law enforcement agents by groups, each of which has a unique approach to police

work. The purpose of such classifications is to demonstrate that the police are not a cohesive, homogeneous group, as many believe, but rather are individuals with differing approaches to their work.[23] The way police approach their task and their attitude toward the police role, as well as their peers and superior officers, have been shown to affect police work. Somewhat surprisingly, officers who have the most negative attitudes toward peers and superiors may be the most likely to be aggressive and quick to make formal arrests.[24]

An examination of the literature suggests that four styles of police work seem to fit the current behavior patterns of most police agents: the crime fighter, the social agent, the law enforcer, and the watchman.

The Crime Fighter. To the **crime fighter,** the most important police work is investigating serious crimes and apprehending criminals. This type of police officer believes that murder, rape, and other major personal crimes should be the primary concerns of police agencies. They consider property crimes to be less significant, while such matters as misdemeanors, traffic control, and social service functions would be better handled by other agencies of government. This type of police officer believes that the ability to investigate criminal behavior that poses a serious threat to life and safety, combined with the power to arrest criminals, separates a police department from other municipal agencies. They see diluting these functions with minor social service and nonenforcement duties as harmful to police efforts to create a secure society.[25]

The Social Agent. Strongly opposed to the crime fighter is the sort of police officer described as the **social agent.** The social agent believes that police should be involved in a wide range of activities without regard for their connection to law enforcement. Rather than viewing themselves as criminal catchers, social agents consider themselves problem solvers. They are troubleshooters who patch the holes that appear where the social fabric wears thin. They are happy to work with special-needs populations, such as the homeless, schoolkids, and those in need of emergency services. The social agent fits well within a community policing unit.

The Law Enforcer. Like the crime fighter, the **law enforcer** tends to emphasize the detection and apprehension aspects of police work. Unlike the crime fighter, this police officer does not distinguish between major and minor crimes. Although a

Figure 7.1
Four police styles.

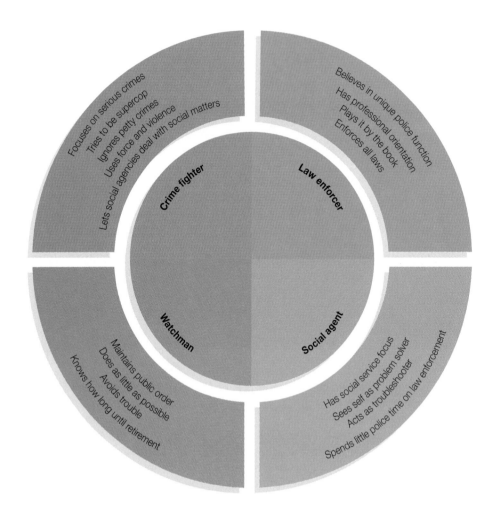

law enforcer may prefer working on serious crimes—they are more intriguing and rewarding in terms of achievement, prestige, and status—he or she sees the police role as one of enforcing all statutes and ordinances. According to this officer's view, duty is clearly set out in law, and the law enforcer stresses playing it "by the book." Since the police are specifically charged with apprehending all types of lawbreakers, they see themselves as generalized law enforcement agents. They do not perceive themselves as lawmakers or as judges of whether existing laws are fair; quite simply, legislators legislate, courts judge, and police officers perform the functions of detecting violations, identifying culprits, and taking the lawbreakers before a court. The law enforcer is devoted to the profession of police work and is the officer most likely to aspire to command rank.

The Watchman. The **watchman** style is characterized by an emphasis on the maintenance of public order as the police goal, rather than on law enforcement or general service.[26] Watchmen choose to ignore many infractions and requests for service unless they believe that the social or political order is jeopardized. Juveniles are "expected" to misbehave and are best ignored or treated informally. Motorists will often be left alone if their driving does not endanger or annoy others. Vice and gambling are problems only when the currently accepted standards of public order are violated.[27] The watchman is the most passive officer, more concerned with retirement benefits than crime rates.

Do Police Styles Actually Exist? As you may recall, the police role involves a great deal of time spent in noncrime service-related activities, ranging from providing emergency medical care to directing traffic. Although officers who admire one style of policing may emphasize one area of law enforcement over another, their daily activities will likely require them to engage in police duties they consider trivial or unimportant. While some pure types exist, an officer probably cannot specialize in one area of policing while ignoring the others.[28]

It is possible that today's police officer is more of a generalist than ever before and that future police recruits understand that they will be required to engage in a great variety of police tasks. Figure 7.1 summarizes the four police styles.

Style and role orientation may influence how police officers carry out their duties and the way they may use their **discretion**.[29] Police have the ability to deprive people of their liberty, to arrest them and take them away in handcuffs, and even to use deadly force to subdue them. A critical aspect of this professional responsibility is the personal discretion each officer has in carrying out his or her daily activities. Discretion can involve the selective enforcement of the law, as when a vice squad plainclothes officer decides not to take action against a tavern that is serving drinks after hours. Patrol officers use discretion when they decide to arrest one suspect for disorderly conduct but escort another home.

The majority of police officers use a high degree of personal discretion in carrying out daily tasks, sometimes referred to as "low visibility decision making" in criminal justice.[30] This terminology suggests that, unlike members of almost every other criminal justice agency, police are neither regulated in their daily procedures by administrative scrutiny nor subject to judicial review (except when their behavior clearly violates an offender's constitutional rights). As a result, the exercise of discretion by police may sometimes deteriorate into discrimination, violence, and other abusive practices. The following sections describe the factors that influence police discretion and review suggestions for its control.

Environment and Discretion

The degree of discretion an officer will exercise is at least partially defined by the living and working environment.[31] Police officers may work or dwell within a community culture that either tolerates eccentricities and personal freedoms or expects extremely conservative, professional, no-nonsense behavior on the part of its civil servants. The police officer who lives in the community he or she serves is probably strongly influenced by and shares a large part of the community's beliefs and values and is likely to be sensitive to and respect the wishes of neighbors, friends, and relatives. Conflict may arise, however, when the police officer commutes to an assigned area of jurisdiction, as is often the case in inner-city precincts. The officer who holds personal values in opposition to those of the community can exercise discretion in ways that conflict with the community's values and result in ineffective law enforcement.[32]

Another environmental factor affecting the police officer's performance is his or her perception of community alternatives to police intervention. A police officer may exercise discretion to arrest an individual in a particular circumstance if it seems that nothing else can be done, even if the officer does not believe that an arrest is the best possible example of good police work. In an environment that has a proliferation of social agencies—detoxification units, drug control centers, and childcare services, for example—a police officer will obviously have more alternatives to choose from in deciding whether to make the arrest. In fact, referring cases to these alternative agencies saves the officer both time and effort—records do not have to be made out and court appearances can be avoided. Thus, social agencies provide greater latitude in police decision making.

Departmental Influences

The policies, practices, and customs of the local police department are another influence on discretion. These conditions vary from department to department and strongly depend on the judgment of the chief and others in the organizational hierarchy. For example, departments can issue directives aimed at influencing

The policies, practices, and customs of the local police department influence discretion. A directive can instruct officers to be particularly alert for certain types of violations or to make some sort of interagency referral when specific events occur. For example, the department may order patrol officers to crack down on kids on the street who are violating a curfew ordinance. Without the directive, the officers might ignore such a minor infraction.

police conduct. Patrol officers may be asked to issue more tickets and make more arrests or to refrain from arresting under certain circumstances. Occasionally, a directive will instruct officers to be particularly alert for certain types of violations or to make some sort of interagency referral when specific events occur. For example, the department may order patrol officers to crack down on street panhandlers or to take formal action in domestic violence cases. These factors affect the decisions of the police officer, who has to produce appropriate performance statistics by the end of the month or be prepared to offer justification for following a course of action other than that officially prescribed.

The ratio of supervisory personnel to subordinates may also influence discretion: Departments with a high ratio of sergeants to patrol officers may experience fewer officer-initiated actions than one in which fewer eyes are observing the action in the streets. The size of the department may also determine the level of officer discretion. In larger departments, looser control by supervisors seems to encourage a level of discretion unknown in smaller, more tightly run police agencies.

Police discretion is also subject to peer pressure.[33] Police officers suffer a degree of social isolation because the job involves strange working conditions and hours, including being on 24-hour call, and their authority and responsibility to enforce the law cause embarrassment during social encounters. At the same time, officers must handle irregular and emotionally demanding encounters involving the most personal and private aspects of people's lives. As a result, police officers turn to their peers for both on-the-job advice and off-the-job companionship, essentially forming a subculture to provide a source of status, prestige, and reward.

The peer group affects how police officers exercise discretion on two distinct levels. In an obvious, direct manner, other police officers dictate acceptable responses to street-level problems by displaying or withholding approval in office discussions. Second, the officer who takes the job seriously and desires the respect and friendship of others will take their advice, abide by their norms, and seek out the most experienced and most influential patrol officers on the force and follow their behavior models.

Situational Influences

The situational factors attached to a particular crime provide another extremely important influence on police actions and behavior. Regardless of departmental or community influences, the officer's immediate interaction with a criminal act, offender, citizen, or victim will weigh heavily on the use of discretionary powers. While it is difficult to catalog every situational factor influencing police discretion, two stand out as having major significance.

Demeanor. Some early research efforts found that police officers rely heavily on **demeanor** (the attitude and appearance of the offender) in making decisions. If an offender was surly, talked back, or otherwise challenged the officer's authority, formal action was more likely to be taken.[34] Some recent research by David Klinger has challenged the influence of demeanor on police decision making, suggesting that it is criminal behavior and actions that occur during police detention and not negative attitude that influence the police decision to take formal action.[35] For example, a person who struggles or touches police during a confrontation is a likely candidate for arrest; merely having a "bad attitude" is not enough to generate police retaliation. Although Klinger's data are persuasive, the weight of the evidence seems to show that in many police-citizen interactions, a negative demeanor will result in formal police action.[36]

Encountering Crime. Another set of situational influences on police discretion concerns the manner in which a crime or situation is encountered. If, for example, a police officer stumbles on an altercation or break-in, the discretionary response may be quite different from a situation in which the officer is summoned by police radio. If an act has received official police recognition, such as the dispatch of a patrol car, police action must be taken or an explanation made as to why it was not. Or if a matter is brought to an officer's attention by a citizen observer, the officer can ignore the request and risk a complaint, or take discretionary action. When an officer chooses to become involved in a situation, without benefit of a summons or complaint, maximum discretion can be used. Even in this circumstance, however, the presence of a crowd or of witnesses may influence the officer's decision making.

And, of course, the officer who acts alone is also affected by personal matters—physical condition, mental state, police style, and whether he or she has other duties to perform.

Legal Factors

The likelihood of a police officer taking legal action may depend on how the individual views offense severity. Obviously, a serious felony will be handled much more formally than a petty offense. The relationship between the parties involved might also influence discretion. An altercation between two friends or relatives may be handled quite differently than an assault on a stranger. For example, research shows that at least in some jurisdictions, police are likely to treat domestic violence cases more casually than other assault cases.[37] There is evidence that police intentionally delay responding to domestic disputes hoping that by the time they get there the problem will be settled.[38]

Other legal factors that might influence police are the use of a weapon, seriousness of injury, and the presence of alcohol or drugs.

Extralegal Factors

One often-debated issue is whether police take race, class, and gender into account when making arrest decisions. The question is whether police discretion works against the young, males, the poor, and minority-group members and favors the wealthy, the politically connected, and majority-group members. Research has uncovered evidence supporting both sides of this argument.[39] Some research indicates that women, minorities, and the poor are victims of police discretion, while others indicate that gender, race, and income have little effect on police decision making.[40] This confusion is illustrated by two recent reviews of the literature that reached opposing conclusions. The first, by Ronald Weitzer, found that while police are involved in "at least some discrimination" against racial minorities "the frequency and scope of police discrimination may be less than anticipated." [41] In contrast, Samuel Walker, Cassia Spohn, and Miriam De-Lone concluded that police discriminate against racial minorities and that "significant problems persist between the police and racial and ethnic communities in the United States."[42] The Walker research concluded that despite progress, significant racial and ethnic disparities remain the norm.

One reason for this confusion is that extralegal influences on police decision making are often quite subtle and hard to detect. For example, there are some indications that the victim's race, and not the criminal's, is the key to racial bias: Police officers are more likely to take formal action when the victim of crime is white than when the victim is a minority-group member.[43] This finding suggests that any study of police discretion must take into account both victim and offender characteristics if it is to be truly valid.

Whether or not police discriminate against minorities in their use of discretion, minority citizens are much more likely to perceive that police are more apt to "hassle them": stop them or watch them closely when they have done nothing wrong. They are also more likely to know someone who has been mistreated by police. Perceptions of "hassling" may erode an individual's future relations with police and affect the police-community relations of a community as a whole.[44] For example, Darlene Conley found evidence that police frequently stop and question youths of color walking down the streets of their neighborhoods or standing on corners. Neighborhood kids told her how suspicion produces crime: If you're going to be harassed and "messed with," you might as well not care and commit crime.[45]

Police discretion is one of the most often debated issues in criminal justice (see Figure 7.2). On its face, the unequal enforcement of the law smacks of unfair-

Figure 7.2
Influences on police discretion.

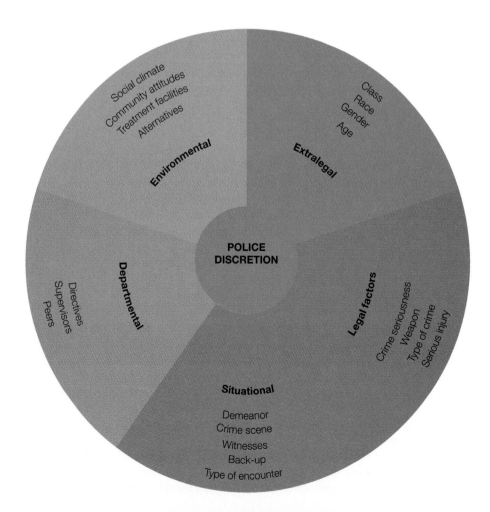

ness and violates the Constitution's doctrines of due process and equal protection. Yet if some discretion were not exercised, police would be forced to function as robots merely following the book. Administrators have sought to control discretion so that its exercise may be both beneficial to citizens and nondiscriminatory.[46]

The composition of the nation's police forces is changing. Traditionally, police agencies were comprised of white males with a high school education who viewed policing as a secure position that brought them the respect of their family and friends and a step up the social ladder. It was not uncommon to see police families in which one member of each new generation would enter the force. This picture has been changing and will continue to change. As criminal justice programs turn out thousands of graduates every year, an increasing number of police officers have at least some college education. In addition, affirmative action programs have helped slowly change the racial and gender composition of police departments to reflect community makeup. The following sections explore these changes in detail.

Police Education

In recent years, many police experts have argued that police recruits should have a college education. This development is not unexpected, considering that higher education for police officers has been recommended by national commissions on policing since 1931.[47] Although the great majority of U.S. police departments do not require a college education of their recruits, the trend for police officers to seek post–high school training has been spurred by the development of law enforcement and criminal justice academic programs and the availability of federal and state tuition aid. Yet, the most recent surveys indicate that only 1% of departments require a college degree and 7% an associates (AA) degree.

What are the benefits of higher education for police officers? Better communication with the public, especially minority and ethnic groups, is believed to be one benefit. Educated officers write better and more clearly and are more likely to be promoted. Police administrators believe that education enables officers to perform more effectively, generate fewer citizen complaints, show more initiative in performing police tasks, and generally act more professionally.[48] In addition, educated officers are less likely to have disciplinary problems and are viewed as better decision makers.[49] Studies have shown that college-educated police officers generate fewer citizen complaints and have better behavioral and performance characteristics than their less-educated peers.[50] Recent research by John Krimmel indicates that educated officers are more likely to rate themselves higher on most performance indicators, indicating that if nothing else higher education is associated with greater self-confidence and assurance.[51]

There is little evidence, however, that educated cops are more effective crime fighters; education appears to have relatively little influence on police officer behavior.[52] The diversity of the police role, the need for split-second decision making, and the often boring and mundane tasks police are required to do are all considered reasons formal education for police officers may be a waste of time.[53] For example, superiors find educated officers to be more reliable employees and better report writers, and citizens find them to be exceptional in the use of good judgment and problem solving.[54]

Although they may not require officers to have a college education, most police departments seem to value academic experience. A national survey of police education requirements found that 62% had at least one formal policy in support of officers pursuing higher education, and 58% required course work to be job-related.[55] While the scope of job-related education included a variety of subjects, about half of the surveyed departments expressed a preference for criminal justice majors, most often because of their enhanced knowledge of the entire criminal justice system and issues in policing. Another promising trend: While they did not require college credits for promotion, 82% of the departments recognized that college education is an important element in promotion decisions.

For the past two decades, U.S. police departments have made a concerted effort to attract female and minority police officers. The reasons for this effort are varied. Viewed in its most positive light, police departments recruit minority citizens to field a more balanced force that truly represents the communities they serve. A heterogeneous police force can be instrumental in gaining the public's confidence by helping dispel the view that police departments are generally bigoted or biased organizations. Furthermore, minority police officers possess special qualities that can serve to improve police performance. For example, Spanish-speaking officers can help with investigations in Hispanic neighborhoods, while Asian officers are essential for undercover or surveillance work with Asian gangs and drug importers. Figure 7.3 shows the racial and gender breakdown of the nation's largest police departments.

Minority Police Officers. The earliest known date of when an African American was hired as a police officer was 1861 in Washington, D.C.; Chicago hired its first black officer in 1872.[56] By 1890, an estimated 2,000 minority police officers were employed in the United States. At first, black officers suffered a great deal of discrimination. Their work assignments were restricted, as were their chances for promotion. Minority officers were often assigned solely to the patrol of black neighborhoods, and in some cities they were required to call a white officer to make an arrest. White officers held highly prejudicial attitudes, and as late as the 1950s some refused to ride with blacks in patrol cars.[57]

The experience of African American police officers has not been an easy one. In his classic 1969 book, *Black in Blue,* Nicholas Alex pointed out that black police officers of the time suffered from what he called **double marginality.**[58] On the one hand, black officers had to deal with the expectation that they would give members of their own race a break. On the other hand, they often experienced overt racism from their police colleagues. Alex found that black officers' adaptation to these pressures ranged from denying that black suspects should be treated differently from whites to treating black offenders more harshly than white offenders did to prove their lack of bias. Alex offered several reasons for some black police officers being tougher on black offenders: They desired acceptance from their white colleagues; they were particularly sensitive to any disrespect given them by black teenagers; and they viewed themselves as protectors of the black community.

These conflicts have become more muted. Minority officers now seem more aggressive and self-assured, less willing to accept any discriminatory practices by the police department.[59] They now appear to be experiencing some of the same

Figure 7.3
Women and minority local police officers, 1987, 1990, and 1993.

*Includes blacks, Hispanics, Asians, Pacific Islanders, American Indians, and Alaska Natives.

SOURCE: Brian Reaves, *Local Police Departments, 1993* (Washington, D.C.: Bureau of Justice Statistics, 1996).

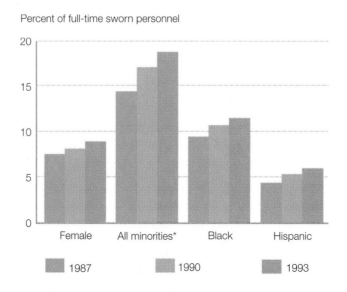

Percent of full-time sworn personnel

problems and issues encountered by white officers.[60] For example, minority police officers report feeling similar if somewhat higher rates of job-related stress and strain than white officers.[61] African American and white police officers share similar attitudes toward community policing (although minority police report being even more favorable toward it than white officers).[62] African American police officers may today be far less detached and alienated from the local community than white or Hispanic police officers.[63] Also helping is the fact that the number of African American officers in some of the nation's largest cities is now proportionate to minority representation in the population. For example, Los Angeles, Washington, D.C., Boston, and Pittsburgh, among other cities, now have police forces that represent their population.[64] So while minority police officers report feeling somewhat more job-related stress and strain than white officers do, it appears that they are on the path to overcoming the problems of double marginality.[65]

Affirmative Action. Despite these positive changes, minority police officers have been victims of intentional and sometimes unintentional departmental discrimination. For example, some departments, in an effort to provide representative coverage to minority areas of the city, assign all their black, Hispanic, or Asian officers to a single patrol area or beat, a practice ruled discriminatory by federal courts.[66] Minority police officers have resorted to lawsuits to seek relief from what they consider to be discriminatory or demeaning activity.[67]

A series of legal actions brought by minority representatives has resulted in local, state, and federal courts ordering police departments to create affirmative action programs to increase minority representation in police departments. One method has been to reformulate entrance exams and requirements to increase minority hiring. Court-ordered hiring was deemed necessary because as late as 1940, less than 1% of all police officers were minorities, and by 1950 the numbers had increased to only 2%.[68]

Numerous hiring plans have been implemented under court supervision. Sometimes the drive to recruit and promote minority officers forces police and city officials to reevaluate the results of normal testing procedures.[69] In 1987, in the case of **United States v. Paradise,** the Supreme Court upheld racial quotas as a means of reversing the effects of past discrimination. Ordering the Alabama Department of Public Safety to promote an equal number of black and white highway patrol officers, the Court said, "Discrimination at the entry level necessarily precluded blacks from competing and resulted in a departmental hierarchy dominated exclusively by nonminorities." The Alabama state patrol had no minority majors, captains, lieutenants, or sergeants, and only 4 of 66 corporals were black. The Court justified its ruling on the grounds that only qualified people would be promoted, the restriction was temporary, and it did not require layoffs of white officers.[70]

Court-ordered hiring has sometimes generated resentment among white officers who view affirmative action hiring and promotion programs as a threat to their job security. Despite the presence of such attitudes, many departments have voluntarily complied with minority hiring plans.[71] Minorities will continue to increase their presence on police forces, especially if the recruitment mechanisms ordered by courts are used. At the same time, police administrators will be challenged to encourage minority youth to consider careers in law enforcement, considering the fact that many hold negative attitudes about police.[72]

Female Police Officers. In 1910 Alice Stebbins Wells became the first woman to hold the title of police officer (in Los Angeles) and to have arrest powers.[73] For more than half a century, female officers endured separate criteria for selection, were given menial tasks, and were denied the opportunity for advancement.[74] Some relief was gained with the passage of the Civil Rights Act of 1964 and its subsequent amendments. Courts have consistently supported the addition of women to police forces by striking down entrance requirements that eliminated almost all female candidates but could not be proven to predict job performance (such as height and upper-body strength).[75] Females do not do as well as males on strength tests and are much more likely to fail the entrance physical than male recruits; critics contend that many of these tests do not reflect the actual tasks police do on the job.[76] Nonetheless, the role of women in police work is still restricted by social and administrative barriers that have been difficult to remove. Today, about 6% of all sworn officers are women.

Women continue to be underrepresented in the senior administrative ranks, and many believe they are assigned duties that underutilize their skills and training.[77] Policewomen become frustrated if they aspire to rise in police organizations when they begin to recognize that few women get promoted to command positions. Female recruits often lack successful female role models on which to shape their career aspirations.[78]

Gender bias is certainly not supported by existing research that indicates that female officers are highly successful police officers.[79] In an important study of recruits in the Metropolitan Police Department of Washington, D.C., policewomen were found to display extremely satisfactory work performances.[80] Compared to male officers, women were found to respond to similar types of calls, and the arrests they made were as likely to result in conviction. Women were more likely than their male colleagues to receive support from the community and were less likely to be charged with improper conduct. Policewomen seem to be more understanding and sympathetic to crime victims than male officers and are more likely to offer them treatment.[81]

Research has also debunked another enduring myth about female officers: that because they are less capable of subduing a suspect physically, they will be more likely to use their firearms. Actually, the opposite is true: Policewomen are less likely to use a firearm in violent confrontations than their male partners, are more emotionally stable, are less likely to seriously injure a citizen, and are no more likely to suffer injuries than their male partners.[82] These generally positive results are similar to findings developed in other studies conducted in major U.S. cities.[83]

Gender Conflicts.

On the surface, women have all the opportunities that the men have. They are, for the most part, in every unit in the police department. [But] have all the discrimi-

Despite the overwhelming evidence supporting their performance, policewomen have not always been fully accepted by their male peers or the general public. Nonetheless, policewomen have been promoted to advanced rank. Beverly Harvard, shown here when she was a captain, has been appointed chief of police of the Atlanta Police Department.

Chapter 7

—

Issues in Policing

208

nation fences been knocked down? Absolutely not, not until the last dinosaur's bones are buried.—Kathleen Burke, New York City police lieutenant, retired[84]

Despite the overwhelming evidence supporting their performance, police-women have not always been fully accepted by their male peers or the general public. Male officers complain that policewomen lack the emotional and physical strength to perform well in situations involving violence.[85] Some officers' wives resent their husbands having a female partner because they consider the police-woman not only a sexual threat but inadequate support in a violent encounter.[86] Studies of policewomen indicate that they are still struggling for acceptance, believe that they do not receive equal credit for their job performance, and report that it is common for them to be sexually harassed by their co-workers.[87] Recent surveys of male officers show that only one-third actually accept a woman on patrol and that more than half do not think that women can handle the physical requirements of the job as well as men.[88]

Gender conflict, jealousy, and stereotyping may be responsible in part for the spate of sexual harassment incidents involving some of the nation's largest police departments. In 1994, for example, the FBI compensated two female agents who had brought charges of being verbally harassed and physically assaulted by their supervisor.[89]

If evidence of gender equality could be proven beyond a doubt, it would be a blow to some male officers who have long been schooled in a macho police culture that is disrespectful of women; they could no longer regard police work as the "manly" profession they entered.[90] It is ironic that research now indicates that despite gender conflict, both male and female police officers share similar attitudes toward their role and occupational duties.[91]

Those female officers who fail to catch on to the unwritten police subculture are often written off as "bad police material."[92] Women who prove themselves tough enough to gain respect as police officers are then labeled as "lesbians" or "bitches" to neutralize their threat to male dominance, a process referred to as **defeminization**.[93] Male officers also generally assume that female officers who adopt an aggressive style of policing will be quicker to use deadly force than their male counterparts. Women working in this male-dominated culture can experience stress and anxiety.[94] It is not surprising, then, that significantly more female than male officers report being the victim of discrimination on the job. And the male officers who claim to have experienced gender-based discrimination suggest that it comes at the hands of female police officers who use their "sexuality" for job-related benefits.[95]

These perceptions of female officers are often based on gender stereotypes and are consequently incorrect.[96] Nonetheless, female officers are frequently caught in the classic catch-22 dilemma: If they are physically weak, male partners view them as a risk in street confrontations; if they are actually more powerful and aggressive than their male partners, they are regarded as an affront to the policeman's manhood.

Minority Female Officers. Black women, who account for only about 2%, occupy a unique status. In a recent study of black women police serving in five large municipal departments, Susan Martin found that they do in fact perceive significantly more racial discrimination than both other female officers and African American male officers.[97] However, white female officers were significantly more likely to perceive sexual discrimination than African American female officers were.

Martin found that black female officers often incur the hostility of both white women and African American men who feel threatened that they will take their place. On patrol, black female officers are treated differently than white females by male officers: Although neither group of females are viewed as equals, the white female officers are protected and coddled while black females are viewed as passive, lazy, and unequal. In the stationhouse, male officers show little respect for black females, who face "widespread racial stereotypes as well as outright racial harassment."[98] Black women also report having difficult relationships with black male officers, their relationships strained by tensions and dilemmas "associated with sexuality and competition for desirable assignments and promotions."[99] Surprisingly, there was little unity among the female officers. Martin concludes:

> Despite changes in the past two decades, the idealized image of the representative of the forces of "law and order" and protector who maintains "the thin blue line" between "them" and "us" remains white and male.[100]

The Future of Women in Policing. What does the future hold for female police officers? One of the main concerns is the low number of female officers in supervisory positions. So far, women, especially African American officers, have been woefully underrepresented in the police command hierarchy. A number of lawsuits have been filed to reverse this situation.[101] However, change in this area continues to be slow. Male officers may find it difficult to take orders from female supervisors; some female officers may not seek promotion because they fear rejection from their male colleagues.[102]

Another area of concern is the development of an effective maternity policy. Most departments do not have policies that identify when pregnant officers are unfit for patrol or other duties and whether they should be reassigned to lighter duties and what these duties should entail. If the number of women on police forces continues to grow, maternity issues are bound to become an important staffing issue for police administrators.[103]

Despite these problems, the future of women in policing grows continually brighter.[104] Female officers want to remain in policing because it pays a good salary, offers job security, and is a challenging and exciting occupation.[105] These factors should continue to bring women to policing for years to come.

Problems of Policing

Law enforcement is not an easy job. The role ambiguity, social isolation, and threat of danger present in "working the street" are the police officer's constant companions. What effects do these strains have on police? This section discusses three of the most significant problems: stress, violence, and corruption.

Stress

The complexity of their role, the need to exercise prudent discretion, the threat of using violence and having violence used against them, and isolation from the rest of society all take a toll on law enforcement officers. It is not surprising, then, that police officers experience tremendous stress, a factor that leads to alcoholism, divorce, depression, and even suicide. Even civilian employees, such as dispatchers, have been found to exhibit elevated stress levels.[106] Stress may not be constant, but at some time during their career (usually the middle years), most officers will feel the effects of stress.[107]

The Cause of Stress. A number of factors have been associated with police stress.[108] The pressure of being on duty 24 hours a day leads to stress and emotional detachment from both work and public needs. Police stress has been related to internal conflict with administrative policies that deny officers support and a meaningful role in decision making. In addition, police suffer stress in their personal lives when they bring the job home or when their work hours are shifted, causing family disruptions.[109] Other stressors include poor training, substandard equipment, inadequate pay, lack of opportunity, job dissatisfaction, role conflict, exposure to brutality, and fears about competence, success, and safety.[110] Some officers may feel stress because they believe that the court system favors the rights of the criminal and "handcuffs" the police; others might be sensitive to a perceived lack of support from government officials and the general public.[111] Some officers believe that their superiors care little about their welfare.[112]

Police psychologists have divided these stressors into four distinct categories:

1. *External stressors,* such as verbal abuse from the public, justice system inefficiency, and liberal court decisions that favor the criminal

2. *Organizational stressors,* such as low pay, excessive paperwork, arbitrary rules, and limited opportunity for advancement

3. *Duty stressors,* such as rotating shifts, work overload, boredom, fear, and danger

4. *Individual stressors,* such as discrimination, marital difficulties, and personality problems[113]

The effects of stress can be shocking. Police work has been related to both physical and psychological ailments. Police have a significantly high rate of premature death caused by such conditions as coronary heart disease and diabetes. They also experience a disproportionate number of divorces and other marital problems. Research indicates that police officers in some departments, but not all, have higher suicide rates than the general public.[114] Police who feel stress may not be open to adopting new ideas and programs such as community policing.[115]

How Can Stress Be Combated? Research efforts have shown that the more support police officers get in the workplace, the lower their feelings of stress and anxiety.[116] Consequently, departments have attempted to fight job-related stress by training officers to cope with its effects. Today, stress training includes diet information, biofeedback, relaxation and meditation, and exercise. Some programs have included family members because if they have more knowledge about the difficulties of police work, they may be better able to help the officer cope. Still other efforts promote "total wellness programming," which enhances the physical and emotional well-being of officers by emphasizing preventive physical and psychological measures.[117] Research also shows that since police perceive many benefits of their job and enjoy the quality of life it provides, stress reduction programs might help officers focus on the positive aspects of police work.[118]

Stress is a critically important aspect of police work. Further research is needed to create valid methods of identifying police officers under considerable stress and to devise effective stress-reduction programs.[119]

Violence and the Police

Since their creation, U.S. police departments have wrestled with the charge that they are brutal, physically violent organizations. Early police officers resorted to violence and intimidation to gain the respect that was not freely given by citizens. In the 1920s, the Wickersham Commission detailed numerous instances of police brutality, including the use of the third degree to extract confessions.

Police violence first became a major topic for discussion in the 1940s, when rioting provoked serious police backlash. Retired Supreme Court Justice Thurgood Marshall, when he was chief counsel of the National Association for the Advancement of Colored People's Legal Defense Fund, referred to the Detroit police as a "gestapo" after a 1943 race riot left 34 people dead.[120] Twenty-five years later, excessive police force was again an issue when television cameras captured police violence against protestors at the Democratic National Convention in Chicago.

Today, police brutality continues to be a concern, especially when police use excessive violence against members of the minority community. The nation looked on in disgust when a videotape was aired on network newscasts showing members of the Los Angeles Police Department beating, kicking, and using electric stun guns on Rodney King. Earlier, Los Angeles police stopped using a restraining choke hold that cuts off circulation of blood to the brain after minority citizens complained that it caused permanent damage and may have killed as many as 17 people.

The question of police use of force has two main aspects: (1) Are typical police officers generally brutal, violent, and disrespectful to the citizens with whom they come in daily contact? (2) Are the police overzealous and discriminatory in their use of deadly force when apprehending suspected felons? Let us examine each of these issues separately.

Police Brutality. **Police brutality** usually involves such actions as using abusive language, unnecessarily using force or coercion, making threats, prodding with nightsticks, stopping and searching people to harass them, and so on. Charges of generalized police brutality were common between the 1940s and 1960s. Surveys undertaken by the President's Commission on Law Enforcement and the Administration of Justice and other national commissions found that many citizens believed that police discriminated against minorities when they used excessive force in handling suspects, displayed disrespect to innocent bystanders, and so on.[121] However, by 1967 the President's Commission on Law Enforcement and the Administration of Justice concluded that the police use of physical brutality had somewhat abated.[122]

While charges of police brutality continue to be made in many jurisdictions, the evidence suggests that actual instances of physical abuse of citizens by police officers are less frequent than commonly imagined. One classic study employed college students to observe police-citizen interactions in high-crime areas in Washington, D.C., Chicago, and Boston.[123] While verbal abuse of citizens was quite common, the excessive use of physical force was relatively rare, occurring in 44 cases out of the 5,360 observations made. There appeared to be little difference in the way police treated blacks and whites; when force was used, it was against more selective groups—those who showed disrespect or disregard for police authority once they were arrested.

Other studies have also found that violent interactions are actually quite atypical.[124] When force is used, it usually involves grabbing and restraining; weapons are rarely used.[125] For example, a recent study of the Phoenix, Arizona police found that physical force was used in only 22% of arrests and that when force was used it was typically at a minimal level; weapons of any kind, such as flashlights, were used in only 2% of arrests. When force was used, it typically involved situations where suspects used force themselves.[126] A national survey on police use of force, conducted by Anthony Pate and Lorie Fridell, also found the use of weapons to be quite rare. Each year for every 1,000 police officers, (a) 4 shoot at a civilian, (b) 500 handcuff a suspect, and (c) 250 use bodily force of some kind.[127] However, the force used is mostly grappling and shoving and not serious confrontation.

Who Are the Problem Cops? Despite such reassuring research findings, widely publicized incidents of police brutality have continued to plague departments around the country. Some of these incidents have been captured on film and later viewed by the public, giving people the impression that there has been an increase in urban police brutality.[128] Police officers in a number of cities have been sentenced to prison for assault and battery on citizens.

What kind of police officer gets involved in problem behavior? Are some officers "chronic offenders"? Recent research conducted in a southeastern city by Kim Michelle Lersch and Tom Mieczkowski found that a few officers (7%) were in fact chronic offenders who accounted for a significant portion of all citizen complaints (33%). Those officers receiving the bulk of the complaints tended to be younger and less experienced and had been accused of harassment or violence after a proactive encounter that they had initiated. While repeat offenders were more likely to be accused of misconduct by minority citizens, there was little evidence that attacks were racially motivated.[129]

Curbing Brutality. Because incidents of brutality undermine efforts to build a bridge between police and the public, police departments around the United

The U.S. Supreme Court has prohibited police from shooting unarmed felons unless they are considered to be a significant threat to society. Thus, it would be illegal for the police to shoot at the unarmed suspect shown here, even if he tried to escape.

States have instituted specialized training programs to reduce them. Departments in such cities as New York and Boston are now implementing or considering implementing neighborhood and community policing models to improve relations with the public. In addition, detailed rules of engagement that limit the use of force are now common in major cities. However, the creation of departmental rules limiting behavior is often haphazard and is usually a reaction to a crisis situation (for example, a citizen is seriously injured) rather than part of a systematic effort to improve police-citizen interactions.[130]

What may be the greatest single factor that can control the use of police brutality is the threat of civil judgments against individual officers who use excessive force, police chiefs who ignore or condone violent behavior, and the cities and towns in which they are employed. This issue is discussed further in the Analyzing Criminal Justice Issues box on "Suing the Police."

Deadly Force. As commonly used, the term **deadly force** refers to the actions of a police officer who shoots and kills a suspect who is fleeing from arrest, assaulting a victim, or attacking the officer.[131] The justification for the use of deadly force can be traced to English common law, in which almost every criminal offense was a felony and bore the death penalty. The use of deadly force in the course of arresting a felon was considered expedient, saving the state the burden of trial (the "fleeing felon" rule).[132]

While the media depict hero cops in a constant stream of deadly shoot-outs in which scores of "bad guys" are killed, the actual number of people killed by the police each year is most likely between 250 and 300.[133] Although these data are encouraging, some researchers believe that the actual number of police shootings is far greater and may be hidden or masked by a number of factors. For example, coroners may be intentionally or accidentally underreporting police homicides by almost half.[134]

Factors Related to Police Shootings. Is police use of deadly force a random occurrence, or are there social, legal, and environmental factors associated with its use? The following patterns have been related to police shootings:

Suing the Police

There is perhaps no sizable police department in the country that has not been sued in state or federal court for damages or injunctive relief.—Rolando del Carmen (1993)

In March 1991, the nation was shaken by media coverage of a home video showing a large group of Los Angeles cops brutally beating a handcuffed African American later identified as Rodney King. The beating, which had taken place on the night of March 3, 1991, involved punches, kicks, clubbings, and the use of an electric shock device. King suffered nine skull fractures and a shattered eye socket, among other injuries. Later, the police involved were heard joking about the incident on their car radios. Most of us know that the acquittal of these officers in state court sparked rioting in Los Angeles and that later the ringleaders were convicted on federal civil rights charges and imprisoned. What may also be a critical outcome is that on April 17, 1994, a Los Angeles jury awarded King $3.8 million in damages stemming from his arrest and beating; his legal fees cost the county millions more.

The King case is the most visible symbol of the growing number of civil lawsuits being filed and won against individual officers and agencies. An estimated 30,000-plus civil suits are now being brought annually, and about 1 in every 30 officers is sued each year! Some cities are averaging over $10,000 per officer in civil compensation. Although the amount of the average award is disputed, a review of studies in the area finds that estimates of average awards is about $187,500.

Why Police Are Sued

In a number of areas of police behavior, legal action has been common. Officers have been sued when, while in "hot pursuit" of a vehicle, they use excessive speed and their negligent behavior results in the death or injury of the suspects or innocent bystanders. Police may be sued when they arrest a person although a reasonable officer should have known there were no legal grounds for an arrest (false arrest).

It is common for people to sue the police if they believe that excessive force was used during their arrest or custody. They may collect damages if they can show that the force used was unreasonable, considering all the circumstances known to the officer at the time he or she acted. Excessive force suits commonly occur when police use a weapon, such as a gun or baton, to subdue an unarmed person who is protesting his or her treatment.

A suit can also be brought if the police fail to act in a matter, as when despite a (court) restraining order, they fail to arrest a husband who is battering his wife or if they fail to give aid to the victim of a crime.

It is also possible to sue the police for abandonment. This occurs when individuals who should be taken into custody by the police are left to fend for themselves and consequently suffer injuries. For example, police have been held liable when a parent is taken into custody and minor children, left at the scene of the crime without care, suffer injury. The police have also been found liable when they have taken a drunk driver into custody while leaving an obviously intoxicated passenger in possession of the car and the passenger becomes a drunk driver. Liability has also attached when law enforcement officers abandon an individual who is in the process of being assaulted, especially when the victim pleads for the officers' help. Courts seem willing to assess damages if an officer's actions (or inaction) enhanced or created the danger or if departmental policies contributed to the injuries.

Legal Rights

Civil suits became common after the Supreme Court ruled in 1978 (*Monell v. Department of Social Services*) that local agencies could be held liable under the federal Civil Rights Act (42 U.S.C. 1983) for actions of their employees if it was part of an official custom or practice. Before *Monell,* attorneys were reluctant to file civil actions against police officers because even if the case could be won, there was often no way to collect damages from individuals who in most instances were without attachable financial resources. After *Monell,* police agencies, with their "deep pockets," could be held liable if in some way the officer's behavior could be attributed to an official policy or behavior. Liability increases if the policy or behavior is sanctioned by a high-ranking official, such as the chief.

A victim can seek redress against the department and the municipality it serves if he or she can show that the incident stemmed from a practice that, although not necessarily an official policy, was so widespread that it had become a "custom" that fairly represented official policy. To make the department liable under this standard, the victim might show that the actions that led to his or her injury were practices accepted by supervisors, that many police officers frequently engaged in these practices, that the police department failed to investigate or discipline officers involved in similar incidents, and that the department knew about such practices and did little to prohibit them. For example, a municipality could be held liable under the Civil Rights Act if police officers made it a custom to use excessive force in making arrests, police officials ignored the problem despite many complaints and incidents, brutality complaints were rarely investigated, and neither rules to limit force nor special training programs to aid police in making arrests were created.

Training

One area of particular concern has been the failure of police departments to properly train officers. Municipalities have been held liable if an officer uses excessive force and that officer has not been trained in the use of force or the training was forgotten, obsolete, and inadequate. The Supreme Court in *Canton v. Harris* ruled that to be liable for their failure to train, police departments must be "deliberately indifferent" to the needs of people injured by the untrained officers. Some commentators believe that *Harris* made suing police more difficult because of the need to prove **deliberate indifference** and not mere negligence or misconduct. Although it is difficult to define deliberate indifference, it would most likely include situations in which the need for training was so obvious that its absence seems a clear-cut violation of constitutional rights, as when police are not given any firearms training after they leave the police academy, even though the department has switched its standard weapon from the .38-caliber revolver to the 9mm automatic. Deliberate indifference might also involve failure to train officers in dealing with a particular crime problem, such as domestic abuse, even though police officials should recognize it as a significant area of concern.

The Threat of Civil Litigation

The threat to police departments posed by civil litigation is significant. Not only are they liable for large dollar awards to victims, but they must also pay hefty legal fees. It is not uncommon for a plaintiff in a civil rights case to be awarded a nominal amount of damages, with ten times that amount going to his or her attorney in legal fees. Recent research by Victor Kappeler and his associates found that litigation filed against the police in federal courts is on the increase. In addition,

this research found that plaintiffs are more successful when they sue the police than previously thought, winning just about half the cases brought. Awards ranged from $1 to $1,650,000; findings of liability based on claims of excessive force averaged $187,503!

Today relatively few citizen complaints against the police are sustained by internal police investigations. A study conducted by the Police Foundation, an organization that does research on policing, found that fewer than 13% of citizen complaints about excessive force were sustained by the departments themselves. In about one-fourth of the city departments, officers were not required to provide information to investigators. The threat of large civil penalties generated from civilian judges and juries may prove the most effective deterrent yet to the police use of excessive force. It will certainly cause police departments to carefully consider whom they hire, how they train, when they investigate, and what action they take against officers who are brutal or negligent.

Critical Thinking Questions

1. Policing is a dangerous, stressful job. Is it fair to hold officers and towns liable for the occasional use of excessive force?

2. Many offenders are disrespectful to officers and provoke violent responses. Even Rodney King, who was brutally beaten by police, resisted being handcuffed and flailed his arms around, rather than meekly consenting to arrest. Would the threat of civil suits prevent officers from taking the necessary steps to subdue dangerous criminals?

3. People want police to make neighborhoods safe, even if it means putting their lives at risk. Research has found that many officers have a real fear of lawsuits and maintain an "us versus them" mentality. Will these concerns undermine police-community relations at a time when they are seen as critical to effective policing? Should officers be immune from punishment if they use too much force in this dangerous undertaking?

SOURCES: David Griswold, "Complaints Against the Police: Predicting Dispositions," *Journal of Criminal Justice* 22 (1994): 215–221; Michael Vaughn, "Police Civil Liability for Abandonment in High-Crime Areas and Other High-Risk Situations," *Journal of Criminal Justice* 22 (1994): 407–424; Victor Kappeler, Stephen Kappeler, and Rolando Del Carmen, "A Content Analysis of Police Civil Liability Cases: Decisions of the Federal District Courts, 1978–1990," *Journal of Criminal Justice* 21 (1993): 325–337; Police Foundation, *Police Use of Force: Official Reports, Citizen Complaints, and Legal Consequences* (Washington, D.C.: Police Foundation, 1993).

1. *Variation by jurisdiction.* Research indicates that cities differ markedly in percentage of police shootings. For example, one study found that police in Portland, Oregon annually shoot 0.81 civilians per 1,000 population; New York City police shoot 1.4; Oakland, California police shoot 5.2; and Jacksonville, Florida police shoot 7.1.[135] Scholars are still uncertain about the reasons for these differences. Police practices, population characteristics, social trends, and so on may be responsible.

2. *Exposure to violence.* Most police shootings involve suspects who are armed and who either attack the officer or are engaged in violent crimes. A number of studies have found that fatal police shootings were closely related to reported violent crime rates and criminal homicide rates; police officers kill civilians at a higher rate in years when the general level of violence in the nation is higher.[136]

3. *Workload.* A relationship exists among police violence and the number of police on the street, the number of calls for service, the number and nature of police dispatches, the number of arrests made in a given jurisdiction, and police exposure to stressful situations.[137]

4. *Firearms availability.* Cities that experience a large number of crimes committed with firearms are also likely to have high police violence rates. In a study of 48 cities, Lawrence Sherman and Robert Langworthy found a strong association between police use of force and "gun density" (the proportion of suicides and murders committed with a gun).[138]

5. *Social variables.* Research suggests that many individuals shot by police are transients or nonresidents caught at or near the scenes of robberies or burglaries of commercial establishments.[139] The greatest number of police shootings occur in areas that have great disparities in economic opportunity and a resulting high level of income inequality.[140]

6. *Administrative policies.* The philosophy, policies, and practices of individual police chiefs and departments significantly influence the police use of deadly force.[141] Departments that stress restrictive policies on the use of force generally have lower shooting rates than those that favor tough law enforcement and encourage officers to shoot when necessary. Poorly written or ambivalent policies encourage shootings because they allow the officer at the scene to decide when deadly force is warranted, often under conditions of high stress and tension.

7. *Race and police shootings.* No other issue is as important to the study of the police use of deadly force as that of racial discrimination. A number of critics have claimed that police are more likely to shoot and kill minority offenders than they are whites. In a famous statement, Paul Takagi charged that police have "one trigger finger for whites and another for blacks."[142] Takagi's complaint was supported by a number of research studies that showed that a disproportionate number of police killings involved minority citizens—almost 80% in some of the cities surveyed.[143]

    Do these findings alone indicate that police discriminate in the use of deadly force? Some pioneering research by James Fyfe helps provide an answer to this question. In his study of New York City shootings over a five-year period, Fyfe found that police officers were most likely to shoot suspects who were armed and with whom they became involved in violent confrontations. Once such factors as being armed with a weapon, being involved in a violent crime, and attacking an officer were considered, the racial differences in the police use of force ceased to be significant. In fact, Fyfe found that black officers were almost twice as likely as white officers to have shot citizens. Fyfe attributes this finding to the fact that (1) black officers work and live in high-crime, high-violence areas where shootings are more common and (2) black officers hold proportionately more line positions and fewer administrative posts than white officers, which would place them more often on the street and less often behind a desk.[144]

Shootings of Police. Although police officers are often taken to task for being too violent, the public sometimes forgets that police are all too often injured and killed by armed assailants. More than 65,000 are attacked and 23,000 seriously injured each year.[145]

This situation has not been improved by the fact that professional criminals and drug dealers are armed with automatic weapons, such as Uzi machine guns, while police officers carry .38-caliber revolvers. The danger in this disparity made national headlines on February 28, 1997 when two bank robbers using high-powered automatic weapons wounded five Los Angeles police officers in a gun battle captured on video camera as it unfolded; both robbers were eventually killed during the melee, which was rebroadcast on national TV.[146]

In the past decade, between 50 and 100 law enforcement and public safety officers have been feloniously killed in the line of duty each year; about 90% of these are shooting victims. An additional 70 officers are killed each year in job-related incidents, such as traffic accidents.

A long-held belief has been that police officers who answer domestic violence calls are at risk of violence against them; when confronted, one of the two battling parties turns on the outsider who dares interfere in a "private matter." Recent research conducted in Charlotte, North Carolina, however, indicates that domestic violence calls may be no more dangerous than many other routine police interactions.[147] So while police officers should be on their guard when investigating a call for assistance from an abused spouse, the risk of violence against them may be no greater than when they answer a call for a burglary or car theft.

The majority of fatal incidents are initiated by the officers themselves, as opposed to an unexpected attack by a hidden assailant. In addition, black officers have a greater risk of getting killed than white officers. Police officers face the greatest danger when they are attempting to arrest an armed assailant.[148] Ecological patterns may also be present when a police officer becomes the victim of violent crime. Southern cities, with high violence and gun-ownership rates, experience the highest numbers of police officer fatalities.[149] Research also shows that off-duty police and plainclothes officers are at high risk. One reason is that off-duty officers, who are usually armed, are expected to take appropriate action yet suffer tactical disadvantages, such as a lack of communication and backup. Plainclothes officers may also be mistaken for perpetrators or unwanted interveners.

Controlling Deadly Force. Since the police use of deadly force is such a serious problem, ongoing efforts have been made to control its use.

One of the most difficult problems that influenced its control was the continued use of the fleeing felon rule in a number of states. However, in 1985 the Supreme Court outlawed the indiscriminate use of deadly force with its decision in the case of *Tennessee v. Garner.* In this case, the Court ruled that the use of deadly force against apparently unarmed and nondangerous fleeing felons is an illegal seizure of their person under the Fourth Amendment. Deadly force may not be used unless it is necessary to prevent the escape and the officer has probable cause to believe that the suspect poses a significant threat of death or serious injury to the officer or others. The majority opinion stated that where the suspect poses no immediate threat to the officer and no threat to others, the harm resulting from failing to apprehend the suspect does not justify the use of deadly force to do so: "A police officer may not seize an unarmed, nondangerous suspect by shooting him dead."[150]

With *Garner,* the Supreme Court effectively put an end to any local police policy that allowed officers to shoot unarmed or otherwise nondangerous offenders if they resisted arrest or attempted to flee from police custody. However, the Court did not ban the use of deadly force or otherwise control police shooting policy. Consequently, in *Graham v. Connor,* the Supreme Court created a reasonableness standard for the use of force: Force is excessive when, considering all the circumstances known to the officer at the time he or she acted, the force used was unreasonable.[151] For example, a police officer is approached in a threatening manner by someone wielding a knife. The assailant fails to stop when warned and is killed by the officer. The officer would not be held liable if it turns out that the shooting victim was deaf and could not hear the officer's command and if the officer at the time of the incident had no way of knowing the person's disability.

Individual state jurisdictions still control police shooting policy. Some states have adopted statutory policies that restrict the police use of violence. Others have upgraded training in the use of force. The Federal Law Enforcement Training Center has developed the FLETC use-of-force model, illustrated in Figure 7.4, to teach officers the proper method to escalate force in response to the threat they face. As the figure shows, resistance ranges from compliant and cooperative to assaultive with the threat of serious bodily harm or death. Officers are taught via lecture, demonstration, computer-based instruction, and training scenarios to assess the suspect's behavior and apply an appropriate and corresponding amount of force.[152]

Another method of controlling police shootings is through internal review and policymaking by police administrative review boards. For example, New York's Firearm Discharge Review Board was established to investigate and adjudicate all police firearm discharges. Among the dispositions available to the board are

1. The discharge was in accordance with law and department policy.

2. The discharge was justifiable, but the officer should be given additional training in the use of firearms or in the law and department policy.

3. The shooting was justifiable under law but violated department policy and warrants department disciplinary action.

Figure 7.4
The Federal Law Enforcement Training Center's use of force model.
SOURCE: Franklin Graves and Gregory Connor, The Federal Law Enforcement Training Center, Glynco, Georgia.

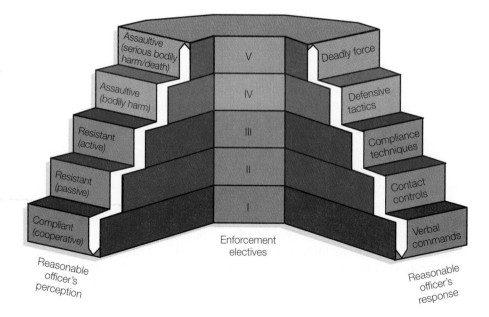

4. The shooting was in apparent violation of law and should be referred to the appropriate prosecutor if criminal charges have not already been filed.

5. The officer involved should be transferred (or offered the opportunity to transfer) to a less sensitive assignment.

6. The officer involved should receive testing or alcoholism counseling.[153]

The review board approach is controversial because it can mean that the department recommends that one of its own officers be turned over for criminal prosecution, an outcome with which some legal scholars disagree.[154] In an analysis of the effect of the firearm review board (and the development of a restrictive shooting policy based on the Model Penal Code), James Fyfe found that "fleeing felon" shootings, warning shots, and opponent and officer deaths had decreased significantly.[155] Because of the positive results of instituting administrative reform, an increasing number of police departments are turning to administrative guidelines and policy reform, such as those formulated by the Commission for Accreditation for Law Enforcement Agencies, as a means of reducing civilian complaints about violence and the legal judgments and increases in liability insurance payments that soon follow.[156]

While police use of force continues to be an important issue, there is little question that control measures seem to be working.[157] It appears that fewer people are being killed by police and fewer officers are being killed than ever before. In 1996, for example, 61 officers were killed by felonious assaults, down from the 82 killed in 1995; a total of 116 law enforcement personnel were killed in the line of duty in 1996, 56 in auto accidents.[158]

From their creation, U.S. police departments have wrestled with the problem of controlling illegal and unprofessional behavior by their officers. Corruption pervaded the American police when the early departments were first formed. In the 19th century, police officers systematically ignored violations of laws related to drinking, gambling, and prostitution in return for regular payoffs. Some actually entered into relationships with professional criminals, especially pickpockets. Illegal behavior was tolerated in return for goods or information. Police officers helped politicians gain office by allowing electoral fraud to flourish; some senior officers sold promotions to higher rank within the department.[159]

Corruption

Since the early 19th century, scandals involving police abuse of power have occurred in many urban cities, and elaborate methods have been devised to control or eliminate the problem. Although most police officers are not corrupt, the few who are dishonest bring discredit to the entire profession (see Table 7.1).

Varieties of Police Corruption. Police deviance can include a number of activities. In a general sense, it involves misuse of authority by police officers in a manner designed to produce personal gain for themselves or others.[160] However, debate continues over whether a desire for personal gain is an essential part of corruption. Some experts argue that police misconduct also involves such issues as the unnecessary use of force, unreasonable searches, or an immoral personal life and that these should be considered as serious as corruption devoted to economic gain.

Scholars have attempted to create typologies categorizing the forms that the abuse of police powers can take. For example, when investigating corruption among police officers in New York, the **Knapp Commission** classified abusers into two categories: "meat eaters" and "grass eaters."[161] **Meat eaters** aggressively misuse police power for personal gain by demanding bribes, threatening legal action, or cooperating with criminals. Across the country, police officers have been accused, indicted, and convicted of shaking down club owners and other businesspeople.[162] In contrast, **grass eaters** accept payoffs when their everyday duties place them in a position to be solicited by the public. For example, police officers

Table 7.1
Recent Police Corruption
Scandals in New York City
SOURCE: "Pockets of Corruption," *New York Times,* 9 April 1995, p. 43.

48th Precinct, the Bronx

The 48th Precinct is the latest focus of corruption inquiries, with two dozen officers under investigation, police officials say. After sting operations involving undercover officers posing as drug dealers, eight officers from the 48th have been indicted. One of the officers has also been charged by the Rockland County District Attorney with participating in a suburban cocaine ring. Officers from the 48th are believed to have robbed drug dealers, sold narcotics, and beat up suspects.

73d Precinct, Brooklyn

During the summer of 1993 a former police officer told investigators about officers who broke down the doors of drug dealers and divided the booty in an abandoned coffin factory. Thus began the Morgue Boys' investigation and trial. Jurors acquitted three officers of extortion charges but deadlocked on civil rights charges stemming from what prosecutors said were illegal searches and arrests based on false evidence.

109th Precinct, Queens

In 1994 the Police Department received a series of complaints from residents in and around Flushing that several officers were using drugs on the job. Four officers were ordered to take drug tests; one resigned and the other three failed their tests and were dismissed. The department also set up a series of corruption stings, resulting in the arrests of two officers and one former officer, who are accused of stealing $1,400 while responding to a false report of a kidnapping. Police officials say more officers are under investigation.

30th Precinct, Harlem

In August 1993 several Harlem police officers were videotaped breaking into an apartment that had been set up by undercover officers as a phony drug den. The sting operation, which followed reports that officers had been shaking down drug dealers and stealing property on their beats, opened up one of the city's biggest police corruption scandals in decades. In the days and months that followed, more than two dozen other officers and supervisors were arrested. The most recent arrests came in May 1995, when two officers and a sergeant were accused of falsifying arrest records and lying in court to win convictions.

have been investigated for taking bribes to look the other way while neighborhood bookmakers ply their trade.[163] The Knapp Commission concluded that the vast majority of police officers on the take are grass eaters, although the few meat eaters who are caught capture all the headlines. In 1993, another police scandal prompted formation of the **Mollen Commission,** which found that some New York cops were actively involved in violence and drug dealing.

Other police experts have attempted to create models to better understand police corruption. It may be possible to divide police corruption into four major categories:[164]

1. *Internal corruption.* This is corruption that takes place among police officers themselves, involving both the bending of departmental rules and the outright performance of illegal acts. For example, in Chicago police officers conspired to sell relatively new police cars to other officers at cut-rate prices, forcing the department to purchase new cars unnecessarily. In Boston, a major scandal hit the police department when a police captain was indicted in an exam tampering and selling scheme. Numerous officers bought promotion exams from the captain, while others had him lower the scores of rivals who were competing for the same job.[165]

2. *Selective enforcement or nonenforcement.* This form occurs when police abuse or exploit their discretion. If an officer frees a drug dealer in return for valuable information, that would be considered a legitimate use of discretion; if the police officer did so for money, that would be an abuse of police power.

3. *Active criminality.* This is participation by police in serious criminal behavior. Police may use their positions of trust and power to commit the very crimes they are entrusted with controlling. For example, a police burglary ring in Denver was so large it prompted one commentator to coin the phrase "burglars in blue." During the past 20 years, police burglary rings have been uncovered in Chicago, Reno, Nashville, Cleveland, and Burlington, Vermont, among other cities.[166] Another disturbing trend has been police use of drugs and alcohol. Police departments have been active in referring officers to treatment programs when substance abuse problems are detected.[167]

4. *Bribery and extortion.* This includes practices in which law enforcement roles are exploited specifically to raise money. Bribery is initiated by the citizen; extortion is initiated by the officer. Bribery or extortion can be a one-shot transaction, as when a traffic violator offers a police officer $20 to forget about issuing a summons. Or the relationship can be an ongoing one, in which the officer solicits (or is offered) regular payoffs to ignore criminal activities, such as gambling or narcotics dealing. This is known as "being on the pad."

Sometimes police officers accept routine bribes and engage in petty extortion without considering themselves corrupt; they consider these payments as some of the unwritten "benefits" of police work. For example, *mooching* involves receiving free gifts of coffee, cigarettes, meals, and so on in exchange for possible future acts of favoritism; *chiseling* occurs when officers demand admission to entertainment events or price discounts; *shopping* involves taking small items, such as cigarettes, from a store whose door was accidentally left unlocked after business hours.[168]

It has also been suggested that entire police departments can be categorized on the basis of the level and type of corruption existing within them.[169] Three types of departments may exist:

1. *Rotten apples and rotten pockets.* This type of police department has a few corrupt officers who use their position for personal gain. When these corrupt officers band together, they form a "rotten pocket." Robert Daley described the activities of such a group in his book *Prince of the City.*[170] Agents of New York City's Special Investigations Unit kept money they confiscated during narcotics raids and used illegal drugs to pay off informers. *Prince of the City* tells the story of New York Detective Frank Leuci, whose testimony against his partners before investigating committees made him an outcast in the police department. Rotten pockets help institutionalize corruption because their members expect newcomers to conform to their illegal practices and to a code of secrecy.

2. *Pervasive unorganized corruption.* This type of department contains a majority of personnel who are corrupt but have little relationship to one another. Though many officers are involved in taking bribes and extortion, they are not cooperating with one another for personal gain.

3. *Pervasive organized corruption.* This describes a department in which almost all members are involved in systematic and organized corruption. The Knapp Commission found this type of relationship in New York City's vice divisions, where payoffs and bribes were an organized and accepted way of police life.

The Causes and Control of Corruption. No single explanation satisfactorily accounts for the various forms the abuse of power takes. One view puts the blame on the type of person who becomes a police officer. This position holds that policing tends to attract lower-class individuals who do not have the financial means to maintain a coveted middle-class lifestyle. As they develop the cynical, authoritarian police personality, accepting graft seems an all-too-easy method of achieving financial security.

A second view is that the wide discretion police enjoy, coupled with the low visibility they maintain with the public and their own supervisors, makes them likely candidates for corruption. In addition, the "code of secrecy" maintained by the police subculture helps insulate corrupt officers from the law. Similarly, police managers, most of whom have risen through the ranks, are reluctant to investigate corruption or punish wrongdoers. Thus, corruption may also be viewed as a function of police institutions and practices.[171]

A third position holds that corruption is a function of society's ambivalence toward many forms of vice-related criminal behavior that police officers are sworn to control. Unenforceable laws governing moral standards promote corruption because they create large groups with an interest in undermining law enforcement. These include consumers—people who gamble, wish to drink after the legal closing hour, or patronize a prostitute—who do not want to be deprived of their chosen form of recreation. Even though the consumers may not actively corrupt police officers, their existence creates a climate that tolerates active corruption by others.[172] Since vice cannot be controlled and the public apparently wants it to continue, the police officer may have little resistance to inducements for monetary gain offered by law violators.

How can police corruption be controlled? One approach is to strengthen the internal administrative review process within police departments. A strong and well-supported internal affairs division has been linked to lowered corruption rates.[173] Another approach, instituted by then New York Commissioner Patrick Murphy in the wake of the Knapp Commission, is the **accountability system.** This holds that supervisors at each level are directly accountable for the illegal behaviors of the officers under them. Consequently, a commander can be demoted or forced to resign if one of his or her command is found guilty of corruption.[174] Close scrutiny by a department, however, can lower officer morale and create the suspicion that the officers' own supervisors distrust them.

In 1996 the city of Philadelphia agreed to implement a set of reforms to combat corruption in order to settle a lawsuit brought by civil rights organizations. Among the measures taken to reduce corruption were

- A policy mandating that all citizens' complaints be forwarded for investigation by the internal affairs division

- Development of computer files that contain all types of complaints and suits against individual officers that could be easily accessed during investigations

- A policy requiring that internal affairs give a high priority to any police officer's claim that another officer was corrupt or used excessive force

- Mandatory reporting and recording of all incidents in which an officer used more than incidental force

- Training of officers to treat citizens without racial bias; a deputy commissioner will be assigned to monitor charges of race discrimination

- Review of all policies and practices to ensure they do not involve or have the potential for race bias[175]

Another approach is to create outside review boards or special prosecutors, such as the Mollen Commission in New York and the Christopher Commission in Los Angeles, to investigate reported incidents of corruption. However, outside investigators and special prosecutors are often limited by their lack of intimate knowledge of day-to-day police operations. As a result, they depend on the testimony of a few officers who are willing to cooperate, either to save themselves from prosecution or because they have a compelling moral commitment. Outside evaluators also face the problem of the blue curtain, which is quickly closed when police officers feel their department is under scrutiny.

Another approach to controlling police corruption is through court review of police behavior. In the past decade, courts have tended to remove restrictions limiting litigation against the police. While it is difficult to analyze the precise effects of legal action on police behavior, the resulting higher insurance rates caused by large settlements and increased media coverage have almost certainly caused police administrators to take corruption quite seriously.[176]

It is also possible that corruption can be controlled by intensive training and education programs begun when a police officer first enters a training academy. Recruits can be made aware of the enticements to police deviance and the steps that can be taken to control it.

A more realistic solution to police corruption, albeit a difficult one, might be to change the social context of policing. Police operations must be made more visible, and the public must be given freer access to controlling police operations. All too often, the public finds out about police problems only when a scandal hits the newspaper. Some of the vice-related crimes the police now deal with might be decriminalized or referred to other agencies. Although decriminalization of vice cannot in itself end the problem, it could lower the pressure placed on individual police officers and help eliminate their moral dilemmas.

Criminal Justice on the Net

Community policing models are certainly influencing police role, discretion, and style. The Community Policing Consortium, a partnership of five of the leading police organizations in the United States, maintains its own web site. The Consortium play a principal role in the development of community policing research, training, and technical assistance and is firmly committed to the advancement of this policing philosophy. To find out more about their efforts, log onto their page at

http://www.communitypolicing.org/

One way of reducing police violence is through improved training. The Federal Law Enforcement Training Center (FLETC) provides quality, cost-effective training for law enforcement professionals. They utilize law enforcement and training experts; provide quality facilities, support services, and technical assistance; conduct law enforcement research and development; and share law enforcement technology. FLETC has been instrumental in helping train law enforcement officers to control violence. Their homepage is

http://www.ustreas.gov/treasury/bureaus/fletc/

Summary

Police departments today are faced with many critical problems in their development and relationship with the public.

Police are believed to be insulated from the rest of society. Some experts hold that police officers have distinct personality characteristics marked by authoritarianism and cynicism. It is also alleged that police maintain a separate culture with distinct rules and loyalties. A police personality also influences their working style. Four distinct police styles have been identified, and each influences police decision making. The complexity and danger of the police role produce an enormous amount of stress that harms police effectiveness.

Social concerns also affect police operations. Today, many police officers are seeking higher education. The jury is still out on whether educated police officers are actually more effective. Women and minorities are now being recruited into the police in increasing numbers. Research indicates that, with few exceptions, they perform as well or even better than other officers. The percentage of minorities on police forces reflects their representation in the general population, but the number of female officers still lags behind. Of greater importance is increasing the number of women and minorities in supervisory positions.

Police departments have also been concerned about limiting police stress and improving police-community relations. One critical concern is the police use of deadly force. Research indicates that anti-shooting policies can limit deaths resulting from police action. Another effort has been to identify and eliminate police corruption, which still mars the reputation of police forces.

Key Terms

blue curtain	discretion	deliberate indifference
cynicism	demeanor	Knapp Commission
style	double marginality	meat eaters
crime fighter	*United States v. Paradise*	grass eaters
social agent	defeminization	Mollen Commission
law enforcer	police brutality	accountability system
watchman	deadly force	

Questions

1. Should male and female officers have exactly the same duties in a police department?
2. Do you think that an officer's working the street will eventually produce a cynical personality and distrust for civilians?
3. How can education help police officers?
4. Should a police officer who accepts a free meal from a restaurant owner be dismissed from the force?
5. A police officer orders an unarmed person running away from a burglary to stop; the suspect keeps running and is shot and killed by the officer. Has the officer committed murder?
6. Would you like to live in a society that abolished police discretion and used a full enforcement policy?

Notes

1. John Hoffman, "Society's Trashy Behavior Winds Up in Cop's Hands: An Interview with Former Drug Czar William J. Bennett," *Law and Order* 42 (1994): 28–33.

2. Kathleen Maguire and Ann Pastore, *Sourcebook of Criminal Justice Statistics, 1995* (Washington, D.C.: Bureau of Justice Statistics, 1996), p. 133.

3. See, for example, Richard Harris, *The Police Academy: An Inside View* (New York: Wiley, 1973); John Van Maanen, "Observations on the Making of a Policeman," in *Order Under Law,* ed. R. Culbertson and M. Tezak (Prospect Heights, Ill.: Waveland Press, 1981), pp. 111–126; Jonathan Rubenstein, *City Police* (New York: Ballantine Books, 1973); John Broderick, *Police in a Time of Change* (Morristown, N.J.: General Learning Press, 1977).

4. Malcolm Sparrow, Mark Moore, and David Kennedy, *Beyond 911, A New Era for Policing* (New York: Basic Books, 1990), p. 51.

5. M. Steven Meagher and Nancy Yentes, "Choosing a Career in Policing: A Comparison of Male and Female Perceptions," *Journal of Police Science and Administration* 16 (1986): 320–327.

6. Michael K. Brown, *Working the Street* (New York: Russell Sage Foundation, 1981), p. 82.

7. Stan Shernock, "An Empirical Examination of the Relationship Between Police Solidarity and Community Orientation," *Journal of Police Science and Administration* 18 (1988):182–198.

8. Egon Bittner, *The Functions of Police in Modern Society* (Cambridge, Mass.: Oelgeschlager, Gunn & Hain, 1980), p. 63.

9. Richard Lundman, *Police and Policing* (New York: Holt, Rinehart & Winston, 1980); see also Jerome Skolnick, *Justice Without Trial* (New York: Wiley, 1966).

10. Robert Regoli, Robert Culbertson, John Crank, and James Powell, "Career Stage and Cynicism Among Police Chiefs," *Justice Quarterly* 7 (1990): 592–614.

11. William Westly, *Violence and the Police: A Sociological Study of Law, Custom, and Morality* (Cambridge: MIT Press, 1970).

12. Skolnick, *Justice Without Trial,* pp. 42–68.

13. Milton Rokeach, Martin Miller, and John Snyder, "The Value Gap Between Police and Policed," *Journal of Social Issues* 27 (1971): 155–171.

14. Bruce Carpenter and Susan Raza, "Personality Characteristics of Police Applicants: Comparisons Across Subgroups and with Other Populations," *Journal of Police Science and Administration* 15 (1987): 10–17.

15. Larry Tifft, "The 'Cop Personality' Reconsidered," *Journal of Police Science and Administration* 2 (1974): 268; David Bayley and Harold Mendelsohn, *Minorities and the Police* (New York: Free

Press, 1969); Robert Balch, "The Police Personality: Fact or Fiction?" *Journal of Criminal Law, Criminology, and Police Science* 63 (1972): 117.

16. Lowell Storms, Nolan Penn, and James Tenzell, "Policemen's Perception of Real and Ideal Policemen," *Journal of Police Science and Administration* 17 (1990): 40–43.

17. Arthur Niederhoffer, *Behind the Shield: The Police in Urban Society* (Garden City, N.Y.: Doubleday, 1967).

18. Ibid., pp. 216–220.

19. Robert Regoli and Eric Poole, "Measurement of Police Cynicism: A Factor Scaling Approach," *Journal of Criminal Justice* 7 (1979): 37–52.

20. Ibid., p. 43.

21. Ibid., p. 44.

22. Carl Klockars, "The Dirty Harry Problem," *Annals* 452 (1980): 33–47.

23. Jack Kuykendall and Roy Roberg, "Police Manager's Perceptions of Employee Types: A Conceptual Model," *Journal of Criminal Justice* 16 (1988): 131–135.

24. Stephen Matrofski, R. Richard Ritti, and Jeffrey Snipes, "Expectancy Theory and Police Productivity in DUI Enforcement," *Law and Society Review* 28 (1994): 113–138.

25. William Muir, *Police: Streetcorner Politicians* (Chicago: University of Chicago Press, 1977).

26. James Q. Wilson, *Varieties of Police Behavior* (Cambridge, Mass.: Harvard University Press, 1968), chap. 7

27. Ibid., p. 141.

28. Ellen Hochstedler, "Testing Types: A Review and Test of Police Types," *Journal of Criminal Justice* 9 (1981): 451–466.

29. For a thorough review, see Eric Riksheim and Steven Chermak, "Causes of Police Behavior Revisited," *Journal of Criminal Justice* 21 (1993): 353–383.

30. Skolnick, *Justice Without Trial.*

31. Gregory Howard Williams, *The Law and Politics of Police Discretion* (Westport, Conn.: Greenwood Press, 1984).

32. Douglas Smith and Jody Klein, "Police Control of Interpersonal Disputes," *Social Problems* 31 (1984): 468–481.

33. Westly, *Violence and the Police.*

34. Nathan Goldman, *The Differential Selection of Juvenile Offenders for Court Appearance* (New York: National Council on Crime and Delinquency, 1963).

35. David Klinger, "Demeanor or Crime? Why 'Hostile' Citizens Are More Likely to Be Arrested," *Criminology* 32 (1994): 475–493.

36. Richard Lundman, "Demeanor or Crime? The Midwest City Police-Citizen Encounters Study," *Criminology* 32 (1994): 631–653; Robert Worden and Robin Shepard, "On the Meaning, Measurement, and Estimated Effects of Suspects' Demeanor Toward the Police," paper presented at the American Society of Criminology meeting, Miami, November 1994.

37. Helen Eigenberg, Kathryn Scarborough, and Victor Kappeler, "Contributory Factors Affecting Arrest in Domestic and Nondomestic Assaults," *American Journal of Police* 15 (1996): 27–51.

38. Leonore Simon, "A Therapeutic Jurisprudence Approach to the Legal Processing of Domestic Violence Cases," *Psychology, Public Policy and Law* 1 (1995): 43–79.

39. Dennis Powell, "Race, Rank, and Police Discretion," *Journal of Police Science and Administration* 9 (1981): 383–389.

40. Riksheim and Chermak, "Causes of Police Behavior Revisited," pp. 374–380.

41. Ronald Weitzer, "Racial Discrimination in the Criminal Justice System: Findings and Problems in the Literature," *Journal of Criminal Justice* 24 (1996): 309–322.

42. Samuel Walker, Cassia Spohn, and Miriam DeLone, *The Color of Justice, Race, Ethnicity and Crime in America* (Belmont, Calif.: Wadsworth, 1996), p. 115.

43. Douglas Smith, Christy Visher, and Laura Davidson, "Equity and Discretionary Justice: The Influence of Race on Police Arrest Decisions," *Journal of Criminal Law and Criminology* 75 (1984): 234–249.

44. Sandra Lee Browning, Francis Cullen, Liqun Cao, Renee Kopache, and Thomas Stevenson, "Race and Getting Hassled by the Police: A Research Note," *Police Studies* 17 (1994): 1–11.

45. Darlene Conley, "Adding Color to a Black and White Picture: Using Qualitative Data to Explain Racial Disproportionality in the Juvenile Justice System," *Journal of Research in Crime and Delinquency* 31 (1994): 135–148.

46. Brown, *Working the Street,* p. 290.

47. See Larry Hoover, *Police Educational Characteristics and Curricula* (Washington, D.C.: U.S. Government Printing Office, 1975).

48. Bruce Berg, "Who Should Teach Police: A Typology and Assessment of Police Academy Instructors," *American Journal of Police* 9 (1990): 79–100.

49. David Carter and Allen Sapp, *The State of Police Education: Critical Findings* (Washington, D.C.: Police Executive Research Forum, 1988), p. 6.

50. See, for example, B. E. Sanderson, "Police Officers: The Relationship of a College Education to Job Performance," *Police Chief* 44 (1977): 62.

51. John Krimmel, "The Performance of College-Educated Police: A Study of Self-Rated Police Performance Measures," *American Journal of Police* 15 (1996): 85–95.

52. Robert Worden, "A Badge and a Baccalaureate: Policies, Hypotheses, and Further Evidence," *Justice Quarterly* 7 (1990): 565–592.

53. See Lawrence Sherman and Warren Bennis, "Higher Education for Police Officers: The Central Issues," *Police Chief* 44 (1977): 32.

54. Worden, "A Badge and a Baccalaureate," pp. 587–589.

55. Carter and Sapp, *The State of Police Education.*

56. Jack Kuykendall and David Burns, "The Black Police Officer: An Historical Perspective," *Journal of Contemporary Criminal Justice* 1 (1980): 4–13.

57. Ibid.

58. Nicholas Alex, *Black in Blue: A Study of the Negro Policeman* (New York: Appleton-Century-Crofts, 1969).

59. Nicholas Alex, *New York Cops Talk Back* (New York: Wiley, 1976).

60. Stephen Leinen, *Black Police, White Society* (New York: New York University Press, 1984).

61. Donald Yates and Vijayan Pillai, "Frustration and Strain Among Fort Worth Police Officers," *Sociology and Social Research* 76 (1992): 145–149.

62. Donald Yates and Vijayan Pillai, "Race and Police Commitment to Community Policing," *The Journal of Intergroup Relations* 19 (1993): 14–23.

63. Bruce Berg, Edmond True, and Marc Gertz, "Police, Riots, and Alienation," *Journal of Police Science and Administration* 12 (1984): 186–190.

64. Samuel Walker and K. B. Turner, "A Decade of Modest Progress: Employment of Black and Hispanic Police Officers, 1983–1992" (Omaha: Department of Criminal Justice, University of Nebraska, mimeo, 1993).

65. Yates and Pillai, "Frustration and Strain Among Fort Worth Police Officers."

66. *Baker v. City of St. Petersburg,* 400 F.2d 294 (5th Cir. 1968).

67. See, for example, *Allen v. City of Mobile,* 331 F.Supp. 1134 (1971), affirmed 466 F.2d 122 (5th Cir. 1972).

68. Kuykendall and Burns, "The Black Police Officer."

69. "The Police Exam That Flunked," *New York Times,* 24 November 1985, p. 20.

70. *United States v. Paradise,* 480 U.S. 149, 107 S.Ct. 1053, 94 L.Ed.2d 203 (1987).

71. Michael Charles, "Resolving Discrimination in the Promotion of Fort Wayne Police Officers," *American Journal of Police* 10 (1991): 67–87.

72. Robert Kaminski, "Police Minority Recruitment: Predicting Who Will Say Yes to an Offer for a Job as a Cop," *Journal of Criminal Justice* 21 (1993): 395–409.

73. For a review of the history of women in policing, see Dorothy Moses Schulz, "From Policewoman to Police Officer: An Unfinished Revolution," *Police Studies* 16 (1993): 90–99; Cathryn House, "The Changing Role of Women in Law Enforcement," *Police Chief* 60 (1993): 139–144.

74. Susan Martin, "Female Officers on the Move? A Status Report on Women in Policing," in *Critical Issues in Policing,* ed. Roger Dunham and Geoffery Alpert (Grove Park, Ill.: Waveland Press, 1988), pp. 312–331.

75. *Le Bouef v. Ramsey,* 26 FEP Cases 884 (9/16/80).

76. Michael Birzer and Delores Craig, "Gender Differences in Police Physical Ability Test Performance," *American Journal of Police* 15 (1996): 93–106.

77. Carole Garrison, Nancy Grant, and Kenneth McCormick, "Utilization of Police Women," *Police Chief* 55 (1988): 32–33.

78. Eric Poole and Mark Pogrebin, "Factors Affecting the Decision to Remain in Policing: A Study of Women Officers," *Journal of Police Science and Administration* 16 (1988): 49–55.

79. Merry Morash and Jack Greene, "Evaluating Women on Patrol: A Critique of Contemporary Wisdom," *Evaluation Review* 10 (1986): 230–255.

80. Peter Bloch and Deborah Anderson, *Policewomen on Patrol: Final Report* (Washington, D.C.: Police Foundation, 1974).

81. Robert Homant and Daniel Kennedy, "Police Perceptions of Spouse Abuse: A Comparison of Male and Female Officers," *Journal of Criminal Justice* 13 (1985): 49–64.

82. Sean Grennan, "Findings on the Role of Officer Gender in Violent Encounters with Citizens," *Journal of Police Science and Administration* 15 (1988): 78–85.

83. See, for example, Jack Molden, "Female Police Officers: Training Implications," *Law and Order* 33 (1985): 62–63.

84. Cited in House, "The Changing Role of Women in Law Enforcement," p. 144.

85. Joseph Balkin, "Why Policemen Don't Like Policewomen," *Journal of Police Science and Administration* 16 (1988): 29–38.

86. Anthony Bouza, "Women in Policing," *FBI Law Enforcement Bulletin* 44 (1975): 2–7.

87. James Daum and Cindy Johns, "Police Work from a Woman's Perspective," *Police Chief* 61 (1994): 46–49.

88. Mary Brown, "The Plight of Female Police: A Survey of NW Patrolmen," *Police Chief* 61 (1994): 50–53.

89. Associated Press, "Two Female Agents Settle FBI Suit," *Boston Globe,* 19 May 1994, p. 8.

90. Balkin, "Why Policemen Don't Like Police-women," p. 36.

91. Alissa Pollitz Worden, "The Attitudes of Women and Men in Policing: Testing Conventional and Contemporary Wisdom," *Criminology* 31 (1993): 203–243.

92. Adriane Kinnane, *Policing* (Chicago: Nelson-Hall, 1979), p. 58.

93. Bruce Berg and Kimberly Budnick, "Defeminization of Women in Law Enforcement: A New Twist in the Traditional Police Personality," *Journal of Police Science and Administration* 14 (1986): 314–319.

94. Curt Bartol, George Bergen, Julie Seager Volckens, and Kathleen Knoras, "Women in Small-Town Policing, Job Performance and Stress," *Criminal Justice and Behavior* 19 (1992): 245–259.

95. Susan Martin, "'Outsider Within' the Station House: The Impact of Race and Gender on Black Women Police," *Social Problems* 41 (1994): 383–400.

96. Michael Charles, "Women in Policing: The Physical Aspects," *Journal of Police Science and Administration* 10 (1982): 194–205.

97. Martin, "'Outsider Within' the Station House," p. 387.

98. Ibid., p. 392.

99. Ibid., p. 394.

100. Ibid., p. 397.

101. Roi Dianne Townsey, "Black Women in American Policing: An Advancement Display," *Journal of Criminal Justice* 10 (1982): 455–468.

102. J. G. Wexler and V. Quinn, "Considerations in the Training and Development of Women Sergeants," *Journal of Police Science and Administration* 13 (1985): 98–105.

103. Martin, "Female Officers on the Move?" pp. 325–326.

104. Ibid.

105. Poole and Pogrebin, "Factors Affecting the Decision to Remain in Policing," pp. 54–55.

106. Roy Roberg, David Hayhurst, and Harry Allen, "Job Burnout in Law Enforcement Dispatchers: A Comparative Analysis," *Journal of Criminal Justice* 16 (1988): 385–394.

107. Yates and Pillai, "Frustration and Strain Among Fort Worth Police Officers."

108. For an impressive review, see Richard Farmer, "Clinical and Managerial Implication of Stress Research on the Police," *Journal of Police Science and Administration* 17 (1990): 205–217.

109. Francis Cullen, Terrence Lemming, Bruce Link, and John Wozniak, "The Impact of Social Supports on Police Stress," *Criminology* 23 (1985): 503–522.

110. Farmer, "Clinical and Managerial Implications of Stress Research on the Police"; Nancy Norvell, Dale Belles, and Holly Hills, "Perceived Stress Levels and Physical Symptoms in Supervisory Law Enforcement Personnel," *Journal of Police Science and Administration* 16 (1988): 75–79.

111. Donald Yates and Vijayan Pillai, "Attitudes Toward Community Policing: A Causal Analysis," *Social Science Journal* 33 (1996): 193–209.

112. Harvey McMurray, "Attitudes of Assaulted Police Officers and Their Policy Implications," *Journal of Police Science and Administration* 17 (1990): 44–48.

113. John Blackmore, "Police Stress," in *Policing Society*, ed. Clinton Terry (New York: Wiley, 1985), p. 395.

114. Rose Lee Josephson and Martin Reiser, "Officer Suicide in the Los Angeles Police Department: A Twelve-Year Follow-Up," *Journal of Police Science and Administration* 17 (1990): 227–230.

115. Yates and Pillai, "Attitudes Toward Community Policing," pp. 205–206.

116. Ibid.

117. Farmer, "Clinical and Managerial Implications of Stress Research on the Police," p. 215.

118. Peter Hart, Alexander Wearing, and Bruce Headey, "Assessing Police Work Experiences: Development of the Police Daily Hassles and Uplifts Scales," *Journal of Criminal Justice* 21 (1993): 553–573.

119. Vivian Lord, Denis Gray, and Samuel Pond, "The Police Stress Inventory: Does It Measure Stress?" *Journal of Criminal Justice* 19 (1991): 139–149.

120. Samuel Walker, *Popular Justice* (New York: Oxford University Press, 1980), p. 197.

121. See, for example, President's Commission on Law Enforcement and the Administration of Justice, *Task Force Report: The Police* (Washington, D.C.: U.S. Government Printing Office, 1967), pp. 181–182; National Advisory Commission on Civil Disorders, *Police and the Community* (Washington, D.C.: U.S. Government Printing Office, 1968), pp. 158–159.

122. President's Commission on Law Enforcement and the Administration of Justice, *Task Force Report: The Police*, pp. 181–182.

123. Albert Reiss, *The Police and the Public* (New Haven, Conn.: Yale University Press, 1972).

124. Lawrence Sherman, "Causes of Police Behavior: The Current State of Quantitative Research," *Journal of Research in Crime and Delinquency* 17 (1980): 80–81.

125. David Bayley and James Garofalo, "The Management of Violence by Police Patrol Officers," *Criminology* 27 (1989): 1–27.

126. Joel Garner, John Buchanan, Tom Schade, and John Hepburn, *Understanding the Use of Force by and Against the Police* (Washington, D.C.: National Institute of Justice, 1996).

127. Antony Pate and Lorie Fridell, *Police Use of Force: Official Reports, Citizen Complaints, and Legal Consequences* (Washington, D.C.: Police Foundation, 1993).

128. Bill Girdner, "Charge of Racism by California Police Is Latest in Long Line," *Boston Globe*, 19 January 1989, p. 3.

129. Kim Michelle Lersch and Tom Mieczkowski, "Who Are the Problem-Prone Officers? An Analysis of Citizen Complaints," *American Journal of Police* 15 (1996): 23–42.

130. Samuel Walker, "The Rule Revolution: Reflections on the Transformation of American Criminal Justice, 1950–1988," *Working Papers, Series 3* (Madison: Institute for Legal Studies, University of Wisconsin Law School, December 1988).

131. Lawrence Sherman and Robert Langworthy, "Measuring Homicide by Police Officers," *Journal of Criminal Law and Criminology* 4 (1979): 546–560.

132. Ibid.

133. James Fyfe, "Police Use of Deadly Force: Research and Reform," *Justice Quarterly* 5 (1988): 165–205.

134. Sherman and Langworthy, "Measuring Homicide by Police Officers."

135. Ibid., pp. 178–179.

136. Richard Kania and Wade Mackey, "Police Violence as a Function of Community Characteristics," *Criminology* 15 (1977): 27–48.

137. Ibid.

138. Sherman and Langworthy, "Measuring Homicide by Police Officers."

139. Ibid.

140. David Lester, "Predicting the Rate of Justifiable Homicide by Police Officers," *Police Studies* 16 (1993): 43; Jonathan Sorenson, James Marquart, and Deon Brock, "Factors Related to Killings of Felons by Police Officers: A Test of the Community Violence and Conflict Hypotheses," *Justice Quarterly* 10 (1993): 417–440; David Jacobs and David Britt, "Inequality and Police Use of Deadly Force: An Empirical Assessment of a Conflict Hypothesis," *Social Problems* 26 (1979): 403–412.

141. Fyfe, "Police Use of Deadly Force," p. 181.

142. Paul Takagi, "A Garrison State in a 'Democratic' Society," *Crime and Social Justice* 5 (1974): 34–43.

143. Mark Blumberg, "Race and Police Shootings: An Analysis in Two Cities," *Contemporary Issues in Law Enforcement*, ed. James Fyfe (Beverly Hills, Calif.: Sage 1981), pp. 152–166.

144. James Fyfe, "Shots Fired" (Ph.D. diss., State University of New York, Albany, 1978).

145. National Law Enforcement Officers Memorial Fund, press release, Washington, D.C, 7 February 1996.

146. S. C. Gwymme, "Bloodshed in the Banks," *Time*, 31 March 1997, pp. 19–21.

147. J. David Hirschel, Charles Dean, and Richard Lumb, "The Relative Contribution of Domestic Violence to Assault and Injury of Police Officers," *Justice Quarterly* 11 (1994): 99–118.

148. David Konstantin, "Law Enforcement Officers Feloniously Killed in the Line of Duty: An Exploratory Study," *Justice Quarterly* 1 (1984): 29–45.

149. David Lester, "The Murder of Police Officers in American Cities," *Criminal Justice and Behavior* 11 (1984): 101–113.

150. *Tennessee v. Garner*, 471 U.S. 1, 105 S.Ct. 1694, 85 L.Ed.2d 889 (1985).

151. *Graham v. Connor*, 490 U.S. 386, 109 S.Ct. 1865, 104 L.Ed.2d 443 (1989).

152. Franklin Graves and Gregory Connor, "The FLETC Use-of-Force Model," *Police Chief* 59 (1992): 56–58.

153. See James Fyfe, "Administrative Interventions on Police Shooting Discretion: An Empirical Examination," *Journal of Criminal Justice* 7 (1979): 313–325.

154. Frank Zarb, "Police Liability for Creating the Need to Use Deadly Force in Self-Defense," *Michigan Law Review* 86 (1988): 1982–2009.

155. Ibid.; for an opposing finding, see William Waegel, "The Use of Lethal Force by Police: The Effect of Statutory Change," *Crime and Delinquency* 30 (1984):121–140.

156. For information, contact Commission for Accreditation for Law Enforcement Agencies, 4242B Chain Bridge Road, Fairfax, Virginia 22030.

157. Estimate based on Geller and Scott, "Deadly Force: What We Know," p. 452.

158. "Sharp Decline in Officer Deaths Reported for 1996," *Criminal Justice Newsletter* 27, 16 January 1997, p. 6.

159. Walker, *Popular Justice*, p. 64.

160. Herman Goldstein, *Police Corruption* (Washington, D.C.: Police Foundation, 1975), p. 3.

161. Knapp Commission, *Report on Police Corruption* (New York: George Braziller, 1973), pp. 1–34.

162. Elizabeth Neuffer, "Seven Additional Detectives Linked to Extortion Scheme," *Boston Globe*, 25 October 1988, p. 60.

163. Kevin Cullen, "U.S. Probe Eyes Bookie Protection," *Boston Globe,* 25 October 1988.

164. Michael Johnston, *Political Corruption and Public Policy in America* (Monterey, Calif.: Brooks/Cole, 1982), p. 75.

165. William Doherty, "Ex-Sergeant Says He Aided Bid to Sell Exam," *Boston Globe,* 26 February 1987, p. 61.

166. Anthony Simpson, *The Literature of Police Corruption,* vol. 1 (New York: John Jay Press, 1977), p. 53.

167. Peter Kraska and Victor Kappeler, "Police On-Duty Drug Use: A Theoretical and Descriptive Examination," *American Journal of Police* 7 (1988): 1–28.

168. Ellwyn Stoddard, "Blue Coat Crime," in *Thinking About Police,* ed. Carl Klockars (New York: McGraw-Hill, 1983), pp. 338–349.

169. Lawrence Sherman, *Police Corruption: A Sociological Perspective* (Garden City, N.Y.: Doubleday, 1974).

170. Robert Daley, *Prince of the City* (New York: Houghton Mifflin, 1978).

171. Sherman, *Police Corruption,* pp. 40–41.

172. Samuel Walker, *Police in Society* (New York: McGraw-Hill, 1983), p. 181.

173. Sherman, *Police Corruption,* p. 194.

174. Barbara Gelb, *Tarnished Brass: The Decade After Serpico* (New York: Putnam, 1983); Candace McCoy, "Lawsuits Against Police: What Impact Do They Have?" *Criminal Law Bulletin* 20 (1984): 49–56.

175. "Philadelphia Police Corruption Brings Major Reform Initiative," *Criminal Justice Newsletter* 27, 1 October 1996, pp. 4–5.

176. Thomas Barker, "Rookie Police Officers' Perceptions of Police Occupational Deviance," *Police Studies* 6 (1983): 30–38.

Police and the Rule of Law

The police are charged with both preventing crime before it occurs and identifying and arresting criminals who have broken the law. To carry out these tasks, police officers want a free hand to search for evidence, to seize contraband such as guns and drugs, to interrogate suspects, and to have witnesses and victims identify suspects. They know their investigation must be thorough. For trial, they will need to provide the prosecutor with sufficient evidence to prove guilt "beyond a reasonable doubt." Therefore, soon after the crime is committed, they must make every effort to gather physical evidence, obtain confessions, and take witness statements that will be adequate to prove the case in court. Police officers also realize that evidence the prosecutor is counting on to prove the case, such as the testimony of a witness or co-conspirator, may evaporate before the trial begins. Then the case outcome may depend on some piece of physical evidence or a suspect's statement taken early during the investigation.

The need for police officers to gather conclusive evidence can conflict with the constitutional rights of citizens. For example, although police want a free hand to search homes and cars for evidence, the Fourth Amendment restricts police activities by requiring that they obtain a warrant before conducting a search.

When police wish to vigorously interrogate a suspect, they are bound to honor the Fifth Amendment's prohibition against forcing people to incriminate themselves.

Over the years, the confrontation between police and the criminal suspect has been moderated by the courts. Most important, the U.S. Supreme Court has used its power of case review and constitutional interpretation to set limits on police operations. At one time, the Court did little to curb police, leaving their authority unchecked. In the 1960s, the Warren Court moved vigorously to restrict police activities, going so far as to "punish" police by excluding from trial any evidence obtained in violation of the suspect's constitutional rights (the so-called *exclusionary rule*). Some critics charged that Court decisions "handcuffed" the police while giving criminal suspects free rein to continue their law-violating activities; the rising crime rate in the 1960s and 1970s was blamed on the Warren Court's "submissiveness." Since then, under the leadership of the Court by Chief Justices Warren Burger (1969 to 1985) and William Rehnquist (1985 to present), the balance has shifted: criminal suspects have received fewer protections, and police officers find it easier to obtain search warrants, interrogate suspects, and conduct lineups. Many appellate courts reverse a smaller percentage

Although courts have curtailed suspects' rights in the 1990s, arrestees are still protected against illegal searches and interrogations. Before police can question this suspect, they must give him his Miranda warning.

of convictions appealed to them than they did a few decades ago. Getting tough with criminals also seems to be the trend in the 1990s. There is often tension between the police, who desire a free hand to investigate crimes and interrogate suspects, and the courts, which seek to uphold civil liberties and to protect the rights of the accused.

Some experts believe that search and seizure rules are too complex for the police to understand. The search warrant requirement, for example, has more than a dozen exceptions, and when the police apply the wrong rules, the legality of the search could result in a guilty defendant going free. On the other hand, it is uncertain whether rules regulating police investigation result in suppression of evidence and the release of the guilty. Some studies show that prosecutions are lost because of suppression rulings less than 1% of the time.[1] (See the discussion of the exclusionary rule at the end of this chapter).

In sum, police are controlled in their investigatory activities by the rule of law. At some junctures in the nation's history the Court has sided with the police, while at others it has put the civil liberties of criminal suspects first. This chapter reviews these issues and shows how the changes in Court rulings have influenced police operations and investigations.

Identification of Criminal Behavior

Once a crime has been committed and the purpose of the investigation has been determined, the police may use various means to collect the evidence needed for criminal prosecution. With each crime, police must decide how best to investigate it. Should surveillance techniques be used to secure information? Is there reasonable suspicion to justify stopping and frisking a suspect? Has the investigation shifted from a general inquiry and begun to focus on a particular suspect so that the police can start a legally appropriate interrogation? Depending on the circumstances, one investigative technique may be more appropriate than another.

Lethal Weapon

Do police officers often get to shoot scores of people, destroy property, and engage in wild, high-speed car chases? If the *Lethal Weapon* series of movies is to be believed, such violent action would be commonplace for a big-city police officer.

The extremely popular *Lethal Weapon* films team the explosive Sgt. Griggs (Mel Gibson) with solid family man Sgt. Murtagh (Danny Glover). These two single-handedly take on international drug cartels and high-powered domestic criminals. Although they are shot at, beaten, and tortured, they emerge unscathed and un-bowed. During the course of a film, they dispatch dozens of bad guys without the need to file a report, face a tribunal, or explain their activities to a board of inquiry. In one famous scene in *Lethal Weapon II*, a corrupt South African official claims diplomatic immunity to save himself from arrest; Murtagh calmly shoots him, claiming that his immunity has been "revoked." While the South African was not the nicest person in the world, the kindly Murtagh committed first-degree murder!

While exciting and entertaining, the *Lethal Weapon* films bear little resemblance to real police work. Any officer who suffered one-tenth the injuries that Griggs and Murtagh sustain would be placed on a disability leave as soon as he got out of intensive care. Yet despite being severely tortured and stabbed, partially drowned and blown up, Griggs and Murtagh never seem to miss a day of work. Even more dubious is the unrestrained use of violence by these officers. The typical police offi-

cer would have to be on the job for more than 500 years before he or she shot and killed a criminal (given that there are 500,000 officers and about 1,000 offenders are killed each year). We also know that in real life, the typical tour of duty results in no serious arrests.

However, hardly a day goes by in the career of Griggs and Murtagh without their making numerous felony arrests, breaking up international drug cartels, and shooting multiple perpetrators who get in their way. In the real world, any time an officer pulls and uses his or her weapon, he or she is required to fill out an extensive shooting incidence report that is reviewed by senior officers. Detectives who shoot as much as Murtagh and Griggs would be spending their entire career writing reports and going before review boards, leaving them precious little time for police work.

Griggs is also considered a psychological basket case because his wife was killed in an automobile accident (which was actually the work of a South African drug dealer). Yet Los Angeles police commanders consider it appropriate to assign this disturbed officer, despite his killing sprees, to cases where he can wreak havoc and endanger civilians. Big-city police officials might try to save the career of officers with psychological problems, but they would assign them to the property room or communications, where they would be less likely to shoot someone. What would a plaintiff's lawyer do to someone like Griggs on cross-examination in an excessive force lawsuit after he admits that he has shot 200 to 300 people during his career? If Griggs were a real Los Angeles cop, his number would have been retired long ago.

Criminal detection, apprehension, and arrest are the primary investigative functions performed by law enforcement officers.[2] Proper police investigations involve collecting facts and information that will lead to the identification, arrest, and conviction of the criminal. Many police operations are informational—such as referring an alcoholic to a hospital or resolving a family dispute—and based on agency policy or police discretion. In contrast, the primary techniques of investigation—such as stopping and questioning people or interrogating a suspect—are controlled by statute and constitutional case law and are subject to review by the courts.

The U.S. Supreme Court has taken an active role in considering the legality of police operations. The Court has reviewed numerous appeals charging that police violated a suspect's rights during the investigation, arrest, and custody stages of the justice process. Of primary concern has been police conduct in obtaining and serving search and arrest warrants and in conducting postarrest interrogations and lineups. In some instances, the Court has expanded police power—for example, by increasing the occasions when police can search without a warrant. In other cases, the Court has restricted police operations—for example, by ruling that every criminal suspect has a right to an attorney when being interrogated by police. Changes in the law often reflect such factors as the justices' legal philosophy, their emphasis on the ability of police to control crime, their views on public safety, and their commitment to the civil liberties of criminal defendants. The issues and cases discussed in the following sections reflect the endless ebb and flow of judicial decision making and its impact on the law enforcement process.

Search and Seizure

Evidence collected by the police is governed by the **search and seizure** requirements of the Fourth Amendment of the U.S. Constitution.[3] The **Fourth Amendment** protects the defendant against unreasonable searches and seizures resulting from unlawful activities. Although there are exceptions, the general rule regarding the application of the Fourth Amendment is that any search or seizure undertaken without a validly obtained search warrant is unlawful. Furthermore, the amendment provides that no warrant shall be issued unless there is probable cause to believe that an offense has been or is being committed. A police officer concerned with investigating a crime can undertake a proper search and seizure if a valid search warrant has been obtained from the court or if the officer is functioning under one of the many exceptions to the search warrant requirement.

A **search warrant** is an order from a court authorizing and directing the police to search a designated place for property stated in the order and to bring that property to court. The order must be based on the sworn testimony of the police officer that the facts on which the request for the search warrant is made are trustworthy.

Search Warrant Requirements

Three critical concepts in the Fourth Amendment are directly related to the search warrant: unreasonableness, probable cause, and particularity.

Unreasonableness in searches and seizures generally refers to whether an officer has exceeded the scope of police authority. Most unreasonable actions are those in which the police officer did not have sufficient information to justify the search. In discussing **probable cause,** the Fourth Amendment provides clearly that no warrants shall be issued unless probable cause is supported by oath or affirmation; in other words, a search warrant can be obtained only if the request for it is supported by facts that convince the court that a crime has been or is being committed.

Particularity generally refers to the search warrant itself; the Fourth Amendment requires that a search warrant specify the place to be searched and the reasons for searching it. When the police request a search warrant, the warrant must identify the premises and the personal property to be seized, and it must be signed under oath by the officer requesting it. The essential facts and information justifying the need for the search warrant are set out in an affidavit requesting the warrant.

In practice, law enforcement officers do not often rely on a search warrant to enter a home or search a person, but in certain kinds of cases—such as investigations of organized crime, gambling, drug, and pornography cases—search warrants are particularly useful. Police also request warrants during investigations of other offenses when they are reasonably sure that the evidence sought cannot be removed from the premises, destroyed, or damaged by the suspect. The police are generally reluctant to seek a warrant, however, because of the stringent evidentiary standards courts require for obtaining one and the availability of search-and-seizure alternatives.

Use of Informers

The U.S. Supreme Court has played an active role in interpreting the legal requirements of a search warrant. One of the major issues considered by the Court has been the reliability of the evidence contained in the affidavit. In many instances, the evidence used by the police in requesting a search warrant originates with a police informer, rather than with the police officer. Such information is normally referred to as **hearsay evidence.**

The Supreme Court has determined that such evidence must be corroborated to serve as a basis for probable cause and thereby justify the issuance of a warrant. In *Illinois v. Gates* (1983), the Court established a "totality of the circumstances" test to determine probable cause for issuing a search warrant.[4] This means that to obtain a warrant, the police must prove to a judge that, considering the "totality of the circumstances," an informant has relevant and factual knowledge that a fair probability exists that evidence of a crime will be found in a certain place.

In sum, to obtain a search warrant, the following procedural requirements must be met: (1) the police officer must request the warrant from the court; (2) the officer must submit an affidavit establishing the proper grounds for the warrant; and (3) the affidavit must state the place to be searched and the property to be seized. Whether the affidavit contains sufficient information to justify issuing the warrant is what determines its validity once it is issued.

Warrantless Searches

There are some significant exceptions to the search warrant requirement of the Fourth Amendment. Two critical exceptions are searches incident to a lawful arrest and field interrogations. Other specialized warrantless searches include automobile searches, consent searches, and drug courier profiles. These exceptions, as well as the doctrine of plain view and the law of electric surveillance, are discussed below.

Searches Incident to a Lawful Arrest

Traditionally, a search without a search warrant is permissible if it is a **search incident to a lawful arrest.** For example, if shortly after the armed robbery of a grocery store, officers arrest a suspect with a briefcase who is hiding in the basement, a search of the suspect's person and of the briefcase would be a proper search incident to a lawful arrest and without a warrant. The legality of this type of search depends almost entirely on the lawfulness of the arrest. The arrest will be upheld if the police officer observed the crime being committed or had probable cause to believe that the suspect committed the offense. If the arrest is found to have been invalid, then any warrantless search made incident to the arrest would be considered illegal, and the evidence obtained from the search would be excluded from trial.

The police officer who searches a suspect incident to a lawful arrest must generally observe two rules. First, it is important that the officer search the suspect at the time of or immediately following the arrest. Second, the police may search only the suspect and the area within the suspect's immediate control; that is, when a police officer searches a person incident to a lawful arrest, such a search may not legally go beyond the area where the person can reach for a

Chimel v. California (1969)

This case illustrates how the U.S. Supreme Court changed its legal position with regard to the scope of a search incident to a lawful arrest.

Facts

On the afternoon of September 13, 1965, three police officers arrived at the Santa Ana, California, home of Ted Chimel with a warrant authorizing his arrest for the burglary of a coin shop. The officers knocked on the door, identified themselves to Chimel's wife, and asked if they could come inside. She admitted the officers into the house, where they waited 10 or 15 minutes until Chimel returned home from work. When he entered the house, one of the officers handed him the arrest warrant and asked for permission to look around. Chimel objected but was advised that the officers could conduct a search on the basis of the lawful arrest. No search warrant had been issued.

Accompanied by Chimel's wife, the officers then looked through the entire three-bedroom house. The officers told Chimel's wife to open drawers in the master bedroom and sewing room and "to physically move contents of the drawers from side to side so that [they] might view any items that would have come from [the] burglary." After completing the search, the officers seized numerous items, including some coins. The entire search took between 45 minutes and an hour.

At the defendant's subsequent state trial on two charges of burglary, the coins taken from his house were admitted into evidence against him over his objection that they had been unconstitutionally seized. He was convicted, and the judgment was affirmed by the California Supreme Court.

Decision

The U.S. Supreme Court decided that the search of Chimel's home went far beyond any area where he might conceivably have obtained a weapon or destroyed any evidence and that no constitutional basis existed for extending the search to all areas of the house. The Court concluded that the scope of the search was unreasonable under the Fourth Amendment as applied through the Fourteenth Amendment, and Chimel's conviction was overturned.

Significance of the Case

The Chimel case changed the policy with regard to the scope of a search made by an officer incident to a lawful arrest. In the past, a police officer was permitted to search all areas under the control of the defendant. The Court's ruling in the Chimel case allows the officer to search only the defendant and the immediate physical surroundings under the defendant's control, generally interpreted as an arm's length distance around the defendant. No longer can a police officer who arrests a person in that person's home search the entire house without a valid search warrant.

weapon or destroy any evidence. The U.S. Supreme Court dealt with the problem of the permissible scope of a search incident to a lawful arrest in the important case of **Chimel v. California,** which is summarized in the accompanying Law in Review.[5] According to the *Chimel* doctrine, the police can search a suspect without a warrant after a lawful arrest to protect themselves from danger and to secure evidence.

One of the problems with the exception of search incident to a lawful arrest is defining what is a "lawful arrest." In common law, an arrest ordinarily occurs if a person believes he or she cannot leave the scene and the police officer conveys this information to the subject. In the case of **California v. Hodari** (1991), the subject, Hodari, fled when police approached and, before being apprehended, threw down a rock of crack cocaine.[6] The question in the case was whether Hodari, after fleeing from police, was under their control and therefore "seized" at the time he dropped the drugs. The Supreme Court ruled that the crack was admissible evidence because it had been abandoned by the suspect and was not obtained by an illegal search and seizure. The *Hodari* case stands for the proposition that a person is not seized under the Fourth Amendment until he or she has either been subjected to physical force or has submitted to the assertion of governmental control.

Another important exception to the rule requiring a search warrant is the **threshold inquiry,** or the **stop-and-frisk** procedure. Police examination of a suspect on the street does not always occur during or after arrest; officers frequently stop persons who appear to be behaving in a suspicious manner or about whom complaints are being made. Ordinarily, police are not required to have sufficient evidence for an arrest in order to stop a person for brief questioning. If the only way in which the police could stop a person was by making an arrest, they would be prevented from investigating many potentially criminal situations. For this reason, the courts have given the police the authority to stop a person, ask questions, and search the person in a limited way, such as frisking for a concealed weapon. The courts have concluded that it is unreasonable to expect a police officer to decide immediately whether to arrest a suspect. With a limited power to stop and frisk, the police officer is able to investigate suspicious persons and situations without having to meet the probable cause standard for arrest. If the police officer did not have this authority, many innocent individuals would probably be arrested.

In the case of **Terry v. Ohio** (1968), the Supreme Court upheld the right of the police to conduct brief threshold inquiries of suspicious persons when they have reason to believe that such persons may be armed and dangerous to the police or others.[7] The Court's intention was to allow the officer, who interacts with members of the community many times each day, to conduct proper investigations where necessary, while keeping invasions of personal rights to a minimum and protecting the officer from harm.[8]

The **field interrogation** process is based primarily on the ability of the police officer to determine whether suspicious conduct exists that gives the officer reason to believe a crime is about to be committed. Some jurisdictions have enacted legislation authorizing the stop-and-frisk procedure, thereby codifying the standard established in *Terry v. Ohio*. Courts have ruled that frisking must be limited to instances in which the police officer determines that his or her safety or that of others is at stake. The stop-and-frisk exception cannot be used to harass citizens or conduct exploratory searches. But the valid pat-down under the *Terry* case must be based on a reasonable belief that the person is armed and presently dangerous.

The U.S. Supreme Court has also established that certain situations justify the warrantless search of an automobile on a public street or highway. For example, evidence can be seized from an automobile when a suspect is taken into custody subject to a lawful arrest. In *Carroll v. United States,* which was decided in 1925, the Supreme Court ruled that distinctions should be made between searches of automobiles, persons, and homes. The Court also concluded that a warrantless search of an automobile is valid if the police have probable cause to believe that the car contains evidence they are seeking.[9]

The legality of searching automobiles without a warrant has always been a trouble spot for police and the courts. Should the search be limited to the interior of the car, or can the police search the trunk? What about a suitcase in the trunk? What about the glove compartment? Does a traffic citation give the police the right to search an automobile? These questions have produced significant litigation over the years. To clear up the matter, the Supreme Court decided the landmark case of **United States v. Ross** in 1982.[10]

In *Ross,* the Court held that if probable cause exists to believe that an automobile contains criminal evidence, a warrantless search by the police is permissible, including a search of closed containers in the vehicle (see the Law in Review on page 237 for a detailed discussion). In sum, the most important requirement for a warrantless search of an automobile is that it must be based on the legal standard of probable cause that a crime related to the automobile has been or is being committed. Police who undertake the search of a vehicle must have reason to believe that it contains evidence pertaining to the crime.

Field Interrogation: Stop and Frisk

Automobile Searches

The legality of searching automobiles without a warrant has always been a trouble spot for police and the courts. Should the search be limited to the interior of the car, or can the police search the trunk? The Supreme Court has ruled that a warrantless search of an automobile is permitted if there is probable cause that a crime related to the automobile has been or is being committed and that the vehicle contains evidence pertaining to the crime.

To substantiate this position further, the Court, in the case of *California v. Acevedo,* stated that the Fourth Amendment does not require the police to obtain a warrant to open a container in a vehicle simply because they lack probable cause to search the entire car.[11] Like the ruling in *Ross,* the police may search an automobile and containers within it when they have probable cause to believe evidence is located there. As a result of *Acevedo,* there is virtually no validity left to the so-called container exception when it is in the automobile.

In sum, beginning with *United States v. Ross* (1982) up to the current time, Court decisions regarding auto searches started going decidedly in favor of greater police latitude.

Consent Searches

Police officers may also undertake warrantless searches when the person in control of the area or object voluntarily consents to the search. Those who consent to a search essentially waive their constitutional rights under the Fourth Amendment. Ordinarily, courts are reluctant to accept such waivers and require the state to prove that the **consent** was voluntarily given. In addition, the consent must be given intelligently, and in some jurisdictions, consent searches are valid only after the suspect is informed of the option to refuse consent.

The major legal issue in most consent searches is whether the police can prove that consent was given voluntarily. For example, in the case of *Bumper v. North Carolina* (1968), police officers searched the home of an elderly woman

United States v. Ross (1982)

Facts

Acting on information from an informant that a described individual was selling narcotics kept in the trunk of a certain car parked at a specified location, District of Columbia police officers immediately drove to the location, found the car there, and a short while later stopped the car and arrested the driver, who matched the informant's description. One of the officers opened the car's trunk, found a closed brown paper bag, and, after opening the bag, discovered glassine bags containing white powder (later determined to be heroin). The officer then drove the car to headquarters, where another warrantless search of the trunk revealed a zippered leather pouch containing cash. The defendant was subsequently convicted of possession of heroin with intent to distribute, the heroin and currency found in the searches having been introduced in evidence after a pretrial motion to suppress the evidence had been denied. The court of appeals reversed the decision, holding that while the officers had probable cause to stop and search the car, including the trunk, without a warrant, they should not have opened either the paper bag or the leather pouch found in the trunk without first obtaining a warrant.

Decision

The U.S. Supreme Court reversed the lower-court ruling, stating, "Police officers who have legitimately stopped an automobile and who have probable cause to believe that contraband is concealed somewhere within it may conduct a warrantless search of the vehicle as thoroughly as a magistrate could authorize by warrant." Furthermore, the rationale justifying the automobile exception does not apply so as to permit a warrantless search of any movable container that is believed to be carrying an illicit substance and that is found in a public place, even when the container is placed in a vehicle not otherwise believed to be carrying contraband. However, where police officers have probable cause to search an entire vehicle, they may conduct a warrantless search of every part of the vehicle and its contents, including all containers and packages, that may conceal the object of the search. The scope of the search is not defined by the nature of the container in which the contraband is secreted. Rather, it is defined by the object of the search and the places in which there is probable cause to believe that it may be found. For example, probable cause to believe that undocumented aliens are being transported in a van will not justify a warrantless search of a suitcase.

Significance of the Case

The U.S. Supreme Court has attempted to clarify the law of warrantless searches of automobiles by applying the singular concept of probable cause to the search of the vehicle and any material, including closed containers, found in the vehicle. The Court emphasized that police officers who have legitimately stopped an automobile and who have probable cause to believe that contraband is concealed somewhere within it may conduct a warrantless search of the vehicle as thoroughly as a magistrate could authorize by warrant. Also, the automobile exception to the Fourth Amendment's warrant requirement established in *Carroll v. United States,* 267 U.S. 132, 45 S.Ct. 280, 69 L.Ed. 543 (1925), applies to searches of vehicles that are supported by probable cause to believe that the vehicles contain contraband. In this kind of case, a search is not unreasonable if based on objective facts that would justify the issuance of a warrant, even though a warrant has not actually been obtained.

This decision should result in some order in the area of legal decision making on warrantless automobile searches, but at a loss of privacy to the individual.

---

after informing her that they possessed a search warrant.[12] At the trial, the prosecutor informed the court that the search was valid because the woman had given her consent. When the government was unable to produce the warrant, the court decided that the search was invalid because the woman's consent was not given voluntarily. On appeal, the U.S. Supreme Court upheld the lower court's finding that the consent had been illegally obtained by the false claim of the police that they had a search warrant.

In most consent searches, however, voluntariness is a question of fact to be determined from all the circumstances of the case. In *Schneckloth v. Bustamonte* (1973), for example, where the defendant actually helped the police by opening the trunk and glove compartment of the car, the Court said this demonstrated that the consent was voluntarily given.[13] Furthermore, the police are usually under no obligation to inform a suspect of the right to refuse consent. Failure to tell a suspect of this right does not make the search illegal, but it may be a factor used by courts to decide whether the suspect gave consent voluntarily.

The Bus Sweep

Today, consent searches have additional significance because of their use in drug control programs. On June 20, 1991 the U.S. Supreme Court, in **Florida v. Bostick,** upheld the police drug interdiction technique of boarding buses and, without suspicion of illegal activity, questioning passengers, asking for identification, and requesting permission to search luggage.[14] Using what is known as the **bus sweep,** police in the *Bostick* case boarded a bus bound from Miami to Atlanta during a stopover in Fort Lauderdale. Without suspicion, the officers picked out the defendant and asked to inspect his ticket and identification. After identifying themselves as narcotics officers looking for illegal drugs, they asked to inspect the defendant's luggage. Although there was some uncertainty about whether the defendant consented to the search in which contraband was found and whether he was informed of his right to refuse to consent to the search, the defendant was convicted.

The Supreme Court was faced with deciding whether consent was freely given or whether the nature of the bus sweep search negated the defendant's consent. Justice Sandra Day O'Connor, writing for the majority, said that police may approach individuals without any suspicion and that asking questions and requesting to search luggage does not constitute a "seizure" in every instance.[15] In other words, drug enforcement officers, after obtaining consent, may search luggage on a crowded bus without meeting the Fourth Amendment requirements for a search warrant or probable cause.

This case raises fundamental questions about the legality of new techniques used to discourage drug trafficking. Law enforcement officials are concerned about intercepting large amounts of drugs and money. Bus sweeps are one answer to the drug menace. But is the Supreme Court compromising individual Fourth Amendment rights when it considers these encounters between police and citizens to be consensual in nature?

A similar issue involves expanding police officers' searches in public housing projects. Supporters of "gun sweeps" argue that the danger of gun violence in the projects constitutes an emergency circumstance in which the Supreme Court may uphold such a warrantless search.

The Doctrine of Plain View

Another instance in which police can search for and seize evidence without benefit of a warrant is if it is in **plain view.** For example, if a police officer is conducting an investigation and notices while questioning some individuals that one person has drugs in her pocket, the officer could seize the evidence and arrest the suspect. Or, if the police are conducting a search under a warrant enabling them to look for narcotics in a person's home and they come upon a gun, the police can seize the gun, even though it is not mentioned in the warrant. The 1986 case of *New York v. Class* illustrates the plain view doctrine.[16] A police officer stopped a car for a traffic violation. Wishing to check the vehicle identification number (VIN) on the dashboard, he reached into the car to clear away material that was obstructing his view. While clearing the dash, he noticed a gun under the seat—"in plain view." The U.S. Supreme Court upheld the seizure of the gun as evidence because the police officer had the right to check the VIN; therefore, the sighting of the gun was legal.

The doctrine of plain view was applied and further developed in *Arizona v. Hicks* in 1987.[17] Here, the Court held that moving a stereo component in plain view a few inches in order to record the serial number constituted a search under the Fourth Amendment. When a check with police headquarters revealed the item had been stolen, the equipment was seized and offered for evidence at Hicks' trial. The Court held that a plain view search and seizure could only be justified by probable cause, not reasonable suspicion, and suppressed the evidence against the defendant. In this case, the Court decided to take a firm stance on protecting Fourth Amendment rights. The standard of reasonable suspicion, as opposed to probable cause, was not enough in this case. The *Hicks* decision is uncharacteristic in an era when most decisions have tended to expand the exceptions to the search warrant requirement.

By way of analogy, the concept of the plain view doctrine has been extended to the plain-feel doctrine. In *Minnesota v. Dickerson,* a police officer patting down a suspect who had been validly stopped under *Terry v. Ohio* may seize an object whose contour and mass make it apparent it is a sizeable object.[18] The patdown must be limited to a search for weapons. The case seems to expand the idea of plain view to embrace all of the senses and not merely that of sight.

An issue long associated with plain view is whether police can search **open fields,** which are fenced in but are otherwise open to view. In *Oliver v. United States* (1984), the U.S. Supreme Court distinguished between the privacy granted persons in their own home or its adjacent grounds (curtilage) and a field. The Court ruled that police can use airplane surveillance to spot marijuana fields and then send in squads to seize the crops, or they can peer into fields from cars for the same purpose.[19]

These cases illustrate how the concepts of curtilage, plain feel and open fields have added significance in defining the scope of the Fourth Amendment in terms of the doctrine of plain view.

Electronic Surveillance

The use of wiretapping to intercept conversations between parties has significantly affected police investigative procedures. Electronic devices allow people to listen to and record the private conversations of others over telephones, through walls and windows, and even over long-distance phone lines. Using these devices, police are able to intercept communications secretly and obtain information related to criminal activity.

The earliest and most widely used form of electronic surveillance is **wiretapping.** With approval from the court and a search warrant, law enforcement officers place listening devices on telephones to overhear oral communications of suspects. Such devices are also often placed in homes and automobiles. The evidence collected is admissible and used in the defendant's trial.

Electronic eavesdropping by law enforcement personnel, however, represents an invasion of an individual's right to privacy unless a court gives prior permission to intercept conversations in this manner. Police can obtain criminal evidence by eavesdropping only if such activities are controlled under rigid guidelines established under the Fourth Amendment, and they must normally request a court order based on probable cause before using electronic eavesdropping equipment.

Many citizens believe that electronic eavesdropping through hidden microphones, radio transmitters, and telephone taps and bugs represents a grave threat to personal privacy.[20] Although the use of such devices is controversial, the police are generally convinced of their value in investigating criminal activity. Others, however, believe that these techniques are often used beyond their lawful intent to monitor political figures, harass suspects, or investigate cases involving questionable issues of national security.

In response to concerns about invasions of privacy, the U.S. Supreme Court has increasingly limited the use of electronic eavesdropping in the criminal justice system. *Katz v. United States* (1967) is an example of a case in which the government failed to meet the requirements necessary to justify electronic surveillance.[21] The *Katz* doctrine is usually interpreted to mean that the government must obtain a court order if it wishes to listen into conversations in which the parties have a reasonable expectation of privacy, such as in their own homes or on the telephone; public utterances or actions are fair game. *Katz* concluded that electronic eavesdropping is a search, even though there is no actual trespass. Therefore, it is unreasonable and a warrant is needed. Katz was convicted of transmitting wagering information by telephone in violation of a federal statute. This case is significant because the Supreme Court declared that the Fourth Amendment was not to apply solely to protected places involving privacy but that such protections also relate to the privacy of individuals.

As a result of the controversy surrounding the use of electronic eavesdropping over the last 25 years, Congress has passed legislation to control the interception of oral communications. The Omnibus Crime Control Act (Title III) of 1968 initially prohibited lawful interceptions except by warrant or with consent.[22] The federal electronic surveillance law was modified by the Electronic Communications Privacy Act of 1986.[23] In light of technological changes, Title III of the new act was expanded to include not only all forms of wire and oral communications but also virtually all types of nonaural electronic communication. The law added new offenses to the previous list of crimes for which electronic surveillance could be used and liberalized court procedures for permitting such surveillance and issuing court orders.

This Act set the minimum legal standards for electronic surveillance for federal and state law enforcement officers. Three of the key provisions of Title III are (1) all electric interceptions are criminal and subject to a $10,000 fine and 5 years in prison unless authorized by statute; (2) application for warrant must be authorized by the U.S. Attorney General; and (3) a neutral and impartial judge must grant the application on the basis of probable cause.

In general, the basic principle of the law of electronic surveillance is that wiretapping and other devices that violate privacy are contrary to the Fourth Amendment. As a result of technological advances, such devices probably pose a greater threat to personal privacy than physical searches. The U.S. Supreme Court has permitted only narrow exceptions, such as court-ordered warrants and consensual monitoring.[24]

Arrest

The **arrest** power of the police involves taking a person into custody in accordance with lawful authority and holding that person to answer for a violation of the criminal law. For all practical purposes, the authority of the police to arrest a suspect is the basis for crime control; without such authority, the police would be powerless to implement the criminal law.

The arrest power is used primarily by law enforcement officers. Generally, law enforcement personnel are employed by public police agencies, derive their authority from statutory laws, and take an oath to uphold the laws of their jurisdiction. Most police officers have complete law enforcement responsibility and unrestricted powers of arrest in their jurisdictions; they carry firearms, and they give evidence in criminal trials.

An arrest, the first formal police procedure in the criminal justice process, occurs when a police officer takes a person into custody or deprives a person of freedom for having allegedly committed a criminal offense. Because the police stop large numbers of people each day for a variety of reasons, the time when an arrest actually occurs may be hard to pinpoint. Some persons are stopped for short periods of questioning, others are informally detained and released, and still others are formally placed under arrest. An actual arrest occurs when the following conditions exist:

1. The police officer believes that sufficient legal evidence exists that a crime is being or has been committed and intends to restrain the suspect.

2. The police officer deprives the individual of freedom.

3. The suspect believes that he or she is in the custody of the police officer and cannot voluntarily leave.

The police officer is not required to use the term *arrest* or some similar word to initiate an arrest, nor does the officer first have to bring the suspect to the stationhouse. For all practical purposes, a person who has been deprived of liberty is under arrest.

Arrests can be initiated with or without an arrest warrant and must be based on probable cause. The arrest warrant, an order issued by the court, determines that an arrest should be made and directs the police to bring the named person before the court. An arrest warrant must be based on probable cause that the person to be arrested has committed or is attempting to commit a crime. The police will ordinarily go before a judge and obtain a warrant where no danger exists that the suspect will leave the area, where a long-term investigation of organized crime is underway, or where probable cause exists to arrest the suspect.

Most arrests are made without a warrant. The decision to arrest is often made by the police officer during contact with the suspect. An arrest may be made without a warrant only in the following two circumstances:

1. Where the arresting officer is able to establish probable cause that a crime has been committed and that the defendant is the person who committed it

2. Where the law of a given jurisdiction allows for arrest without a warrant

In the case of a felony, most jurisdictions provide that a police officer may arrest a suspect without a warrant where probable cause exists even if the officer was not present when the offense was committed. In the case of a misdemeanor, probable cause and the officer's presence at the time of the offense are required. When there is some question as to the legality of an arrest, it usually involves whether the police officer has probable cause or a reasonable belief based on reliable evidence that the suspect has committed a crime. The issue is reviewed by the judge when the suspect is brought before the court for a hearing.

As a general rule, if the police make an arrest without a warrant, the person arrested must be brought before a magistrate promptly for a probable cause hearing. The U.S. Supreme Court dealt with the meaning of promptness in the 1991 case of *Riverside County v. McLaughlin*.[25] The Court said that the police may detain an individual arrested without a warrant for up to 48 hours without a court hearing on whether the arrest was justified. This decision takes into account the state's interest in taking suspects into custody and the individual's concern about prolonged custody affecting employment and family relations.

One of the long-running issues in the area of arrest and search and seizure is the propriety of the so-called pretextual stops and arrests of motorists. These stops and arrests are generally for traffic infractions in which the police officer has a motive for his or her actions unrelated to traffic (usually drug enforcement). In the 1996 case of **Whren v. U.S.,** the Supreme Court ruled that if the stop is objectively supported by probable cause to believe a traffic violation occurred, the pretextual stop and arrest does not violate the Fourth Amendment, regardless of the officer's motivation.[26] Often defendants argue that such police actions are racially motivated, but the Court said racial discrimination issues should be raised in an equal protection context.

Custodial Interrogation

A suspect who comes into police custody at the time of arrest—on the street, in a police car, or in the police station—must be warned of his or her right under the Fifth Amendment to be free from self-incrimination before police conduct any questioning. In the landmark case of **Miranda v. Arizona** (1966), the Supreme Court held that the police must give the *Miranda* warning to a person in custody before questioning begins.[27] Suspects in custody must be told that they have the following rights:

1. They have the right to remain silent.

2. If they decide to make a statement, the statement can and will be used against them in a court of law.

3. They have the right to have an attorney present at the time of the interrogation, or they will have an opportunity to consult with an attorney.

4. If they cannot afford an attorney, one will be appointed for them by the state.

Most suspects choose to remain silent, and since oral as well as written statements are admissible in court, police officers often do not elicit any statements without making certain a defense attorney is present. If an accused decides to answer any questions, he or she may also stop at any time and refuse to answer further questions. A suspect's constitutional rights under *Miranda* can be given up (waived), however. Consequently, a suspect should give careful consideration before abrogating any custodial rights under the *Miranda* warning.

Thirty years have passed since this warning was established by the Warren Court. During this time, U.S. appellate courts have heard literally thousands of cases involving alleged violations of *Miranda* rights, custodial interrogation, right to counsel, and statements made to persons other than the police, among others. Some experts believe felons have been freed because of the *Miranda* decision. What follows is a detailed analysis of this often litigated and hotly contested legal issue.

Historical Perspective on Miranda

Prior to the *Miranda* safeguards, confessions could be obtained from a suspect who had not consulted with an attorney. An early ruling in *Brown v. Mississippi* (1936) held that statements obtained by physical coercion were inadmissible evidence, but it also limited the use of counsel to aid the accused at this early stage of the criminal process.[28] Not until 1964 in **Escobedo v. Illinois** was the groundwork laid for the landmark *Miranda* decision. In *Escobedo,* the Supreme Court finally recognized the critical relationship between the Fifth Amendment privilege against self-incrimination and the Sixth Amendment right to counsel. Danny Escobedo was a convicted murderer who maintained that the police interrogation forced him to make incriminating statements that were regarded as a voluntary confession. In *Escobedo,* the Court recognized that he had been denied the assistance of counsel, which was critical during police interrogation. With this

Miranda v. Arizona (1966)

Miranda v. Arizona is a landmark decision that climaxed a long line of self-incrimination cases in which the police used unlawful methods to obtain confessions from suspects accused of committing a crime.

Facts

Ernesto Miranda, a 25-year-old mentally retarded man, was arrested in Phoenix, Arizona and charged with kidnapping and rape. Miranda was taken from his home to a police station, where he was identified by a complaining witness. He was then interrogated and, after about two hours, signed a written confession. Miranda was subsequently convicted and sentenced to 20 to 30 years in prison. His conviction was affirmed by the Arizona Supreme Court, and he appealed to the U.S. Supreme Court, claiming that he had not been warned that any statement he made would be used against him and that he had not been advised of any right to have counsel present at his interrogation.

The Miranda case was one of four cases heard simultaneously by the U.S. Supreme Court, which dealt with the legality of confessions obtained by the police from a suspect in custody. In Vignera v. New York (1966), the defendant was arrested in connection with a robbery and taken to two different detective headquarters, where he was interrogated and subsequently confessed after eight hours in custody. In Westover v. United States (1966), the suspect was arrested by the Kansas City police, placed in a lineup, and booked on a felony charge. He was interrogated by the police during the evening and the morning and by the FBI in the afternoon, when he signed two confessions. In California v. Stewart (1966), the defendant was arrested at his home for being involved in a robbery. He was taken to a police station and placed in a cell, where over a period of five days he was interrogated nine times. The Supreme Court in Miranda described the common characteristics of these four cases:

In each, the defendant was questioned by the police in a room in which he was cut off from the outside world. In none of these cases was the defendant given a full and effective warning of his rights at the outset of the interrogation process. In all the cases, the questioning elicited oral admissions, and in three of them, signed statements as well which were admitted at their trials. They all thus share salient features—incommunicado interrogation of individuals in a police-dominated atmosphere, resulting in self-incriminating statements without full warnings of constitutional rights.

Decision

The major constitutional issue in Miranda, as in the other three cases, was the admissibility of statements obtained from a defendant questioned while in custody or while otherwise deprived of his freedom. The Fifth Amendment provides that no person shall be compelled to be a witness against himself or herself. This means that a defendant cannot be required to testify at his or her trial and that a suspect who is questioned before trial cannot be subjected to any physical or psychological pressure to confess.

In the opinion of Chief Justice Earl Warren in the Miranda case, "the third degree method was still 'sufficiently widespread to be the object of concern.'" Of greater concern, he believed, was the increased use of sophisticated psychological pressures on suspects during interrogation. Thus, in a 5-to-4 decision, Miranda's conviction was overturned, and the Court established specific procedural guidelines for police to follow before eliciting statements from persons in police custody.

The Court's own summary of its decision is

Our holding will be spelled out with some specificity in the pages which follow but briefly it is this: the prosecution may not use statements, whether exculpatory or inculpatory, stemming from custodial interrogation of the defendant unless it demonstrates the use of procedural safeguards effective to secure the privilege against self-incrimination. By custodial interrogation, we mean questioning initiated by law enforcement officers after a person has been taken into custody or otherwise deprived of his freedom of action in any significant way. As for the procedural safeguards to be employed, unless fully effective means are devised to inform accused persons of their right of silence and to assure a continuous opportunity to exercise it, the following measures are required. Prior to any questioning the person must be warned that he has a right to remain silent, that any statement he does make may be used as evidence against him, and that he has a right to the presence of an attorney, either retained or appointed. The defendant may waive effectuation of these rights, provided the waiver is made voluntarily, knowingly, and intelligently. If, however, he indicates in any manner and at any stage of the process that he wishes to consult with an attorney before speaking, there can be no questioning. Likewise, if the individual is alone and indicates in any manner that he does not wish to be interrogated, the police may not question him. The mere fact that he may have answered some questions or volunteered some statements on his own does not deprive him of the right to refrain from answering any further inquiries until he has consulted with an attorney and thereafter consents to be questioned.

Significance of the Case

The Miranda decision established that the Fifth Amendment privilege against self-incrimination requires that a criminal suspect in custody or in any other manner deprived of freedom must be informed of his or her rights. If the suspect is not warned, then any evidence given is not admissible by the government to prove its case.

decision, the Court made clear its concern that the accused should be permitted certain due process rights during interrogation.[29]

Two years later came the *Miranda* decision, which has had an historic impact on police interrogation practices at the arrest stage of the criminal justice process. Prior to *Miranda,* the police often obtained confessions through questioning methods that violated the constitutional privilege against self-incrimination. The Supreme Court declared in *Miranda* that the police have a duty to inform defendants of their rights. Certain specific procedures (that is, the *Miranda* warning) must be followed, or any statements by a defendant will be excluded from evidence. The purpose of the warning is to implement the basic Fifth Amendment right to be free from self-incrimination.

As a result, the interrogation process is protected by the Fifth Amendment, and if the accused is not given the *Miranda* warning, any evidence obtained during interrogation is not admissible to prove the state's case. It is important to note, however, that the *Miranda* decision does not deny the police the opportunity to ask a suspect general questions as a witness at the scene of an unsolved crime, as long as the person is not in custody and the questioning is of an investigative and nonaccusatory nature. In addition, a suspect can still offer a voluntary confession after the *Miranda* warning has been issued. The *Miranda* decision is summarized in the Law in Review box on page 243.

After the *Miranda* decision, many people became concerned that the Supreme Court under Chief Justice Earl Warren had gone too far in providing procedural protections to the defendant. Some nationally prominent persons expressed opinions that made it seem as if the Supreme Court was emptying the prisons of criminals, and law enforcement officers throughout the nation generally have been disturbed by the *Miranda* decision, believing that it seriously hampers their efforts to obtain confessions and other self-incriminating statements from defendants. Early research indicates, however, that the decision had little or no effect on the number of confessions obtained by the police and that it has not affected the rate of convictions.[30] Since *Miranda,* little empirical evidence has been produced showing that the decision has had a detrimental impact on law enforcement efforts.

Table 8.1 summarizes some of the most significant Fourth and Fifth Amendment Supreme Court decisions that have an impact on law enforcement practices and individual rights.

The Pretrial Identification Process

After the accused is arrested, he or she is ordinarily brought to the police station, where the police list the possible criminal charges. At the same time, they obtain other information, such as a description of the offender and the circumstances of the offense, for booking purposes. The **booking process** is a police administrative procedure in which generally the date and time of the arrest are recorded; arrangements are made for bail, detention, or removal to court; and any other information needed for identification is obtained. The defendant may be fingerprinted, photographed, and required to participate in a lineup. In a lineup, a suspect is placed in a group for the purpose of being viewed and identified by a witness. In accordance with the U.S. Supreme Court decisions in *United States v. Wade* (1967)[31] and *Kirby v. Illinois* (1972),[32] the accused has the right to have counsel present at this postindictment lineup or identification procedure.

In the *Wade* case, the Supreme Court held that a defendant has a right to counsel if the lineup takes place after the suspect has been formally charged with a crime. This decision was based on the Court's belief that the postindictment lineup procedure is a critical stage of the criminal justice process. In contrast, the suspect does not have a comparable right to counsel at a pretrial lineup when a complaint or indictment has not been issued. When the right to counsel is violated, the evidence of any pretrial identification must be excluded from the trial.

Fourth Amendment Doctrine	Case Decision	Holding
Expectation of privacy	*Katz v. United States* (1968)	Electronic eavesdropping is a search.
Plain view	*Arizona v. Hicks* (1967)	Fourth Amendment may not apply when the object is in plain view.
Open fields	*Oliver v. United States* (1984)	To what extent can police search a field and curtilage?
Exigent or emergency	*Mincey v. Arizona* (1978)	There is no "murder scene" exception to the requirement of a warrant for search absent an emergency. The emergency dealt with by this exception is often life-related.

Warrant Requirements	Case Decision	Holding
Probable cause	*Brinegar v. United States* (1949)	Probable cause exists where the facts and circumstances within the officers' knowledge and of which they have trustworthy information are sufficient for a man of reasonable caution to believe that an offense has been committed. Best definition of probable cause.
	Illinois v. Gates (1983)	Probable cause to issue a warrant is based on a "totality of circumstances."

Exceptions to the Warrant Requirement	Case Decision	Holding
Federal requirement of exclusionary rule	*Weeks v. United States* (1914)	U.S. Supreme Court applied the exclusionary rule to federal prosecutions.
State application	*Mapp v. Ohio* (1961)	U.S. Supreme Court applied the exclusionary rule to state prosecutions.
Automobile search	*United States v. Ross* (1982)	Warrantless search of an auto is permissible when it is based on probable cause.
Search incident to arrest	*Chimel v. California* (1969)	Permissible scope for a search is the area "within the arrestee's immediate control."

Fourth Amendment Doctrine	Case Decision	Holding
Stop and frisk	*Terry v. Ohio* (1967)	Police are authorized to stop and frisk suspicious persons.
Consent	*Schneckloth v. Bustamonte* (1973)	Consent to search must be voluntarily given.
Bus sweep	*Florida v. Bostick* (1991)	Police, after obtaining consent, may conduct a search of luggage without a search warrant or probable cause.

Exceptions to the Exclusionary Rule	Case Decisions	Holding
Good faith	*United States v. Leon* (1984)	When police rely on "good faith" in a warrant, the evidence seized is admissible even if the warrant is subsequently deemed defective.
	Arizona v. Evans (1995)	Evidence seized incident to an arrest, based on a patrol car's computer showing an outstanding arrest warrant which was in error due to mistake of court employees, need not be excluded from trial.

Fifth Amendment Doctrine	Case Decisions	Holding
Self-incrimination	*Miranda v. Arizona* (1966)	Defendant must be given the *Miranda* warning before questioning begins.

Table 8.1
Notable Case Doctrines and Exceptions to the Fourth Amendment (Search and Seizure) and Fifth Amendment (Self-Incrimination) Clauses

One of the most difficult legal issues in this area is determining whether the identification procedure is "suggestive" and consequently in violation of the due process clause of the Fifth and Fourteenth Amendments. In S*immons v. United States* (1968), the Supreme Court said, "The primary evil to be avoided is a very substantial likelihood of irreparable misidentification."[33] In its decision in *Neil v. Biggers* (1972), the Court established the following general criteria to judge the suggestiveness of a pretrial identification procedure: (1) the opportunity of the witness to view the criminal at the time of the crime; (2) the degree of attention by the witness and the accuracy of the prior description by the witness; (3) the level of certainty demonstrated by the witness; and (4) the length of time between the crime and the confrontation.[34]

The Exclusionary Rule

No review of the legal aspects of policing would be complete without a discussion of the exclusionary rule, the principal means used to restrain police conduct. As previously mentioned, the Fourth Amendment guarantees individuals the right to be secure in their persons, homes, papers, and effects against unreasonable searches and seizures. The **exclusionary rule** provides that all evidence obtained by illegal searches and seizures is inadmissible in criminal trials. Similarly, it excluded the use of illegal confessions under Fifth Amendment prohibitions.

For many years, evidence obtained by unreasonable searches and seizures that should consequently have been considered illegal was admitted by state and federal governments in criminal trials. The only criteria for admissibility was whether the evidence was incriminating and whether it would assist the judge or jury in ascertaining the innocence or guilt of the defendant. How the evidence was obtained was unimportant; its admissibility was determined by its relevance to the criminal case.

In 1914, however, the rules on the admissibility of evidence underwent a change of direction when the Supreme Court decided the case of *Weeks v. United States*.[35] The defendant, Freemont Weeks, was accused by federal law enforcement authorities of using the mails for illegal purposes. After his arrest, the home in which Weeks was staying was searched without a valid search warrant. Evidence in the form of letters and other materials was found in his room and admitted at the trial. Weeks was then convicted of the federal offense based on incriminating evidence. On appeal, the Supreme Court held that evidence obtained by unreasonable search and seizure must be excluded in a federal criminal trial.

Thus, for the first time, the Court held that the Fourth Amendment barred the use in a federal prosecution of evidence obtained through illegal search and seizure. With this ruling, the Court established the exclusionary rule. The rule was based not on legislation but on judicial decision making. Can the criminal go free because the constable blunders? That became the question.

Over the years, subsequent federal and state court decisions have gradually applied the exclusionary rule to state court systems. In 1961 the Supreme Court made the exclusionary rule applicable to state courts in the landmark decision of **Mapp v. Ohio** (1961).[36] Because of the importance of the *Mapp* case, it is discussed in the accompanying Law in Review.

Current Status and Controversy

The U.S. Supreme Court, with its conservative bent of recent years, has been diminishing the scope of the exclusionary rule. In *Illinois v. Gates* (1983), the Court made it easier for police to search a suspect's home by allowing an anonymous letter to be used as evidence in support of a warrant.[37] In another critical case, *United States v. Leon* (1984), the Court ruled that evidence seized by police relying on a warrant issued by a detached and neutral magistrate can be used in a court proceeding, even if the judge who issued the warrant may have relied on less than sufficient evidence.[38] In this case, the Court articulated a **good faith exception** to the exclusionary rule: Evidence obtained with less than an adequate

Mapp v. Ohio (1961)

In this historic case, the U.S. Supreme Court held that all law enforcement agents, federal and state, are affected by the exclusionary rule, which bars the admission of illegally obtained evidence in a criminal trial.

Facts

On May 23, 1957, three police officers arrived at Dolree Mapp's residence pursuant to information that "a person [was] hiding out in the home, who was wanted for questioning in connection with a recent bombing and that there was a large amount of police paraphernalia being hidden in the home." Mapp and her daughter by a former marriage lived on the top floor of the two-family dwelling. Upon their arrival at the house, the officers knocked on the door and demanded entrance, but Mapp, after telephoning her attorney, refused to admit them without a search warrant.

The officers again sought entrance three hours later when four or more additional officers arrived on the scene. When Mapp did not immediately come to the door, the police forcibly opened one of the doors to the house and gained admittance. Meanwhile, Mapp's attorney arrived, but the officers would not permit him to see Mapp or to enter the house. Mapp was halfway down the stairs from the upper floor to the front door when the officers broke into the hall. She demanded to see the search warrant. A paper, claimed to be a search warrant, was held up by one of the officers. She grabbed the "warrant" and placed it in her bosom. A struggle ensued in which the officers recovered the piece of paper and handcuffed Mapp because she had ostensibly been belligerent.

Mapp was then forcibly taken upstairs to her bedroom, where the officers searched a dresser, a chest of drawers, a closet, and some suitcases. They also looked into a photo album and through personal papers belonging to her. The search spread to the rest of the second floor, including the child's bedroom, the living room, the kitchen, and the dinette. In the course of the search, the police officers found pornographic literature. Mapp was arrested and subsequently convicted in an Ohio court of possessing obscene materials.

Decision

The question in the *Mapp* case was whether the evidence was seized in violation of the search and seizure provisions of the Fourth Amendment and therefore inadmissible in the state trial, which resulted in an obscenity conviction. The Supreme Court of Ohio found the conviction valid. However, the U.S. Supreme Court overturned it, stating that the Fourth Amendment's prohibition against unreasonable searches and seizures, enforceable against the states through the due process clause, had been violated by the police. Justice Tom Clark, delivering the majority opinion of the Court, made clear the importance of this constitutional right in the administration of criminal justice when he stated:

There are those who say, as did Justice [then Judge] Cardozo, that under our constitutional exclusionary doctrine "[t]he criminal is to go free because the constable has blundered." In some cases this will undoubtedly be the result. But . . . there is another consideration—the imperative of judicial integrity. . . . The criminal goes free, if he must, but it is the law that sets him free. Nothing can destroy a government more quickly than its failure to observe its own laws, or worse its disregard of the charter of its own existence.

Significance of the Case

In previous decisions, the U.S. Supreme Court had refused to exclude evidence in state court proceedings based on Fourth Amendment violations of search and seizure. The *Mapp* case overruled such decisions, including that of *Wolf v. Colorado,* and held that evidence gathered in violation of the Fourth Amendment would be inadmissible in a state prosecution. For the first time, the Court imposed federal constitutional standards on state law enforcement personnel. In addition, the Court reemphasized the point that a relationship exists between the Fourth and Fifth Amendments, which forms the constitutional basis for the exclusionary rule.

search warrant may be admissible in court if the police officers acted in good faith in obtaining court approval for their search. However, deliberately misleading a judge or using a warrant that the police know is unreasonably deficient would be grounds to invoke the exclusionary rule. A 1988 empirical study of the effects of *United States v. Leon* on police warrant practices found virtually no impact on the judicial suppression of evidence.[39] Although prosecutors initially applauded the decision and defense lawyers feared that the police would be inclined to secure warrants from sympathetic judges, both groups agree that *Leon* has had little practical effect on the processing of criminal cases. Further, most experts believe that no important data exist to prove that the exclusionary rule has had a direct impact on police behavior.

In the latest federal court approach, the Supreme Court addressed the exclusionary rule in 1995 in **Arizona v. Evans.**[40] The case raised the question again as to whether the rule is appropriate when the police act in good faith believing they are in conformity with the Fourth Amendment.

The facts in *Evans* were relatively simple. Phoenix police officers stopped the defendant for a vehicular violation and in so doing ran a computer check that showed an outstanding arrest warrant for Evans. As he was being arrested, he dropped a marijuana cigarette, and more of the drug was seized after being found in the car. There was one problem with the seizure. Seventeen days earlier, the Phoenix Justice Court had quashed the arrest warrant. The Supreme Court ruled that the evidence did not have to be suppressed under the exclusionary rule. The rule was designed as a means of deterring police misconduct, not mistakes by employees, and it doesn't apply where the police acted in reasonable reliance on an apparently valid warrant.

The Future of the Exclusionary Rule

The exclusionary rule has long been a controversial subject in the administration of criminal justice. It was originally conceived to control illegitimate police practices, and that remains its primary purpose today. It is justified on the basis that it deters illegal searches and seizures. Yet most experts believe that no impartial data exist to prove that the rule has a direct impact on police behavior. This is by far the most significant criticism of the rule. By excluding evidence, the rule has a more direct effect on the criminal trial than on the police officer on the street. Furthermore, the rule is powerless when the police have no interest in prosecuting the accused or in obtaining a conviction. In addition, it does not control the wholesale harassment of individuals by law enforcement officials bent on disregarding constitutional rights.

The most popular criticism of the exclusionary rule, however, is that it allows guilty defendants to go free. Because courts frequently decide in many types of cases (particularly those involving victimless offenses, such as gambling and drug use) that certain evidence should be excluded, the rule is believed to result in excessive court delays and to negatively affect plea-bargaining negotiations. However, the rule appears to result in relatively few case dismissals.

Because the exclusionary rule may not deter illegal police action and because its use may result in some offenders escaping conviction, proposals for modifying the rule have been suggested. The American Law Institute's Model Code of Pre-Arraignment Procedure limits the use of the exclusionary rule to substantial violations by law enforcement officials.[41] This means that evidence should be suppressed only if the court finds that the constitutional violations are substantial.

Although the code is only a proposed model, its modification of the exclusionary rule would seem to offer some relief from the problem of having to free criminals due to minor Fourth Amendment violations by police officials. On the other hand, modification of the rule could lead police to become sloppy in their application of constitutional rights and cause them to care more about developing excuses for their actions, such as "we acted in good faith" or "the evidence would have been discovered anyway," than about individuals' rights.[42]

Another approach has been to legislate the exclusionary rule out of existence. In 1988 the U.S. Supreme Court considered this issue in the case of *California v. Greenwood.*[43] Concerned that the defendant Greenwood might be involved in selling drugs, the police collected Greenwood's trash bags from the curb of his home, searched them without a warrant, and found items indicating the defendant used drugs. A subsequent search of Greenwood's home with a warrant disclosed additional drugs. The California Supreme Court held that the police officers' conduct was an impermissible and illegal search. The U.S.

Supreme Court, however, took cognizance of the 1982 amendment to the California State Constitution that provided that evidence was not to be excluded in criminal trials on this basis. Greenwood argued that since state law prohibited the police from examining the trash, this gave him a right of privacy protected by the Fourth Amendment. But the Supreme Court rejected Greenwood's argument, holding that the state could establish the scope of its exclusionary rule and weigh the benefits of controlling police misconduct against the price of excluding reliable evidence. The *Greenwood* case suggests that the exclusionary rule could be modified so long as it pertains to police parameters established by the U.S. Supreme Court.

Other suggested approaches to dealing with violations of the exclusionary rule include (1) criminal prosecution of police officers who violate constitutional rights; (2) internal police control; (3) civil lawsuits against state or municipal police officers; and (4) federal lawsuits against the government under the Federal Tort Claims Act. An individual using any of these alternatives, however, would be faced with such obstacles as the cost of bringing a lawsuit, proving damages, and dealing with a bureaucratic law enforcement system. In the end, of all the civilized countries in the world, only the United States applies an exclusionary rule to illegal searches and seizures of material evidence.[44] Whether the Supreme Court or legislative bodies adopt any more significant changes to the rule will depend largely on efforts by police to discipline themselves. It will also depend on a tough civil tort remedy that allows lawsuits and claims for damages against offending police officers.

The fate of the exclusionary rule will remain difficult to predict. Although it is a simple rule of evidence, it involves complex issues of fairness, justice, and crime control.[45]

Judge Harold Rothwax, in his 1996 book *The Collapse of Criminal Justice,* is convinced that formalistic rules and technicalities like the exclusionary rule cause criminals to go free. Search rules, he states, are too complex for the police to understand, and the search warrant requirement has too many exceptions.[46] Many legal experts believe the time has come again to reexamine and reform the rule. Modifications to the exclusionary rule are a perennial issue before the U.S. Congress.[47]

Criminal Justice on the Net

To better understand the rules governing police conduct, it is important to have access to current criminal procedure law materials. Criminal procedure consists of the law governing the series of proceedings through which the substantive criminal law is enforced. In the United States, most criminal law is set by the states, although the federal government has adopted its own criminal code, Title 18, to deal with activities that extend beyond state boundaries or have special impact on federal government operations.

Cornell University Law School's Legal Information Institute maintains an Internet web site consisting of recent and historic Supreme Court decisions, hypertext versions of the full U.S. Code, the U.S. Constitution, Federal Rules of Evidence and Civil Procedure, recent opinions of the New York Court of Appeals, and other important legal materials—federal, state, foreign and international. Accessing this site is a good way to keep up on decisions influencing police behavior:

http://www.law.cornell.edu/

Summary

Law enforcement officers use many investigatory techniques to detect and apprehend criminal offenders. These include searches, electronic eavesdropping, interrogation, the use of informants, surveillance, and witness identification procedures. Over the past three decades, in particular through U.S. Supreme Court decisions, serious constitutional limitations have been placed on the pretrial process. Under interpretations of the Fourth Amendment, for example, police are required to use warrants to conduct searches except in some clearly defined situations. The exceptions to the search warrant rule include searches of automobiles used in a crime, stop and frisks, searches incident to an arrest, searches of material in plain view, and some instances of electronic eavesdropping.

Police interrogation procedures have also been reviewed extensively. Through the *Miranda* rule, the Supreme Court established an affirmative procedure as a requirement for all custodial interrogations. Many issues concerning *Miranda* continue to be litigated. For instance, in 1994 the Supreme Court held that the police are not obliged to stop questioning a suspect who makes an ambiguous request to have a lawyer present.[48] Lineups and other suspect identification practices have also been subject to court review.

The exclusionary rule continues to be one of the most controversial issues in the criminal justice system. Even though the courts have curtailed its application in recent years, it still generally prohibits the admission of evidence that violates the defendant's constitutional rights.

Key Terms

search and seizure	threshold inquiry	wiretapping
Fourth Amendment	stop and frisk	arrest
search warrant	*Terry v. Ohio*	*Whren v. U.S.*
unreasonableness	field interrogation	*Miranda v. Arizona*
probable cause	*United States v. Ross*	*Escobedo v. Illinois*
particularity	consent	booking process
hearsay evidence	*Florida v. Bostick*	exclusionary rule
searches incident to a lawful arrest	bus sweep	*Mapp v. Ohio*
Chimel v. California	plain view	good faith exception
California v. Hodari	open fields	*Arizona v. Evans*

Questions

1. Should obviously guilty persons go free because police originally arrested them with less than probable cause?

2. Should illegally seized evidence be excluded from trial, even though it is conclusive proof of a person's criminal acts?

3. Should police be personally liable if they violate a person's constitutional rights? How might this influence their investigations?

4. Should a person be put in a lineup without the benefit of counsel?

5. Have criminals been given too many rights? Should courts be more concerned with the rights of victims or the rights of offenders?

6. Does the exclusionary rule effectively deter police misconduct?

7. Do you agree or disagree with the *Mapp v. Ohio* decision?

Notes

1. William Greenhalgh, *The Fourth Amendment Handbook: A Chronological Survey of Supreme Court Decisions* (Chicago: American Bar Association Section on Criminal Justice, 1995).

2. See, generally, American Bar Association, *Standards Relating to the Urban Police Function,* 2nd ed. (Chicago: American Bar Association, 1988); see also Herman Goldstein, *Policing a Free Society* (Cambridge, Mass.: Ballinger, 1977).

3. See classic works of: Wayne R. LaFave, *Arrest: The Decision to Take a Suspect into Custody* (Boston: Little, Brown, 1965); Lawrence P. Tiffany, Donald McIntyre, and Daniel Rotenberg, *Detection of Crime: Stopping and Questioning, Search and Seizure* (Boston: Little, Brown, 1967); Wayne R. LaFave, *Search and Seizure: A Treatise on the Fourth Amendment* (St. Paul: West Publishing, 1978).

4. *Illinois v. Gates,* 462 U.S. 213, 103 S.Ct. 2317, 76 L.Ed.2d 527 (1983).

5. *Chimel v. California,* 395 U.S. 752, 89 S.Ct. 2034, 23 L.Ed.2d 685 (1969).

6. *California v. Hodari,* 499 U.S. 621, 111 S.Ct. 1547, 113 L.Ed.2d 690 (1991).

7. *Terry v. Ohio,* 392 U.S. 1, 88 S.Ct. 1868, 20 L.Ed.2d 889 (1968).

8. Ibid., at 20–27, 88 S.Ct. at 1879–1883.

9. *Carroll v. United States,* 267 U.S. 132, 45 S.Ct. 280, 69 L.Ed. 543 (1925).

10. *United States v. Ross,* 20.456 U.S. 798, 102 S.Ct. 2157, 72 L.Ed.2d 572 (1982); see also Barry Latzer, "Searching Cars and Their Contents: *U.S. v. Ross,*" *Criminal Law Bulletin* 6 (1982): 220; Joseph Grano, "Rethinking the Fourth Amendment Warrant Requirements," *Criminal Law Review* 19 (1982):603.

11. *California v. Acevedo,* 500 U.S. 565, 111 S.Ct. 1982, 114 L.Ed.2d 619 (1991).

12. *Bumper v. North Carolina,* 391 U.S. 543, 88 S.Ct. 1788, 20 L.Ed.2d 797 (1968).

13. *Schneckloth v. Bustamonte,* 412 U.S. 218, 93 S.Ct. 2041, 36 L.Ed.2d 854 (1973).

14. *Florida v. Bostick,* 500 U.S. 167, 111 S.Ct. 2382, 115 L.Ed.2d 389 (1991).

15. Joseph Cronin, "Working the Buses: Leave the Searching to Us," *Suffolk University Law School Journal* 22 (1991): 31–37; see also Edward Felsenthal, "High Court May Back Gun Sweeps," *Wall Street Journal,* 21 April 1994, p. B12.

16. *New York v. Class,* 475 U.S. 106, 106 S.Ct. 960, 89 L.Ed.2d 81 (1986).

17. *Arizona v. Hicks,* 480 U.S. 321, 107 S.Ct. 1149, 94 L.Ed.2d 347 (1987); see also Note, "Fourth Amendment Requires Probable Cause for Search and Seizure Under Plain View Doctrine," *Journal of Criminal Law and Criminology* 78 (1988): 763.

18. *Minnesota v. Dickerson*, 508 U.S. 366, 113 S.Ct. 2130, 124 L.Ed.2d 334 (1993).

19. *Oliver v. United States,* 466 U.S. 170, 104 S.Ct. 1735, 80 L.Ed.2d 214 (1984).

20. Gary T. Marx, *Undercover: Police Surveillance in America* (Berkeley: University of California Press, 1988).

21. *Katz v. United States,* 389 U.S. 347, 88 S.Ct. 507, 19 L.Ed.2d 576 (1967).

22. Omnibus Crime Control Act, Title III, 90th Congress 1968; 18 U.S.C. §§ 2511-2520.

23. Electronic Communications and Privacy Act of 1986, Public Law No. 99-508, Title 18 U.S.C. § 2510.

24. See Michael Goldsmith, "The Supreme Court and Title III: Rewriting the Law of Electronic Surveillance," *Journal of Criminal Law and Criminology* 74 (1983): 76–85.

25. *Riverside County v. McLaughlin,* 500 U.S. 44, 111 S.Ct. 1661, 114 L.Ed.2d 49 (1991).

26. *Whren v. U.S.,* 116 S.Ct. 1769 (1996); see also Kathryn R. Urbonya, "The Fishing Gets Easier," *ABA Journal* 83 (1997): 46.

27. *Miranda v. Arizona,* 384 U.S. 436, 86 S.Ct. 1602, 16 L.Ed.2d 694 (1966).

28. *Brown v. Mississippi,* 297 U.S. 278, 56 S.Ct. 461, 80 L.Ed. 682 (1936).

29. *Escobedo v. Illinois,* 378 U.S. 478, 84 S.Ct. 1758, 12 L.Ed.2d 977 (1964).

30. Michael Wald, "Interrogations in New Haven: The Impact of *Miranda,*" *Yale Law Journal* 76 (1967): 1519.

31. *United States v. Wade,* 388 U.S. 218, 87 S.Ct. 1926, 18 L.Ed.2d 1149 (1967).

32. *Kirby v. Illinois,* 406 U.S. 682, 92 S.Ct. 1877, 32 L.Ed.2d 411 (1972).

33. *Simmons v. United States,* 390 U.S. 377, 88 S.Ct. 967, 19 L.Ed.2d 1247 (1968).

34. *Neil v. Biggers,* 409 U.S. 188, 93 S.Ct. 375, 34 L.Ed.2d 401 (1972).

35. *Weeks v. United States,* 232 U.S. 383, 34 S.Ct. 341, 58 L.Ed. 652 (1914).

36. *Mapp v. Ohio,* 367 U.S. 643, 81 S.Ct. 1684, 6 L.Ed.2d 1081 (1961).

37. *Illinois v. Gates,* 462 U.S. 213, 103 S.Ct. 2317, 76 L.Ed.2d 527 (1983).

38. *U.S. v. Leon,* 468 U.S. 897, 104 S.Ct. 3405, 82 L.Ed.2d 677 (1984).

39. Craig V. Chida, *The Effects of* U.S. v. Leon *on Police Search Warrant Practices* (Washington, D.C.: U.S. Government Printing Office, 1988).

40. *Arizona v. Evans,* 514 U.S., 115 S.Ct. 1185, 131 L.Ed.2d 34 (1995).

41. American Law Institute, *A Model Code of Pre-Arraignment Procedure* (Washington, D.C.: American Law Institute, 1975), Articles 290 and 290.2(4).

42. See, generally, James Fyfe, "In Search of the 'Bad Faith' Search," *Criminal Law Bulletin* 18 (1982): 260–264.

43. *California v. Greenwood,* 486 U.S. 35, 108 S.Ct. 1625, 100 L.Ed.2d 30 (1988).

44. See "The Exclusionary Rule," *American Bar Association Journal* 19 (February 1983): 3; "Rule Prohibiting Illegal Evidence Faces Limitation," *Wall Street Journal,* 30 November 1982.

45. See Bradford Wilson, *Exclusionary Rule* (Washington, D.C.: U.S. Government Printing Office, 1986); see also Jana Nestlerode, "Distinguishing the Exclusionary Rule Exceptions," *Journal of National Association of District Attorneys* 24 (1991): 29–35; see also Lawrence Crocker, "Can the Exclusionary Rule Be Saved?" *Journal of Criminal Law and Criminology* 84 (1993): 310.

46. Harold Rothwax, *The Collapse of Criminal Justice* (New York: Random House, 1996).

47. Tom Smith, "Legislative and Legal Developments," *American Bar Association Journal of Criminal Justice,* 11(1996): 46–47.

48. *Davis v. U.S.,* 512 U.S., 114 S.Ct. 2350, 129 L.Ed.2d 362 (1994).

CHAPTER 9

Courts, Prosecution, and the Defense

The criminal court is the setting in which many of the most important decisions in the criminal justice system are made: Bail, trial, plea negotiations, and sentencing all involve court-made decisions. Within the confines of the court, those accused of crime (defendants) call on the tools of the legal system to provide them with a fair and just hearing, with the burden of proof resting on the state; crime victims ask the government to provide them with justice for the wrongs done them and the injuries they have suffered; and agents of the criminal justice system attempt to find solutions that benefit the victim, the defendant, and society in general. The court process is designed to provide an open and impartial forum for deciding the truth of the matter and reaching a solution that, although punitive, is fairly arrived at and satisfies the rule of law.

As we already know, in today's crowded court system, such abstract goals are often impossible to achieve. In reality, the U.S. court system is often the scene of accommodation and "working things out" rather than an arena for a vigorous criminal defense. Plea negotiations and other nonjudicial alternatives, such as diversion, are far more common than the formal trial process.

In this chapter, we examine the structure and function of the court system, as well as the roles of the judge, the prosecutor, and the defense attorney in the criminal process. Each state, like the federal government, has an independent judicial branch. The prosecutor, to a great extent, is the person who single-handedly controls the "charging" decision in the judicial system. To charge or not, and for what offense, is the prosecutor's great discretionary authority. The defense attorney acts in a different capacity. Although defendants have a right to defend themselves, most are represented by a lawyer who is knowledgeable about the criminal law. The criminal lawyer has a legal obligation to make every effort to provide a competent and adequate defense.

The court is a complex social agency with many independent but interrelated subsystems, each of which has a role in the court's operation: police, prosecutor, defense attorney, judge, and probation department. It is also the scene of many important elements of criminal justice decision making: bail, detention, charging, jury selection, trial, and sentencing.

The Criminal Court Process

As you may recall, there are two ways to view the criminal court process. In the traditional model, the court is seen as a setting for an adversarial procedure that pits the defendant against the state, the defense counsel against the prosecutor. Procedures are fair and formalized, controlled by the laws of criminal procedure and the rule of evidence.

In the second model, the court is viewed as a system that encourages settling matters in the simplest, quickest, and most efficient manner possible. Rather than being adversaries, prosecutors and defense attorneys form a "work group" with the judge and other court personnel that tries to handle the situation with as little fuss as possible. This usually involves dropping the case if the defendant agrees to make restitution or enter a treatment or diversion program, plea bargaining, or using some other "quick fix." In Malcolm Feeley's early study of a lower court in Connecticut, not one defendant in 1,640 cases analyzed insisted on having a jury trial, and only half made use of legal counsel. Because cases dragged on endlessly, people were encouraged to plea bargain. And the haphazard nature of justice produced a situation in which the defendant's prior criminal record and the seriousness of the current charge had little influence on case outcome. Felons with prior records fared as well as first-time misdemeanants.[1]

The U.S. court system has evolved over the years into an intricately balanced legal process that has recently come under siege because of the sheer numbers of cases it must consider and the ways in which it is forced to handle such overcrowding. Overloaded court dockets have given rise to charges of "assembly-line justice," in which a majority of defendants are induced to plead guilty, jury trials are rare, and the speedy trial is highly desired but unattainable.

Overcrowding causes the poor to languish in detention, while the wealthier go free on bail. The possibility increases that an innocent person may be frightened into pleading guilty and, conversely, a guilty person released because a trial has been delayed too long.[2] Whether providing more judges or new or enlarged courts will solve the problem of overcrowding remains to be seen. Meanwhile, diversion programs, decriminalization of certain offenses, and bail reform provide other avenues of possible relief. More efficient court management and administration is also seen as a step that might ease the congestion of the courts. The introduction of professional trial court managers—administrators, clerks, and judges with management skills—is one of the more significant waves of change in the nation's courts in recent decades.

Another emphasis today is on the jury. The role of the grand jury has diminished in favor of the preliminary hearing in felony court cases. Trial court juries have changed in how they are selected, as have size and verdict rules. The U.S. Supreme Court has relaxed the requirements that verdicts be unanimous and be rendered by 12-person juries (see Chapter 11). A major effort is also underway to increase the representativeness of jury pools.

These issues are extremely important if defendants are going to view their experience as a fair one in which they were able to present their side of the case and influence its outcome. Ironically, there is evidence that the informal justice system, which is often deplored by experts, may provide criminal suspects a greater degree of satisfaction than the more formal criminal trial.[3]

To house this rather complex process, each state maintains its own state court organization and structure. American courts basically have two systems: state and federal. There are 50 state trial and appellate systems and separate courts for the District of Columbia and the Commonwealth of Puerto Rico. Usually three (or more) separate court systems exist within each state jurisdiction. These are described next.

State Courts

The state court system alone handled 86 million new cases in 1995. That total included nearly 20 million civil and domestic cases, over 13 million criminal cases, almost 2 million juvenile cases, and 51 million traffic and ordinance viola-

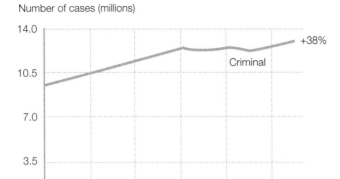

Number of cases (millions)

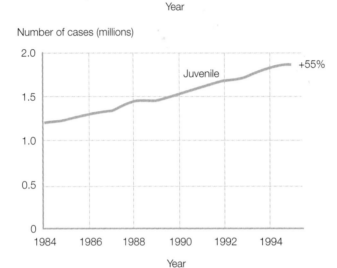

Number of cases (millions)

Figure 9.1

Criminal and juvenile cases filed in state courts, 1984–1995.

SOURCE: Brian Ostrom and Neal Kauder, "Examining the Work of State Courts, 1995: A National Perspective from the Court Statistics Project" (Williamsburg, Va.: National Center for State Courts, 1996).

tions. Significant growth characterized the states' criminal caseloads, which rose 38% from 1984 to 1995. Juvenile delinquency and status offense cases were up 55% during the same period,[4] as shown in Figure 9.1.

There are approximately 14,000 courts of limited jurisdiction in the United States. Most are organized along town, municipal, and county lines of government; the rest are controlled by state governments. Limited jurisdiction courts outnumber general jurisdiction courts approximately five to one (14,000 to 3,000).[5]

Courts of limited jurisdiction (sometimes called municipal courts, or **lower courts**) are restricted in the types of cases they may hear. Usually, they will handle misdemeanor criminal infractions, violations of municipal ordinances, traffic violations, and civil suits where the damages involve less than a certain amount of money (usually $10,000). These courts also conduct preliminary hearings for felony criminal cases.

The lower criminal courts are restricted in the criminal penalties they can impose. Most can levy a fine of $1,000 or less and incarcerate a person for 12 months or less in the local jail.

Included within the category of courts of limited jurisdictions are special courts, such as juvenile and family courts and probate (divorce, estate issues, and custody) courts. Some states separate limited courts into those that handle civil cases only and those that settle criminal cases. A particular problem, such as drug use, may cause states to even create specialized juvenile and adult drug courts.

Courts of Limited Jurisdiction

The nation's lower courts are the ones most often accused of providing assembly-line justice. Because the matters they decide involve minor personal confrontations and conflicts—family disputes, divorces, landlord-tenant conflicts, barroom brawls—the rule of the day is "handling the situation" and resolving the dispute.

Courts of General Jurisdiction

Approximately 3,000 courts of general jurisdiction, or **felony courts,** exist in the United States and process about 1.5 million felony cases each year.[6] Courts of general jurisdiction handle the more serious felony cases (such as murder, rape, and robbery), while courts of limited jurisdiction handle misdemeanors (for example, simple assault, shoplifting, bad checks). About 90% of the general courts are state-administered, and the remainder are controlled by counties or municipalities. The overwhelming majority of general courts hear both serious civil and criminal matters (felonies). A general jurisdiction trial court is the highest state trial court where felony criminal cases are adjudicated.

Courts of general jurisdiction may also be responsible for reviewing cases on appeal from courts of limited jurisdiction. In some cases, they will base their decision on a review of the transcript of the case, while in others, they can actually grant a new trial; this latter procedure is known as the *trial de novo* process. Changes in the courts of general jurisdiction, such as increases in felony filing rates, are watched closely because serious crime is of great public concern. The number of felony filings increased 64% from 1984 to an all-time high in 1995 (see Figure 9.2).[7]

Appellate Courts

If defendants believe that the procedures used in their case were in violation of their constitutional rights, they may appeal the outcome of their case. For example, defendants can file an appeal if they believe that the law they were tried under violates constitutional standards (for example, it was too vague) or if the procedures used in the case contravened principles of due process and equal protection or were in direct opposition to a constitutional guarantee (for example, the defendants were denied the right to have competent legal representation). **Appellate courts** do not try cases; they review the procedures of the case to determine whether an error was made by judicial authorities. Judicial error can include admitting into evidence illegally seized material, improperly charging a jury, allowing a prosecutor to ask witnesses improper questions, and so on. The appellate court can order a new trial, allow the defendant to go free, or uphold the original verdict.

Most criminal appeals are limited to trial convictions, sentences, and guilty plea convictions. The most basic feature of the appellate system is the distinction between mandated appeals by right and discretionary review of certain cases. For example, appeals of trial convictions are ordinarily under the courts' manda-

Figure 9.2
Felony filings in unified and general jurisdiction courts in 38 states, 1984–1995.

SOURCE: Brian Ostrom and Neal Kauder, "Examining the Work of State Courts, 1995: A National Perspective from the Court Statistics Project" (Williamsburg, Va.: National Center for State Courts, 1996).

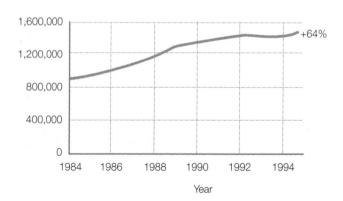

If defendants believe that the procedures used in prosecuting their case were in violation of their constitutional rights, they may appeal the outcome. Pam Smart, shown here, has tried twice to appeal her murder conviction. Smart, a high school teacher, was convicted of conspiring with her teenage student/lover in the murder of her husband, Greg. She appealed her conviction on the grounds that pretrial publicity prevented her from getting a fair hearing.

tory jurisdiction. The most famous appellate court with discretionary jurisdiction—the U.S. Supreme Court—requires four justices to agree to accept a case for review at the nation's highest court.

State criminal appeals are heard in one of the appellate courts in the 50 states and the District of Columbia. Each state has at least one **court of last resort,** usually called a state supreme court, which reviews issues of law and fact appealed from the trial courts; a few states have two high courts, one for civil appeals and the other for criminal cases. In addition, many states have established intermediate appellate courts to review decisions by trial courts and administrative agencies before they reach the supreme court stage. A great deal of diversity exists in the organizational features of the state appellate court system.

Many people believe that criminal appeals clog the nation's court system because so many convicted criminals try to "beat the rap" on a technicality. Actually, criminal appeals represent a small percentage of the total number of cases processed by the nation's appellate courts. All types of appeals, including criminal ones, continue to inundate the courts, so most courts are having problems processing cases expeditiously.[8]

State courts have witnessed an increase in the number of appellate cases each year. From 1984 to 1995, state criminal appeals increased 32%. In the meantime, the number of judges and support staff has not kept pace. The resulting imbalance has led to the increased use of intermediate courts to screen cases.

Although criminal cases do in fact make up only a small percentage of appellate cases, they are still of concern to the judiciary. Steps have been taken to make appealing more difficult. For example, the Supreme Court has tried to limit access to federal courts by prisoners being held in state prisons who have complaints arising out of the conditions of their captivity.

Figure 9.3 illustrates the interrelationship of appellate and trial courts in a model state court structure. Of course, each state's court organization varies

Chapter 9

Courts, Prosecution, and the Defense

257

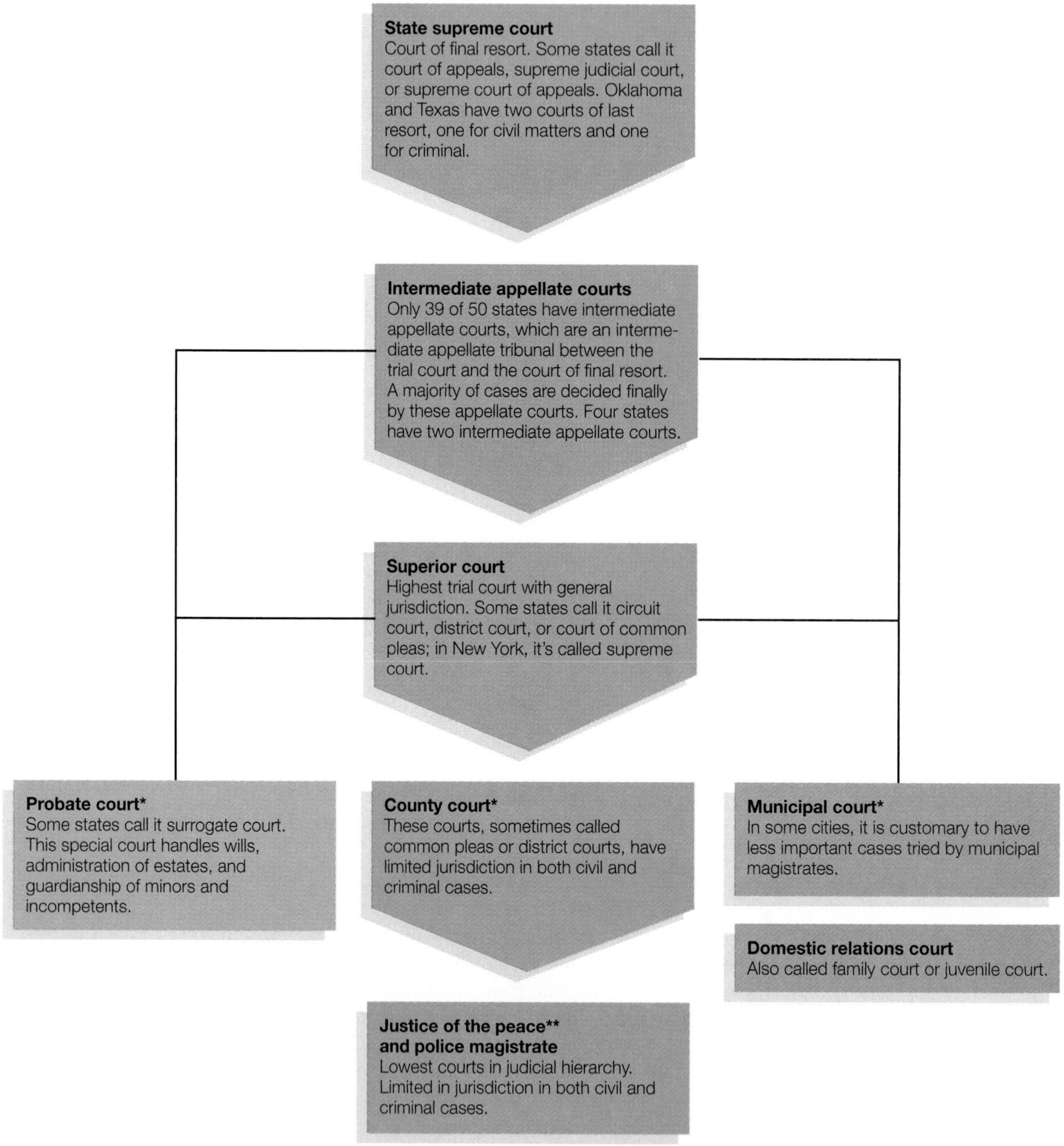

State supreme court
Court of final resort. Some states call it court of appeals, supreme judicial court, or supreme court of appeals. Oklahoma and Texas have two courts of last resort, one for civil matters and one for criminal.

Intermediate appellate courts
Only 39 of 50 states have intermediate appellate courts, which are an intermediate appellate tribunal between the trial court and the court of final resort. A majority of cases are decided finally by these appellate courts. Four states have two intermediate appellate courts.

Superior court
Highest trial court with general jurisdiction. Some states call it circuit court, district court, or court of common pleas; in New York, it's called supreme court.

Probate court*
Some states call it surrogate court. This special court handles wills, administration of estates, and guardianship of minors and incompetents.

County court*
These courts, sometimes called common pleas or district courts, have limited jurisdiction in both civil and criminal cases.

Municipal court*
In some cities, it is customary to have less important cases tried by municipal magistrates.

Domestic relations court
Also called family court or juvenile court.

Justice of the peace**
and police magistrate
Lowest courts in judicial hierarchy. Limited in jurisdiction in both civil and criminal cases.

*Courts of special jurisdiction, such as probate, family, or juvenile courts, and the so-called inferior courts, such as common pleas or municipal courts, may be separate courts or part of the trial court of general jurisdiction.

**Justices of the peace do not exist in all states. Where they do exist, their jurisdictions vary greatly from state to state.

Figure 9.3
A model of a state judicial system.

SOURCES: American Bar Association, *Law and the Courts* (Chicago: American Bar Association, 1974), p. 20; Bureau of Justice Statistics, *State Court Organization—1993* (Washington, D.C.: U.S. Department of Justice, 1995).

from this standard pattern. All states have a tiered court organization (lower, upper, and appellate courts), but they vary somewhat in the way they have delegated responsibility to a particular court system.

In sum, most states have at least two trial courts and two appellate courts, but they differ as to where jurisdiction over such matters as juvenile cases and felony versus misdemeanor offenses is found. Such matters vary from state to state and between the state courts and the federal system. According to the National Center For State Courts, there is no single uniform court system in the United States.[9]

The legal basis for the federal court system is contained in Article 3, section 1, of the U.S. Constitution, which provides that "the judicial power of the United States shall be vested in one Supreme Court, and in such inferior courts as Congress may from time to time ordain and establish." The important clauses in Article 3 indicate that the federal courts have jurisdiction over the laws of the United States and treaties and cases involving admiralty and maritime jurisdiction, as well as over controversies between two or more states and citizens of different states.[10] This complex language generally means that state courts have jurisdiction over all legal matters, unless they involve a violation of a federal criminal statute or a civil suit between citizens of different states or between a citizen and an agency of the federal government.

Within this authority, the federal government has established a three-tiered hierarchy of court jurisdiction that, in order of ascendancy, consists of the (1) U.S. district courts, (2) U.S. courts of appeals (circuit courts), and (3) the U.S. Supreme Court (see Figure 9.4).

U.S. district courts are the trial courts of the federal system. They have jurisdiction over cases involving violations of federal laws, including civil rights abuses, interstate transportation of stolen vehicles, and kidnappings. They may also hear cases on questions involving citizenship and the rights of aliens. The jurisdiction of the U.S. district court will occasionally overlap that of state courts. For example, citizens who reside in separate states and are involved in litigation of an amount in excess of $10,000 may choose to have their cases heard in either of the states or the federal court. Finally, federal district courts hear cases in which one state sues a resident (or firm) in another state, where one state sues another, or where the federal government is a party in a suit. A single judge ordinarily presides over criminal trials; a defendant may also request a jury trial.

Federal district courts were organized by Congress in the Judicial Act of 1789, and today 94 independent courts are in operation. Originally, each state was

The Federal Courts

District Courts

Figure 9.4
The federal judicial system.
SOURCE: American Bar Association, *Law and the Courts* (Chicago: American Bar Association, 1974), p. 21. Updated information provided by the Federal Courts Improvement Act of 1982 and West Publishing Company, St. Paul, Minnesota.

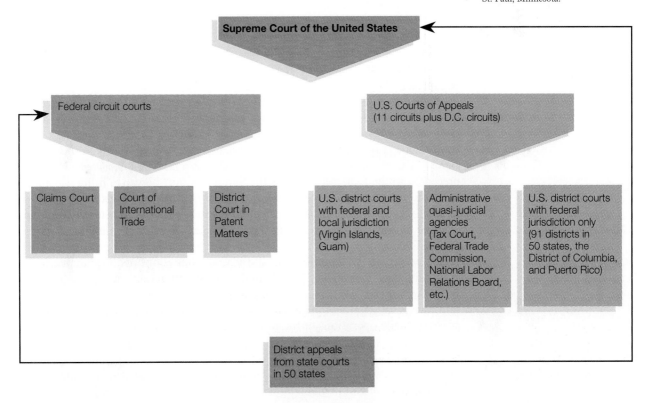

259

allowed one court; as the population grew, however, so did the need for courts. Now each state has from 1 to 4 district courts, and the District of Columbia has 1 for itself. The generally stable federal criminal trial caseload reached a low in 1980 of about 30,000 cases, down from 40,000 in 1972. Since that time, criminal filings have increased, to about 44,000 in 1995. The number of drug cases has contributed to the upward trend in criminal filings.

Federal Appeals Courts

Approximately 35,000 appeals from the district courts are heard each year in the 12 federal courts of appeals, sometimes referred to as U.S. circuit courts. This name is derived from the historical practice of having judges ride the circuit and regularly hear cases in the judicial seats of their various jurisdictions. Today, appellate judges are not required to travel (although some may sit in more than one court), and each federal appellate court jurisdiction contains a number of associate justices who share the caseload. Circuit court offices are usually located in major cities, such as San Francisco and New York, and cases must be brought to these locations by attorneys to be heard.

The circuit court is empowered to review federal and state appellate court cases on substantive and procedural issues involving rights guaranteed by the Constitution. Circuit courts do not actually retry cases, nor do they determine whether the facts brought out during trial support conviction or dismissal. Instead, they analyze judicial interpretations of the law, such as the charge (or instructions) to the jury, and reflect on the constitutional issues involved in each case they hear.

The U.S. Supreme Court

The U.S. Supreme Court is the nation's highest appellate body and the court of last resort for all cases tried in the various federal and state courts.

The Supreme Court is composed of nine members appointed for lifetime terms by the president with the approval of Congress. The Court has discretion over most of the cases it will consider and may choose to hear only those it deems important, appropriate, and worthy of its attention. The Court chooses around 300 of the 5,000 cases that are appealed each year; only half of these receive full opinions.

When the Court decides to hear a case, it grants a **writ of certiorari,** requesting a transcript of the proceedings of the case for review. However, the Supreme Court must grant jurisdiction in a few instances, such as decisions from a three-judge federal district court on reapportionment or cases involving the Voting Rights Act.

When the U.S. Supreme Court rules on a case, usually by majority decision (at least five votes), its rule becomes a precedent that must be honored by all lower courts. For example, if the Court grants a particular litigant the right to counsel at a police lineup, all similarly situated clients must be given the same right. This type of ruling is usually referred to as a **landmark decision.** The use of precedent in the legal system gives the Supreme Court power to influence and mold the everyday operating procedures of the police, trial courts, and corrections agencies. This influence became particularly pronounced during the tenure of Chief Justices Earl Warren and Warren Burger, who greatly amplified and extended the power of the Court to influence criminal justice policies. Under current Chief Justice William Rehnquist, the Court has continued to influence criminal justice matters, ranging from the investigation of crimes to the execution of criminals. The personal legal philosophy of the justices and their orientation toward the civil and personal rights of victims and criminals significantly affect the daily operations of the justice system. (See Chapter 3).

How a Case Gets to the Supreme Court

The Supreme Court is unique in many ways. First, it is the only court established by constitutional mandate, rather than federal legislation. Second, it decides basic social and political issues of grave consequence and importance to the nation. Third, the Court's nine justices shape the future meaning of the U.S. Constitution. Their decisions identify the rights and liberties of citizens throughout the United States.

When our nation was first established, the Supreme Court did not review state court decisions involving issues of federal law. Even though Congress had given the Supreme Court jurisdiction to review state decisions, much resistance and controversy surrounded the relationship between the states and the federal government. However, in a famous decision, *Martin v. Hunter's Lessee* (1816), the Supreme Court reaffirmed the legitimacy of its jurisdiction over state court decisions when such courts handled issues of federal or constitutional law.[11] This decision allowed the Court to actively review actions by states and their courts and reinforced the Court's power to make the supreme law of the land. Since that time, a defendant who indicates that governmental action—whether state or federal—violates a constitutional law is in a position to have the Supreme Court review such action.

To carry out its responsibilities, the Court had to develop a method for dealing with the large volume of cases coming from the state and federal courts for final review. In the early years of its history, the Court sought to review every case brought before it. Since the middle of the 20th century, however, the court has used the writ of certiorari to decide what cases it should hear. *Certiorari* is a Latin term meaning "to bring the record of a case from a lower court up to a higher court for immediate review." When applied, it means that an accused in a criminal case is requesting the U.S. Supreme Court to hear the case. More than 90% of the cases heard by the Court are brought by petition for a writ of certiorari. Under this procedure, the justices have discretion to select the cases they will review for a decision. Of the thousands of cases filed before the Court every year, only 100 to 150 receive a full opinion. Four of the nine justices sitting on the Court must vote to hear a case brought by a writ of certiorari for review. Generally, these votes are cast in a secret meeting attended only by the justices.

After the Supreme Court decides to hear a case, it reviews written and oral arguments. The written materials are referred to as legal briefs, and oral arguments are normally presented to the justices at the Court in Washington, D.C.

After the material is reviewed and the oral arguments heard, the justices normally meet in what is known as a case conference. At this case conference, they discuss the case and vote to reach a decision. The cases voted on by the Court generally come from the judicial systems of the various states or the U.S. courts of appeals, and they represent the entire spectrum of law.

In reaching a decision, the Supreme Court reevaluates and reinterprets state statutes, the U.S. Constitution, and previous case decisions. Based on a review of the case, the Court either affirms or reverses the decision of the lower court. When the justices reach a decision, the chief justice of the Court assigns someone of the majority group to write the opinion. Another justice normally writes a dissent or minority opinion. In the final analysis, the justices join with either the majority opinion or the dissenting opinion. When the case is finished, it is submitted to the public and becomes the law of the land. The decision represents the legal precedents that add to the existing body of law on a given subject, change it, and guide its future development.

In the area of criminal justice, the decisions of the U.S. Supreme Court have had the broadest impact on the reform of the system. The Court's action is the final step in settling constitutional criminal disputes throughout the nation. By discretionary review through a petition for certiorari, the U.S. Supreme Court requires state courts to accept its interpretation of the Constitution. In doing so, the Court has changed the day-by-day operations of the criminal justice system (see the Analyzing Criminal Justice Issues box for an example of the Court's role in the federal and state partnership).

The Role of the High Court and States' Rights

In 1993 the U.S. Congress passed the Brady Handgun Violence Prevention Act. One requirement of the law was that local officials check the backgrounds of handgun purchasers. As a result, the law has been credited with keeping thousands of convicted criminals from purchasing handguns in the past four years. President Clinton considered this legislation one of the most important accomplishments of his first term in office.

In 1997, however, the U.S. Supreme Court struck down the use of background checks by ruling that Congress does not have the power to order the states to conduct such checks on prospective gun buyers. While not addressing the other main provision of the law—the requirement that gun buyers face a five-day waiting period, the Court affirmed the principle of states' rights over federal regulatory power. In a 5–4 decision, the Court said the federal gun law violated the Tenth Amendment of the U.S. Constitution (see *Prince v. United States* and *Mack v. United States,* June 28, 1997). The Tenth Amendment gives states all powers that are not specifically given to the federal government by the Constitution. The Court ruled that Congress went too far in passing a law that required local law enforcement to carry out a federal mandate.

In recent years, the Supreme Court has been sympathetic to the states' rights argument. Two years ago the Court declared unconstitutional a federal law that prohibited the possession of guns near schools because it believed that states, not Congress, had the power to enact such a law. The Brady Law ruling marks another case in which law enforcement is viewed as a state and local function.

As a practical matter, by striking down the handgun check, the Supreme Court used its power to press the federal government to complete a national computerization system for gun checks. The Brady Law required the federal government to establish a national computer bank containing criminal records for each state so that local police can have access to information to block felons from buying handguns. However, the Court's decision is not expected to change substantially the way checks are conducted since the majority of states already require their own handgun checks.

What about the role of the Court in policing the relationships among the three branches of government? It appears that the Court is more skeptical of federal authority than any Court in recent history. The decision represented the Court's recognition that Congress cannot infringe on state powers and that the Brady Law was a major encroachment on states' rights. Underlying this decision is the fear that the Brady Law ruling could threaten federal domestic abuse laws. This ruling highlights the role of the Supreme Court in balancing power between the federal government and the states. According to Justice Antonin Scalia, "The federal government may neither issue directives requiring states to address particular problems, nor command state officials to administer or enforce a federal regulatory program."

Critical Thinking Questions

1. Is it fair for the Supreme Court to strike down a key provision of the Brady Law? Do you think this ruling seems like constitutional common sense to the average person?

2. How do we continue to keep handguns out of the hands of criminals?

SOURCES: *Prince v. United States,* 95–103, July 28, 1997; *United States v. Lopez,* 115 S.Ct. 1624 (1995).

The nation's courts handle over 100 million civil, criminal, and traffic cases each year, resulting in backlogs, delays, and "assembly-line justice."[12] Of these cases, approximately 13 million are criminal matters, an all-time high in 1995. In addition, the federal district courts hear approximately 45,000 criminal and 200,000 civil cases a year.[13] While these figures seem overwhelming, they are even more disturbing because of the sharp increase in both civil and criminal litigation in the past few years. For example, in 1980 federal district courts disposed of 29,000 criminal cases; by 1990 the number had increased to 42,000; in 1995 the number had risen to about 45,000. In 1980 about 19,000 appeals were heard in federal circuit courts; by 1990 the number had grown to almost 35,000 and to

40,000 in 1995.[14] In state courts, the number of felony case filings increased from 690,000 in 1984 to more than 1 million by 1990 and 1.17 million in 1992, an increase of almost 65% in six years. In 1995 the figure stood at 1.5 million (see Figure 9.5). As we noted, the state criminal court caseload rose 38% between 1984 and 1995, while the U.S. population increased by only 10% during the same period. Criminal cases are increasing at least four times faster than the national population.[15] The increasing volume of criminal court cases filed in state courts is one important measure of the amount of criminal activity in our society (see Chapter 2).

Criminal cases are clearly on the rise. The significant increases in both criminal and civil litigation has forced state and local governments to seek ever greater resources for the courts. Court services, including the judiciary, prosecution, legal services such as public defenders, and other court-related matters (juries, stenographers, clerks, bailiffs, maintenance), continue to run in the billions of dollars per year.

What causes court caseloads to overflow? In a survey of judges and trial court administrators, two factors that stood out were the excessive number of continuances demanded by attorneys and the increasing number of pretrial motions on evidence and procedural issues. As the law becomes more complex and involves such issues as computer crimes, the need for a more involved court process has escalated. Ironically, efforts being made to reform the criminal law may also be helping to overload the courts. For example, the increase of mandatory prison sentences for some crimes may reduce the use of plea bargaining and increase the number of jury trials because defendants fear that a conviction will lead to an incarceration sentence and thus must be avoided at all costs. Second, the recent explosion in civil litigation has added to the backlog because most courts handle both criminal and civil matters.

Some courts give criminal cases priority. But the National Center for State Courts still reports that roughly two-thirds of the states do not keep up with the flow of criminal cases since their clearance rates are less than 100%.[16] A state court's clearance rate is a key measure of the adequacy of the court's resources. A clearance rate of 100% means that cases are disposed of by the court at the same rate that new cases are filed. The processing of felony cases poses considerable problems for general jurisdiction courts because the offenses (1) often involve violent or drug crimes; (2) receive a great deal of public attention; (3) generate substantial prosecutorial cost; (4) impose tremendous burdens on the victims; and (5) involve serious evidentiary issues, such as DNA or blood analysis.

If relief is to be found, it will probably be in the form of better administrative and management techniques that improve the use of existing resources. Most courts, however, are not keeping pace with increasing numbers of criminal trial and appellate cases.[17] Another possible method of creating a more efficient court system is to unify existing state courts into a single administrative structure using modern management principles. A third solution would be the appointment of additional judges to the court. The Clinton administration has been criticized for its slow pace in filling vacancies on the federal bench.[18]

The judge is the senior officer in a court of criminal law. His or her duties are quite varied and far more extensive than might be expected. During trials, the judge rules on the appropriateness of conduct, settles questions of evidence and procedure, and guides the questioning of witnesses. In a **jury trial,** the judge must instruct jurors on which evidence is proper to examine and which should be ignored. The judge also formally charges the jury by instructing its members on

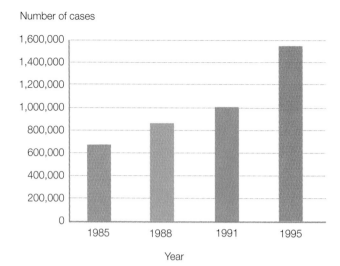

Number of cases

**Figure 9.5
Total felony case filings from 33 states.**

SOURCES: Brian J. Ostrom et al. *State Court Caseload Statistics: Annual Report, 1992* (Williamsburg, Va.: National Center for State Courts, 1994), p. 39; B. Ostrom and N. Kauder, "Examining the Work of State Courts, 1995" (Williamsburg, Va.: National Center for State Courts, 1996).

what points of law and evidence they must consider to reach a decision of either guilty or not guilty. When a jury trial is waived, the judge must decide whether to hold for the complainant or the defendant. Finally, if a defendant is found guilty, the judge must decide on the sentence (in some cases, this is legislatively determined), which includes choosing the type of sentence, its length, and in the case of probation, the conditions under which it may be revoked.

Other Judicial Functions

Beyond these stated duties, the trial judge has extensive control and influence over the other agencies of the court: probation, the court clerk, the police, and the district attorney's office. Probation and the clerk may be under the judge's explicit control. In some courts, the operations, philosophy, and procedures of these agencies are within the magistrate's administrative domain. In others—for example, where a state agency controls the probation department—the attitudes of the county or district court judge greatly influence the way a probation department is run and how its decisions are made. Judges often consult with probation staff on treatment decisions, and many judges are interested in providing the most innovative and up-to-date care possible.

Police and prosecutors are also directly influenced by the judge, whose sentencing discretion affects the arrest and charging processes. For example, if a judge usually chooses minimal sentences—such as a fine for a particular offense—the police may be reluctant to arrest offenders for that crime, knowing that doing so will basically be a waste of their time. Similarly, if a judge is known to have a liberal attitude toward police discretion, the local department may be more inclined to engage in practices that border on entrapment or to pursue cases through easily obtained wiretaps. However, a magistrate oriented toward strict use of due process guarantees would stifle such activities by dismissing all cases involving apparent police abuses of personal freedoms. The district attorney's office may also be sensitive to judicial attitudes. The district attorney might forgo indictments in cases that the presiding magistrate expressly considers trivial or quasi-criminal and in which the judge has been known to take only token action, such as the prosecution of pornographers.

Finally, the judge considers requests by police and prosecutors for leniency (or severity) in sentencing. The judge's reaction to these requests is important if the police and the district attorney are to honor the bargains they may have made with defendants to secure information, cooperation, or guilty pleas. For example, when police tell informers that they will try to convince the judge to go easy on them to secure required information, they will often discuss the terms of the promised leniency with representatives of the court. If a judge ignores police demands, the department's bargaining power is severely diminished, and communication within the criminal justice system is impaired.

Judicial Qualifications

The qualifications for appointment to one of the existing 30,000 judgeships vary from state to state and court to court. Most typically, the potential judge must be a resident of the state, licensed to practice law, a member of the state bar association, and at least 25 and less than 70 years of age. However, a significant degree of diversity exists in the basic qualification, depending on the level of court jurisdiction. While almost every state requires judges to have a law degree if they are to serve on appellate courts or courts of general jurisdiction, it is not uncommon for municipal or town court judges to lack a legal background, even though they maintain the power to incarcerate criminal defendants.

Many methods are used to select judges, depending on the level of court jurisdiction. In some jurisdictions, the governor simply appoints judges. In others, the governor's recommendations must be confirmed by (1) the state senate, (2) the governor's council, (3) a special confirmation committee, (4) an executive council elected by the state assembly, or (5) an elected review board. Some states employ a judicial nominating commission that submits names to the governor for approval.

Another form of judicial selection is popular election. In some jurisdictions, judges run as members of the Republican, Democratic, or other parties, while in others they run without party affiliation. In 13 states partisan elections are used for selecting judges in courts of general jurisdiction, in 17 states nonpartisan elections are used, and in the remainder upper trial-court judges are appointed by the governor or the legislature.

Many states have adopted some form of what is known as the **Missouri Plan** to select appellate court judges, and six states also use it to select trial-court judges. This plan consists of three parts: (1) a judicial nominating commission to nominate candidates for the bench, (2) an elected official (usually from the executive branch) to make appointments from the list submitted by the commission, and (3) subsequent nonpartisan and noncompetitive elections in which incumbent judges run on their records and voters can choose either their retention or dismissal.[19]

The quality of the judiciary is a concern. Although merit plans, screening committees, and popular elections are designed to ensure a competent judiciary, it has often been charged that many judicial appointments are made to pay off political debts or to reward cronies and loyal friends. Also not uncommon are charges that those desiring to be nominated for judgeships are required to make significant political contributions.

The Prosecutor

In 1994 about 2,400 chief state court prosecutors employed about 65,000 attorneys, investigators, and support staff to handle felony cases in the state trial courts. Hundreds of municipal and county attorneys prosecute criminal cases in courts of limited jurisdiction, while others work in the federal court system. The personnel and workload of prosecutors' offices (county-state-federal) has increased by 14% since 1992.[20]

Depending on the level of government and the jurisdiction in which he or she functions, the **prosecutor** may be known as a district attorney, a county attorney, a state's attorney, or a U.S. attorney. Whatever the title, the prosecutor is ordinarily a member of the practicing bar who has been appointed or elected to be a public prosecutor.

Although the prosecutor participates with the judge and defense attorney in the adversary process, the prosecutor is responsible for bringing the state's case against the accused. The prosecutor focuses the power of the state on those who

In the adversary process, the prosecutor is responsible for focusing the power of the state on those who disobey the law by charging them with a crime, releasing them from prosecution, or eventually bringing them to trial. Here Los Angeles prosecutor Pamela Bozanich is shown cross-examining Lyle Menendez, who was on trial for murdering his parents.

Chapter 9

Courts, Prosecution, and the Defense

are accused of disobeying the law by charging them with a crime, releasing them from prosecution, or eventually bringing them to trial.

Although the prosecutor's primary duty is to enforce the criminal law, his or her fundamental obligation as an attorney is to seek justice, as well as to convict those who are guilty. For example, if the prosecutor discovers facts suggesting that the accused is innocent, he or she must bring this information to the attention of the court.

The senior prosecutor must make policy decisions on the exercise of prosecutorial enforcement powers in a wide range of cases in criminal law, consumer protection, housing, and other areas of the law. In so doing, the prosecutor determines and ultimately shapes the manner in which justice is exercised in society.

Many individual prosecutors are caught between being compelled by their supervisors to do everything possible to obtain a guilty verdict and acting as a concerned public official to ensure that justice is done. Sometimes this conflict can lead to prosecutorial misconduct. According to some legal authorities, unethical prosecutorial behavior is often motivated by the desire to obtain a conviction and by the fact that prosecutorial misbehavior is rarely punished by the courts.[21] Some prosecutors may conceal evidence or misrepresent it or influence juries by impugning the character of opposing witnesses. Even where a court may instruct a jury to ignore certain evidence, a prosecutor may attempt to sway the jury or the judge by simply mentioning the tainted evidence. Since appellate courts generally uphold convictions in cases where such misconduct is not considered serious (the harmless error doctrine), prosecutors are not penalized for their misbehavior, nor are they personally liable for their conduct. Overzealous, excessive, and even cruel prosecutors, motivated by a desire for political gain or notoriety, produce wrongful convictions, thereby abusing their office and the public trust.[22] According to legal expert Stanley Fisher, prosecutorial excesses appear when the government (1) always seeks the highest charges, (2) interprets the criminal law expansively, (3) wins as many convictions as possible, and (4) obtains the severest penalties.[23]

Duties of the Prosecutor

The prosecutor is the chief law enforcement officer of a particular jurisdiction. His or her participation spans the entire gamut of the justice system, from the time search and arrest warrants are issued or a grand jury is empaneled to the final sentencing decision and appeal. The general duties of a prosecutor include (1) enforcing the law, (2) representing the government, (3) maintaining proper standards of conduct as an attorney and court officer, (4) developing programs and legislation for law and criminal justice reform, and (5) being a public spokesperson for the field of law. Of these, representing the government while presenting the state's case to the court is the prosecutor's most frequent task. In this regard, the prosecutor does many of the following:

1. Investigates possible violations of the law

2. Cooperates with police in investigating a crime

3. Determines what the charge will be

4. Interviews witnesses in criminal cases

5. Reviews applications for arrest and search warrants

6. Subpoenas witnesses

7. Represents the government in pretrial hearings and in motion procedures

8. Enters into plea-bargaining negotiations

9. Tries criminal cases

10. Recommends sentences to courts upon convictions

11. Represents the government in appeals

Many jurisdictions have also established special prosecution programs aimed at seeking indictments and convictions of those committing major felonies, violent offenses, rapes, and white-collar crimes. In a recent national survey of prosecutorial practices, Michael Benson and his colleagues found an apparent increase in the local prosecution of corporate offenders.[24] According to Benson, the federal government historically played the dominant role in controlling white-collar crime. But there appears to be an increased willingness to prosecute corporate misconduct on a local level if an offense causes substantial harm. The National District Attorneys Association has responded to the concerns of prosecutors faced with the need to enforce complex environmental laws by creating the National Environmental Crime Prosecution Center. This center, modeled after the National Center for Prosecution of Child Abuse, lends assistance to district attorneys who are prosecuting environmental crimes.

In addition, a form of priority prosecutions commonly known as the career criminal prosecution program is popular in many jurisdictions. This program involves identifying dangerous adult and juvenile offenders who commit a high number of crimes so that prosecutors can target them for swift prosecution.[25]

In the federal system, prosecutors are known as U.S. attorneys and are appointed by the president. They are responsible for representing the government in federal district courts. The chief prosecutor is usually an administrator, while assistants normally handle the actual preparation and trial work. Federal prosecutors are professional civil service employees with reasonable salaries and job security.

Types of Prosecutors

On the state and county levels, the attorney general and the district attorney, respectively, are the chief prosecutorial officers. Again, the bulk of the criminal prosecution and staff work is performed by scores of full- and part-time attorneys, police investigators, and clerical personnel. Most attorneys who work for prosecutors on the state and county levels are political appointees who earn low salaries, handle many cases, and, in some jurisdictions, maintain private law practices. Many young lawyers take these staff positions to gain the trial experience that will qualify them for better opportunities. In most state, county, and municipal jurisdictions, however, the office of the prosecutor can be described as having the highest standards of professional skill, personal integrity, and working conditions.

In urban jurisdictions, the structure of the district attorney's office is often specialized, with separate divisions for felonies, misdemeanors, and trial and appeal assignments. In rural offices, chief prosecutors handle many of the criminal cases themselves. Where assistant prosecutors are employed, they often work part-time, have limited professional opportunities, and depend on the political patronage of chief prosecutors for their positions.

The personnel practices, organizational structures, and political atmospheres of many prosecutors' offices often restrict the effectiveness of individual prosecutors in investigating and prosecuting criminal offenses. For many years, prosecutors have been criticized for bargaining justice away, using their position as a stepping stone to higher political office, and often failing to investigate or simply dismissing criminal cases. Lately, however, the prosecutor's public image has improved. Violations of federal laws, such as white-collar crime, drug peddling, and corruption, are being more aggressively investigated by the 94 U.S. attorneys and the nearly 2,000 assistant U.S. attorneys. The National Drug Prosecution Center of the National District Attorneys Association, for instance, is assisting state and federal prosecutors in enforcing complex drug laws.

Aggressive federal prosecutors in New York have also made extraordinary progress in the war against insider trading and security fraud on Wall Street, using informants, wiretaps, and federal racketeering laws. Through RICO (Racketeer Influenced and Corrupt Organization Act, detailed in Chapter 3), the government has successfully obtained convictions of important Mafia gangsters.[26]

At Least One Case of	All Offices	Full-Time Office (population served)		Part-Time Office
		500,000 or More	Less than 500,000	
Case type				
Domestic violence	88%	100%	92%	79%
Stalking	68	94	73	50
Elder abuse	41	82	50	15
Hate crime	29	85	32	13
Environmental pollution	26	68	28	13
Gang membership	12	46	15	0
HIV exposure	10	27	13	0
Child related				
Child abuse	88	100	91	80
Nonpayment of child support	57	58	63	45
Parental abduction of children	41	81	54	6
Fraud				
Bank/thrift fraud	34	58	43	11
Health care fraud	21	49	27	4
Computer fraud/tampering	16	64	19	0
Number of offices	2,336	120	1,533	683

State crimes ranging from murder to larceny are prosecuted in state courts by district attorneys, who are stepping up their efforts against career criminals, shortening the time it takes to bring serious cases to trial, and addressing the long-neglected problems of victims and witnesses. With such actions, the prosecutor will continue to be one of the most powerful and visible professionals in the justice system. Table 9.1 identifies the special categories of felony prosecutions today involving some newly defined crimes.

Prosecutorial Discretion

One might expect that after the police arrest and bring a suspect to court, the entire criminal court process would be mobilized. This is often not the case, however. For a variety of reasons, a substantial percentage of defendants are never brought to trial. The prosecutor decides whether to bring a case to trial or to dismiss it outright. Even if the prosecutor decides to pursue a case, the charges may later be dropped if conditions are not favorable for a conviction, in a process called *nolle prosequi*.

Even in felony cases, the prosecutor ordinarily exercises much discretion in deciding whether to charge the accused with a crime.[27] After a police investigation, the prosecutor may be asked to review the sufficiency of the evidence to determine whether a criminal complaint should be filed. In some jurisdictions, this may involve presenting the evidence at a preliminary hearing. In other cases, the prosecutor may decide to seek a criminal complaint through the grand jury or other information procedure.

There is little question that prosecutors exercise a great deal of discretion in even the most serious cases. Barbara Boland studied the flow of felony cases through three jurisdictions in the United States: Golden, Colorado; Manhattan, New York; and Salt Lake City, Utah.[28] Although procedures were different in the three districts, prosecutors used their discretion to dismiss a high percentage of the cases before trial. When cases were forwarded for trial, very few defendants were actually acquitted, indicating that the prosecutorial discretion was exercised to screen out the weakest cases. In addition, of those cases accepted for prosecution, a high percentage ended with the defendant pleading guilty. All the evidence here points to the conclusion that prosecutorial discretion is used to reduce potential trial cases to a minimum.

The prosecutor may also play a limited role in exercising discretion in minor offenses. This role may consist of simply consulting with the police after their investigation results in a complaint being filed against the accused. In such instances, the decision to charge a person with a crime may be left primarily to the discretion of the law enforcement agency. The prosecutor may decide to enter this type of case after an arrest has been made and a complaint has been filed with the court, and he or she may subsequently determine whether to adjust the matter or proceed to trial. In some minor crimes, the prosecutor may not even appear until the trial stage of the process (or not at all); the police officer sometimes handles the entire case, including its prosecution.

The power to institute formal charges against the defendant is the key to the prosecutorial function. The ability to initiate or discontinue charges against a defendant is the control and power the prosecutor has over an individual's liberty. Over 50 years ago, Newman Baker commented on the problems of prosecutorial decision making:

> "To prosecute or not to prosecute?" is a question which comes to the mind of this official scores of times each day. A law has been contravened and the statute says he is bound to commence proceedings. His legal duty is clear. But what will be the result? Will it be a waste of time? Will it be expensive to the state? Will it be unfair to the defendant (the prosecutor applying his own ideas of justice)? Will it serve any good purpose to society in general? Will it have good publicity value? Will it cause a political squabble? Will it prevent the prosecutor from carrying the offender's home precinct when he, the prosecutor, runs for Congress after his term as prosecutor? Was the law violated a foolish piece of legislation? If the offender is a friend, is it the square thing to do to reward friendship by initiating criminal proceedings? These and many similar considerations are bound to come to the mind of the man responsible for setting the wheels of criminal justice in motion.[29]

Because they are ultimately responsible for deciding whether to prosecute, prosecutors must be aware of the wide variety of circumstances that affect their decisions. Frank Miller has identified a number of factors that affect discretion and the charging decision. Some of these include (1) the attitude of the victim, (2) the cost of prosecution to the criminal justice system, (3) the avoidance of undue harm to the suspect, (4) the availability of alternative procedures, (5) the use of civil sanctions, and (6) the willingness of the suspect to cooperate with law enforcement authorities.[30]

The Role of Prosecutorial Discretion

Regardless of its source, the proper exercise of prosecutorial discretion can improve the criminal justice process. For example, its use can prevent unnecessarily rigid implementation of the criminal law. Discretion allows the prosecutor to consider alternative decisions and humanize the operation of the criminal justice system. If prosecutors had little or no discretion, they would be forced to prosecute all cases brought to their attention. Judge Charles Breitel has stated, "If every policeman, every prosecutor, every court, and every postsentence agency performed his or its responsibility in strict accordance with rules of law, precisely and narrowly laid down, the criminal law would be ordered but intolerable."[31]

On the other hand, too much discretion can lead to abuses that result in the abandonment of law. One of the nation's most eminent legal scholars, Roscoe Pound, has defined discretion as:

> an authority conferred by law to act in certain conditions or situations in accordance with an official's or an official agency's considered judgment and conscience. It is an idea of morals, belonging to the twilight between law and morals.[32]

In terms of prosecutorial practices, this definition of discretion implies the need to select and choose among alternative decisions—to remove cases from the criminal process, to modify criminal charges, or to prosecute to the fullest intent of legal authority. Because there is no easy way to make these decisions, it has been recommended that the prosecutor establish standards for evaluating whether criminal proceedings should be brought against an accused.

Prosecutorial discretion is also influenced by the types of problems that exist in serious felony cases. The main reasons for not prosecuting a defendant include (1) search or seizure problems; (2) unavailability of prosecution's witness; (3) speedy trial restrictions; and (4) victim reluctance.

Judicial Restraints

The prosecutor's charging discretion has been considered and examined by the U.S. Supreme Court. For example, in **Town of Newton v. Rumery** (1987), a defendant entered into an agreement with a prosecutor under which the criminal charges against him would be dropped in exchange for his agreeing not to file a civil suit against the town police. The defendant later filed the suit anyway, maintaining that the original agreement was coercive and interfered with his right to legal process. He lost the case when the trial court ruled that his earlier agreement not to file suit against the town was binding. On appeal, the Supreme Court found for the town. It upheld the legality of the prosecutor's actions because the idea for the bargain had originated with the defense and therefore was not inherently coercive. *Rumery* illustrates that prosecutors maintain significant discretion to work out bargains and deals as long as they do not deprive defendants of their legal rights.[33]

The courts have also reviewed such prosecutorial behavior issues as (1) disciplining a prosecutor for making disruptive statements in court, (2) the failure of a prosecutor to adhere to sentence recommendations pursuant to a plea bargain, (3) disqualifying a prosecutor who represented a criminal defendant currently under indictment, and (4) removing a prosecutor for making public statements harmful to the office of the district attorney not constitutionally protected under the First Amendment.

Prosecutors need to exercise control and discretion. In accordance with the national prosecution standards of the National District Attorneys Association and the American Bar Association, the broad discretion given to the prosecutor necessitates that the greatest effort be made to use this power fairly.[34]

Courts have also been more concerned about prosecutors who use their discretion in a vindictive manner to punish defendants who exercise their legal rights. For example, in *North Carolina v. Pearce* (1969), the U.S. Supreme Court held that a judge in a retrial cannot impose a sentence more severe than that originally imposed. In other words, a prosecutor cannot seek a stricter sentence for a defendant who succeeds in getting his or her first conviction set aside.[35] In *Blackledge v. Perry* (1974), the Court dealt with the issue of vindictiveness on the part of the prosecutor and found that imposing a penalty on a defendant for having successfully pursued a statutory right of appeal is a violation of due process of law.[36] But in *Bordenkircher v. Hayes* (1978), the Court allowed the prosecutor to carry out threats of increased charges made during plea negotiations when the defendant refused to plead guilty to the original charge.[37]

These decisions provide the framework of the "prosecutorial vindictiveness" doctrine: Due process of law may be violated if the prosecutor retaliates against a defendant and there is proof of actual vindictiveness. The prosecutor's legitimate exercise of discretion must be balanced against the defendant's legal rights.

The Defense Attorney

The defense attorney is the counterpart of the prosecuting attorney in the criminal process. The accused has a constitutional right to counsel, and when the defendant cannot afford an attorney, the state must provide one. The accused may obtain counsel from the private bar if he or she can afford to do so; if the defendant is indigent, private counsel or a **public defender** may be assigned by the court (see the discussion on the defense of the indigent later in this chapter).

For many years, much of the legal community looked down on the criminal defense attorney and the practice of criminal law. This attitude stemmed from the kinds of legal work a defense attorney was forced to do: working with shady characters, negotiating for the release of known thugs and hoods, and often overzealously defending alleged criminals in the criminal trial. Lawyers have been reluctant to specialize in criminal law because defense attorneys receive comparatively low pay and often provide services without any compensation. In addition, law schools in the past seldom offered more than one or two courses in criminal law and trial practices.

In recent years, however, with the advent of constitutional requirements regarding the assistance of counsel, interest has grown in criminal law. Almost all law schools today have clinical programs that employ students as voluntary defense attorneys. They also offer courses in trial tactics, brief writing, and appellate procedures. In addition, such legal organizations as the American Bar Association, the National Legal Aid and Defenders Association, and the National Association of Criminal Defense Lawyers have assisted in recruiting able lawyers to do criminal defense work. As the American Bar Association has noted, "An almost indispensable condition to fundamental improvement of American criminal justice is the active and knowledgeable support of the bar as a whole."[38]

The defense counsel is an attorney as well as an officer of the court. As an attorney, the defense counsel is obligated to uphold the integrity of the legal profession and to observe the requirements of the American Bar Association's Code of Professional Responsibility in the defense of a client. In the code, the duties of the lawyer to the adversary system of justice are stated as follows:

The Role of the Criminal Defense Attorney

> Our legal system provides for the adjudication of disputes governed by the rules of substantive, evidentiary, and procedural law. An adversary presentation counters the natural human tendency to judge too swiftly in terms of the familiar that which is not yet fully known; the advocate, by his zealous preparation of facts and law, enables the tribunal to come to the hearing with an open and neutral mind and to render impartial judgments. The duty of a lawyer to his client and his duty to the legal system are the same: To represent his client zealously within the boundaries of the law.[39]

The defense counsel performs many functions while representing the accused in the criminal process. These functions include but are not limited to

1. Investigating the incident

2. Interviewing the client, police, and other witnesses

3. Discussing the matter with the prosecutor

4. Representing the defendant at the various pretrial procedures, such as arrest, interrogation, lineup, and arraignment

5. Entering into plea negotiations

6. Preparing the case for trial, including developing tactics and strategy

7. Filing and arguing legal motions with the court

8. Representing the defendant at trial

9. Providing assistance at sentencing

10. Determining the appropriate basis for appeal

Because of the way the U.S. system of justice operates today, criminal defense attorneys face many role conflicts. They are viewed as the prime movers in what is essentially an **adversarial process:** The prosecution and the defense engage in conflict over the facts of the case at hand, with the prosecutor arguing the case for the state and the defense counsel using all the means at his or her disposal to aid the client.

However, as members of the legal profession, defense counsels must be aware of their role as officers of the court. As an attorney, the defense counsel is obligated to uphold the integrity of the legal profession and to rely on constitutional ideals of fair play and professional ethics (discussed next) to provide adequate representation for a client.

Ethical Issues

As an officer of the court, along with the judge, prosecutors, and other trial participants, the defense attorney seeks to uncover the basic facts and elements of the criminal act. In this dual capacity of being both a defensive advocate and an officer of the court, the attorney is often confronted with conflicting obligations to his or her client and profession. Monroe Freedman identifies three of the most difficult problems involving the professional responsibility of the criminal defense lawyer:

1. Is it proper to cross-examine for the purpose of discrediting the reliability or credibility of an adverse witness who you know to be telling the truth?

2. Is it proper to put a witness on the stand when you know he will commit perjury?

3. Is it proper to give your client legal advice when you have reason to believe that the knowledge you give him will tempt him to commit perjury?[40]

There are other, equally important issues with respect to a lawyer's ethical responsibilities. Suppose, for example, a client confides that he is planning to commit a crime. What are the defense attorney's ethical responsibilities in this case? Obviously, the lawyer would have to counsel the client to obey the law; if the lawyer assisted the client in engaging in illegal behavior, the lawyer would be subject to charges of unprofessional conduct and even criminal liability. In another area, suppose the defense attorney is aware that the police made a procedural error and that the guilty client could be let off on a technicality. What are the attorney's ethical responsibilities in this case? The criminal lawyer needs to be aware of these troublesome situations to properly balance the duties of being an attorney with those of being an officer of the court.

Because the defense attorney and the prosecutor have different roles, their ethical dilemmas may also vary. The defense attorney must maintain confidentiality and advise his or her client of the constitutional requirements of counsel, the privilege against self-incrimination, and the right to trial. On the other hand, the prosecutor represents the public and is not required to abide by such restrictions in the same way. In some cases, the defense counsel may even be justified in withholding evidence by keeping the defendant from testifying at the trial. In addition, while prosecutors are prohibited from expressing a personal opinion as to the defendant's guilt on summation of a case, defense attorneys are not altogether barred from expressing their belief about a client's innocence.

In 1995 the American Bar Association produced an ethics guide for public and private criminal defense attorneys.[41] It focused primarily on (1) conflict-of-interest issues, (2) confidentiality, and (3) the proper allocation of decision-making responsibility by the defense counsel. At a time when society is tough on crime, the conduct of the defense attorney is subject to heightened scrutiny. This guide assists lawyers in making ethical choices without compromising the defendants' right to competent and zealous representation under the Sixth Amendment.

The Right to Counsel

Over the past decade, the rules and procedures of criminal justice administration have become extremely complex. Bringing a case to court involves a detailed investigation of a crime, knowledge of court procedures, the use of rules of evidence, and skills in criminal advocacy. Both the state and the defense must have this specialized expertise, particularly when an individual's freedom is at stake. Consequently, the right to the assistance of counsel in the criminal justice system is essential if the defendant is to have a fair chance of presenting a case in the adversary process.

One of the most critical issues in the criminal justice system has been whether an **indigent defendant** has the right to counsel. Can the accused who is poor and cannot afford an attorney have a fair trial without the assistance of counsel? Is counsel required at preliminary hearings? Should the convicted indigent offender be given counsel at state expense in appeals of the case? Questions such as these have arisen constantly in recent years. The federal court system has long provided counsel to the indigent defendant on the basis of the **Sixth Amendment** to the U.S. Constitution, unless he or she waived this right.[42] This constitutional mandate clearly applies to the federal courts, but its application to state criminal proceedings has been less certain.

In the landmark case of **Gideon v. Wainwright** in 1963, the U.S. Supreme Court took the first major step on the issue of right to counsel by holding that state courts must provide counsel to indigent defendants in felony prosecutions.[43] Almost ten years later, in the case of *Argersinger v. Hamlin* in 1972, the Court extended the obligation to provide counsel to all criminal cases where the penalty includes imprisonment—regardless of whether the offense is a felony or misdemeanor.[44] These two major decisions relate to the Sixth Amendment right to counsel as it applies to the presentation of a defense at the trial stages of the criminal justice system.

In numerous Supreme Court decisions since *Gideon v. Wainwright,* the states have been required to provide counsel for indigent defendants at virtually all other stages of the criminal process, beginning with arrest and concluding with the defendant's release from the system. Today, the Sixth Amendment right to counsel and the Fifth and Fourteenth Amendment guarantee of due process of law have been judicially interpreted together to provide the defendant with counsel by the state in all types of criminal proceedings.

In addition to guaranteeing the right of counsel at the earliest stages of the justice system, as well as at trials, the Supreme Court has moved to extend the right to counsel to postconviction and other collateral proceedings, such as probation and parole revocation and appeal. When, for example, the court intends to revoke a defendant's probation and impose a sentence, the probationer has a right to counsel at the deferred sentence hearing.[45] Where the state provides for an appellate review of the criminal conviction, the defendant is entitled to the assistance of counsel for this initial appeal.[46] The defendant does not have the right to counsel for an appellate review beyond the original appeal or for a discretionary review to the U.S. Supreme Court. The Supreme Court has also required the states to provide counsel in other proceedings that involve the loss of personal liberty, such as juvenile delinquency hearings[47] and mental health commitments.[48]

Areas still remain in the criminal justice system where the courts have not required assistance of counsel for the accused. These include (1) preindictment lineups; (2) booking procedures, including the taking of fingerprints and other forms of identification; (3) grand jury investigations; (4) appeals beyond the first review; (5) disciplinary proceedings in correctional institutions; and (6) postrelease revocation hearings. Nevertheless, the general rule of thumb is that no person can be deprived of freedom or lose a "liberty interest" without representation by counsel.

The right to counsel can also be spelled out in particular federal or state statutes. For example, beyond abiding by current constitutional requirements, a state may provide counsel by statute at all stages of juvenile proceedings, in dealing with inmate prison infractions or pretrial release hearings, or when considering temporary confinement of drug or sex offenders for psychiatric examination.

Today, the scope of representation for the indigent defendant is believed to cover virtually all areas of the criminal process and most certainly those critical points at which a person's liberty is at stake. Table 9.2 summarizes the major U.S. Supreme Court decisions granting defendants counsel throughout the criminal justice system.

Table 9.2
Major U.S. Supreme Court Cases Granting Right to Counsel

Case	Stage and Ruling
Escobedo v. Illinois, 378 U.S. 478 (1964)	The defendant has the right to counsel during the course of any police interrogation.
Miranda v. Arizona, 384 U.S. 436 (1966)	Procedural safeguards, including the right to counsel, must be followed at custodial interrogation to secure the privilege against self-incrimination.
Massiah v. United States, 377 U.S. 201 (1964)	The defendant has the right to counsel during post-indictment interrogation.
Hamilton v. Alabama, 368 U.S. 52 (1961)	The arraignment is a critical stage in the criminal process, so that denial of the right to counsel is a violation of due process of law.
Coleman v. Alabama, 399 U.S. 1 (1970)	The preliminary hearing is a critical stage in a criminal prosecution requiring the state to provide the indigent defendant with counsel.
United States v. Wade, 388 U.S. 218 (1967)	A defendant in a pretrial, postindictment lineup for identification purposes has the right to assistance of counsel.
Moore v. Michigan, 355 U.S. 155 (1957)	The defendant has the right to counsel when submitting a guilty plea to the court.
Brady v. United States, 397 U.S. 742 (1970)	Counsel is required during the plea bargaining process.
Powell v. Alabama, 287 U.S. 45 (1932)	Defendants have the right to counsel at their trial in a state capital case.
Gideon v. Wainwright, 372 U.S. 335 (1963)	An indigent defendant charged in a state court with a noncapital felony has the right to the assistance of free counsel at trial under the due process clause of the Fourteenth Amendment.
Argersinger v. Hamlin, 407 U.S. 25 (1972)	A defendant has the right to counsel at trial whenever he or she may be imprisoned for any offense, even for one day, whether classified as a misdemeanor or a felony.
Faretta v. California, 422 U.S. 806 (1975)	The defendant has a constitutional right to defend herself or himself if her or his waiver of right to counsel is knowing and intelligent.
In re Gault, 387 U.S. 1 (1967)	Procedural due process, including the right to counsel, applies to juvenile delinquency adjudication that may lead to a child's commitment to a state institution.
Townsend v. Burke, 334 U.S. 736 (1948)	A convicted offender has a right to counsel at the time of sentencing.
Douglas v. California, 372 U.S. 353 (1963)	An indigent defendant granted a first appeal from a criminal conviction has the right to be represented by counsel on appeal.
Mempa v. Rhay, 389 U.S. 128 (1967)	A convicted offender has the right to assistance of counsel at probation revocation hearings where the sentence has been deferred.
Gagnon v. Scarpelli, 411 U.S. 778 (1973) *Morrissey v. Brewer,* 408 U.S. 471 (1972)	The defendant has a right to counsel in the court's discretion at probation revocation and parole board revocation hearings.

Today, the lawyer whose practice involves a substantial proportion of criminal cases is often considered a specialist in the field. Since most lawyers are not prepared in law school for criminal work, their skill often results from their experience in the trial courts. Such lawyers as Robert Shapiro, Alan Dershowitz, John Cochran, F. Lee Bailey, James St. Claire, Gerry Spence, and Roy Black of William Kennedy Smith fame are the elite of the private criminal bar; they are nationally known criminal defense attorneys who often represent defendants for large fees in celebrated and widely publicized cases. Attorneys like these are relatively few in number and do not regularly handle the ordinary criminal defendant.

In addition to this limited group of well-known criminal lawyers, some lawyers and law firms serve as house counsel for such professional criminals as narcotics dealers, gamblers, prostitutes, and even big-time burglars. These lawyers, however, constitute a very small percentage of the private bar practicing criminal law.

A large number of criminal defendants are represented by lawyers who often accept many cases for small fees. These lawyers may belong to small law firms or work alone, but a sizable portion of their practice involves representing those accused of crime. Other private practitioners occasionally take on criminal matters as part of their general practice.

Associated with the private practice of criminal law is the fact that the fee system can create a conflict of interest. Because private attorneys are usually paid in advance and do not expect additional funds if their client is convicted, and because many are aware of the guilt of their client before the trial begins, they earn the greatest profit if they get the case settled as quickly as possible. This usually means bargaining with the prosecutor rather than going to trial. Even if attorneys win the case at trial, they may lose personally, since the time expended will not be compensated by more than the gratitude of their client. And, of course, many criminal defendants cannot afford even a modest legal fee and therefore cannot avail themselves of the services of a private attorney. For these reasons, an elaborate, publicly funded legal system has developed.

Legal Services for the Indigent

To satisfy the constitutional requirements that indigent defendants be provided with the assistance of counsel at various stages of the criminal process, the federal government and the states have had to evaluate and expand criminal defense services. Prior to the Supreme Court's mandate in *Gideon v. Wainwright,* public defendant services were provided mainly by local private attorneys appointed and paid for by the court—called *assigned counsels*—or by limited public defendant programs. In 1961, for example, public defender services existed in only 3% of the counties in the United States, serving only about a quarter of the country's population.[49] The general lack of defense services for indigents traditionally stemmed from these causes, among others:

1. Until fairly recently, the laws of most jurisdictions did not require the assistance of counsel for felony offenders and others.

2. Only a few attorneys were interested in criminal law practice.

3. The organized legal bar was generally indifferent to the need for criminal defense assistance.

4. The caseloads of lawyers working in public defender agencies were staggering.

5. Financial resources for courts and defense programs were limited.

Today, virtually all jurisdictions have public defender systems in one form or another.

However, beginning with the *Gideon* case in 1963 and continuing through the *Argersinger* decision in 1972, the criminal justice system has been forced to increase public defender services. Today, about 3,000 state and local agencies are providing indigent legal services in the United States.

The Client

Most defense attorneys would be willing to drop everything and take a client for no fee, risk life and limb to help them, and threaten federal agents to get their way. Sure they would—if you are a fan of John Grisham and his best-selling books. The 1994 movie *The Client,* based on the Grisham best-seller, would have us believe that defense attorneys are selfless champions of the poor who care little for their own personal safety, let alone their legal fees.

The Client is the story of an 11-year-old Memphis boy, Mark Sway, who along with his younger brother Ricky, witnesses the suicide of a New Orleans attorney, Jerome Clifford. Before he dies Clifford tells Mark a secret that can implicate his client, organized crime figure Barry Muldanno, in the murder of a U.S. senator. The police and federal agents, led by the U.S. attorney for the Southern District of Louisiana, J. Roy Foltrigg (Tommy Lee Jones), pressure the boy to tell what he knows and testify at trial. Knowing that his cooperation in a case against a powerful organized crime figure could lead to his death, Mark refuses to cooperate. He escapes from custody and locates (by accident) a defense attorney named Reggie Love, who is willing to take on his case for one dollar! Tough and feisty, Reggie (Susan Sarandon) protects Mark from both the law and the Mafia. They hatch a plan to go to New Orleans

and dig up the body of the senator, which is resting under a boat in attorney Clifford's house. They break in, fight off thugs, locate the body, and turn the information over to the Feds in return for a new identity and a new life for Mark and his family. Everything turns out okay!

The Client is part of the media genre that glorifies the legal profession as champions of the poor and downtrodden. Attorney Love is able to drop all her cases (how did her other clients feel?) to concentrate on the indigent Mark Sway. She cares little for fees or retainers, movie deals, or any other form of compensation. In reality, most attorneys are concerned about the "bottom line," and firms are looking to find partners who are "rainmakers," able to bring in lots of paying clients.

Reggie will stop at nothing to help her client. She violates federal law by illegally helping her client to escape from federal custody and also conspires to tape a conversation, which is in violation of most state laws. She is willing to take on the Mafia and sneaks around at night without a thought for her personal safety. At the end, when Mark Sway gets a new identity, Reggie Love goes back to her legal practice and, potentially, Mafia revenge. While most of us would like to find an attorney like Reggie Love in the Yellow Pages, they are for the most part only found in John Grisham's imagination.

Providing legal services for the indigent offender is a huge undertaking. Almost 5 million offenders are given free legal services annually. And although most states have a formal set of rules to signify who is an indigent, and many require indigents to repay the state for at least part of their legal services (known as recoupment), indigent legal services still cost over $1.5 billion annually.

Programs providing assistance of counsel to indigent defendants can be divided into three major categories: public defender systems, assigned counsel systems, and contract systems. In addition, other approaches to the delivery of legal services include the use of mixed systems, such as representation by both the public defender and the private bar, law school clinical programs, and prepaid legal services. Of the three major approaches, assigned counsel systems dominate defender programs, with the majority of U.S. courts using this method; 34% use public defenders, and 6% use contract attorneys.[50] Although many jurisdictions have a combination of these programs, statewide public defender programs seem to be on the increase.

Public Defenders. Approximately 1,100 public defender offices are located in about 40% of the counties in the United States.[51] However, since public defender services are housed in 43 of the 50 largest counties, they serve a majority (68%) of the population. The first public defender program in the United States opened in 1913 in Los Angeles. Over the years, primarily as a result of efforts by judicial leaders and bar groups, the public defender program has become the model for the delivery of legal services to indigent defendants in criminal cases throughout the country.

Most public defender offices can be thought of as law firms whose only clients are criminal offenders. However, there is a major division in the administration of public defender services. Many states have a statewide public defender's office headed by a chief public defender who administers the operation. In some of these states, the chief defender establishes offices in all the counties around the state, while in others, the chief defender relies on part-time private attorneys to provide indigent legal services in rural counties. Statewide public defenders are organized as part of the judicial branch, as part of the executive branch, as an independent state agency, or even as a private, nonprofit organization.

Lawyers doing criminal defense work have discovered an increasing need for their services, not only at trial but also at the pretrial and postjudicial stages of the criminal justice system. Public defenders may be called on to provide a variety of services to their clients. Here a public defender meets with a client at the client's home.

In the majority of states, the public defender's office is organized on the county level of government, and each office is autonomous. For example, in Florida elected public defenders operate separately in each of the judicial circuits in the state. In Pennsylvania, a local public defender is legislatively mandated in each of the state's counties. In Illinois, each county with a population above a certain level has a legislatively mandated public defender's office.

Assigned Counsel System. In contrast to the public defender system, the **assigned counsel system** involves the use of private attorneys appointed by the court to represent indigent defendants. The private attorney is selected from a list of attorneys established by the court and is reimbursed by the state for any legal services rendered to the client. Assigned counsels are usually used in rural areas, which do not have sufficient criminal caseloads to justify a full-time public defender staff.

There are two main types of assigned counsel systems. In the first, which makes up about 75% of all assigned counsel systems, the presiding judge appoints attorneys on a case-by-case basis; this is referred to as an *ad hoc assigned counsel system.* In a *coordinated assigned counsel system,* an administrator oversees the appointment of counsel and sets up guidelines for the administration of indigent legal services. The fees awarded to assigned counsels can vary widely, ranging from a low of $10 per hour for handling a misdemeanor out of court to over $100 per hour for a serious felony handled in court. Some jurisdictions may establish a maximum allowance per case of $750 for a misdemeanor and $1,500 for a felony. Average rates seem to be between $40 and $80 per hour, depending on the nature of the case. Restructuring the attorney fee system is undoubtedly needed to maintain fair standards for the payment of such legal services.

The assigned counsel system, unless organized properly, suffers from such problems as unequal assignments, inadequate legal fees, and the lack of supportive or supervisory services. Other disadvantages are the frequent use of inexperienced attorneys and the tendency to use the guilty plea too quickly. Some judicial experts believe the assigned counsel system is still no more than an ad hoc approach that presents serious questions about the quality of representation. However, the system is simple to operate. It also offers the private bar an important role in providing indigent legal services, since most public defender systems cannot represent all needy criminal defendants. Thus, the appointed counsel system gives attorneys the opportunity to do criminal defense work.

Contract System. The **contract system** is a relative newcomer to providing legal services to the indigent. In this system, a block grant is given to a lawyer or law firm to handle indigent defense cases. In some instances, the attorney is given a set amount of money and is required to handle all cases assigned. In other jurisdictions, contract lawyers agree to provide legal representation for a set number of cases at a fixed fee. A third system involves representation at an estimated cost per case until the dollar amount of the contract is reached. At that point, the contract may be renegotiated, but the lawyers are not obligated to take new cases.

The contract system is used quite often in counties that also have public defenders. Such counties may need independent counsel when a conflict of interests arises or when there is a constant overflow of cases. It is also used in sparsely populated states that cannot justify the structure and costs of full-time public defender programs. Pauline Houlden and Steven Balkin found that contract attorneys were at least as effective as assigned counsel and were most cost-effective.[52] The per case cost in any jurisdiction for indigent defense services is determined largely by the type of program offered. In most public defender programs, funds are obtained through annual appropriations; assigned counsel costs relate to legal charges for appointed counsel; and contract programs negotiate a fee for the entire service. No research currently available indicates which method is the most effective way to represent the indigent on a cost-per-case basis. Advantages of the contract system include the provision of comprehensive legal services, controlled costs, and improved coordination in counsel programs.[53]

Mixed Systems. A mixed system uses both public defenders and private attorneys in an attempt to draw on the strengths of both. In this approach, the public defender system operates simultaneously with the assigned counsel system or contract system to offer total coverage to the indigent defendant. This need occurs when the caseload increases beyond the capacity of the pubic defender's office. In addition, many counties supply independent counsel to all co-defendants in a single case to prevent a conflict of interest. In most others, separate counsel will be provided if a co-defendant requests it or if the judge or public defender perceives a conflict of interest. Because all lawyers in a public defender's office are considered to be working for the same firm, outside counsel is required if co-defendants are in conflict with one another. Many counties having public defenders also have a program to assign counsel in overflow and conflict-of-interest cases. Public defender services supplemented by contract programs and an assigned counsel system often provide the best model to uphold the Sixth Amendment right to counsel for indigent defendants.

Other methods of providing counsel to the indigent include the use of law school students and prepaid legal service programs (similar to comprehensive medical insurance). Most jurisdictions have a student practice rule of procedure; third-year law school students in clinical programs provide supervised counsel to defendants in nonserious offenses. In *Argersinger v. Hamlin,* Supreme Court Justice William Brennan suggested that law students are an important resource in fulfilling constitutional defense requirements.[54]

Costs of Defending the Poor. Over the past decade, the justice system has been faced with extreme pressure to provide counsel for all indigent criminal defendants. Inadequate funding has made implementation of this Sixth Amendment right an impossible task. The chief reasons for underfunded defender programs are (1) caseload problems, (2) lack of available attorneys, and (3) legislative restraints. Increasing numbers of drug cases, mandatory sentencing, and even overcharging have put tremendous stress on defender services. The system is also overloaded with appeals by indigent defendants convicted at the trial level whose representation involves filing complex briefs and making oral arguments. Such postconviction actions often consume a great deal of time and result in additional backlog problems. Death penalty litigation is another area where legal resources for the poor are strained.

In some jurisdictions, attorneys are just not available to provide defense work. Burnout due to heavy caseloads, low salaries, and poor working conditions is generally the major cause for the limited supply of attorneys interested in representing the indigent defendant. Some attorneys even refuse to accept appointments in criminal cases because the fees are too low.

Lack of government funding is the most significant problem today. While the entire justice system is often underfunded, the prosecutor-defense system is usually in the worst shape. Ordinarily, providing funding for indigent criminal defendants is not the most politically popular thing to do.

Obviously, the Sixth Amendment means little without counsel. The constitutional mandate that calls for legal representation requires adequate funding for these services. The National Center for State Courts, the National Legal Aid and Defenders Association, the American Bar Association, and many other legal and citizen groups indicate that the public defender system is losing the battle for funding to the enormous increase in drug cases.[55]

Funding for defender programs is ordinarily the responsibility of state and local government. As a result of an amendment to the Crime Control Act of 1990, however, federal funds are also available through the Drug Control Act of

1988.[56] According to most experts on defense funding, jurisdictions whose legislatures have been relatively generous in funding such programs in the past have continued to do so, while underfunded programs have become more seriously hampered. The Anti-Terrorism Act of 1996 authorizes over $300 million to improve the federal judiciary's Defender Program.[57]

Over the years, the quality of legal representation for indigent defendants has often been criticized by criminal justice experts. Yet, despite that assertion, a recent study of felony dispositions in nine state trial courts by the National Center for State Courts proves otherwise.[58] The study found that public defenders are consistently as successful as private counsel in resolving cases expeditiously and providing effective representation. There are few differences in conviction rates, charge reduction rates, incarceration rates, and lengths of prison sentences in cases represented by different types of criminal defense attorneys. Other implications of the study included (1) indigent defenders constituted an experienced group of attorneys who were part of an emerging subprofession; (2) financial resources are essential to effective public defense work; and (3) the type of organizational structure (public defender, contract attorney, assigned counsel, or private counsel) must be based on the circumstances of each jurisdiction.

The Competence of Defense Lawyers

The presence of competent and effective counsel has long been a basic principle of the adversary system. With the Sixth Amendment's guarantee of counsel for virtually all defendants, the performance of today's attorneys has come into question.

Inadequacy of counsel may occur in a variety of instances. The attorney may refuse to meet regularly with his or her client, fail to cross-examine key government witnesses, or fail to investigate the case properly. A defendant's plea of guilty may be based on poor advice, where the attorney may misjudge the admissibility of evidence. When co-defendants have separate counsel, conflicts of interest between the defense attorneys may arise. On an appellate level, the lawyer may decline to file a brief, instead relying on a brief submitted for one of the co-appellants. Such problems as these are being raised with increasing frequency.

The concept of attorney competence was defined by the U.S. Supreme Court in the case of **Strickland v. Washington** in 1984.[59] Strickland had been arrested for committing a string of extremely serious crimes, including murder, torture, and kidnapping. Against his lawyer's advice, Strickland pleaded guilty and threw himself on the mercy of the trial judge at a capital sentencing hearing. He also ignored his attorney's recommendation that he exercise his right to have an advisory jury at his sentencing hearing.

In preparing for the hearing, the lawyer spoke with Strickland's wife and mother but did not otherwise seek character witnesses. Nor was a psychiatric examination requested since, in the attorney's opinion, Strickland did not have psychological problems. The attorney also did not ask for a presentence investigation because he felt such a report would contain information damaging to his client.

Although the presiding judge had a reputation for leniency in cases where the defendant confessed, he sentenced Strickland to death. Strickland appealed on the grounds that his attorney had rendered ineffective counsel, citing his failure to seek psychiatric testimony and present character witnesses.

The case eventually went to the Supreme Court, which upheld Strickland's sentence. The justices found that a defendant's claim of attorney incompetence must have two components. First, the defendant must show that the counsel's performance was deficient and that such serious errors were made as to eliminate the presence of counsel guaranteed by the Sixth Amendment. Second, the defendant must also show that the deficient performance prejudiced the case to an extent that the defendant was deprived of a fair trial. In the case at hand, the Court found insufficient evidence that the attorney had acted beyond the boundaries of professional competence. The Strickland case established the two-pronged test for determining effectiveness of counsel.

The U.S. Supreme Court dealt with the issue of conflict of interest between defense lawyers in **Burger v. Kemp** (1987).[60] Two defendants charged with murder were represented by law partners. Each defendant was tried separately, but the attorneys conferred and assisted each other in the trial process. One defendant, who was found guilty and sentenced to death, claimed ineffective legal representation because he believed his attorney failed to present mitigating circumstances to show that he was less culpable than the co-defendant. But the Supreme Court said this view was unfounded because the defendant claiming the conflict of interest actually perpetrated the crime. The Court also said it is not per se a violation of constitutional guarantees of effective assistance of counsel when a single attorney represents two defendants or when two partners supplement each other in the trial defense.

The key issue is the level of competence that should be required of defense counsel in criminal cases. This question concerns appointed counsel, as well as counsel chosen by the accused. Some appellate court decisions have overturned lower court convictions when it was judged that the performance of counsel had reduced the trial to a farce or a mockery. Other appellate courts have held that there was ineffective counsel where gross incompetence had the effect of eliminating the basis for a substantial defense.

In recent years, the courts have adopted a **reasonable competence standard,** but differences exist on the formulation and application of this standard. For example, is it necessary for defense counsel to answer on appeal every nonfrivolous issue requested by his or her convicted client? What if counsel does not provide the court with all the information at the sentencing stage and the defendant feels counsel's performance is inadequate? Whether any of these instances is an appropriate situation for stating that counsel is incompetent requires court review.

Criminal Justice on the Net

There are many good sources on the Internet to learn more about the courts and the legal system. The American Bar Association's General Information Center contains information on a variety of topics:

http://www.abanet.org/

Another good source of law-related information is the Emory University Law Library electronic reference desk. This site allows you to review law by country and subject. It also contains career information, entertainment and culture, journals and periodicals, law firms and lawyers, law schools/education, and reference materials:

**http://www.law.emory.edu/LAW/
refdesk/toc.html**

The National Center for State Courts is an independent, nonprofit organization dedicated to the improvement of justice. It was founded in 1971 at the urging of Chief Justice Warren E. Burger. NCSC accomplishes its mission by providing leadership and service to the state courts. Leadership activities include developing policies to enhance state courts, advancing state courts' interests within the federal government, fostering state court adaptation to future changes, securing sufficient resources for state courts, strengthening state court leadership, facilitating state court collaboration, and providing a model for organizational administration. You can access their home page at:

http://www.ncsc.dni.us/

Summary

The U.S. court system is a complex social institution. There is no set pattern of court organization. Courts are organized on federal, state, county, and local levels of government. The judge, the prosecutor, and the defense attorney are the major officers of justice in the judicial system. The judge approves plea bargains, tries cases, and determines the sentence given the offender. The prosecutor, who is the people's attorney, has discretion to decide the criminal charge and disposition. The prosecutor's daily decisions significantly affect police and court operations.

The role of the defense attorney in the criminal justice system has grown dramatically during the past 30 years. Today, providing defense services to the indigent criminal defendant is an everyday practice. Under landmark decisions of the U.S. Supreme Court, particularly *Gideon v. Wainwright* and *Argersinger v. Hamlin,* all defendants who may be imprisoned for any offense must be afforded counsel at trials. Methods of providing counsel include systems for assigned counsel, where an attorney is selected by the court to represent the accused, and public defender programs, where public employees provide legal services. Lawyers doing criminal defense work have discovered an increasing need for their services, not only at trial but also at the pre- and postjudicial stages of the criminal justice system.

Key Terms

lower courts
felony courts
appellate courts
court of last resort
writ of certiorari
landmark decision
jury trial

Missouri Plan
prosecutor
Town of Newton v. Rumery
public defender
adversarial process
indigent defendant
Sixth Amendment

Gideon v. Wainwright
assigned counsel system
contract system
Strickland v. Washington
Burger v. Kemp
reasonable competence standard

Questions

1. Should attorneys disclose information given them by their clients concerning participation in an earlier unsolved crime?

2. Should defense attorneys cooperate with a prosecutor if it means that their clients will go to jail?

3. Should a prosecutor have absolute discretion over which cases to proceed on and which to drop?

4. Should clients be made aware of an attorney's track record in court?

5. Does the assigned counsel system present an inherent conflict of interest, since attorneys are hired and paid by the institution they are to oppose?

6. Do you believe prosecutors have a great deal of discretion? Why?

Notes

1. Malcolm Feeley, *The Process Is the Punishment* (New York: Russell Sage Foundation, 1979), pp. 9–11.

2. Thomas Henderson, *The Significance of Judicial Structure: The Effect of Unification on Trial Court Operations* (Washington, D.C.: National Institute of Justice, 1984).

3. Johnathan Casper, Tom Tyler, and Bonnie Fisher, "Procedural Justice in Felony Cases," *Law and Society Review* 22 (1988): 497–505.

4. Brian Ostrom and Neal Kauder, "Examining the Work of State Courts, 1995: A National Perspective from the Court Statistics Project" (Williamsburg, Va.: National Center for State Courts, 1996).

5. This section relies heavily on Conference of State Court Administrators and National Center for State Courts, *State Court Caseload Statistics, Annual Report, 1990* (Williamsburg, Va.: National Center for State Courts, 1992) and Brian J. Ostrom, *State Court Caseload Statistics, Annual Report, 1992* (Williamsburg, Va.: National Center for State Courts, 1994), herein cited as *State Court Statistics.*

6. Patrick Langan, *State Felony Courts and Felony Laws* (Washington, D.C.: Bureau of Justice Statistics, 1987). See also Ostrom, *State Court Statistics, 1992,* and Ostrom and Kauder, "Examining the Work of State Courts, 1995."

7. Ostrom and Kauder, "Examining the Work of State Courts, 1995," p. 58.

8. Timothy Flanagan and Katherine Jamieson, *Sourcebook of Criminal Justice Statistics, 1989* (Washington, D.C.: U.S. Government Printing Office, 1990), p. 450; *State Court Statistics, 1992,* p. 64.

9. David B. Rottman et al., *State Court Organization, 1993* (Washington, D.C.: U.S. Department of Justice, Bureau of Justice Statistics, 1995).

10. U.S. Constitution, Art. 3, secs. 1 and 2.

11. 1 Wharton 304, 4 L.Ed. 97 (1816).

12. *State Court Statistics, 1992*; see also Ostrom and Kauder, "Examining the Work of State Courts, 1995."

13. Administrative Office of the United States Courts, *Annual Report of the Director, 1990* (Washington, D.C.: Administrative Office of the United States Courts, 1991).

14. Kathleen Maguire and Timothy Flanagan, *Sourcebook of Criminal Justice Statistics, 1990* (Washington, D.C.: U.S. Government Printing Office, 1991), p. 529; *State Court Statistics, 1992* and 1994.

15. Ostrom and Kauder, "Examining the Work of State Courts, 1995," p. 50.

16. Ibid.

17. American Bar Association, *The State of Criminal Justice, Annual Report, 1993* (Chicago: American Bar Association), p. 13.

18. "A Report on Clinton's Judges," *American Bar Association Journal* 80 (1994): 16.

19. Sari Escovitz with Fred Kurland and Nan Gold, *Judicial Selection and Tenure* (Chicago: American Judicature Society, 1974), pp. 3–16.

20. Bureau of Justice Statistics Bulletin, "Prosecutors in State Courts—1994" (Washington, D.C.: Office of Justice Programs, 1996).

21. See Bennett Gershman, "Why Prosecutors Misbehave," *Criminal Law Bulletin* 22 (1986):131–143.

22. American Bar Association, *Model Rules of Professional Conduct* (Chicago: American Bar Association, 1983), Rule 3.8; see also Stanley Fisher, "In Search of the Virtuous Prosecutor: A Conceptual Framework," *American Journal of Criminal Law* 15 (1988): 197.

23. Stanley Fisher, "Zealousness and Overzealousness: Making Sense of the Prosecutor's Duty to Seek Justice," *Prosecutor* 22 (1989): 9; see also Bruce Green, "The Ethical Prosecutor and the Adversary System," *Criminal Law Bulletin* 24 (1988): 126–145.

24. Michael Benson, Francis Cullen, and William Maakestad, "Local Prosecutors and Corporate Crime," *Crime and Delinquency* 36 (July 1990): 356–372; see also Neil Weiner, "Priority Prosecution of Juveniles," *NIJ Journal,* November 1993.

25. "NDAA Establishes Environmental Center," *National District Attorneys Association Bulletin* 10 (October 1991): 1; Marcia Chaiken and Jan Chaiken, *Priority Prosecutors of High-Rate Dangerous Offenders* (Washington, D.C.: National Institute of Justice, 1991).

26. "Litigator's Legacy," *Wall Street Journal,* 11 January 1989, p. 1; Selwyn Raab, "A Battered and Ailing Mafia Is Losing Its Grip on America," *New York Times,* 22 October 1990, p. 1.

27. Kenneth C. Davis, *Discretionary Justice* (Baton Rouge: Louisiana State University Press, 1969), p. 180; see also James B. Stewart, *The Prosecutor* (New York: Simon & Schuster, 1987).

28. Barbara Boland, *The Prosecution of Felony Arrests* (Washington, D.C.: U.S. Government Printing Office, 1983).

29. Newman Baker, "The Prosecutor—Initiation of Prosecution," *Journal of Criminal Law, Criminology, and Police Science* 23 (1933): 770–771; see also Joan Jacoby, *The American Prosecutor: A Search for Identity* (Lexington, Mass.: Lexington Books, 1980).

30. Frank W. Miller, *Prosecution: The Decision to Charge a Suspect with a Crime* (Boston: Little, Brown, 1970).

31. Charles D. Breitel, "Controls in Criminal Law Enforcement," *University of Chicago Law Review* 27 (1960): 427.

32. Roscoe Pound, "Discretion, Dispensation, and Mitigation: The Problem of the Individual Special Case," *New York University Law Review* 35 (1960): 925; "Unleashing the Prosecutor's Discretion: *United States v. Goodwin,*" *American Criminal Law Review* 20 (1983): 507.

33. *Town of Newton v. Rumery* 480 U.S. 386, 107 S.Ct. 1187, 94 L.Ed.2d 405 (1987); see also American Bar Association, *Standards for Prosecution and Defense Function,* 3rd ed. (Washington, D.C.: American Bar Association Criminal Justice Project, 1993).

34. National District Attorneys Association, *National Prosecution Standards* (Alexandria, Va.: NDAA, 1991).

35. *North Carolina v. Pearce* 395 U.S. 711, 89 S.Ct. 2072, 23 L.Ed.2d 656 (1969).

36. *Blackledge v. Perry* 417 U.S. 21, 94 S.Ct. 2098, 40 L.Ed.2d 628 (1974).

37. *Bordenkircher v. Hayes* 434 U.S. 357, 98 S.Ct. 663, 54 L.Ed.2d 604 (1978).

38. President's Commission on Law Enforcement and the Administration of Justice, *The Challenge of Crime in a Free Society* (Washington, D.C.: U.S. Government Printing Office, 1968), p. 150; American Bar Association, *Report of Standing Committee on Legal Aid and Indigent Defendants* (Chicago: American Bar Association, 1991).

39. American Bar Association Model Rules of Professional Conduct (Chicago: ABA, 1983), Rule 3.8.

40. Monroe H. Freedman, "Professional Responsibility of the Criminal Defense Lawyer: The Three Hardest Questions," *Michigan Law Review* 64 (1966): 1468.

41. Rodney Uphoff, Editor, "Ethical Problems Facing the Criminal Defense Lawyer: Practical Answers to Tough Questions" (Chicago: American Bar Association, 1995).

42. The Sixth Amendment provides: "In all criminal prosecutions, the accused shall enjoy the right . . . to have the assistance of counsel for his defense."

43. *Gideon v. Wainwright,* 372 U.S. 335, 83 S.Ct. 792, 9 L.Ed.2d 799 (1963).

44. *Argersinger v. Hamlin,* 407 U.S. 25, 92 S.Ct. 2006, 32 L.Ed.2d 530 (1972).

45. *Mempa v. Rhay,* 389 U.S. 128, 88 S.Ct. 254, 19 L.Ed.2d 336 (1967).

46. *Douglas v. California,* 372 U.S. 353, 83 S.Ct. 814, 9 L.Ed.2d 811 (1963).

47. *In re Gault,* 387 U.S. 1, 875 S.Ct. 1428, 18 L.Ed.2d 527 (1967).

48. *Specht v. Patterson,* 386 U.S. 605, 87 S.Ct. 1209, 18 L.Ed.2d 326 (1967).

49. See F. Brownell, *Legal Aid in the United States* (Chicago: National Legal Aid and Defender Association, 1961); for an interesting study of the Cook County, Illinois, Office of Public Defenders, see Lisa McIntyre, *Public Defenders—Practice of Law in Shadows of Dispute* (Chicago: University of Chicago Press, 1987).

50. Carla Gaskins, *Criminal Defense for the Poor—1986* (Washington, D.C.: Bureau of Justice Statistics, September 1988), p. 2; see also Robert L. Spangenberg and Tessa Schwartz, "The Indigent Defense Crisis Is Chronic," *American Bar Association Journal on Criminal Justice* 9 (1994): 12.

51. Gaskins, *Criminal Defense for the Poor—1986,* pp. 1–8.

52. Pauline Houlden and Steven Balkin, "Quality and Cost Comparisons of Private Bar Indigent Defense Systems: Contract vs. Ordered Assigned Counsel," *Journal of Criminal Law and Criminology* 76 (1985): 176–200.

53. Lawrence Spears, "Contract Counsel: A Different Way to Defend the Poor—How It's Working in North Dakota," *American Bar Association Journal on Criminal Justice* 6 (1991): 24–31.

54. *Argersinger v. Hamlin,* 407 U.S. 25, 92 S.Ct. 2006, 32 L.Ed.2d 530 (1972).

55. Timothy Murphy, "Indigent Defense and the War on Drugs—The Public Defender's Losing Battle," *American Bar Association Journal on Criminal Justice* 26(6) (1991): 14–20.

56. See Drug Control Act of 1988, 42 U.S.C. § 375(G)(10).

57. Anti-Terrorism Act of 1996 (Public Law No. 104-132, 1996).

58. Roger Hanson et al., "Indigent Defenders—Get the Job Done and Done Well" (Williamsburg, Va.: National Center for State Courts, 1992).

59. *Strickland v. Washington,* 466 U.S. 668, 104 S.Ct. 2052, 80 L.Ed.2d 674 (1984).

60. *Burger v. Kemp,* 483 U.S. 776, 107 S.Ct. 3114, 97 L.Ed.2d 638 (1987).

Pretrial Procedures

Between arrest and trial a series of events occur that are critical links in the chain of justice. These include arraignments, grand jury investigations, bail hearings, plea-bargaining negotiations, and predisposition treatment efforts. These **pretrial procedures** are critically important components of the justice process because the great majority of all criminal cases are resolved informally at this stage and never come before the courts. Although the media like to focus on the elaborate jury trial with its dramatic elements and impressive setting, formal criminal trials are relatively infrequent. Consequently, understanding the events that take place during the pretrial period is essential in grasping the reality of criminal justice policy.

Cases are settled during the pretrial stage in a number of ways. Prosecutors can use their discretion to drop cases before formal charges are filed, because of insufficient evidence, office policy, witness conflicts, or similar problems. Even if charges are filed, the prosecutor can decide not to proceed against the defendant (*nolle prosequi*) because of a change in the circumstances of the case.

In addition, the prosecution and the defense almost always meet to try to arrange a nonjudicial settlement for the case. Plea bargaining, in which the defendant exchanges a guilty plea for some consideration, such as a reduced sen-

tence, is commonly used to terminate the formal processing of the case. The prosecution or the defense may believe, for example, that a trial is not in the best interests of the victim, the defendant, or society because the defendant is incapable of understanding the charges or controlling his or her behavior. In this instance, the defendant may have a competency hearing before a judge and be placed in a secure treatment facility until ready to stand trial. Or the prosecutor may waive further action so that the defendant can be placed in a special treatment program, such as a detoxification unit at a local hospital.

After arrest, the accused is ordinarily taken to the police station, where the police list the possible criminal charges against him or her and obtain other information for **booking** purposes. This may include recording a description of the suspect and the circumstances of the offense. The suspect may then be finger-printed, photographed, and required to participate in a lineup.

Individuals arrested on a misdemeanor charge are ordinarily released from the police station on their own recognizance to answer the criminal charge before the court at a later date. They are usually detained by the police until it is decided whether a criminal complaint will be filed. The **complaint** is the formal written

After arrest, the accused is ordinarily taken to the police station, where the police list the possible criminal charges against him or her and obtain other data for booking purposes. This information may include a description of the suspect and the circumstances of the offense. The suspect may then be fingerprinted, photographed, and required to participate in a lineup.

document identifying the criminal charge, the date and place where the crime occurred, and the circumstances of the arrest. The complaint is sworn to and signed under oath by the complainant, usually a police officer. The complaint will request that the defendant be present at an **initial hearing** held soon after the arrest is made; in some jurisdictions, this may be referred to by other names, such as *arraignment.* The defendant may plead guilty at the initial hearing, and the case may be disposed of immediately. Defendants who plead not guilty to a minor offense have been informed of the formal charge, provided with counsel if they are unable to afford a private attorney, and asked to plead guilty or not guilty as charged. A date in the near future is set for trial, and the defendant is generally released on bail or on his or her own recognizance to await trial.

Where a felony or a more serious crime is involved, the U.S. Constitution requires an intermediate step before a person can be tried. This involves proving to an objective body that there is probable cause to believe that a crime has taken place and that the accused should be tried on the matter. This step of the formal charging process is ordinarily an *indictment* from a grand jury or an *information* issued by a lower court.

An **indictment** is a written accusation charging a person with a crime; it is drawn up by a prosecutor and submitted to a **grand jury,** which, after considering the evidence presented by the prosecutor, votes to endorse or deny the indictment. An **information** is a charging document drawn up by a prosecutor in jurisdictions that do not use the grand jury system. The information is brought before a lower-court judge in a **preliminary hearing** (sometimes called a **probable cause hearing**). The purpose of this hearing is to require the prosecutor to present the case so that the judge can determine whether the defendant should be held to answer for the charge in a felony court.

After an indictment or information is filed, the accused is brought before the trial court for arraignment, during which the judge informs the defendant of the charge, ensures that the accused is properly represented by counsel, and determines whether he or she should be released on bail or some other form of release pending a hearing or trial.

The defendant who is arraigned on an indictment or information can ordinarily plead guilty, not guilty, or *nolo contendere,* which is equivalent to a guilty plea, but it cannot be used as evidence against the defendant in a civil case on

Law and Order

The long-running TV show *Law and Order* claims to be an honest attempt to depict the workings of the criminal justice system. Every week, the first half hour of the program is devoted to police investigation, and the second half to charging and prosecution. After more than five years on the air, how accurate is *Law and Order*'s portrayal of the criminal process?

Law and Order seems accurate when it pairs up experienced detectives who almost always seem to be white males (played at various times by George Dzunda, Paul Sorvino, Chris Noth, Jerry Orbach, and Benjamin Bratt). Their supervisor, Lt. Anita Van Buren (played by S. Epatha Merkerson), is an African-American female, so the show does give a nod to the emerging diversity in American policing.

The show accurately portrays the working style of many police officers. The detectives are world-weary and cynical, quick to mistrust what people tell them, and suspicious of anyone who appears too cooperative. While they sometimes get angry when suspects or witnesses fail to cooperate, they never get so out of control that they beat a suspect or are forced to use their weapons. You won't see a high-speed chase or a shoot-out on *Law and Order*. These detectives are civil servants who value their police careers and professional abilities. Their personal problems are also realistically portrayed. For example, Detective Lenny Briscoe, played by Jerry Orbach, is a recovering alcoholic and is divorced, two social problems not uncommon to police officers. (Showing divorce and alcoholism among police officers is now common in the media. For example, the character Detective Sipowicz on *NYPD Blue,* played by Dennis Franz, shares these problems.) While these characters are compelling, the show is misleading when it implies that detectives routinely solve complex criminal investigations.

The show is also accurate when it shows how Assistant District Attorneys Claire Kincaid (Jill Hennessy) and Jack McCoy (Sam Waterson) are often forced to face unpleasant political realities, deal with media pressure, and plea-bargain cases. They sometimes even lose jury trials! *Law and Order* is one of the first TV shows to routinely portray such pretrial issues as evidentiary hearings, arraignments, bail, and plea bargaining. The show recognizes that criminal procedure is often determined by the outcome of the early court process.

Though perhaps no different from many media versions of the justice system, *Law and Order* bends reality in one significant way: Every character is so attractive and every case so interesting that one would wonder why all attorneys do not aspire to become Manhattan County DA's.

the same matter. In cases where a guilty plea is entered, the defendant admits to all the elements of the crime, and the court begins a review of the person's background for sentencing purposes. A plea of not guilty sets the stage for a trial on the merits or for negotiations, known as plea bargaining, between the prosecutor and the defense attorney.

Before discussing these issues, it is important to address the question of pretrial release and bail, which may arise at the police station, at the initial court appearance in a misdemeanor, or at the arraignment in most felony cases.

As we have described, many jurisdictions today are faced with significant increases in the number of criminal cases, particularly those involving drugs. The police have responded with an unprecedented number of arrests, clogging an already overburdened jail system. Of these arrestees, the justice system must

Pretrial Services

determine which can safely be released pending trial. Pretrial services help courts deal with this problem. At the pretrial stage, the system is required to balance the often conflicting goals of ensuring community safety and respecting the rights of the arrestee.

Often, there is some confusion about the meaning of *pretrial services.* These are the practices and programs that screen arrestees to provide the bail-setting magistrate with concise summaries of the arrestee's personal background as it relates to bail.[1] This definition is distinguished from *diversion,* in which criminal prosecution is bypassed for alternative measures, such as treatment or counseling; diversion is discussed at the end of this chapter.

Pretrial service programs seek to

1. Improve the release/detention decision process in criminal courts by providing complete, accurate, nonadversarial information to judicial officers

2. Identify those for whom alternative forms of supervision may be more appropriate than incarceration

3. Monitor released pretrial arrestees to ensure they comply with the conditions of release imposed by the judicial officer for the benefit of public safety[2]

Virtually all jurisdictions in the United States have pretrial release in one form or another. Court-administered programs make up the greatest percentage of pretrial programs (38%), while probation-administered programs constitute the next largest segment (24%). The general criteria used to assess eligibility for release center on the defendant's community ties and prior criminal justice involvement. Over three-fourths of the programs in the United States have a wide variety of release options.[3] Many jurisdictions have conditional and supervised release and third-party custody release, in addition to release on a person's own recognizance.

In recent years, many states have also begun to rely on programs to detect illicit drug use by defendants. The aim is to provide a judge with an objective measure of a defendant's drug use for pretrial release determination and to serve as a tool for controlling possible misconduct during the pretrial release period. A recent demonstration program of mandatory drug testing of criminal defendants in eight federal judicial districts revealed that over 31% of the defendants who submitted to urinalysis provided positive samples.[4] Judges and magistrates generally believe that pretrial drug testing is a valuable tool in implementing the statutory requirements of any pretrial release program. The validity of judicial predictions of dangerousness of future crimes based on drug testing remains uncertain.[5] Recent studies show that urine test results have no consistent power to predict pretrial misconduct.[6]

Effective pretrial release programs benefit the justice system in many ways. Judicial officers are able to make more effective decisions about who may be released safely. The compliance of pretrial arrestees with their conditions of release can be monitored. In addition, pretrial programs can operate at different stages of the judicial process, thereby increasing the number of release options available to the courts. Table 10.1 provides a list of such pretrial release mechanisms.

Bail

Bail is money or some other security provided to the court to ensure the appearance of the defendant at every subsequent stage of the criminal justice process. Its purpose is to obtain the release from custody of a person charged with a crime. Once the amount of bail is set by the court, the defendant is required to deposit all or a percentage of the entire amount in cash or security (or to pay a professional bonding agent to submit a bond). If the defendant is released on bail but fails to appear in court at the stipulated time, the bail deposit is forfeited. A defendant who fails to make bail is confined in jail until the court appearance.

Table 10.1
Pretrial Release
Alternatives

Stage	Release Mechanism
1. Police	**Field citation release**—An arresting officer releases the arrestee on a written promise to appear in court, made at or near the actual time and location of the arrest. This procedure is commonly used for misdemeanor charges and is similar to issuing a traffic ticket.
2. Police	**Stationhouse citation release**—The determination of an arrestee's eligibility and suitability for release and the actual release of the arrestee are deferred until after he or she has been removed from the scene of an arrest and brought to the stationhouse or police headquarters.
3. Police/pretrial	**Jail citation release**—The determination of an arrestee's eligibility and suitability for citation release and the actual release of the arrestee are deferred until after he or she has been delivered by the arresting department to a jail or other pretrial detention facility for screening, booking, and admission.
4. Pretrial/court	**Direct release authority by pretrial program**—To streamline release processes and reduce the length of stay in detention, courts may authorize pretrial programs to release defendants without direct judicial involvement. Where court rule delegates such authority, the practice is generally limited to misdemeanor charges, but felony release authority has been granted in some jurisdictions.
5. Police/court	**Bail schedule**—An arrestee can post bail at the stationhouse or jail according to amounts specified in a bail schedule. The schedule is a list of all bailable charges and a corresponding dollar amount for each. Schedules may vary widely from jurisdiction to jurisdiction.
6. Court	**Judicial release**—Arrestees who have not been released by either the police or the jailer and who have not posted bail appear at the hearing before a judge, magistrate, or bail commissioner within a set period of time. In jurisdictions with pretrial release programs, program staff often interview arrestees detained at the jail prior to the first hearing, verify the background information, and present recommendations to the court at arraignment.

The Legal Right to Bail

The Eighth Amendment to the U.S. Constitution does not guarantee a constitutional right to bail but rather prohibits "excessive bail." Since many state statutes place no precise limit on the amount of bail a judge may impose, many defendants who cannot make bail are placed in detention while awaiting trial. It has become apparent over the years that the bail system is discriminatory because defendants who are financially well-off are able to make bail, while indigent defendants languish in pretrial detention in the county jail. In addition, keeping a person in jail imposes serious financial burdens on local and state governments—and, in turn, on taxpayers—who must pay for the cost of confinement. These factors have given rise to bail reform programs that depend on the defendant's personal promise to appear in court for trial (recognizance), rather than on financial ability to meet bail. While these reforms have enabled many deserving but indigent offenders to go free, another trend has been to deny people bail on the grounds that they are a danger to themselves or to others in the community.

The Eighth Amendment restriction on excessive bail may also be interpreted to mean that the sole purpose of bail is to ensure that the defendant return for trial; bail may not be used as a form of punishment, nor may it be used to coerce or threaten a defendant. In most cases, a defendant has the right to be released on reasonable bail. Many jurisdictions also require a bail review hearing by a higher court in cases in which the initial judge set what might be considered excessive bail.

The U.S. Supreme Court's interpretation of the Eighth Amendment's provisions on bail was set out in the case of *Stack v. Boyle* (1951).[7] In that case, the Supreme Court found bail to be a traditional right to freedom before trial that permits unhampered preparation of a defense and prevents the criminal defendant from being punished prior to conviction. The Court held that bail is excessive when it exceeds an amount reasonably calculated to ensure that the defendant will return for trial. The Court indicated that bail should be in the amount that is generally set for similar offenses. Higher bail can be imposed when evidence supporting the increase is presented at a hearing at which the defendant's constitutional rights can be protected. Although *Stack* did not mandate an absolute right to bail, it did set guidelines for state courts to follow: If a crime is bailable, the amount set should not be frivolous, unusual, or beyond a person's ability to pay.

Receiving Bail

Whether a defendant can be expected to appear at the next stage of the criminal proceeding is a key issue in determining bail. Bail cannot be used to punish an accused, nor can it be denied or revoked at the indulgence of the court. Many experts believe that money bail is one of the most unacceptable aspects of the criminal justice system: It is discriminatory because it works against the poor; it is costly because the government must pay to detain those offenders who are unable to make bail but who would otherwise be in the community; it is unfair because a higher proportion of detainees receive longer sentences than people released on bail; and it is dehumanizing because innocent people who cannot make bail suffer in the nation's deteriorated jail system.[8]

How successful are bail and pretrial release? A study of bail procedures in eight urban jurisdictions (including Baltimore, Washington, D.C., Miami, Tucson, Louisville, and San Jose) found that about 85% of all defendants received bail. Of these, about 15% did not return for trial because they had absconded. An additional 15% were rearrested for another crime before their trial date. Thus, about 30% of those released on bail could be considered failures for one reason or another.[9]

A study found that about 10% of the defendants released by federal trial courts failed to honor their bail; the reasons included rearrest, failure to appear, and violation of the conditions of bail.[10] Those rearrested tended to (1) be on bail longer (nine months or more); (2) have a serious prior record; (3) abuse drugs; (4) have a poor work record; and (5) be disproportionately young, male, and minority-group members.

The differences between the state and federal studies may be attributed to the types of offenders who pass through their jurisdictions. The federal courts probably see more white-collar offenders and fewer violent offenders. Thus, although the state statistics are less than encouraging, the 10% failure rate recorded by the federal government indicates that pretrial release has been quite successful in some jurisdictions.

A comprehensive 1990 study of the National Pretrial Reporting Program found that about 24% of the released defendants failed to appear in court, while about 18% were rearrested for a felony while on pretrial release. These findings were drawn from a sample of felony cases in 1988, representing the 75 most populous counties in the United States and involving 44,719 defendants, of which over two-thirds, or almost 30,000, were released prior to trial.[11] Some of the conclusions resulting from this important study are that (1) significant numbers of defendants are given pretrial release; (2) the failure-to-appear rate varies according to the type of arrest charge and the type of release; and (3) defendants in different age groups and those with different criminal backgrounds are rearrested at different rates. The rates of rearrest and of failure to appear, which range from 18% to 24%, respectively, are similar to the results of previous research in the area. The study presents new and convincing evidence that pretrial release continues to be a successful component in the criminal justice system, providing pivotal services at key stages of the criminal process.

The most recent Justice Department study of pretrial release programs in the 75 largest counties found that nearly 40% of defendants failed bail because (1) they didn't appear for scheduled court hearings; (2) they remained fugitives one year after their court date; and (3) they committed new felonies while out on bail.[12] Thus, contradictory data exist about the viability and success of pretrial release programs in America.

One of the collateral developments of the bail system is the practice of **bail bonding.** For a fee, bonding agents lend money to people who cannot make bail on their own. Powerful ties often exist between bonding agents and the court, with the result that defendants are steered toward particular bonding agents. Charges of kickbacks and cooperation accompany such arrangements. Allegations of corruption associated with the bail-bonding system have long been made. Consequently, many states have abolished bonding agents, replacing them with bail systems in which the state itself acts as a bonding agency. Defendants put up 10% of the total bail but are responsible for paying the entire amount if they abscond; this is referred to as the "10% cash match," or **deposit bail,** system. Nevertheless, an estimated 5,000 professional bail-bonding agents operate in the United States today.[13] The potential for abuse inherent in the system has led many critics to suggest that in many instances, the traditional bail system is an unsatisfactory pretrial release procedure.[14]

Efforts have been made to reform and even eliminate money bail and reduce the importance of bonding agents. Until the early 1960s, the justice system relied primarily on money bonds as the principal form of pretrial release. Many states now allow defendants to be released on their own recognizance without any money bail. **Release on recognizance (ROR)** was pioneered by the Vera Institute of Justice in an experiment called the **Manhattan Bail Project,** which began in 1961 with the cooperation of the New York City criminal courts and local law students.[15] It came about because defendants with financial means were able to post bail to secure pretrial release, while indigent defendants remained in custody.

The Eighth Amendment to the U.S. Constitution does not guarantee a constitutional right to bail but rather prohibits "excessive bail." Most defendants do in fact make bail. One was John Kelly, a defendant in a highly publicized rape trial. Kelly, who was accused of raping a 16-year-old girl, fled to Europe, where he remained for ten years before being tried. Kelly was found guilty as charged in June 1997 and was rereleased on bail to await sentencing.

Chapter 10
—
Pretrial Procedures

The project found that if the court had sufficient background information about the defendant, it could make a reasonably good judgment as to whether the accused would return to court. When release decisions were based on such information as the nature of the offense, family ties, and employment record, most defendants returned to court when released on their own recognizance. The results of the Vera Institute's initial operation showed a default rate of less than .7%. The bail project's experience suggested that releasing a person on the basis of verified information more effectively guaranteed appearance in court than did money bail. Highly successful ROR projects were set up in major cities around the country, including Philadelphia and San Francisco. By 1980 more than 120 formal programs were in operation, and today they exist in almost every major jurisdiction.[16]

The success of ROR programs in the early 1960s resulted in bail reforms that culminated with the enactment of the federal Bail Reform Act of 1966, the first change in federal bail laws since 1789.[17] This legislation sought to ensure that release would be granted in all noncapital cases in which there was sufficient reason to believe that the defendant would return to court. The law clearly established the presumption of ROR that must be overcome before money bail is required, authorized 10%-deposit bail, introduced the concept of conditional release, and stressed the philosophy that release should be under the least restrictive method necessary to ensure court appearance.

During the 1970s and early 1980s, the pretrial release movement was hampered by public pressure over pretrial increases in crime. As a result, the more recent federal legislation, the **Bail Reform Act of 1984,** mandated that no defendants shall be kept in pretrial detention simply because they cannot afford money bail, established the presumption for ROR in all cases in which a person is bailable, and formalized restrictive preventive detention provisions, which are explained later in this chapter. The 1984 act required that community safety, as well as the risk of flight, be considered in the release decision. Consequently, such criminal justice factors as the seriousness of the charged offense, the weight of the evidence, the sentence that may be imposed upon conviction, court appearance history, and prior convictions are likely to influence the release decisions of the federal court.

During 1990, the U.S. district courts released 27,000, or 62%, of 44,000 defendants facing federal felony charges.[18] Rates of pretrial release for felons in state courts are nearly identical (two-thirds of both federal and state arrestees are released prior to case disposition). A number of innovative alternative bail programs are described in Table 10.2. The most often used are (1) personal recognizance, (2) unsecured or personal bond, (3) surety or cash bond, and (4) percentage or deposit bail. Release on recognizance and conditional release have nearly replaced the traditional cash bail system.

Bail reform is considered one of the most successful programs in the recent history of the criminal justice system. Yet it is not without critics who suggest that emphasis should be put on controlling the behavior of serious criminals rather than on making sure that nondangerous defendants are released before their trials. Criminal defendants released without bail and those who commit crimes awaiting trial fuel the constant debate over pretrial release versus community protection.

The Preventive Detention Controversy

Those who promote bail reform point to the Eighth Amendment of the Constitution as evidence that bail should be made available to almost all people accused of crime. The presumption of bail is challenged by those who believe that releasing dangerous criminals before trial poses a threat to public safety. They point to evidence showing that many people released on bail commit new crimes while at large and often fail to appear for trial. One response to the alleged failure of the bail system to protect citizens is the adoption of preventive detention statutes. These laws require that certain dangerous defendants be confined before trial for

Table 10.2
Innovative Bail Systems
SOURCE: Adapted from Andy Hall,
Pretrial Release Program Options
(Washington, D.C.: National Institute
of Justice, 1984), pp. 32–33.

Program	Description
Nonfinancial Release	
Release on recognizance	The defendant is released on a promise to appear, without any requirement of money bond. This form of release is unconditional—that is, without imposition of special conditions, supervision, or specially provided services.
Conditional release	The defendant is released on a promise to fulfill some stated requirements that go beyond those associated with release on recognizance. Four types of conditions are placed on defendants: (1) status quo conditions, such as requiring that the defendant maintain residence or employment status; (2) restrictive conditions, such as requiring that the defendant remain in the jurisdiction; (3) contact conditions, such as requiring that the defendant report by telephone or in person to the release program; and (4) problem-oriented conditions, such as requiring that the defendant participate in drug or alcohol treatment programs.
Financial Release	
Unsecured bail	The defendant is released with no immediate requirement of payment. However, if the defendant fails to appear, he or she is liable for the full amount.
Privately secured bail	A private organization or individual posts the bail amount, which is returned when the defendant appears in court.
Property bail	The defendant may post evidence of real property in lieu of money.
Deposit bail	The defendant deposits a percentage of the bail amount, typically 10%, with the court. When the defendant appears in court, the deposit is returned, sometimes minus an administrative fee. If the defendant fails to appear, he or she is liable for the full amount of the bail.
Surety bail	The defendant pays a percentage of the bond, usually 10%, to a bonding agent who posts the full bail. The fee paid to the bonding agent is not returned to the defendant if he or she appears in court. The bonding agent is liable for the full amount of the bond should the defendant fail to appear. Bonding agents often require posting of collateral to cover the full bail amount.
Cash bail	The defendant pays the entire amount of bail set by the judge to secure release. The bail is returned to the defendant when he or she appears in court.

their own protection and that of the community. Preventive detention is an important manifestation of the crime control perspective on justice, since it favors the use of incapacitation to control the future behavior of suspected criminals. Often, the key question is whether preventive detention is punishment before trial.

The most striking use of preventive detention can be found in the federal Bail Reform Act of 1984, which contrasted sharply with previous law.[19] Although the act does contain provisions for ROR, it also allows judges to order preventive detention if they determine "that no condition or combination of conditions will reasonably assure the appearance of the person as required and the safety of any other person and the community."[20]

A number of state jurisdictions have incorporated elements of preventive detention into their bail systems. Although most of the restrictions do not constitute

United States v. Salerno (1987)

In this case, the U.S. Supreme Court held that the use of preventive detention is constitutionally permissible.

Facts

On March 21, 1986 Anthony Salerno and co-defendant Vincent Cafaro were charged in a 29-count indictment alleging various racketeering violations, including gambling, wire fraud, extortion, and conspiracy to commit murder. At their arraignment, the government moved to have them detained on the grounds that no condition of release could ensure community safety. At a detention hearing, the prosecution presented evidence that Salerno was the "boss" of the Genovese crime family and that Cafaro was a "captain." Wiretap evidence indicated that the two men had participated in criminal conspiracies, including murder. The court heard testimony from two witnesses who had personally participated in the murder conspiracies. In rebuttal, Salerno provided character statements, presented evidence that he had a heart condition, and challenged the veracity of the government's witnesses. Cafaro claimed the wiretaps had merely recorded "tough talk." The trial court allowed the detention on the grounds that the defendants wanted to use their pretrial freedom to continue their "family" business and "when business as usual involves threats, beatings, and murder, the present danger such people pose to the community is self-evident."

On appeal, the U.S. Court of Appeals for the Second Circuit agreed with the defendants' claim that the government could not detain suspects simply because they were thought to represent a danger to the community. The circuit court found that the criminal law system holds people accountable for their past deeds, not their anticipated future actions. The government then reappealed the case to the Supreme Court.

Decision

The Supreme Court held that the preventive detention act had a legitimate and compelling regulatory purpose and did not violate the due process clause. Preventive detention was not designed to punish dangerous individuals but to find a solution for the social problem of people committing crimes while on bail; preventing danger to the community is a legitimate societal goal.

The Court also stated that society's need for protection can outweigh an individual's liberty interest: Under some circumstances, individuals can be held without bail. The act provides that only the most serious criminals can be held and mandates careful procedures to ensure that the judgment of future dangerousness is made after careful deliberation. Finally, the Court found that the Eighth Amendment does not limit the setting (or denial) of bail simply to prohibit defendants' flight to avoid trial and held that considerations of dangerousness are a valid reason to deny pretrial release.

Significance of the Case

Salerno legitimizes the use of preventive detention as a crime control method. It permits the limitations on bail already in place in many state jurisdictions to continue. *Salerno* further illustrates the concern for community protection that has developed in the past decade. It is a good example of the recent efforts by the Court to give the justice system greater control over criminal defendants. At this time, it is still unclear how often judges will rely on preventive detention statutes that require a hearing on the facts or whether they will simply continue to set extremely high bail for defendants they wish to remain in pretrial custody.

outright preventive detention, they serve to narrow the scope of bail eligibility. These provisions include (1) exclusion of certain crimes from bail eligibility; (2) definition of bail to include appearance in court and community safety; and (3) the limitations on right to bail for those previously convicted.

Preventive detention has also been a source of concern for civil libertarians who believe it violates the due process clause of the U.S. Constitution, since it means that a person will be held in custody before proven guilty. In two recent important cases, the U.S. Supreme Court disagreed with this analysis. In *Schall v. Martin,* the Court upheld the application of preventive detention statutes to juvenile defendants on the grounds that such detention is useful to protect the welfare of the minor and society as a whole.[21] In **United States v. Salerno,** the Court upheld the Bail Reform Act's provision on preventive detention.[22] According to Chief Justice William Rehnquist, the statute conforms to the principle that "[i]n our society liberty is the norm, and detention prior to trial or without trial is the carefully limited exception."[23] Because of the importance of this case, it is analyzed in the accompanying Law in Review box.

The criminal defendant who is not eligible for bail or ROR is subject to **pretrial detention** in the local county jail. The jail has long been a trouble spot for the criminal justice system. Conditions tend to be poor and rehabilitation nonexistent.

Pretrial Detention

In terms of the number of persons affected per year, pretrial custody accounts for more incarceration in the United States than does imprisonment after sentencing.[24] In the 1990s, on any given day in the United States almost 300,000 people were held in more than 3,500 local jails. Over the course of a year, many times that number pass through these jails. More than 50% of those held in local jails have been accused of crimes but not convicted. They are pretrial detainees. In the United States, people are detained at a rate twice that of neighboring Canada and three times that of Great Britain. Hundreds of jails are overcrowded, and many are under court orders to reduce their populations and improve conditions.

This national jail-crowding crisis has worsened over the years. Nationwide, local jails held about 210,000 persons on June 30, 1982, and 405,000 on June 29, 1990—an increase of 93%. There were nearly 20 million admissions and releases from local jails during the year ending 1990, compared to about 14 million just eight years earlier, an increase of 43%. The occupancy rate of jails rose from 85% in 1982 to 104% in 1990. Experts believe that 500 new jail beds per week, or 26,000 per year, will be needed just to keep up with the current rate of growth in the jail population.[25]

The latest data indicate local jails held approximately 485,000 adults awaiting trial or serving a sentence at the end of 1994. According to the Bureau of Justice Statistics, the jail population in the United States has increased dramatically in the past decade; the number of inmates on any given day has more than doubled during that period (see Figure 10.1).[26]

Jails are often considered the weakest link in the criminal justice process: They are frequently dangerous, harmful, decrepit, and filled with the poor and friendless. The costs of holding a person in jail range up to more than $85 per day and $30,000 per year.[27] In addition, detainees are often confined with those convicted of crimes and those who have been transferred from other institutions because of overcrowding. Many felons are transferred to jails from state prisons to ease crowding. It is possible to have in close quarters a convicted rapist, a father jailed for nonpayment of child support, and a person awaiting trial for a crime that he did not actually commit. Thus, jails contain a mix of inmates that can lead to violence, brutality, and suicide.

Why does the jail crisis persist? Societal problems—such as drug use, the needs of the mentally ill, and cutbacks in federal and state social service funding—provide a partial answer. To a large degree, jails are in poor condition because the public does not care about them.

What happens to people who do not get bail or who cannot afford to put up bail money? Traditionally, they find themselves getting a long prison sentence if they are convicted at trial.[28] Data on cases processed through the federal court system indicate that detainees received significantly longer sentences than those who had been released on bail; for some crime categories, the detainees' sentences were double that of bailees.[29]

Figure 10.1
Jail, prison, probation, and parole population, 1985–1994. The total number of persons increased from 3 to 5 million.

SOURCE: U.S. Department of Justice, Bureau of Justice Statistics, *Fiscal Year 1996 at a Glance* (Washington, D.C.: Office of Justice Programs, 1996), p. 35.

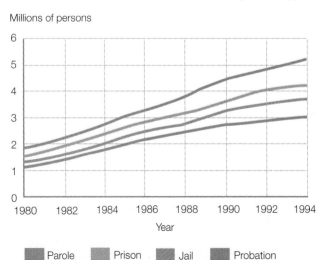

Millions of persons

Parole   Prison   Jail   Probation

The Pretrial Release Debate

While pretrial release advocates believe that accused individuals should not be incarcerated before their trial just because they can't afford bail, opponents charge that pretrial release programs put too many potentially dangerous people back on the street without supervision. Which position is correct?

The Eighth Amendment of the U.S. Constitution prohibits excessive bail. Even prosecutors and victims' groups agree that bail shouldn't be used to punish suspects. But others argue that defendants who don't have to raise their own bail have no incentive to return for trial.

In 1994 a Department of Justice study of pretrial release found that one-third of defendants accused of violent crimes were released without paying bail. Of that number, 25% failed to appear in court and 11% committed new felonies while awaiting trial. Other studies of federal data suggest that possibly half of the defendants released under pretrial release programs have previously jumped bail, and many others have prior felony convictions.

On the other hand, pretrial release programs, which began during the 1960s, were originally designed for indigent defendants. Based on personal history, prior criminal record, and risk of flight, a judge could set a defendant free on personal recognizance and monitor him or her until trial. Over the years, caseloads expanded, and court rulings and statutes now provide the opportunity for pretrial release to virtually all defendants. Also, judges use pretrial release to relieve jail overcrowding. As a result, more time elapses before a defendant is brought to trial, which increases the likelihood of trial default and the commission of additional crimes while under pretrial release. Using new monitoring devices such as electronic bracelets and telephone contacts, pretrial release officials still defend their programs as needed for poor defendants and as cost-effective for taxpayers.

Critical Thinking Questions

1. Historically, bail statutes were designed to assure the defendant's appearance at court proceedings. Bail reform was needed, however, because of the unregulated and discriminatory use of pretrial detention, primarily among poor defendants in urban jails. The solution was to establish pretrial release programs. But isn't it true that many people released today often commit crimes while awaiting trial? Why?

2. *United States v. Salerno* upheld the federal Bail Reform Act of 1984, which authorized the use of preventive detention in federal criminal prosecutions. Preventive detention is used before trial solely to prevent an accused from committing further crimes during the pretrial period. Can we really predict a person's future behavior? Isn't a prediction of dangerousness so unreliable as to pose due process violations? Should people be punished because their past actions indicate a risk of criminality? Compare preventive detention with money bail.

3. Despite such reservations, legislatures have increasingly relied on preventive detention as an instrument of social control. According to the *Salerno* case, the detention of dangerous individuals is not punishment but regulation. To civil libertarians, restrictions on liberty and freedom constitute a form of punishment. To what degree does preventive detention further community safety?

SOURCES: Andrea Gerlin, "Criminal Defendants Released Without Bail Spark Heated Debate," *Wall Street Journal*, 9 July 1996, p. A; see also Jeffrey Fagan and Martin Guggenheim, "Preventive Detention and Judicial Prediction of Dangerousness for Juveniles: A Natural Experiment," *Journal of Criminal Law and Criminology* 86 (1996): 415.

In sum, the first stage of bail reform began in the 1960s because reformers were critical of the discriminatory setting of unaffordable bail for the urban poor and deplored the conditions of jail confinement. The second stage involved the passage of the federal Bail Reform Act of 1984, which moved the emphasis in bail decisions toward denial of bail for community protection. This transformation was completed with the *Schall* and *Salerno* decisions, which gave approval to the use of preventive detention. Today, most states and the federal system have changed their laws to allow judges to detain suspects who are a danger to the community if released during the pretrial period.[30] The debate on pretrial release versus community safety is discussed in the accompanying Analyzing Criminal Justice Issues box.

Charging a defendant with a crime is a process that varies somewhat depending on whether it occurs via a grand jury or a preliminary hearing.

The grand jury was an early development of the English common law. Under the Magna Carta (1215), no freeman could be seized and imprisoned unless he had been judged by his peers. To determine fairly who was eligible to be tried, a group of freemen from the district where the crime was committed would be brought together to examine the facts of the case and determine whether the charges had merit. Thus, the grand jury was created as a check against arbitrary prosecution by a judge who might be a puppet of the government.

The Indictment Process—The Grand Jury

The concept of the grand jury was brought to the American colonies by early settlers and later incorporated into the Fifth Amendment of the U.S. Constitution, which states that "no person shall be held to answer for a capital, or otherwise infamous crime, unless on presentment or indictment of a grand jury."

Today, the use of the grand jury is diminishing. In 1961, 33 states required grand jury indictments. As of 1987, 14 states required a grand jury indictment to begin all felony proceedings.[31] About 25 states allow a grand jury to be called at the option of the prosecutor. The federal government uses both the grand jury and the preliminary hearing systems.

What is the role of the grand jury today? First, the grand jury has the power to act as an independent investigating body. In this capacity, it examines the possibility of criminal activity within its jurisdiction. These investigative efforts are directed toward general rather than individual criminal conduct. After an investigation is completed, a report called a *presentment* is issued. The presentment contains not only information concerning the findings of the grand jury but also usually a recommendation of indictment.

The grand jury's second and better known role is accusatory in nature. In this capacity, the grand jury acts as the community's conscience in determining whether the accusation of the state (the prosecution) justifies a trial. The grand jury relies on the testimony of witnesses called by the prosecution through its subpoena power. After examining the evidence and the testimony of witnesses, the grand jury decides whether probable cause exists for prosecution. If it does, an indictment, or *true bill,* is affirmed. If the grand jury fails to find probable cause, a *no bill* (meaning that the indictment is ignored) is passed. In some states, a prosecutor can present evidence to a different grand jury if a no bill is returned; in other states, this action is prohibited by statute.

The grand jury usually meets at the request of the prosecution. Hearings are closed and secret. The prosecuting attorney presents the charges and calls witnesses who testify under oath to support the indictment. Usually, the accused individuals are not allowed to attend the hearing unless they are asked to testify by the prosecutor or grand jury.

The preliminary hearing is used in about half the states as an alternative to the grand jury. Although the purpose of preliminary and grand jury hearings is the same—to establish whether probable cause is sufficient to merit a trial—the procedures differ significantly.

The Preliminary Hearing

The preliminary hearing is conducted before a magistrate or inferior court judge and, unlike the grand jury hearing, is open to the public unless the defendant requests otherwise. Present at the preliminary hearing are the prosecuting attorney, the defendant, and the defendant's counsel, if already retained. The prosecution presents its evidence and witnesses to the judge. The defendant or the defense counsel then has the right to cross-examine witnesses and to challenge the prosecutor's evidence.

After hearing the evidence, the judge decides whether there is sufficient probable cause to believe that the defendant committed the alleged crime. If so, the defendant is bound over for trial, and the prosecuting attorney's information

An arraignment takes place after an indictment or information is filed following a grand jury or preliminary hearing. At the arraignment, the judge informs the defendant of the charges against him or her and appoints counsel if it has not yet been retained. Here John Salvi is shown at his arraignment on charges that he killed two women when he attacked a reproductive clinic in Boston. Salvi, who was later convicted, committed suicide while in prison.

(same as an indictment) is filed with the superior court, usually within 15 days. When the judge does not find sufficient probable cause, the charges are dismissed, and the defendant is released from custody.

A unique aspect of the preliminary hearing is the defendant's right to waive the proceeding. In most states, the prosecutor and the judge must agree to this **waiver.** A waiver has advantages and disadvantages for both the prosecutor and the defendant. In most situations, a prosecutor will agree to a waiver because it avoids revealing evidence to the defense before trial. However, if the state believes it is necessary to obtain a record of witness testimony because of the possibility that a witness or witnesses may be unavailable for the trial or unable to remember the facts clearly, the prosecutor might override the waiver. In this situation, the record of the preliminary hearing can be used at the trial.

The defendant will most likely waive the preliminary hearing for one of three reasons: (1) he or she has already decided to plead guilty; (2) he or she wants to speed up the criminal justice process; or (3) he or she hopes to avoid the negative publicity that might result from the hearing. On the other hand, the preliminary hearing is of obvious advantage to the defendant who believes that it will result in a dismissal of the charges. In addition, the preliminary hearing gives the defense the opportunity to learn what evidence the prosecution has. Figure 10.2 outlines the significant differences between the grand jury and the preliminary hearing process.

Arraignment

An arraignment takes place after an indictment or information is filed following a grand jury or preliminary hearing. At the arraignment, the judge informs the defendant of the charges against him or her and appoints counsel if one has not yet been retained. According to the Sixth Amendment of the U.S. Constitution, the accused has the right to be informed of the nature and cause of the accusation; thus, the judge at the arraignment must make sure that the defendant clearly understands the charges.

After the charges are read and explained, the defendant is asked to enter a plea. If a plea of not guilty or not guilty by reason of insanity is entered, a trial date is set. When the defendant pleads guilty or *nolo contendere,* a date for sentencing is arranged. The magistrate then either sets bail or releases the defendant on personal recognizance.

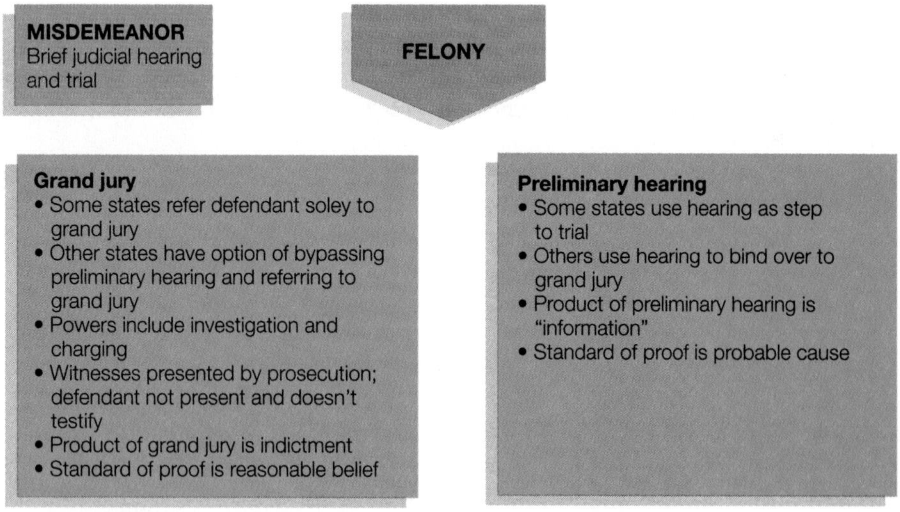

MISDEMEANOR
Brief judicial hearing and trial

FELONY

Grand jury
- Some states refer defendant soley to grand jury
- Other states have option of bypassing preliminary hearing and referring to grand jury
- Powers include investigation and charging
- Witnesses presented by prosecution; defendant not present and doesn't testify
- Product of grand jury is indictment
- Standard of proof is reasonable belief

Preliminary hearing
- Some states use hearing as step to trial
- Others use hearing to bind over to grand jury
- Product of preliminary hearing is "information"
- Standard of proof is probable cause

Figure 10.2
Charging the defendant with a crime: Note the differences between the grand jury and preliminary hearing.

Ordinarily, a defendant in a criminal trial will enter one of three pleas: guilty, not guilty, or *nolo contendere.*

The Plea

Guilty. More than 90% of defendants appearing before the courts plead guilty prior to the trial stage. A guilty plea has several consequences. It functions not only as an admission of guilt but also as a surrender of the entire array of constitutional rights designed to protect a criminal defendant against unjustified conviction, including the right to remain silent, the right to confront witnesses against him or her, the right to a trial by jury, and the right to be proven guilty by proof beyond a reasonable doubt.

As a result, judges must take certain procedures when accepting a plea of guilty. First, the judge must clearly state to the defendant the constitutional guarantees automatically waived by this plea. Second, the judge must believe that the facts of the case establish a basis for the plea and that the plea is made voluntarily. Third, the defendant must be informed of the right to counsel during the pleading process. In many felony cases, the judge will insist on the presence of defense counsel. Finally, the judge must inform the defendant of the possible sentencing outcomes, including the maximum sentence that can be imposed.

After a guilty plea has been entered, a sentencing date is arranged. In a majority of states, a guilty plea may be withdrawn and replaced with a not guilty plea at any time prior to sentencing if good cause is shown.

Not Guilty. At the arraignment or before the trial, a not guilty plea is entered in two ways: (1) it is verbally stated by the defendant or the defense counsel, or (2) it is entered for the defendant by the court when the defendant stands mute before the bench.

Once a plea of not guilty is recorded, a trial date is set. In misdemeanor cases, trials take place in the lower-court system, whereas felony cases are normally transferred to the superior court. At this time, a continuance or issuance of bail is once again considered.

Nolo Contendere. The plea *nolo contendere,* which means "no contest," is essentially a plea of guilty. This plea has the same consequences as a guilty plea, with one exception: It may not be held against the defendant as proof in a subsequent civil matter because technically there has been no admission of guilt. This plea is accepted at the discretion of the trial court and must be voluntarily and intelligently made by the defendant.

One of the most common practices in the criminal justice system today, and a cornerstone of the "informal justice" system, is **plea bargaining.** More than 90% of criminal convictions are estimated to result from negotiated pleas of guilty. Even in serious felony cases, some jurisdictions will have several plea-bargaining arrangements for every trial.

Plea bargaining has been defined concisely as the exchange of prosecutorial and judicial concessions for pleas of guilty.[32] Normally, a bargain can be made between the prosecutor and the defense attorney in four ways: (1) the initial charges may be reduced to those of a lesser offense, thus automatically reducing the sentence imposed; (2) in cases where many counts are charged, the prosecutor may reduce the number of counts; (3) the prosecutor may promise to recommend a lenient sentence, such as probation; and (4) when the charge imposed has a negative label attached (for example, child molester), the prosecutor may alter the charge to a more "socially acceptable" one (such as assault) in exchange for a plea of guilty. In a jurisdiction where sentencing disparities exist between judges, the prosecutor may even agree to arrange for a defendant to appear before a lenient judge in exchange for a plea; this practice is known as "judge shopping."

Because of excessive criminal court caseloads and the personal and professional needs of the prosecution and the defense (to get the case over with in the shortest amount of time), plea bargaining has become an essential yet controversial part of the administration of justice. Proponents contend that plea bargaining actually benefits both the state and the defendant in the following ways:

1. The overall costs of the criminal prosecution are reduced.

2. The administrative efficiency of the courts is greatly improved.

3. The prosecution is able to devote more time to more serious cases.

4. The defendant avoids possible detention and an extended trial and may receive a reduced sentence.[33]

Those who favor plea bargaining believe it is appropriate to enter into plea discussions when the interests of the state in the effective administration of justice will be served. Opponents of the plea-bargaining process believe that the negotiated plea should be eliminated. Some argue that plea bargaining is objectionable because it encourages defendants to waive their constitutional right to trial. In addition, some experts suggest that sentences tend to be less severe when a defendant enters a guilty plea than in actual trials and that plea bargains result in even greater sentencing disparity. Particularly in the eyes of the general public, this allows the defendant to beat the system and further tarnishes the criminal process. Plea bargaining also raises the danger that an innocent person will be convicted of a crime if he or she is convinced that the lighter treatment from a guilty plea is preferable to the risk of conviction with a harsher sentence following a formal trial.

It is unlikely that plea negotiations will be eliminated or severely curtailed in the near future. Supporters of the total abolition of plea bargaining are in the minority. As a result of abuses, however, efforts are being made to improve plea-bargaining operations. Such reforms include (1) development of uniform plea practices, (2) representation of counsel during plea negotiations, and (3) establishment of time limits on plea negotiations.

Legal Issues in Plea Bargaining

The U.S. Supreme Court has reviewed the propriety of plea bargaining in several decisions, particularly in regard to the voluntariness of guilty pleas. Defendants are entitled to the effective assistance of counsel to protect them from pressure and influence. The Court ruled in *Hill v. Lockhart* (1985) that to prove ineffectiveness, the defendant must show a "reasonable probability that, but for counsel's errors, he would not have pleaded guilty and would have insisted on going to trial."[34]

In **Boykin v. Alabama** (1969), the Court held that an affirmative action (such as a verbal statement) that the plea was made voluntarily must exist on the record before a trial judge may accept a guilty plea.[35] This is essential because a guilty plea basically constitutes a waiver of the defendant's Fifth Amendment privilege against self-incrimination and Sixth Amendment right to a jury trial. Subsequent to *Boykin,* the Court ruled in *Brady v. United States* (1970) that a guilty plea is not invalid merely because it is entered to avoid the possibility of the death penalty.[36]

When the question arose about whether a guilty plea may be accepted by a defendant maintaining his or her innocence, the Supreme Court, in *North Carolina v. Alford* (1970), said that such action was appropriate where a defendant was seeking a lesser sentence. In other words, a defendant could plead guilty without admitting guilt.[37]

In **Santobello v. New York** (1971), the Court held that the promise of the prosecutor must be kept and that a prosecutor's breaking of a plea-bargaining agreement required a reversal for the defendant.[38] In *Ricketts v. Adamson* (1987), the Court ruled that defendants must also keep their side of a bargain to receive the promised offer of leniency. In this case, the defendant was charged with first-degree murder but was allowed to plead guilty to second-degree murder in exchange for testifying against his accomplices. The testimony was given, but the co-defendants' conviction was later reversed on appeal. Ricketts refused to testify a second time, and the prosecutor withdrew the offer of leniency. On appeal, the Supreme Court allowed the recharging and held that Ricketts had to suffer the consequences of his voluntary choice not to testify again.[39]

How far can prosecutors go to convince a defendant to plead guilty? The Supreme Court ruled in the 1978 case of *Bordenkircher v. Hayes* that a defendant's due process rights are not violated when a prosecutor threatens to reindict the accused on more serious charges if the defendant does not plead guilty to the original offense.[40]

In 1995, the U.S. Supreme Court decided the case of **United States v. Mezzanatto,** which may cause the plea-bargaining process to change in state courts. In *Mezzanatto,* the Court declared that statements made by the defendant during plea bargaining can be used at trial for impeachment purposes. This means that a prosecutor can refuse to plea bargain with a defendant unless the defendant agrees that any statements made during the negotiations can be used to impeach him at trial. The Court narrowly interpreted Rule 410 of the Federal Rules of Evidence, which says that statements made during plea bargaining are inadmissible at trial. Although the ruling applies only to federal trials, it is likely to be adopted by many state court systems that watch Supreme Court decisions and follow suit.[41]

From repeated actions by the Supreme Court, we realize that plea bargaining is a constitutionally accepted practice in the United States. Table 10.3 summarizes the major Supreme Court decisions regulating plea-bargaining practices.

Plea-Bargaining Decision Making

Because the plea-bargaining process is largely informal, lacking in guidelines, and discretionary, some effort has been made to determine what kinds of information and how much is used by the prosecutor to make plea-bargaining decisions. Research has found that certain information weighs heavily in the prosecutorial decision to accept a plea negotiation.[42] Such factors as the offense, the defendant's prior record and age, and the type, strength, and admissibility of evidence are considered important in the plea-bargaining decision. It was also discovered that the attitude of the complainant is an important factor in the decision-making process; for example, in victimless cases, such as heroin possession, the police attitude is most often considered, whereas in victim-related crimes, such as rape, the attitude of the victim is a primary concern. The study also revealed that prosecutors in low-population or rural jurisdictions not only use more information while making their decisions but also seem more likely

Table 10.3
Notable U.S. Supreme
Court Cases on the Regula-
tion of Plea Bargaining

Case	Ruling
Boykin v. Alabama (1969)	The defendant must make an affirmative statement that the plea is voluntary before the judge can accept it.
Brady v. United States (1970)	Avoiding the possibility of the death penalty is not grounds to invalidate a guilty plea.
North Carolina v. Alford (1970)	Accepting a guilty plea from a defendant who maintains his or her innocence is valid.
Santobello v. New York (1971)	The promise of a prosecutor that rests on a guilty plea must be kept in a plea-bargaining agreement.
Bordenkircher v. Hayes (1978)	A defendant's constitutional rights are not violated when a prosecutor threatens to reindict the accused on more serious charges if he or she is not willing to plead guilty to the original offense.
Hill v. Lockhart (1985)	To prove ineffectiveness of defense counsel, the defendant needs to show a reasonable probability that, except for counsel's errors, the defendant would not have pleaded guilty.
Ricketts v. Adamson (1987)	The defendant is required to keep his or her side of the bargain to receive the promised offer of leniency, since plea bargaining rests on an agreement between the parties.
United States v. Mezzanatto (1995)	A defendant who wants to plea bargain in federal court can be required to agree that if he testifies at trial his statements during the plea-bargain negotiations can be used against him.

than their urban counterparts to accept bargains. It was suggested that "this finding tends to dispute the notion that plea bargaining is a response to overcrowding in large urban courts."[43] It appears that where caseload pressures are less, the acceptance of a plea bargain is actually more probable.

The Role of the Prosecutor in Plea Bargaining

The major players in the plea negotiations are (1) the prosecutor, (2) the defense attorney, (3) the judge, and (4) the defendant. The prosecutor in the U.S. system of criminal justice has broad discretion in the exercise of his or her responsibilities. Such discretion includes deciding whether to initiate a criminal prosecution, determining the nature and number of the criminal charges, and choosing whether to plea bargain a case and under what conditions. Plea bargaining is one of the major tools the prosecutor uses to control and influence the criminal justice system (the other two are the decision to initiate a charge and the ability to take the case to trial). Few states have placed limits on the discretion of prosecutors in plea-bargaining situations. Instead, in making a plea-bargaining decision, the prosecutor is generally free to weigh competing alternatives and factors, such as the seriousness of the crime, the attitude of the victim, the police report of the incident, and applicable sentencing provisions. Plea bargaining frequently occurs in cases where the government believes the evidence is weak, as when a key witness seems unreliable or unwilling to testify. Bargaining permits a compromise settlement in a weak case where the criminal trial outcome is in doubt.

On a case-by-case basis, the prosecutor determines the concessions to be offered in the plea bargain and seeks to dispose of each case quickly and efficiently. On the broader scale, however, the role of the chief prosecutor as an administrator also affects plea bargaining. While the assistant prosecutor evaluates and moves individual cases, the chief prosecutor must establish plea-bargaining guidelines for the entire office. In this regard, the prosecutor may be acting as an administrator.[44] Guidelines cover such aspects as avoiding overindictment and controlling nonprovable indictments, reducing felonies to misdemeanors, and bargaining with defendants.

Some jurisdictions have established guidelines to provide consistency in plea-bargaining cases. For instance, a given office may be required to define the kinds and types of cases and offenders that may be suitable for plea bargaining. In other jurisdictions, approval to plea bargain may be required. Other controls might include procedures for internally reviewing decisions by the chief prosecutor and the use of written memorandums to document the need and acceptability for a plea bargain in a given case. For example, pleas may be offered on a "take it or leave it" basis. In each case, a special prosecutor, whose job it is to screen cases, sets the bargaining terms. If the defense counsel cannot accept the agreement, there is no negotiation, and the case must go to trial. Only if complications arise in the case, such as witnesses changing their testimony, can negotiations be reopened.[45]

The prosecutor's role in plea bargaining is also important on a statewide or systemwide basis because it involves exercising leadership in setting policy. The most extreme example of a chief prosecutor influencing the plea negotiation process has occurred where the prosecutor has attempted to eliminate plea bargaining. In Alaska, such efforts met with resistance from assistant prosecutors and others in the system, particularly judges and defense attorneys.[46]

Both the U.S. Supreme Court and such organizations as the American Bar Association in its *Standards Relating to Pleas of Guilty* have established guidelines for the court receiving a guilty plea and for the defense counsel representing the accused in plea negotiations.[47] No court should accept a guilty plea unless the defendant has been properly advised by counsel and the court has determined that the plea is voluntary and has a factual basis; the court has the discretion to reject a plea if it is inappropriately offered. The defense counsel—a public defender or a private attorney—is required to play an advisory role in plea negotiations. The

The Role of the Defense Counsel in Plea Bargaining

There are a number of reasons that prosecutors will grant a plea bargain. For one, they may want a suspect to testify against fellow conspirators or co-defendants. Here Jennifer McVeigh, sister of Tim McVeigh, is seen with her attorney. She was given immunity as part of a plea bargain in which she agreed to testify at her brother's Oklahoma City bombing trial.

defendant's counsel is expected to be aware of the facts of the case and of the law and to advise the defendant of the alternatives available. The defense attorney is basically responsible for making certain that the accused understands the nature of the plea-bargaining process and the guilty plea. This means that the defense counsel should explain to the defendant that by pleading guilty, he or she is waiving certain rights that would be available on going to trial. In addition, the defense attorney has the duty to keep the defendant informed of developments and discussions with the prosecutor regarding plea bargaining. While doing so, the attorney for the accused cannot misrepresent evidence or mislead the client into making a detrimental agreement.

According to Keith Bystrom, the defense counsel is not only ethically but constitutionally required to communicate all plea bargain offers to a client even if counsel believes the offers to be unacceptable.[48]

In reality, most plea negotiations occur in the chambers of the judge, in the prosecutor's office, or in the courthouse hallway. Under these conditions, it is often difficult to assess the actual roles played by the prosecutor and the defense attorney. Even so, it is fundamental that a defendant not be required to plead guilty until advised by counsel and that a guilty plea should not be made unless it is done with the consent of the accused.

<table>
<tr><td>

The Judge's Role in Plea Bargaining

</td><td>

One of the most confusing problems in the plea-bargaining process has been the proper role of the judge. Should the judge act only in a supervisory capacity or actually enter into the negotiation process? The leading national legal organization, the American Bar Association, is opposed to judicial participation in plea negotiations.[49] The American Bar Association sets out its position on the role of the judge in the plea-bargaining process by clearly stating that the trial judge should not participate in plea discussions. In addition, the Federal Rules of Criminal Procedure prohibit federal judges from participating in plea negotiations.[50] A few states disallow any form of judicial involvement in plea bargaining, but others permit the judge to participate.

The American Bar Association objects in general to the judge participating in plea negotiations because of his or her position as chief judicial officer. A judge should not be a party to arrangements for the determination of a sentence, whether as a result of a guilty plea or a finding of guilty based on proof. Furthermore, judicial participation in plea negotiations (1) creates the impression in the mind of the defendant that he or she could not receive a fair trial; (2) lessens the ability of the judge to make an objective determination of the voluntariness of the plea; (3) is inconsistent with the theory behind the use of presentence investigation reports; and (4) may induce an innocent defendant to plead guilty because he or she is afraid to reject the disposition desired by the judge.[51]

On the other hand, those who suggest that the judge should participate directly in plea bargaining argue that such an approach would make sentencing more uniform and ensure that the plea-bargaining process would be fairer and more efficient.

</td></tr>
<tr><td>

The Victim and Plea Bargaining

</td><td>

Related to the issue of the prosecutor's exercise of discretion is the proper role of the victim in influencing plea bargaining. Often defense attorneys criticize prosecutors for treating victims' interests as paramount and oppose the practice of seeking approval for the proposed plea from a victim or family member. Some suggest that the system today is too "victim driven." Others maintain that the victim plays an almost secondary role in the process.

In reality, the victim is not "empowered" at the pretrial stage of the criminal process. Statutes do not require that the prosecutor defer to the victim's wishes, and there are no legal consequences for ignoring the victim in a plea bargaining decision. Even the American Bar Association Model Uniform Victims of Crime Act only suggests that the prosecutor "confer" with the victim.[52]

</td></tr>
</table>

Victims are certainly not in a position to veto a plea bargain. Most of the work of the victims' rights movement in the justice system is devoted to securing financial compensation from the state and some restitution when possible from the defendant. At the current time it is at the trial stage where the victim has the greatest influence. Here, the victim often has the right to offer a victim-impact statement after a guilty determination and before the court imposes a sentence.

There is no question that the prosecutor should consider the impact that a plea bargain may have on the victim or victim's family. Some victims' groups even suggest that the victim's family have statutory authority to approve or disapprove any plea bargain between the prosecutor and defense attorney in criminal homicide cases. Given the volume of plea bargains, it appears that the victim should have greater control and participation.

As we have mentioned, over 90% of all criminal cases are generally disposed of without a trial. Plea bargaining is an inevitable result and essential to the continued functioning of the criminal justice process. If that is so, then it must be conducted fairly, and as George Fletcher, a noted legal scholar at Columbia Law School indicates, "with due consideration of the victim whose complaint initiates the action."[53]

Plea bargaining is so widespread that it is recognized as one of the major elements of the criminal justice system. Despite its prevalence, its merits are hotly debated. Those opposed to the widespread use of plea bargaining assert that it is coercive in its inducement of guilty pleas, that it encourages the unequal exercise of prosecutorial discretion, and that it complicates sentencing as well as the job of correctional authorities. Others argue that it is unconstitutional and that it results in cynicism and disrespect for the entire system.

Plea-Bargaining Reform

On the other hand, its proponents contend that the practice ensures the flow of guilty pleas essential to administration efficiency. It allows the system the flexibility to individualize justice and inspires respect for the system because it is associated with certain and prompt punishment.[54]

In recent years, efforts have been made to convert plea bargaining into a more visible, understandable, and fair dispositional process. Many jurisdictions have developed safeguards and guidelines to prevent violations of due process and to ensure that innocent defendants do not plead guilty under coercion. Such safeguards include the following: (1) the judge questions the defendant about the facts of the guilty plea before accepting the plea; (2) the defense counsel is present and able to advise the defendant of his or her rights; (3) the prosecutor and the defense attorney openly discuss the plea; and (4) full and frank information about the defendant and the offenses is made available at this stage of the process. In addition, judicial supervision ensures that plea bargaining is conducted in a fair manner.

What would happen if plea bargaining were banned outright, as its critics advocate? Numerous jurisdictions throughout the United States have experimented with bans on plea bargaining. In 1975 Alaska eliminated the practice. Honolulu, Hawaii has also attempted to abolish plea bargaining. Other jurisdictions, including Iowa, Arizona, Delaware, and the District of Columbia, have sought to limit the use of plea bargaining.[55] In theory, eliminating plea bargains means that prosecutors in these jurisdictions give no consideration or concessions to a defendant in exchange for a guilty plea.

In reality, however, in these and most jurisdictions, sentence-related concessions, charge-reduction concessions, and alternative methods for prosecution continue to be used in one fashion or another.[56] Where plea bargaining is limited or abolished, the number of trials may increase, the sentence severity may change, and more questions regarding the right to a speedy trial may arise. Discretion may also be shifted farther up the system. Instead of spending countless hours preparing for and conducting a trial, prosecutors may dismiss more cases outright or decide not to prosecute them after initial action has been taken.

In 1993 Candace McCoy published a well-documented book, *Politics and Plea Bargaining: Victims' Rights in California,* in which she describes legislative efforts to eliminate the plea bargaining process in California. Instead of achieving a ban on plea bargaining, the process shifted from the superior to the municipal courts. McCoy found that the majority of defendants pled guilty after some negotiations and that the new law actually accelerated the guilty plea process. McCoy's prescription is not to ban plea bargaining, but make it better. This includes (1) emphasizing public scrutiny of plea bargaining, (2) adhering to standards of professionalism, and (3) making a greater commitment to due process procedures.[57]

Pretrial Diversion

Another important feature in the early court process is placing offenders into noncriminal **diversion** programs before their formal trial or conviction. Pretrial diversion programs were first established in the late 1960s and early 1970s, when it became apparent that a viable alternative to the highly stigmatized criminal sentence was needed. In diversion programs, formal criminal proceedings against an accused are suspended while that person participates in a community treatment program under court supervision. Diversion helps the offender avoid the stigma of a criminal conviction and enables the justice system to reduce costs and alleviate prison overcrowding.

Many diversion programs exist throughout the United States. These programs vary in size and emphasis but generally pursue the same goal: to constructively bypass criminal prosecution by providing a reasonable alternative in the form of treatment, counseling, or employment programs.

The prosecutor often plays the central role in the diversion process. Decisions about nondispositional alternatives are based on (1) the nature of the crime, (2) special characteristics of the offender, (3) whether the defendant is a first-time offender, (4) whether the defendant will cooperate with a diversion program, (5) the impact of diversion on the community, and (6) consideration for the opinion of the victim.[58]

Diversion programs can take many forms. Some are separate, independent agencies that were originally set up with federal funds but are now being continued with county or state assistance. Others are organized as part of a police, prosecutor, or probation department's internal structure. Still others are a joint venture between the county government and a private, nonprofit organization that actually carries out the treatment process.

First viewed as a panacea that could reduce court congestion and help treat minor offenders, diversion programs have come under fire for their alleged failures. Some national evaluations have concluded that diversion programs are no more successful at avoiding stigma and reducing recidivism than traditional justice processing.[59] The most prominent criticism is that they help "widen the net" of the justice system. By this, critics mean that the people placed in diversion programs are the ones most likely to have otherwise been dismissed after a brief hearing with a warning or small fine.[60]

Those who would have ordinarily received a more serious sentence are not eligible for diversion anyway. Thus, rather than limiting contact with the system, the diversion programs actually increase it. Of course, not all justice experts agree with this charge, and some have championed diversion as a worthwhile exercise of the criminal justice system's rehabilitation responsibility. Although diversion may not be a cure-all for criminal behavior, it is an important effort that continues to be made in most jurisdictions across the United States. Originally proposed by the well-known President's Commission on Law Enforcement in 1967, and supported by federal funds, most existing programs are now underwritten with state funds.[61]

Criminal Justice on the Net

The Pretrial Services Resource Center is an independent, nonprofit clearinghouse for information on pretrial issues and a technical assistance provider for pretrial practitioners, criminal justice officials, academicians, and community leaders nationwide. The Resource Center offers assistance regarding pretrial services agencies, pretrial services programming and management, and jail overcrowding. Since its inception in 1976, the Resource Center has helped criminal justice professionals achieve the often conflicting goals of maintaining the rights of defendants, ensuring public safety, and maintaining the integrity of the criminal justice system by providing information, publications, training, and assistance on pretrial services at the federal, state, and local levels.

The Resource Center's web site provides information on the following topics: technical assistance, jurisdictional on-site consulting, national projects, cooperative projects with other criminal justice agencies, the pretrial reporter, and Resource Center publications. You'll find all this at:

http://www.gslink.com/~pretrial/psrc.html

Summary

Many important decisions about what happens to a defendant are made prior to trial. Hearings, such as before the grand jury and the preliminary hearing, are held to determine if probable cause exists to charge the accused with a crime. If so, the defendant is arraigned, enters a plea, is informed of his or her constitutional rights, particularly the right to the assistance of counsel, and is considered for pretrial diversion. The use of money bail and other alternatives, such as release on recognizance, allows most defendants to be free pending their trial. Bail provisions are beginning to be toughened, resulting in the preventive detention of people awaiting trial. Preventive detention has been implemented because many believe that significant numbers of criminals violate their bail and commit further crimes while on pretrial release.

The issue of discretion plays a major role at this stage of the criminal process. Since only a small percentage of criminal cases eventually go to trial, many defendants agree to plea bargains or are placed in diversion programs. Not enough judges, prosecutors, defense attorneys, and courts exist to try every defendant accused of a crime. As a result, such subsystems as plea bargaining and diversion are essential elements in the administration of the criminal justice system. Research indicates that most cases never go to trial but are bargained out of the system. Although plea bargaining has been criticized, efforts to control it have not met with success. Similarly, diversion programs have not been overly successful, yet they continue to be used throughout the United States.

Key Terms

pretrial procedures
booking
complaint
initial hearing
indictment
grand jury
information
preliminary hearing

probable cause hearing
bail
bail bonding
deposit bail
release on recognizance (ROR)
Manhattan Bail Project
Bail Reform Act of 1984
United States v. Salerno

pretrial detention
waiver
plea bargaining
Boykin v. Alabama
Santobello v. New York
United States v. Mezzanatto
diversion

1. Should criminal defendants be allowed to bargain for a reduced sentence in exchange for a guilty plea?
2. Should those accused of violent acts be subjected to preventive detention instead of bail, even though they have not been convicted of a crime?
3. What purpose does a grand jury or preliminary hearing serve in adjudicating felony offenses?
4. What is the purpose of bail? Of preventive detention?
5. Is plea bargaining constitutional?

Notes

1. D. Alan Henry, "Pretrial Services: Today and Yesterday," *Federal Probation,* June 1991, 54.

2. Bureau of Justice Assistance, *Pretrial Services Program* (Washington, D.C.: U.S. Government Printing Office, 1990), p. 3.

3. Kristen Segebarth, *Pretrial Services and Practices in the 1990s* (Washington, D.C.: Pretrial Resource Center, March 1991), p. 3.

4. Director of Administrative Office of the United States Courts, *The Demonstration Program of Mandatory Drug Testing of Criminal Defendants* (Washington, D.C.: Bureau of Justice Assistance, 29 March 1991).

5. U. S. Department of Justice, *Predicting Pretrial Misconduct with Drug Tests of Arrestees* (Washington, D.C.: National Institute of Justice Research in Brief, 1996), p. 1.

6. William Rhodes, Raymond Hyatt, and Paul Scheiman, "Predicting Pretrial Misconduct with Drug Tests of Arrestees: Evidence from Eight Settings," *Journal of Quantitative Criminology* 12 (1996): 315–347.

7. *Stack v. Boyle,* 342 U.S. 1, 72 S.Ct. 1, 96 L.Ed. 3 (1951).

8. Andy Hall, *Pretrial Release Program Options* (Washington, D.C.: National Institute of Justice, 1984), pp. 30–31.

9. Mary Toborg, *Pretrial Release: A National Evaluation of Practices and Outcomes* (Washington, D.C.: National Institute of Justice, 1982).

10. William Rhodes, *Pretrial Release and Misconduct* (Washinton, D.C.: Bureau of Justice Statistics, 1985).

11. Bureau of Justice Statistics, *Pretrial Release of Felony Defendants, 1988* (Washington, D.C.: U.S. Government Printing Office, February 1991), p. 1.

12. Andrea Gerlin, "Criminal Defendants Released Without Bail Spark a Heated Debate," *Wall Street Journal,* 9 July 1996, p. A1.

13. Hall, *Pretrial Release Program Options.*

14. President's Commission on Law Enforcement and the Administration of Justice, *Task Force Report: The Courts* (Washington, D.C.: U.S. Government Printing Office, 1967), p. 38.

15. Vera Institute of Justice, *1961–1971: Programs in Criminal Justice* (New York: Vera Institute of Justice, 1972).

16. Chris Eskridge, *Pretrial Release Programming* (New York: Clark Boardman, 1983), p. 27.

17. 4 Public Law 89-465, 18 U.S.C. § 3146 (1966).

18. Brian Reaves, *Pretrial Release of Federal Felony Defendants* (Washington, D.C.: Bureau of Justice Statistics, 1994), p. 1.

19. 18 U.S.C. § 3142 (1984).

20. See, generally, Fred Cohen, "The New Federal Crime Control Act," *Criminal Law Bulletin* 21 (1985): 330–337.

21. *Schall v. Martin,* 467 U.S. 253, 104 S.Ct. 2403, 81 L.Ed.2d 207 (1984).

22. *United States v. Salerno,* 481 U.S. 739, 107 S.Ct. 2095, 95 L.Ed.2d 697 (1987).

23. Ibid. at 742, 107 S.Ct. at 2098 (1992).

24. Susan Kline, *Jail Inmates, 1987* (Washington, D.C.: Bureau of Justice Statistics, 1988).

25. "Jail Crowding," *Pretrial Reporter,* October–November 1993, pp. 8–9.

26. U. S. Department of Justice, Bureau of Justice Statistics, *Fiscal Year 1996 at a Glance* (Washington, D.C.: Office of Justice Programs, 1996), p. 34.

27. *Pretrial Reporter,* October 1991, p. 4.

28. Two excellent studies are Caleb Foote, "Compelling Appearance in Court: Administration of Bail in Philadelphia," *University of Pennsylvania Law Review* 102 (1956): 1056, and idem, "A Study of Administration of Bail in New York City," *University of Pennsylvania Law Review* 106 (1960): 693–730.

29. Rhodes, *Pretrial Release and Misconduct;* see also Foote, "A Study of Administration of Bail in New York City"; Ellen Steury and Nancy Frank, "Gender Bias and Pretrial Release," *Journal of Criminal Justice* 18 (1990): 417–432.

30. Michael Corrado, "Punishment and the Wild Beast of Prey: The Problem of Preventive Detention," *Journal of Criminal Law and Criminology* 86 (1996): 778–792.

31. David B. Rottman et al., *State Court Organization, 1993* (Washington, D.C.: U.S. Department of Justice, Bureau of Justice Statistics).

32. Alan Alschuler, "The Prosecutor's Role in Plea Bargaining," *University of Chicago Law Review* (1968): 50–112.

33. For the most cogent arguments favoring plea bargaining, see John Wheatley, "Plea Bargaining—A Case for Its Continuance," *Massachusetts Law Quarterly* 59 (1974): 31.

34. *Hill v. Lockhart,* 474 U.S. 52, 106 S.Ct. 366, 88 L.Ed.2d 203 (1985).

35. *Boykin v. Alabama,* 395 U.S. 238, 89 S.Ct. 1709, 23 L.Ed.2d 274 (1969).

36. *Brady v. United States,* 397 U.S. 742, 90 S.Ct. 1463, 25 L.Ed.2d 747 (1970).

37. *North Carolina v. Alford,* 400 U.S. 25, 91 S.Ct. 160, 27 L.Ed.2d 162 (1970).

38. *Santobello v. New York,* 404 U.S. 257, 92 S.Ct. 495, 30 L.Ed.2d 427 (1971).

39. *Ricketts v. Adamson,* 483 U.S. 1, 107 S.Ct. 2680, 97 L.Ed.2d 1 (1987).

40. *Bordenkircher v. Hayes,* 434 U.S. 357, 98 S.Ct. 663, 54 L.Ed.2d 604 (1978).

41. *United States v. Mezzanatto,* 116 S. Ct. 1480, 134 L.Ed.2d 687 (1995).

42. Stephen P. Lagoy, Joseph J. Senna, and Larry J. Siegel, "An Empirical Study on Information Usage for Prosecutorial Decision Making in Plea Negotiations," *American Criminal Law Review* 13 (1976): 435–471.

43. Ibid., p. 462.

44. Alschuler, "The Prosecutor's Role in Plea Bargaining."

45. Barbara Boland and Brian Forst, *The Prevalence of Guilty Pleas* (Washington, D.C.: Bureau of Justice Statistics, 1984), p. 3; see also Gary Hengstler, "The Troubled Justice System," *American Bar Association Journal* 80 (1994): 44.

46. National Institute of Law Enforcement and Criminal Justice, *Plea Bargaining in the United States* (Washington, D.C.: Georgetown University, 1978), p. 8.

47. See American Bar Association, *Standards Relating to Pleas of Guilty,* 2nd ed. (Chicago: ABA, 1988); see also *North Carolina v. Alford,* 400 U.S. 25, 91 S.Ct. 160, 27 L.Ed.2d 162 (1970).

48. Keith Bystrom, "Communicating Plea Offers to the Client" in *Ethical Problems Facing the Criminal Defense Lawyer,* ed. Rodney Uphoff (Chicago: American Bar Association Section on Criminal Justice, 1995), p. 84.

49. American Bar Association, *Standards Relating to Pleas of Guilty,* standard 3.3; National Advisory Commission on Criminal Justice Standards and Goals, *Task Force Report on Courts* (Washington, D.C.: U.S. Government Printing Office, 1973), p. 42.

50. Federal Rules of Criminal Procedure, rule 11.

51. American Bar Association, *Standards Relating to Pleas of Guilty,* p. 73; see also Alan Alschuler, "The Trial Judge's Role in Plea Bargaining," *Columbia Law Review* 76 (1976): 1059.

52. American Bar Association, Model Uniform Victims of Crime Act (Chicago: ABA, 1992).

53. George P. Fletcher, *With Justice for Some— Victims' Rights in Criminal Trials* (New York: Addison-Wesley, 1995), pp. 190–193.

54. *Santobello v. New York,* 404 U.S. 257, 92 S.Ct. 495, 30 L.Ed.2d 427 (1971).

55. National Institute of Law Enforcement and Criminal Justice, *Plea Bargaining in the United States,* pp. 37–40.

56. For a discussion of this issue, see Michael Tonry, "Plea Bargaining Bans and Rules" in *Sentencing Reform Impacts* (Washington, D.C.: U.S. Government Printing Office, 1987).

57. Candace McCoy, *Politics and Plea Bargaining: Victims' Rights in California* (Philadelphia: University of Pennsylvania Press, 1993).

58. National District Attorneys Association, *National Prosecution Standards,* 2nd ed. (Alexandria, Va.: NDAA, 1991), p. 130.

59. Franklyn Dunford, D. Wayne Osgood, and Hart Weichselbaum, *National Evaluation of Diversion Programs* (Washington, D.C.: U.S. Government Printing Office, 1982).

60. Sharla Rausch and Charles Logan, "Diversion from Juvenile Court, Panacea or Pandora's Box?" in *Evaluating Juvenile Justice,* ed. James Kleugel (Beverly Hills, Calif.: Sage, 1983), pp. 19–30.

61. See Malcolm Feeley, *Court Reform on Trial* (New York: Basic Books, 1983).

The Criminal Trial

The **adjudication** stage of the criminal justice process begins with a hearing that seeks to determine the truth of the facts of a case. This process is usually referred to as the criminal *trial.* As we have mentioned, the classic jury trial of a criminal case is an uncommon occurrence. The greatest proportion of individuals charged with crimes plead guilty. Others have their cases dismissed by the judge for a variety of reasons: The government may decide not to prosecute (*nolle prosequi*); the accused may be found emotionally disturbed and unable to stand trial; or the court may be unwilling to attach the stigma of a criminal record to a particular defendant.

Still other defendants waive their constitutional right to a jury trial. In this situation, which occurs daily in the lower criminal courts, the judge may initiate a number of formal or informal dispositions, including dismissing the case, finding the defendant not guilty, finding the defendant guilty and imposing a sentence, or even continuing the case indefinitely. The decision the judge makes often depends on the seriousness of the offense, the background and previous record of the defendant, and the judgment of the court as to whether the case can be properly dealt with in the criminal process.

In a minor case in some jurisdictions, for example, the *continuance* is a frequently used disposition. In this instance, the court holds a case in abeyance without a finding of guilt to induce the accused to improve his or her behavior in the community; if the defendant's behavior does improve, the case is ordinarily closed within a specific amount of time.

The number of actual criminal jury trials is small in comparison to all the cases processed through the criminal justice system, since upward of 90% of all defendants plead guilty and about 5% are dealt with by other methods, it appears that fewer than 5% ever reach the trial stage. Those cases that are actually tried before a jury often involve serious crimes. Such crimes require a formal inquiry into the facts to determine the guilt or innocence of the accused.

Even though proportionately few cases are actually tried by juries, the trial process remains a focal point in the criminal justice system. It symbolizes the U.S. system of jurisprudence, in which an accused person can choose to present a defense against the government's charges. The fact that the defendant has the option of going to trial significantly affects the operation of the criminal justice system.

Underlying every trial are constitutional principles, complex legal procedures, rules of court, and interpretations of statutes, all designed to ensure that the accused will receive a fair trial. This section discusses the most important constitutional rights of the accused at the trial stage of the criminal justice system and reviews the legal nature of the trial process. Here we examine the major legal decisions and statutes involving the right to confront witnesses and the rights to jury trial, counsel, self-representation, and speedy and public trial.

The Right to Confront Witnesses

The Sixth Amendment states, "In all criminal prosecutions, the accused shall enjoy the right . . . to be confronted with the witnesses against him."[1] The **confrontation clause** is essential to a fair criminal trial because it restricts and controls the admissibility of hearsay evidence. In other words, secondhand evidence, which depends on a witness not available in court, is ordinarily limited in preference to the personal knowledge of a witness or victim of a crime. The framers of the Constitution sought face-to-face accusations in which the defendant has a right to see and cross-examine all witnesses against him or her. The idea that it is always more difficult to tell lies about people to their face than behind their back illustrates the meaning of the confrontation clause. In other words, a witness in a criminal trial may have more difficulty repeating his or her testimony when facing the accused in a trial than in providing information to the police during an investigation.

The accused has the right to confront the witnesses and challenge their assertions and perceptions: Did they really see what they believe? Are they biased? Can they be trusted? What about the veracity of their testimony? Generally speaking, the courts have been nearly unanimous in their belief that the right of confrontation and cross-examination is an essential requirement for a fair trial.[2]

This face-to-face presence has been reviewed recently by the Supreme Court in matters involving a child as a witness in criminal proceedings. In the case of *Coy v. Iowa* (1988), the Supreme Court limited the protection available to child sex abuse victims at the trial stage.[3] In *Coy,* two girls were allowed to be cross-examined behind a screen that separated them from the defendant. The Court ruled that the screen violated the defendant's right to confront witnesses and overturned his conviction. However, in her supporting opinion, Justice Sandra Day O'Connor made it clear that ruling out the protective screen did not bar the states from using videotapes or closed-circuit television.

In *Maryland v. Craig* (1990), the second case in this area, the Supreme Court carved out an exception to the Sixth Amendment confrontation clause by deciding that alleged child abuse victims could testify by closed-circuit television if face-to-face confrontation would cause them trauma.[4] In allowing the states to take testimony via closed-circuit television, the Supreme Court has found that circumstances exist in child sex abuse cases that override the defendant's right of confrontation.

As a result of these decisions, it appears that the confrontation clause does not guarantee criminal defendants the absolute right to a face-to-face meeting with witnesses at their trial. This right may be denied when necessary to further an important public policy, such as protecting a child from trauma in a criminal trial.

The Right to a Jury Trial

The defendant has the right to choose whether the trial will be before a judge or a jury. Although the Sixth Amendment to the U.S. Constitution guarantees the right to a jury trial, the defendant can and often does waive this right. In fact, a substantial proportion of defendants, particularly those charged with misdemeanors, are tried before the court without a jury.

The major legal issue surrounding jury trial has been the question of whether all offenders, both misdemeanants and felons, have an absolute right to a jury trial. Because the U.S. Constitution is silent on this point, the Supreme Court has ruled that all defendants in felony cases have this right. In *Duncan v. Louisiana* (1968), the Court held that the Sixth Amendment right to a jury trial is applicable to the states as well as to the federal government and that it can be interpreted to apply to all defendants accused of serious crimes.[5] The Court in

Perry Mason

One thing we know from watching *Perry Mason* on television is that if you get a good criminal lawyer, you are bound to "beat the rap." In both the long-running TV show and made-for-TV movies, Mason (played by the late Raymond Burr), his loyal secretary Della Street, and investigator Paul Drake had an astounding record of success. Mason's clients were never convicted, and more often than not his relentless questioning and astute legal mind convinced the real culprit to get up in the courtroom and make a full confession.

The exploits of Perry Mason, duplicated by other TV lawyers such as the wily Matlock, have become such a time-tested standard that people sometimes refer to their own attorney as a "real Perry Mason" when they recommend the lawyer to friends. How accurate is the model of the attorney-client relationship portrayed on *Perry Mason*? Not very. All of Perry's clients are articulate, attractive people, none of whom seems to have substance abuse or psychological problems; most seem to talk and act like alumni of exclusive, private prep schools and universities. Few fit the profile of what we know to be the "typical" criminal: a young male who is most likely an educational underachiever, unemployed, and a substance abuser. These are hardly the characteristics of the clients who find their way to Perry's office.

Ironically, while Mason's clients are invariably affluent, Perry seems reluctant to ask them for a retainer, bill them when he wins the case, or negotiate rights to any TV or film treatments of their case. While commendable, Perry's laissez faire attitude toward legal fees is hardly the behavior you would expect from a successful criminal lawyer who earns enough to support an in-house private investigator.

Another media fiction is that Perry's courtroom opponent, District Attorney Hamilton Burger, never wins a case. Even though supported by the able police Lt. Tragg, Burger is constantly backing the wrong horse in the race. Luckily for him, he has Perry Mason to identify the real criminal. Had the unfortunate Burger been employed in a real big-city district attorney's office, he would have long been relegated to answering appeals or working on misdemeanors. If *Perry Mason* were more accurate, the district attorney would win most of the cases, many through plea bargains.

Does hiring a high-powered attorney guarantee that you can beat the rap? Ask Mike Tyson, Leona Helmsley, Ivan Boesky, and Michael Milken. They probably wish they had saved their money.

Duncan based its holding on the premise that in the American states, as in the federal judicial system, a general grant of jury trial for serious offenses is a fundamental right, essential for preventing miscarriages of justice and for assuring that fair trials are provided for all defendants.[6]

The *Duncan* decision did not settle whether all defendants charged with crimes in state courts are constitutionally entitled to jury trials. It seemed to draw the line at only those charged with serious offenses, leaving the decision to grant jury trials to defendants in minor cases to the discretion of the individual states.

In 1970, in the case of *Baldwin v. New York,* the Supreme Court departed from the distinction of serious versus minor offenses and decided that a defendant has a constitutional right to a jury trial when facing a prison sentence of six months or more, regardless of whether the crime committed was a felony or a misdemeanor.[7] Where the possible sentence is six months or less, the accused is not entitled to a jury trial unless it is authorized by state statute.

Chapter 11

The Criminal Trial

In the case of *Blanton v. North Las Vegas,* the Court ruled unanimously that when a state defines the crime of drunk driving as a petty offense,[8] the U.S. Constitution does not require that the defendant receive a jury trial. If, however, a state treats driving under the influence as a serious crime, a jury trial would be required. This decision upheld a Nevada law classifying drunk driving as a petty offense and similar procedures in at least five other jurisdictions in the United States. In most jurisdictions, the more serious the charge, the greater likelihood of trial—and of a trial by jury.

The latest U.S. Supreme Court decision on jury trials occurred in 1996 in the case of *Lewis v. United States.*[9] As noted above, the Supreme Court has used six months' potential imprisonment as the dividing line between petty offenses for which the Sixth Amendment gives no right to jury trial and "serious" offenses that enjoy such a legal right. In the *Lewis* case, the Court faced the unusual problem of multiple petty offenses which had an aggregate potential imprisonment in excess of six months. The defendant argued that he was constitutionally entitled to a jury trial. But the Supreme Court said there was no Sixth Amendment right to a jury trial for a string of petty offenses tried together even where the potential aggregate sentence could exceed six months. The reasons were (1) the Court believed the legislature was responsible for the design of an offense with a maximum possible penalty, and (2) the prosecutor has the right to exercise discretion to join different offenses in one trial without defeating the legislative intent to distinguish between petty and serious offenses.

Other important issues related to the defendant's rights in a criminal jury trial include the right to a jury consisting of 12 people or fewer and the right to a unanimous verdict.

Jury Size. The actual size of the jury has been a matter of great concern. Can a defendant be tried and convicted of a crime by a jury of fewer than 12 persons? Traditionally, 12 jurors have deliberated as the triers of fact in criminal cases involving misdemeanors or felonies. However, the U.S. Constitution does not specifically require a jury of 12 persons. As a result, in *Williams v. Florida* in 1970, the Supreme Court held that a **6-person jury** in a criminal trial does not deprive a defendant of the constitutional right to a jury trial.[10] The Court made clear that the 12-person panel is not a necessary ingredient of a trial by jury, and it upheld a Florida statute permitting the use of a 6-person jury in a robbery trial.

Justice Byron White, writing for the majority, said, "In short, while sometime in the 14th century the size of the jury came to be fixed generally at 12, that particular feature of the jury system appears to have been a historical accident, unrelated to the great purpose which gave rise to the jury in the first place."[11] *Williams v. Florida* has offered a welcome measure of relief to an overburdened crime control system. Today, jury size may be reduced for all but the most serious criminal cases.

Unanimous Verdict. In addition to the convention of 12-person juries in criminal trials, tradition also had been that the jurors' decision must be unanimous. However, in the case of *Apodica v. Oregon* (1972), the Supreme Court held that the Sixth and Fourteenth Amendments do not prohibit criminal convictions by less than unanimous jury verdicts in noncapital cases.[12] In the *Apodica* case, the Court upheld an Oregon statute requiring only 10 of 12 jurors to convict the defendant of assault with a deadly weapon, burglary, and grand larceny. It is not unusual to have such verdicts in civil matters, but much controversy remains regarding their place in the criminal process.

The Right to Counsel at Trial

Mention has already been made in previous chapters of the defendant's right to counsel at numerous points in the criminal justice system. Through a series of leading U.S. Supreme Court decisions (*Powell v. Alabama* in 1932,[13] *Gideon v. Wainwright* in 1963,[14] and *Argersinger v. Hamlin* in 1972[15]), the right of a criminal defendant to have counsel in state trials has become a fundamental right in the U.S. criminal justice system. Today, state courts must provide counsel at trial to indigent defendants who face the possibility of incarceration.

It is interesting to note the historical development of the law regarding right to counsel, for it shows the gradual process of decision making in the Supreme Court, as well as reiterating the relationship between the Bill of Rights and the Fourteenth Amendment. The Bill of Rights protects citizens against federal encroachment, while the Fourteenth Amendment provides that no state shall deprive any person of life, liberty, or property without due process of law. A difficult constitutional question has been whether the Fourteenth Amendment incorporates the Bill of Rights and makes its provisions binding on individual states. In *Powell v. Alabama* (also known as the *Scottsboro Boys* case), for example, nine young black men were charged in an Alabama court with raping two young white women. They were tried and convicted without the benefit of counsel. The U.S. Supreme Court concluded that the presence of a defense attorney is so vital to a fair trial that the failure of the Alabama trial court to appoint counsel was a denial of due process of law under the Fourteenth Amendment. In this instance, due process meant the right to counsel for defendants accused of committing a capital offense.

Then, in the case of *Gideon v. Wainwright* almost 30 years later, the Supreme Court in a unanimous and historic decision stated that while the Sixth Amendment does not explicitly lay down a rule binding on the states, right to counsel is so fundamental and ethical to a fair trial that states are obligated to abide by it under the Fourteenth Amendment's due process clause. Thus, the Sixth Amendment requirement regarding the right to counsel in the federal court system is also binding on the states. The accompanying Law in Review box on page 316 examines the *Gideon* case.

The *Gideon* decision made it clear that a person charged with a felony in a state court has an absolute constitutional right to counsel. But while some states applied the *Gideon* ruling to all criminal trials, others did not provide a defendant with an attorney in misdemeanor cases. Then, in 1972, in the momentous decision of *Argersinger v. Hamlin,* the Supreme Court held that no person can be imprisoned for any offense—whether classified as a petty offense, a misdemeanor, or a felony—unless he or she is offered representation by counsel at trial. The right to counsel in misdemeanor cases is limited to cases where the defendant is actually sentenced to jail, as decided by *Scott v. Illinois* in 1979.[16] The decision extended this right to virtually all defendants in state criminal prosecutions. The timeline in Figure 11.1 indicates how it has taken over 200 years to

Figure 11.1
Timeline for right to counsel at criminal trials.
SOURCE: The idea for this timeline was adapted from Edward Monahan, "Who Is Trying to Kill the Sixth Amendment?" *American Bar Association Journal of Criminal Justice* 6 (1991): 26, reprinted with permission.

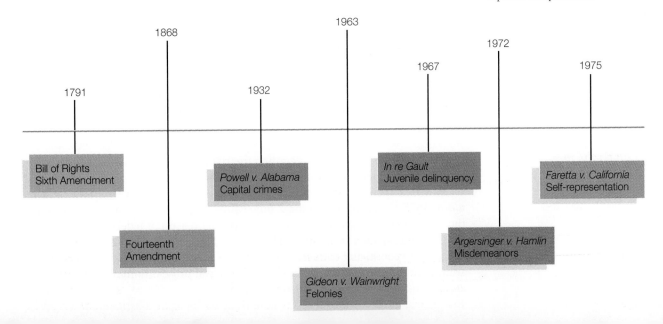

Gideon v. Wainwright (1963)

Facts

Clarence Gideon was charged in a Florida state court with having broken into and entered a poolroom with intent to commit a misdemeanor. This offense is a felony under Florida law. Appearing in court without funds and without a lawyer, the petitioner asked the court to appoint him counsel. The court replied that it could not appoint counsel because under Florida law, the only time the court can appoint counsel for a defendant is when that person is charged with a capital offense.

Put to a trial before a jury, Gideon conducted his defense about as well as could be expected from a layperson. He made an opening statement to the jury, cross-examined the state's witnesses, presented witnesses in his own defense, declined to testify himself, and made a short argument emphasizing his innocence of the charge contained in the information filed in the case. The jury returned a verdict of guilty, and Gideon was sentenced to serve five years in the Florida state prison.

Gideon filed a habeas corpus petition in the Florida Supreme Court attacking his conviction and sentence on the ground that the trial court's refusal to appoint counsel for him denied him rights guaranteed by the Constitution and the Bill of Rights. Relief was denied.

Gideon then filed an *in forma pauperis* appeal to the U.S. Supreme Court, which granted certiorari and appointed counsel to represent him. The Supreme Court took on this case to review its earlier decision in *Betts v. Brady* (1942), which held that the refusal to appoint counsel is not so "offensive to the common and fundamental ideas of fairness" as to amount to a denial of due process.

The issues faced by the Supreme Court were simple but of gigantic importance: (1) Is an indigent defendant charged in a state court with a noncapital felony entitled to the assistance of a lawyer under the due process clause of the Fourteenth Amendment? (2) Should *Betts v. Brady* be overruled?

Decision

Justice Hugo Black delivered the opinion of the Court:

We accept *Betts v. Brady*'s assumption, based as it was on our prior cases, that a provision of the Bill of Rights which is fundamental and essential to a fair trial is made obligatory upon the States by the Fourteenth Amendment. We think the Court in *Betts v. Brady* was wrong, however, in concluding that the Sixth Amendment's guarantee is not one of the fundamental rights. In our adversary system of criminal justice, any person brought into court, who is too poor to hire a lawyer, cannot be assured a fair trial unless counsel is provided for him. That government hires lawyers to prosecute and defendants who have the money to hire lawyers to defend, are the strongest indications of the widespread belief that lawyers in criminal court are necessities, not luxuries. The right of one charged with crime to counsel may not be deemed essential to fair trial in some countries, but it is in ours.

Significance of the Case

The U.S. Supreme Court unanimously overruled its earlier decision in *Betts v. Brady* and explicitly held that the right to counsel in criminal cases is fundamental and essential to a fair trial and as such applicable to the states by way of the Fourteenth Amendment. The *Gideon* decision thus guarantees the right to counsel in criminal cases in both federal and state proceedings. The refusal to appoint counsel for indigent defendants consequently violates the due process clause of the Fourteenth Amendment and the right to counsel of the Sixth Amendment.

establish what the U.S. Constitution stated in 1791—namely that "in all criminal prosecutions, the accused shall enjoy the right . . . to have the assistance of counsel for his defense."[17]

The Right to Self-Representation

Another important question regarding the right to counsel is whether criminal defendants are guaranteed the right to represent themselves—that is, to act as their own lawyers. Before the U.S. Supreme Court decision in *Faretta v. California* in 1975,[18] defendants in most state courts and in the federal system claimed the right to proceed **pro se,** or for themselves, by reason of federal and state statutes and on state constitutional grounds. This permitted defendants to choose between hiring counsel or conducting their own defense. Whether a constitutional right to represent oneself in a criminal prosecution existed remained an open question until the *Faretta* decision.

The defendant, Anthony Faretta, was charged with grand theft in Los Angeles County. Before his trial, he requested that he be permitted to represent himself. The judge told Faretta that he believed this would be a mistake but accepted his waiver of counsel. The judge then held a hearing to inquire into Faretta's ability to conduct his own defense and subsequently ruled that Faretta had not made an intelligent and knowing waiver of his right to the assistance of counsel. As a result, the judge appointed a public defender to represent Faretta, who was brought to trial, found guilty, and sentenced to prison. He appealed, claiming that he had a constitutional right to self-representation.

Upon review, the U.S. Supreme Court recognized Faretta's *pro se* right on a constitutional basis, while making it conditional on a showing that the defendant could competently, knowingly, and intelligently waive his right to counsel. The Court's decision was based on the belief that the right of self-representation finds support in the structure of the Sixth Amendment, as well as in English and colonial jurisprudence from which the amendment emerged.[19] Thus, in forcing Faretta to accept counsel against his will, the California trial court deprived him of his constitutional right to conduct his own defense.

It is important to recognize that the *Faretta* case dealt only with the constitutional right to self-representation. It did not provide guidelines for administering the right during the criminal process.[20]

Today, a defendant in a criminal trial is able to waive the right to the assistance of counsel. In other words, the defendant has a constitutional right to defend himself if his or her waiver of right to counsel is knowing and intelligent. Generally, however, the courts have encouraged defendants to accept counsel so that criminal trials may proceed in an orderly and fair manner.

Faretta v. California (1975) allowed qualified defendants to proceed pro se—that is, to choose between hiring counsel or conducting their own defense if they are found competent to do so. One defendant who chose to conduct his own defense was Colin Ferguson, who had killed six passengers on a New York commuter train and wounded 19 others. He was found guilty of murder. Should a person as deeply disturbed as Ferguson be allowed to conduct his own defense?

The requirement of the right to counsel at trial in virtually all criminal cases often causes delays in the formal processing of defendants through the court system. Counsel usually seeks to safeguard the interests of the accused and in so doing may employ a variety of legal devices—pretrial motions, plea negotiations, trial procedures, and appeals—that require time and extend the decision-making period in a particular case. The involvement of counsel, along with inefficiencies in the court process—such as the frequent granting of continuances, poor scheduling procedures, and the abuse of time by court personnel—has made the problem of delay in criminal cases a serious and constitutional issue. As the American Bar Association's *Standards Relating to Speedy Trial* state, "Congestion in the trial courts of this country, particularly in urban centers, is currently one of the major problems of judicial administration."[21]

The Sixth Amendment guarantees a criminal defendant the right to a speedy trial in federal prosecutions. This right has been made applicable to the states by the decision in *Klopfer v. North Carolina* (1967).[22] In this case, the defendant Klopfer was charged with criminal trespass. His original trial ended in a mistrial, and he sought to determine whether and when the government intended to retry him. The prosecutor asked the court to take a "*nolle prosequi* with leave," a legal device discharging the defendant but allowing the government to prosecute him in the future. The U.S. Supreme Court held that the effort by the government to postpone Klopfer's trial indefinitely without reason denied him the right to a speedy trial guaranteed by the Sixth and Fourteenth Amendments.

In *Klopfer,* the Supreme Court emphasized the importance of the speedy trial in the criminal process by stating that this right was "as fundamental as any of the rights secured by the Sixth Amendment."[23] Its primary purposes are

The Right to a Speedy Trial

1. To improve the credibility of the trial by seeking to have witnesses available for testimony as early as possible

2. To reduce the anxiety for the defendant in awaiting trial, as well as to avoid pretrial detention

3. To avoid extensive pretrial publicity and questionable conduct of public officials that would influence the defendant's right to a fair trial

4. To avoid any delay that could affect the defendant's ability to defend himself or herself

Since the *Klopfer* case in 1967, the Supreme Court has dealt with the speedy trial guarantee on numerous occasions. One such recent example is the case of *Doggett v. United States,* in which the Court found that a delay of eight and a half years between indictment and arrest was prejudicial to the defendant and required a dismissal of the charges against the defendant.[24]

We have reviewed some of the major constitutional rights surrounding the jury trial in this chapter as well as in Chapter 8 (Police and the Rule of Law). The conflict between the defendant's legal rights and public safety is discussed in the Issues box titled "What's Wrong with the Criminal Trial?"

The Right to a Fair Trial

Every person charged with a crime also has a fundamental right to a fair trial. What does it mean to have a fair trial in the criminal justice system? A fair trial is one before an impartial judge and jury, in an environment of judicial restraint, orderliness, and fair decision making. Although it is not expressly stated in the U.S. Constitution, the right of the accused to a fair trial is guaranteed by the due process clauses of the Fifth and Fourteenth Amendments. This fair trial right may be violated in a number of ways. A hostile courtroom crowd, improper pressure on witnesses, or any behavior that produces prejudice toward the accused, among other things, can preclude a fair trial. When, for example, a defendant was required to go to trial in prison clothing, the U.S. Supreme Court found a violation of the due process clause of the Fourteenth Amendment.[25] Adverse pretrial publicity can also deny a defendant a fair trial. The release of premature evidence by the prosecutor, extensive and critical reporting by the news media, and vivid and uncalled for details in indictments can all prejudice a defendant's case.

Recently, one of the controversial issues involving the conduct of a trial has been the apparent conflict between the constitutional guarantees of fair trial and freedom of the press. When there is wide pretrial publicity, as in the Jean Harris murder case, the Atlanta child killings, and the Rodney King police-brutality case, whether an accused can have a fair trial as guaranteed by the Fifth, Sixth, and Fourteenth Amendments has been a matter of great concern. Think, for instance, of the intense media coverage in the Pamela Smart murder case, the William Kennedy Smith rape case, and the O. J. Simpson double murder case.

Publicity is essential to preserving confidence in the trial system. This principle may occasionally clash with the defendant's right to a fair trial. The murder conviction of Dr. Sam Sheppard over 25 years ago was reversed by the U.S. Supreme Court because negative publicity generated by the government had denied Sheppard a fair trial.[26] In one of the most highly publicized trials in U.S. history, Claus von Bulow was acquitted of the attempted murder of his wife after two trials.[27] Both the prosecution and the defense used the media to reflect their side. Press conferences, leaked news stories, and daily television and radio coverage all contributed to a media sideshow. Even jury sequestration was not successful, as many of the jurors had prior knowledge of the case. In the end, the media played a critical role in both the initial conviction and the subsequent acquittal on retrial of the defendant. More recently, the sensational and unending TV and press coverage of the O. J. Simpson case raised the issue of whether pretrial publicity violated Simpson's constitutional right to a fair trial.

What's Wrong with the Criminal Trial?

Although most criminal prosecutions do not involve the adversary determination of guilt or innocence that occurs at a formal criminal trial, the trial process remains a matter of vital importance to the criminal justice system. It represents to the defendant a legal option guaranteed by the U.S. Constitution. It is also a critical fact-finding process that seeks the truth, in addition to determining guilt or innocence. Does the criminal trial accomplish this goal?

In 1996 Judge Harold Rothwax published his book *The Collapse of Criminal Justice,* in which he answers this question and sets out a conservative agenda for reforming the legal principles of the criminal trial. Based on 25 years of presiding over criminal trials in New York City, Rothwax argues that procedural formalism and technicalities have taken over the criminal trial. Truth is an elusive idea, and the system is constructed of elaborate barriers to achieving it.

Rothwax recommends the following changes be made to the trial process:

1. Reform the exclusionary rule and make it discretionary instead of mandatory. The Supreme Court has ruled that evidence seized in violation of the Fourth Amendment must be excluded from the criminal trial. Rothwax believes that when you exclude or suppress evidence needed at trial, you hinder the fact-finding process.
2. The right to a lawyer provided by the Sixth Amendment should not be applicable in the investigative stage but only in the pretrial and trial stages of the criminal justice system. The famous *Miranda v. Arizona* case protects arrestees from overbearing police interrogation. Yet Rothwax wants the suspect to receive no warnings, even when locked in the back room of the stationhouse under interrogation.
3. The Fifth Amendment states that no person shall be forced to testify against himself. Rothwax objects to the jury instruction that indicates that the jury cannot draw any negative conclusions if the defendant refuses to take the witness stand. Rothwax believes that this aspect of the Fifth Amendment does not imply that one might not draw reasonable inferences from the silence of a defendant.

4. Unanimous jury verdicts should no longer be required. If criminal verdicts were decided by less than a unanimous verdict, there would be a reduced risk that one juror could cause a retrial.
5. Limit or abolish the peremptory challenge. This process enables attorneys to excuse jurors for no particular reason. Rothwax thinks peremptory challenges make it possible to stack juries and manipulate jury decision making (see the discussion on peremptory challenges later in this chapter).

Critical Thinking Questions

1. Judge Rothwax's most serious efforts at proving the collapse of criminal justice revolve around the critique of search and seizure law, the "terrible" *Miranda* decision, and the technicalities and rules of jury decision making. Are his solutions troubling to civil libertarians? Why? Might not some defendants be unfairly convicted?
2. To some legal experts, Judge Rothwax's criticism of search rules is right on target because they believe that such rules assist the courts in letting dangerous criminals go free. Others believe that the many exceptions to the Fourth Amendment adequately protect the defendant and the public. What are the most significant exceptions?
3. According to Rothwax, the *Miranda* warning urges suspects not to confess. Yet confession rates are as high as ever, and courts rarely throw out confessions obtained after warnings are given. What are the implications of this apparent conflict?
4. Despite the many reservations about the criminal trial process raised by Rothwax, isn't it likely that the justice system will continue to utilize the same procedures if studies show that prosecutions are rarely lost because of suppression rulings? Why are search rules so complex, and in what kinds of cases do they usually result in suppression of evidence?

SOURCES: Harold J. Rothwax, *The Collapse of Criminal Justice* (New York: Random House, 1996); see also William Grimes, *Criminal Law Outline* (Reno, Nev.: National Judicial College—University of Nevada, 1995).

Judges involved in newsworthy criminal cases have attempted to place restraints on media coverage to preserve the defendant's right to a fair trial; at the same time, it is generally believed that the media have a constitutional right to provide news coverage.

Chapter 11

The Criminal Trial

The U.S. Supreme Court dealt with the fair trial–free press issue in the case of *Nebraska Press Association v. Stuart* (1976).[28] The Court ruled unconstitutional a trial judge's order prohibiting the press from reporting the confessions implicating the defendant in the crime. The Court's decision was based primarily on the fact that "prior restraints on speech and publication are the most serious and least tolerable infringement on First Amendment rights."[29]

In *Gannett Co. v. DePasquale* (1979), the Court was asked to decide whether the public had an independent constitutional right of access to a pretrial judicial hearing, even though all the parties had agreed to closure to guarantee a fair trial.[30] Justice Potter Stewart, writing for the Court, said that the trial court was correct in finding that the press had a right of access of constitutional dimensions but that this right was outweighed by the defendant's right to a fair trial.[31] In other words, the Court balanced competing social interests and found that denial of access by the public did not violate the First, Sixth, or Fourteenth Amendment rights of the defendant. The interest of justice requires that the defendant's case not be jeopardized, and the desire for a fair trial far outweighs the public's right of access to a pretrial suppression hearing. The *Gannett* decision is not ordinarily cited as precedent to determine whether a right of access to trials is constitutionally guaranteed, since the Court believes that motion hearings are not trials.

The question of the **First Amendment** right of access to preliminary hearings was raised again in the case of *Press-Enterprise Co. v. Superior Court* (1986).[32] The defendant, charged with murder, agreed to have the preliminary hearing closed to the press and the public. But the Supreme Court said that closure is permissible under the First Amendment only if there is a substantial probability that the defendant's right to a fair trial would be prejudiced by publicity that closed proceedings would prevent. According to the Court, preliminary hearings have traditionally been open to the public and should remain so.

In the most recent case involving pretrial hearings (1993), a reporter for the largest newspaper in Puerto Rico was denied access to a probable cause hearing because of a rule in the Commonwealth of Puerto Rico requiring that the hearings be held privately. The Supreme Court held that this rule violated the First Amendment to the Constitution based on the *Press Enterprise* case and indicated that a pretrial hearing cannot be closed to the press except if prejudice will result to the accused.[33]

The Right to a Public Trial

The U.S. Supreme Court has also interpreted the First Amendment to mean that members of the press (and the public) have a right to attend trials. The most important case on this issue is *Richmond Newspapers, Inc. v. Virginia* (1980).[34] Here, the Supreme Court clearly established that criminal trials must remain public. Following the *Richmond Newspapers* case, the Supreme Court extended the right of the press to attend trials involving even highly sensitive, sexually related matters in which the victim is under 18 years of age.[35]

Although the Court has ruled that criminal trials are open to the press, the right to a public trial is basically for the benefit of the accused. The familiar language of the Sixth Amendment clearly states that "the accused shall enjoy the right to a speedy and public trial." Underlying this provision is the belief that a trial in the criminal justice system must be a public activity. The amendment is rooted in the principle that justice cannot survive behind walls of silence.[36] It was enacted because the framers of the Constitution distrusted secret trials and arbitrary proceedings. In the 1948 case of *In re Oliver*, for instance, the Supreme Court held that the secrecy of a criminal contempt trial violated the right of the defendant to a public trial under the Fourteenth Amendment.[37] In *Oliver*, the Court recognized the constitutional guarantee of a public trial for the defendant in state and federal courts. Three decades later, the *Richmond Newspapers* decision clearly affirmed the right of the public and the press to attend criminal trials.

Should TV Cameras Be Permitted in Criminal Courts?

Three major concerns arise in televising criminal trials: (1) jurors and potential jurors are exposed to media coverage that may cause prejudgment; (2) in-court media coverage, especially cameras and television, can increase community and political pressure on participants and even cause grandstanding by participants; and (3) media coverage can erode the dignity and decorum of the courtroom.

In addition, many experts believe that courtrooms should not be rented to commercial enterprises to sell products. A noncommercial court TV network could focus on educational trials and expose the judicial process to proper public scrutiny. Some say the tabloid approach seeks only to televise sensational trials that shock the public.

Cameras are now allowed in the courtroom in even greater numbers. Here a cameraman focuses on a defense attorney's cross-examination during the O. J. Simpson criminal murder trial. Do cameras in the courtroom change or affect trial outcomes? Do they make it impossible for a defendant to get a fair trial if, for example, the case ends in a hung jury and the person must be retried before a new jury whose members may have watched part or all of the first trial on TV?

Critical Thinking Questions

1. Most state court systems allow television cameras in courts with some restrictions. In light of the belief that television coverage of trials may be worthwhile for educational purposes, do you consider the case of *Florida v. William Kennedy Smith* to be a valuable learning experience? What about the role of television in the O. J. Simpson trial? Critics argue that the Simpson case embodies what is wrong with televising trials.

2. Since 1990 there has been a surge in media-type trials that present popular drama in the criminal justice system. In 1991 we had the Rodney King police brutality case and the William Kennedy Smith rape trial; in 1992 Mike Tyson was tried for rape and Pamela Smart plotted the murder of her husband; in 1993 the trial of those accused of bombing the World Trade Center occurred; in 1994–1996 O. J. Simpson was tried for double murder and wrongful death, Colin Ferguson was found guilty in the Long Island murders of commuter train passengers; and Susan Smith was convicted of murdering her two small children. Timothy McVeigh was tried and convicted in 1997 of the Oklahoma bombing. Did these trials provide the public with an accurate and fair representation of the criminal justice system?

3. Cameras are not allowed in the federal courts. Why? Is it because the federal judiciary believes that

the defendant's ability to obtain a fair trial outweighs the public interest? In a democratic society, should the public have access to all trials, even those of a scandalous nature, through the television medium? Because of the importance of the First Amendment, should the ban against TV cameras in the federal courts be reviewed? Although prohibited in federal trials, the use of television cameras does not violate the Constitution. Also, keep in mind that there is no per se rule that prohibits television cameras from state court trials. (See *Chandler v. Florida* for an excellent discussion regarding cable television and electronic media coverage in state courts.)

SOURCE: *Chandler v. Florida,* 449 U.S. 560, 101 S.Ct. 802, 66 L.Ed.2d 740 (1981); "Rally for Court Cameras Falls Short," *American Bar Association Journal,* 81 (1995): 30.

Because of the public interest in high-profile criminal cases, whether jury trials should be televised is one of the most controversial questions in the criminal justice system. The legal community is divided over the use of TV cameras in the courtroom. Today many state courts permit such coverage, often at the judge's discretion, while the federal courts prohibit TV coverage altogether. In 1981 the U.S. Supreme Court, in *Chandler v. Florida,* removed any constitutional obstacles to the use of electronic media coverage and still-photography of public criminal proceedings over the objections of a criminal defendant.[38] To be certain, the defendant has a constitutional right to a public trial, but it is equally imperative that the media be allowed to exercise its First Amendment rights. "Media circus" has been used to describe the intense media coverage of the Simpson case. If you turned on ABC, CNN, or Court TV, the topic was usually the same: the *People v. O. J. Simpson.* In this type of trial, the Court is required to protect the rights of the accused by providing him or her with a fair trial by an unbiased jury. Unfortunately, many legal experts feel that the media circus generated by highly publicized cases makes it difficult, if not impossible, to provide famous defendants with an unbiased jury.

In sum, the defendant's right to an impartial trial and jury under the Fifth and Sixth Amendments often runs into direct conflict with the First Amendment's guarantee of freedom of the press and public access. In the Analyzing Criminal Issues box on page 321, the issue of televising criminal trials is reviewed. This is one example of the fair trial–free press dilemma.

The Trial Process

The trial of a criminal case is a formal process conducted in a specific and orderly fashion in accordance with rules of criminal law, procedure, and evidence. Unlike what transpires in popular television programs involving lawyers—where witnesses are often asked leading and prejudicial questions and where judges go far beyond their supervisory role—the modern criminal trial is a complicated and often time-consuming, technical affair. It is a structured adversary proceeding in which both the prosecution and defense follow specific procedures and argue the merits of their cases before the judge and jury. Each side seeks to present its case in the most favorable light. When possible, the prosecutor and the defense attorney will object to evidence they consider damaging to their positions. The prosecutor will use direct testimony, physical evidence, and a confession, if available, to convince the jury that the accused is guilty beyond a reasonable doubt. On the other hand, the defense attorney will rebut the government's case with his or her own evidence, make certain that the rights of the criminal defendant under the federal and state constitutions are considered during all phases of the trial, and determine whether an appeal is appropriate if the client is found guilty.

Although each jurisdiction in the United States has its own trial procedures, all jurisdictions conduct criminal trials in a generally similar fashion. The basic steps of the criminal trial, which proceed in an established order, are described in this section and outlined in Figure 11.2.

Jury Selection

In both civil and criminal cases jurors are selected randomly from tax assessment or voter registration lists within each court's jurisdiction.

Few states impose qualifications on those called for jury service. Over 30 states mandate a residency requirement.[39] There is also little uniformity in the amount of time served by jurors, with the term ranging from one day to months, depending on the nature of the trial. In addition, most jurisdictions prohibit convicted felons from serving on juries, as well as others exempted by statute, such as public officials, medical doctors, and attorneys. The initial list of persons chosen, which is called **venire,** or jury array, provides the state with a group of potentially capable citizens able to serve on a jury. Many states, by rule of law, review the venire to eliminate unqualified persons and to exempt those who by reason of their professions are not allowed to be jurors. The actual jury selection process begins with those remaining on the list.

The court clerk, who handles the administrative affairs of the trial—including the processing of the complaint, evidence, and other documents—randomly selects enough names (sometimes from a box) to fill the required number of

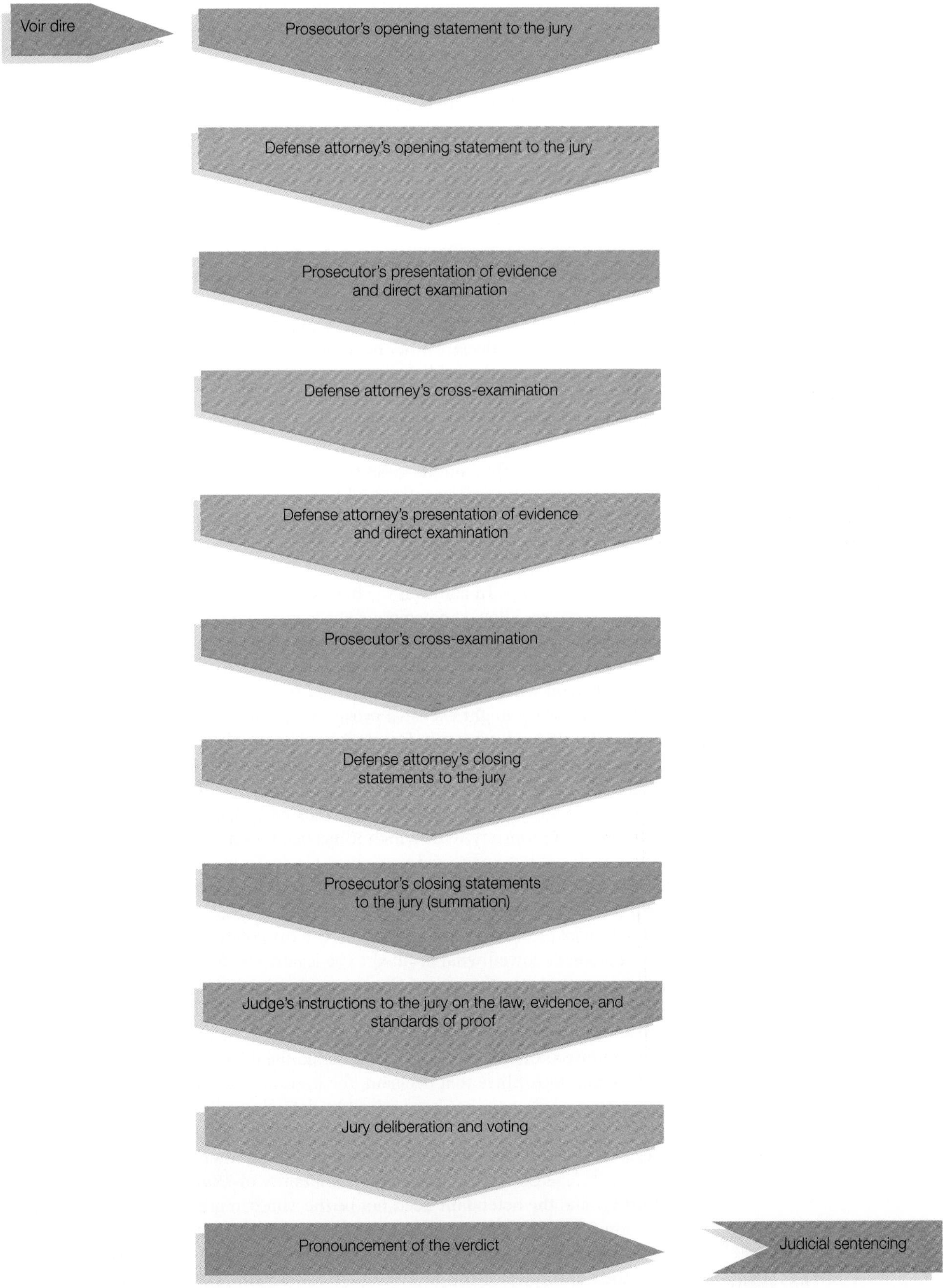

Figure 11.2
The steps in a jury trial.

Source: Marvin Zalman and Larry Siegel, *Criminal Procedure: Constitution and Society* (St. Paul: West Publishing, 1991), p. 655.

places on the jury. In most cases, the jury in a criminal trial consists of 12 persons, with 2 alternate jurors standing by to serve should any of the regular jurors be unable to complete the trial.

Voir Dire. Once the prospective jurors are chosen, the process of **voir dire** is begun, in which all persons selected are questioned by both the prosecution and the defense to determine their appropriateness to sit on the jury. The lengthy process of questioning and selecting jurors is called the *voir dire,* from the French for "to tell the truth." Prospective jurors are examined under oath by the government, the defense, and sometimes the judge about their backgrounds, occupations, residences, and possible knowledge of or interest in the case. A juror who acknowledges any bias for or prejudice against the defendant—if the defendant is a friend or relative, for example, or if the juror has already formed an opinion about the case—is removed for "cause" and replaced with another. Thus, any prospective juror who declares that he or she is unable to be impartial and render a verdict solely on the evidence to be presented at the trial may be removed by either the prosecution or the defense. Because normally no limit is placed on the number of **challenges for cause** that can be exercised, it often takes considerable time to select a jury for controversial and highly publicized criminal cases.

Jury selection in the famous 1989 Iran-Contra trial of Oliver North, for example, lasted for over three months, and hundreds of prospective jurors were examined. It took over two months for jurors to be selected for the O. J. Simpson criminal trial.

Peremptory Challenges. In addition to challenges for cause, both the prosecution and the defense are allowed **peremptory challenges,** which enable the attorneys to excuse jurors for no particular reason or for undisclosed reasons. For example, a prosecutor might not want a bartender as a juror in a drunk driving case, believing that a person with that occupation would be sympathetic to the accused. Or the defense attorney might excuse a prospective male juror because the attorney prefers to have a predominantly female jury. The number of peremptory challenges permitted is limited by state statute and often varies by case and jurisdiction.

The peremptory challenge has been criticized by legal experts who question the fairness and propriety with which it has been used.[40] The most significant criticism is that it has been used to exclude blacks from hearing cases in which the defendant is also black. In *Swain v. Alabama* (1964), the U.S. Supreme Court upheld the use of peremptory challenges in isolated cases to exclude jurors by reason of racial or other group affiliations.[41] This policy was extremely troublesome because it allowed what seemed to be legally condoned discrimination against minority-group members. Consequently, in 1986 the Court struck down the *Swain* doctrine in *Batson v. Kentucky.*[42]

The *Batson* case held that the use of peremptory challenges against potential jurors by prosecutors in criminal cases violated the Constitution if the challenges were based on race. Since that decision, the issue of race discrimination in the use of peremptory challenges has been raised by defendants in numerous cases. In 1991, in *Powers v. Ohio,* for instance, the Supreme Court was faced with deciding the legality of peremptory challenges involving jurors not of the same race as the defendant.[43] The Court held that the racial identity of "*Batson*-excluded prospective jurors" and the defendant need not be the same. In other words, the Equal Protection Clause prohibits a prosecutor from using the peremptory challenge to exclude qualified and unbiased persons from a jury solely by reason of race. In so ruling, the Court rejected the government's contention that the jurors be of the same race as the defendant. Similarly, in the 1992 case of *Georgia v. McCollum,* the Supreme Court said that criminal defendants may not seek to exclude potential jurors strictly on the basis of race. Race-based peremptory challenges to potential jurors in civil lawsuits have also been declared unconstitutional.[44]

Table 11.1
Evolution of *Batson v. Kentucky* and Its Progeny

Case	Ruling
Batson v. Kentucky (1986)	Under the Fourteenth Amendment, the Supreme Court ruled that prosecutors were barred from using peremptory challenges to remove black jurors because of their race.
Powers v. Ohio (1991)	The Court concluded that a defendant has the standing to object to the race-based exclusion by the use of peremptory challenges of jurors on the grounds of equal protection, even if not of the same race as the challenged jurors.
Edmonson v. Leesville Concrete Co. (1991)	The *Batson* ruling applies to attorneys in civil lawsuits. In other words, a private party in a civil action may not raise peremptory challenges to exclude jurors on the basis of race.
Georgia v. McCollum (1992)	On the basis of *Batson,* the *Georgia* decision prohibited the exercise of peremptory challenges that are race-based by defense attorneys in criminal cases.
J.E.B. v. Alabama (1994)	The Supreme Court held that the equal protection clause of the Fourteenth Amendment bars discrimination in jury selection on the basis of sex. Discrimination in jury selection, whether based on race or gender, causes harm to the litigants, the community, and the individual jurors who are wrongfully excluded from participation in the judicial process.

Batson strikes down a legal procedure that was "out of synch" with modern ideas of justice and fairness. It prevents an element of racial discrimination from entering into the trial stage of justice, which is one of the cornerstones of American freedom. Yet it preserves, under controlled circumstances, the use of the peremptory challenge, which is an integral part of the jury selection process. While some argue that the *Batson* rule should be limited to race and ethnicity, the Supreme Court declared in 1994 that the rule also bars gender-based peremptory challenges. In other words, both sides in a civil or criminal case should be required to provide a nondiscriminatory reason for removing a large number of prospective male or female jurors (*J.E.B. v. Alabama*).[45]

Some legal scholars would like to take the 1986 *Batson* decision a step further and grant minority defendants a right to juries with minority representation. Table 11.1 highlights the evolution of the *Batson v. Kentucky* peremptory challenge cases.

Once the jury has been selected and the criminal complaint has been read to the jurors by the court clerk, the prosecutor and the defense attorney may each make an opening statement about the case. The purpose of the prosecutor's statement is to introduce the judge and the jury to the particular criminal charges, to outline the facts, and to describe how the government will prove the defendant guilty beyond a reasonable doubt. The defense attorney reviews the case and indicates how the defense intends to show that the accused is not guilty.

Usually, the defense attorney makes an opening statement after the government reads its case. In some jurisdictions, the court in its discretion can permit the defense to make opening remarks before any evidence is introduced. But, for the most part, current rules dictate that the prosecutor is entitled to offer an opening statement first.

Opening Statements

The opening statement gives the jury a concise overview of the evidence that is to follow. In the opening statement, neither attorney is allowed to make prejudicial remarks or inflammatory statements or mention irrelevant facts. Both are free, however, to identify what they will eventually prove by way of evidence, which includes witnesses, physical evidence, and the use of expert testimony. As a general rule, the opening statements used in jury trials are important because they provide the finders of fact (the jury) with an initial summary of the case. They are infrequently used and less effective in **bench trials,** however, where juries are not used. Most lower-court judges have handled hundreds of similar cases and do not need the benefit of an opening statement.

Presentation of the Prosecutor's Evidence

Witness Testimony. Following the opening statements, the government begins its case by presenting evidence to the court through its witnesses. Those called as witnesses—such as police officers, victims, or experts—provide testimony via **direct examination.** During direct examination, the prosecutor questions the witness to reveal the facts believed pertinent to the government's case. Testimony involves what the witness actually saw, heard, or touched and does not include opinions. However, a witness's opinion can be given in certain situations, such as when describing the motion of a vehicle or indicating whether a defendant appeared to act intoxicated or insane. Witnesses may also qualify to give opinions because they are experts on a particular subject relevant to the case; for example, a psychiatrist may testify as to a defendant's mental capacity at the time of the crime.

After the prosecutor finishes questioning a witness, the defense conducts a **cross-examination** of the same witness by asking questions in an attempt to clarify the defendant's role in the crime. The right to cross-examine witnesses is an essential part of a trial, and unless extremely unusual circumstances exist (such as a person's being hospitalized), witness statements will not be considered unless they are made in court and open for question. For example, in *Lee v. Illinois* (1986), the U.S. Supreme Court ruled that a confession made to police by a co-defendant in a criminal trial cannot be used in court unless the person making the confession is available for cross-examination.[46] If desired, the prosecutor may seek a second direct examination after the defense attorney has completed cross-examination; this allows the prosecutor to ask additional questions about information brought out during cross-examination. Finally, the defense attorney

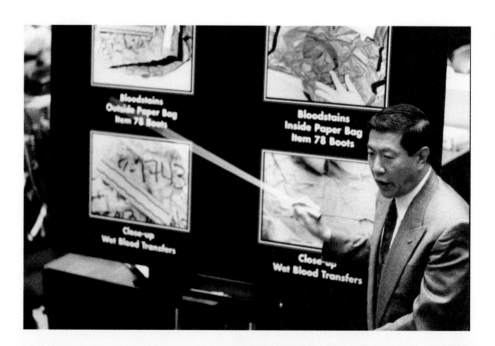

Real evidence consists of the exhibits taken into the jury room for review by the jury. Photographs, maps, diagrams, and crime scene displays are types of real evidence. Here criminologist Harry Lee makes his famous presentation of blood stain evidence to the jury in the O. J. Simpson case. The presentation of this evidence may have been a key element in Simpson's acquittal.

may then question or cross-examine the witness once again. All witnesses for the trial are sworn in and questioned in the same basic manner.

Types of Evidence at a Criminal Trial. In addition to testimonial evidence given by police officers, citizens, and experts, the court also acts on real, or nonverbal, evidence.[47] **Real evidence** often consists of the exhibits taken into the jury room for review by the jury. A revolver that may have been in the defendant's control at the time of a murder, tools in the possession of a suspect charged with a burglary, and a bottle allegedly holding narcotics are all examples of real or physical evidence. Photographs, maps, diagrams, and crime scene displays are further types of real evidence. The criminal court judge will also review documentary evidence, such as writings, government reports, public records, and business or hospital records.

In general, the primary test for the admissibility of evidence in either a criminal or civil proceeding is its relevance.[48] In other words, the court must ask itself whether the gun, shirt, or photograph, for instance, has relevant evidentiary value in determining the issues in the case. Ordinarily, evidence that establishes an element of the crime is acceptable to the court. For example, in a prosecution for possession of drugs, evidence that shows the defendant to be a known drug user might be relevant. In a prosecution for bribery, monies received in the form of a cancelled check identified as the amount received would clearly be found relevant to the case.

Circumstantial, or indirect, **evidence** is also often used in trial proceedings. Such evidence is often inferred or indirectly used to prove a fact in question. On the issue of malice in a criminal murder trial, for instance, it would be appropriate to use circumstantial evidence to prove the defendant's state of mind. Such evidence has often been the controversial issue in many celebrated criminal cases. The Dr. George Parkman case, more than a century ago, attracted national attention when Parkman's colleague at Harvard University, Dr. Webster, was convicted of murder after Parkman disappeared.[49] Because no body was found, Webster's conviction was based on circumstantial evidence.

Once the prosecution has provided all the government's evidence against a defendant, it will inform the court that it rests the people's case. The defense attorney at this point may enter a motion for a **directed verdict.** This is a procedural device by means of which the defense attorney asks the judge to order the jury to return a verdict of not guilty. The judge must rule on the motion and will either sustain it or overrule it, depending on whether he or she believes that the prosecution proved all the elements of the alleged crime. In essence, the defense attorney argues in the directed verdict that the prosecutor's case against the defendant is insufficient to prove the defendant guilty beyond a reasonable doubt. If the motion is sustained, the trial is terminated. If it is rejected by the court, the case continues with the defense portion of the trial.

Motion for a Directed Verdict

The defense attorney has the option of presenting many, some, or no witnesses on behalf of the defendant. In addition, the defense attorney must decide whether the defendant should take the stand and testify in his or her own behalf. In a criminal trial, the defendant is protected by the Fifth Amendment right to be free from self-incrimination, which means that a person cannot be forced by the state to testify against himself or herself in a criminal trial. However, defendants who choose voluntarily to tell their side of the story can be subject to cross-examination by the prosecutor.

Presentation of Evidence by the Defense Attorney

After the defense concludes its case, the government may then present rebuttal evidence. This normally involves bringing evidence forward that was not used when the prosecution initially presented its case. The defense may examine the rebuttal witnesses and introduce new witnesses in a process called a *surrebuttal.* After all the evidence has been presented to the court, the defense attorney may again submit a motion for a directed verdict. If the motion is denied, both the prosecution and the defense prepare to make closing arguments, and the case on the evidence is ready for consideration by the jury.

Closing Arguments

Closing arguments are used by the attorneys to review the facts and evidence of the case in a manner favorable to each of their positions. At this stage of the trial, both prosecution and defense are permitted to draw reasonable inferences and to show how the facts prove or refute the defendant's guilt. Often both attorneys have a free hand in arguing about the facts, issues, and evidence, including the applicable law. They cannot comment on matters not in evidence, however, or on the defendant's failure to testify in a criminal case. Normally, the defense attorney will make a closing statement first, followed by the prosecutor. Either party can elect to forgo the right to make a final summation to the jury.

Instructions to the Jury

In a criminal trial, the judge will instruct, or **charge,** the jury members on the principles of law that ought to guide and control their decision on the defendant's innocence or guilt. Included in the charge will be information about the elements of the alleged offense, the type of evidence needed to prove each element, and the burden of proof required to obtain a guilty verdict. Although the judge commonly provides the instruction, he or she may ask the prosecutor and the defense attorney to submit instructions for consideration; the judge will then use discretion in determining whether to use any of their instructions. The instructions that cover the law applicable to the case are extremely important because they may serve as the basis for a subsequent appeal. Procedurally, in highly publicized and celebrated cases the judge may have sequestered the jury overnight to prevent them from having contact with the outside world. This process, called *sequestration,* is discretionary with the trial judge, and most courts believe "locking a jury up" is needed only in sensational cases.

The Verdict

Once the charge is given to the jury members, they retire to deliberate on a verdict. As previously mentioned, the **verdict** in a criminal case—regardless of whether the trial involves a 6-person or a 12-person jury—is usually required to be unanimous. Unanimity of 12 is not required by the U.S. Constitution in state cases but is the rule in federal criminal trials. Unanimity is required with 6-person juries. A review of the case by the jury may take hours or even days. The jurors are always sequestered during their deliberations, and in certain lengthy and highly publicized cases, they are kept overnight in a hotel until the verdict is reached. In less sensational cases, the jurors may be allowed to go home, but they are cautioned not to discuss the case with anyone.

If a verdict cannot be reached, the trial may result in a *hung jury,* after which the prosecutor must bring the defendant to trial again if the prosecution desires a conviction. If found not guilty, the defendant is released from the criminal process. On the other hand, if the defendant is convicted, the judge will normally order a presentence investigation by the probation department before imposing a sentence. Before sentencing, the defense attorney will probably submit a motion for a new trial, alleging that legal errors occurred in the trial proceedings. The judge may deny the motion and impose a sentence immediately, a practice quite common in most misdemeanor offenses. In felony cases, however, the judge will set a date for sentencing, and the defendant will either be placed on bail or held in custody until that time.

The Sentence

The imposition of the criminal sentence is normally the responsibility of the trial judge. In some jurisdictions, the jury may determine the sentence or make recommendations involving leniency for certain offenses. Often, the sentencing decision is based on information and recommendations given to the court by the probation department after a presentence investigation of the defendant. The sentence itself is determined by the statutory requirements for the particular

crime as established by the legislature; in addition, the judge ordinarily has a great deal of discretion in reaching a sentencing decision. The different criminal sanctions available include fines, probation, imprisonment, and even commitment to a state hospital. The sentence may be a combination of all these. Sentencing is discussed in detail in Chapter 12.

Defendants have as many as three possible avenues of appeal: the direct appeal, postconviction remedy, and federal court review.[50] Both the direct appeal and federal court review provide the convicted person with the opportunity to appeal to a higher state or federal court on the basis of an error that affected the conviction in the trial court. Extraordinary trial court errors, such as the denial of the right to counsel or the inability to provide a fair trial, are subject to the "plain error" rule of the federal courts.[51] "Harmless errors," such as the use of innocuous identification procedures or the denial of counsel at a noncritical stage of the proceeding, would not necessarily result in the overturning of a criminal conviction. A postconviction appeal, on the other hand, or what is often referred to as "collateral attack," takes the form of a legal petition, such as habeas corpus, and is the primary means by which state prisoners have their convictions or sentence reviewed in the federal court. A **writ of habeas corpus** (meaning "you have the body") seeks to determine the validity of a detention by asking the court to release the person or give legal reasons for the incarceration.

In most jurisdictions, direct criminal appeal to an appellate court is a matter of right. This means that the defendant has an automatic right to appeal a conviction based on errors that may have occurred during the trial proceedings. A substantial number of criminal appeals are the result of disputes over points of law, such as the introduction at the trial of illegal evidence detrimental to the defendant or statements made during the trial that were prejudicial to the defendant. Through objections made at the pretrial and trial stages of the criminal process, the defense counsel will reserve specific legal issues on the record as the basis for appeal. A copy of the transcript of these proceedings will serve as the basis on which the appellate court will review any errors that may have occurred during the lower court proceedings.

The Appeal

Because an appeal is an expensive, time-consuming, and technical process involving a review of the lower-court record, the research and drafting of briefs, and the presentation of oral arguments to the appellate court, the defendant has been granted the right to counsel at this stage of the criminal process. In the case of *Douglas v. California* (1963), the Supreme Court held that an indigent defendant has a constitutional right to the assistance of counsel on a direct first appeal.[52] If the defendant appeals to a higher court, the defendant must have private counsel or apply for permission to proceed **in forma pauperis,** meaning that the defendant may be granted counsel at public expense if the court believes the appeal has merit. There is no right to free counsel beyond the first appeal as a matter of constitutional right.[53] In order to ensure effective counsel, the Supreme Court has ruled that counsel must act as an advocate and support his or her client completely.[54]

After an appeal has been fully heard, the appeals court renders an opinion on the procedures used in the case. If an error of law is found—such as an improper introduction of evidence or an improper statement by the prosecutor that was prejudicial to the defendant—the appeals court may reverse the decision of the trial court and order a new trial. If the lower court's decision is upheld, the case is finished, unless the defendant seeks a discretionary appeal to a higher state or federal court.

Over the last decade, criminal appeals have increased significantly in almost every state and the federal courts. Criminal case appeals make up close to 50% of the state appellate caseload and over 35% of the total federal caseload, which includes prisoner petitions and ordinary criminal appeals.[55] Today, a substantial number of these appeals involve drug-related cases and appeals of sentences where the offender was institutionalized. Most appeals usually occur after final trial court decisions on convictions and sentencing of the defendant.

Evidentiary Standards

Proof **beyond reasonable doubt** is the standard required to convict a defendant charged with a crime at the adjudicatory stage of the criminal process. This requirement dates back to early American history and over the years has become the accepted measure of persuasion needed by the prosecutor to convince the judge or jury of the defendant's guilt. Many 20th-century U.S. Supreme Court decisions have reinforced this standard by making "beyond a reasonable doubt a due process and constitutional requirement."[56] In *Brinegar v. United States* (1948), for instance, the Supreme Court stated:

> Guilt in a criminal case must be proven beyond a reasonable doubt and by evidence confined to that which long experience in the common-law tradition, to some extent embodied in the Constitution, has crystallized into rules of evidence consistent with that standard. These rules are historically grounded rights of our system, developed to safeguard men from dubious and unjust convictions with resulting forfeitures of life, liberty, and property.[57]

The reasonable doubt standard is an essential ingredient of the criminal justice process. It is the prime instrument for reducing the risk of convictions based on factual errors.[58] The underlying premise of this standard is that it is better to release a guilty person than to convict someone who is innocent. Since the defendant is presumed innocent until proven guilty, this standard forces the prosecution to overcome this presumption with the highest standard of proof. Unlike the civil law, where a mere **preponderance of the evidence** is the standard, the criminal process requires proof beyond a reasonable doubt for each element of the offense. As the Supreme Court pointed out in *In re Winship* (1970), where the reasonable doubt standard was applied to juvenile trials, "If the standard of proof for a criminal trial were a preponderance of the evidence rather than proof beyond a reasonable doubt, there would be a smaller risk of factual errors that result in freeing guilty persons, but a far greater risk of factual errors that result in convicting the innocent."[59] The various evidentiary standards of proof are analyzed and compared in Table 11.2.

Standard	Definition	Where Used
Absolute certainty	No possibility of error; 100% certainty	Not used in civil or criminal law
Beyond reasonable doubt; moral certainty	Conclusive and complete proof, while leaving any reasonable doubt as to the innocence or guilt of the defendant; allowing the defendant the benefit of any possibility of innocence	Criminal trial
Clear and convincing evidence	Prevailing and persuasive to the trier of fact	Civil commitments, insanity defense
Preponderance of evidence	Greater weight of evidence in terms of credibility; more convincing than an opposite point of view	Civil trial
Probable cause	U.S. constitutional standard for arrest and search warrants, requiring existence of facts sufficient to warrant that a crime has been committed	Arrest, preliminary hearing, motions
Sufficient evidence	Adequate evidence to reverse a trial court	Appellate review
Reasonable suspicion	Rational, reasonable belief that facts warrant investigation of a crime on less than probable cause	Police investigations
Less than probable cause	Mere suspicion; less than reasonable belief to conclude criminal activity exists	Prudent police investigation where safety of an officer or others is endangered

Table 11.2
Evidentiary Standards of Proof—Degrees of Certainty

Criminal Justice on the Net

Would you like to learn more about trials in other nations? In Britain, unlike many other jurisdictions, including the United States, there is no entrenched Bill of Rights. The rights and duties of the public have evolved from documents such as the Magna Carta (1215), parliamentary legislation, custom and practice (common law), and precedent (judge-made law). Added to this, piecemeal, have been the more recent structures of European law with its developments in human rights.

Almost all courts operate on an adversarial system in Europe. That means the opposing parties in a case conduct a "fight" overseen by the judge, who ensures that the fight is fair. This is in direct contrast to the inquisitorial system adopted by many other countries, where a case is conducted very much like an inquiry or investigation.

To learn more about British trials and courts log on to:

http://www.dircon.co.uk/belmarsh/ cort.html

Summary

The number of cases disposed of by trials is relatively small in comparison to the total number that enter the criminal justice system. Nevertheless, the criminal trial provides the defendant with an important option. Unlike other steps in the system, the U.S. criminal trial allows the accused to assert the right to a day in court.

The defendant may choose between a trial before a judge alone or a trial by jury. In either case, the purpose of the trial is to adjudicate the facts, ascertain the truth, and determine the guilt or innocence of the accused.

Criminal trials represent the adversary system at work. The state uses its authority to seek a conviction, and the defendant is protected by constitutional rights, particularly those under the Fifth and Sixth Amendments. When they involve serious crimes, criminal trials are complex legal affairs. Each jurisdiction relies on rules and procedures that have developed over many years to resolve legal issues. As the U.S. Supreme Court has extended the rights of the accused, as described in this chapter, the procedures have undoubtedly contributed to the complexities and delays within the system. Some solutions have included smaller juries, more efficient control of police misconduct, and reduced time delays between arrest, indictment, and trial. But the right to a fair trial, trial by jury, and the due process rights to counsel and confrontation need to be guarded and protected in our society.

An established order of steps is followed throughout a criminal trial, beginning with the selection of a jury, proceeding through opening statements and the introduction of evidence, and concluding with closing arguments and a verdict. The criminal trial serves both a symbolic and a pragmatic function for defendants who require a forum of last resort to adjudicate their differences with the state. The trial is the central test of the facts and law involved in a criminal case.

Key Terms

adjudication
confrontation clause
6-person jury
pro se
First Amendment
venire
voir dire

challenges for cause
peremptory challenges
bench trials
direct examination
cross-examination
real evidence
circumstantial evidence

directed verdict
charge
verdict
writ of habeas corpus
in forma pauperis
beyond reasonable doubt
preponderance of the evidence

Questions

1. What are the steps involved in the criminal trial?
2. What are the pros and cons of a jury trial versus a bench trial?
3. What are the legal rights of the defendant in the trial process?
4. Trace the historical development of the right to counsel at the trial stage of the criminal justice system.
5. What is the significance of the Supreme Court decision in *Gideon v. Wainwright*?
6. "The burden of proof in a criminal trial to show that the defendant is guilty beyond a reasonable doubt is on the government in the adversary system of criminal justice." Explain the meaning of this statement in terms of other legal standards of proof.
7. What is evidence?

Notes

1. U.S. Constitution, Sixth Amendment.
2. *Pointer v. State of Texas,* 380 U.S. 400, 85 S.Ct. 1065, 13 L.Ed.2d 923 (1965).
3. *Coy v. Iowa,* 487 U.S. 1012, 108 S.Ct. 2798, 101 L.Ed.2d 857 (1988).
4. *Maryland v. Craig,* 497 U.S. 836, 110 S.Ct. 3157, 111 L.Ed.2d 666 (1990).
5. *Duncan v. Louisiana,* 391 U.S. 145, 88 S.Ct. 1444, 20 L.Ed.2d 491 (1968).
6. Ibid., at 157–158, 88 S.Ct. at 1451–1452.
7. *Baldwin v. New York,* 399 U.S. 66, 90 S.Ct. 1886, 26 L.Ed.2d 437 (1970).

8. *Blanton v. North Las Vegas,* 489 U.S. 538, 109 S.Ct. 1289, 103 L.Ed.2d 550 (1989).
9. *Lewis v. United States,* 116 S.Ct. 2163 (1996).
10. *Williams v. Florida,* 399 U.S. 78, 90 S.Ct. 1893, 26 L.Ed.2d 446 (1970).
11. Ibid., at 101, 90 S.Ct. at 1906.
12. *Apodica v. Oregon,* 406 U.S. 404, 92 S.Ct. 1628, 32 L.Ed.2d 184 (1972).
13. *Powell v. Alabama,* 287 U.S. 45, 53 S.Ct. 55, 77 L.Ed. 158 (1932).
14. *Gideon v. Wainwright,* 372 U.S. 335, 83 S.Ct. 792, 9 L.Ed.2d 799 (1963); see also Yale Kamisar,

"Gideon v. Wainwright, a Quarter Century Later," *Pace Law Review* 10 (1990): 343.
15. *Argersinger v. Hamlin,* 407 U.S. 25, 92 S.Ct. 2006, 32 L.Ed.2d 530 (1972).
16. *Scott v. Illinois,* 440 U.S. 367, 99 S.Ct. 1158, 59 L.Ed.2d 383 (1979).
17. U.S. Constitution, Sixth Amendment.
18. *Faretta v. California,* 422 U.S. 806, 95 S.Ct. 2525, 45 L.Ed.2d 562 (1975).
19. Ibid.
20. Ibid., at 592.

21. See American Bar Association, *Standards Relating to Speedy Trial* (Chicago: ABA, 1995).

22. *Klopfer v. North Carolina,* 386 U.S. 213, 87 S.Ct. 988, 18 L.Ed.2d 1 (1967).

23. Ibid., at 223, 87 S.Ct. at 993.

24. *Doggett v. United States,* 505 U.S. 162, 112 S.Ct. 2686, 120 L.Ed.2d 520 (1992).

25. *Estelle v. Williams,* 425 U.S. 501, 96 S.Ct. 1691, 48 L.Ed.2d 126 (1976); see also American Bar Association, "Fair Trial and Free Press," in *Standards for Criminal Justice* (Washington, D.C.: ABA, 1993).

26. *Sheppard v. Maxwell,* 384 U.S. 333, 86 S.Ct. 1507, 16 L.Ed.2d 600 (1966).

27. See *State v. von Bulow,* 475 A.2d 995 (R.I. 1984); see also Alan Dershowitz, *Reversal of Fortune: The Von Bulow Affair* (New York: Random House, 1986).

28. *Nebraska Press Association v. Stuart,* 427 U.S. 539, 96 S.Ct. 2791, 49 L.Ed.2d 683 (1976).

29. Ibid., at 547, 96 S.Ct. at 2797.

30. *Gannett Co. v. De Pasquale,* 443 U.S. 368, 99 S.Ct. 2898, 61 L.Ed.2d 608 (1979).

31. Ibid., at 370, 99 S.Ct. at 2900.

32. *Press-Enterprise Co. v. Superior Court,* 478 U.S. 1, 106 S.Ct. 2735, 92 L.Ed.2d 1 (1986).

33. *El Vocero de Puerto Rico (Caribbean International News Corp. v. Puerto Rico),* 508 U.S. 147, 113 S.Ct. 2004, 124 L.Ed.2d 60 (1993).

34. *Richmond Newspapers, Inc. v. Virginia,* 448 U.S. 555, 100 S.Ct. 2814, 65 L.Ed.2d 973 (1980).

35. *Globe Newspaper Co. v. Superior Court for County of Norfolk,* 457 U.S. 596, 102 S.Ct. 2613, 73 L.Ed.2d 248 (1982).

36. Nicholas A. Pellegrini, "Extension of Criminal Defendant's Right to Public Trial," *St. John's University Law Review* 611 (1987): 277–289.

37. *In re Oliver,* 333 U.S. 257, 68 S.Ct. 499, 92 L.Ed. 682 (1948).

38. *Chandler v. Florida,* 449 U.S. 560 (1981); also American Bar Association, *Criminal Justice Standards, Fair Trial and Free Press* (Washington, D.C.: ABA, 1992).

39. Conference of State Court Administrators, *State Court Organization, 1987* (Williamsburg, Va.: National Center for State Courts, 1988), p. 10.

40. George Hayden, Joseph Senna, and Larry Siegel, "Prosecutorial Discretion in Peremptory Challenges: An Empirical Investigation of Information Use in the Massachusetts Jury Selection Process," *New England Law Review* 13 (1978): 768.

41. *Swain v. Alabama,* 380 U.S. 202, 85 S.Ct. 824, 13 L.Ed.2d 759 (1964).

42. *Batson v. Kentucky,* 476 U.S. 79, 106 S.Ct. 1712, 90 L.Ed.2d 69 (1986); see also Albert Alschuler and Randall Kennedy, "Equal Justice— Would Color-Conscious Jury Selection Help?" *American Bar Association Journal* 81 (1995): 36–37.

43. *Powers v. Ohio,* 479 U.S. 400, 111 S.Ct. 1364, 113 L.Ed.2d 411 (1991).

44. *Georgia v. McCollum,* 505 U.S. 42, 112 S.Ct. 2348, 120 L.Ed.2d 33 (1992).

45. *J.E.B. v. Alabama,* 511 U.S., 114 S.Ct. 1419, 128 L.Ed.2d 89 (1994).

46. *Lee v. Illinois,* 476 U.S. 530, 106 S.Ct. 2056, 90 L.Ed.2d 514 (1986).

47. See Charles McCormick, Frank Elliott, and John Sutton, Jr., *Evidence—Cases and Materials* (St. Paul: West Publishing, 1981), chap. 1.

48. Ibid.

49. See the fascinating case study of the *State's Case v. Dr. Webster* in Helen Thomson, *Murder at Harvard* (Boston: Houghton-Mifflin, 1971).

50. Bureau of Justice Statistics, *Report to the Nation on Crime and Justice,* 2nd ed. (Washington, D.C.: U.S. Government Printing Office, 1988), p. 88.

51. *Chapman v. California,* 386 U.S. 18, 87 S.Ct. 824, 17 L.Ed.2d 705 (1967).

52. *Douglas v. California,* 372 U.S. 353, 83 S.Ct. 814, 9 L.Ed.2d 811 (1963).

53. *Ross v. Moffitt,* 417 U.S. 600, 94 S.Ct. 2437, 41 L.Ed.2d 341 (1974).

54. *Anders v. California,* 386 U.S. 738, 87 S.Ct. 1396, 18 L.Ed.2d 493 (1967).

55. Brian J. Ostrom, *State Court Caseload Statistics, Annual Report, 1992* (Williamsburg, Va.: National Center for State Courts, 1994).

56. See *Brinegar v. United States,* 338 U.S. 160, 69 S.Ct. 1302, 93 L.Ed. 1879 (1949); *In re Winship,* 397 U.S. 358, 90 S.Ct. 1068, 25 L.Ed.2d 368 (1970).

57. *Brinegar v. United States,* 338 U.S. 160, 174, 69 S.Ct. 1302, 1310, 93 L.Ed. 1879 (1949).

58. See *In re Winship,* at 397.

59. Ibid., at 371, 90 S.Ct. at 1076.

CHAPTER 12

Punishment and Sentencing

After a defendant has been found guilty of a crime by a jury, a judge, or his or her own admission of guilt, the state has the right to impose a criminal **sanction** or **punishment** in what is referred to as the sentencing process.

Historically, a full range of punishments were inflicted on criminal defendants, including physical torture, branding, whipping, and, for most felony offenses, death. During the Middle Ages, the philosophy of punishment was to "torment the body for the sins of the soul."[1] People who violated the law were considered morally corrupt and in need of strong discipline. If punishment was harsh enough, it was assumed, they would never repeat their mistakes. Punishment was also viewed as a spectacle that taught a moral lesson. The more gruesome and public the sentence, the greater the impact it would have on the local populace.[2] Harsh physical punishments would control any thoughts of rebellion and dissent against the central government and those who held political and economic control. Such barbaric use of state power is, of course, no longer tolerated in the United States.

In modern U.S. society, the most important forms of criminal punishment are

- *Fines*—monetary payments made to the court reflecting the costs to society of the criminal act

- *Community sentences*—periods of supervision in the community during which the criminal is required to obey predetermined rules of behavior and may be asked to perform tasks, such as make restitution to the victim

- *Incarceration*—a period of confinement in a state or federal prison, jail, or community-based treatment facility

- *Capital punishment*—death in the electric chair or gas chamber or by lethal injection

Punishing criminal offenders continues to be one of the most complex and controversial issues in the criminal justice system. Its complexity stems from the wide variety of sentences available and the discretion judges have in applying them. The proper sanction for a particular criminal defendant is often difficult to determine. The controversy over punishment involves both its nature and extent: Are too many people being sent to prison? Do people get widely different sentences for very similar crimes? Is there discrimination in sentencing based on race, gender, or social class?[3] These are but a few of the most significant issues in the sentencing process.

This chapter first examines the history of punishment and then focuses on incarceration and capital punishment, the two most traditional and punitive forms of criminal sanctions used today. Chapter 13 reviews alternative sentences that have been developed to reduce the strain on the overburdened correctional system; these sentences provide intermediate sanctions designed to control people whose behavior and personality make an incarceration sentence unnecessary. Such sanctions include probation and other forms of community correction.

History of Punishment

The punishment and correction of criminals has changed considerably through the ages, reflecting custom, economic conditions, and religious and political ideals.[4]

From Exile to Fines and Forfeiture to Torture

In early Greece and Rome, the most common state-administered punishment was banishment or exile. Only slaves were commonly subjected to harsh physical punishment for their misdeeds. Interpersonal violence, even attacks that resulted in death, were viewed as a private matter. These ancient peoples typically used economic punishments, such as fines, for such crimes as assault on a slave, arson, or housebreaking.

During the Middle Ages (5th to 11th centuries), there was little law or government control. Offenses were settled by blood feuds carried out by the families of the injured parties. When possible, the Roman custom of settling disputes by fine or an exchange of property was adopted as a means of resolving interpersonal conflicts with a minimum of bloodshed. After the 11th century, during the feudal period, forfeiture of land and property was common punishment for persons who violated law and custom or who failed to fulfill their feudal obligations to their lord. The word **felony** actually comes from the 12th century, when the term *felonia* referred to a breach of faith with one's feudal lord.

During this period, the main emphasis of criminal law and punishment was on maintaining public order. If in the heat of passion or while intoxicated a person severely injured or killed his or her neighbor, freemen in the area would gather to pronounce a judgment and make the culprit do penance or pay compensation called **wergild.** The purpose of the fine was to pacify the injured party and ensure that the conflict would not develop into a blood feud and anarchy. The inability of the peasantry to pay a fine led to the use of corporal punishment, such as whipping or branding, as a substitute penalty.

The development of the common law in the 11th century brought some standardization to penal practices. However, corrections remained an amalgam of fines and brutal physical punishments. Capital and corporal punishment were used to control the criminal poor. While the wealthy could buy their way out of punishment and into exile, the poor were executed and mutilated at ever-increasing rates. Execution, banishment, mutilation, branding, and flogging were used on a whole range of offenders, from murderers and robbers to vagrants and gypsies. Punishments became unmatched in their cruelty, featuring a gruesome variety of physical tortures often part of a public spectacle, presumably so that the sadistic sanctions would act as deterrents. But the variety and imagination of the tortures inflicted on even minor criminals before their death suggest that retribution, sadism, and spectacle were more important than any presumed deterrent effect.

Public Work and Transportation

By the end of the 16th century, the rise of the city and overseas colonization provided tremendous markets for manufactured goods and spurred the need for labor. Punishment of criminals changed to meet the demands created by these social conditions. Instead of being tortured or executed, many offenders were made to do hard labor for their crimes. **Poor laws,** developed at the end of the 16th century, required that the poor, vagrants, and vagabonds be put to work in public or private enterprise. Houses of correction were developed to make it convenient to assign petty law violators to work details. In London, a workhouse was developed at Brideswell in 1557; its use became so popular that by 1576, Parliament ordered a Brideswell-type workhouse be built in every county in England. Many convicted offenders were pressed into sea duty as galley slaves, a fate considered so loathsome that many convicts mutilated themselves rather than submit.

The constant shortage of labor in the European colonies also prompted authorities to transport convicts overseas. In England, an Order in Council of 1617 granted a reprieve and stay of execution to people convicted of robbery and other felonies who were strong enough to be employed overseas. Similar measures were used in France and Italy to recruit galley slaves and workers.

Transporting convicts to the colonies became popular; it supplied labor, cost little, and was actually profitable for the government, since manufacturers and plantation owners paid for convicts' services. The Old Bailey Court in London supplied at least 10,000 convicts between 1717 and 1775. Convicts would serve a period as workers and then become free again.

The American Revolution ended the transportation of felons to North America, although it continued in Australia and New Zealand. Between 1787 and 1875, when the practice was finally abandoned, over 135,000 felons were transported to Australia.

While transportation in lieu of a death sentence may at first glance seem advantageous, transported prisoners endured enormous hardships. Those who were sent to Australia suffered incredible physical abuse, including severe whippings and mutilation. Many of the British prison officials placed in charge of the Australian penal colonies could best be described as sociopaths or sadists.

Between the American Revolution in 1776 and the first decades of the 19th century, the population of Europe and the United States increased rapidly. Transportation of convicts to North America was no longer an option. The increased use of machinery made industry capital- and not labor-intensive. As a result, there was less need for unskilled laborers in England, and many workers could not find suitable employment.

The gulf between poor workers and wealthy landowners and merchants widened. The crime rate rose significantly, prompting a return to physical punishment and increased use of the death penalty. During the later part of the 18th century, 350 types of crime in England were punishable by death. While many people sentenced to death for trivial offenses were spared the gallows, the use of capital punishment was extremely common in England during the mid-18th century. Prompted by the excessive use of physical and capital punishment, legal philosophers argued that physical punishment should be replaced by periods of confinement and incapacitation. Jails and workhouses were commonly used to hold petty offenders, vagabonds, the homeless, and debtors. However, these institutions were not meant for hard-core criminals. One solution to imprisoning a growing criminal population was to keep prisoners in abandoned ships anchored in rivers and harbors throughout England. The degradation under which prisoners lived in these ships inspired John Howard, the sheriff of Bedfordshire, to write *The State of the Prisons* in 1777, which inspired Parliament to pass legislation mandating the construction of secure and sanitary structures to house prisoners.

By 1820, long periods of incarceration in walled institutions called reformatories or **penitentiaries** began to replace physical punishment in England and the United States. These institutions were considered liberal reforms during a time when harsh physical punishment and incarceration in filthy holding facilities were the norm. The history of correctional institutions will be discussed further

The Rise of the Prison

in Chapter 14. Incarceration has remained the primary mode of punishment for serious offenses in the United States since it was introduced early in the 19th century. Ironically in our high-tech society, some of the institutions constructed soon after the Revolutionary War are still in use today. In recent times, prison as a method of punishment has been supplemented by a sentence to community supervision for less serious offenders, while the death penalty is reserved for those considered to be the most serious and dangerous.

The Goals of Criminal Punishment

When we hear about a notorious criminal, such as serial killer Jeffery Dahmer or Ted Bundy, receiving a long prison sentence or the death penalty for a particularly heinous crime, each of us has a distinct reaction. Some of us are gratified that a truly evil person "got just what he deserved"; many people feel safer because a dangerous person is now "where he can't harm any other innocent victims"; others hope the punishment serves as a warning to potential criminals that "everyone gets caught in the end"; some may actually feel sorry for the defendant—"He got a raw deal, he needs help, not punishment"; and still others hope that "when he gets out, he'll have learned his lesson." And when an offender is forced to pay a large fine, we say, "What goes around comes around."

Each of these sentiments may be at work when criminal sentences are formulated. After all, sentences are devised and implemented by judges, many of whom are elected officials and share the general public's sentiments and fears. The objectives of criminal sentencing today can usually be grouped into six distinct areas: general deterrence, incapacitation, specific deterrence, retribution or just desert, rehabilitation, and restitution (equity).

General Deterrence

What effect does the impact of punishing a criminal offender have on the community? By punishing an offender severely, the state can demonstrate its determination to control crime and deter potential offenders. Too lenient a sentence might encourage criminal conduct; too severe a sentence might reduce the system's ability to dispense fair and impartial justice and may actually encourage criminality. For example, if the crime of rape were punished with death, rapists might be encouraged to kill their victims to dispose of the one person who could identify them; since they would already be facing the death penalty for rape, they would have nothing more to lose. Maintaining a balance between fear and justice is an ongoing quest in the justice system.

Sentencing for the purposes of **general deterrence,** then, is designed to give a signal to the community at large: Crime does not pay! While the message is impressive, it may also be a case of wishful thinking. There is actually little clear-cut evidence that severe punishments actually influence criminal behavior trends. Nonetheless, criminal penalties have been toughened for many crimes and, as Table 12.1 shows, once arrested people have a greater chance of being convicted today than in the past. As a result, prison sentences are lengthening and the prison population is increasing. Despite these stern measures, there is still a lot of crime.

Why does the threat of punishment have a less than expected influence on crime? Criminals may be too desperate or psychologically impaired by drugs and alcohol to be deterred by the threat of distant criminal punishment; their economic circumstances may be too desperate for the threat of punishment to have an effect.

Table 12.1
Approximate Likelihood of Felony Arrest Leading to Felony Conviction

SOURCE: Patrick A. Langan and Jodi M. Brown, *Felony Sentences in State Courts, 1994* (Washington, D.C.: Bureau of Justice Statistics, 1997).

Felony	1988	1990	1992	1994
Murder	48%	55%	65%	65%
Robbery	32	37	41	39
Aggravated assault	10	13	14	14
Burglary	33	38	41	39
Drug trafficking	39	53	55	52

Nonetheless, some experts believe that severe and draconian sentences can eventually bring crime rates down. They call for a "get tough" policy featuring long, mandatory prison terms with little chance for early release.

Incapacitation

If an offender is a risk to society, he or she may be sentenced to a period of secure confinement. **Incapacitation** of criminals is a justifiable goal of sentencing because inmates will not be able to repeat their criminal acts while they are under state control. For some offenders, this means a period in a high-security state prison where behavior is closely monitored. Fixing sentence length involves determining how long a particular offender needs to be incarcerated to ensure that society is protected.

To some critics, incapacitation strategies seem of questionable utility because little association seems to exist between the number of criminals behind bars and the crime rate: Although the prison population jumped between 1980 and 1990, the crime rate also increased. Those who favor an incapacitation policy claim that the recent decline in the crime rate can be attributed to the fact that there are more than 1.7 million people behind bars. Opponents counter that crime rates have little to do with incarceration trends and that reductions in crime are related to the number of teens in the population, police effectiveness, drug use trends, and other unrelated factors.

Although the merits of incarcerating criminals are still open to debate, there is no question that sentences designed to incapacitate convicted offenders are certainly in vogue. Mandatory life sentences for three-time felons—the so-called "three strikes and you're out" model—have been adopted in a number of states, including California. In addition, sentences that require a mandatory prison stay for people convicted of drug- and gun-related crimes are quite common. States have also toughened juvenile laws, and many more young people who in the past would have been treated in the juvenile justice system are now being sent to adult courts and, if convicted, incarcerated in adult prisons.

Specific Deterrence

Specific deterrence refers to the ability of criminal punishment to convince convicted offenders that **recidivism** would not be in their best interests. The theory is that the suffering caused by punishment, such as an extended prison stay or a large fine, should inhibit future law violations.

While a few research efforts have found that punishment can have a significant specific deterrent effect on future criminality, they are more than matched by others that have failed to find specific deterrent effects.[5] The specific deterrence goal of punishment is weakened by the fact that about 70% of prison inmates have had prior convictions and more than 60% return to prison within three years of their release.[6]

Retribution/Just Desert

According to the retributive goal of sentencing, the essential purpose of the criminal process is to punish deserving offenders—fairly and justly—in a manner that is proportionate to the gravity of their crimes.[7]

Offenders are punished simply and solely because they deserve to be disciplined for what they have done; "the punishment should fit the crime."[8] It would be wrong to punish people to set an example for others or to deter would-be criminals, as the general deterrence goal demands. Punishment should be no more or less than the offender's actions deserve; it must be based on how **blameworthy** the person is; this is referred to as the concept of **just desert**.[9]

According to this view, punishments must be equally and fairly distributed to all people who commit similar illegal acts. Determining just punishments can be difficult, because there is generally little consensus about the treatment of criminals, the seriousness of crimes, and the proper response to criminal acts.[10] Nonetheless, there has been an ongoing effort to calculate fair and just sentences by creating guidelines to control judicial decision making. This effort will be discussed in greater detail later in the chapter.

Rehabilitation

Can criminal offenders be effectively treated so that they can eventually readjust to society? It may be fairer to offer offenders an opportunity for rehabilitation rather than harsh criminal punishments. In a sense, society has failed criminal offenders, many of whom have grown up in disorganized neighborhoods and dysfunctional families. Society is therefore obligated to help these unfortunate people who, through no fault of their own, experience social and emotional problems that are often the root of their criminal behavior.

The rehabilitation aspect of sentencing is based on a prediction of the future needs of the offender and not on the gravity of the current offense. For example, if a judge sentences a person convicted of a felony to a period of community supervision, the judge's actions reflect his or her belief that the offender can be successfully treated and presents no future threat to society.

The rehabilitation goal of sentencing has been criticized because, according to skeptics, little conclusive evidence exists that correctional treatment programs can prevent future criminality.[11] While the rehabilitative ideal has been undermined by such attacks, surveys indicate that the general public still supports the treatment goal of sentencing.[12] Numerous studies show that under the right circumstances rehabilitation efforts can be quite effective.[13]

Equity

Because criminals gain from their misdeeds, it seems both fair and just to demand that they reimburse society for its loss caused by their crimes. In the early common law, wergild and fines represented the concept of creating an equitable solution to crime by requiring the convicted offender to make restitution to both the victim and the state. Today, judges continue to require that offenders pay victims for their losses.

The **equity** goal of punishment means that convicted criminals must pay back their victims for their loss, the justice system for the costs of processing their case, and society for any disruption they may have caused. In a so-called victimless crime, such as drug trafficking, the social costs might include the expense of drug enforcement efforts, drug treatment centers, and care for infants born to drug-addicted mothers. In predatory crimes, the costs might include the services of emergency room doctors, lost work days and productivity, and treatment for long-term psychological problems. To help defray these costs, convicted offenders might be required to pay a fine, forfeit the property they acquired through illegal gain, do community service work, make financial restitution to their victim, and reimburse the state for the costs of the criminal process. Because the criminals' actions helped expand their personal gains, rights, and privileges at society's expense, justice demands that they lose rights and privileges to restore the social balance.[14]

Each of the factors that influence sentencing decisions is illustrated in Figure 12.1.

Imposing the Sentence

Regardless of the factors that influence the sentence, it is generally imposed by the judge, and sentencing is one of the most crucial functions of judgeship. Sentencing authority may also be exercised by the jury, or it may be mandated by statute (for example, a mandatory prison sentence for a certain crime).

In most felony cases, except where the law provides for mandatory prison terms, sentencing is usually based on a variety of information available to the judge. Some jurisdictions allow victims to make impact statements that are considered at sentencing hearings. Most judges also consider a presentence investigation report by the probation department in making a sentencing decision. This report is a social and personal history as well as an evaluation of the defendant's chances for rehabilitation within the community. Some judges give the presentence investigation report great weight; others may dismiss it completely or rely on only certain portions.

When an accused is convicted of two or more charges, he or she must be sentenced on each charge. If the sentences are **concurrent,** they begin the same day and are completed when the longest term has been served. For example, a defendant is convicted of burglarizing an apartment and assaulting its occupant; he is sentenced to 3 years on a charge of assault and 10 years for burglary, the sentences to be served concurrently. After 10 years in prison, the sentences would be completed.

In contrast, receiving a **consecutive sentence** means that on completion of the sentence for one crime, the offender begins serving time for the second of multiple crimes. If the defendant in the above example had been sentenced consecutively, he would serve 3 years on the assault charge and then 10 for the burglary. Therefore, the total term on the two charges would be 13 years. Concurrent sentences are the norm; consecutive sentences are requested for the most serious criminals and for those who are unwilling to cooperate with authorities.

When a convicted offender is sentenced to prison, the statutes of the jurisdiction in which the crime was committed determine the penalties that may be imposed by the court. Over the years, a variety of sentencing structures have been used in the United States. They include indeterminate sentences, determinate sentences, and mandatory sentences.

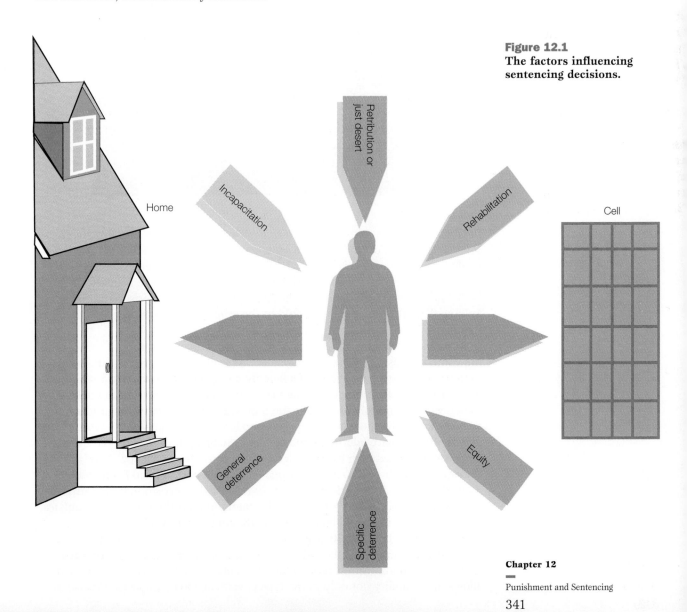

Figure 12.1
The factors influencing sentencing decisions.

Sentencing decisions are based on an amalgam of information available to the judge. Younger offenders may be given a more lenient sentence than hardened older criminals. The three teens shown on the monitor were charged with murdering an elderly man during a Florida hold-up. They were sentenced to life in prison. Should their age have been taken into consideration when punishment was considered?

Indeterminate Sentences

In the 1870s prison reformers, such as Enoch Wines and Zebulon Brockway, called for creation of **indeterminate sentences**, tailored to fit individual needs. Offenders, the argument went, should only be placed in confinement until they were rehabilitated and then released on parole. Criminals were believed to be "sick" rather than bad; they could be successfully treated in prison. Rather than holding that "the punishment should fit the crime," reformers believed "the treatment should fit the offender."

The indeterminate sentence is still the most widely used type of sentence in the United States. Convicted offenders are typically given a "light" minimum sentence that must be served and a lengthy maximum sentence that is the outer boundary of the time that can be served. For example, the legislature might set a sentence of a minimum of 3 years and a maximum of 20 years for burglary; the convicted offender must be sentenced to no less than 3 years but no more than 20 years in prison. Under this scheme, the actual length of time served by the offender is controlled both by the judge and the correctional agency. A judge could sentence a burglar to 3 to 20. The inmate could then be paroled from confinement soon after serving the minimum sentence if the correctional authorities believe that he or she is ready to live in the community. If the inmate accumulates good time, he or she could be released in 18 months; a troublesome inmate would be forced to do all 20 years.

The basic purpose of the indeterminate sentence is to individualize each sentence in the interests of rehabilitating the offender. This type of sentencing allows for flexibility not only in the type of sentence to be imposed but also in the length of time to be served. Following are some possible variations on the indeterminate sentence:

- The maximum sentence is set by the legislature and cannot be changed; the minimum is determined by the judge. For example, offender A receives 1 to 20 years for burglary; offender B, 16 to 20; offender C, 10 to 20; and so on.

- The judge sets both the maximum and the minimum sentence within guidelines set up by the legislature. For example, the minimum and maximum sentence for burglary is 1 to 20 years. Offender A gets 1 to 20; offender B, 4 to 10; offender C, 3 to 6. The maximum the judge uses cannot exceed 20 years; the minimum cannot be less than 1.

- The maximum sentence is set by the judge within the upper limit, and the minimum is determined by the legislature. For example, all sentenced burglars do at least 1 year in prison but no more than 20. Offender A receives 1 to 10; offender B, 1 to 20; offender C, 1 to 5.

Most jurisdictions that use indeterminate sentences employ statutes that specify minimum and maximum terms but allow judges discretion to fix the actual sentence within those limits. The typical minimum sentence is at least 1 year; a few state jurisdictions require at least a 2-year minimum sentence for felons.[15]

The indeterminate sentence has come under attack in recent years for a variety of reasons. It is alleged to produce great disparity in the way people are treated in the correctional system. For example, one offender may serve 1 year and another may serve 20 for the same crime. Further, the indeterminate sentence is believed to take control of sentencing out of the hands of the judiciary and place it within the framework of corrections, especially when the minimum sentence is quite short. Every time an inmate granted early release via discretionary parole commits a violent crime, the call goes up to get tough on prison inmates. In contrast, many inmates feel cheated by the system when they are denied parole despite having a good prison record. The protections of due process maintained in the courtroom are absent in the correctional setting. Dissatisfaction with the disparity and uncertainty of indeterminate sentencing has prompted some states and the federal government to abandon it in favor of determinate or structured sentencing models.

Determinate sentences were actually the first kind used in the United States and are today employed in about ten jurisdictions. As originally conceived, a determinate sentence was a fixed term of years, the maximum set in law by the legislature, to be served by the offender sentenced to prison for a particular crime. For example, if the law provided for a sentence of up to 20 years for robbery, the judge might sentence a repeat offender to a 15-year term; another, less experienced felon might receive a more lenient sentence of 5 years.

Although determinate sentences provide a single term of years to be served without benefit of parole, the actual time spent in prison is reduced by the implementation of "time off for good behavior." This concept was first used in 1817 in New York, and it was quickly adopted in most other jurisdictions. Good time is still in use today; inmates can accrue good time at a rate ranging from 10 to 15 days per month. In addition, some correctional authorities grant earned sentence reductions to inmates who participate in treatment programs, such as educational and vocational training, or who volunteer for experimental medical testing programs. More than half of a determinate sentence can be erased by accumulating standard and earned good time.

Good-time laws allow inmates to calculate their release date at the time they enter prison by subtracting the expected good time from their sentence. However, good time can be lost if inmates break prison rules, get into fights, or disobey correctional officers. In some jurisdictions, former inmates can be returned

Determinate Sentences

to prison to serve the balance of their unexpired sentence when their good time is revoked for failing to conform to conditions set down for their release (for example, not reporting to a postrelease supervisor or abusing drugs).

Structured Sentencing. Today determinate sentencing states usually use some procedure to control judicial discretion. Some use **presumptive sentences,** which mandate a certain term of years for a particular crime and allow judges to deviate slightly from this term if there are either aggravating or mitigating circumstances. For example, the recommended sentence for robbery is 5 years; the sentence can be increased if the offender used unnecessary violence or carried a weapon; it can be reduced if there were mitigating circumstances such as the offender's youth, mental state, or substance abuse. California and Indiana are examples of states that use this type of sentence.

Another approach to determinate sentencing is referred to as **structured sentencing,** which uses written standards or guidelines to control the sentencing decision. Forms of **sentencing guidelines** are used by the federal government and by various state jurisdictions, including Minnesota, Washington, Florida, and Pennsylvania.

Guidelines classify offenses on the basis of (a) the seriousness of the crime and (b) the offender's prior offense history. Sentences are then calculated based on these characteristics so that offenders who commit similar crimes and have comparable criminal histories receive identical sentences. Both presumptive and guideline sentences must be served in their entirety (minus time off for good behavior); there is no parole or early release.

Some guidelines are voluntary and others mandatory. Voluntary guidelines are used to give judges a suggested benchmark from which to sentence an offender; research indicates that judges often diverge from the recommended sentence.[16] In contrast, mandatory guidelines require that the sentence fall within a narrow range and that any deviation from the mandated sentence must be explained in writing. In all, nine states now have some form of mandatory guidelines, eight more are developing them, and four have voluntary guidelines, which are recommendations that help guide judicial discretion.[17]

Figure 12.2 shows Minnesota's guidelines. Note that as prior record and offense severity increase, so does recommended sentence length. After a certain point, probation is no longer an option, and the defendant must do prison time. A burglar with no prior convictions can expect to receive probation or an 18-month sentence for a house break-in; an experienced burglar with six or more prior convictions can get 54 months for the same crime, and probation is not an option.

The Federal Guidelines. The federal government's Crime Control Act of 1984 created the U.S. Sentencing Commission, an independent body in the judicial branch of the government charged with establishing federal sentencing policy.

The guidelines themselves are quite extensive and detailed. To determine the actual sentence, a magistrate must first determine the base penalty that a particular charge is given in the guidelines. Table 12.2 (p. 346) gives the base score (18) and mitigation factors for robbery. The base level can be adjusted upward if the crime was particularly serious or violent. For example, 7 points could be added to the robbery base if a firearm was discharged during the crime, and 5 points if the weapon was simply in the offender's possession. Similarly, points can be added to a robbery if a large amount of money was taken, a victim was injured, a person was abducted or restrained in order to facilitate an escape, or the object of the robbery was to steal weapons or drugs. Upward adjustments can also be made if the defendant was a ringleader in the crime, obstructed justice, or used a professional skill or position of trust (such as doctor, lawyer, or politician) to commit the crime. Offenders designated as "career criminals" by a court can likewise receive longer sentences.

Severity level of conviction offense (common offenses listed in italics)		Criminal history score						
		0	1	2	3	4	5	6 or more
Murder, 2nd degree (intentional murder; drive-by-shootings)	X	306 *299–313*	326 *319–333*	346 *339–353*	366 *359–373*	386 *379–393*	406 *399–413*	426 *419–433*
Murder 3rd degree Murder 2nd degree (unintentional murder)	IX	150 *144–156*	165 *159–171*	180 *174–186*	195 *189–201*	210 *204–216*	225 *219–231*	240 *234–246*
Criminal sexual conduct, 1st degree Assault, 1st degree	VIII	86 *81–91*	98 *93–103*	110 *105–115*	122 *117–127*	134 *129–139*	146 *141–151*	158 *153–163*
Aggravated robbery, 1st degree	VII	48 *44–52*	58 *54–62*	68 *64–72*	78 *74–82*	88 *84–92*	98 *94–102*	108 *104–112*
Criminal sexual conduct, 2nd degree (a) & (b)	VI	21	26	30	34 *33–35*	44 *42–46*	54 *50–58*	65 *60–70*
Residential burglary Simple robbery	V	18	23	27	30 *29–31*	38 *36–40*	46 *43–49*	54 *50–58*
Nonresidential burglary	IV	12¹	15	18	21	25 *24–26*	32 *30–34*	41 *37–45*
Theft crimes (over $2,500)	III	12¹	13	15	17	19 *18–20*	22 *21–23*	25 *24–26*
Theft crimes ($2,500 or less) Check forgery ($200–$2,500)	II	12¹	12¹	13	15	17	19	21 *20–22*
Sale of simulated controlled substance	I	12¹	12¹	12¹	13	15	17	19 *18–20*

Presumptive commitment to state imprisonment. First-degree murder is excluded from the guidelines by law and continues to have a mandatory life sentence.

Presumptive stayed sentence; at the discretion of the judge, up to a year in jail and/or other nonjail sanctions can be imposed as conditions of probation. However, certain offenses in this section of the grid always carry a presumptive commitment to a state prison. These offenses include 3rd degree controlled substance crimes when the offender has a prior felony drug conviction, burglary of an occupied dwelling when the offender has a prior felony burglary conviction, second and subsequent criminal sexual conduct offenses, and offenses carrying a mandatory minimum prison term due to the use of a dangerous weapon (e.g., 2nd degree assault).

¹One year and one day.

Figure 12.2
Sentencing guidelines grid.
Italicized numbers within the grid denote the range of months within which a judge may sentence without the sentence being deemed a departure. Offenders with nonimprisonment felony sentences are subject to jail time according to law.
SOURCE: Minnesota Sentencing Guidelines Commission, 1996.

Once the base score is computed, judges determine the sentence by consulting a sentencing table that converts scores into months to be served. Offense levels are set out in the vertical column, and the criminal history (ranging from one to six prior offenses) is displayed in a horizontal column, forming a grid that contains the various sentencing ranges (similar to the Minnesota guidelines grid). By matching the applicable offense level and the criminal history, the judge can determine the sentence that applies to the particular offender.

Are the Federal Guidelines Useful? Harmful? While decreasing sentencing disparity, the guidelines have had and will continue to have some dubious effects. The federal guidelines have diminished the use of probation. They require incarceration sentences for minor offenders who in preguideline days would have been

Table 12.2

Base Score and Mitigation Factors for Robbery

Source: U.S. Sentencing Commission.

§ 2B3.1. *Robbery*

(a) Base offense level: 18

(b) Specific offense characteristics

(1) If the value of the property taken or destroyed exceeded $2,500, increase the offense level as follows:

Loss	Increase in level
(A) $2,500 or less	no increase
(B) $2,501–$10,000	add 1
(C) $10,001–$50,000	add 2
(D) $50,001–$250,000	add 3
(E) $250,001–$1,000,000	add 4
(F) $1,000,001–$5,000,000	add 5
(G) more than $5,000,000	add 6

Treat the loss for a financial institution or post office as at least $5,000.

(2) (A) If a firearm was discharged increase by 7 levels; (B) if a firearm or a dangerous weapon was otherwise used, increase by 6 levels; (C) if a firearm or other dangerous weapon was brandished, displayed, or possessed, increase by 5 levels.

(3) If any victim sustained bodily injury, increase the offense level according to the seriousness of the injury:

Degree of bodily injury	Increase in level
(A) Bodily injury	add 2
(B) Serious bodily injury	add 4
(C) Permanent or life-threatening bodily injury	add 6

Provided, however, that the cumulative adjustments from (2) and (3) shall not exceed 9 levels.

(4) (A) If any person was abducted to facilitate commission of the offense or to facilitate escape, increase by 4 levels; or (B) if any person was physically restrained to facilitate commission of the offense or to facilitate escape, increase by 2 levels.

(5) If obtaining a firearm, destructive device, or controlled substance was the object of the offense, increase by 1 level.

given community release; many of these petty offenders might be better served with cheaper alternative sanctions.[18]

The size of the federal prison population has increased because guideline sentences are tougher and defendants have little incentive to plea bargain. The prison time added by the federal guidelines is compounded by other statutes increasing penalties for particular crimes, such as drug dealing (the Anti-Drug Abuse Act of 1986), and for career offenders with multiple convictions. The guidelines adjust for these sentencing provisions by giving base scores commensurate with the crime's seriousness; crimes that call for mandatory minimum sentences of at least 10 years are assigned a base score of 32. The amount of time served by offenders will almost double in the future because of the impact of guidelines coupled with sentencing enhancement statutes. For example, robbers who served approximately 45 months before the guidelines were implemented now serve 75; drug offenders will see their sentences increase on average from 23 months to 57 months. These sentencing enhancements will boost the federal prison population by up to 60,000 inmates over preguideline estimates by the year 2002.

Because guidelines control sentence length, they were supposed to reduce any disparity in the sentencing process. Yet the federal guidelines have also been criticized because they punish possession of "crack" cocaine much more heavily than powdered cocaine, when the former is a crime associated with African American offenders and the latter with white offenders.[19]

These problems are not lost on the federal judiciary, many of whom dislike the guidelines, feeling they are too harsh, rigid, and mechanical. Some judges believe that the guidelines give too much power to prosecutors who make the charging decision. The judges may even engage in "hidden" plea bargaining to manipulate the guidelines and allow offenders to plead to a lesser charge that they and the prosecutor believe is more fair. Because of these problems, sentencing expert Michael Tonry calls the guidelines "the most controversial and disliked sentencing reform initiative in United States history."[20]

The Future of Guidelines. There has been support for structured sentencing. The U.S. Supreme Court has ruled that these sentences do not violate the constitutional rights of defendants and are therefore a valid exercise of justice.[21] State guidelines have received praise from sentencing experts. Michael Tonry found that the Minnesota guidelines helped conserve state resources, were resistant to political pressures, and increased overall fairness in the sentencing system.[22] While at first it was feared that guidelines would dramatically increase prison populations, there is little evidence that this has occurred, and in at least two states that use guidelines, Minnesota and Washington, prison populations have been reduced.[23] There is also evidence that the Minnesota guidelines effectively reduced the effect nonlegal variables have on the length of sentences.[24]

Despite the widespread acceptance of guidelines, some nagging problems remain. Research indicates that judges diverge from sentences established by the guidelines.[25] There are also instances where legislators have backtracked on guidelines, creating loopholes that undercut their determinacy, such as allowing for early release from prison by administrative order.[26]

Others suggest that race and economic status continue to influence sentencing.[27] Guidelines that provide long sentences for some drug offenses, such as possession of crack cocaine, almost invariably result in disparate sentences for African Americans.[28]

Some defense attorneys oppose the use of guidelines because they result in longer prison terms, prevent judges from considering mitigating circumstances, and reduce the use of probation.[29]

Despite initial success, the guideline "movement" has not taken off. Although it was predicted that that most states would have adopted structured sentencing by now, the majority have resisted such radical change. And some guideline states, such as Pennsylvania, are proposing overhauling their guidelines because of their effect on prison crowding.[30] While a get-tough approach makes good political sense to gain votes, getting taxpayers to foot the bill is extremely difficult. The ultimate test of guideline or any other determinate sentencing model is whether it can ease crime rates, and so far there is little evidence that these laws can alone reduce the incidence of crime.[31]

In his important book *Sentencing Matters,* Michael Tonry offers a prescription to improve structured sentencing guidelines, calling in part for the creation of ongoing sentencing commissions, creation of realistic guidelines, reliance on alternative sanctions, and a sentencing philosophy that stresses the "least punitive and intrusive appropriate sentence."[32]

Mandatory Sentences

Another effort to limit judicial discretion and at the same time "get tough" on crime has been the development of the **mandatory sentence.** Some states, for example, prohibit people convicted of certain offenses, such as violent crimes, and multiple offenders (recidivists) from being placed on probation; they must serve at least some time in prison. Other statutes bar certain offenders from being considered for parole. Mandatory sentencing legislation may impose minimum and maximum terms, but typically it requires a fixed prison sentence.

Mandatory sentencing generally limits the judge's discretionary power to impose any disposition but that authorized by the legislature; as a result, it limits individualized sentencing and restricts sentencing disparity. Mandatory sentencing

Three Strikes and You're Out!

Public concern over crime has convinced lawmakers to toughen sentences for repeat offenders. One new group of laws mandates lengthy periods of incarceration for repeat offenders, which in some cases can mean a life sentence for a minor felony. The new "three strikes and you're out" laws provide these lengthy terms for any person convicted of three felony offenses, even if the third crime is relatively trivial. California's statute "three strike" law is aimed at getting habitual criminals off the street. Anyone convicted of a third serious felony must do a minimum term of 25 years to life; the third felony does not have to be serious or violent. The Federal Crime Bill of 1994 also adopted a three-strikes provision, requiring a mandatory life sentence for any offender convicted of three felony offenses; 22 states have so far followed suit and passed some form of the three-strikes law.

While welcomed by conservatives looking for a remedy for violent crime, the three-strikes policy is quite controversial because it can mean that a person convicted of a minor felony can receive a life sentence. There are reports that some judges are defying three-strikes provisions because they consider them unduly harsh. Much to the chagrin of three-strikes advocates, a recent California court decision, *People v. Romero*, allows judges to disregard an earlier conviction if the judge believes a life term is unjustified.

Three-strikes laws may in fact help put some chronic offenders behind bars, but can they realistically be expected to lower the crime rate? Marc Mauer of the Sentencing Project, a private group that conducts research on justice-related issues, finds that the three-strikes approach may satisfy the public's hunger for retribution but makes little practical sense. First, "three-time losers" are at the brink of aging out of crime; locking them up for life should have little effect on the crime rate. Second, current sentences for chronic violent offenders are already quite severe, yet their punishment seems to have had little influence on reducing national violence rates. Mauer also suggests that a three-strikes policy will enlarge an already overburdened prison system, driving up costs and, presumably, reducing resources available to house non-three-strikes inmates. Mauer also warns that African Americans face an increased risk of being sentenced under three-strikes statutes, expanding the racial disparity in sentencing. More ominous is the fact that police officers may be put at risk because two-time offenders would violently resist arrest, knowing that they face a life sentence.

Costs Are High

Three-strikes laws have undeniable political appeal to legislators being pressured by their constituents to "do something about crime." Yet even if possibly effective against crime, any effort to deter criminal behavior through tough laws is not without costs. A study by the Rand Corporation, a California-based think tank, concluded that the state's three-strikes law may actually reduce serious felonies between 22% and 34%. However, the price of this reduction is an extra $4.5 to $6.5 billion per year in correctional costs in California

provides equal treatment for all offenders who commit the same crime, regardless of age, sex, or other individual characteristics.

More than 35 states have already replaced discretionary sentencing with fixed-term mandatory sentences for such crimes as the sale of hard drugs, kidnapping, gun possession, and arson. The results have been mixed. Mandatory sentences have helped increase the size of the correctional population to record levels. They have also failed to eliminate racial disparity from the sentencing process.[33] Some state courts have ruled such practices unconstitutional. A survey conducted for the American Bar Association found that judges are unhappy with such laws because they are unfair to first-time offenders and limit judicial discretion.[34] As a result many offenders who in the past might have received probation are now being incarcerated. For example, in 1994 a federal survey found that 21% of all federal prison inmates were "low level" drug offenders alone. To put that in perspective, just the *additional* cost of the three-strikes policy would be sufficient to give more than *1 million* students a full-tuition scholarship to the state university system!

While many states have passed three-strikes laws, most have rarely invoked the penalty. California is one of the few to have used it with thousands of offenders, and while many of these have committed serious crimes, as of 1996, 192 people had been sentenced to life for possession of marijuana. Because of its use with petty offenders, there are ongoing legal challenges to the use of three-strikes laws, and their future is still uncertain.

Can Three Strikes Work?

While California officials attribute reduced crime rates to its three-strikes policy, others are skeptical about the approach. The Rand researchers argue that an alternative scheme would be to guarantee a full term in prison for serious felons without the possibility of probation, parole, or time off for good behavior. Their research shows that a guaranteed full-term policy would achieve the same benefits at a much lower cost.

As Mark Mauer points out, "Three-strikes policies tend to incarcerate people at the tail end of their offending career, at a point when they may be on the verge of spontaneously 'aging out' of crime." A three-strikes policy also suffers because criminals typically underestimate their risk of apprehension while overestimating the rewards of crime. Given their inflated view of the benefits of crime, coupled with a seeming disregard of the risks of apprehension and punishment, it is unlikely a three-strikes policy can have a measurable deterrent effect on the crime rate. And even if such a policy could reduce the number of career offenders on the street, the drain in economic resources that might have gone for education and social welfare ensures that a new generation of young criminals will fill the offending shoes of their incarcerated brethren.

Critical Thinking Questions

1. Is a policy that calls for spending billions on incarceration throwing money into the wind? After all, the number of people in prison already exceeds 1 million, and there is little conclusive evidence that incarceration alone can reduce crime rates. Might the funds earmarked for prison construction be used elsewhere with greater effect?

2. A large portion of the prison population consists of drug offenders, and this group has had the greatest overall increase during the past decade. While the number of people incarcerated for violent and property crimes has actually decreased in recent years, the number of incarcerated drug offenders has skyrocketed. Are the nation's interests best served by giving a life sentence to someone convicted of their third drug trafficking charge, even if the crime involves selling a small amount of cocaine?

SOURCES: "California Supreme Court Undercuts Three-Strikes Law," *Criminal Justice Newsletter*, 1 July 1996, p. 2; "Three-Strikes Laws Rarely Used, Except California's, Study Finds," *Criminal Justice Newsletter*, 17 September 1996, p. 4; "California Passes a Tough Three-Strikes-You're-Out Law," *Criminal Justice Newsletter*, 4 April 1993, p. 6; Rand Research Brief, *California's New Three-Strikes Law: Benefits, Costs and Alternatives* (Santa Monica, Calif.: Rand Corp., 1994); Marc Mauer, testimony before the U.S. Congress House Judiciary Committee on "Three Strikes and You're Out," 1 March 1994 (Washington, D.C.: The Sentencing Project, 1994); Lois Forer, *A Rage to Punish: The Unintended Consequences of Mandatory Sentencing* (New York: Norton, 1994).

with no involvement in sophisticated criminal enterprise and no prior prison record who had been sentenced under mandatory sentencing statutes. These nonviolent offenders will average 6 years in prison at a cost to taxpayers of over $20,000 per year before they are released.[35]

Another type of mandatory sentence is designed for chronic, multiple, or career criminals. Habitual offender statutes can be found in the criminal codes of most states. They are employed at the discretion of the prosecutor when an offender is found to have been convicted for previous felony offenses. If found guilty when charged as a habitual felon, the defendant is given a long prison sentence, sometimes life in prison without hope of parole. For example, California passed a "three strikes and you're out" type of law aimed at getting habitual criminals off the street. Anyone convicted of a third serious felony must do a minimum term of 25 years to life; the third felony does not have to be serious or violent.[36] Habitual

Police take serial killer Joel Rifkin into custody. Fear of such predatory criminals has prompted legislators to enact tough new sentencing laws.

offender statutes are aimed at career criminals and represent the dominance of the conservative incapacitation philosophy in the nation's sentencing policies. The Analyzing Criminal Issues box on page 348 discusses these laws.

The Analyzing Criminal Issues box on page 348 discusses these laws.

How People Are Sentenced

What sentences do people actually receive for their criminal behavior? A recent analysis of sentencing practices using data from 300 jurisdictions around the United States found that the likelihood of going to prison on conviction for crime has been relatively stable since the mid-1980s. The one exception is drug trafficking: The likelihood of being incarcerated is about 20 % higher today than it was in 1988.

As Table 12.3 shows, many people convicted of serious felonies do not receive incarceration sentences (about 29 % of all convicted felons receive probation only). For example, of 12,000 murder convictions in 1994, 3 % of offenders received a sentence of community supervision. This means that about 360 people convicted of killing another person received no prison or jail time at all. Similarly, of the 20,000 people convicted of rape, 12 % or 2,400 offenders, totally avoided an incarceration sentence.[37] How could such serious offenders avoid prison or jail? Most likely they cooperated with the prosecution and were willing to testify against other people.

Other key findings from the national sentencing survey include:

- In 1994 the mean length of sentences to state prison was almost 6 years; the median term was 4 years.

Table 12.3
The Likelihood of Getting an Incarceration Sentence
SOURCE: Patrick A. Langan and Jodi M. Brown, *Felony Sentences in State Courts, 1994* (Washington, D.C.: Bureau of Justice Statistics, 1997).

Offenses	Convicted Felons Who Received a Prison Sentence (%)				Probation-Only Sentences (1994)
	1988	*1990*	*1992*	*1994*	
All offenses	44	46	44	45	29
Murder	91	91	93	95	3
Rape	69	67	68	71	12
Robbery	75	73	74	77	12
Aggravated assault	45	45	44	48	25
Burglary	54	54	52	53	25
Larceny	39	40	38	38	34
Drug trafficking	41	49	48	48	29

- Felons sentenced to a state prison in 1994 had an average sentence of 6 years but were likely to serve roughly a third of that sentence—or about 2 years—before release.

- The average sentence to local jail was 6 months. The average probation sentence was just over 3 years. In addition, a fine was imposed on 21% of convicted felons, restitution on 18%, and community service on 7%; treatment was ordered for 7%.

- Of the total number of convicted felons in 1994, 89% had pleaded guilty to their crime. The remaining 11% had been found guilty at trial.

- Nationally, of the felons convicted in 1994, 51% were white, 48% were black, and 1% were of other races.

Extralegal Factors in Sentencing

One suspected cause of sentencing disparity is the consideration of age, race, gender, and economic factors when sentencing decisions are made. Considerations of such variables would be a direct violation of constitutional due process and equal protection, as well as of federal statutes, such as the Civil Rights Act. Limiting judicial bias is one of the reasons that states have adopted determinate and mandatory sentencing statutes. Do extralegal factors actually influence judges when they make sentencing decisions?

Social Class. Evidence supports an association between social class and sentencing outcomes: Members of the lower class may expect to get longer prison sentences than more affluent defendants. Not all research efforts have found a consistent class-crime relationship, however, and the relationship may be more robust for violent and victimless crimes than for property offenses.[38] Where economic status has been found to be related to sentence length, the relationship has been influenced by the inability of poor defendants to obtain quality legal representation and to make bail and their reluctance to plea bargain.[39]

Gender. Does a defendant's gender influence how he or she is sentenced? Some theorists believe females benefit from sentence disparity because the criminal justice system is dominated by males who have a paternalistic or protective attitude toward women; this is referred to as the **chivalry hypothesis.** Others argue that female criminals can be the victim of bias because their behavior violates what males believe is "proper" female behavior.[40]

Women are less likely to receive incarceration sentences than men. One national survey of sentencing practices in 300 counties found that while 74% of convicted males were incarcerated, only 57% of women were similarly punished.

Most research indicates that women receive more favorable outcomes the farther they go in the criminal justice system: They are more likely to receive prefer-

Susan Smith, shown here in a detention facility, received life in prison rather than the death penalty after being convicted of killing her two young sons. Was her sentence an example of the "chivalry hypothesis"?

making the arrest or the prosecutor seeking the indictment.[41] Gender bias may be present because judges perceive women as better risks than men. Females have been granted more lenient pretrial release conditions and lower bail amounts than males; women are also more likely to spend less time in pretrial detention.[42]

Age. Another extralegal factor that may play a role in sentencing is age. Judges may be more lenient with elderly defendants and more punitive toward younger ones.[43] While sentencing leniency may be a result of judges' perception that the elderly pose little risk to society, such practices are a violation of the civil rights of younger defendants. On the other hand, they may also wish to protect the youngest defendants, sparing them the pains of a prison experience.

Research by Darrell Steffensmeier and his associates found that in fact judges often give the oldest and youngest offenders a break on their prison sentence while imposing the harshest terms on those ages 21–29.[44]

Victim Statements. Sentencing can also involve **victim impact statements,** which are made in court after conviction and allow those affected by the crime to tell of their experiences. The victims can describe their ordeal, and in the case of a murder trial the surviving family can recount the effect the crime has had on their lives and well-being.[45] The effect of witness statements on sentencing has been the topic of some debate: Do they cause offenders to be sentenced on the basis of the victims' ability to express their pain and suffering and on the judge's sympathy for them? In homicide cases, are offenders whose victims have surviving families more likely to be punished than those whose victims are family-less? Research to test these issues has been inconclusive. Edna Erez and Pamela Tontodonato found that victim statements result in a higher rate of incarceration; in contrast, Robert Davis and Barbara Smith found that the effect of witness statements is insignificant.[46]

Race. No issue concerning sentencing is more important than the suspicion that race influences sentencing outcomes. Racial disparity in sentencing has been suspected because a disproportionate number of African American inmates are in state prisons and on death row. Research efforts show that black defendants suffer discrimination in a variety of court actions: They are more likely to be detained before trial than whites and, on conviction, are more likely to receive jail sentences than fines.[47] Prosecutors are less likely to divert African Americans from the legal system than whites who commit the same crimes; further, African Americans are less likely to win *appeals* than white appellants.[48] If African Americans suffer discrimination in these decisions, why not sentencing?

While such findings are disturbing, research on sentencing has in fact failed to show a definitive pattern of racial discrimination. Some studies do indicate that a defendant's race has a direct impact on sentencing outcomes, while others fail to show that racial disparity controls the application of criminal punishments. For example, Stephen Klein, Joan Petersilia, and Susan Turner found that after relevant legal factors were considered, race had little effect on sentencing outcomes.[49] Another national survey of sentencing in state courts shows that African Americans receive somewhat longer sentences than whites; nonetheless, the average difference was only about five months, far less than what critics of the sentencing process would expect.[50]

In contrast, a recent extensive analysis of sentencing in 300 jurisdictions conducted by the federal government's Bureau of Justice Statistics indicates that more African Americans are sent to prison (54%) than whites (42%) and that African Americans have a greater chance than whites of being incarcerated for violent, property, and drug crimes.[51]

As these studies suggest, the actual impact of race on sentencing decisions is often ambiguous: Some studies find a racial effect, others do not.[52] One reason is that the association between race and sentencing may not be constant and unidirectional—that is, African American defendants may be punished more severely for some crimes, while in other circumstances they are treated more leniently.[53] For example, when James Nelson studied misdemeanant sentencing in New York State, he found that African Americans were given more lenient sentences than whites if they had no prior arrest record; in contrast, African Americans with a prior arrest record received harsher sentences than whites with similar criminal backgrounds.[54] Some jurisdictions, then, may exhibit little racial bias while others demonstrate a great deal. Studies that combine data from multiple courts and jurisdictions in their analysis may therefore miss the effects of race on sentencing. [55]

In a thorough review of sentencing disparity, Samuel Walker, Cassia Spohn, and Miriam DeLone identified what they call **contextual discrimination.** This term refers to the practices of judges in some jurisdictions to impose harsher sentences on some African Americans, such as those who victimize whites. These judges may also give racial minorities prison sentences in "borderline" cases for which whites get probation.[56] According to these researchers, racism is subtle and hard to detect but still exerts an influence in the court setting.

It is also possible that sentencing disparity may be related to economic and legal factors and not judicial bias and discrimination. For example, the greatest percentage of the African American population lives in the South, where prison sentences tend to be highest for all races.[57] There is also evidence that the association between race and legal factors, such as plea bargaining, crime seriousness, prior record, and use of a weapon, all help explain interracial sentencing disparity.[58] Probation presentence reports may favor white over black defendants, causing judges to award whites probation more often than African Americans. Defendants who can afford bail receive more lenient sentences than those who remain in pretrial detention; black defendants are less likely to make bail because they suffer a higher degree of poverty. Sentencing outcome is also affected by the defendant's ability to afford a private attorney and put on a vigorous legal defense that makes use of high-paid expert witnesses. These factors place the poor and minority-group members at a disadvantage in the sentencing process and result in sentencing disparity.[59] And while considerations of prior record may be legitimate in forming sentencing decisions, there is evidence that African Americans are more likely to have prior records because of organizational and individual bias on the part of police.[60]

In sum, the evidence seems to show that whereas judicial bias may have been an important factor in the past, its direct influence on sentencing has decreased and flagrant racism has been eliminated. Nonetheless, race still affects sentencing outcomes. New forms of sentencing such as guidelines may also have helped curtail discrimination.[61]

The Future of Sentencing

Because of the lingering problem of racial and class bias in the sentencing process, one primary goal of the criminal justice system in the 1990s has been to reduce disparity by creating new forms of criminal sentences that limit judicial discretion and are aimed at uniformity and fairness. Efforts are now being made to limit the ability of correctional authorities to grant inmates early release from prison. The three-strikes laws are an example of a sentencing provision that limits discretion. In addition, "truth in sentencing laws," such as one recently adopted in Virginia, reduce defendants' ability to circumvent sentences through early release from prison. Virginia's law demands that offenders serve a large percentage of their sentence behind bars (85%) without the option of parole. This get-tough approach will double Virginia's prison population within ten years.[62]

While crime control advocates applaud these efforts, critics fear that they will swell prison populations, costing taxpayers billions in extra dollars and taking money away from more important public needs, such as health care and education. Others fear that these sentencing policies will further exacerbate racial disparity in the prison population. Mandatory minimum sentences for drug crimes have resulted in a significant portion (more than 30%) of all minority males ages 20–29 being under some form of correctional care today.[63] The war on drugs has been centered in African American communities, and politically motivated punitive sentencing policies aimed at crack cocaine have had a devastating effect on young African American men. If, charges Michael Tonry, such punitive measures are allowed to continue or are even expanded, an entire cohort of young African Americans may be placed in jeopardy.[64]

Capital Punishment

The most severe sentence used in our nation is capital punishment, or execution. More than 14,500 confirmed executions have been carried out in America under civil authority, starting with the execution of Captain George Kendall in 1608. Most of these executions were for murder and rape. However, federal, state, and military laws have conferred the death penalty for other crimes, including robbery, kidnapping, treason (offenses against the federal government), espionage, and desertion from military service.

In recent years, the Supreme Court has limited the death penalty to first-degree murder and only then when aggravating circumstances, such as murder for profit or murder using extreme cruelty, are present.[65] The federal government still has provisions for granting the death penalty for espionage by a member of the armed forces, treason, and killing during a criminal conspiracy, such as drug trafficking. Some states continue to have laws on their books that provide capital punishment for such crimes as aircraft piracy, ransom kidnapping, and the aggravated rape of a child, but it remains to be seen whether the courts will allow criminals to be executed today for any crime less than aggravated first-degree murder.

Today, the death penalty for murder is used in 38 states and by the federal government with the approval of about 75% of the population. After many years of abolition, New York reinstated the use of the death penalty in 1995 and expanded its use to cover numerous acts, including serial murder, contract killing, and the use of torture.[66] There are currently more than 3,000 people on death row. Between 50 and 60 people are now executed each year, most having served 10 years on death row before their execution.[67] As of 1996, lethal injection was the predominant method of execution (32 states); 11 states used electrocution; 7 states, lethal gas; 4 states, hanging; and 3 states, a firing squad. In 16 states more than one method—lethal injection and an alternative method—is used, generally at the election of the condemned prisoner, although 5 of these 16 stipulate which method must be used, depending on the date of sentencing, 1 authorizes hanging only if lethal injection cannot be given, and—if lethal injection is ever ruled unconstitutional—1 authorizes lethal gas and 1 authorizes electrocution.[68]

No issue in the criminal justice system is more controversial or emotional than the implementation of the death penalty. Opponents and proponents have formulated a number of powerful arguments in support of their positions; these arguments are reviewed in the following sections.

Let's look at some of the most common arguments for retaining the death penalty in the United States.

Arguments for the Death Penalty

Incapacitation. Supporters argue that death is the "ultimate incapacitation" and the only one that can ensure that convicted killers can never be pardoned or paroled or escape. Most states that do not have capital punishment provide the sentence of "life in prison without the chance of parole." However, 48 states grant their chief executive the right to grant clemency and commute a life sentence and may give "lifers" eligibility for various furlough and release programs.

Death penalty advocates believe that the potential for recidivism is a serious enough threat to require that murderers be denied further access to the public. Stephen Markman and Paul Cassell analyzed the records of 52,000 state prison inmates serving time for murder and found that 810 had previously been convicted of homicide and that these recidivists had killed 821 people following their first convictions.[69] More than 250 inmates on death row today had prior homicide convictions; if they had been executed for their first offense, close to 250 innocent people would still be alive.[70]

Deterrent. Proponents of capital punishment argue that executions serve as a strong deterrent for serious crimes. While capital punishment could probably not deter the few mentally unstable criminals, it could have an effect on the cold, calculating murderer, such as the hired killer or someone who kills for profit; the fear of death may convince felons not to risk using handguns during armed robberies. The deterrent effect of an execution can produce a substantial decline in the murder rate.[71]

Morally Correct. Advocates of capital punishment justify its use on the grounds that it is morally correct because it is mentioned in the Bible and other religious works. While the Constitution forbids "cruel and unusual punishments," this prohibition could not include the death penalty since capital punishment was widely used at the time the Constitution was drafted. The "original intent" of the Founding Fathers was to allow the states to use the death penalty; capital punishment may be cruel, but it is not unusual.

The death penalty is "morally correct" because it provides the greatest justice for the victim and helps alleviate the psychic pain of the victim's family and friends. It has even been accepted by criminal justice experts who consider themselves "humanists," concerned with the value and dignity of human beings. As David Friedrichs, a noted humanist argues, a civilized society has no choice but to hold responsible those who commit horrendous crimes. The implementation of the death penalty provides the greatest justice for the victim and helps alleviate the psychic pain of the victim's family and friends. The death penalty makes a moral statement: there is behavior that is so unacceptable to a community of human beings that one who engages in such behavior forfeits his or her right to live.[72]

Proportional. Putting dangerous criminals to death also conforms to the requirement that the punishment must be proportional to the seriousness of the crime. Since we use a system of escalating punishments, it follows that the most serious punishment should be used to sanction the most serious crime. And before the brutality of the death penalty is considered, the cruelty with which the victim was treated should not be forgotten.

Reflects Public Opinion. Those who favor capital punishment charge that a majority of the public believes that criminals who kill innocent victims should forfeit their own lives. Recent public opinion polls show that up to 80% of the public favors the death penalty, almost double the percentage of 20 years ago.[73] Public approval is based on the rational belief that the death penalty is an important instrument of social control, can deter crime, and is less costly than maintaining a murderer in prison for his or her life.[74] A recent research study by Alexis Durham and his associates found that the 80% approval rating may actually be low, that almost everyone (95%) would give criminals the death penalty under some circumstances, and the most heinous crimes are those for which the public is most likely to approve capital punishment.[75]

Unlikely Chance of Error. The many legal controls and appeals currently in use make it almost impossible for an innocent person to be executed or for the death penalty to be used in a racist or capricious manner. While some unfortunate mistakes may have been made in the past, the current system makes it virtually impossible to execute an innocent person. Federal courts closely scrutinize all death penalty cases and rule for the defendant in an estimated 60%–70% of the appeals. Such judicial care should ensure that only those who are both truly guilty and deserving of death are executed.

In sum, those who favor the death penalty find it to be traditional punishment for serious crimes, one that can help prevent criminality, is in keeping with the traditional moral values of fairness and equity, and is highly favored by the public.

Arguments Against the Death Penalty

Arguments for the death penalty are matched by those that support its abolition.

Possibility of Error. Critics of the death penalty believe capital punishment has no place in a mature democratic society.[76] They point to the finality of the act and the real possibility that innocent persons can be executed. Examples of people wrongfully convicted of murder abound. Critics point to miscarriages of justice such as the case of Rolando Cruz and Alejandro Hernandez who, wrongfully convicted of murder, were released in 1995 after spending more than a decade on death row in the Illinois prison system; three former prosecutors and four deputy sheriffs who worked on the case were charged with fabricating evidence against the pair.[77] Their wrongful conviction would have been even more tragic if they had been executed for their crimes. A congressional report cited 48 cases in the past two decades in which people who served time on death row were released because of evidence of their innocence; one Maryland man served 9 years on death row before DNA testing proved that he could not have committed the crime.[78] These findings show that even with the best intentions there is grave risk that an innocent person can be executed.[79]

According to research by Michael Radelet and Hugo Bedeau, there have been about 350 wrongful murder convictions this century, of which 23 led to executions. They estimate that about three death sentences are returned every two years in cases where the defendant has been falsely accused. More than half the errors stem from perjured testimony, false identifications, coerced confessions, and suppression of evidence. In addition to the 23 who were executed, 128 of the falsely convicted served more than 6 years in prison; 39 served more than 16 years in confinement; and 8 died while serving their sentence.[80] It is their view that even though the system attempts to be especially cautious in capital cases, unacceptable mistakes can occur. And while there is careful review of death

Opponents of the death penalty argue that there is a significant chance of executing an innocent person. Here Missouri inmate Lloyd Schlup is seen conferring with his lawyer, Sean O'Brien. Schlup, who had been condemned to death for a prison murder, had presented a late claim of innocence, partially based on a video that showed him in another location at the time of the incident. Many witnesses claimed he was in the cafeteria at the time a fellow inmate was stabbed; nonetheless, he was sentenced to death. Schlup narrowly avoided execution in 1994 when the U.S. Supreme Court reversed its rigid standard on late claims of innocence and remanded the case for an evidentiary hearing. In an earlier Texas case, the Court let the execution proceed, saying that claims of "actual innocence" belong before a clemency board, not in the courts. A Missouri judge granted Schlup a new trial on May 2, 1997.

penalty sentences relatively few stays of execution are actually granted (about 2 out of 50); obviously there is room for judicial error.[81]

Unfair Use of Discretion. Critics also frown on the tremendous discretion used in seeking the death penalty and the arbitrary manner in which it is imposed. Of the approximately 10,000 persons convicted each year on homicide charges, only 250 to 300 are sentenced to death, while an equal number receive a sentence of probation or community supervision only.[82] While it is true that many convicted murderers do not commit first-degree murder and therefore are ineligible for execution, it is also likely that many serious criminals who could have received the death penalty are not sentenced to death because of prosecutorial discretion. Some escape death by cooperating or giving testimony against their partners in the crime. A person who commits a particularly heinous crime and knows full well that he will receive the death penalty if convicted may be the one most likely to plea bargain to avoid capital punishment. Is it fair to spare the life of a dangerous killer who cooperates with the prosecutor while executing another who does not?

Vicious Criminals Often Go Free. Some vicious criminals who grievously injure victims during murder attempts are spared death because of a physician's skill. Some notable cases come to mind. Lawrence Singleton used an axe to cut off the arms of a woman he raped, yet he served only 8 years in prison because the victim's life was saved by prompt medical care (after being released from prison, Singleton killed a female companion in 1997). "David," a boy severely burned in a murder attempt, lives in fear because his assailant, his father, Charles Rothenberg, was paroled from prison after serving a short sentence.[83] Although these horrific crimes received national attention and the intent to kill the victim was present, the death penalty could not be applied because of the availability of effective medical treatment. Research shows that areas that have superior medical resources actually have lower murder rates than less well-equipped areas; for example, ambulance response time can reduce the death rate by expeditiously transporting victims to an appropriate treatment center.[84] It makes little sense to punish someone for an impulsive murder while sparing the life of those who intentionally maim and torture victims who happen by chance to live because of prompt medical care.

Misplaced Vengeance. While critics acknowledge that the use of the death penalty is approved by the general public, they maintain that prevailing attitudes reflect a primitive desire for revenge and not "just desert." Public acceptance of capital punishment has been compared to the approval of human sacrifices practiced by the Aztecs in Mexico 500 years ago.[85] Even if the majority of the general public favors the death penalty, support has been associated with prejudice against racial minorities and the approval of revenge as a rationale for punishment.[86] Public support is not as strong as death penalty advocates believe: When surveys ask about a *choice of punishments,* such as life without parole, support for the death penalty declines from 80% to 50%.[87]

Marla Sandys and Edmund McGarrell show that legislators in a death penalty state (Indiana) are swayed by their perception of their constituents' attitudes; most of the officials surveyed do not personally favor capital punishment.[88] Should the taking of life be a function of political expedience and public opinion polls? The Supreme Court's justification of the death penalty on the basis that it reflects public opinion should be reassessed.[89] The Media box on *Dead Man Walking* focuses on the efforts of a crusading nun who believes that capital punishment is truly "misplaced vengeance."

No Deterrent Effect. Those opposed to the death penalty also find little merit in the argument that capital punishment deters crime. They charge that insufficient evidence exists that the threat of a death sentence can convince potential murderers to forgo their criminal activity. Most murders involve people who knew each other, very often friends and family members. Since murderers are often under the influence of alcohol or drugs or are suffering severe psychological turmoil, no penalty will likely be a deterrent. Most research concludes that the death penalty is not an effective deterrent.[90]

Hope of Rehabilitation. The death sentence also rules out any hope of offender rehabilitation. There is evidence that convicted killers actually make good parole risks; convicted murderers are actually model inmates and, once released, commit fewer crimes than other parolees.

Racial Bias. One of the most compelling arguments against the use of the death penalty is that it is employed in a racially discriminatory fashion. Since the death penalty was first instituted in the United States, a disproportionate number of minorities have been executed. Charges of racial bias are supported by the disproportionate numbers of blacks who have received the death sentence, are currently on death row, and who have been executed (53.5% of all executions). Racism was particularly blatant when the death penalty was invoked in rape cases: 90% of those receiving death for rape in the South and 63% of those in the North and West were black.[91] Today, about 40% of the inmates on death row are black, a number disproportionate to the minority representation in the population.

White criminals arrested for homicide actually have a slightly greater chance of getting the death penalty than blacks do, and a majority of murderers executed since 1980 have also been white.[92] Does this statistical anomaly mean that discrimination in the use of the death penalty has either ended or that it never actually existed? The answer may be that simply calculating the relative propor-

Dead Man Walking

Hollywood has produced a long line of anti–death penalty films, ranging from the 1958 *I Want to Live* with Susan Hayward (who received the Oscar for best actress for her efforts portraying a woman sent to the gas chamber) to *In Cold Blood,* a 1967 film based on Truman Capote's powerful account of the capture and execution of two drifters (Perry Smith and Dick Hicock) who had killed a family in Holcomb, Kansas during a botched burglary. More recent efforts include *The Chamber* (based on the John Grisham novel) and *Last Dance,* starring Sharon Stone as Cindy Ligget, a death row inmate denied a pardon despite the feverish efforts of her idealistic attorney, Rick Hayes (Rob Morrow).

Dead Man Walking tells the story of the unusual relationship between Sister Helen Prejean (Susan Sarandon) and Matthew Poncelet (Sean Penn), a condemned killer of two teenagers. When the date is set for his execution, Matthew asks Sister Helen to be his spiritual adviser, and she complies. During their meetings, Sister Helen learns that beneath Matthew's "tough guy" exterior is a terrified human being. At first he denies his

guilt, but with her guidance he learns to come to terms with his culpability and admit his role in the gruesome murders. Sister Helen helps Matthew cope with his guilt, his family's pain, and the rage of the victims' families, who seek retribution for their terrible loss.

To its credit, the film does not try to gloss over the pain caused by a sympathetic character who waits on death row. Sister Helen is less concerned with trying to sway the government to reconsider the death penalty than with helping a confused and angry man find dignity, understanding, and sufficient courage to face his final ordeal.

Like other anti–death penalty films, *Dead Man Walking* encourages the audience to sympathize with the condemned criminal. By the time Matthew Poncelet is executed, he has grown and matured. The demons that drove him to commit crime have been exorcised; there seems to be little point in carrying out the execution. *Dead Man Walking* makes a powerful statement against the death penalty and is a chilling account of the tragedy that violent crime visits upon not only the victim but society as a whole.

tion of each racial group sentenced to death may not tell the whole story. A number of researchers have found that the death penalty is associated with the race of the *victim* rather than the race of the offender. In most instances, prosecutors are more likely to ask for the death penalty if the victim was white. The fact that most murders involving a white victim also involve a white attacker (86%) accounts for the higher death sentence rate for white murderers.[93] With few exceptions, the relatively infrequent interracial murder cases involving a black criminal and a white victim (14%) are the most likely to result in the death penalty.[94] In contrast, since 1976 only two white criminals have been executed for murdering a black victim, the most recent being Kermit Smith, who was executed on January 24, 1995 in North Carolina for the kidnap, rape, and murder of a 20-year-old college cheerleader.[95]

Brutality. Abolitionists believe that executions are unnecessarily cruel and inhuman and come at a high moral and social cost. Our society does not punish criminals by subjecting them to the same acts they themselves committed. Rapists are not sexually assaulted, and arsonists do not have their house burned down; why, then, should murderers be killed?

Robert Johnson has described the execution process as a form of torture in which the condemned are first tormented psychologically by being made to feel powerless and alone while on death row; suicide is a constant problem among those on death row.[96] The execution itself is a barbaric affair marked by the smell of burning flesh and stiffened bodies. The executioners suffer from delayed stress reactions, including anxiety and a dehumanized personal identity.

The brutality of the death penalty may actually produce more violence than it prevents—the so-called **brutalization effect.**[97] Executions may increase murder rates because they raise the general violence level in society and because violence-prone people actually identify with the executioner, not with the target of the death penalty. When someone gets in a conflict with such individuals or challenges their authority, they execute them in the same manner the state executes people who violates its rules.[98] The brutalization effect was recently encountered by John Cochran, Mitchell Chamlin, and Mark Seth when they studied the influence of a well-publicized execution in Oklahoma: After the execution, murders of strangers actually increased by one per month.[99]

Because of its brutality, many enlightened nations have abandoned the death penalty with few ill effects. Abolitionists point out that such nations as Denmark and Sweden have long abandoned the death penalty and that 40% of the countries with a death penalty have active abolitionist movements.[100]

Expense. Some people complain that they do not want to support "some killer in prison for 30 years." Abolitionists counter that legal appeals drive the cost of executions far higher than years in prison. If the money spent on the judicial process were invested, the interest would more than pay for the lifetime upkeep of death row inmates. At least 30 states now have a sentence of life in prison without parole, and this can more than make up for an execution. Being locked up in a hellish prison without any chance of release (barring a rare executive reprieve) may be a worse punishment than a painless death by lethal injection. If vengeance is the goal, life without parole may eliminate the need for capital punishment. The various arguments for and against capital punishment are summarized in Figure 12.3.

The Law of Capital Punishment

In recent years, the constitutionality of the death penalty has been a major concern to both the nation's courts and its concerned social scientists. In 1972, the Supreme Court in *Furman v. Georgia*[101] decided that the discretionary imposition of the death penalty was cruel and unusual punishment under the Eighth and Fourteenth Amendments of the Constitution. This case not only questioned whether capital punishment is a more effective deterrent than life imprisonment but also challenged the very existence of the death penalty on the grounds of its brutality and finality. The Court did not completely rule out the use of capital punishment as a penalty; rather, it objected to the arbitrary and capricious manner in which it was imposed. After *Furman,* many states changed statutes that had allowed jury discretion in imposing the death penalty.

In some states, this was accomplished by enacting statutory guidelines for jury decisions; in others, the death penalty was made mandatory for certain crimes only. Despite these changes in statutory law, no further executions were carried out while the Supreme Court pondered additional cases concerning the death penalty.

Figure 12.3
Arguments about the death penalty.

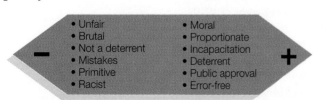

- Unfair
- Brutal
- Not a deterrent
- Mistakes
- Primitive
- Racist

- Moral
- Proportionate
- Incapacitation
- Deterrent
- Public approval
- Error-free

Then, in July 1976, the Supreme Court ruled on the constitutionality of five state death penalty statutes. In the first case, *Gregg v. Georgia*,[102] the Court found valid the Georgia statute holding that a finding by the jury of at least one "aggravating circumstance" out of ten is required in pronouncing the death penalty in murder cases. In the *Gregg* case, for example, the jury imposed the death penalty after finding beyond a reasonable doubt two aggravating circumstances: (1) the offender was engaged in the commission of two other capital felonies, and (2) the offender committed the offense of murder for the purpose of receiving money and other financial gains (e.g., an automobile).[103]

In probably the most important death penalty case of the past few years, *McLesky v. Kemp,* the Court upheld the conviction of a black defendant in Georgia despite social science evidence that black criminals who kill white victims have a significantly greater chance of receiving the death penalty than white offenders who kill black victims. The Court ruled that the evidence of racial patterns in capital sentencing was not persuasive without a finding of racial bias in the immediate case.[104] Many observers believe that *McLesky* presented the last significant legal obstacle that death penalty advocates had to overcome and that, as a result, capital punishment will be a sentence in the United States for years to come (McLesky was executed in 1991).

Limiting Capital Punishment

While the Court has generally supported the death penalty, it has also placed some limitations on its use. Rulings have promoted procedural fairness in the capital sentencing process. For example, the Court has limited the death penalty sentence to capital murder cases, ruling that it is not permissible to punish rapists with death.[105] It has prohibited prosecutors from presenting damaging evidence about the defendant's background unless it is directly relevant to the case.[106]

The Court has also reinforced the idea that mental and physical conditions such as age, while not excusing criminal behavior, can be considered as mitigating factors in capital sentencing decisions. In *Wilkins v. Missouri* and *Stanford v. Kentucky* the Court set a limit of 16 on the age of defendants who could be sentenced to death.[107] (Eight inmates are currently on death row who committed their crime at age 17 or younger.) These rulings effectively barred the use of capital punishment from minors under the age of 16 who have been waived or transferred from the juvenile to the adult court system.

The Court also moved to make sure that the aggravating circumstances needed to qualify an offender for the death penalty be clearly stated and carefully considered. In *Clemons v. Mississippi,* the Court mandated that aggravating circumstances be defined precisely and that terms such as "especially heinous, atrocious and cruel" are so vague that they fail to adequately guide the sentencing judge's discretion.[108] The Court has ruled that appellate courts must carefully consider the presence of mitigating evidence when they review capital sentencing decisions.[109]

The Court seems committed to maintaining the death penalty within boundaries of fairness and due process. It has reduced a defendant's ability to reappeal in a capital case by raising claims that were not included in the original legal motion.[110] It now allows victim impact statements to be made and gives prosecutors the right to include such statements in their closing argument describing how the victims will be missed by their family and friends.[111] A judge now may, when the law allows, ignore a jury's recommendation for leniency, and impose the death penalty.[112] These rulings, plus the failure to grant stays in numerous capital cases, underscore the Court's willingness to retain the death sentence.

Death-qualified juries are ones in which any person opposed in concept to capital punishment has been removed during voir dire. Defense attorneys are opposed to death qualification because it bars citizens who oppose the death penalty and who may also be more liberal and less likely to convict defendants from serving

Death-Qualified Juries

on juries. Death qualification creates juries that are nonrepresentative of the 20% of the public that opposes capital punishment.

In *Witherspoon v. Illinois* (1968), the Supreme Court upheld the practice of excusing jurors who are opposed to the death penalty.[113] The Court has made it easier to convict people in death penalty cases by ruling that any juror can be excused if his or her views on capital punishment are deemed by a trial judge to "prevent or substantially impair the performance of their duties."[114] The Court has also ruled that jurors can be removed because of their opposition to the death penalty at the guilt phase of a trial, even though they would not have to consider the issue of capital punishment until a separate sentencing hearing. In *Lockhart v. McCree* (1986), the Court also ruled that removing anti–capital punishment jurors does not violate the Sixth Amendment's provision that juries represent a fair cross-section of the community, nor does it unfairly tip the scale toward juries who are prone to convict people in capital cases.[115] So, it appears that for the present, prosecutors will be able to excuse jurors who feel that the death penalty is wrong or immoral.

Does the Death Penalty Deter Murder?

The key issue in the capital punishment debate is whether it can acutally lower the murder rate and save lives. Despite its inherent cruelty, capital punishment might be justified if it proved to be an effective crime deterrent that could save many innocent lives. Abolitionists claim it has no real deterrent value; advocates claim it does. Who is correct?

Considerable empirical research has been carried out on the effectiveness of capital punishment as a deterrent. In particular, studies have tried to discover whether the death sentence serves as a more effective deterrent than life imprisonment for capital crimes such as homicide. Three methods have been used:

- Immediate impact studies, which calculate the effect a well-publicized execution has on the short-term murder rate

- Time-series analysis, which compares long-term trends in murder and capital punishment rates

- Contiguous-state analysis, which compares murder rates in states that have the death penalty with a similar state that has abolished capital punishment

Using these three methods over a 60-year period, most researchers have failed to show any deterrent effect of capital punishment.[116] These studies show that murder rates do not seem to rise when a state abolishes capital punishment any more so than they decrease when the death penalty is adopted. The murder rate is also quite similar in both states that use the death penalty and neighboring states that have abolished capital punishment. Finally, there is little evidence that a well-publicized execution has an immediate impact on the murder rate.

Only a few studies have found that the long-term application of capital punishment may actually reduce the murder rate.[117] However, these have been disputed by researchers who have questioned the methodology used and indicate that the deterrent effects the studies uncover are an artifact of the statistical techniques used in the research.[118]

The general consensus among death penalty researchers today is that the threat of capital punishment has little effect on murder rates. While it is still unknown why capital punishment fails as a deterrent, the cause may lie in the nature of homicide itself: As noted earlier, murder is often a crime of passion involving people who knew each other, and many murders are committed by people under the influence of drugs and alcohol—more than 50% of all people arrested for murder test positively for drug use. People involved in interpersonal conflict with friends, acquaintances, and family members and who may be under the influence of drugs and alcohol are not likely to be capable of considering the threat of the death penalty.

Murder rates have also been linked to the burdens of poverty and income inequality. Desperate adolescents caught up in the cycle of urban violence and who become members of criminal groups and gangs may find that their life situation gives them little choice except to engage in violent and deadly behavior; they have few chances to ponder the deterrent impact of the death penalty.

The failure of the "ultimate deterrent" to deter the "ultimate crime" has been used by critics to question the value of capital punishment.

Despite the less than conclusive empirical evidence, many people still hold to the efficacy of the death penalty as a crime deterrent, and recent Supreme Court decisions seem to justify its use. Of course, even if the death penalty were no greater a deterrent than a life sentence, some people would still advocate its use on the grounds that it is the only way to permanently rid society of dangerous criminals who deserve to die.

Criminal Justice on the Net

One of the most important sources of sentencing guideline information on the net is maintained by the United States Sentencing Commission, an independent agency in the judicial branch of government. Its principal purpose is to establish sentencing policies and practices for the federal courts, including detailed guidelines prescribing the appropriate form and severity of punishment for offenders convicted of federal crimes. While the development, monitoring, and amendment of the sentencing guidelines is the centerpiece of the agency's work, the commission provides training, conducts research on sentencing-related issues, and serves as an information resource for Congress, criminal justice practitioners, and the public. The commission is charged with the ongoing responsibilities of evaluating the effects of the sentencing guidelines on the criminal justice system, recommending to Congress appropriate modifications of substantive criminal law and sentencing procedures, and establishing a research and development program on sentencing issues. Visit the commission's site at

http://www.ussc.gov/

If your interest is capital punishment, you might want to look at the most recent data on capital punishment put out by the Bureau of Justice Statistics. Its annual reports provide numerical tables that present data on offenders' sex, race, ethnic origin, education, marital status, age at time of arrest for capital offense, legal status at time of capital offense, methods of execution, trends, and time between imposition of death sentence and execution. Historical tables present sentencing since 1973. Obtain this information at

http://www.ncjrs.org/cp95/ index.html

Summary

Punishment and sentencing have gone through various phases throughout the history of Western civilization. Initially, punishment was characterized by retribution and the need to fix sentences for convicted offenders. Throughout the middle years of the 20th century, individualized sentencing was widely accepted, and the concept of rehabilitation was used in sentencing and penal codes. During the 1960s, however, experts began to become disenchanted with rehabilitation and concepts related to treating the individual offender. There was less emphasis on treatment and more on the legal rights of offenders. A number of states returned to the concept of punishment in terms of mandatory and fixed sentences.

Theorists suggest that the philosophy of sentencing has thus changed from a concentration on rehabilitation to a focus on incapacitation and deterrence, where the goal is to achieve equality of punishment and justice in the law and to lock up dangerous criminals for as long as possible.

Sentencing in today's criminal justice system is based on deterrence, incapacitation, and rehabilitation. Traditional dispositions include fines, probation, and incarceration, with probation being the most common choice.

A number of states have developed determinate sentences that eliminate parole and attempt to restrict judicial discretion. Methods for making dispositions more uniform include the institution of sentencing guidelines that create uniform sentences based on offender background and crime characteristics. Despite these changes, most states continue to use indeterminate sentences, which give convicted offenders a short minimum sentence after which they can be released on parole if they are considered "rehabilitated." Jurisdictions that use either determinate or indeterminate sentences allow inmates to be released early on good behavior.

The death penalty continues to be the most controversial sentence, with over half the states reinstituting capital punishment laws since the *Furman v. Georgia* decision of 1972. Although there is little evidence that the death penalty deters murder, supporters still view it as necessary in terms of incapacitation and retribution and cite the public's support for the death penalty and the low chance of error in its application. Opponents point out that mistakes can be made, that capital sentences are apportioned in a racially biased manner, and that the practice is cruel and barbaric. Nonetheless, the courts have generally supported the legality of capital punishment, and it has been used more frequently in recent years.

Key Terms

sanction	recidivism	structured sentencing
punishment	blameworthy	sentencing guidelines
felony	just desert	mandatory sentence
wergild	equity	chivalry hypothesis
poor laws	concurrent sentence	victim impact statements
penitentiaries	consecutive sentence	contextual discrimination
general deterrence	indeterminate sentence	brutalization effect
incapacitation	determinate sentence	death-qualified juries
specific deterrence	presumptive sentence	

Questions

1. Discuss the sentencing dispositions in your jurisdiction. What are the pros and cons of each?
2. Compare the various types of incarceration sentences. What are the similarities and differences? Why are many jurisdictions considering the passage of mandatory sentencing laws?
3. Discuss the issue of capital punishment. In your opinion, does it serve as a deterrent? What new rulings has the U.S. Supreme Court made on the legality of the death penalty?
4. Why does the problem of sentencing disparity exist? Do programs exist that can reduce disparate sentences? If so, what are they? Should all people who commit the same crime receive the same sentence?
5. Should convicted criminals be released from prison when correctional authorities are convinced they are rehabilitated?

1. Michel Foucault, *Discipline and Punishment* (New York: Vintage Books, 1978).

2. Graeme Newman, *The Punishment Response* (Philadelphia: Lippincott, 1978), p. 13.

3. Kathleen Daly, "Neither Conflict nor Labeling nor Paternalism Will Suffice: Intersections of Race, Ethnicity, Gender, and Family in Criminal Court Decisions," *Crime and Delinquency* 35 (1989): 136–168.

4. Among the most helpful sources for this section are Benedict Alper, *Prisons Inside-Out* (Cambridge, Mass.: Ballinger, 1974); Gustave de Beaumont and Alexis de Tocqueville, *On the Penitentiary System in the United States and Its Applications in France* (Carbondale: Southern Illinois University Press, 1964); Orlando Lewis, *The Development of American Prisons and Prison Customs, 1776–1845* (Montclair, N.J.: Patterson-Smith, 1967); Leonard Orland, ed., *Justice, Punishment, and Treatment* (New York: Free Press, 1973); J. Goebel, *Felony and Misdemeanor* (Philadelphia: University of Pennsylvania Press, 1976); George Rusche and Otto Kircheimer, *Punishment and Social Structure* (New York: Russell & Russell, 1939); Samuel Walker, *Popular Justice* (New York: Oxford University Press, 1980); Newman, *The Punishment Response;* David Rothman, *Conscience and Convenience* (Boston: Little, Brown, 1980); George Ives, *A History of Penal Methods* (Montclair, N.J.: Patterson-Smith, 1970); Robert Hughes, *The Fatal Shore* (New York: Knopf, 1986); Leon Radzinowicz, *A History of English Criminal Law,* vol. 1 (London: Stevens, 1943), p. 5.

5. Gerald Wheeler and Rodney Hissong, "Effects of Sanctions on Drunk Drivers: Beyond Incarceration," *Crime and Delinquency* 34 (1988): 29–42; Jeffrey Fagan, "Cessation of Family Violence: Deterrence and Dissuasion" in *Crime and Justice,* vol. 11, ed. Lloyd Ohlin and Michael Tonry (Chicago: University of Chicago Press, 1989), pp. 100–151.

6. Allen Beck and Bernard Shipley, *Recidivism of Prisoners Released in 1983* (Washington, D.C.: Bureau of Justice Statistics, 1989).

7. Charles Logan, *Criminal Justice Performance Measures for Prisons* (Washington, D.C.: Bureau of Justice Statistics, 1993), p. 3.

8. Alexis Durham, "The Justice Model in Historical Context: Early Law, the Emergence of Science, and the Rise of Incarceration," *Journal of Criminal Justice* 16 (1988): 331–346.

9. Andrew von Hirsh, *Doing Justice: The Choice of Punishments* (New York: Hill and Wang, 1976).

10. Alexis Durham, "Crime Seriousness and Punitive Severity: An Assessment of Social Attitudes," *Justice Quarterly* 5 (1988): 131–153.

11. Charles Logan and Gerald Gaes, "Meta-Analysis and the Rehabilitation of Punishment," *Justice Quarterly* 10 (1993): 245–264.

12. Richard McCorkle, "Research Note: Punish and Rehabilitate? Public Attitudes Toward Six Common Crimes," *Crime and Delinquency* 39 (1993): 240–252; D. A. Andrews, Ivan Zinger, Robert Hoge, James Bonta, Paul Gendreau, and Francis Cullen, "Does Correctional Treatment Work? A Clinically Relevant and Psychologically Informed Meta-Analysis," *Criminology* 28 (1990): 369–404; Francis Cullen, John Cullen, and John Wozniak, "Is Rehabilitation Dead? The Myth of the Punitive Public," *Journal of Criminal Justice* 16 (1988): 303–316.

13. For a review, see Arnulf Kolstad, "Imprisonment as Rehabilitation: Offenders' Assessment of Why It Does Not Work," *Journal of Criminal Justice* 24 (1996): 323–335.

14. Jacob Adler, *The Urgings of Conscience: A Theory of Punishment* (Philadelphia: Temple University Press, 1991).

15. Langan, *State Felony Courts and Felony Laws,* p. 6.

16. Michael Tonry, "The Politics and Processes of Sentencing Commissions," *Crime and Delinquency* 37 (1991): 307–329.

17. "Sentencing Guides Said to Work—If Judges Must Use Them," *Criminal Justice Newsletter* 27, 16 December 1996, p.4.

18. Elaine Wolf and Marsha Weissman, "Revising Federal Sentencing Policy: Some Consequences of Expanding Eligibility for Alternative Sanctions," *Crime and Delinquency* 42 (1996): 192–205.

19. Samuel Walker, Cassia Spohn, and Miriam DeLone, *The Color of Justice: Race, Ethnicity, and Crime in America* (Belmont, Calif.: Wadsworth, 1996), p. 159.

20. Michael Tonry, "The Failure of the U.S. Sentencing Commission's Guidelines," *Crime and Delinquency* 39 (1993): 131–149.

21. *Mistretta v. United States,* 488 U.S. 361 (1989); 109 S.Ct. 647 (1989).

22. Tonry, "The Politics and Process of Sentencing Commissions."

23. Marvell and Moody, "Determinate Sentencing and Abolishing Parole," p. 123.

24. Lisa Stolzenberg and Stewart D'Alessio, "Sentencing and Unwarranted Disparity: An Empirical Assessment of the Long-Term Impact of Sentencing Guidelines in Minnesota," *Criminology* 32 (1994): 301–310.

25. David Griswold, "Deviation from Sentencing Guidelines: The Issue of Unwarranted Disparity," *Journal of Criminal Justice* 16 (1988): 317–329; Minnesota Sentencing Guidelines Commission, *The Impact of the Minnesota Sentencing Guidelines: Three-Year Evaluation* (St. Paul: Minnesota Sentencing Guidelines Commission, 1984), p. 162.

26. Pamala Griset, "Determinate Sentencing and Administrative Control Over Time Served in Prison: A Case Study of Florida," *Crime and Delinquency* 42 (1996): 127–143.

27. Terence Miethe and Charles Moore, "Socioeconomic Disparities Under Determinate Sentencing Systems: A Comparison of Preguideline and Postguideline Practices in Minnesota," *Criminology* 23 (1985): 337–363; Richard Frase, "Implementing Commission-Based Sentencing Guidelines: The Lessons of the First Ten Years in Minnesota," paper presented at the annual meeting of the American Society of Criminology, San Francisco, November 1991, p. 5.

28. Michael Tonry, "Racial Politics, Racial Disparities, and the War on Crime," *Crime and Delinquency* 40 (1994): 475–494.

29. Chris Eskridge, "Sentencing Guidelines: To Be or Not to Be," *Federal Probation* 50 (1986): 70–76.

30. "Pennsylvania Begins Overhaul of Sentencing Guidelines," *Criminal Justice Newsletter* 24 (1 October 1993): 1–2.

31. Ibid., p. 122.

32. Michael Tonry, *Sentencing Matters* (New York: Oxford University Press, 1996), p. 5.

33. Henry Scott Wallace, "Mandatory Minimums and the Betrayal of Sentencing Reform: A Legislative Dr. Jekyll and Mr. Hyde," *Federal Probation* 57 (1993): 9–16.

34. "Survey Finds Judges Unhappy with Mandatory Sentencing," *Criminal Justice Newsletter* 24 (1 October 1993): 3.

35. "21% of Federal Prisoners Found to Be Low-Level Drug Offenders," *Criminal Justice Newsletter* 25 (2 January 1994): 7.

36. "California Passes a Tough Three-Strikes-You're-Out Law," *Criminal Justice Newsletter* 24 (4 April 1993): 6.

37. Patrick A. Langan and Jodi M. Brown, *Felony Sentences in State Courts, 1994* (Washington, D.C.: Bureau of Justice Statistics, 1997).

38. Stewart D'Alessio and Lisa Stolzenberg, "Socioeconomic Status and the Sentencing of the Traditional Offender," *Journal of Criminal Justice* 21 (1993): 61–77.

39. For a general look at the factors that affect sentencing, see Susan Welch, Cassia Spohn, and John Gruhl, "Convicting and Sentencing Differences Among Black, Hispanic, and White Males in Six Localities," *Justice Quarterly* 2 (1985): 67–80.

40. Cecilia Saulters-Tubbs, "Prosecutorial and Judicial Treatment of Female Offenders," *Federal Probation* 57 (1993): 37–41.

41. See, generally, Janet Johnston, Thomas Kennedy, and I. Gayle Shuman, "Gender Differences in the Sentencing of Felony Offenders," *Federal Probation* 87 (1987): 49–56; Cassia Spohn and Susan Welch, "The Effect of Prior Record in Sentencing Research: An Examination of the Assumption That Any Measure Is Adequate," *Justice Quarterly* 4 (1987): 286–302; David Willison, "The Effects of Counsel on the Severity of Criminal Sentences: A Statistical Assessment," *Justice System Journal* 9 (1984): 87–101.

42. Ellen Hochstedler Steury and Nancy Frank, "Gender Bias and Pretrial Release: More Pieces of the Puzzle," *Journal of Criminal Justice* 18 (1990): 417–432.

43. Dean Champion, "Elderly Felons and Sentencing Severity: Interregional Variations in Leniency and Sentencing Trends," *Criminal Justice Review* 12 (1987): 7–15.

44. Darrell Steffensmeier, John Kramer, and Jeffry Ulmer, "Age Differences in Sentencing," *Justice Quarterly* 12 (1995): 583–601.

45. *Payne v. Tennessee,* 111 S.Ct. 2597, 115 L.Ed.2d 720 (1991).

46. Robert Davis and Barbara Smith, "The Effects of Victim Impact Statements on Sentencing Decisions: A Test in an Urban Setting," *Justice Quarterly* 11 (1994): 453–469; Edna Erez and Pamela Tontodonato, "The Effect of Victim Participation in Sentencing on Sentence Outcome," *Criminology* 28 (1990): 451–474.

47. Madeline Wordes, Timothy Bynum, and Charles Corley, "Locking Up Youth: The Impact of Race on Detention Decisions," *Journal of Research in Crime and Delinquency* 31 (1994): 149–165; Darlene Conley, "Adding Color to a Black and White Picture: Using Qualitative Data to Explain Racial Disproportionality in the Juvenile Justice System," *Journal of Research in Crime and Delinquency* 31 (1994): 135–148.

48. Celesta Albonetti and John Hepburn, "Prosecutorial Discretion to Defer Criminalization: The Effects of Defendant's Ascribed and Achieved Status Characteristics," *Journal of Quantitative Criminology* 12 (1996): 63–81; Jimmy Williams, "Race of Appellant, Sentencing Guidelines, and Decision Making in Criminal Appeals: A Research Note," *Journal of Criminal Justice* 23 (1995): 83–91.

49. Stephen Klein, Joan Petersilia, and Susan Turner, "Race and Imprisonment Decisions in California," *Science* 247 (1990): 812–816.

50. Patrick Langan and Richard Solari, *National Judicial Reporting Program, 1990* (Washington, D.C.: National Institute of Justice, 1993), p. 23.

51. Ibid., p. 15.

52. Spohn and Welch, "The Effect of Prior Record in Sentencing Research."

53. Darnell Hawkins, "Race, Crime Type and Imprisonment," *Justice Quarterly* 3 (1986): 251–269; James Unnever and Larry Hembroff, "The Prediction of Racial/Ethnic Sentencing Disparities: An Expectation States Approach," *Journal of Research in Crime and Delinquency* 25 (1988): 53–82.

54. James Nelson, "A Dollar or a Day: Sentencing Misdemeanants in New York State," *Journal of Research in Crime and Delinquency* 31 (1994): 183–201.

55. Robert Crutchfield, George Bridges, and Susan Pitchford, "Analytical and Aggregation Biases in Analyses of Imprisonment: Reconciling Discrepancies in Studies of Racial Disparity," *Journal of Research in Crime and Delinquency* 31 (1994): 166–182.

56. Walker, Spohn, and DeLone, *The Color of Justice,* pp. 145–146.

57. Ibid.

58. Alan Lizotte, "Extra-Legal Factors in Chicago's Criminal Courts: Testing the Conflict Model of Criminal Justice," *Social Problems* 25 (1978): 564–580; P. Burke and A. Turk, "Factors Affecting Post-Arrest Dispositions: A Model for Analysis," *Social Problems* 22 (1975): 313–332; Terence Thornberry, "Race, Socioeconomic Status and Sentencing in the Juvenile Justice System," *Journal of Criminal Law and Criminology* 64 (1973): 90–98.

59. William Rhodes, *Pretrial Release and Misconduct* (Washington, D.C.: U.S. Government Printing Office, 1985).

60. Dale Dannefer and Russell Schutt, "Race and Juvenile Justice Processing in Court and Police Agencies," *American Journal of Sociology* 87 (1982): 1113–1132; Douglas Smith and Christy Visher, "Street-Level Justice: Situational Determinants of Police Arrest Decisions," *Social Problems* 29 (1981): 267–277.

61. Jo Dixon, "The Organizational Context of Sentencing," *American Journal of Sociology* 100 (1995): 1157–1198.

62. "Virginia OKs Tougher Sentences, Ends Parole in Landmark Bill," *Criminal Justice Newsletter,* 3 October 1994, p. 5.

63. For a review of this issue, see Marc Mauer and Tracy Huling, *Young Black Americans and the Criminal Justice System: Five Years Later* (Washington, D.C.: Sentencing Project, 1995).

64. Michael Tonry, *Malign Neglect: Race, Crime and Punishment in America* (New York: Oxford University Press, 1995), pp. 105–109.

65. *Coker v. Georgia,* 433 U.S. 584, 97 S.Ct. 2861, 53 L.Ed.2d 982 (1977).

66. "Many State Legislatures Focused on Crime in 1995, Study Finds," *Criminal Justice Newsletter* 27, 2 January 1996, p.2.

67. Tracy Snell, *Capital Punishment, 1995* (Washington, D.C.: Bureau of Justice Statistics, 1996).

68. Ibid.

69. Stephen Markman and Paul Cassell, "Protecting the Innocent: A Response to the Bedeau-Radelet Study," *Stanford Law Review* 41 (1988): 121–170.

70. Snell, *Capital Punishment 1995,* p. 2.

71. Stephen Layson, "United States Time-Series Homicide Regressions with Adaptive Expectations," *Bulletin of the New York Academy of Medicine* 62 (1986): 589–619.

72. David Friedrichs, "Comment—Humanism and the Death Penalty: An Alternative Perspective," *Justice Quarterly* 6 (1989): 197–209.

73. Kathleen Maguire and Ann Pastore, *Sourcebook of Criminal Justice Statistics, 1995* (Washington, D.C.: U.S. Government Printing Office, 1996), p. 183.

74. For an analysis of the formation of public opinion on the death penalty, see Kimberly Cook, "Public Support for the Death Penalty: A Cultural Analysis," paper presented at the annual meeting of the American Society of Criminology, San Francisco, November 1991.

75. Alexis Durham, H. Preston Elrod, and Patrick Kinkade, "Public Support to the Death Penalty: Beyond Gallup," *Justice Quarterly* 13 (1996): 705–736.

76. See, generally, Hugo Bedeau, *Death Is Different: Studies in the Morality, Law, and Politics of Capital Punishment* (Boston: Northeastern University Press, 1987); Keith Otterbein, *The Ultimate Coercive Sanction* (New Haven, Conn.: HRAF Press, 1986).

77. "Illinois Ex-Prosecutors Charged with Framing Murder Defendants," *Criminal Justice Newsletter* 28 1997: p. 3.

78. House Subcommittee on Civil and Constitutional Rights, *Innocence and the Death Penalty: Assessing the Danger of Mistaken Executions* (Washington, D.C.: U.S. Government Printing Office, 1993).

79. David Stewart, "Dealing with Death," *ABA Journal* (1994): 53.

80. Michael Radelet and Hugo Bedeau, "Miscarriages of Justice in Potentially Capital Cases," *Stanford Law Review* 40 (1987): 121–181.

81. Stewart, "Dealing with Death."

82. Patrick Langan and John Dawson, *Felony Sentences in State Courts, 1988* (Washington, D.C.: Bureau of Justice Statistics, 1990), p. 2.

83. "A Victim's Progress," *Newsweek,* 12 June 1989, p. 5.

84. William Doerner, "The Impact of Medical Resources on Criminally Induced Lethality: A Further Examination," *Criminology* 26 (1988): 171–177.

85. Elizabeth Purdom and J. Anthony Paredes, "Capital Punishment and Human Sacrifice," in *Facing the Death Penalty: Essays on Cruel and Unusual Punishment,* ed. Michael Radelet (Philadelphia: Temple University Press, 1989), pp. 152–153.

86. Steven Barkan and Steven Cohn, "Racial Prejudice and Support for the Death Penalty by Whites," *Journal of Research in Crime and Delinquency* 31 (1994): 202–209; Robert Bohm and Ronald Vogel, "A Comparison of Factors Associated with Uninformed and Informed Death Penalty Opinions," *Journal of Criminal Justice* 22 (1994): 125–143.

87. Kathleen Maguire and Ann Pastore, *Sourcebook of Criminal Justice Statistics, 1995* (Washington, D.C.: U. S. Government Printing Office, 1996), p. 183.

88. Marla Sandys and Edmund McGarrell, "Attitudes Toward Capital Punishment Among Indiana Legislators: Diminished Support in Light of Alternative Sentencing Options," *Justice Quarterly* 11 (1994): 651–675.

89. See, generally, Bohm, ed., *The Death Penalty in America.*

90. William Bowers and Glenn Pierce, "Deterrence or Brutalization: What Is the Effect of Executions?" *Crime and Delinquency* 26 (1980): 453–484.

91. Lawrence Greenfield and David Hinners, *Capital Punishment, 1984* (Washington, D.C.: Bureau of Justice Statistics, 1985).

92. Gennaro Vito and Thomas Keil, "Capital Sentencing in Kentucky: An Analysis of the Factors Influencing Decision Making in the Post-Gregg Period," *Journal of Criminal Law and Criminology* 79 (1988): 493–503; David Baldus, C. Pulaski, and G. Woodworth, "Comparative Review of Death Sentences: An Empirical Study of the Georgia Experience," *Journal of Criminal Law and Criminology* 74 (1983): 661–685; Raymond Paternoster, "Race of the Victim and Location of Crime: The Decision to Seek the Death Penalty in South Carolina," *Journal of Criminal Law and Criminology* 74 (1983): 754–785.

93. Raymond Paternoster, "Prosecutorial Discretion and Capital Sentencing in North and South Carolina," in *The Death Penalty in America: Current Research,* ed. Robert Bohm (Cincinnati: Anderson Publishing, 1991), pp. 39–52.

94. Vito and Keil, "Capital Sentencing in Kentucky," pp. 502–503.

95. David Brown, "Man is Executed in Carolina; Second of a White Who Killed Black," *Boston Globe,* 25 January 1995, p. 3.

96. Robert Johnson, *Death Work: A Study of the Modern Execution Process* (Belmont, Calif.: Brooks/Cole, 1990).

97. William Bailey, "Disaggregation in Deterrence and Death Penalty Research: The Case of Murder in Chicago," *Journal of Criminal Law and Criminology* 74 (1986): 827–859.

98. Gennaro Vito, Pat Koester, and Deborah Wilson, "Return of the Dead: An Update on the Status of Furman-Commuted Death Row Inmates," in *The Death Penalty in America: Current Research,* ed. Robert Bohm (Cincinnati: Anderson Publishing, 1991), pp. 89–100; Gennaro Vito, Deborah Wilson, and Edward Latessa, "Comparison of the Dead: Attributes and Outcomes of Furman-Commuted Death Row Inmates in Kentucky and Ohio," *The Death Penalty in America: Current Research,* ed. Robert Bohm (Cincinnati: Anderson Publishing, 1991), pp. 101–112.

99. John Cochran, Mitchell Chamlin, and Mark Seth, "Deterrence or Brutalization? An Impact Assessment of Oklahoma's Return to Capital Punishment," *Criminology* 32 (1994): 107–134.

100. Joseph Schumacher, "An International Look at the Death Penalty," *International Journal of Comparative and Applied Criminal Justice* 14 (1990): 307–315.

101. *Furman v. Georgia,* 408 U.S. 238, 92 S.Ct. 2726, 33 L.Ed.2d 346 (1972).

102. *Gregg v. Georgia,* 428 U.S. 153, 96 S.Ct. 2909, 49 L.Ed.2d 859 (1976).

103. Ibid., at 205–207, 96 S.Ct. at 2940–2941.

104. *McLesky v. Kemp,* 428 U.S. 262, 96 S.Ct. 2950, 49 L.Ed.2d 929 (1976).

105. *Coker v. Georgia,* 430 U.S. 349, 97 S.Ct. 1197, 51 L.Ed.2d 393 (1977).

106. *Dawson v. Delaware,* 503 U.S. 159, 112 S.Ct. 1093, 117 L.Ed.2d 309 (1992).

107. *Wilkins v. Missouri* and *Stanford v. Kentucky,* 492 U.S. 361, 109 S.Ct. 2969, 106 L.Ed.2d 306 (1989).

108. *Clemons v. Mississippi,* 494 U.S. 738, 110 S.Ct. 1441, 108 L.Ed.2d 725 (1990).

109. *Stringer v. Black,* 503 U.S. 222, 112 S.Ct. 1130, 117 L.Ed.2d 367 (1992); see also *Parker v. Duggen,* 498 U.S. 308, 111 S.Ct. 731, 112 L.Ed. 2d 812.

110. *McKlesky v. Zant,* 49 Cr.L. 2031 (1991).

111. *Payne v. Tennessee,* 501 U.S. 808, 111 S.Ct. 2597, 115 L.Ed.2d 720 (1991).

112. *Harris v. Alabama,* U.S., 115 S.Ct. 1031, 130 L.Ed.2d. 1004 (1995).

113. *Witherspoon v. Illinois,* 391 U.S. 510, 88 S.Ct. 1770, 20 L.Ed.2d 776 (1968).

114. *Wainwright v. Witt,* 469 U.S. 412, 105 S.Ct. 844, 83 L.Ed.2d 841 (1985).

115. *Lockhart v. McCree,* 476 U.S. 162, 106 S.Ct. 1758, 90 L.Ed.2d 137 (1986).

116. Walter C. Reckless, "Use of the Death Penalty," *Crime and Delinquency* 15 (1969): 43; Thorsten Sellin, "Effect of Repeal and Reintroduction of the Death Penalty on Homicide Rates," in *The Death Penalty,* ed. Thorsten Sellin (Philadelphia: American Law Institute, 1959). Robert H. Dann, "The Deterrent Effect of Capital Punishment," *Friends Social Service Series* 29 (1935): 1; William Bailey and Ruth Peterson, "Murder and Capital Punishment: A Monthly Time-Series Analysis of Execution Publicity," *American Sociological Review* 54 (1989): 722–743; David Phillips, "The Deterrent Effect of Capital Punishment," *American Journal of Sociology* 86 (1980): 139–148; Sam McFarland, "Is Capital Punishment a Short-Term Deterrent to Homicide? A Study of the Effects of Four Recent American Executions," *Journal of Criminal Law and Criminology* 74 (1984): 1014–1032; Richard Lempert, "The Effect of Executions on Homicides: A New Look in an Old Light," *Crime and Delinquency* 29 (1983): 88-115.

117. Isaac Ehrlich, "The Deterrent Effect of Capital Punishment: A Question of Life or Death," *American Economic Review* 65 (1975): 397.

118. For a review, see William Bailey, "The General Prevention Effect of Capital Punishment for Non-Capital Felonies," in *The Death Penalty in America: Current Research,* ed. Robert Bohm (Cincinnati: Anderson Publishing, 1991), pp. 21–38.

Probation and Intermediate Sanctions

Although many people would like to see dangerous offenders do "hard time," incarcerating every convicted criminal is both expensive and unworkable. The prison system is already overcrowded and dangerous. New prison construction is a costly option for cash-strapped states. Little evidence exists that a prison stay can effectively rehabilitate many inmates; more than 60% of parolees are rearrested within six years of their release.[1] Inmates describe institutions as "criminal universities" where their deviant identities become reinforced.[2]

The failure of traditional correctional models has prompted criminal justice policymakers to create alternatives to incarceration that are both effective and economical. The most traditional and common alternative sanction, probation, involves maintaining an offender in the community under a set of behavioral rules created and administered by judicial authority. Considering the potential benefits and cost effectiveness of a probation sentence, it is not surprising that the number of probationers is at an all-time high.

The need to create effective and efficient methods of controlling offenders in the community has also prompted correctional policymakers to develop and

amplify the use of new forms of community-based intermediate sanctions: fines, forfeiture, restitution, shock probation and split sentencing, intensive probation supervision, house arrest, electronic monitoring, and residential community corrections. These programs are designed to provide greater control over an offender and increase the level of sanction without resorting to a prison sentence.

Both traditional probation and the newer intermediate sanctions have the potential to become reasonable answers to many of the economic and social problems faced by correctional administrators: They are less costly than jail or prison sentences; they help the offender maintain family and community ties; they can be structured to maximize security and maintain public safety; and they can be scaled in severity to correspond to the seriousness of the crime. No area of the criminal justice system is undergoing more change and greater expansion than probation and intermediate sanctions.

This chapter reviews these criminal sanctions. It begins with a brief history of probation and covers probation as an organization, sentence, and correctional practice. Then we focus attention on such intermediate sanctions as intensive supervision, house arrest, and electronic monitoring.

Probation is a criminal sentence mandating that a convicted offender be placed and maintained in the community under the supervision of a duly authorized agent of the court. Once on probation, the offender is subject to certain rules and conditions that must be followed to remain in the community. The probation sentence is managed by a probation department that supervises offenders' behavior and treatment and carries out other tasks for the court. Although the term has many meanings, *probation* usually indicates a nonpunitive form of sentencing for convicted criminal offenders and delinquent youth, emphasizing maintenance in the community and treatment without institutionalization or other forms of punishment.[3]

The History of Probation

The roots of probation can be traced back to the traditions of the English common law. During the Middle Ages, judges wishing to spare deserving offenders from the pains of the then commonly used punishments of torture, mutilation, and death used their power to grant clemency and stays of execution. The common law practice of **judicial reprieve** allowed judges to suspend punishment so that convicted offenders could seek a pardon, gather new evidence, or demonstrate that they had reformed their behavior. Similarly, the practice of **recognizance** enabled convicted offenders to remain free if they agreed to enter into a debt obligation with the state. The debt would have to be paid only if the offender was caught engaging in further criminal behavior. Sometimes **sureties** were required—these were people who made themselves responsible for the behavior of an offender after he was released.

Early U.S. courts continued the practice of indefinitely suspending sentences of criminals who seemed deserving of a second chance, but it was John Augustus of Boston who is usually credited with originating the modern probation concept.[4] As a private citizen, Augustus began in 1841 to supervise offenders released to his custody by a Boston judge. Over an 18-year period, Augustus supervised close to 2,000 probationers and helped them get jobs and establish themselves in the community. Augustus had an amazingly high success rate, and few of his charges became involved in crime again.

In 1878 Augustus's work inspired the Massachusetts Legislature to pass a law authorizing appointment of a paid probation officer for the city of Boston. In 1880 probation was extended to other jurisdictions in Massachusetts, and by 1898 the probation movement had spread to the superior (felony) courts.[5] The Massachusetts experience was copied by Missouri (1887), by Vermont (1898), and soon after by most other states. In 1925 the federal government established a probation system for the U.S. district courts. The probation concept soon became the most widely used correctional mechanism in the United States.[6]

The Concept of Probation

The philosophy of probation is that the average offender is not actually a dangerous criminal or a menace to society. Advocates of probation suggest that when offenders are institutionalized instead of being granted community release, the prison community becomes their new reference point, they are forced to interact with hardened criminals, and the "ex-con" label prohibits them from making successful adjustments to society. Probation provides offenders with the opportunity to prove themselves, gives them a second chance, and allows them to be closely supervised by trained personnel who can help them reestablish proper forms of behavior in the community. The media box on the movie *Sleepers* illustrates why probation is the choice of sentence for juveniles who must be protected from the pains of imprisonment.

Probation usually involves suspension of the offender's sentence in return for the promise of good behavior in the community under the supervision of the probation department. As practiced in all 50 states and by the federal government, probation implies a contract between the court and the offender in which the former promises to hold a prison term in abeyance while the latter promises to adhere to a set of rules or conditions mandated by the court. If the rules are

Sleepers

In Hell's Kitchen, a tough part of New York City in the 1960s, Lorenzo (Joe Perrino), also known as Shakes, hangs out with his friends Michael (Brad Renfro), John (Geoff Wigdor), and Tommy (Jonathan Tucker). They play ball, go swimming, roam the streets, and serve as altar boys for Father Bobby, the neighborhood priest (Robert de Niro). One day, on a prank they swipe a hot-dog vendor's cart. Things go tragically awry, and before they are caught, the cart falls down a flight of subway stairs and almost kills a man.

Charged with assault and reckless endangerment, they are sentenced to 9–18 months at a reform school in upstate New York (the title *Sleepers* refers to the length of their term).

Although the boys are experienced street kids, they are not prepared for the physical, sexual, and emotional abuse heaped on them at the Wilkinson Home for Boys. They are beaten mercilessly, starved, tortured, and raped by a gang of guards led by Sean Nokes (Kevin Bacon). The four friends are damaged for the rest of their lives.

It's now 15 years later. Lorenzo (played as an adult by Jason Patric) has left the neighborhood to become a reporter at the *New York Daily News*. Michael (Brad Pitt) has earned a law degree and is an assistant dis-

trict attorney. Tommy (Billy Crudup) and John (Ron Eldard), permanently damaged by their reform school experience, have turned into hardened killers and drug addicts. One night, the pair enter a local restaurant and notice that none other than Sean Nokes is eating in a corner booth. They impulsively gun him down. In a secret plan, Michael handles the case as prosecutor without revealing his past associations. In a dramatic and controversial turn, Father Bobby lies on the stand to protect Tommy and John, and they go free.

Sleepers is a film that is riveting not only because of its violence, but also because it is supposedly factual. The accuracy of the book by Lorenzo Carcaterra on which it is based has been questioned—some critics do not believe that the events actually took place. There is little question, however, that rape and assaults were not uncommon in juvenile justice correctional institutions. A number of books, including the widely read *Weeping in the Play Time of Others* by Kenneth Wooden, exposed the harsh reality of reform schools and prompted some states such as Massachusetts to close institutions. *Sleepers* depicts the type of events that solidify the need for community corrections and probation. If innocent boys can be turned into hardened criminals by their correctional experiences, the entire purpose of secure confinement is discredited.

violated, and especially if the probationer commits another criminal offense, probation may be revoked; **revocation** means that the contract is terminated and the original sentence is enforced. If an offender on probation commits a second offense that is more serious than the first, he or she may also be indicted, tried, and sentenced on that second offense. However, probation may be revoked simply because the rules and conditions of probation have not been met; it is not necessary for an offender to commit another crime.

Each probationary sentence is for a fixed period of time, depending on the seriousness of the offense and the statutory law of the jurisdiction. Probation is considered served when offenders fulfill the conditions set by the court for that period of time; they can then live without state supervision.

Awarding Probation

Probationary sentences may be granted by state and federal district courts and state superior (felony) courts. In some states, juries may recommend probation if the case meets certain legally regulated criteria (for example, if it falls within a certain class of offenses as determined by statute). Even in those jurisdictions that allow juries to recommend probation, judges have the final say in the matter and may grant probation at their discretion. In nonjury trials, probation is granted solely by judicial mandate.

In most jurisdictions, all juvenile offenders are eligible for probation, as are most adults. Some state statutes prohibit probation for certain types of adult offenders, usually those who have engaged in repeated and serious violent crimes, such as murder or rape, or those who have committed crimes for which mandatory prison sentences have been legislated.

The most common manner in which a probationary sentence is imposed is for the judge to formulate a prison sentence and then suspend it if the offender agrees to obey the rules of probation while living in the community (a **suspended sentence**). About 50% of all probationary sentences are imposed in this manner.[7] The term of a probationary sentence may extend to the limit of the suspended prison term, or the court may set a time limit that reflects the sentencing period. For misdemeanors, probation usually extends for the entire period of the jail sentence, while felonies are more likely to warrant probationary periods that are actually shorter than their prison sentences would have been.

Probation may also be granted to an offender whose sentence is deferred pending successful completion of his or her probationary period (about 6% of all cases).[8] This step is usually taken to encourage the defendant to pursue a specific rehabilitation program, such as treatment for alcohol abuse. If the program is successfully completed, further legal action is not usually taken. Probation can also be a sole sentence with no prison sentence imposed or contemplated, but if the rules are violated, the probationer can be brought in for resentencing.

The Extent of Probation

There are approximately 2,000 adult probation agencies in the United States. Slightly more than half are associated with a state-level agency, while the remainder are organized at the county or municipal level of government. About 30 states combine probation and parole supervision into a single agency.

About two-thirds of all adults under some form of correctional supervision are on probation; at last count there were more than 3 million adults under federal, state, or local jurisdiction.[9] Little more than half of all offenders on probation have been convicted of a felony; one-fourth are on probation for a misdemeanor. One in every six probationers has been convicted of driving while intoxicated or under the influence of alcohol.

During any given year, about 1.5 million people are placed on probation, and somewhat fewer (1.3 million) complete their probationary sentence; this imbalance has resulted in a steadily increasing probation population. In 1980, there were 1.1 million people on probation, so the number of probationers *has tripled* in a decade and a half. In all, almost two-thirds of the correctional population is on probation. During 1995, five states reported increases of at least 10% in their probation populations. Arkansas led the nation with a 14.2% rise in its probation population in a single year.

Who Is on Probation?

Women make up about 21% of the nation's probationers, and men 79%. Approximately 64% of the adults on probation are white, and 34% are black; Hispanics represent 14% of probationers.

Most of those on probation (78%) are being actively supervised by a probation officer; about 8% are classified as inactive. In addition, probation officers are unaware of the whereabouts of 10% of their cases, who are classified as "absconded."

The extensive use of probation is probably a reflection of its low cost and its importance. Without probation, the correctional system would rapidly become overcrowded.

Eligibility for Probation

Several criteria are used in granting probation. On one level, the statutes of many states determine the factors that a judge should take into account when deciding whether to grant probation. Some states limit the use of probation in serious felony cases and for specific crimes whose penalties are controlled by mandatory sentencing laws. However, the granting of probation to serious felons is quite common.

Some states have attempted to control judicial discretion by creating guidelines for granting probation. While these guidelines are often followed by judges, probation decision making is quite varied: An individual offender granted probation in one jurisdiction might not be if tried in another. Probation is most often granted by a discretionary decision based on the beliefs and attitudes of the presiding judge and the probation staff.

A significant issue involving eligibility for probation is community supervision of convicted felons. Many people believe that probation is given to minor or first offenders who are deserving of a break. This is not actually the case. Many serious criminal offenders are given probation sentences (see Figure 13.1). About 29% of all convicted felons are granted probation, including people convicted on homicide (3%), rape (12%), and robbery (12%) charges. In short, while originally conceived as a way to provide a second chance for young offenders, probation today is also a means of reducing the population pressures on an overcrowded and underfunded correctional system.

Conditions of Probation

A probation sentence reflects the rehabilitative aspects of criminal sentencing. Yet there are two distinct sides to the probationary contract drawn up between the offender and the court. One side involves the treatment and rehabilitation of the offender through regular meetings with trained probation staff or other

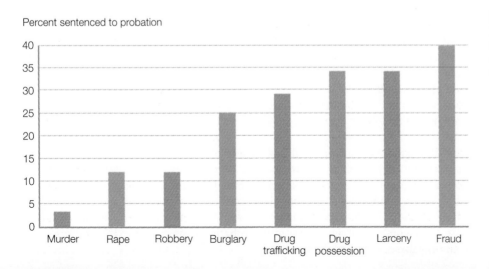

Percent sentenced to probation

Figure 13.1
Receiving probation. Overall, about 29% of all people convicted of serious crimes receive probation only.

treatment personnel; the other side reflects the supervision and enforcement aspects of probation. Probation as practiced today often saddles the probationer with rules and conditions that may impede achieving the stated treatment goals of the probation department by emphasizing the punitive aspects of criminal justice.

When probation is fixed as a sentence, the court sets down certain conditions for qualifying for community treatment. In many jurisdictions, statutory law mandates that certain conditions be applied in every probation case; the sentencing judge usually has broad discretion to add to or lessen these standard conditions on a case-by-case basis. A presiding judge may not, of course, impose capricious or cruel conditions, such as requiring an offender to make restitution out of proportion to the seriousness of the criminal act.[10]

In addition to standard conditions, judges may legally impose on a probationer restrictions tailored both to fit his or her individual needs and to protect society from additional harm.[11] The most common of these special conditions include residential placement, alcohol- or drug-abuse treatment and testing, mental health counseling, house arrest, and community service (the last two conditions are discussed later in this chapter); almost half of all probationers are given one or more special conditions.[12]

Some special conditions are tailored to the particular needs of the probationer. A judge may limit the interpersonal relationships a probationer may have if they are potential threats to society; for example, a child molester can be forbidden to associate with minor children.[13] In one case, a probationer was actually banished from the county in which he lived on the grounds that he was a popular figure among drug-using adolescents to whom he sold cocaine; barring him from his residence also gave him an opportunity for a fresh start.[14] Probationers' community supervision may be revoked if they fail to comply with these conditions and to obey the reasonable requests of the probation staff to meet their treatment obligations.[15]

Probationers can be ordered to abstain from using alcohol and illegal drugs and to take chemical tests at the request of their probation officer to determine whether they have recently used controlled substances.[16] Some courts have permitted probation officers to demand drug tests even though such testing was not part of the original conditions of probation.[17] Probationers can be required to cooperate with legal authorities; for instance, they may be required to testify against others in grand jury hearings.[18] Similarly, probation rules can require periodic reporting of personal practices; for example, tax violators can be required to submit their tax returns.[19] A common procedure today is to require probationers to make restitution to the victims of their crimes (restitution will be discussed later in this chapter). However, an Illinois appeals court ruled that requiring a probationer to make a public apology in the local newspaper for driving drunk was too punitive and a more drastic requirement than those authorized by the state's probation laws.[20]

Courts have upheld probation conditions as long as they are reasonably related to the purposes of probation. Probation conditions may even infringe on some constitutional rights, as long as they are not capricious or cruel.[21] Probationers have a right to challenge rules imposed at the time of sentencing or others imposed later by the court (for example, if the original rules are violated). Some courts have ruled that probationers may bring legal challenges to rules even before they have been charged with their violation.[22]

Administration of Probation Services

Probation services are organized in a variety of ways, depending on the state and the jurisdiction in which they are located. Some states have a statewide probation service, but each court jurisdiction actually controls its local department. Other states maintain a strong statewide authority with centralized control and administration. Thirty states combine probation and parole services in a single unit; some combine juvenile and adult probation departments, while others maintain these departments separately.

The typical probation department is situated in a single court district, such as a juvenile, superior, district, or municipal court. The relationship between the department and court personnel (especially the judge) is extremely close.

In the typical department, the **chief probation officer** (CPO) sets policy, supervises hiring, determines training needs, and may personally discuss with or recommend sentencing to the judge. In state-controlled departments, some of the CPO's duties are mandated by the central office; training guidelines, for example, may be determined at the state level. If, on the other hand, the department is locally controlled, the CPO is invested with great discretion in the management of the department.

Most large probation departments also have one or more assistant chiefs. Sometimes, in departments of moderate size, each of these middle managers will be responsible for a particular aspect of probation services: One assistant chief will oversee training; another will supervise treatment and counseling services; another will act as a liaison with police or other agencies. In smaller departments, the CPO and the executive officers may also maintain a caseload or investigate cases for the court. For example, the chief may handle a few of the most difficult cases personally and concentrate on these. In larger municipal departments, however, the probation chief is a purely administrative figure.

The line staff, or the probation officers (POs), may be in direct and personal contact with the entire supervisory staff, or they may be independent of the chief and answer mainly to the assistant chiefs. Line staff perform the following major functions:

1. They supervise or monitor cases assigned to them to ensure that the rules of probation are followed.

2. They attempt to rehabilitate their cases through specialized treatment techniques.

3. They investigate the lives of convicted offenders to enable the court to make intelligent sentencing decisions.

4. They occasionally collect fines due the court or oversee the collection of delinquent payments, such as child support.

5. They interview complainants and defendants to determine whether criminal action should be taken, whether cases can be decided informally, whether diversion should be advocated, and so on. This last procedure, called intake, is common in juvenile probation.

Some officers view themselves as "social workers" and maintain a treatment orientation; their goal is to help offenders adjust in the community. Others are "law enforcers" who are more concerned with supervision, control, and public safety. An officer's style is influenced by both personal values and the department's general policies and orientation toward the goals of probation.[23] In some major cities, the probation department is quite complex, controlling detention facilities, treatment programs, research, and evaluation staffs. In such a setting, the CPO's role is similar to that of a director of a multiservice public facility. This CPO rarely comes into direct contact with clients, and his or her behavior, attitudes, and values are quite different from those of the rural CPO who maintains a full caseload.

Duties of Probation Officers. Staff officers in probation departments are usually charged with four primary tasks: investigation, intake, diagnosis, and treatment supervision.

In the investigative stage, the probation officer conducts an inquiry within the community to discover the factors related to the criminality of the offender. The **presentence investigation** is conducted primarily to gain information for judicial sentences, but in the event that the offender is placed on probation, the investigation becomes a useful testimony on which to base treatment and supervision.

Intake is a process by which probation officers interview cases that have been summoned to the court for initial appearances. Intake is most commonly used with juvenile offenders but may also be used with adult misdemeanant cases. During juvenile court intake, the petitioner (the juvenile) and the complainant (the private citizen or the police officer) may work with the probation officer to determine an equitable resolution of the case. The PO may settle the case without further court action, recommend restitution or other compensation, initiate actions that result in a court hearing, or recommend unofficial or informal probation.

Diagnosis is the analysis of the probationer's personality and the subsequent development of a personality profile that may be helpful in treating the offender. Diagnosis involves evaluating the probationer based on information from an initial interview (intake) or the presentence investigation for the purpose of planning a proper treatment program. The diagnosis should not merely reflect the desire or purpose of labeling the offender neurotic or psychopathic, for example, but should "codify all that has been learned about the individual, organized in such a way as to provide a means for the establishment of future treatment goals."[24]

Treatment Supervision. Based on a knowledge of psychology, social work, or counseling and the diagnosis of the offender, the probation officer plans a treatment program that will, it is hoped, allow the probationer to fulfill the probation contract and make a reasonable adjustment to the community.

In years past, the probation staff had primary responsibility for supervision and treatment. Probation officers today rarely have hands-on treatment responsibility and instead employ the resources of the community to carry out this function. Attitudes toward treatment also seem to be changing. Probation officers seem less interested today in treating clients than in controlling their behavior.[25] Some experts have called for totally eliminating the personal involvement of probation officers in supervising treatment.[26] However, the increasing number of narcotics abusers in probation caseloads often overwhelms the availability of community-based substance abuse programs.[27] Probation officers have been forced to rely on their own skills to provide treatment services. One survey of 231 probation departments found that more than half continue to use hands-on counseling and behavior modification techniques with drug abusers.[28]

The treatment function is a product of both the investigative and diagnostic aspects of probation. It is based on the PO's perceptions of the probationer, including family problems, peer relationships, and employment background. Treatment may also involve the use of community resources. For example, a probation officer who discovers that a client has a drinking problem may find a detoxification center willing to accept the client, while a chronically underemployed offender may be given job counseling or training and a person undergoing severe psychological stress may be placed in a therapeutic treatment program. Or in the case of juvenile delinquency, a probation officer may work with teachers and other school officials to help a young offender stay in school. Of course, most cases do not (or cannot) receive such individualized treatment.

Failure to adequately supervise probationers and determine whether they are obeying the rules of probation can result in the officer and the department being held legally liable for civil damages. For example, if a probationer with a history of child molestation attacks a child while working as a school custodian, the probationer's case supervisor could be held legally responsible for failing to check on the probationer's employment activities.[29]

The proper diagnostic, treatment, and investigative skills needed for effective probation work are difficult to find in a single individual. Probation officers often have social work backgrounds, and a master's degree may be a prerequisite for ad-

vancement in large departments. Today, most jurisdictions require officers to have a background in the social sciences and to hold at least a bachelor's degree.

Presentence Investigations. An important task of probation officers is the investigation and evaluation of defendants coming before the court for sentencing. The court uses presentence investigation reports in deciding whether to grant probation, incarcerate, or use other forms of treatment.

The style and content of presentence investigations may vary among jurisdictions and also among individual probation officers within the same jurisdiction. Some departments require voluminous reports covering every aspect of the defendant's life; other departments, which may be rule-oriented, require that officers stick to the basic facts, such as the defendant's age, race, sex, and previous offense record. Each department also has its own standards for presentence investigations.

At the conclusion of most presentence investigations, a recommendation is made to the presiding judge that reflects the department's sentencing posture on the case at hand. This is a crucial aspect of the report because the probation department's recommendation is followed in many but not all cases. Probation officers make critical decisions when recommending sentences to a judge, and a number of environmental and situational factors are thought to influence their decisions.

One obvious influence on presentence recommendations is the working environment of the department and the court. Close working relationships between the probation department's staff and the chief and between the chief and the trial judge will greatly influence the decision making of junior officers. Dissonance within a department, either among staff members or between staff and administration, may lead to the department having less influence on the kinds of recommendations POs make. In larger departments, where the chief may be functionally separated from the staff and where close personal supervision is rare, guidance in decision making may come from middle managers (assistant chiefs) or more experienced staff.

The personal and individual characteristics of offenders and the clients' relationship to probation officers are also believed to significantly affect the probation officer's recommendations. Among the factors that have been found to influence probation decision making are the probationer's attitude, family data, prior arrest record, interview impression, educational achievement, psychological profile, interests and activities, and involvement in religious activities, as well as the gravity of the present offense. Of course, the crime and the offender's prior record play particularly important roles in this decision making.

Presentence investigations are extremely important, as the recommendations developed out of them are followed closely by the sentencing judge. Thus, the probation officer exercises discretion similar to that used by a judge in making sentencing decisions.[30] Federal courts have prohibited defendants from suing probation officers who have made errors in their presentence investigations on the grounds that liability "would seriously erode the officers' independent fact-finding function and would as a result impair the sentencing judge's ability to carry out his judicial duties."[31]

Risk Classification. **Risk classification** involves classifying and assigning cases to a level and type of supervision on the basis of the clients' particular needs and the risks they present to the community. For example, some clients may receive frequent (intensive) supervision, while others are assigned to minimum monitoring by a probation officer.

While a number of risk assessment approaches are used, most employ such objective measures as the offender's age, employment status, drug abuse history, prior felony convictions, and number of address changes in the year prior to sentencing (see Table 13.1).[32] Efforts are under way to create more effective instruments using subjective information obtained through face-to-face interviews and encounters.[33]

Does classification make a dramatic difference in the success of probation? There is little clear-cut evidence that classification has a substantial impact on reducing recidivism. But while probation administrators are often skeptical about their validity, they continue to use these scales and believe that may be a useful tool in case management and treatment delivery. The scales may validate the probation officer's self-perception of being a rational and scientific decision maker.[34] The classification of offenders aids the most important goal of supervision: reducing the risk the probationer presents to the community. In addition, classification schemes are in synch with desert-based sentencing models: The most serious cases get the most intensive supervision.[35]

Table 13.1
Risk Prediction Scale

SOURCE: Adapted from the Classification and Supervision Planning System, Probation Division, Administrative Office, U.S. Courts, January 1981.

Automatic Component: Automatically places an individual in low-activity supervision if two conditions are satisfied:
  A. Offender has a 12th-grade education or better.
  B. Individual has a history free of opiate usage.
If the two conditions are not met, the remaining items are scored:
  C. 28 years of age or older at time of offense: 7 points. If not, score as 0.
  D. Arrest-free period of five or more consecutive years: 4 points. If not, score as 0.
  E. Few prior arrests (none, one, or two = 10 points). If not, score as 0.
  F. History free of opiate usage: 9 points. If not, score as 0.
  G. At least four months of steady employment immediately prior to arraignment for present offense: 3 points. If not, score as 0.

Risk Score	Supervisor Level	Minimum Personal Contacts	Maximum Personal Contacts	Collateral Contacts
Automatic assignment or 20–33	Low activity	1 per quarter	1 per quarter	Unlimited
0–19	High activity	1 per month	No maximum	Unlimited

Probation is the most commonly used alternative sentence for a number of reasons: It is humane, it helps offenders maintain community and family ties, and it is cost-effective. Incarcerating an inmate costs over $20,000 per year, while probation costs about $2,000 per year.[36]

While unquestionably inexpensive, is probation successful? If most probation orders fail, the costs of repeated criminality would certainly outweigh the cost savings of a probation sentence. Overall, most probation orders do seem successful. A federal survey of probation practices in 37 states found that about 81% of all people who complete their probation orders could be classified as "successful." Of the 19% classified as "failures," about 11% have been incarcerated for a new offense, while the remaining 8% violated rules, absconded, were discharged to another jurisdiction, or were released because a warrant had been issued against them.[37]

Felony Probation. While the typical client completes probation successfully, the most serious felony offenders may be the ones most likely to commit new crimes. Since felons are commonly granted probation today, this issue is an important one. Tracking the outcome of felony probation was the goal of Joan Petersilia and her colleagues at the Rand Corporation, a private think tank, when they traced 1,672 men convicted of felonies who had been granted probation in Los Angeles and Alameda counties in California.[38] They found that 1,087 (65%) were rearrested; of those rearrested, 853 (51%) were convicted; and of those convicted, 568 (34%) were sentenced to jail or prison! Of the probationers who had new charges filed against them, 75% were charged with burglary, theft, robbery, and other predatory crimes; 18% were convicted of serious, violent crimes.

The Rand researchers found that probation is by far the most common sentencing alternative to prison, used in about 60%–80% of all criminal convictions. What is disturbing, however, is that the crimes and criminal records of about 25% of all probationers are indistinguishable from those of offenders who go to prison.

The Rand data are supported by the results of a federally sponsored, 17-state analysis of felony probation.[39] About 62% of the probationers in the sample either had a disciplinary hearing for violating a condition of probation or were arrested for another serious criminal offense within three years of their release on probation. In fact, within three years, 46% of the probationers had been sent to prison or jail or had absconded from the jurisdiction. This pattern is illustrated in Figure 13.2. Although murderers and rapists were the least likely of all probationers to lapse into criminal behavior, they were the most likely to commit new murders and rapes while on probation. Probationers who were frequent drug abusers were arrested at a far higher rate (55%) than nonabusers (36%); drug treatment and testing efforts did not seem to lower recidivism rates.

Who Fails on Probation? These results are not dissimilar to other findings showing that those most likely to fail on probation are those considered to have the highest risk potential.[40] Young males who are unemployed or who have a very low income, a prior criminal record, and a history of instability are most likely to be rearrested. In contrast, probationers who are married with children, have lived in the area for two or more years, and are adequately employed are the most likely to be successful on probation.[41] Among female probationers, those who have stable marriages, who are better educated, and who are employed full- or part-time are more likely to successfully complete probation orders than male probationers or those who are single, less educated, and unemployed. Prior record also is related to probation success: Clients who have a history of criminal behavior, prior probation, and previous incarceration are the most likely to fail.[42]

While the recidivism rate of probationers seems high, it is still somewhat lower than the recidivism rate of prison inmates.[43] To improve probation

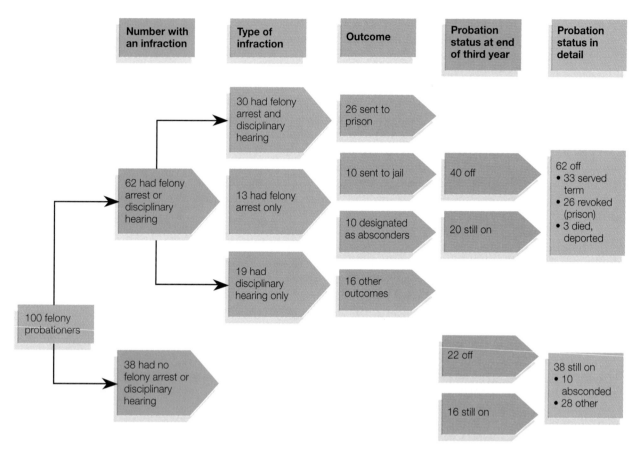

Number with an infraction	Type of infraction	Outcome	Probation status at end of third year	Probation status in detail

- 100 felony probationers
  - 62 had felony arrest or disciplinary hearing
    - 30 had felony arrest and disciplinary hearing → 26 sent to prison
    - 13 had felony arrest only → 10 sent to jail → 40 off
    - → 10 designated as absconders → 20 still on
    - 19 had disciplinary hearing only → 16 other outcomes
    - 62 off
      - 33 served term
      - 26 revoked (prison)
      - 3 died, deported
  - 38 had no felony arrest or disciplinary hearing
    - 22 off
    - 16 still on
    - 38 still on
      - 10 absconded
      - 28 other

Figure 13.2
Probation outcomes of 100 felons.

SOURCE: Patrick Langan and Mark Cuniff, *Recidivism of Felons on Probation, 1986–1989* (Washington, D.C.: Bureau of Justice Statistics, 1992).

effectiveness, it could be supplemented with more stringent rules, such as curfews, and closer supervision. Even though such measures can dramatically increase the cost of probation, they would still be far less expensive than the cost of incarceration.

Probationers in Prison. A survey of prison inmates estimates that there are more than 162,000 probation violators in prison; 74% had been convicted of a new offense, and the remaining 26% had violated a technical condition.[44] What type of acts caused their probation to be terminated? Most (87%) had been arrested for a new offense (but not charged or convicted). Others had tested positive for drug use, failed to report for drug testing/treatment, failed to report for counseling, left the jurisdiction without telling their probation officer, neglected to make restitution payment, made contact with known offenders, or failed to report a change in address.

The survey of probationers in prison inmates showed that based on the offense that brought them to prison, the 162,000 violators committed at least 6,400 murders, 7,400 rapes, 10,400 assaults, and 17,000 robberies while under supervision in the community an average of 17 months.[45] Probation failures, then, were responsible for a significant number of highly serious crimes. These offenders are referred to as **avertable recidivists,** people whose crimes could have been avoided had they been harshly punished—in this case sent to prison—in the first place.

Legal Rights of Probationers

A number of important legal issues surround probation, one set involving the civil rights of probationers and another involving the rights of probationers during the revocation process.

Civil Rights. The Supreme Court has ruled that probationers have a unique status and therefore are entitled to fewer constitutional protections than other citizens. One area of law involves the Fifth Amendment right of freedom from self-incrimination. The Court dealt with this issue in the case of *Minnesota v. Murphy* (1984).[46] In this case, Murphy was ordered to seek psychological counseling. During his therapy session, he admitted to his counselor that he had committed a rape and murder. Murphy's counselor reported this admission to Murphy's probation officer. Although Murphy had earlier been suspected of these crimes, the evidence had been insufficient to try him on those charges; his conviction had been on a lesser offense. The probation officer confronted Murphy about the rape and murder, and Murphy admitted that he had committed them. The probation officer brought the information to the police, who then had sufficient evidence to bring the case to the prosecutor.

Murphy contested his subsequent conviction on rape and murder on the grounds that the information he gave the probation officer was an in-custody interrogation and that therefore he should have been given the *Miranda* warning. However, the Supreme Court disagreed and held that the interrogation was noncustodial and that a probation officer has every right to turn information over to the police. That a probation officer can require a probationer to show up for an interview does not constitute a police arrest; therefore, the self-incrimination protections do not apply.

This case holds that the probation officer–client relationship is not confidential, like doctor-patient or attorney-client relationships. Furthermore, the *Murphy* decision held that a probation officer could even use trickery or psychological pressure to get information and turn it over to police.

A second area of law involving probationers is search and seizure. In *Griffin v. Wisconsin,* the Supreme Court held that a probationer's home may be searched without a warrant on the grounds that probation departments "have in mind the welfare of the probationer" and must "respond quickly to evidence of misconduct." The usual legal standards were deemed inapplicable to probation because to do so "would reduce the deterrent effect of the supervisory arrangement" and "the probation agency must be able to act based upon a lesser degree of certainty than the Fourth Amendment would otherwise require in order to intervene before a probationer does damage to himself or society."[47]

Revocation Rights. During the course of a probationary term, a violation of the rules or terms of probation or the commitment of a new crime can result in probation being revoked, at which time the offender may be placed in an institution. Revocation is not often an easy decision, since it conflicts with the treatment philosophy of most probation departments.

When revocation is chosen, the offender is notified and a formal hearing is scheduled. If the charges against the probationer are upheld, the offender can then be placed in an institution to serve the remainder of the sentence. Most departments will not revoke probation unless the offender commits another crime or seriously violates the rules of probation.

Because placing a person on probation implies that probation will continue unless the probationer commits some major violation, the defendant has been given certain procedural due process rights at this stage of the criminal process. In three significant decisions, the U.S. Supreme Court provided procedural safeguards to apply at proceedings to revoke probation (and parole). In *Mempa v. Rhay* (1967), the Court unanimously held that a probationer was constitutionally entitled to counsel in a revocation-of-probation proceeding where the imposition of sentence had been suspended.[48] Then, in 1972, the Supreme Court in the case of *Morrissey v. Brewer* handed down an important decision detailing the procedures required for parole revocation.[49] Because the revocations of probation and parole are similar, the standards in the *Morrissey* case affected the probation process as well. In *Morrissey,* the Court required an informal inquiry to determine whether there was probable cause to believe the arrested parolee had violated the conditions of parole, as well as a formal revocation hearing with minimum due process requirements. However, in *Morrissey* the Court did not deal with the issue of right to counsel. Chief Justice Warren Burger stated, "We do not reach or decide the question whether the parolee is entitled to the assistance of retained counsel or to appointed counsel if he is indigent."

The question of the right to counsel in revocation proceedings came up again in the 1973 case of *Gagnon v. Scarpelli.*[50] In that decision, which involved a probationer, the Supreme Court held that both probationers and parolees have a constitutionally limited right to counsel in revocation proceedings.

The *Gagnon* case can be viewed as a step forward in the application of constitutional safeguards to the correctional process. The provision of counsel helped give control over the unlimited discretion exercised in the past by probation and parole personnel in revocation proceedings.

With the development of innovative probation programs, courts have had to review the legality of changing probation rules and their effect on revocation. For example, courts have, in general, upheld the demand that restitution be made to the victim of crime.[51] Because restitution is designed to punish and reform the offender, rather than simply repay the victim, the probationer can be made legally responsible for paying restitution.

In a recent case, *United States v. Granderson* (1994), the Supreme Court helped clarify what can happen to a probationer whose community sentence is revoked. Granderson was eligible for a 6-month prison sentence but instead was given 60 months of probation. When he tested positively for drugs, his probation was revoked. The statute he was sentenced under required that he serve one-third his *original sentence* in prison. When the trial court sentenced him to 20 months, he appealed. Was his original sentence six months or sixty months? The Court found that it would be unfair to force a probationer to serve more time in prison than he would have if originally incarcerated and ruled that the proper term should have been one-third the 6 months, or 2 months.[52]

The Future of Probation

Probation will likely continue to be the most popular alternative sentence used by U.S. courts, and if anything, its use as a community-based correction will continue to grow as it has in the 1990s. Part of its appeal stems from its flexibility, which allows it to be coupled with a wide variety of treatment programs, including residential care. As prison overcrowding has grown worse, more than half the states have taken some measures to change their probation guidelines to help reduce the prison population.[53] It is unlikely that the treatment and rehabilitation potential of probation will be abandoned in the 21st century.[54]

Probation will continue to be a sentence of choice in both felony and misdemeanor cases because it holds the promise of great savings in cost at a time when many state budgets are being reduced. In fact, it is possible to help defray the cost of probation by asking clients to pay fees for probation services, a concept that would be impossible with prison inmates. At least 25 states now impose some form of fee on probationers to defray the cost of community corrections. Massachusetts has initiated day fees, which are based on the probationer's wages (the usual fee is between one and three days' wages each month).[55] An analysis of the probation fee system found that it may actually improve the quality of services afforded clients.[56] Texas requires judges to impose supervision fees unless the offender is truly unable to pay; fees make up more than half the probation department's annual budget.[57]

Probation is unquestionably undergoing dramatic changes. During the past decade, it has been supplemented and used as a restrictive correctional alternative. Expanding the scope of probation has created a new term, *intermediate sanctions,* to signify penalties that fall between traditional community supervision and confinement in jail or prison. These new correctional services are discussed in detail in the remainder of this chapter.

Community corrections has traditionally emphasized offender rehabilitation. The probation officer has been viewed as a caseworker or counselor whose primary job is to help the offender adjust to society. Offender surveillance and control has seemed more appropriate for law enforcement, jails, and prisons, than for community corrections.[58]

But since 1980, a more conservative justice system has reoriented toward social control. While the rehabilitative ideals of probation have not been abandoned, new programs have been developed that add a control dimension to community corrections. These programs can be viewed as "probation plus," since they add restrictive penalties and conditions to community service orders. Being more punitive than probation, intermediate sanctions can be sold to conservatives, while they remain attractive to liberals as alternatives to incarceration.[59]

Intermediate sanctions include programs typically administered by probation departments: intensive probation supervision, house arrest, electronic monitoring, restitution orders, shock probation or split sentences, and residential community corrections.[60] Some experts also include high-impact shock incarceration, or "boot camp" experiences, within the definition of intermediate sanctions, but since these programs are typically operated by correctional departments, they are discussed separately in Chapter 14. Intermediate sanctions also involve sentences administered independently of probation staffs: fines and forfeiture, pretrial programs, and pretrial and posttrial residential programs. Intermediate sanctions therefore range from the barely intrusive, such as restitution orders, to the highly restrictive, such as house arrest accompanied by electronic monitoring and a stay in a community correctional center.

The popularity of alternative sanctions is not limited to the United States, and they have been used around the world. For example, since 1950, in Germany the emphasis on incarceration sentences has given way to alternative measures: suspensions, probation, community service, and fines. Between 1982 and 1990, incarceration of juveniles decreased more than 50%—from 9,500 to 4,500 cases; during the same period, adult imprisonment dropped from 39,000 to 33,000. Research indicates that youthful offenders sent to prison in Germany had higher rates of recidivism than those given alternative sanctions. Removing youths from society—even when incarceration included job training—appeared (a) to negatively affect their ability to find employment when released and (b) to increase their chances of reoffending. [61]

What are the advantages of creating a system of intermediate sanctions? Primary is the need to develop alternatives to prisons and jails, which have proved to be costly, ineffective, and injurious. Research indicates that more than 60% of all prison inmates are rearrested and returned to prison, many within a short period after their release.[62] Little evidence exists that incapacitation is either a general deterrent to crime or a specific deterrent against future criminality. Some correctional systems have become inundated with new inmates. Even states that have extensively used alternative sanctions have experienced rapid increases in their prison population; the pressure on the correctional system if alternative sanctions had not been an option is almost inconceivable.[63]

Intermediate sanctions also have the potential to save money. While they are more expensive than traditional probation, they are far less costly than incarceration. If those offenders given alternative sanctions would have otherwise been incarcerated, the extra cost would be significant. In addition, offenders given intermediate sanctions generate income, pay taxes, reimburse victims, perform community service, and provide other cost savings that would be nonexistent had they been incarcerated. Although it is unlikely that intermediate sanctions

*The Advantages of
Intermediate Sanctions*

Figure 13.3
The punishment ladder.

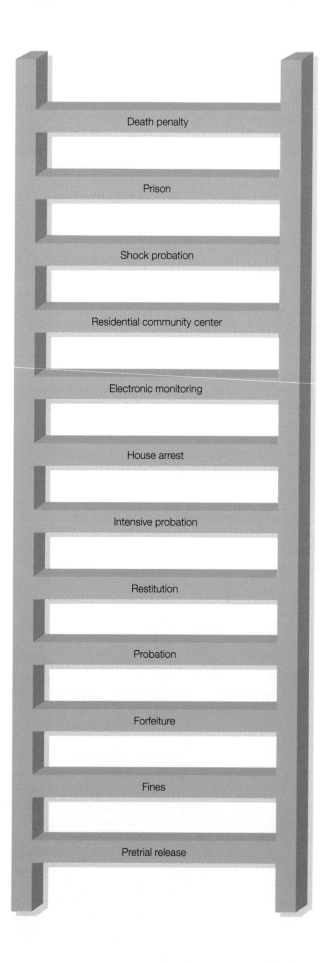

Death penalty

Prison

Shock probation

Residential community center

Electronic monitoring

House arrest

Intensive probation

Restitution

Probation

Forfeiture

Fines

Pretrial release

will pay an immediate "corrections dividend," as many correctional costs are fixed, they may reduce the need for future prison and jail construction.

Intermediate sanctions also help meet the need for developing community sentences that are fair, equitable, and proportional.[64] It seems unfair to treat both a rapist and a shoplifter with the same type of probationary sentence, considering the differences in their crimes. As Figure 13.3 illustrates, intermediate sanctions can form the successive steps of a meaningful "ladder" of scaled punishments outside of prison, thereby restoring fairness and equity to nonincarceration sentences.[65] For example, while forgers may be ordered to make restitution to their victims, rapists can be placed in a community correctional facility while they receive counseling at a local psychiatric center. This feature of intermediate sanctions allows judges to fit the punishment to the crime without resorting to a prison sentence. Intermediate sentences can be designed to increase punishment for people whose serious or repeat crimes make a straight probation sentence inappropriate yet for whom a prison sentence would be unduly harsh and counterproductive.[66]

Target Populations

In the broadest sense, intermediate sanctions can serve the needs of a number of offender groups. The most likely candidates are convicted criminals who would normally be sent to prison but who pose either a low risk of recidivism or who are of little threat to society (such as nonviolent property offenders). Used in this sense, intermediate sanctions are a viable solution to the critical problem of prison overcrowding.

Intermediate sanctions can also reduce overcrowding in jails by providing alternatives to incarceration for misdemeanants and cut the number of pretrial detainees who currently make up about half the inmate population.[67] Some forms of bail already require conditions, such as supervision by court officers and periods of home confinement (conditional bail), that are a form of intermediate sanctions.

Intermediate sanctions can also potentially be used as "halfway back" strategies for probation and parole violators. Probationers who violate the conditions of their community release could be placed under increasingly more intensive supervision before actual incarceration is required. Parolees who pose the greatest risk of recidivism might receive conditions that require close monitoring or home confinement. Parole violators could be returned to a community correctional center rather than a walled institution.

In the following sections, the forms of intermediate sanctions currently in use are more thoroughly discussed.

Fines

Fines are monetary payments imposed on offenders as an intermediate punishment for their criminal acts. They are a direct offshoot of the early common law practice of requiring compensation be paid to the victim and the state (wergild) for criminal acts. Fines are still commonly used in Europe, where they are often the sole penalty, even in cases involving chronic offenders who commit fairly serious crimes.[68]

In the United States, fines are most commonly used in cases involving misdemeanors and lesser offenses. Fines are also frequently used in felony cases where the offender benefited financially. Investor Ivan Boesky paid over $100 million for violating insider stock trading rules; the firm of Drexel Burnham Lambert paid a fine of $650 million in 1988 for securities violations.[69] A study sponsored by the federal government found that lower-court judges impose fines alone or in tandem with other penalties in 86% of their cases; superior court judges imposed fines in 42% of their cases.[70]

Fines may be used as a sole sanction or combined with other punishments, such as probation or confinement. Quite commonly, judges levy other monetary sanctions along with fines, such as court costs, public defender fees, probation and treatment fees, and victim restitution, to increase the force of the financial punishment.[71] However, there is evidence that many offenders fail to pay fines and that courts are negligent in their efforts to collect unpaid fees; it has been estimated that defendants fail to pay upwards of $2 billion in fines each year.[72]

Are Fines Fair?

In most jurisdictions, little guidance is given to the sentencing judge directing the imposition of the fine. Judges often have inadequate information on the offender's ability to pay, resulting in defaults and contempt charges. Because the standard sanction for nonpayment is incarceration, many offenders held in local jails are confined for nonpayment of criminal fines. Although the U.S. Supreme Court in *Tate v. Short* (1971) recognized that incarcerating a person who is financially unable to pay a fine discriminates against the poor, many judges continue to incarcerate offenders for noncompliance with financial orders.[73]

Research indicates that, given the facts of a case, judges do seem to use fines in a rational manner: Low-risk offenders are the ones most likely to receive fines instead of a jail sentence; the more serious the crime, the higher the amount of the fine. Offenders who are fined seem less likely to commit new crimes than those who receive a jail sentence.[74]

Day Fines

Because judges rely so heavily on offense seriousness to fix the level of fines, financial penalties may have a negative impact on success rates. The more serious the offense and the higher the fine, the greater the chances that the offender will fail to pay the fine and risk probation revocation. To overcome this sort of problem, some jurisdictions, such as New York City, are experimenting with **day fines.**[75]

A concept originated in Europe, day fines are geared to an offender's net daily income. In an effort to make them equitable and fairly distributed, fines are based on the severity of the crime weighted by a daily-income value taken from a chart similar to an income tax table; the number of the offender's dependents are also taken into account. The day fine concept means that the severity of punishment is geared to the offender's ability to pay.

Several demonstration programs have been set up recently to determine the effectiveness of the day fine concept. An evaluation of the Staten Island, New York, project indicates that it is generally successful, enabling judges to increase the amount of fines collected while reducing the number of arrest warrants issued for failure to appear at postsentencing hearings; even if the fine could not be paid in full, more offenders paid something as opposed to nothing.[76] Day fines hold the promise of becoming an equitable solution to the problem of setting the amount of a fine according to the offender's ability to pay.

Forfeiture

Another alternative sanction with a financial basis is criminal (*in personam*) and civil (*in rem*) **forfeiture.** Both involve the seizure of goods and instrumentalities related to the commission or outcome of a criminal act. For example, federal law provides that after arresting drug traffickers, the government may seize the boats they used to import the narcotics, the cars they used to carry the drugs overland, the warehouses in which the drugs were stored, and the homes paid for with the drug profits; on conviction, the drug dealers lose permanent ownership of these "instrumentalities" of crime.

Forfeiture is not a new sanction. During the Middle Ages, "forfeiture of estate" was a mandatory result of most felony convictions. The Crown could seize all of a felon's real and personal property. Forfeiture derived from the common law concept of "corruption of blood" or "attaint," which prohibited a felon's family from inheriting or receiving his or her property or estate. The common law mandated that descendants could not inherit property from a relative who may have attained the property illegally: "[T]he Corruption of Blood stops the Course of Regular Descent, as to Estates, over which the Criminal could have no Power, because he never enjoyed them."[77]

Forfeiture was reintroduced to U.S. law with the passage of the Racketeer Influenced and Corrupt Organizations (RICO) and the Continuing Criminal Enterprises acts, both of which allow the seizure of any property derived from illegal enterprises or conspiracies. While these acts were designed to apply to ongoing criminal conspiracies, such as drug or pornography rings, they are now being applied to a far-ranging series of criminal acts, including white-collar crimes. More than 100 federal statutes use forfeiture of property as a punishment.

Although law enforcement officials at first applauded the use of forfeiture as a hard-hitting way of seizing the illegal profits of drug law violators, the practice has been criticized because the government has often been overzealous in its application. For example, million-dollar yachts have been seized because someone aboard possessed a small amount of marijuana; this confiscatory practice is referred to as **zero tolerance.** This strict interpretation of the forfeiture statutes has come under fire because it is often used capriciously, the penalty is sometimes disproportionate to the crime involved, and it makes the government a "partner in crime."[78]

The Supreme Court has expanded the ability of government agents to seize property in some instances and restricted it in others. For example, in the recent case of *United States v. Ursery* (1996), the Court settled the issue of whether a person can both have his assets seized and be persecuted for a criminal offense. Jerome Ursery paid a fine of $13,250 to settle a civil forfeiture claim against his home after police seized 147 marijuana plants on the premises. He was later criminally prosecuted and sentenced to prison. In its opinion, the Court argued that the Constitution bars successive prosecutions for the same crime, not successive punishments.[79] In another case that expanded police power to seize property, *Bennis v. Michigan,* the Supreme Court ruled that a person's property could be seized and confiscated if used in a crime even if the owner had no knowledge of the crime; an "innocent owner" cannot recover his or her property. [80]

Some commentators, such as Eric Jensen and Jurg Gerber, maintain that the use of (civil) forfeiture has allowed the government to impose what in essence are fines that are "unreasonable and severely disproportionate to the seriousness of the offense, a condition that is unacceptable in a society based on the rule of law."[81] And, in fact, the Supreme Court limited confiscatory practices in two recent cases, *Austin v. United States* and *Alexander v. United States,* in which it held that the seizure of property must be proportional to the seriousness of the crime in both civil and criminal forfeitures.[82] In the *Alexander* case, the government seized an entire chain of adult bookstores and ordered the destruction of the entire inventory of 100,000 items after the owner had been convicted of selling 7 obscene items; *Austin* involved the civil seizure of the defendant's home and business after he was convicted of possessing 2 grams of cocaine. Despite this setback, it is likely that forfeiture will continue to be used as an alternative sanction against such selective targets as drug dealers and white-collar criminals.

Another popular intermediate sanction is **restitution,** which can take the form of requiring offenders either to pay back the victims of crime (**monetary restitution**) or serve the community to compensate for their criminal acts (**community service restitution**).[83] Restitution programs offer offenders a chance to avoid a jail or prison sentence or a lengthier probationary period. It may help them develop a sense of allegiance to society, better work habits, and some degree of gratitude for being given a second chance. Restitution serves many other purposes, including giving the community something of value without asking it to foot the bill for an incarceration stay and helping victims regain lost property and income.[84]

Surveys on financial restitution indicate that

- Financial restitution is ordered in about 30% of all probation cases.

- The average award is about $3,400 per case.

- About 60% of all orders are paid in full within three years.

- In an additional 11% of cases, at least something is paid.[85]

Restitution

If monetary restitution is called for, the probation department typically makes a determination of victim loss and develops a plan for paying fair compensation. To avoid the situation in which a well-heeled offender can fill a restitution order by merely writing a check, judges will sometimes order that compensation be paid out of income derived from a low-paid social service or public works job.

Community service orders usually require duty in a public nursing home, shelter, hospital, drug treatment unit, or works program; some young vandals may find that they must clean up the damage they caused to the school or the park. Judges sometimes have difficulty gauging the length of community service orders. One suggestion is that the maximum order should be no more than 240 hours and that this should be considered the equivalent of a 6- to 12-month jail term.[86] Whether these terms are truly equivalent remains a matter of personal opinion.

Judges and probation officers have embraced the concept of restitution because it appears to benefit the victim of crime, the offender, the criminal justice system, and society.[87] Financial restitution is inexpensive to administer, helps avoid stigma, and provides compensation for victims of crime. Offenders ordered to do community service work have been placed in schools, hospitals, and nursing homes. Helping them avoid a jail sentence can mean saving the public thousands of dollars that would have gone to maintaining them in a secure institution, frees up needed resources, and gives the community the feeling that equity has been returned to the justice system.

Does restitution work? Most reviews rate it as a qualified success.[88] It is estimated that almost 90% of the clients successfully complete their restitution orders and that 86% have no subsequent contact with the justice system. Most restitution orders are met by a majority of program clients.[89] Other research indicates that those receiving restitution sentences have equal or lower recidivism rates compared to control groups that include those receiving incarceration sentences.[90] One evaluation of community service orders in a federal district court in northern California found that groups of offenders receiving community service were no more likely to commit new crimes than equivalent groups who had suffered incarceration. If this finding is valid, community service would be an effective and less expensive alternative to a jail or prison sentence.[91]

While these findings are encouraging, the original enthusiasm for the restitution concept has been dampened somewhat by concern that it has not lived up to its promise of being a true alternative to incarceration. Critics charge that restitution merely serves to "widen the net" and increase the proportion of persons whose behavior is regulated and controlled by the state.[92] Instead of helping defendants avoid the pains of imprisonment, restitution orders are believed to add to the burden of people who would ordinarily have been given a relatively lenient probation sentence instead of a prison term.[93]

Shock probation and **split sentences** are alternative sanctions designed to allow judges to grant offenders community release only after they have sampled prison life. These sanctions are based on the premise that if offenders are given a taste of incarceration sufficient to shock them into law-abiding behavior, they will be reluctant to violate the rules of probation or commit another crime.

In a number of states and in the Federal Criminal Code, a jail term can actually be a condition of probation, known as split sentencing. Under current federal practices, about 15% of all convicted federal offenders receive some form of split sentence, including both prison and jail as a condition of probation; this number is expected to rise to 25% as tougher sentencing laws take effect.[94] In state courts, about half of all probationers are believed to receive a jail term as a condition of probation. California and New York routinely include a jail term as a condition of probation, and in one California jurisdiction (Orange County), almost all felony probationers receive jail sentences.[95]

The shock probation approach involves resentencing an offender to probation after a short prison stay. The shock comes because the offender originally receives a long maximum sentence but is then eligible for release to community supervision at the discretion of the judge (usually within 90 days of incarceration). About one-third of all probationers in the 14 states that use the program (including Ohio, Kentucky, Idaho, New Jersey, Tennessee, Utah, and Vermont) receive a period of confinement.[96] Evaluations of shock probation have shown it to be quite effective.[97]

Some states have linked the short prison stay with a boot camp experience, referred to as *shock incarceration,* in which young inmates undergo a brief but intense period of militarylike training and hard labor designed to impress them with the vigors of prison life.[98] Boot camp programs will be discussed in greater detail in Chapter 14. Shock probation and split sentencing have been praised as ways to limit prison time, reintegrate the client quickly into the community, maintain family ties, and reduce prison populations and the costs of corrections.[99] An initial jail sentence probably makes offenders more receptive to the conditions of probation, since it amply illustrates the problems they will face if probation is violated.

Split sentences and shock probation programs have been criticized by those who believe that even a brief period of incarceration can interfere with the purpose of probation, which is to provide the offender with nonstigmatizing, community-based treatment. Even a short-term commitment subjects probationers to the destructive effects of institutionalization, disrupts their life in the community, and stigmatizes them for having been in jail.

Intensive probation supervision (IPS) programs are another important form of intermediate sanction (these programs are also referred to as intensive supervision programs). IPS programs, which have been implemented in some form in about 45 states and today include more than 50,000 clients, involve small caseloads of 15 to 40 clients who are kept under close watch by probation officers.[100]

The primary goal of IPS is decarceration: Without intensive supervision, clients would normally be sent to already overcrowded prisons or jails.[101] The second goal is control: High-risk offenders can be maintained in the community under much closer security than traditional probation efforts can provide. A

Shock Probation and Split Sentencing

Intensive Probation Supervision (IPS)

third goal is reintegration: Offenders can maintain community ties and be reoriented toward a more productive life while avoiding the pains of imprisonment.

In general, IPS programs rely on a great degree of client contact to achieve the goals of diversion, control, and reintegration.[102] Most programs have admissions criteria based on the nature of the offense and the offender's criminal background. Some programs, such as New Jersey's, exclude violent offenders; others will not take substance abusers. In contrast, some jurisdictions, such as Massachusetts, do not exclude offenders based on their prior criminal history. About 60% of existing programs exclude offenders who have already violated probation orders or who otherwise failed on probation.

Types of IPS Programs

Intensive probation supervision programs are used in several ways. In some states, IPS is a direct sentence imposed by a judge; in others, it is a postsentencing alternative used to divert offenders from the correctional system. A third practice is to use IPS as a case management tool to give the local probation staff flexibility in dealing with clients. Other jurisdictions use IPS in all three ways in addition to applying it to probation violators to bring them "halfway back" into the community without resorting to a prison term.

Numerous IPS programs operate around the United States. The best known is Georgia's, which serves as a model for many other states' efforts. Georgia's program includes such measures as

- Five face-to-face contacts per week

- 132 hours of mandatory community service

- Mandatory curfew

- Mandatory employment

- Weekly check of local arrest records

- Automatic notification of arrest via the State Crime Information Network listing

- Routine and unannounced drug and alcohol testing[103]

An evaluation of the Georgia program gave it generally high marks: it reached its target audience and resulted in a 10% reduction in the number of felons incarcerated without a significant increase in the recidivism rate.[104] While an IPS program is more expensive than a straight probation sentence, it is far less costly than prison. IPS averages about $16 per day, while prison costs about $60; in addition, IPS clients are employed, which allows them to save the state additional revenues by paying taxes, making victim restitution, and supporting families.[105]

How Effective Is IPS?

Evaluations indicate that IPS programs are generally successful, deliver more services than would normally be received by probationers, are cost-effective, and produce recidivism rates equal to or better than those of offenders who have been confined.[106] However, evaluations have so far not been definitive, often ignoring such issues as whether the program met its stated goals, whether IPS is more attractive than other alternative sanctions, and which types of offenders are particularly suited for IPS. For example, IPS seems to work better for offenders with good employment records than it does for the underemployed or unemployed.[107] Younger offenders who commit petty crimes are the most likely to fail on IPS; ironically, people with these characteristics are the ones most likely to be included in IPS programs.[108]

Indications also exist that the failure rate in IPS caseloads is quite high, in some cases approaching 50%; IPS clients may even have a higher rearrest rate than other probationers.[109] It should come as no surprise that IPS clients fail more often because, after all, they are more serious criminals who might otherwise have been incarcerated and are now being watched and supervised more closely than probationers. Probation officers may also be more willing to revoke the probation of IPS clients because they believe the clients are a risk to the community and, under normal circumstances, would have been incarcerated. Why risk the program to save a few "bad apples"?

In an important analysis of IPS programs in three California counties, Joan Petersilia and Susan Turner found that IPS clients were less dangerous than those sent to prison and just as likely to commit new crimes as clients in traditional probation caseloads.[110] Another nationwide study also found that IPS clients were just as likely to get arrested for new offenses as those in traditional correctional caseloads and more likely to have probation revoked for a technical violation; IPS is a waste of taxpayers' money if it works no better than traditional probation and serves a similar clientele.[111]

Although evidence that it can significantly reduce offending rates is still insufficient, IPS might be an attractive alternative to traditional correctional methods if it can be restricted to offenders who would most likely have been incarcerated without the availability of the IPS program. These programs can succeed only if they are supported both within the probation organization and by the criminal justice system and the community.[112] While effective leadership is important, IPS cannot survive in an atmosphere where people believe it is a device that allows dangerous offenders to remain in the community essentially unsupervised.

House Arrest

A number of states, including Florida, Oklahoma, Oregon, Kentucky, and California, have developed **house arrest** programs as an intermediate sanction. The house arrest concept requires convicted offenders to spend extended periods of time in their own home as an alternative to an incarceration sentence. For example, persons convicted on a drunk driving charge might be sentenced to spend between 6 P.M. Friday and 8 A.M. Monday and every weekday after 5:30 P.M. in their home for six months. Current estimates indicate that more than 10,000 people are under house arrest; Florida alone has placed 40,000 offenders under house arrest during the past decade.[113]

As with IPS programs, there is a great deal of variation in house arrest initiatives: Some are administered by probation departments, while others are simply judicial sentences monitored by **surveillance officers.** Some check clients 20 or more times a month (such as the Florida Community Control Program), while others do only a few curfew checks. Some use 24-hour confinement, while others allow offenders to attend work or school. Regardless of the model used, house arrest programs are designed to be more punitive than IPS or any other community supervision alternative and are considered a "last chance" before prison.[114]

No definitive data exist indicating that house arrest is an effective crime deterrent, nor is there sufficient evidence to conclude that it has utility as a device to lower the recidivism rate. One evaluation of the Florida program found that nearly 10% of the house arrest sample had their probation revoked for technical violations within 18 months of their sentencing.[115] Another evaluation of the same program found that recidivism rates were almost identical to a matched sample of inmates released from secure correctional facilities; four out of five offenders in both forms of correction recidivated within five years.[116]

Criticisms of house arrest also include charges that it has little deterrent value and seems more like being "grounded" than real punishment. They point to such cases as that of convicted Saudi arms dealer Adnan Khashoggi, whose "punishment" required him to be in his 30,000-square-foot luxury home—with its own swimming pool—between the hours of 1 A.M. and 8 A.M. with permission to take trips to Aspen and Fort Lauderdale.[117] While these findings are troublesome, the advantages of house arrest in reducing costs and overcrowding in the correctional system probably make further experimentation inevitable.

For house arrest to work, sentencing authorities must be assured that arrestees are actually at home during their assigned times. Random calls and visits are one way to check on compliance with house arrest orders. However, one of the more interesting developments in the criminal justice system has been the introduction of **electronic monitoring (EM)** devices to manage offender obedience to home confinement orders. Electronic monitoring programs have been around since 1964, when Ralph Schwitzgabel of Harvard University experimented with linking offenders with a central monitoring station.[118] As Figure 13.4 shows, electronic monitoring can be used with offenders at a variety of points in the criminal justice system, ranging from pretrial release to parole.

Electronically monitored offenders wear devices around their ankles, wrists, or necks that send signals back to a control office. Two basic types of systems are used: active and passive. Active systems constantly monitor offenders by continuously sending a signal back to the central office. If offenders leave their home at an unauthorized time, the signal is broken and the "failure" recorded. In some cases, the control officer is automatically notified electronically through a beeper. In contrast, passive systems usually involve random phone calls generated by computers to which the offenders have to respond within a particular time (such as 30 seconds). Some passive systems require offenders to place their monitoring device into a verifier box that then sends a signal back to the control computer; another approach is to have the arrestee repeat words that are analyzed by a voice verifier and compared to tapes of the client's voice. Other systems use radio transmitters that receive a signal from a device worn by the offenders and relay it back to the computer monitoring system via telephone lines.

The Benefits of EM

Electronic monitoring combined with house arrest is being hailed as one of the most important developments in correctional policy.[119] Its supporters claim the EM has the benefits of relatively low cost and high security, while helping offenders avoid the pains of imprisonment in overcrowded, dangerous state facilities. Electronic monitoring is capital- rather than labor-intensive. Since offenders are monitored by computers, an initial investment in hardware rules out the need for hiring many more supervisory officers to handle large numbers of clients.

There are some indications that EM can be an effective addition to the galaxy of alternative sanctions, providing the judiciary with an enhanced supervision tool.[120] Program evaluations with pretrial, probation, and parole groups indicate that recidivism rates are no higher than in traditional programs, costs are lower, and system overcrowding is reduced.[121] Research shows that while

Figure 13.4
Key decision points where electronic monitoring programs are being used.
SOURCE: James Byrne, Arthur Lurigio, and Christopher Baird, *The Effectiveness of the New Intensive Supervision Programs,* Research in Corrections Series, vol. 2, no. 2 (preliminary unpublished draft; Washington, D.C.: National Institute of Corrections, 1989).

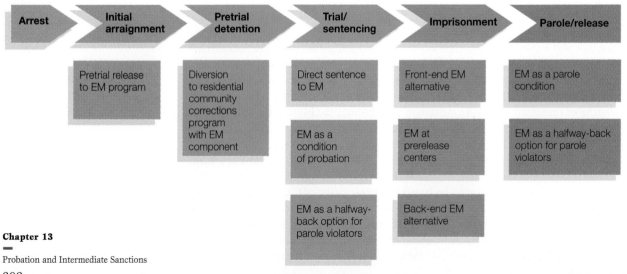

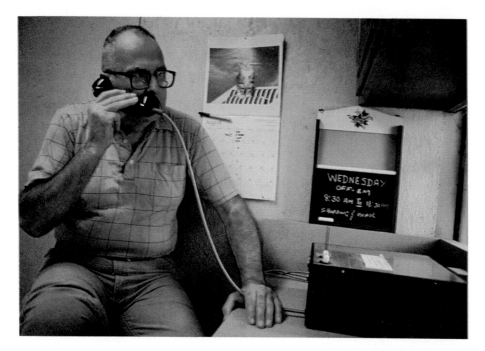

Larry Ingles, convicted of drunk driving, answers a home electronic monitoring call in his home. Advocates suggest that EM allows nondangerous offenders such as Ingles to avoid a jail sentence, freeing up space for more violent criminals. Opponents charge that EM is an invasion of privacy and represents the triumph of "big brother" government over the general public.

many EM clients are cited for program violations, recidivism rates are quite low, clients find the program valuable, and many use the opportunity to obtain jobs and improve family relationships.[122] If the program can service defendants who definitely would have been confined without the option of EM (for example, people convicted of driving while intoxicated in jurisdictions that have mandatory incarceration sentences), it will prove to be an efficient correctional option that works as well as if not better than a probation sentence.[123]

Electronic monitoring holds the promise of becoming a widely used intermediate sanction in the 1990s. Nevertheless, a few critics charge that the concept has drawbacks that can counterbalance the advantages gained from its provision of low-cost confinement.

    First, current technology is limited. Existing systems can be affected by faulty telephone equipment, by radio beams from powerful transmitters, such as those located at airports or radio stations, by storms and weather disturbances, and even by large concentrations of iron and steel, which can block signals or cause electromagnetic interference. There have also been cases when EM has been "defeated" by people using call-forwarding systems and prerecorded messages to fool monitors.[124] Assessing what the proper response should be when tracking equipment reveals a breach of home confinement is difficult: Can we incarcerate someone for what might be an equipment failure?

    It may also be inaccurate to assume that electronic monitoring can provide secure confinement at a relatively low cost. In addition to the initial outlay for the cost of equipment, other expenses involved with electronic monitoring include overtime pay for control officers who must be on duty nights or weekends, the cost of training personnel to use the sophisticated equipment, and the cost of educating judges in the legality of home confinement. The cost of home confinement with electronic monitoring is estimated to be four times greater than that of traditional probation.[125]

    Most electronic monitoring or house arrest programs do not provide for rehabilitation services, since the focus is on guaranteeing the secure incapacitation of offenders and not their treatment. Ultimately, electronic monitoring may lack the deterrent power of a prison sentence while offering little of the rehabilitative effects of traditional probation.

The Limits of EM

It is assumed that EM will be used as a cost-saving alternative to jail or prison. Unfortunately, alternative sanctions are often directed at offenders who might have received more lenient sentences in the past, thereby "widening the net" of the criminal system of justice.[126] Electronic monitoring will not save money unless it eliminates the need for new jail and prison construction, as it is unlikely that staff in existing institutions will be let go because offenders are being monitored in their homes.[127]

Some civil libertarians are troubled by the fact that electronic monitoring can erode privacy and liberty. Do we really want U.S. citizens watched over by a computer? What are the limits of electronic monitoring? Can it be used with mental patients? HIV carriers? Suicidal teenagers? Those considered high-risk future offenders? While promising to reduce the correctional population, EM actually has the potential to substantially increase it by turning homes into prisons.[128]

While EM seems to hold great promise, both its effectiveness and its virtue have not been determined. It is not yet clear whether EM is a correctional savior or a temporary fad.[129]

Residential Community Corrections (RCC)

The most secure intermediate sanction is a sentence to a **residential community corrections (RCC)** facility. Such a facility has been defined as

> a freestanding nonsecure building that is not part of a prison or jail and houses pretrial and adjudicated adults. The residents regularly depart to work, to attend school, and/or participate in treatment activities and programs.[130]

Traditionally, the role of community corrections was supplied by the nonsecure halfway house, designed to reintegrate soon-to-be-paroled prison inmates back into the community. Inmates spend the last few months in the halfway house acquiring suitable employment, building up cash reserves, obtaining an apartment, and developing a job-related wardrobe.

The traditional concept of community corrections has expanded recently. Today, the community correctional facility is a vehicle to provide intermediate sanctions as well as a prerelease center for those about to be paroled from the prison system. For example, RCC has been used as a direct sentencing option for judges who believe particular offenders need a correctional alternative halfway between traditional probation and a stay in prison. Placement in an RCC center can be used as a condition of probation for offenders who need a nonsecure

Placement in an RCC center can be used as a condition of probation for offenders who need a nonsecure community facility that provides a more structured treatment environment than traditional probation. Here some residents are at dinner at the Outreach Home in Coney Island, New York.

community facility that provides a more structured treatment environment than traditional probation. It is quite commonly used in the juvenile justice system for youths who need a more secure environment than can be provided by traditional probation yet who are not deemed a threat to the community requiring a secure placement.

Probation departments and other correctional authorities have been charged with running RCC centers that serve as a preprison sentencing alternative. In addition, some RCC centers are operated by private, nonprofit groups that receive referrals from the county or district courts and from probation or parole departments. For example, Portland House, a private residential center in Minneapolis, operates as an alternative to incarceration for young adult felony offenders. The 25 residents regularly receive group therapy and financial, vocational, educational, family, and personal counseling. Residents may work to earn a high school equivalency degree. With funds withheld from their earnings at work-release employment, residents pay room and board, family and self support, and income taxes. Portland House appears to be successful. It is significantly cheaper to run than a state institution, and the recidivism rate of clients is much lower than that of those who have gone through traditional correctional programs.[131]

Functions of RCC Programs

Another well-known RCC program is Nexus, in Onamia, Minnesota. Nexus accepts males ages 13 to 18 who have an intensive history of involvement in the criminal justice system. The Nexus program has a mixed population but provides primary treatment for young sex offenders. Services include treatment for chemical dependency as well as educational, financial, and vocational counseling. Each resident receives a comprehensive individual diagnosis of his treatment needs. The program philosophy stresses adoption of treatments that have a proven record of success. Residents are often asked to make restitution to the victims of their crime. Nexus is currently expanding. A new residential program has opened in Dupage County, Illinois, and the Nexus approach is being adapted to a nonresidential program developed in conjunction with social services, court services, mental health agencies, and the schools in the Chicago suburbs.[132]

In addition to being sole sentence and halfway houses, RCC facilities have also been residential pretrial release centers for offenders who are in immediate need of social services before their trial and as halfway-back alternatives for both parole and probation violators who might otherwise have to be imprisoned. In this capacity, RCC programs serve as a base from which offenders can be placed in outpatient psychiatric facilities, drug and alcohol treatment programs, job training, and so on. Some programs make use of both in-patient and out-patient programs to provide clients with specialized treatment, such as substance abuse management.[133]

One recent development has been the use of RCC facilities as **day reporting centers (DRCs)**.[134] Day reporting centers provide a single location to which a variety of clients can report for supervision and treatment. Used in Massachusetts, Connecticut, Minnesota, and other states, DRCs utilize existing RCC facilities to service nonresidential clients. They can be used as a step up for probationers who have failed in the community and a step down in security for jail or prison inmates.[135] For example, Genesis II in Minneapolis serves female clients with multiple problems who attend the program five days a week for up to six hours a day. The women have been involved in prostitution and child abuse and may be drug dependent. Genesis II operates a licensed day care center to both care for children while their mothers are in treatment and monitor the youngsters for signs of child abuse. Day reporting centers report better success rates with inmates released from secure confinement (70%–80%) and average success with probationers (50%). However, the former may be among the best risks in their groups, while the latter are generally program failures.

Day Reporting Centers (DRCs)

Can Alternative Sanctions Work?

Some criminal justice professionals welcome the use of intermediate sanctions as a practical alternative to prison, while others are skeptical about the ability of community sentences to significantly reduce the correctional population.

Against Alternative Sanctions

Skeptics John Dilulio and Charles Logan argue that it is a "myth" that prison crowding can be reduced, that new construction can be avoided, and that annual operating costs can be cut if greater advantage is taken of intensive probation, fines, electronic monitoring, community service, boot camps, wilderness programs, and placement in nonsecure settings such as halfway houses.

The myth, they suggest, is that we need more sanctions to use as alternatives to imprisonment because we do not already make the maximum possible use of existing alternatives to imprisonment. This is a false premise. There are already millions of people on probation and parole. About two-thirds of convicted felons are already sentenced to at least some period of incarceration. However, at any time after sentencing and prior to final discharge from the criminal justice system, the great majority of those under correctional supervision will be in the community and not incarcerated. In other words, most convicted criminals are already experiencing an "alternative sanction" for at least some part of their sentence.

If one-third of convicted felons receive no incarceration at all, and three-quarters receive at least some time on probation or parole, how much room is left for expanding the use of alternatives to imprisonment? Some, perhaps, but probably not much, especially if you look at offenders' prior records when searching for additional convicts to divert or remove from prison. Two-thirds of inmates currently in state prisons were given probation as an alternative sanction one or more times on prior convictions, and over 80% have had prior convictions resulting in either probation or incarceration. After how many failures for a given offender do we say that alternatives to imprisonment have been exhausted?

In sum, the idea that we have not given alternatives to imprisonment a fair chance is a myth. Any day of the week you will find three times as many convicts under alternative supervision as you will find under the watchful eye of a warden. And most of those in the warden's custody are probably there at least partly because they did not do well under some prior alternative.

For Alternative Sanctions

While they recognize that intermediate punishments have not worked as designed, Michael Tonry and Mary Lynch still believe that can be a useful correctional tool. To create credible alternatives to prison three obstacles must be overcome: (1) Lawmakers must reject the current obsession with strict sentences that has made the

The Effectiveness of RCC

More than 2,000 state-run community-based facilities are in use today. In addition, up to 2,500 private, nonprofit RCC programs operate in the United States. About half also have inmates who have been released from prison (halfway houses) and use the RCC placement to ease back into returning to society. The remainder are true intermediate sanctions, including about 400 federally sponsored programs.[136]

Despite the thousands of traditional and innovative RCC programs in operation around the United States, relatively few efforts have been made to evaluate their effectiveness. Those evaluations that do exist suggest that many residents do not complete their treatment regimen in RCC facilities, violating the rules or committing new offenses. Those that do complete the program have lower recidivism rates than the unsuccessful discharges.[137]

One reason that it is so difficult to assess RCC is that programs differ considerably with respect to target population, treatment alternatives, and goals. While some are rehabilitation-oriented and operate under loose security, others are control-oriented and use such security measures as random drug and alcohol testing. Although critics question their overall effectiveness, RCC facilities appear to work for some types of offenders, and some treatment orientations seem to work better than others. It is possible that rather than being used as a "last re-

United States far more punitive than other Western nations; 30-year sentences for drug crimes would be unimaginable in most countries. (2) The widespread commitment to "just desert" must be softened. In the effort to make sure that sentences are fair and equal, the differences between crimes have become blurred. Not everyone who commits a robbery is the same and they should not receive identical punishments. One robber may require a prison sentence while another warrants a nonsecure intermediate sanction. (3) Judges are more likely to sentence people to intermediate sanctions who heretofore had been given a probation sentence, which results in "widening the net."

To overcome these obstacles, a number of solutions might be tried. Clients for alternative sanction programs might be chosen from those already incarcerated, eliminating the threat of net widening. Judges' discretion could be modified by creating guidelines that mandate alternative sanctions for certain crimes or groups of offenders. It might also be possible to create "exchange rates" that create equivalent sentences for prison and community alternatives, such as three days in home confinement instead of one day in jail. While intermediate sanctions are not a panacea for all offenders (as Tonry and Lynch put it, "there is no free lunch"), they conclude

. . . for offenders who do not present unacceptable risks of violence, well-managed intermediate sanctions offer a cost-effective way to keep them in the community at less cost than imprisonment and with no worse later prospects for criminality.

Critical Thinking Questions

1. Alternative sanctions seem to work as well as prison at a much lower cost. If nonviolent offenders could be monitored in the community as effectively as they are in prison, would it not free up more cells to house dangerous predatory criminals for longer periods of time?

2. The fact that two-thirds of all inmates have already served probation sentences before their current incarceration is not conclusive evidence that most inmates have failed in the community and that increasing the frequency of intermediate sanctions would be to no avail. It is unlikely that these inmates were placed in new alternative sanction programs or were subject to a mix of community control and treatment. While probation has certainly been given a chance, the true value of intermediate sanctions has yet to be measured. Should they be used with all nonviolent criminals?

SOURCES: John Dilulio and Charles Logan, "The Ten Deadly Myths About Crime and Punishment in the U.S.," *Wisconsin Interest* 1 (1992): 21–35; Michael Tonry and Mary Lynch, "Intermediate Sanctions," *Crime and Justice, A Review of Research*, vol. 20, ed. Michael Tonry (Chicago: University of Chicago Press, 1996), pp. 99–144, quote, p. 137.

sort" community alternative before sentence to a jail or prison, RCC placement might actually work better with first-time offenders who have relatively little experience with the criminal or juvenile justice systems.[138]

The rapid increase in the use of community corrections and the variety of alternative sanctions now available reflect the dual correctional concerns of economy and control. On the one hand, the public is concerned about the expense of the criminal justice system. Existing facilities are overcrowded, and budget cutbacks in many states promise little chance of relief. On the other hand, the public wants to feel safe in their homes and protected from predatory criminals. This dilemma is the subject of the accompanying Analyzing Criminal Issues box, "Can Alternative Sanctions Work?"

Alternative, community-based sanctions hold the promise of satisfying both needs by being cost-effective crime control strategies without widening the net of the criminal justice system.[139] They reduce overreliance on incarceration and exploding correctional construction costs.[140] Nonetheless, there are indications that as currently situated, alternative sanctions are no more effective in reducing recidivism than traditional forms of probation and, because of the more intense monitoring involved, may result in more offenders being discovered to have

The Future of Intermediate Sanctions

committed technical violations.[141] Revocation for technical reasons helps increase rather than decrease the correctional population, an outcome in opposition to the stated goals of alternative sentencing.[142]

One approach to improve alternative sentencing may be to meet offender needs with a market basket of community corrections approaches. Already there are indications that intermediate sanctions can be made more effective if they are used collectively. For example, program evaluations indicate that electronic monitoring is highly successful when clients are also placed in treatment programs.[143] One evaluation of a community-based drug treatment program for electronically monitored offenders in Oregon found that it was a highly successful alternative to incarceration. Electronic monitoring plus treatment helped lower recidivism rates for a client group that has typically resisted rehabilitation efforts.[144] Another effort in 22 Colorado jurisdictions combines electronic monitoring with intensive probation supervision. The program, which also features on-site drug testing, seems to be a successful alternative to prison at a reasonable cost.[145] Intensive probation is also being combined with intensive drug treatment programs so that it can be successfully used with high-risk substance abusers. Such a substance abuse program for probationers shows promise of being a more successful strategy to produce a drug- and crime-free lifestyle than traditional probation.

A number of important documents can be accessed on the Internet that provide information about probation and intermediate sanctions. For example, the National Institute of Justice (NIJ) conducts the National Assessment Program (NAP) survey approximately every three years to identify the needs and problems for state and local probation and parole agency directors. The survey asks participants about their workload problems and initiatives to solve them, as well as about special concerns and needs. Find out more at:

http://www.ncjrs.org/txtfiles/ppa.txt

The Internet contains a number of important documents on developing intermediate sanctions. A 1997 report titled *Key Legislative Issues in Criminal Intermediate Sanctions Justice: Intermediate Sanctions* addresses the pros and cons of the principal forms of intermediate sanctions, including intensive supervision programs, home confinement (with or without electronic monitoring), community service orders, prison boot camps, day fines, and day reporting centers. You can read this report at:

**http://www.ncjrs.org/
txtfiles/161838.txt**

Summary

Probation can be traced to the common-law practice of granting clemency to deserving offenders. The modern probation concept was developed by John Augustus of Boston, who personally sponsored 2,000 convicted inmates over an 18-year period. Today, probation is the community supervision of convicted offenders by order of the court. It is a sentence reserved for defendants who the magistrate views as having potential for rehabilitation without needing to serve prison or jail terms. Probation is practiced in every state and by the federal government and includes both adult and juvenile offenders.

In the decision to grant probation, most judges are influenced by their personal views and the presentence reports of the probation staff. Once on probation, the offender must follow a set of rules or conditions, the violation of which may lead to revocation of probation and reinstatement of a prison sentence. These rules vary from state to state but usually involve such demands as refraining from using alcohol or drugs, obeying curfews, and terminating past criminal associations.

Probation officers are usually organized into countywide departments, although some agencies are statewide and others are combined parole-probation departments. Probation departments have instituted a number of innovative programs designed to bring better services to their clients. These include restitution and diversionary programs, intensive probation, and residential probation.

In recent years, the U.S. Supreme Court has granted probationers greater due process rights; today, when the state wishes to revoke probation, it must conduct a full hearing on the matter and pro- vide the probationer with an attorney when that assistance is warranted.

To supplement probation, a whole new family of alternative sanctions have been developed. These range from pretrial diversion to residential community corrections. Other widely used alternative sanctions include fines and forfeiture, house arrest, and intensive probation supervision. Electronic monitoring (EM) involves a device worn by an offender under home confinement. While some critics complain that EM smacks of a "Big Brother Is Watching You" mentality, it would seem an attractive alternative to a stay in a dangerous and deteriorated secure correctional facility. A stay in a community correctional center is one of the most intrusive alternative sentencing options. Residents may be eligible for work and educational release during the day while attending group sessions in the evening. Residential community correction is less costly than more secure institutions while being equally effective.

While it is too soon to determine whether these programs are successful, they provide the hope of being low-cost, high-security alternatives to traditional corrections. Alternatives to incarceration can help reduce overcrowding in the prison system and spare nonviolent offenders the pains of a prison experience. While alternatives may not be much more effective than a prison sentence in reducing recidivism rates, they are far less costly and can free up needed space for more violent offenders.

Key Terms

probation
judicial reprieve
recognizance
sureties
revocation
suspended sentence
chief probation officer
presentence investigation
intake
diagnosis

risk classification
avertable recidivists
intermediate sanctions
fines
day fines
forfeiture
zero tolerance
restitution
monetary restitution
community service restitution

shock probation
split sentences
intensive probation supervision (IPS)
house arrest
surveillance officers
electronic monitoring (EM)
residential community correction (RCC)
day reporting centers (DRCs)

Questions

1. What is the purpose of probation? Identify some conditions of probation, and discuss the responsibilities of the probation officer.
2. Discuss the procedures involved in probation revocation. What are the rights of the probationer?
3. Is probation a privilege or a right?
4. Should a convicted criminal make restitution to the victim? When is restitution inappropriate?
5. Should offenders be fined based on the severity of what they did or according to their ability to pay? Is it fair to gear day fines to wages? Should offenders be punished more severely because they are financially successful?
6. Does house arrest involve a violation of personal freedom? Does wearing an ankle bracelet smack of "Big Brother"? Would you want the government monitoring your daily activities? Could this be expanded, for example, to monitor the whereabouts of AIDS patients?
7. Would you want a community correctional center located in your neighborhood?

Notes

1. Allen Beck and Bernard Shipley, *Recidivism of Young Parolees* (Washington, D.C.: Bureau of Justice Statistics, 1987), p. 1.

2. Arnulf Kolstad, "Imprisonment as Rehabilitation: Offenders' Assessment of Why It Does Not Work," *Journal of Criminal Justice* 24 (1996): 323–335.

3. See, generally, Todd Clear and Vincent O'Leary, *Controlling the Offender in the Community* (Lexington, Mass.: Lexington Books, 1983).

4. For a history of probation, see Edward Sieh, "From Augustus to the Progressives: A Study of Probation's Formative Years," *Federal Probation* 57 (1993): 67–72.

5. Ibid.

6. David Rothman, *Conscience and Convenience* (Boston: Little, Brown, 1980), pp. 82–117.

7. Lawrence Greenfield, *Probation and Parole, 1987* (Washington, D.C.: Bureau of Justice Statistics, 1988), p. 20.

8. Ibid.

9. Bureau of Justice Statistics, "Probation and Parole Population Reaches Almost 3.8 Million," press release, 30 June 1996.

10. *Higdon v. United States,* 627 F.2d 893 (9th Cir. 1980).

11. Jerome Weissman, "Constitutional Primer on Modern Probation Conditions," *New England Journal on Prison Law* 8 (1982): 367–393.

12. Patrick Langan and Mark Cuniff, *Recidivism of Felons on Probation, 1986–1989* (Washington, D.C.: Bureau of Justice Statistics, 1992).

13. *Ramaker v. State,* 73 Wis.2d 563, 243 N.W.2d 534 (1976).

14. *United States v. Cothran,* 855 F.2d 749 (11th Cir. 1988).

15. *United States v. Gallo,* 20 F.3d 7(1st. Cir., 1994).

16. *State v. McCoy,* 45 N.C.App. 686, 263 S.E.2d 801 (1980).

17. *United States v. Duff,* 831 F.2d 176 (9th Cir. 1987).

18. *United States v. Pierce,* 561 F.2d 735 (9th Cir. 1977), *cert. denied* 435 U.S. 923, 98 S.Ct.1486, 55 L.Ed.2d 516 (1978).

19. *United States v. Kahl,* 583 F.2d 1351 (5th Cir. 1978); see also Harvey Jaffe, "Probation with a Flair: A Look at Some Out-of-the-Ordinary Conditions," *Federal Probation* 33 (1979): 29.

20. *People v. Johnson,* 175 Ill.App.3d 908, 125 Ill. Dec. 469, 530 N.E.2d 627 (1988).

21. *United States v. Williams,* 787 F.2d 1182 (7th Cir. 1986).

22. *United States v. Ofchinick,* 937 F.2d 892 (1991).

23. Todd Clear and Edward Latessa, "Probation Officers' Roles in Intensive Supervision: Surveillance Versus Treatment," *Justice Quarterly* 10 (1993): 441–462.

24. Ibid.

25. Patricia Harris, Todd Clear, and S. Christopher Baird, "Have Community Supervision Officers Changed Their Attitudes Toward Their Work?" *Justice Quarterly* 6 (1989): 233–246.

26. John Rosencrance, "Probation Supervision: Mission Impossible," *Federal Probation* 50 (1986): 25–31.

27. David Duffee and Bonnie Carlson, "Competing Value Premises for the Provision of Drug Treatment to Probationers," *Crime and Delinquency* 42 (1996): 574–592.

28. "Drug Treatment Role Increasing for Probation, Parole Agencies," *Criminal Justice Newsletter,* 9 September 1988, p. 6.

29. Richard Sluder and Rolando Del Carmen, "Are Probation and Parole Officers Liable for Injuries Caused by Probationers and Parolees?" *Federal Probation* 54 (1990): 3–12.

30. *Turner v. Barry,* 856 F.2d 1539 (D.C. Cir. 1988).

31. Ibid., at 1538.

32. Mark Cuniff, Dale Sechrest, and Robert Cushman, "Redefining Probation for the Coming Decade," paper presented at the annual meeting of the American Society of Criminology, San Francisco, November 1991.

33. Patricia Harris, "Client Management Classification and Prediction of Probation Outcome," *Crime and Delinquency* 40 (1994): 154–174.

34. Anne Schneider, Laurie Ervin, and Zoann Snyder-Joy, "Further Exploration of the Flight from Discretion: The Role of Risk/Need Instruments in Probation Supervision Decisions," *Journal of Criminal Justice* 24 (1996): 109–121.

35. Clear and O'Leary, *Controlling the Offender in the Community,* pp. 11–29, 77–100.

36. Joan Petersilia, "An Evaluation of Intensive Probation in California," *Journal of Criminal Law and Criminology* 82 (1992): 610–658.

37. Greenfield, *Probation and Parole, 1987.*

38. Joan Petersilia, Susan Turner, James Kahan, and Joyce Peterson, *Granting Felons Probation: Public Risks and Alternatives* (Santa Monica, Calif.: Rand Corporation, 1985).

39. Langan and Cuniff, *Recidivism of Felons on Probation, 1986–1989.*

40. Cuniff, Sechrest, and Cushman, "Redefining Probation for the Coming Decade," pp. 7–8.

41. Kathryn Morgan, "Factors Influencing Probation Outcome: A Review of the Literature," *Federal Probation* 57 (1993): 23–29.

42. Kathryn Morgan, "Factors Associated with Probation Outcome," *Journal of Criminal Justice* 22 (1994): 341–353.

43. Langan and Cuniff, *Recidivism of Felons on Probation, 1986–1989;* Allen Beck and Bernard Shipley, *Recidivism of Prisoners Released in 1983* (Washington, D.C.: Bureau of Justice Statistics, 1989).

44. Robyn L. Cohen, *Probation and Parole Violators in State Prison, 1991* (Washington, D.C.: Bureau of Justice Statistics, 1995).

45. Ibid.

46. *Minnesota v. Murphy,* 465 U.S. 420, 104 S.Ct. 1136, 79 L.Ed.2d 409 (1984).

47. *Griffin v. Wisconsin,* 483 U.S. 868, 107 S.Ct. 3164, 97 L.Ed.2d 709 (1987).

48. *Mempa v. Rhay,* 389 U.S. 128, 88 S.Ct. 254, 19 L.Ed.2d 336 (1967).

49. *Morrissey v. Brewer,* 408 U.S. 471, 92 S.Ct. 2593, 33 L.Ed.2d 484 (1972).

50. *Gagnon v. Scarpelli,* 411 U.S. 778, 93 S.Ct. 1756, 36 L.Ed.2d 656 (1973).

51. *United States v. Carson,* 669 F.2d 216 (5th Cir. 1982).

52. *United States v. Granderson,* 114 Ct. 1259, 127 L.Ed.2d 611 (1994).

53. Peter Finn, "Prison Crowding: The Response of Probation and Parole," *Crime and Delinquency* 30 (1984): 141–153.

54. Richard Sluder, Allen Sapp, and Denny Langston, "Guiding Philosophies for Probation in the 21st Century," *Federal Probation* 58 (1994): 3–7.

55. "Law in Massachusetts Requires Probationers to Pay 'Day Fees,'" *Criminal Justice Newsletter,* 15 September 1988, p. 1.

56. Gerald Wheeler, Therese Macan, Rodney Hissong, and Morgan Slusher, "The Effects of Probation Service Fees on Case Management Strategy and Sanctions," *Journal of Criminal Justice* 17 (1989): 15–24.

57. Peter Finn and Dale Parent, *Making the Offender Foot the Bill, A Texas Program* (Washington, D.C.: National Institute of Justice, 1992).

58. Richard Lawrence, "Reexamining Community Corrections Models," *Crime and Delinquency* 37 (1991): 449–464.

59. Todd Clear and Patricia Hardyman, "The New Intensive Supervision Movement," *Crime and Delinquency* 36 (1990): 42–60.

60. For a thorough review of these programs, see James Byrne, Arthur Lurigio, and Joan Petersilia, eds., *Smart Sentencing: The Emergence of Intermediate Sanctions* (Newbury Park, Calif.: Sage, 1993). Hereinafter cited as *Smart Sentencing.*

61. Christian Pfeiffer, *Alternative Sanctions in Germany: An Overview of Germany's Sentencing Practices* (Washington, D.C.: National Institute of Justice, 1996).

62. Beck and Shipley, *Recidivism of Prisoners Released in 1983* (Washington, D.C.: Bureau of Justice Statistics, 1989).

63. S. Christopher Baird and Dennis Wagner, "Measuring Diversion: The Florida Community Control Program," *Crime and Delinquency* 36 (1990): 112–125.

64. Norval Morris and Michael Tonry, *Between Prison and Probation: Intermediate Punishments in a Rational Sentencing System* (New York: Oxford University Press, 1990).

65. Michael Tonry and Richard Will, *Intermediate Sanctions* (Washington, D.C.: National Institute of Justice, 1990).

66. Ibid., p. 8.

67. Michael Maxfield and Terry Baumer, "Home Detention with Electronic Monitoring: Comparing Pretrial and Postconviction Programs," *Crime and Delinquency* 36 (1990): 521–556.

68. Sally Hillsman and Judith Greene, "Tailoring Fines to the Financial Means of Offenders," *Judicature* 72 (1988): 38–45.

69. David Pauly and Carolyn Friday, "Drexel's Crumbling Defense," *Newsweek,* 19 December 1988, p. 44.

70. George Cole, Barry Mahoney, Marlene Thorton, and Roger Hanson, *The Practices and Attitudes of Trial Court Judges Regarding Fines as a Criminal Sanction* (Washington, D.C.: U.S. Government Printing Office, 1987).

71. Ibid.

72. George Cole, "Monetary Sanctions: The Problem of Compliance," in *Smart Sentencing.*

73. *Tate v. Short,* 401 U.S. 395, 91 S.Ct. 668, 28 L.Ed.2d 130 (1971).

74. Margaret Gordon and Daniel Glaser, "The Use and Effects of Financial Penalties in Municipal Courts," *Criminology* 29 (1991): 651–676.

75. "'Day Fines' Being Tested in a New York City Court," *Criminal Justice Newsletter,* 1 September 1988, pp. 4–5.

76. Laura Winterfield and Sally Hillsman, *The Staten Island Day-Fine Project* (Washington, D.C.: National Institute of Justice, 1993), pp. 5–6.

77. C. Yorke, *Some Consideration on the Law of Forfeiture for High Treason,* 2nd ed. (1746), p. 26; cited in David Freid, "Rationalizing Criminal Forfeiture," *Journal of Criminal Law and Criminology* 79 (1988): 329.

78. Fried, "Rationalizing Criminal Forfeiture," p. 436.

79. *United States v. Ursery,* N. 95-345 (1996).

80. *Bennis v. Michigan,* 116 S.Ct. 994, 58 CrL 2060 (1996).

81. Eric Jensen and Jurg Gerber, "The Civil Forfeiture of Assets and the War on Drugs: Expanding Criminal Sanctions While Reducing Due Process Protections," *Crime and Delinquency* 42 (1996): 421–434.

82. *Austin v. United States* (92-6073, 1993); *Alexander v. United States* (91-1526, 1993).

83. For a general review, see Burt Galaway and Joe Hudson, *Criminal Justice, Restitution, and Reconciliation* (New York: Criminal Justice Press, 1990); Robert Carter, Jay Cocks, and Daniel Glazer, "Community Service: A Review of the Basic Issues," *Federal Probation* 51 (1987): 4–11.

84. Douglas McDonald, "Punishing Labor: Unpaid Community Service as a Criminal Sentence," in *Smart Sentencing.*

85. Langan and Cuniff, *Recidivism of Felons on Probation, 1986–1989,* p. 1.

86. Morris and Tonry, *Between Prison and Probation,* pp. 171–175.

87. Frederick Allen and Harvey Treger, "Community Service Orders in Federal Probation: Perceptions of Probationers and Host Agencies," *Federal Probation* 54 (1990): 8–14.

88. Peter Schneider, Anne Schneider, and William Griffith, *Monthly Report of the National Juvenile Restitution Evaluation Project V* (Eugene, Ore.: Institute for Policy Analysis, 1981).

89. Sudipto Roy, "Two Types of Juvenile Restitution Programs in Two Midwestern Counties: A Comparative Study," *Federal Probation* 57 (1993): 48–53.

90. Anne Schneider, "Restitution and Recidivism Rates of Juvenile Offenders: Four Experimental Studies," *Criminology* 24 (1986): 533–552.

91. Malcolm Feeley, Richard Berk, and Alec Campbell, "Community Service Orders in the Northern District of California," paper presented at the annual meeting of the American Society of Criminology, San Francisco, November 1991.

92. James Austin and Barry Krisberg, "The Unmet Promise of Alternatives to Incarceration," *Crime and Delinquency* 28 (1982): 374–409.

93. Alan Harland, "Court-Ordered Community Service in Criminal Law: The Continuing Tyranny of Benevolence," *Buffalo Law Review* (Summer 1980): 425–486.

94. Michael Block and William Rhodes, *The Impact of Federal Sentencing Guidelines* (Washington, D.C.: National Institute of Justice, 1987).

95. Cuniff, Sechrest, and Cushman, "Redefining Probation for the Coming Decade," p. 6.

96. Louis Jankowski, *Probation and Parole, 1990* (Washington, D.C.: Bureau of Justice Statistics, 1991), p. 2.

97. Harry Allen, Chris Eskridge, Edward Latessa, and Gennaro Vito, *Probation and Parole in America* (New York: Free Press, 1985), p. 88.

98. Joan Petersilia, *The Influence of Criminal Justice Research* (Santa Monica, Calif.: Rand Corporation, 1987).

99. Ibid.

100. James Byrne, Arthur Lurigio, and Christopher Baird, *The Effectiveness of the New Intensive Supervision Programs, Research in Corrections Series,* vol. 2, no. 2 (preliminary unpublished draft; Washington, D.C.: National Institute of Corrections, 1989), p. 16; Jankowski, *Probation and Parole, 1990,* p. 4.

101. Stephen Gettinger, "Intensive Supervision: Can It Rehabilitate Probation?" *Corrections Magazine* 9 (April 1983): 7–18.

102. Byrne, Lurigio, and Baird, *The Effectiveness of the New Intensive Supervision Programs.*

103. Billie Erwin and Lawrence Bennett, *New Dimensions in Probation: Georgia's Experience with Intensive Probation Supervision (IPS)* (Washington, D.C.: National Institute of Justice, 1987).

104. Ibid.

105. Frank Pearson and Alice Glasel Harper, "Contingent Intermediate Sentences: New Jersey's Intensive Supervision Program," *Crime and Delinquency* 36 (1990): 75–86.

106. Edward Latessa and Gennaro Vito, "The Effects of Intensive Supervision on Shock Probationers," *Journal of Criminal Justice* 16 (1988): 319–330.

107. James Byrne and Linda Kelly, "Restructuring Probation as an Intermediate Sanction: An Evaluation of the Massachusetts Intensive Probation Supervision Program," final report to the National Institute of Justice, Research Program on the Punishment and Control of Offenders, Washington, D.C., 1989.

108. James Ryan, "Who Gets Revoked? A Comparison of Intensive Supervision Successes and Failures in Vermont," *Crime and Delinquency* 43 (1997): 104–118.

109. Peter Jones, "Expanding the Use of Noncustodial Sentencing Options: An Evaluation of the Kansas Community Corrections Act," *Howard Journal* 29 (1990): 114–129; Michael Agopian, "The Impact of Intensive Supervision Probation on Gang-Drug Offenders," *Criminal Justice Policy Review* 4 (1990): 214–222.

110. Joan Petersilia, "Comparing Intensive and Regular Supervision for High-Risk Probationers: Early Results from Experiment in California," *Crime and Delinquency* 36 (1990): 87–111.

111. Joan Petersilia and Susan Turner, *Evaluating Intensive Supervision Probation/Parole: Results of a Nationwide Experiment* (Washington, D.C.: National Institute of Justice, 1993).

112. Joan Petersilia, "Conditions That Permit Intensive Supervision Programs to Survive," *Crime and Delinquency* 36 (1990): 126–145.

113. Dennis Wagner and Christopher Baird, *Evaluation of the Florida Community Control Program* (Washington, D.C.: National Institute of Justice, 1993).

114. Joan Petersilia, *Expanding Options for Criminal Sentencing* (Santa Monica, Calif.: Rand Corporation, 1987), p. 32.

115. Wagner and Baird, *Evaluation of the Florida Community Control Program,* p. 4.

116. Linda Smith and Ronald Akers, "A Comparison of Recidivism of Florida's Community Control and Prison: A Five-Year Survival Analysis," *Journal of Research in Crime and Delinquency* 30 (1993): 267–292.

117. Cited in Stephen Rackmill, "An Analysis of Home Confinement as a Sanction," *Federal Probation* 58 (1994): 45.

118. Marc Renzema, "Home Confinement Programs: Development, Implementation, and Impact," in *Smart Sentencing.*

119. Kenneth Moran and Charles Lindner, "Probation and the Hi-Technology Revolution: Is Reconceptualization of the Traditional Probation Officer Role Model Inevitable?" *Criminal Justice Review* 3 (1987): 25–32.

120. Joseph Papy and Richard Nimer, "Electronic Monitoring in Florida," *Federal Probation* 55 (1991): 31–33.

121. James Beck, Jody Klein-Saffran, and Harold Wooten, "Home Confinement and the Use of Electronic Monitoring with Federal Parolees," *Federal Probation* 54 (1990): 22–31.

122. Terry Baumer and Robert Mendelsohn, "Electronically Monitored Home Confinement: Does It Work?" in *Smart Sentencing.*

123. J. Robert Lilly, Richard Ball, G. David Curry, and John McMullen, "Electronic Monitoring of the Drunk Driver: A Seven-Year Study of the Home Confinement Alternative," *Crime and Delinquency* 39 (1993): 462–484.

124. James Davis, "Electronic Monitoring in the Criminal Justice System," paper presented at the American Society of Criminology meeting, Miami, November 1994, p. 3.

125. Joan Petersilia, "Exploring the Option of House Arrest," *Federal Probation* 50 (1986): 50–55.

126. Morris and Tonry, *Between Prison and Probation.*

127. Schmidt, "Electronic Monitors—Realistically, What Can Be Expected?" *Federal Probation* 55 (1991): 51.

128. Richard Rosenfeld, "The Scope and Purposes of Corrections: Exploring Alternative Responses to Crowding," *Crime and Delinquency* 37 (1991): 500.

129. For a more complete analysis of the EM controversy, see Ronald Corbett and Gary Marx, "Critique: No Soul in the New Machine: Technofallacies in the Electronic Monitoring Movement," *Justice Quarterly* 8 (1991): 399–414.

130. See generally, Edward Latessa and Lawrence Travis III, "Residential Community Correctional Programs," in *Smart Sentencing.*

131. Updated with personal correspondence with Jan Cartalucca, administrative assistant, and Tom Hayden, director, 8 January 1992.

132. Personal correspondence with Glen Just, Ph.D., executive director, 15 January 1992.

133. Harvey Siegal, James Fisher, Richard Rapp, Casey Kelliher, Joseph Wagner, William O'Brien, and Phyllis Cole, "Enhancing Substance Abuse Treatment with Case Management," *Journal of Substance Abuse Treatment* 13 (1996): 93–98.

134. Dale Parent, *Day Reporting Centers for Criminal Offenders—A Descriptive Analysis of Existing Programs* (Washington, D.C.: National Institute of Justice, 1990); Jack McDevitt and Robyn Miliano, "Day Reporting Centers: An Innovative Concept in Intermediate Sanctions," in *Smart Sentencing.*

135. David Diggs and Stephen Pieper, "Using Day Reporting Centers as an Alternative to Jail," *Federal Probation* 58 (1994): 9–12.

136. For a description of these programs, see Edward Latessa and Lawrence Travis III, "Residential Community Correctional Programs," in *Smart Sentencing;* see also, Byrne and Kelly, "Restructuring Probation as an Intermediate Sanction."

137. David Hartmann, Paul Friday, and Kevin Minor, "Residential Probation: A Seven-Year Follow-Up of Halfway House Discharges," *Journal of Criminal Justice* 22 (1994): 503–515.

138. Banhram Haghighi and Alma Lopez, "Success/Failure of Group Home Treatment Programs for Juveniles," *Federal Probation* 57 (1993): 53–57.

139. Peter R. Jones, "Community Corrections in Kansas: Extending Community-Based Corrections or Widening the Net?" *Journal of Research in Crime and Delinquency* 27 (1990): 79–101.

140. Richard Rosenfeld and Kimberly Kempf, "The Scope and Purposes of Corrections: Exploring Alternative Responses to Crowding," *Crime and Delinquency* 37 (1991): 481–505.

141. For a thorough review, see Michael Tonry and Mary Lynch, "Intermediate Sanctions," in *Crime and Justice, A Review of Research,* vol. 20, ed. Michael Tonry (Chicago: University of Chicago Press, 1996), pp. 99–144.

142. Francis Cullen, "Control in the Community: The Limits of Reform?" Paper presented at the International Association of Residential and Community Alternatives, Philadelphia, November 1993.

143. Joan Petersilia and Susan Turner, *Intensive Supervision for High-Risk Probationers* (Santa Monica, Calif.: Rand Corporation, 1990).

144. Annette Jolin and Brian Stipak, "Drug Treatment and Electronically Monitored Home Confinement: An Evaluation of a Community-Based Sentencing Option," paper presented at the annual meeting of the American Society of Criminology, San Francisco, November 1984.

145. V. Fogg, "Expanding the Sanction Range of ISP Programs: A Report on Electronic Monitoring," *Journal of Offender Monitoring* 3 (1990): 12–13, 16, 18.

CHAPTER 14

Corrections: History, Institutions, and Populations

When a person is convicted for a criminal offense, state and federal governments through their sentencing authority reserve the right to institutionally confine the offender for a period of time. The system of **secure corrections** comprises the entire range of treatment and punishment options available to the government, including community residential centers, jails, reformatories, and penal institutions (prisons).

Correctional treatment is currently practiced on federal, state, and county levels of government. Felons may be placed in state or federal penitentiaries (**prisons**), which are usually isolated, fortress-like structures. Misdemeanants are housed in county **jails**, sometimes called **reformatories** or houses of correction. And juvenile offenders have their own institutions, sometimes euphemistically called schools, camps, ranches, or homes. Typically, the latter are nonsecure facilities, often located in rural areas, that provide both confinement and rehabilitative services for young offenders.

Other types of correctional institutions include ranches and farms for adult offenders and community correctional settings, such as halfway houses, for inmates who are about to return to society. Today's correctional facilities encom-

pass a wide range, from "maxi-maxi" security institutions, such as the federal prison at Marion, Illinois where the nation's most dangerous felons are confined, to low-security camps that house white-collar criminals convicted of such crimes as insider trading and mail fraud.

One of the great tragedies of our time is that correctional institutions, whatever form they may take, do not seem to correct. They are, in most instances, overcrowded, understaffed, outdated warehouses for social outcasts. The overcrowding crisis is the most significant problem faced by the prison today: Prisons now contain more than 1.2 million inmates. Prisons are more suited to control, punishment, and security than to rehabilitation and treatment. It is a sad but unfortunately accurate observation that today's correctional institution has become a revolving door and that all too many of its residents return time and again. Although no completely accurate statement of the **recidivism** rate is available, it is estimated that more than half of all inmates will be back in prison within six years of their release.[1]

Despite the apparent lack of success of penal institutions, great debate continues over the direction of their future operations. Some penal experts maintain

Chapter 14

Corrections: History, Institutions, and Populations

that prisons and jails are not really places for rehabilitation and treatment but rather should be used to keep dangerous offenders apart from society and give them the "just deserts" for their crimes.[2] In this sense, prison success would be measured by such factors as physical security, length of incapacitation, relationship between the crime rate and the number of incarcerated felons, and inmates' perceptions that their treatment was fair and proportionate. The dominance of this correctional philosophy is illustrated by the facts that (1) presumptive and mandatory sentencing structures are now used in such traditionally progressive states as California, Massachusetts, and Illinois; (2) the number of people under lock and key has risen rapidly in the past few years; and (3) political candidates who are portrayed by their opponents as advocates of inmate rehabilitation soon find themselves on the defensive with voters.

While the conservative tide in corrections is self-evident, many penal experts still maintain that prisons can be useful places for offender rehabilitation.[3] Many examples of the treatment philosophy still flourish in prisons: Educational programs allow inmates to get college credits; vocational training has become more sophisticated; counseling and substance abuse programs are almost universal; and every state maintains some type of early-release and community correctional programs.

In this chapter, we will explore the correctional system, beginning with the history and nature of correctional institutions. Then in Chapter 15, we examine institutional life in some detail.

History of Correctional Institutions

As you may recall, the original legal punishments were typically banishment or slavery, restitution (wergild), corporal punishment, and execution. The concept of incarcerating convicted offenders for long periods of time as a punishment for their misdeeds did not become the norm of corrections until the 19th century.[4]

While the use of incarceration as a routine punishment began much later, some early European institutions were created specifically to detain and punish criminal offenders. Penal institutions were actually constructed in England during the 10th century to hold pretrial detainees and those waiting for their sentence to be carried out.[5] During the 12th century, King Henry II of England constructed a series of county jails to hold thieves and vagrants prior to the disposition of their sentence. In 1557, the workhouse in Brideswell, England, was built to hold people convicted of relatively minor offenses who would work to pay off their debt to society; those committing more serious offenses were held there prior to their execution.

Le Stinche, a prison in Florence, Italy, was used to punish offenders as early as 1301.[6] Prisoners were enclosed in separate cells, classified on the basis of gender, age, mental state, and crime seriousness. Furloughs and conditional release were permitted, and perhaps for the first time, a period of incarceration replaced corporal punishment for some offenses. Although Le Stinche existed for 500 years, relatively little is known about its administration or whether this early example of incarceration was unique to Florence.

The first penal institutions were foul places devoid of proper care, food, or medical treatment. The jailer, usually a shire reeve (sheriff), an official appointed by king or noble landholder as chief law enforcement official of a county, ran the jail under the "fee system." This required inmates to pay for their own food and services. Those who could not pay were fed scraps until they literally starved to death:

> In 1748 the admission to Southwark prison was eleven shillings and four pence. Having got in, the prisoner had to pay for having himself put in irons, for his bed, of whatever sort, for his room if he was able to afford a separate room. He had to pay for his food, and when he had paid his debts and was ready to go out, he had to pay for having his irons struck off, and a discharge fee . . . The gaolers [jailers] were usually "low bred, mercenary and oppressive, barbarous fellows, who think of nothing but enriching themselves by the most cruel extortion, and have less regard for the life of a poor prisoner than for the life of a brute."[7]

Jail conditions were deplorable because jailers ran them for personal gain; the fewer the services provided, the greater their profit. Early jails were catchall institutions that held not only criminal offenders awaiting trial but vagabonds, debtors, the mentally ill, and assorted others.

From 1776 to 1785, a growing inmate population that could no longer be transported to North America forced the English to house prisoners on **hulks,** abandoned ships anchored in harbors. The hulks became infamous for their degrading conditions and brutal punishments but were not totally abandoned until 1858. The writings of John Howard, the reform-oriented sheriff of Bedfordshire, drew attention to the squalid conditions in British penal institutions. His famous book, *The State of Prisons* (1777), condemned the lack of basic care given English inmates awaiting trial or serving sentences.[8] Howard's efforts to create humane standards in the British penal system resulted in the Penitentiary Act, by which Parliament established a more orderly penal system, with periodic inspections, elimination of the fee system, and greater consideration for inmates.

American Developments

Although Europe had jails and a variety of other penal facilities, it was in the United States that correctional reform was first instituted. The first American jail was built in James City in the Virginia colonies in the early 17th century. However, the "modern" American correctional system had its origin in Pennsylvania under the leadership of William Penn.

At the end of the 17th century, Penn revised Pennsylvania's criminal code to forbid torture and the capricious use of mutilation and physical punishment. These penalties were replaced with imprisonment at hard labor, moderate flogging, fines, and forfeiture of property. All lands and goods belonging to felons were to be used to make restitution to the victims of crimes, with restitution being limited to twice the value of the damages. Felons who owned no property were required by law to work in the prison workhouse until the victim was compensated.

Penn ordered that a new type of institution be built to replace the widely used public forms of punishment—stocks, pillories, gallows, and branding irons. Each county was instructed to build a house of corrections similar to today's jails. County trustees or commissioners were responsible for raising money to build the jails and providing for their maintenance, although they were operated by the local sheriff. Penn's reforms remained in effect until his death in 1718, when the criminal penal code was changed back to open public punishment and harsh brutality.

It is difficult to identify the first American prison. Alexis Durham has described the opening of the Newgate Prison of Connecticut in 1773 on the site of an abandoned copper mine. Newgate, which closed in the 1820s, is often ignored by correctional historians.[9] In 1785, Castle Island prison was opened in Massachusetts and operated for about 15 years.

The origin of the modern correctional system, however, is usually traced to 18th-century developments in Pennsylvania. In 1776 postrevolutionary Pennsylvania again adopted William Penn's code, and in 1787 a group of Quakers led by Benjamin Rush formed the Philadelphia Society for Alleviating the Miseries of Public Prisons. The aim of the society was to bring some degree of humane and orderly treatment to the growing penal system. The Quakers' influence on the legislature resulted in limiting the use of the death penalty to cases involving treason, murder, rape, and arson. Their next step was to reform the institutional system so that the prison could serve as a suitable alternative to physical punishment.

The only models of custodial institutions at that time were the local county jails that Penn had established. These facilities were designed to detain offenders, to securely incarcerate convicts awaiting other punishment, or to hold offenders who were working off their crimes. The Pennsylvania jails placed men, women, and children of all ages indiscriminately in one room. Liquor was often freely sold.

Under pressure from the Quakers to improve these conditions, the Pennsylvania State Legislature in 1790 called for the renovation of the prison system. The ultimate result was the creation of a separate wing of Philadelphia's **Walnut Street Jail** to house convicted felons (except those sentenced to death). Prisoners were placed in solitary cells, where they remained in isolation and did not have the right to work.[10] Quarters that contained the solitary or separate cells were called the **penitentiary house,** as was already the custom in England.

The new Pennsylvania prison system took credit for a rapid decrease in the crime rate—from 131 convictions in 1789 to 45 in 1793.[11] The prison became known as a school for reform and a place for public labor. The Walnut Street Jail's equitable conditions were credited with reducing escapes to none in the first four years of its existence (except for 14 on opening day).

The Walnut Street Jail was not a total success. Overcrowding undermined the goal of solitary confinement of serious offenders, and soon more than one inmate was placed in each cell. The isolation had a terrible psychological effect on inmates, and eventually inmates were given in-cell piecework on which they worked up to 8 hours a day. Despite these difficulties, similar institutions were erected in New York (Newgate in 1791) and New Jersey (Trenton in 1798).

The Auburn System

As the 19th century got underway, both the Pennsylvania and the New York prison systems were experiencing difficulties maintaining the ever-increasing numbers of convicted criminals. Initially, administrators dealt with the problem by increasing the use of pardons, relaxing prison discipline, and limiting supervision.

In 1816 New York built a new prison at Auburn, hoping to alleviate some of the overcrowding at Newgate. The Auburn Prison design became known as the **tier system,** because cells were built vertically on five floors of the structure. It was also referred to as the **congregate system,** since most prisoners ate and worked in groups. Later, in 1819, construction was started on a wing of solitary cells to house unruly prisoners. Three classes of prisoners were then created: One group remained continually in solitary confinement as a result of breaches of prison discipline; the second group was allowed labor as an occasional form of recreation; and the third and largest class worked and ate together during the day and were separated only at night.

The philosophy of the **Auburn system** was crime prevention through fear of punishment and silent confinement. The worst felons were to be cut off from all contact with other prisoners, and although they were treated and fed relatively well, they had no hope of pardon to relieve their solitude or isolation. For a time, some of the worst convicts were forced to remain totally alone and silent during the entire day; this practice caused many prisoners to have mental breakdowns, resulting in many suicides and self-mutilations. This practice was abolished in 1823.

The combination of silence and solitude as a method of punishment was not abandoned easily. Prison officials sought to overcome the side effects of total isolation while maintaining the penitentiary system. The solution adopted at Auburn was to keep convicts in separate cells at night but allow them to work together during the day under enforced silence. Hard work and silence became the foundation of the Auburn system wherever it was adopted. Silence was the key to prison discipline; it prohibited the formulation of escape plans, it prevented plots and riots, and it allowed prisoners to contemplate their infractions.

Why did prisons develop at this time? One reason, of course, was that during this period of "enlightenment," a concerted effort was made to alleviate the harsh punishments and torture that had been the norm. The interest of religious groups, such as the Quakers, in prison reform was prompted in part by humanitarian ideals. Another factor was the economic potential of prison industry, viewed as a valuable economic asset in times of a short labor supply.[12]

The concept of using harsh discipline and control to "retrain" the heart and soul of offenders was the subject of an important book on penal philosophy: *Dis-*

cipline and Punish (1978) by French sociologist Michel Foucault.[13] Foucault's thesis is that as societies evolve and become more complex, they create increasingly more elaborate mechanisms to discipline their recalcitrant members and make them docile enough to obey social rules. In the 17th and 18th centuries, discipline was directed toward the human body itself, through torture. However, physical punishment and torture turned some condemned men into heroes and martyrs. Prisons presented the opportunity to rearrange, not diminish, punishment—to make it more effective and regulated. In the development of the 19th-century prison, the object was to discipline the offender psychologically; "the expiation that once rained down on the body must be replaced by a punishment that acts in the depths of the heart."[14]

Regimentation became the standard mode of prison life. Convicts did not simply walk from place to place; rather, they went in close order and single file, each looking over the shoulder of the preceding person, faces inclined to the right, feet moving in unison. The lockstep prison shuffle was developed at Auburn and is still used in some institutions today.[15]

When discipline was breached in the Auburn system, punishment was applied in the form of a rawhide whip on the inmate's back. Immediate and effective, Auburn discipline was so successful that when 100 inmates were used to build the famous Sing Sing Prison in 1825, not one dared try to escape, although they were housed in an open field with only minimal supervision.[16]

The Pennsylvania System

In 1818 Pennsylvania took the radical step of establishing a prison that placed each inmate in a single cell for the duration of his sentence. Classifications were abolished, because each cell was intended as a miniature prison that would prevent the inmates from contaminating one another.

The new Pennsylvania state prison, called the Western Penitentiary, had an unusual architectural design. It was built in a semicircle, with the cells positioned along its circumference. Built back to back, some cells faced the boundary wall while others faced the internal area of the circle. Its inmates were kept in solitary confinement almost constantly, being allowed out for about an hour a day for exercise. In 1820 a second, similar penitentiary using the isolate system was built in Philadelphia and called the Eastern Penitentiary.

Supporters of the **Pennsylvania system** believed that the penitentiary was truly a place to do penance. By advocating totally removing the sinner from society and allowing the prisoner a period of isolation in which to reflect alone on the evils of crime, the supporters of the Pennsylvania system reflected the influence of religion and religious philosophy on corrections. Solitary confinement (with in-cell labor) was believed to make work so attractive that upon release, the inmate would be well suited to resume a productive existence in society.

The Pennsylvania system eliminated the need for large numbers of guards or disciplinary measures. Isolated from one another, inmates could not plan escapes or collectively break rules. When discipline was a problem, however, the whip and the iron gag were used.

Many fiery debates occurred between advocates of the Pennsylvania system and adherents of the Auburn system. Those supporting the latter boasted of its supposed advantages; it was the cheapest and most productive way to reform prisoners. They criticized the Pennsylvania system as cruel and inhumane, suggesting that solitary confinement was both physically and mentally damaging. The Pennsylvania system's devotees, on the other hand, argued that their system was quiet, efficient, humane, and well ordered and provided the ultimate correctional facility.[17] They chided the Auburn system for tempting inmates to talk by putting them together for meals and work and then punishing them when they did talk. Finally, the Auburn system was accused of becoming a breeding place for criminal associations by allowing inmates to get to know one another.

The Auburn system eventually prevailed and spread throughout the United States; many of its features are still used today. Its innovations included congregate working conditions, the use of solitary confinement to punish unruly inmates, military regimentation, and discipline. In Auburn-like institutions, prisoners were marched from place to place; their time was regulated by bells telling them to wake up, sleep, and work. The system was so like the military that many of its early administrators were recruited from the armed services.

Although the prison was viewed as an improvement over capital and corporal punishment, it quickly became the scene of depressed conditions; inmates were treated harshly and routinely whipped and tortured. Prison brutality flourished in these institutions, which had originally been devised as a more humane correctional alternative. In these early penal institutions brutal corporal punishment took place indoors where, hidden from public view, it could become even more savage.[18]

The Civil War Era

The prison of the late 19th century was remarkably similar to that of today. The congregate system was adopted in all states except Pennsylvania. Prisons were overcrowded, and the single-cell principle was often ignored. The prison, like the police department, became the scene of political intrigue and efforts by political administrators to control the hiring of personnel and dispensing of patronage.

Prison industry developed and became the predominant theme around which institutions were organized. Some prisons used the **contract system,** in which officials sold the labor of inmates to private businesses. Sometimes the contractor supervised the inmates inside the prison itself. Under the **convict-lease system,** the state leased its prisoners to a business for a fixed annual fee and gave up supervision and control. Finally, some institutions had prisoners produce goods for the prison's own use.[19]

The development of prison industry quickly led to the abuse of inmates, who were forced to work for almost no wages, and to profiteering by dishonest administrators and businessmen. During the Civil War era, prisons were major manufacturers of clothes, shoes, boots, furniture, and the like. Beginning in the 1870s, opposition by trade unions sparked restrictions on interstate commerce in prison goods.

Prison operations were also reformed. The National Congress of Penitentiary and Reformatory Discipline, held in Cincinnati in 1870, heralded a new era of prison reform. Organized by penologists Enoch Wines and Theodore Dwight, the congress provided a forum for corrections experts from around the nation to call for the treatment, education, and training of inmates.

One of the most famous people to attend the congress, Z. R. Brockway, warden at the Elmira Reformatory in New York, advocated individualized treatment, the indeterminate sentence, and parole. The reformatory program initiated by Brockway included elementary education for illiterates, designated library hours, lectures by faculty members of the local Elmira College, and a group of vocational training shops. From 1888 to 1920, Elmira administrators used military-like training to discipline the inmates and organize the institution. The military organization could be seen in every aspect of the institution: schooling, manual training, sports, supervision of inmates, and even parole decisions.[20] The cost to the state of the institution's operations was to be held to a minimum.

Although Brockway proclaimed Elmira to be an ideal reformatory, his actual achievements were limited. The greatest significance of his contribution was the injection of a degree of humanitarianism into the industrial prisons of that day (although there were accusations that excessive corporal punishment was used and that Brockway personally administered whippings).[21] Although many institutions were constructed across the nation and labeled reformatories based on the Elmira model, most of them continued to be industrially oriented.[22]

Reform Movements

The early 20th century was a time of contrasts in the prison system of the United States.[23] At one extreme were those who advocated reform, such as the Mutual Welfare League led by Thomas Mott Osborne. Prison reform groups proposed better treatment for inmates, an end to harsh corporal punishment, the creation of meaningful prison industries, and educational programs. Reformers argued that prisoners should not be isolated from society and that the best elements of society—education, religion, meaningful work, self-governance—should be brought to the prison. Osborne went so far as to spend one week in New York's notorious Sing Sing Prison to learn firsthand about its conditions.

Opposed to the reformers were conservative prison administrators and state officials who believed that stern disciplinary measures were needed to control dangerous prison inmates. They continued the time-honored system of regimentation and discipline. Although the whip and the lash were eventually abolished, solitary confinement in dark, bare cells became a common penal practice.

In time, some of the more rigid prison rules gave way to liberal reform. By the mid-1930s, few prisons required inmates to wear the red-and-white-striped convict suit and substituted nondescript gray uniforms. The code of silence ended, as did the lockstep shuffle. Prisoners were allowed "the freedom of the yard" to mingle and exercise an hour or two each day.[24] Movies and radio appeared in the 1930s. Visiting policies and mail privileges were liberalized.

A more important trend was the development of specialized prisons designed to treat particular types of offenders. For example, in New York the prisons at Clinton and Auburn were viewed as industrial facilities for hard-core inmates, Great Meadow was an agricultural center to house nondangerous offenders, and Dannemora was a facility for the criminally insane. In California, San Quentin housed inmates considered salvageable by correctional authorities, while Folsom was reserved for hard-core offenders.[25]

Prison industry also evolved. Opposition by organized labor helped put an end to the convict-lease system and forced inmate labor. By 1900, a number of states had restricted the sale of prisoner-made goods on the open market. The worldwide Depression that began in 1929 prompted industry and union leaders to further pressure state legislators to reduce competition from prison industries. A series of ever more restrictive federal legislative initiatives led to the Sumners-Ashurst Act (1940), which made it a federal offense to transport in interstate commerce goods made in prison for private use, regardless of the laws of the state receiving the goods.[26] The restrictions imposed by the federal government helped to severely curtail prison industry for 40 years. Private entrepreneurs shunned prison investments because they were no longer profitable; the result was inmate idleness and make-work jobs.[27]

Despite some changes and reforms, the prison in the mid-20th century remained a destructive total institution. Although some aspects of inmate life improved, severe discipline, harsh rules, and solitary confinement were the way of life in prison. The Criminal Justice and the Media box on *The Shawshank Redemption* (p. 410) focuses on inmate life during this era of corrections.

The Modern Era

The modern era has been a period of change and turmoil in the nation's correctional system. Three trends stand out. First, between 1960 and 1980, what is referred to as the **prisoners' rights movement** occurred. After many years of indifference (a policy referred to as the "hands off doctrine"), state and federal courts ruled in case after case that institutionalized inmates had rights to freedom of religion and speech, medical care, procedural due process, and proper living conditions. Inmates won rights unheard of in the 19th- and early 20th-century prisons. Since 1980, however, an increasingly conservative judiciary has curtailed the growth of inmate rights.

Second, violence within the correctional system became a national concern. Well-publicized riots at New York's Attica Prison and the New Mexico State Penitentiary drew attention to the potential for death and destruction that lurks in every prison. Prison rapes and killings have become commonplace. The locus of control in many prisons shifted from the correctional staff to violent inmate gangs. In reaction, some administrators have tried to improve conditions and provide innovative programs that give inmates a voice in running the institution.

The Shawshank Redemption

The Shawshank Redemption, a film based on a Stephen King novella, tells the story of Andy Defresne (Tim Robbins), a banker falsely accused of his wife's murder. Sentenced to life in a maximum-security prison, he is subjected to vicious beatings and rapes at the hands of both guards and predatory inmates. Andy learns to adjust with the help of his friend Red (Morgan Freeman), a wily prison veteran. Andy's experience with finance comes in handy when he gives the tough guard captain (Clancy Brown) advice on life insurance and then becomes the crooked warden's financial adviser and accountant. When evidence of Andy's innocence turns up, the warden suppresses it and has a friend of Andy's killed rather than risk losing his trusted inmate adviser.

Andy always has a poster of a beautiful actress in his cell (when he first arrives in the 1940s, it's Rita Hayworth), presumably to remind him of what he is missing on the outside. When Andy escapes with the records of the warden's crooked dealings, we find out the true purpose of the poster: It conceals a tunnel he has been digging for twenty years! Andy flees to Mexico, and when Red is released on parole, Andy arranges passage for him so they can be together again.

The Shawshank Redemption is accurate when it shows the brutality of a maximum-security prison in the 1940s, ruled with an iron fist by a corrupt warden and brutal guards. This is the subject of another recent film, *Murder in the First,* in which Kevin Bacon plays an inmate brutalized and killed by guards and wardens at Alcatraz. The era of the "big house" is over today, brought down by the prisoners' rights revolution, which gave inmates access to courts and the ability to sue if subjected to such callous behavior.

The film also shows the victimization of weak inmates by sexual predators, a practice that still goes on today. However, inmates have the right to sue if they are not protected by prison officials, and administrators have taken pains to segregate dangerous inmates from the general population or offer protection to potential victims.

The Shawshank Redemption presents a chilling picture of prison life at midcentury. Although it is fiction, it helps us understand why the federal courts felt it necessary to take control of prisons and empower inmates to seek legal remedies. Without such actions prison brutality might have remained unchecked.

Another reaction has been to tighten discipline and build new super maximum-security prisons to control the most dangerous offenders. The problem of prison overcrowding has made attempts to improve conditions extremely difficult.

Third, the view that traditional correctional rehabilitation efforts have failed has prompted many penologists to reconsider the purpose of incapacitating criminals. Between 1960 and 1980, it was common for correctional administrators to cling to the **medical model,** which viewed inmates as "sick people" who were suffering from some social malady that prevented them from adjusting to society. Correctional treatment could help "cure" them and enable them to live productive lives once they returned to the community. In the 1970s, efforts were also made to help offenders become reintegrated into society by providing them with new career opportunities that relied on work release programs. Inmates were allowed to work outside the institution during the day and return in the evening; some were given extended *furloughs* in the community. Work release became a political issue when Willie Horton, a furloughed inmate from Massachusetts, raped a young woman. Criticism of its "liberal" furlough program helped George Bush defeat Massachusetts Governor Michael Dukakis for the U.S. presidency in 1988; in the aftermath of the Horton case a number of states, including Massachusetts, restricted their furlough policies.

Prisons have come to be viewed as places for control, incapacitation, and punishment, rather than as sites for rehabilitation and reform. Advocates of the "no frills" or "penal harm" movement believe that if prison is a "punishing" experience, would-be criminals will be deterred from crime and current inmates will be encouraged to "go straight." Nonetheless, efforts to use correctional institutions as treatment facilities have not ended, and such innovations as the development of private industries on prison grounds have kept the rehabilitative ideal alive.

The alleged failure of correctional treatment coupled with constantly increasing correctional costs has prompted the development of alternatives to incarceration, such as intensive probation supervision, house arrest, and electronic monitoring. What has developed is a bifurcated correctional policy: Keep as many nonviolent offenders out of the correctional system as possible by means of community-based programs; incarcerate dangerous, violent offenders for long periods of time.[28] These efforts have been compromised by a growing "get-tough" stance in judicial and legislative sentencing policy, accented by mandatory minimum sentences for gun crimes and drug trafficking. Despite the development of alternatives to incarceration, the number of people under lock and key has skyrocketed.

In the following sections, we review the most prominent types of correctional facilities in use today.

The nation's jails are institutional facilities with five primary purposes: (1) they detain accused offenders who cannot make or are not eligible for bail prior to trial; (2) they hold convicted offenders awaiting sentence; (3) they serve as the principal institution of secure confinement for offenders convicted of misdemeanors; (4) they hold probationers and parolees picked up for violations and waiting for a hearing; and (5) they house felons when state prisons are overcrowded.

A number of formats are used to jail offenders. About 15,000 local jurisdictions maintain short-term police or municipal lockups that house offenders for no more than 48 hours before a bail hearing can be held; thereafter, detainees are kept in the county jail. In some jurisdictions, such as New Hampshire and Massachusetts, a house of corrections holds convicted misdemeanants, while a county jail is used for pretrial detainees. Today the jail is a multipurpose correctional institution whose other main functions are set out in Table 14.1.

According to the most recent statistics, about half of jailed inmates are unconvicted, awaiting formal charges (arraignment), bail, or trial. The remaining half are convicted offenders who are serving time, awaiting parole or probation revocation hearings, or transferred from a state prison because of overcrowding.[29]

Jails

Table 14.1

Jail Functions and Services

SOURCE: Darrell K. Gilliard and Allen J. Beck, *Prison and Jail Inmates at Midyear 1996* (Washington, D.C.: Bureau of Justice Statistics, 1997).

Receive individuals pending arraignment and hold them awaiting trial, conviction, or sentencing.

Readmit probation, parole, and bail-bond violators and absconders.

Temporarily detain juveniles pending transfer to juvenile authorities.

Hold mentally ill persons pending their movement to appropriate health facilities.

Hold individuals for the military, for protective custody, for contempt, and for the courts as witnesses.

Release convicted inmates to the community on completion of sentence.

Transfer inmates to federal, state, or other authorities.

House inmates for federal, state, or other authorities because of crowding of their facilities.

Relinquish custody of temporary detainees to juvenile and medical authorities.

Sometimes operate community-based programs as alternatives to incarceration.

Hold inmates sentenced to short terms (generally under one year).

Jails are typically a low-priority item in the criminal justice system. Because they are usually administered on a county level, jail services have not been sufficiently regulated, nor has a unified national policy been developed to mandate what constitutes adequate jail conditions. Many jails have consequently developed into squalid, crumbling holding pens.

Jails are considered to be holding facilities for the county's undesirables, rather than correctional institutions that provide meaningful treatment. They may house indigents who, looking for a respite from the winter's cold, commit a minor offense; the mentally ill who will eventually be hospitalized after a civil commitment hearing; and substance abusers who are suffering the first shocks of confinement. The jail rarely holds professional "criminals," most of whom are able to make bail.[30] Instead, the jail holds the people considered detached from and disreputable in local society and who are frequently arrested because they are considered "offensive" by the local police. The purpose of the jail is to "manage" these persons and keep them separate from the rest of society. By intruding in their lives, jailing them actually increases their involvement with the law.

Jail Populations

A national effort has been made to remove as many people from local jails as possible through the adoption of both bail reform measures and pretrial diversion. Nonetheless, jail populations have been steadily increasing, due in part to the increased use of mandatory jail sentences for such common crimes as drunk driving and the use of local jails to house inmates for whom there is no room in state prisons.

There are approximately 520,000 jail inmates today, split almost equally between sentenced offenders and detainees.[31] In addition, more than 70,000 are supervised outside jail facilities in programs such as community service, work release, weekend reporting, electronic monitoring, and alternative programs. In total, then, almost 600,000 people are under jail authority.

Whereas the number of jails has declined from a high of 4,037 in 1970 to about 3,500 today, the number of inmates has increased about 300% (from 160,683); there is thus a trend toward fewer but larger jails. Figure 14.1 shows the explosive growth of the jail population. On an annual basis, close to 10 million people are admitted to jail. In 1970 there were 79 inmates per 100,000 population; in 1990 that number had risen to 163 per 100,000; today there are 196 per 100,000! The increase in the jail population is a direct function of the nation's "get tough" policy against drug offenders and offenses.

Who Are Jail Inmates?

While the removal of juveniles from adult jails has long been a national priority, it is likely that more than 50,000 youths are admitted to adult jails each year. An estimated 8,100 persons under age 18 are housed in adult jails on a given day.

Male —90%

At time of crime:
- 43% under the influence of alcohol
- 26% on drugs
- 17% on major drug

Offense
- 23% violent
- 30% property
- 22% drug
- 23% public order (DWI)

- 39% white
- 41% black
- 17% Hispanic

Hours spent in cell per day: 14.6

Hours spent on physical exercise: 1.5

Hours spent working: 5.9

Most common jobs:
- maintenance: 28%
- food preparation: 26%

- 28% under 24 years old
- Median age: 28
- High school grads: 46%
- Married: 19%
- Physically or sexually abused: 13%

Female —10%

At time of crime:
- 21% under the influence of alcohol
- 36% on drugs
- 31% on major drug

Offense
- 13% violent
- 32% property
- 34% drug
- 23% public order (DWI)

- 38% white
- 43% black
- 16% Hispanic

Hours spent in cell per day: 16.8

Hours spent on physical exercise: 1.2

Hours spent working: 4.2

Most common jobs:
- maintenance: 39%
- food preparation: 19%

- 35% under 24 years old
- Median age: 28
- High school grads: 50%
- Married: 16%
- Physically or sexually abused: 44%

Figure 14.1
Profile of jail inmates.

SOURCE: Tracy Snell, *Correctional Populations in the United States* (Washington, D.C.: Bureau of Justice Statistics, 1993, updated 1997), pp. 7–19.

Over two-thirds of these young inmates have been convicted or are being held for trial as adults in criminal court.

Male inmates make up about 90% of the local jail population. However, the female population, like the crime rate, has been growing at a faster pace. On average, the female jail population has grown 10.2% annually since 1985, whereas the male inmate population has grown by 6.1% per year.[32]

A majority of local jail inmates are either black or Hispanic. White non-Hispanics made up about 40% of the jail population; black non-Hispanics, 40%; Hispanics, 16%; and other races (Asians, Pacific Islanders, American Indians, and Alaska Natives), 1.7%. Relative to their number of U.S. residents, black non-Hispanics are six times more likely than white non-Hispanics, over twice as likely as Hispanics, and over eight times more likely than persons of other races to have been held in a local jail.

Most inmates were either doing time or awaiting trial on property crime charges, such as burglary, larceny, or motor vehicle theft. However, the number of drug offenders has increased markedly. In 1983, about 9% of the total population was in jail for drug-related crimes; that number has now increased to more than 25% of all inmates.

Women in Jail

Since 1983, the number of women in jail has increased at a much faster pace than that of male inmates. Female inmates suffer many of the social problems that plague U.S. society. Most are substance abusers: More than half had used drugs in the month prior to the current offense; about 40% were daily drug users; about 20% report being under the influence of alcohol; about 25% said they had committed crime to buy drugs.[33] In 1983, about 15% of the female inmates had used cocaine or crack during the month preceding their arrest; by 1990 that number had increased to 39%. More women in jail are drug-involved than men are.

A strong association between child abuse and crime has long been assumed. Female inmates give evidence that this hypothesis is accurate. More than 44% report being physically or sexually abused at some time in their lives before their current incarceration; about one-third had been abused before age 18. Abused women were more likely to be violent recidivists, affirming the view that "violence begets violence."

Jail Conditions

Jails are the oldest and most deteriorated institutions in the criminal justice system. Because they are usually run by the county government (and controlled by

On an annual basis, close to 10 million people are admitted to jail. An increasing jail population is a direct function of the nation's "get tough" policy against drug offenders and offenses. Although there are fewer jails today than ever before, larger jails are now holding more people than ever before, often in severely overcrowded facilities.

a sheriff), it is difficult to encourage taxpayers to appropriate money for improved facilities. In fact, jails are usually administered under the concept of "custodial convenience," which involves giving inmates minimum standards of treatment and benefits while controlling the cost of jail operations. Jail employees are often underpaid, ill-trained, and lacking in professional experience.

Some jails are practically run by violent inmate cliques that terrorize other prisoners; one former IBM executive who served time in jail for writing bad checks relates this story:

> I've seen people raped, especially young kids. You can get a kid as young as . . . 16. These young boys would come in and if they were fresh and young, the guys who run the tank and lived in the first cell, they would take the kid, forcibly hold him and someone would rape him. . . . Some of them go to pieces just right there and then, kids who can't hack it and are torn apart.[34]

A report on incarceration in the United States by the Human Rights Watch found that because they are short-term facilities, jails often lack basic programs and services. Because of insufficient data and record keeping, violence-prone inmates are held in the same cells as first offenders. The report cited the cases of an 18-year-old in California who committed suicide after being raped in a county jail and an AIDS-infected inmate who was denied a change of clothing, bedding, soap, towels, toothbrush, toilet paper, a Bible, or visitors; this inmate was left in a bare room and denied access to a telephone on the grounds that there was no disinfectant with which to clean the phone after he made a call.[35] About 900 people die in jail each year, and more than one-third of these are suicides.[36] Well aware of these problems, some judges are reluctant to sentence offenders to a jail term if they seem weak or vulnerable.[37]

While the number of jail inmates was actually less than the stated capacity of jails as of 1996, some jails are so overcrowded that they simply have no room to put people. A moratorium has been placed on new admissions to some city jails, and many detainees are released on their own recognizance who might ordinarily have been forced to put up cash bail.[38]

Creating Overcrowded Jails

A number of factors lead to jail overcrowding. One is the concerted effort being made to reduce or control particular crime problems, including substance abuse, spousal abuse, and driving while intoxicated (DWI). For example, some jurisdictions have passed legislation requiring that people arrested on suspicion of domestic violence be held in confinement for a number of hours to "cool off" before becoming eligible for bail. Other jurisdictions have attempted to deter drunk driving by passing mandatory jail sentences for people convicted of DWI.

An evaluation of the mandatory jailing of drunk drivers in four jurisdictions (Seattle, Memphis, Minneapolis, and Cincinnati) found that such legislation can quickly result in overcrowded jails.[39] After a well-publicized campaign to alert the public about mandatory jail terms, arrests of drunk drivers began to increase, indicating that police departments were devoting greater resources and effort to controlling the DWI problem. Court caseloads also increased because more of the arrested violators contested their case rather than face a jail term. The number of drunk drivers sent to jail increased dramatically. Whereas before the legislation only 9% of convicted offenders went to jail in the four jurisdictions, the number climbed to 97% after the DWI laws took effect. Jailing DWI violators puts a tremendous strain on the correctional system. Because many drunk drivers did not have criminal histories, they were confined separately from the general jail population; many were entitled by law to special treatment and reform programs, creating additional costs and system overload. Some offenders had to wait six to seven months before serving their sentence because of overcrowding.

The Federal Bureau of Prisons and every state government maintain closed correctional facilities, also called prisons, penitentiaries, or reformatories. Usually, prisons are organized or classified on three levels—maximum, medium, and minimum security—and each has distinct characteristics.

Types of Prisons

Maximum-security prisons are probably the institutions most familiar to the public, since they house the most famous criminals and are often the subject of films and stories. Famous "max prisons" have included Sing Sing, Joliet, Attica, Walpole, and the most fearsome jail of all, the now-closed federal facility on Alcatraz Island known as The Rock.

A typical maximum-security facility is fortresslike, surrounded by stone walls with guard towers at strategic places. These walls may be 25 feet high, and sometimes inner and outer walls divide the prison into courtyards. Barbed wire or electrified fences are used to discourage escapes. High security, armed guards, and stone walls give the inmate the sense that the facility is impregnable and reassure the citizens outside that convicts will be completely incapacitated.

Inmates live in interior, metal-barred cells that contain their own plumbing and sanitary facilities and are locked securely either by key or electronic device. Cells are organized in sections called blocks, and in large prisons, a number of cell blocks make up a wing. During the evening, each cell block is sealed off from the others, as is each wing. Thus, an inmate may be officially located in, for example, Block 3 of E Wing.

Every inmate is assigned a number and a uniform on entering the prison system. Unlike the striped, easily identifiable uniforms of old, the maximum-security inmate today wears khaki attire not unlike military fatigues. Dress codes may be strictly enforced in some institutions, but closely cropped hair and other strict features are vestiges of the past.

During the day, the inmates engage in closely controlled activities: meals, workshops, education, and so on. Rule violators may be confined to their cells, and working and other shared recreational activities are viewed as privileges.

The byword of the maximum-security prison is security. Guards and other correctional workers are made aware that each inmate may be a dangerous criminal or violent and that, as a result, the utmost in security must be maintained. In keeping with this philosophy, prisons are designed to eliminate hidden corners where people can congregate, and passages are constructed so that they can be easily blocked off to quell disturbances.

Ultra-Maximum-Security Prisons

Some states and the federal government have constructed ultra-maximum or "maxi-maxi" prisons to house the most dangerous predatory criminals. These high-security institutions can be independent correctional centers or locked wings of existing prisons.

Maxi-maxi prisons are modeled on the federal penitentiary in Marion, Illinois, which was infamous for its tight security and isolate conditions. Marion has been supplanted by a new 484-bed facility in Florence, Colorado. This new prison has the most sophisticated security measures in the United States, including 168 videocameras and 1,400 electronically controlled gates. Inside the cells all furniture is unmovable; the desk, bed, and TV stand are made of cement. All potential weapons, including soap dishes, toilet seats, and toilet handles, have been removed. The cement walls are 5,000-pound quality, and steel bars are placed so they crisscross every 8 inches inside the walls. Cells are angled so that inmates can see neither each other or the outside scenery (see Figure 14.A). This cuts down on communications and denies inmates a sense of location, in order to prevent escapes.

Getting out of the prison seems impossible. There are six guard towers at different heights to prevent air attacks. To get out, the inmates would have to pass through seven 3-inch-thick steel doors, each of which can be opened only after the previous one has closed. If a guard tower is ever seized, all controls are switched to the next station. If the whole prison is seized, it can be controlled from the outside. It appears that the only way out is via good works and behavior, through which an inmate can earn transfer to another prison within three years.

Threat of transfer to a maxi-maxi institution is used to deter inmate misbehavior in less restrictive institutions. Civil rights watchdog groups charge that these maxi-maxi prisons violate the United Nations standards for the treatment of inmates.

Critical Thinking Questions

1. Ultra-maxi prisons are reminiscent of the old Pennsylvania system, which made use of solitary confinement and high security. Is this inhumane in our more enlightened age? Why or why not?

SOURCES: Federal Bureau of Prisons, *State of the Bureau, 1995* (Washington, D.C.: U.S. Government Printing Office, 1996); Dennis Cauchon, "The Alcatraz of the Rockies," *USA Today,* 16 Novemeber 1994, p. 6a.

Some states have constructed maxi-maxi prisons to house the most predatory criminals. These high-security institutions can be independent correctional centers or locked wings of existing prisons. Some maxi-maxi prisons lock inmates in their cells 22 to 24 hours a day, never allowing them out unless they are shackled. Threat of transfer to the maxi-maxi institution is used to deter inmate misbehavior in less restrictive institutions. Civil rights watchdog groups charge that these maxi-maxi prisons violate the United Nations standards for the treatment of inmates.[40] For example, California's Pelican Bay State Prison is designed to hold the most violent criminals. Inmates have no privileges to hold jobs, attend educational or training sessions, or mingle with other prisoners. They spend almost the entire day in windowless cells. During the 90 minutes allowed outside their cell, inmates can exercise in a concrete space measuring 10×26 that has no athletic equipment. Whenever possible, this maxi prison is designed to limit contact with both staff and other inmates; however, a lawsuit filed by residents charges that overcrowding forces inmates to be housed two to a cell resulting in many violent assaults.[41] The accompanying Issues box discusses these "super maximum" security prisons.

Medium-security prisons may be similar in appearance to maximum-security prisons; however, the security and atmosphere are neither so tense nor so vigilant. Medium-security prisons are also surrounded by walls, but there may be fewer

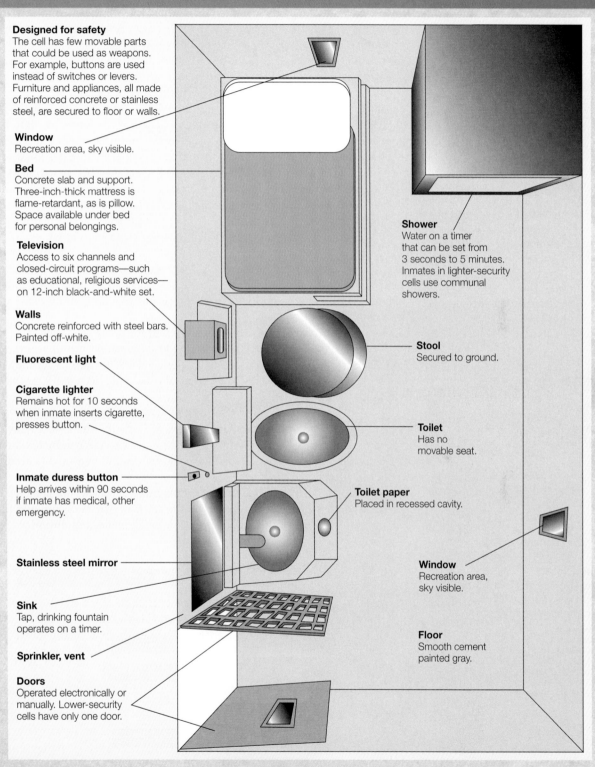

Designed for safety
The cell has few movable parts that could be used as weapons. For example, buttons are used instead of switches or levers. Furniture and appliances, all made of reinforced concrete or stainless steel, are secured to floor or walls.

Window
Recreation area, sky visible.

Bed
Concrete slab and support. Three-inch-thick mattress is flame-retardant, as is pillow. Space available under bed for personal belongings.

Television
Access to six channels and closed-circuit programs—such as educational, religious services—on 12-inch black-and-white set.

Walls
Concrete reinforced with steel bars. Painted off-white.

Fluorescent light

Cigarette lighter
Remains hot for 10 seconds when inmate inserts cigarette, presses button.

Inmate duress button
Help arrives within 90 seconds if inmate has medical, other emergency.

Stainless steel mirror

Sink
Tap, drinking fountain operates on a timer.

Sprinkler, vent

Doors
Operated electronically or manually. Lower-security cells have only one door.

Shower
Water on a timer that can be set from 3 seconds to 5 minutes. Inmates in lighter-security cells use communal showers.

Stool
Secured to ground.

Toilet
Has no movable seat.

Toilet paper
Placed in recessed cavity.

Window
Recreation area, sky visible.

Floor
Smooth cement painted gray.

Figure 14.A
Typical cell in an ultra-maximum-security prison. Some of the toughest felons in the federal prison system are held in a new penitentiary in Florence, Colorado. It is designed to be the most secure ever built by the government. Many inmates live in isolation, except for an hour a day of recreation. A high-security cell in the 575-bed facility has these features.
SOURCE: Louis Winn, United States Penitentiary, Administrative Maximum-Florence, Colorado.

guard towers or other security precautions. For example, visitor privileges may be more extensive and personal contact may be allowed, whereas in a maximum-security prison visitors may be separated from inmates by Plexiglas or other barriers (to prohibit the passing of contraband). While most prisoners are housed in cells, individual honor rooms in medium-security prisons are used to reward those who make exemplary rehabilitation efforts. Finally, medium-security prisons promote greater treatment efforts, and the relaxed atmosphere allows freedom of movement for rehabilitation workers and other therapeutic personnel.

Minimum-security prisons operate without armed guards or walls; usually, they are constructed in compounds surrounded by a Cyclone-type fence. Minimum-security prisons usually house the most trustworthy and least violent offenders; white-collar criminals may be their most common occupants. Inmates are allowed a great deal of personal freedom. Instead of being marched to activities by guards, they are summoned by bells or loudspeaker announcements and assemble on their own. Work furloughs and educational releases are encouraged, and vocational training is of the highest level. Dress codes are lax, and inmates are allowed to grow beards or mustaches or demonstrate other individual characteristics.

Minimum-security facilities may have dormitories or small private rooms for inmates. Prisoners are allowed quite a bit of discretion in acquiring or owning personal possessions that might be deemed dangerous in a maximum-security prison, such as radios.

Minimum-security prisons have been scoffed at for being too much like "country clubs"; some federal facilities catering to white-collar criminals even have tennis courts and pools (they are called derisively "Club Fed"). Yet they remain prisons, and the isolation and loneliness of prison life deeply affects the inmates at these facilities.

Prison Inmates—
A Profile

The Bureau of Justice Statistics conducts a survey of prison inmates every five to seven years.[42] The consistency of findings from prison surveys conducted during the past ten years suggests that the data collected represent a reasonably accurate portrait of today's prison inmate.

The most recent survey indicates that, as might be expected, the personal characteristics of prison inmates reflect common traits of arrestees: Inmates tend to be young, single, poorly educated, disproportionately male, and minority-

Figure 14.2
State inmate profile. Prison inmates are most likely to be male, minority, young, unemployed, and indigent.
SOURCE: Lawrence Greenfield and Allen Beck, *Survey of State Prison Inmates, 1991* (Washington, D.C.: Bureau of Justice Statistics, 1993), p. 21.

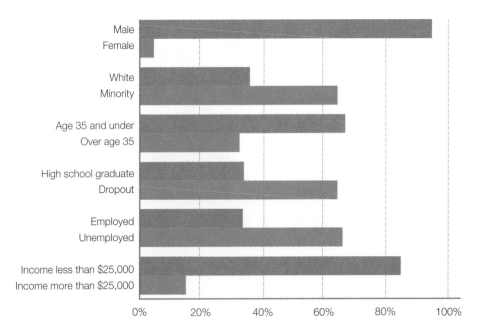

group members (see Figure 14.2). About one-third of all inmates report that they were not employed prior to their arrest, and about one-third had a yearly income of less than $5,000. The picture that emerges is that prisons hold those people who face the toughest social obstacles in society. Only a few members of the educated middle-class wind up behind bars, and these people are usually held in low-security, "country club" institutions.

What did the inmates do to earn their sentence? About half of all inmates are serving time for violent crimes. Many of the violent inmates carried guns or knives, but the majority claim to have carried no weapon during their crime. Only about a quarter of the armed criminals had purchased their weapon at a retail outlet; the rest had stolen them, gotten them from friends and family members, or purchased them on the black market. The fact that far less than half the armed felons had actually purchased their weapon underscores the difficulty of achieving gun control by mandating waiting periods before guns can be bought.

The number of offenders doing time for drug crimes has more than tripled during the past decade This increase probably reflects the effect of mandatory minimum sentences for drug offenders and the increased emphasis that law enforcement agencies are putting on control of the drug trade.

Gender differences in the prison population are considerable. Women are actually underrepresented in prison, and not solely because they commit less serious crimes. The Uniform Crime Reports arrest statistics indicate that the overall male-female arrest ratio is today about three male offenders to one female offender; for violent crimes, the ratio is closer to six males to one female. Yet female inmates account for only about 6% of the prison population. While the typical male inmate was a violent offender, most female inmates committed property offenses.

The prison system is populated disproportionately by minorities; black males in the United States have been incarcerated at a higher rate than in South Africa *before* the election of Nelson Mandela. About one-fourth of African American males ages 20–29 are in some form of correctional treatment. This condition severely decreases the life chances of African American men, has a devastating effect on the black community, and is an ongoing national concern.[43]

The survey also found that many inmates had used drugs and alcohol throughout their life. About 80% of the inmates who reported using drugs sometime during their life were on drugs at the time of their offense, and more than 60% were regular users; about half of the inmates reported being either drunk, high, or both when they committed the crime that landed them in prison.

Drug and Alcohol Abuse

These data support the view that a strong association exists between substance abuse and serious crime (unless one believes that only substance-abusing criminals are caught, convicted, and sent to prison). Considering the rampant drug and alcohol abuse among offenders, it is not surprising that crime control strategies depending on general deterrence often fail to achieve their desired result: A majority of current inmates may have been incapable of appreciating both the severity of the punishments they faced and the certainty of their capture. Substance abuse may be the single greatest obstacle to creating a successful deterrence-based crime control strategy.

In summary, the portrait of the prison inmate developed by the national survey is as follows: young, male, minority, poor, drug and alcohol abuser, undereducated, recidivist, and violent.

In addition to prison and jails, a number of other correctional institutions are operating around the United States. Some have been in use for quite some time, while others have been developed as part of an innovative or experimental program.

Alternative Correctional Institutions

Farms and Camps

Prison farms and camps are used to detain offenders. These types of facilities are found primarily in the South and the West and have been in operation since the 19th century.

Today, about 40 farms, 40 forest camps, 80 road camps, and more than 60 similar facilities (vocational training centers, ranches, and so on) exist in the nation. Prisoners on farms produce dairy products, grain, and vegetable crops that are used in the state correctional system and other government facilities, such as hospitals and schools. Forestry camp inmates maintain state parks, fight forest fires, and do reforestation work. Ranches, primarily a western phenomenon, employ inmates in cattle raising and horse breeding, among other activities. Road gangs repair roads and state highways.

Shock Incarceration

A recent approach to correctional care that is gaining popularity around the United States is **shock incarceration** in **boot camps.** Such programs typically include youthful, first-time offenders and feature military discipline and physical training. The concept is that short periods (90 to 180 days) of high-intensity exercise and work will "shock" the inmate into going straight. Tough physical training is designed to promote responsibility and improve decision-making skills, build self-confidence, and teach socialization skills. Inmates are treated with rough intensity by drill masters who may call them names and punish the entire group for the failure of one of its members (see Figure 14.3).

There is wide variation in the more than 75 programs now operating around the United States.[44] Some programs also include educational and training components, counseling sessions, and treatment for special-needs populations, while others devote little or no time to therapeutic activities. Some receive program participants directly from court sentencing, while others choose potential candidates from the general inmate population. Some allow voluntary participation and others voluntary termination.[45]

Shock incarceration programs can provide some important correctional benefits. New York houses inmates in these programs in separate institutions and provides most (but not all) "graduates" with extensive follow-up supervision. While recidivism rates for these programs in New York are similar to those of traditional prisons, there are indications that both inmates and staff view shock incarceration as a positive experience.[46] It is estimated that the New York program has saved taxpayers hundreds of millions of dollars, because boot camps are cheaper to build and maintain than traditional prisons. Other evaluations have found that a boot camp experience can improve inmates' attitudes and have the potential for enhancing their postcorrection lifestyle.[47]

Shock incarceration has the advantage of being a lower-cost alternative to overcrowded prisons, as inmates are held in nonsecure facilities and sentences are short. Both staff and inmates seem excited by the programs, and even those who fail on parole report that they felt the shock incarceration was a valuable experience.[48] Of course, if shock incarceration is viewed as an exciting or helpful experience by its "graduates," they may be encouraged to recidivate, since the threat of the prison experience has been weakened.

Is shock incarceration a correctional panacea or another fad doomed to failure? The results so far are mixed. The costs of boot camps are no lower than those of traditional prisons, but since sentences are shorter, they do provide long-term savings. Some programs suffer high failure-to-complete rates, which makes program evaluations difficult (even if "graduates" are successful, it is possible that success is achieved because troublesome cases drop out and are placed back in the general inmate population). What evaluations exist indicate that the recidivism rates of inmates who attend shock programs are in some cases no lower than for those released from traditional prisons.[49]

Many of these evaluations have been conducted by Doris Layton Mackenzie and her associates. One study with James Shaw found that while boot camp inmates may have lower recidivism rates than probationers and parolees, they have higher rates of technical violations and revocations.[50] While these results are disappointing, Mackenzie reports that both staff and inmates seem excited by the programs, and even those who fail on parole report they felt boot camp was a valuable experience.[51] She also found, with Alex Piquero, that carefully managed boot camp programs can make a major dent in prison overcrowding.[52] Nonetheless, Mackenzie's extensive evaluations of the boot camp experience generate little evidence that they can significantly lower recidivism rates. Programs that seem to work best, such as those in New York, stress treatment and therapeutic activities, are voluntary, and are longer in duration.[53] It is possible that the therapeutic aspect of the programs and not the military provide any achieved benefits.

One of the goals of correctional treatment is to help reintegrate the offender back into society. Placing offenders in a prison makes them more likely to adapt an inmate lifestyle than to reassimilate conventional social norms. As a result, the **community corrections** concept began to take off in the 1960s. State and federal correctional systems created community-based correctional models as an alternative to closed institutions. Today, hundreds of community-based facilities hold an estimated 12,000 inmates.[54] Many are **halfway houses** to which inmates are transferred just before their release into the community. These facilities are designed to bridge the gap between institutional living and the community.

Rita finishes 50 sit-ups and springs to her feet. At 6 A.M. her platoon begins a 5-mile run, the last portion of this morning's physical training. After 5 months in New York's Lakeview Shock Incarceration Correctional Facility, the morning workout is easy. Rita even enjoys it, taking pride in her physical conditioning.

When Rita graduates and returns to New York City, she will face 6 months of intensive supervision before moving to regular parole. More than two-fifths of Rita's platoon did not make it this far: some withdrew voluntarily, and the rest were removed for misconduct or failure to participate satisfactorily. By completing shock incarceration, she will enter parole 11 months before her minimum release date.

The requirements for completing shock incarceration are the same for male and female inmates. The women live in a separate housing area of Lakeview. Otherwise, men and women participate in the same education, physical training, drill and ceremony, drug education, and counseling programs. Men and women are assigned to separate work details and attend network group meetings held in inmates' living units.

Daily Schedule

A.M.

5:30	Wake up and standing count
5:45–6:30	Calisthenics and drill
6:30–7:00	Run
7:00–8:00	Mandatory breakfast/cleanup
8:15	Standing count and company formation
8:30–11:55	Work/school schedules

P.M.

12:00–12:30	Mandatory lunch and standing count
12:30–3:30	Afternoon work/school schedule
3:30–4:00	Shower
4:00–4:45	Network community meeting
4:45–5:45	Mandatory dinner, prepare for evening
6:00–9:00	School, group counseling, drug counseling, prerelease counseling, decision-making classes
8:00	Count while in programs
9:15–9:30	Squad bay, prepare for bed
9:30	Standing count, lights out

Figure 14.3
Shock incarceration. Typical daily routines and schedule in a boot camp program.
SOURCE: Cherie Clark, David Aziz, and Doris Mackenzie, *Shock Incarceration in New York: Focus on Treatment* (Washington, D.C.: National Institute of Justice, 1994), p. 5.

Community Facilities

Specialized treatment may be offered, and the residents use the experience to cushion the shock of reentering society.

As you may recall, commitment to a community correctional center may also be used as an intermediate sanction and sole mode of treatment. An offender may be assigned to a community treatment center operated by the state department of corrections or to probation. Or the corrections department can contract with a private community center. This practice is common in the treatment of drug addicts and other nonviolent offenders whose special needs can be met in a self-contained community setting that specializes in specific types of treatment.

Halfway houses and community correctional centers can look like residential homes and in many instances were originally residences; in urban centers, older apartment buildings can be adapted for the purpose. Usually, these facilities have a central treatment theme—such as group therapy or reality therapy—that is used to rehabilitate and reintegrate clients.

Another popular approach in community-based corrections is the use of ex-offenders as staff members. These individuals have made the transition between the closed institution and society and can be invaluable in helping residents overcome the many hurdles they face in proper readjustment.

Despite the encouraging philosophical concept presented by the halfway house, evaluation of specific programs has not led to a definite endorsement of this type of treatment.[55] One significant problem has been a lack of support from community residents, who fear the establishment of an institution housing "dangerous offenders" in their neighborhood. Court actions and zoning restrictions have been brought in some areas to foil efforts to create halfway houses.[56] As a result, many halfway houses are located in decrepit neighborhoods in the worst areas of town—certainly a condition that must influence the attitudes and behavior of inmates. Furthermore, the climate of control exercised in most halfway houses, where rule violation can be met with a quick return to the institution, may not be one that the average inmate can distinguish from his or her former high-security penal institution.

Despite these problems, the promise held by community correctional centers, coupled with their low cost of operations, has led to their continued use throughout the 1990s.

Private Institutions

Correctional facilities are now being run by private firms as business enterprises. In some instances a private corporation will finance and build an institution and then contract with correctional authorities to provide services for convicted criminals. Sometimes the private concern will finance and build the institution and then lease it outright to the government. This model has the advantage of allowing the government to circumvent the usually difficult process of getting voters to approve a bond issue and raising funds for prison construction. Another common method of private involvement is with specific service contracts; for example, a private concern might be hired to manage the prison health care system, food services, or staff training.

The federal government has used private companies to run detention centers for illegal aliens who are being held for trial or deportation.[57] One private firm, the Corrections Corporation of America, runs a federal halfway house, two detention centers, and a 370-bed jail in Bay County, Florida. On January 6, 1986, the U.S. Corrections Corporation opened the first private state prison in Marion, Kentucky—a 300-bed minimum-security facility for inmates who are within three years of parole. Today, more than 20 companies are trying to enter the private prison market, five states are contracting with private companies to operate facilities, and more than ten others—including Oregon, New Mexico, and Florida—have recently passed laws authorizing or expanding the use of private prison contractors.[58]

Although privately run institutions have been around for a few years, their increased use may present a number of problems. For example, will private providers be able to effectively evaluate programs, knowing that a negative evaluation might cause them to lose their contract? Will they skimp on services and programs in order to reduce costs? Might they not skim off the "easy" cases and leave the hard-core inmate to the state's care? And will the need to keep business booming require "widening the net" to fill empty cells? Must they maintain state-mandated liability insurance to cover inmate claims?[59] So far, private and state institutions cost about the same to operate.

Private corrections firms also run into opposition from existing state correctional staff and management who fear the loss of jobs and autonomy. Moreover, the public may be skeptical about an untested private concern's ability to provide security and protection.

Private corrections also face administrative problems. How will program quality be controlled? To compete on price, a private facility may have to cut corners to beat out the competition. Determining accountability for problems and mishaps will be difficult when dealing with a corporation that is a legal fiction and protects its officers from personal responsibility for their actions. And legal problems can emerge quickly: Can privately employed guards patrol the perimeter and use deadly force to stop escape attempts? The Supreme Court has recently ruled that private correctional officers have less immunity from law suits than state employees.

The very fact that individuals can profit from running a prison may also prove unpalatable to large segments of the population. Should profit be made from human tragedy and suffering? However, is a private correctional facility really much different from a private hospital or mental health clinic that provides services to the public in competition with state-run institutions? The issue that determines the future of private corrections may be one of efficiency and cost effectiveness, not fairness and morality.

While a private correctional enterprise may be an attractive alternative to a costly correctional system, these legal, administrative, and cost issues need to be resolved before private prisons can become widespread.[60] A balance must be reached between the need for a private business to make a profit and the integrity of a prison administration that must be concerned with such complex issues as security, rehabilitation, and dealing with highly dangerous people in a closed environment.[61] While these issues remain to be settled, evaluations of existing private enterprises seem to suggest that they may provide better services at a lower cost than public facilities.[62]

Correctional Populations

The nation's vast system of penal institutions holds over 1.5 million people (counting jail and community correction populations) and employs more than 250,000 to care for and guard them.

As Figure 14.4 indicates, the nation's prison population has had a number of cycles of growth and decline.[63] Between 1925 and 1939, it increased at about 5% a year, reflecting the nation's concern for the lawlessness of that time. The incarceration rate reached a high of 137 per 100,000 U.S. population in 1939. Then, during World War II, the prison population declined by 50,000, as potential offenders were drafted into the armed services. By 1956 the incarceration rate had dropped to 99 per 100,000 U.S. population.

The postwar era saw a steady increase in the prison population until 1961, when 220,000 people were in custody, a rate of 119 per 100,000. During the Vietnam era (1961–1968), the prison population actually declined by 30,000. The incarceration rate remained rather stable until 1974, when the current dramatic rise began.

One of the most significant problems in the criminal justice system has been the meteoric rise in the prison population; today there are more than 1,200,000

Figure 14.4
Number of sentenced state and federal prisoners, year end, 1925–1997.
SOURCE: Bureau of Justice Statistics, *Prisoners 1925–1981* (Washington, D.C.: U.S. Government Printing Office, 1982, updated, 1997).

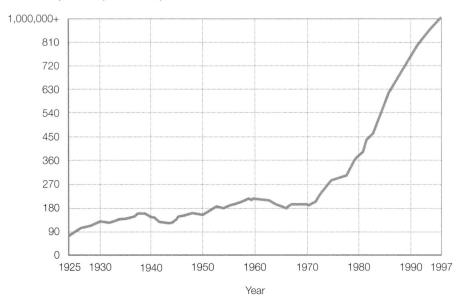

people incarcerated.[64] There are an estimated 420 prison inmates per 100,000 U.S. residents—up from 292 at year end 1990. The average growth in the prison population between 1990 and 1996 was more than 65,000 per year!

The Growth of the Prison Population

How can this significant rise in the prison population be explained? Prison administrators have linked the growth of the correctional population to a change in public opinion, which has demanded a more punitive response to criminal offenders. Public concern about drugs and violent crime has not been lost on state lawmakers. Mandatory sentencing laws, which have been implemented by a majority of states and the federal government, increase eligibility for incarceration and limit the availability for early release via parole. At the same time, arrests for drug and violent crimes, the target of this legislation, have increased significantly; more than 1 million people are now arrested each year on drug-related charges. Although probation and community sentences still predominate, structural changes in criminal codes and crime rates have helped produce an expanding correctional population. The growing punitiveness of sentencing has significantly increased the amount of time served in prison, and efforts are now under way to adopt "truth in sentencing laws" that require inmates to serve at least 85% of their sentence behind bars.[65]

As you may recall from Chapter 12, the conviction rate is increasing for crimes that are traditionally punished with a prison sentence, such as robbery and burglary. In addition, "get tough" policies have helped curtail the use of parole and have reduced judicial discretion to impose nonincarceration sentences.[66]

States fed up with juvenile crime have passed strict laws mandating that violent juveniles be waived or transferred to the adult court for treatment.[67] About 22,500 juveniles are being tried as adults each year and are therefore eligible for incarceration in adult facilities.[68]

The rise in the prison population has also been fueled in part by an increase in the number of inmates serving time for drug offenses. The number of arrests for drug offenses has increased more than 60% in the past decade. This increase is magnified by the fact that since 1988 (a) the number of drug arrestees who are later convicted has increased from 39% to 52%; (b) the number of people convicted for drug offenses sent to prison has increased from 41% to 48%; and (c) a number of states and the federal guidelines require prison sentences for many drug crimes.[69] The result is an increasing portion of the inmate population being admitted for drug law violations.

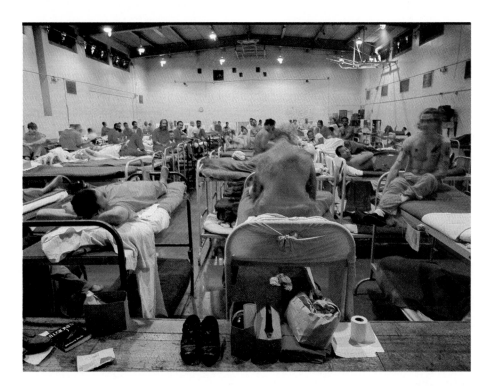

Prison overcrowding has become routine in the nation's correctional systems. Inmates are routinely housed two and three to a cell or in large dormitory-like rooms that hold more than 50. Military bases and even tents have been used to house overflow inmates. Much of the overcrowding has been the result of mandatory sentences for drug crimes. These prisoners are being held in Chino Prison in California.

Prisons today are desperately overcrowded. Prison systems in about 40 states, plus the District of Columbia, Puerto Rico, and the Virgin Islands, are operating under court orders because of conditions relating to overcrowding.[70] The state prison system is now operating at 115% of capacity.[71]

Inmates are routinely housed two and three to a cell or in large dormitory-like rooms that hold more than 50. Military bases and even tents have been used to house overflow inmates. In addition to detainees and misdemeanants, thousands of people convicted of felonies are being held in local jails because of prison crowding. State correctional authorities have attempted to deal with the overcrowding problem by building new facilities using construction techniques that limit expenditures, such as modular or preassembled units. Precast concrete cells are fabricated as fully finished units and can be installed quickly.

At the time of this writing, there is little evidence that the prison population and the incarceration rate will decrease soon. Although crime rates have declined, increasing conviction rates, coupled with tough sentencing laws, have provided a steady supply of inmates. A number of states have undertaken or are planning major correctional building projects. For example, Texas expects to spend more than $1 billion on new prison construction in the 1990s, increasing its existing system by more than 30,000 cells.[72] Florida plans construction of almost 15,000 new beds, bringing the total to about 82,000 in 1998; the cost of expansion will be more than $330 million.[73] In 1996 the states spent about $21 billion on corrections and still could not keep pace with the influx of inmates; the prison population is expanding faster than the government's ability to build cells.[74]

So many people are now going to prison that the federal government estimates that a significant portion of the nation's population will at one time or another be behind prison gates. About 5% of the population, or more than 13 million people, will serve a prison sentence sometime during their life. Men are over eight times more likely than women to be incarcerated in prison at least once during their life. Among men, blacks (28.5%) are about twice as likely as Hispanics (16.0%) and six times more likely than whites (4.4%) to be admitted to prison during their life. Among women, 3.6% of blacks, 1.5% of Hispanics, and 0.5% of whites will enter prison at least once.[75] The extreme racial differences in the imprisonment

Prison Overcrowding

What the Future Holds

Chapter 14
—
Corrections: History, Institutions, and Populations

rate is a key concern of the justice system. Do these differences reflect racial discrimination in the sentencing process? What can be done to reduce or eliminate this significant social problem?

Despite such ominous signs, the nation's prison population may be "maxing out." Budget cutbacks and belt tightening may halt the expansion of prison construction and the housing of ever more prisoners in already crowded prison facilities.[76] While new modular construction techniques and double and triple bunking of inmates make existing prisons expandable, the secure population probably cannot expand endlessly. As costs skyrocket, some states are now spending more on prisons than on higher education. The public may begin to question the wisdom of a strict incarceration policy.

In addition, the supply of offenders may decline if the recent downward trend in the crime rate is maintained over time. The waning of the crack cocaine epidemic in large cities may hasten this decline because street crimes will decline and fewer offenders will be eligible for the long penalties associated with the possession of crack.[77]

In the final analysis, change in the correctional population may depend on the faith judges and legislators place in incarceration as a crime control policy. As long as policymakers believe that incarcerating predatory criminals can bring crime rates down, the likelihood of a significant decrease in the institutional population seems remote. If there is little evidence that this costly system does nothing to lower crime rates, less costly and equally effective alternatives may be sought.

Criminal Justice on the Net

The National Institute of Corrections is located within the U.S. Department of Justice. The institute is headed by a director appointed by the U.S. attorney general. A 16-member Advisory Board, also appointed by the attorney general, was established by the enabling legislation (Public Law 93-415) to provide policy direction to the institute. The NIC provides training, technical assistance, information services, and policy/program development assistance to federal, state, and local corrections agencies. Its website gives information on its history, mission, and goals, and facts about corrections:

http://www.bop.gov/nicpg/ nicmain.html

The Federal Bureau of Prisons webpage is a good source of information on a variety of prison issues, including quick facts and statistics about the inmate population, Inmate Management Directives (Program Statements), employment information, and institutions:

http://www.bop.gov/

Summary

Today's correctional institutions can trace their development from European origins. Punishment methods developed in Europe were modified and improved by American colonists, most notably William Penn. He replaced the whip and other methods of physical punishment with confinement in county institutions or penitentiaries.

Later, as needs grew, the newly formed states created their own large facilities. Discipline was harsh within them, and most enforced a code of total and absolute silence. The Auburn system of congregate working conditions during the day and isolation at night has been adopted in our present penal system.

The current correctional population has grown dramatically in the past few years. Although the number of inmates diminished in the late 1960s and early 1970s, it has since hit an all-time high. This development may reflect a toughening of sentencing procedures nationwide.

A number of institutions currently house convicted offenders. Jails are used for misdemeanants and minor felons. Because conditions are so poor in jails, they have become a major trouble spot for the criminal justice system.

Federal and state prisons—classified as minimum, medium, and maximum security—house most of the nation's incarcerated felons. However, their poor track record has spurred the development of new correctional models, specifically the boot camp, the halfway house, and the community correctional center. Nonetheless, the success of these institutions has been challenged by research efforts indicating that their recidivism rates are equal to those of state prisons. One recent development has been the privately run correctional institution. These are jails and prisons operated by private companies that receive a fee for their services. Used in a limited number of jurisdictions, they have been the center of some controversy: Can a private company provide better management of what has traditionally been a public problem?

The greatest problem facing the correctional system today is overcrowding, which has reached a crisis level. To help deal with the problems of overcrowding, corrections departments have begun to experiment with modular prison construction and the use of alternative sanctions.

Key Terms

secure corrections
prisons
jails
reformatories
recidivism
hulks
Walnut Street Jail
penitentiary house

tier system
congregate system
Auburn system
Pennsylvania system
contract system
convict-lease system
prisoners' rights movement
medical model

maximum-security prisons
medium-security prisons
minimum-security prisons
shock incarceration
boot camps
community corrections
halfway houses

Questions

1. Would you allow a community correctional center to be built in your neighborhood?

2. Should pretrial detainees and convicted offenders be kept in the same institution?

3. What can be done to reduce correctional overcrowding?

4. Should private companies be allowed to run correctional institutions?

5. What are the drawbacks to shock incarceration?

Notes

1. Allen Beck and Bernard Shipley, *Recidivism of Young Parolees* (Washington, D.C.: Bureau of Justice Statistics, 1987); see also John Wallerstedt, *Returning to Prison* (Washington, D.C.: Bureau of Justice Statistics, 1984).

2. See David Fogel, *We Are the Living Proof,* 2nd ed. (Cincinnati: Anderson Publishing, 1978); An-drew von Hirsch, *Doing Justice: The Choice of Punishments* (New York: Hill and Wang, 1976); R. G. Singer, *Just Deserts—Sentencing Based on Equality and Desert* (Cambridge, Mass.: Ballinger Publishing, 1979).

3. Ted Palmer, *Correctional Intervention and Research* (Lexington, Mass.: Lexington Books, 1978); Michael Gottfredson, "The Social Scientist and Rehabilitative Crime Policy," *Criminology* 20 (1982): 29–42. The most widely cited source on the failure of rehabilitation is Robert Martinson; see Robert Martinson, Douglas Lipton, and Judith Wilks, *The Effectiveness of Correctional Treatment* (New York: Praeger Publishers, 1975).

4. Among the most helpful sources in developing this section were David Duffee, *Corrections: Practice and Policy* (New York: Random House, 1989); Harry Allen and Clifford Simonsen, *Correction in America,* 5th ed. (New York: MacMillan, 1989); Benedict Alper, *Prisons Inside-Out* (Cambridge, Mass.: Ballinger Publishing, 1974); Harry Elmer Barnes, *The Story of Punishment,* 2nd ed. (Montclair, N.J.: Patterson-Smith, 1972); Gustave de Beaumont and Alexis de Tocqueville, *On the Penitentiary System in the United States and Its Applications in France* (Carbondale: Southern Illinois University Press, 1964); Orlando Lewis, *The Development of American Prisons and Prison Customs, 1776–1845* (Montclair, N.J.: Patterson-Smith, 1967); Leonard Orland, ed., *Justice, Punishment, and Treatment* (New York: Free Press, 1973); J. Goebel, *Felony and Misdemeanor* (Philadelphia: University of Pennsylvania Press, 1976); Georg Rusche and Otto Kircheimer, *Punishment and Social Structure* (New York: Russell & Russell, 1939); Samuel Walker, *Popular Justice* (New York: Oxford University Press, 1980); Graeme Newman, *The Punishment Response* (Philadelphia: J. B. Lippincott, 1978); David Rothman, *Conscience and Convenience* (Boston: Little, Brown, 1980).

5. F. Pollock and F. Maitland, *History of English Law* (London: Cambridge University Press, 1952).

6. Marvin Wolfgang, "Crime and Punishment in Renaissance Florence," *Journal of Criminal Law and Criminology* 81 (1990): 567–584.

7. Margaret Wilson, *The Crime of Punishment,* Life and Letters Series, no. 64 (London: Johnathon Cape, 1934), p. 186.

8. John Howard, *The State of Prisons,* 4th ed. (1792; reprint ed., Montclair, N.J.: Patterson-Smith, 1973).

9. Alexis Durham III, "Newgate of Connecticut: Origins and Early Days of an Early American Prison," *Justice Quarterly* 6 (1989): 89–116.

10. Lewis, *Development of American Prisons and Prison Customs,* p. 17.

11. Ibid., p. 29.

12. Dario Melossi and Massimo Pavarini, *The Prison and the Factory: Origins of the Penitentiary System* (Totowa, N.J.: Barnes and Noble, 1981).

13. Michel Foucault, *Discipline and Punish* (New York: Vintage Books, 1978).

14. Ibid., p. 16.

15. David Rothman, *The Discovery of the Asylum* (Boston: Little, Brown, 1970).

16. Orland, *Justice, Punishment, and Treatment,* p. 143.

17. Ibid., p. 144.

18. Walker, *Popular Justice,* p. 70.

19. Ibid., p. 71.

20. Beverly Smith, "Military Training at New York's Elmira Reformatory, 1880–1920," *Federal Probation* 52 (1988): 33–41.

21. Ibid.

22. See Z. R. Brockway, "The Ideal of a True Prison System for a State," in *Transactions of the National Congress on Penitentiary and Reformatory Discipline,* reprint ed. (Washington, D.C.: American Correctional Association, 1970), pp. 38–65.

23. This section leans heavily on Rothman, *Conscience and Convenience.*

24. Ibid., p. 23.

25. Ibid., p. 133.

26. 18 U.S.C. § 1761.

27. Barbara Auerbach, George Sexton, Franlin Farrow, and Robert Lawson, *Work in American Prisons: The Private Sector Gets Involved* (Washington, D.C.: National Institute of Justice, 1988), p. 72.

28. See, generally, Jameson Doig, *Criminal Corrections: Ideals and Realities* (Lexington, Mass.: Lexington Books, 1983).

29. Darrell K. Gilliard and Allen J. Beck, *Prison and Jail Inmates at Midyear 1996* (Washington, D.C.: Bureau of Justice Statistics, 1997).

30. John Irwin, *The Jail: Managing the Underclass in American Society* (Berkeley: University of California Press, 1985).

31. Gilliard and Beck, *Prison and Jail Inmates at Midyear 1996.*

32. Tracy Snell, *Correctional Populations in the United States* (Washington, D.C.: Bureau of Justice Statistics, 1993; updated 1997).

33. Tracy Snell, *Women in Jail, 1989* (Washington, D.C.: Bureau of Justice Statistics, 1992).

34. Cited in Ben Bagdikan and Leon Dash, *The Shame of the Prisons* (New York: Pocket Books, 1972), p. 32.

35. Human Rights Watch, *Prison Conditions in the United States* (New York: Human Rights Watch, 1991).

36. Victor Kappeler, Michael Vaughn, and Rolando Del Carmen, "Death in Detention: An Analysis of Police Liability for Negligent Failure to Prevent Suicide," *Journal of Criminal Justice* 19 (1991): 381–393.

37. "Judge Won't Subject Man to Jail 'Brutalities,'" *Omaha World Herald,* 10 April 1981, p. 21.

38. "Philadelphia Frees Defendants to Meet Goal on Jail Crowding," *Criminal Justice Newsletter,* 15 June 1988.

39. Fred Heinzlemann, W. Robert Burkhart, Bernard Gropper, Cheryl Martorana, Lois Felson Mock, Maureen O'Connor, and Walter Philip Travers, *Jailing Drunk Drivers: Impact on the Criminal Justice System* (Washington, D.C.: National Institute of Justice, 1984).

40. Human Rights Watch, *Prison Conditions in the United States.*

41. "Suit Alleges Violations in California's 'Super-Max' Prison," *Criminal Justice Newsletter,* 1 September 1993, p. 2.

42. Allen Beck, Darrell Gilliard, Lawrence Greenfeld, Caroline Harlow, Thomas Hester, Louis Jankowski, Tracy Snell, James Stephan, and Danielle Morton, *Survey of Prison Inmates, 1991* (Washington, D.C.: Bureau of Justice Statistics, 1993).

43. Marc Mauer, "Men in American Prisons: Trends, Causes and Issues," *Men's Studies Review* 9 (1992): 10–12.

44. Doris Layton Mackenzie, Robert Brame, David McDowall, and Claire Souryal, "Boot Camp Prison and Recidivism in Eight States," *Criminology* 33 (1995): 327–357.

45. Ibid., pp. 328–329.

46. "New York Correctional Groups Praises Boot Camp Programs," *Criminal Justice Newsletter,* 1 April 1991, pp. 4–5.

47. Velmer Burton, James Marquart, Steven Cuvelier, Leanne Fiftal Alarid, and Robert Hunter, "A Study of Attitudinal Change Among Boot Camp Participants," *Federal Probation* 57 (1993): 46–52.

48. Doris Layton Mackenzie, "Boot Camp Prisons: Components, Evaluations, and Empirical Issues," *Federal Probation* 54 (1990): 44–52; see also idem, "Boot Camp Programs Grow in Number and Scope," *NIJ Reports,* November/December 1990, pp. 6–8.

49. See, for example, Dale Sechrest, "Prison 'Boot Camps' Do Not Measure Up," *Federal Probation* 53 (1989): 15–20.

50. Doris Layton Mackenzie and James Shaw, "The Impact of Shock Incarceration on Technical Violations and New Criminal Activities," *Justice Quarterly* 10 (1993): 463–487.

51. Doris Layton Mackenzie, "Boot Camp Prisons: Components, Evaluations, and Empirical Issues," *Federal Probation* 54 (1990): 44–52.

52. Doris Layton MacKenzie and Alex Piquero, "The Impact of Shock Incarceration Programs on Prison Crowding," *Crime and Delinquency* 40 (1994): 222–249.

53. Mackenzie et al., "Boot Camp Prisons and Recidivism in Eight States," pp. 352–353.

54. Bureau of Justice Statistics, *Prisons and Prisoners* (Washington, D.C.: U.S. Government Printing Office, 1982).

55. Correctional Research Associates, *Treating Youthful Offenders in the Community, An Evaluation Conducted by A. J. Reiss* (Washington, D.C.: Correctional Research Associates, 1966).

56. Kevin Krajick, "Not on My Block: Local Opposition Impedes the Search for Alternatives," *Corrections Magazine* 6 (1980): 15–27.

57. For a review, see John DiIulio, *Private Prisons* (Washington, D.C.: U.S. Government Printing Office, 1988); Joan Mullen, *Corrections and the Private Sector* (Washington, D.C.: National Institute of Justice, 1984).

58. "Many State Legislatures Focused on Crime in 1995, Study Finds," *Criminal Justice Newsletter* 2 January 1996, p.2.

59. Ira Robbins, *The Legal Dimensions of Private Incarceration* (Chicago: American Bar Foundation, 1988).

60. Lawrence Travis, Edward Latessa, and Gennaro Vito, "Private Enterprise and Institutional Corrections: A Call for Caution," *Federal Probation* 49 (1985): 11–17.

61. Patrick Anderson, Charles Davoli, and Laura Moriarty, "Private Corrections: Feast or Fiasco," *Prison Journal* 65 (1985): 32–41.

62. Charles Logan and Bill McGriff, "Comparing Costs of Public and Private Prisons: A Case Study," *NIJ Reports,* September-October 1989, pp. 2–8.

63. Data in this section come from Bureau of Justice Statistics, *Prisoners, 1925–1981* (Washington, D.C.: U.S. Government Printing Office, 1982).

64. Gilliard and Beck, *Prison and Jail Inmates at Midyear 1996.*

65. Todd Clear, *Harm in American Penology: Offenders, Victims and Their Communities* (Albany: State University of New York Press, 1994).

66. Daniel Nagin, "Criminal Deterrence Research: A Review of the Evidence and a Research Agenda for the Outset of the 21st Century," forthcoming in *Crime and Justice: An Annual Review* (Chicago: University of Chicago Press, 1997).

67. For more on this issue, see Marcy Rasmussen Podkopacz and Barry Feld, "The End of the Line: An Empirical Study of Judicial Waiver," *Journal of Criminal Law and Criminology* 86 (1996): 449–492.

68. Jeffrey Butts et al., *Juvenile Court Statistics, 1993* (Washington, D.C.: Office of Juvenile Justice and Delinquency Prevention, 1993).

69. Patrick A. Langan, and Jodi M. Brown, *Felony Sentences in State Courts, 1994* (Washington, D.C.: Bureau of Justice Statistics, 1997).

70. *Status Report: The Courts and the Prisons* (Washington, D.C.: National Prison Project, 1989).

71. Cohen, *Prisoners in 1990,* p. 6.

428

72. "Texas Legislature Considered More Prisons and Alternatives," *Criminal Justice Newsletter* 1 August 1991, p. 4.

73. "Florida Plans More Prisons For Violent Offenders," *Criminal Justice Newsletter,* 18 January 1994, p. 6.

74. American Bar Association, *The State of Criminal Justice* (Washington, D.C.: American Bar Association, 1996).

75. Thomas P. Bonczar and Allen J. Beck, *Lifetime Likelihood of Going to State or Federal Prison* (Washington, D.C.: Bureau of Justice Statistics, 1997).

76. Timothy Noah, "Prison Population Boom Sputters to Halt as States Lack Funds to House Criminals," *Wall Street Journal,* 3 February 1992, p. A7.

77. Andrew Lang Golub, Farrukh Hakeem, and Bruce Johnson, *Monitoring the Decline in the Crack Epidemic with Data from the Drug Use Forecasting Program, Final Report* (Washington, D.C.: National Institute of Justice, 1996).

CHAPTER 15 Prison Life

To meet the needs of a growing inmate population, a vast and costly state and federal correctional system has developed. A significant percentage of facilities are old, decrepit, archaic structures: 25 prisons were built before 1875, 79 between 1875 and 1924, and 141 between 1925 and 1949. In fact, some of the first prisons ever constructed, such as the Concord Reformatory in Massachusetts, are still in operation.

Although a majority of prisons are classified as medium security, more than half of all inmates are being held in large, maximum-security institutions. Despite the continuous outcry by penologists against the use of fortresslike prisons, institutions holding a thousand or more inmates still predominate. Prison overcrowding is a significant problem. As noted in Chapter 14, the prison system now holds over 1 million people. Some institutions are operating at two or three times their stated capacity. Recreation and workshop facilities have been turned into dormitories housing 30 or more inmates in a single room. While most prison experts agree that a minimum of 60 square feet is needed for each inmate, many prisons fail to reach this standard. In fact, surveys show that not one state has avoided crowding inmates in less than adequate space. It is estimated that

58% of all one-person cells, 90% of all two-person cells, and 20% of all larger living units (dormitories) are overcrowded.

This giant, overcrowded system designed to reform and rehabilitate offenders is instead undergoing a crisis of massive proportions. Institutions are so overcrowded that meaningful treatment efforts are often a matter of wishful thinking; recidivism rates are shockingly high. Inmates are resentful of the deteriorated conditions, and correctional officers fear that the institution is ready to explode. In addition, correctional administrators have begun to adopt a "no-frills" policy in prison, removing privileges and making prisons truly places of punishment. The no-frills movement is a response to lawmakers' claims that crime rates are high because inmates no longer fear imprisonment. This chapter presents a brief review of some of the most important issues confronting the nation's troubled correctional system.

According to prevailing wisdom, prisons in the United States are **total institutions.** This means that inmates locked within their walls are segregated from the outside world, kept under constant scrutiny and surveillance, and forced to obey strict official rules to avoid facing formal sanctions. Their personal possessions are taken from them, and they must conform to institutional dress and personal appearance norms. Many human functions are strictly curtailed—heterosexual relationships and sex, friendships, family relationships, education, and participation in groups become privileges of the past.

Imprisonment is a disheartening experience for most men, one that causes their lives to be disrupted, their relationships to be suspended, their ambitions and dreams to go sour. Few prisoners have experienced comparable stress on the outside and so have not developed coping strategies that can shield them from prison problems. Although prisoners differ from each other and may feel the pressures of confinement somewhat differently, they concur on the extraordinarily stressful nature of life in maximum-security penal institutions.

Living in Prison

Inmates quickly learn what the term *total institution* really means. When they arrive at the prison, they are stripped, searched, shorn, and assigned living quarters. Before they get there, though, their first experience occurs in a classification or reception center, where they are given a series of psychological and other tests and are evaluated on the basis of their personality, background, offense history, and treatment needs. Based on the classification they are given, they will be assigned to a permanent facility. Hard-core, repeat, and violent offenders will go to the maximum-security unit; offenders with learning disabilities may be assigned to an institution that specializes in educational services; mentally disordered offenders will be held in a facility that can provide psychiatric care; and so on.

Once they arrive at the long-term facility, inmates may be granted a short orientation period and then given a permanent cell assignment in the general population. Due to overcrowding, they may be sharing a cell designed for a single inmate with one or more others. All previous concepts of personal privacy and dignity are soon forgotten. Personal losses include the deprivation of liberty, goods, and services, heterosexual relationships, autonomy, and security.[1] Inmates may be subject to verbal and physical attack and threats with little chance of legal redress. While the criminal law applies to inmates as to any other citizen, it is rarely enforced within prison walls.[2] Therefore, part of living in prison involves learning to protect oneself and developing survival instincts.

Prisons have been called "total institutions." They totally envelop inmates within the prison culture. They have a whole new language and moral code to learn. All previous concepts of personal privacy and dignity are soon forgotten. Personal losses include the deprivation of liberty, goods, and services, heterosexual relationships, autonomy, and security. Inmates may be subject to verbal and physical attack and threats, with little chance of legal redress.

Inmates in large, inaccessible prisons may find themselves physically cut off from families, friends, and associates. Visitors may find it difficult to travel great distances to see them; mail is censored and sometimes destroyed.

Inmates may go through a variety of attitude and behavior changes, or cycles, as their sentence unfolds. During the early part of their prison stay, inmates may become easily depressed while considering the long duration of the sentence and the loneliness and dangers of prison life. They must learn the ins and outs of survival in the institution: Which persons can be befriended, and which are best avoided? Who will grant favors and for what repayment? Some inmates will request that regular payments be made to them in exchange for protection from rape and beatings.

Inmates may find that some prisoners have formed cliques or groups based on ethnic backgrounds or personal interests; they are likely to encounter Mafia-like or racial terror groups that must be dealt with. Inmates may be the victim of homosexual attacks. They may find that power in the prison is shared by terrified guards and inmate gangs; the only way to avoid being beaten and raped may be to learn how to beat and rape.[3] If they are weak and unable to defend themselves, new inmates may find that they are considered a "punk"; if they ask a guard for help, they are labeled a "snitch." After that, they may spend the rest of their sentence in protective custody, sacrificing the "freedom of the yard" and rehabilitation services for personal protection.[4]

Despite all these hardships, many inmates learn to adapt to the prison routine. Each prisoner has his own method of coping; he may stay alone, become friends with another inmate, join a group, or seek the advice of treatment personnel. New inmates must learn to deal with the guards and other correctional personnel; these relationships will determine whether the inmates do "hard time" or "easy time." Regardless of adaptation style, the first stage of the inmates' prison cycle is marked by a growing awareness that they can no longer depend on their traditional associates for help and support and that for better or worse, the institution is a new home to which they must adjust. Unfortunately for the goal of rehabilitation, the predominant emotion that inmates must confront is boredom. The absence of anything constructive to do, the forced idleness, is what is often so frustrating and so damaging.[5]

Part of new inmates' early adjustment involves becoming familiar with and perhaps participating in the black market, the hidden economy of the prison— the hustle. Hustling provides inmates with a source of steady income and the satisfaction that they are beating the system.[6] Hustling involves sales of such illegal commodities as drugs (uppers, downers, pot), alcohol, weapons, or illegally obtained food and supplies. When prison officials crack down on hustled goods, it merely serves to drive the price up—giving hustlers greater incentive to promote their activities. Drugs and other contraband are smuggled into prison by visitors, carried in by inmates who are out on furlough or work-release programs, or bought from corrupt prison officials. Control of the prison drug trade is often the spark that creates violence and conflict.

Inmates must also learn to deal with the racial conflict that is a daily fact of life. Prisoners tend to segregate themselves, and if peace is to reign in the institution, they learn to stay out of each other's way. Often racial groupings are quite exact; for example, Hispanics will separate themselves according to their national origin (Mexican, Puerto Rican, Colombian, and so on). Because racial disparity in sentencing is common in many U.S. courts, prisons are one place where "minorities" often hold power.

Inmates may find that the social support of inmate peers can make incarceration somewhat less painful. They may begin to take stock of their situation and enter into educational or vocational training programs, if they are available. Many turn to religion and take Bible classes. They heed the inmate grapevine to

Adjusting to Prison

determine what the parole board considers important in deciding to grant community release. They may become more politically aware in response to the influence of other inmates, and the personal guilt they may have felt may be shifted to society at large. Why should they be in prison when those equally guilty go free? They learn the importance of money and politics. Eventually, they may be called on by new arrivals to aid them in adapting to the system.

Coping Behavior

Even in the harsh prison environment, inmates may learn to find a niche for themselves. Inmates may be able to find a place, activity, or group in which they can feel comfortable and secure.[7] An inmate's niche is a kind of insulation from the pains of imprisonment, enabling him to cope and providing him with a sense of autonomy and freedom. As one prisoner said about his niche, a desirable work detail:

> Now I have to deal with one officer, and I work a very short period each day. The rest of the day is mine to do as I choose with, which gives me a great deal of time for myself. . . . I don't have to lock in for some counts. . . . I'm pretty much free here.[8]

Some inmates are able to cope by dealing with problems head-on, using legitimate resources available to them.[9] Even maximum-security prisons can provide the opportunity for mature change.[10]

Of course, not all inmates learn to cope. Some inmates repeatedly violate institutional rules; more than 10% of all inmates have six or more such infractions yearly.[11] While it is difficult to predict who will become an institutional troublemaker, rule-breaking behavior has been associated with being a younger inmate with a low IQ possessing numerous juvenile convictions, being a repeat offender, and having victimized a stranger. Inmates who have limited intelligence and maintain low self-control may not be able to form adaptive coping mechanisms and manage the stress of being in prison.[12]

Inmate Social Codes

For many years, criminal justice experts maintained that inmates formed their own world with a unique set of norms and rules, known as the **inmate subculture.**[13] A significant aspect of the inmate subculture was a unique **social code,** unwritten guidelines that expressed the values, attitudes, and type of behavior that older inmates demanded of young ones. Passed on from one generation of inmates to another, the inmate social code represented the values of interpersonal relations within the prison.

National attention was first drawn to the inmate social code and subculture by Donald Clemmer's classic book *The Prison Community,* in which he presented a detailed sociological study of life in a maximum-security prison.[14] Referring to thousands of conversations and interviews, as well as to inmate essays and biographies, Clemmer was able to identify a unique language, or *argot,* that prisoners use. In addition, Clemmer found that prisoners tend to group themselves into cliques on the basis of such personal criteria as sexual preference, political beliefs, and offense history. He found complex sexual relationships in prison and concluded that many heterosexual men will turn to homosexual relationships when faced with long sentences and the loneliness of prison life.

Clemmer's most important contribution may have been his identification of the **prisonization** process. This he defined as the inmate's assimilation into the existing prison culture through acceptance of its language, sexual code, and norms of behavior. Those who become the most "prisonized" will be the least likely to reform on the outside.

Using Clemmer's work as a jumping-off point, a number of prominent sociologists have set out to more fully explore the various roles in the prison community. The most important principles of the dominant inmate culture have been identified, including:

1. **Don't interfere with inmates' interests.** Within this area of the code are maxims concerning serving the least amount of time in the greatest possible comfort. For example, inmates are warned never to betray another inmate to authorities; in other words, grievances must be handled personally. Other aspects of the noninterference doctrine include "Don't be nosy," "Don't have a loose lip," "Keep off the other inmates' backs," and "Don't put another inmate on the spot."

2. **Don't lose your head.** Inmates are also cautioned to refrain from arguing, quarreling, or engaging in other emotional displays with fellow inmates. The novice may hear such warnings as "Play it cool" and "Do your own time."

3. **Don't exploit inmates.** Prisoners are warned not to take advantage of one another—"Don't steal from cons," "Don't welsh on a debt," "Be right."

4. Inmates are cautioned to be tough and not lose their dignity. While rule 2 forbids conflict, once it starts, an inmate must be prepared to deal with it effectively and thoroughly. Maxims include "Don't cop out," "Don't weaken," "Be tough; be a man."

5. **Don't be a sucker.** Inmates are cautioned not to make fools of themselves and support the guards or prison administration over the interest of the inmates—"Be sharp."[15]

While some inmates violate the code and exploit their peers, the "right guy" is someone who uses the inmate social code as his personal behavior guide. He is always loyal to his fellow prisoners, keeps his promises, is dependable and trustworthy, and never interferes with inmates who are conniving against the officials.[16] The right guy does not go around looking for a fight, but he never runs away from one; he acts like a man.

The "New" Inmate Culture

While some prison experts believe that the prison experience transforms people and forces them to accept the inmate culture, others argue that the culture is actually imported from the outside world.[17] In other words, inmate culture is affected as much by the values of newcomers and events on the outside as it is by traditional inmate values.

The importation of outside values into the inmate culture has had a dramatic effect on prison life. While the "old" inmate subculture may have been harmful because its norms and values insulated the inmate from change efforts, it also helped create order within the institution and prevented violence among the inmates. People who violated the code and victimized others were sanctioned by their peers. An understanding developed between guards and inmate leaders: The guards would let the inmates have things their own way; the inmates would not let things get out of hand and draw the attention of the administration.

The old system may be dying or already dead in most institutions. The change seems to have been precipitated by the Black Power movement in the 1960s and 1970s. Black inmates were no longer content to fill a subservient role and challenged the power of established white inmates. As the Black Power movement gained prominence, racial tension in prisons created divisions that severely altered the inmate subculture. Older, respected inmates could no longer cross racial lines to mediate disputes. Predatory inmates could victimize others without fear of retaliation. Consequently, more inmates than ever are now assigned to protective custody for their own safety.

In the new culture, African American and Latino inmates are much more cohesively organized than whites.[18] Their groups sometimes form out of religious or political affiliations, such as the Black Muslims; out of efforts to combat discrimination in prison, such as the Latino group La Familia; or from street gangs, such as the Vice Lords or Gangster Disciples in the Illinois prison system and the Crips in California. Where white inmates have successfully organized, it is in the form of a neo-Nazi group called the Aryan Brotherhood. Racially homogenous gangs are so cohesive and powerful that they are able to supplant the original inmate code with one of their own. Consider the oath taken by new members of Nuestra Familia (Our Family), a Latino gang operating in California prisons: "If I go forward, follow me. If I hesitate, push me. If they kill me, avenge me. If I am a traitor, kill me."[19]

These groups not only provide protection to their members but also act as a bloc to make demands on prison administrators. Although their members may adhere to principles of the traditional inmate code (such as "Don't inform"), allegiance is always to members of their own group.

Future research on prison culture will begin to evaluate the role race plays in prison life and how inmate racism influences the "traditional" prisoner culture. This research is particularly important when we consider that hundreds of inmates have been killed and scores wounded in gang warfare.[20] In fact, the situation is so bad and tensions are so high that some respected prison authorities have suggested that it may be humane and appropriate to segregate inmates along racial lines to maintain order and protect individual rights. It is alleged that in some prisons, administrators use integration as a threat to keep inmates in line; to be transferred to a racially mixed setting may mean beatings or death.[21]

Rape has become an ever-increasing problem. While at one time it was suggested that heterosexual men in prison might turn to homosexual relations because of the absence of female partners, rape as a means of expressing dominance, power, and anger is now an accepted prison norm.[22]

Women Imprisoned

Before 1960, few women were in prison. Women's prisons were relatively rare and were usually an outgrowth of male institutions. Only 4 institutions for women were built between 1930 and 1950; in comparison, 34 women's prisons were constructed during the 1980s.

At the turn of the century, female inmates were viewed as morally depraved people who flaunted conventional rules of female behavior. The treatment of white and African American women differed significantly. In some states, white women were placed in female-only reformatories designed to improve their deportment; black women were placed in male prisons, where they were subject to the chain gang and beatings.[23]

The place of women in the correctional system has changed rapidly. Today, approximately 75,000 women are in the state and federal systems, about 6% of the total inmate population.[24] Although still small compared to the male inmate population, the female population has grown at a faster pace since 1980, climbing more than 200%, compared to an increase of slightly more than 100% for males.

The female offender population has increased so rapidly for a number of reasons. Females have accelerated their crime rate at a faster pace than males. The get-tough policies that produced mandatory and determinate sentencing statutes also helped reduce the judicial discretion that has traditionally benefited women. As Meda Chesney-Lind points out, women are swept up in the get-tough movement and no longer receive the benefits of male chivalry. The use of sentencing guidelines means that such factors as family ties and employment record, two elements that usually benefit women during sentencing, can no longer be considered by judges.[25] Chesney-Lind notes that judges seem willing once again to view female offenders as "depraved" and outside the ranks of "true womanhood."

The characteristics of female and male prisoners are compared in Figure 15.1.

Female Institutions

State jurisdictions have been responding to the influx of female offenders into the correctional system by expanding the facilities for housing and treating them.[26] Women's prisons tend to be smaller than those housing male inmates.[27]

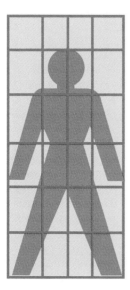

Figure 15.1
Characteristics of male and female inmates.
SOURCE: Tracy Snell and Danielle Morton, *Women in Prison* (Washington, D.C.: Bureau of Justice Statistics, 1994), pp. 1–11.

Males
- About 18% are married.
- Only 12% attended college; 10% had an 8th grade education or less.
- More than half were 35 years old.
- Half victimized strangers; about 10% victimized relatives.
- 37% had family members who were also incarcerated.
- More than a quarter said their parents abused alcohol or drugs.
- 12% claimed physical or sexual abuse.
- Two-thirds had children.
- 80% had abused drugs.
- 2% tested positively for HIV.
- 47% had committed a violent crime.

Females
- Two-thirds had a child under 18.
- 17% were married.
- 16% attended college; 16% had an 8th grade education or less
- More than half were unemployed before prison.
- About 47% had an immediate family member who had been incarcerated.
- Half said they had been high when they committed the crime.
- 35% had victimized strangers; 16% victimized relatives.
- One-third said their parents abused drugs.
- 43% had been physically or sexually abused.

Although some female institutions are strictly penal, with steel bars, concrete floors, and other security measures, the majority are nonsecure institutions similar to college dormitories and group homes in the community. Women's facilities, especially those in the community, commonly offer a great deal of autonomy to inmates and allow them to make decisions affecting their daily life in the institution.

Like men's prisons, women's prisons suffer from a lack of adequate training, health, treatment, and educational facilities. Psychological counseling often takes the form of group sessions conducted by lay people, such as correctional officers. Most trained psychologists and psychiatrists restrict themselves to such activities as conducting intake classifications and court-ordered examinations and prescribing mood-controlling medication. Although many female inmates are parents and had custody of their children before their incarceration, little effort is made to help them develop better parenting skills.

The lack of meaningful work opportunities is also a problem. Where vocational training exists, it is in areas with limited financial reward, hindering adjustment on release. Female inmates, many of whom were on the economic margin before their incarceration began, find little room for improvement during their prison experience.[28]

Like their male counterparts, female inmates are young (most are under age 30), minority-group members, unmarried, undereducated (more than half are high school dropouts), and either unemployed or underemployed.[29]

Incarcerated women also had a troubled family life. Significant numbers were at-risk children, products of "broken homes" and the welfare system; over

The Female Inmate

Female inmates tend to be young, unmarried, undereducated, and either unemployed or underemployed. Incarcerated women also had a troubled family life. Significant numbers were "at-risk" children—products of broken homes and the welfare system who were physically and sexually abused.

half had received welfare at some time during their adult lives. They experienced a pattern of harsh discipline and physical abuse. About 40% claim to have been physically or sexually abused at some point in their life.[30] This pattern continued in their adult life: Many female inmates were victims of domestic violence.

A serious problem for women in prison is the disruption of their families. About three-fourths of all female inmates are mothers, and most were living with their children before their incarceration. Who takes care of the children while their mothers are incarcerated? Most children of incarcerated women are placed with their father, grandparent, other relative, or a family friend. About 10% wind up in foster homes or state facilities.

A significant number of female inmates report having substance abuse problems. About three-fourths had used drugs at some time in their lives, and almost half were involved with addictive drugs, such as cocaine, heroin, or PCP. There is actually little difference in major drug use between male and female offenders when measured over their life span or at the time of their current arrest.

The picture that emerges of the female inmate is troubling. After a lifetime of emotional turmoil, physical and sexual abuse, and drug use, it seems improbable that overcrowded, underfunded correctional institutions can forge a dramatic turnaround in the behavior of at-risk female inmates.

The Culture of the Female Prisoner

Daily life in the women's prison differs somewhat from that in male institutions. For one thing, unlike male inmates women usually do not present an immediate physical danger to staff and fellow inmates. Relatively few engage in violent behavior, and incidents of inmate-initiated sexual aggression, so common in male institutions, are quite rare in women's prisons.[31] Nevertheless, there are numerous reports of female prisoners being sexually abused and exploited by male correctional workers who either use brute force or psychological coercion to gain sexual control over inmates.[32] The situation in women's prison as portrayed in movies is discussed in the accompanying media box.

Nor does there exist the rigid, antiauthority inmate social code found in many male institutions.[33] Confinement for women, however, may produce severe anxiety and anger, because of separation from families and loved ones and the inability to function in normal female roles. Unlike men, who direct their

Chained Heat

Are most female inmates held in fortresslike institutions in which brutal guards terrorize them and gang fights are routine? If you have ever seen one of those sensational "women in prison" films, you have been presented with just that picture of inmate life. Such B-movies as *Women in Chains* and *Chained Heat* typically portray helpless female inmates, usually framed for a crime they did not commit, being victimized by a corrupt prison staff led by a warden of uncertain sexual orientation. To make matters worse (and to appeal to their mostly male audience), these films feature fights in the yard between the heroine and the warden's inmate henchwomen, a shower scene, and brutal male guards who sexually abuse the weaker inmates. At the end, the heroine leads an escape attempt and the warden and her staff get their just deserts.

While popular on late-night cable TV, these films paint a highly distorted picture of women in prison. Few, if any, are held in maximum-security enclaves patrolled by gun-toting guards. Many are coed institutions. Almost all female institutions are minimum security, without high walls and guard towers. If inmates experience violence, it is more likely to come at their own hands than that of other inmates. Prison gangs are less prevalent in female institutions, and most inmates are more worried about maintaining ties with their children and families than they are about violent gang fights. Worries about the care of dependent children are prevalent: Who will take care of their children while they are incarcerated?

anger outward, female prisoners may turn to more self-destructive acts to cope with their problems. Female inmates are more likely than males to mutilate their own bodies and attempt suicide. For example, one common practice among female inmates is self-mutilation or "carving." This ranges from simple scratches to carving the name of their boyfriend on their body or even complex statements or sentences ("To mother, with hate").[34]

Another form of adaptation to prison used by women is the **make-believe family.** This group contains masculine and feminine figures acting as fathers and mothers; some even act as children and take on the role of brother or sister. Formalized marriages and divorces may be conducted. Sometimes one inmate holds multiple roles, so that a "sister" in one family may "marry" and become the "wife" of another inmate. It is estimated that about half of all female inmates are members of make-believe families.[35]

Why do make-believe families exist? Experts suggest that they provide the warm, stable relationships otherwise unobtainable in the prison environment. People both in and out of prison have needs for security, companionship, affection, attention, status, prestige, and acceptance that can be filled only by having primary group relationships. Friends fill many of these needs, but the family better represents the ideal or desire for these things in a stable relationship.

Institutional Treatment Programs

Almost every prison facility uses some mode of treatment for inmates. This may come in the form of individual or group therapy programs or educational or vocational training.

Despite good intentions, rehabilitative treatment within prison walls is extremely difficult to achieve. Trained professional treatment personnel usually command high salaries, and most institutions do not have sufficient budgets to adequately staff therapeutic programs. Usually, a large facility may have a single staff psychiatrist or a few social workers. A second problem revolves around the philosophy of **less eligibility,** which has been interpreted to mean that prisoners should always be treated less well than the most underprivileged law-abiding citizen. Translated into today's terms, less eligibility usually involves the question "Why should inmates be treated to expensive programs denied to the average honest citizen?" Enterprising state legislators use this argument to block expenditures for prison budgets, and some prison administrators may actually agree with them.

Finally, correctional treatment is hampered by the ignorance surrounding the practical effectiveness of one type of treatment program over another. What constitutes proper treatment has not yet been determined, and studies evaluating treatment effectiveness have suggested that few, if any, of the programs currently used in prisons actually produce significant numbers of rehabilitated offenders.

This section discusses a selected number of therapeutic methods that have been used nationally in correctional settings and identifies some of their more salient features.

Counseling Programs

The most common type of institutional treatment is counseling, which is done through a wide variety of programs. The number of clinically trained mental health professionals on a corrections department's payroll is typically inadequate to carry out treatment requirements. Consequently, counseling programs commonly use nonclinical treatment personnel as group leaders.[36] Some counseling is conducted under contract by private, nonprofit agencies that send counselors into the institution.[37]

Group counseling can be directed toward helping inmates solve perplexing personal problems that they are incapable of dealing with alone, such as by helping them to end deviant or violent sexual behaviors. Inmates may also use the group to learn to understand how others view them and how they view themselves.

Many correctional systems use a variety of more intensive individual and group techniques, including behavior modification, aversive therapy, milieu therapy, reality therapy, transactional analysis, and responsibility therapy.

While counseling is a major component of correctional treatment policy, the personnel and resources needed to carry out effective programs are often lacking. Many institutions maintain a unit for the emotionally disturbed and offer psychological services tied in with state hospitals and mental health services. Yet the number of trained mental health professionals employed in the correctional system is far less than what is needed. This problem becomes even more acute when we consider that an estimated 10% of the prison population may be suffering from acute mental problems, such as schizophrenia; an additional 10%–50% may suffer from adaption problems marked by nervousness, sleeplessness, and depression; and another 30% or more suffer from what are termed character disorders or antisocial behavior.[38]

One of the challenges of correctional treatment is to care for the so-called **special-needs inmates.** These individuals can have a variety of social problems. Some are mentally ill but have been assigned to prison because the state has toughened its insanity laws. Others suffer mental problems developed during their imprisonment. It is estimated that about 10% of all inmates suffer from acute mental disorders.[39] An additional 1%–6% of the inmate population is mentally retarded.[40] Treating the mentally ill inmate has required the development and use of new therapies in the prison environment. While some critics warn of the overuse of "chemical straitjackets"—psychotropic medications—to keep disturbed inmates docile, prison administrators have been found to have a genuine concern for these special-needs inmates.[41]

Treating the Special-Needs Inmate

Restrictive crime control policies have also produced another special-needs group, elderly inmates who require health care, diets, and work and recreational opportunities that are quite different from those of the general population. Some correctional systems have responded to the growing number of elderly inmates by creating facilities tailored to their needs.[42] It is now estimated that more than 22,000 inmates are over 55, an increase of more than 40% since 1990.[43]

The Drug-Dependent Inmate. Another special-needs group in prison are drug-dependent inmates. Although most institutions attempt to provide drug and alcohol treatment, these efforts are often inadequate. Government-sponsored surveys have found that an estimated half a million state inmates are in need of drug treatment, but because of lack of funding and inadequate security measures, only 100,000 receive adequate treatment.[44]

While the ideal drug treatment has yet to be identified, experimental efforts around the country use counseling sessions, instruction in coping strategies, employment counseling, and strict security measures featuring random urinalysis.

The AIDS-Infected Inmate. The AIDS-infected prisoner is another acute special-needs inmate. Two groups of people at high risk of contracting the HIV virus are intravenous drug users who share needles and males who engage in homosexual sex, two lifestyles common in prison. Although the numbers are constantly changing, more than 11,000 inmates have been diagnosed as having AIDS, and the incidence is increasing daily. While an estimated 17 people in every 100,000 of the U.S. population may be infected with the AIDS virus, the rate in prison is about ten times higher; imprisoned women are slightly more likely than men to be HIV-positive. Among some correctional populations, such as female inmates in New York, the HIV rate is 25%.[45] About 30% of all inmate deaths are now believed to be AIDS related.

Correctional administrators have found it difficult to arrive at effective policies to confront AIDS. While all state and federal jurisdictions do some AIDS testing, only 15 states and the Federal Bureau of Prisons conduct mass screenings of all inmates. Most states test inmates only if there are significant indications that they are HIV-positive. About 40% of all state prison inmates have never been tested for AIDS.

Most correctional systems are now training staff about AIDS. Educational programs for inmates are often inadequate, because administrators are reluctant to give them information on the proper cleaning of drug paraphernalia and safe sex (since both drug use and homosexual sex are forbidden in prison).

Many questions remain about the proper treatment of AIDS-infected inmates. Should they be given the full range of treatment, including multiple doses of expensive medications, such as AZT? While most jurisdictions report that they provide this care, many fail to provide treatment to all infected inmates. Should AIDS-infected inmates be excluded from the general population and held in restricted areas? While about 30% of state correctional systems have some type of segregation policy, most inmates with AIDS are in the general inmate population. Cases challenging segregation policies have been filed. In one important California case, *Gates v. Deukmejian,* a court upheld a one-year experimental program in which 20 to 30 HIV-infected inmates would live in a closed unit but be mainstreamed with the general population in all programs and activities.[46] Prison administrators have been sued over incidents in which staff or inmates were bitten or spit on by HIV-infected inmates. So far, no cases have been reported of a correctional officer becoming infected as a result of such an incident; at least 33 health care workers have been infected.

What steps should be taken to limit the HIV infection risk to inmates and staff? A majority of institutions now provide AIDS information and education to both groups. Most encourage the proper handling of inmates to reduce risk of infection. Controversy exists over whether condoms should be provided to inmates. Only five correctional systems currently take that step; the majority of officials believe condom distribution encourages and condones behavior that is illegal and—some feel—immoral.

Educational and Vocational Programs

In addition to treatment programs stressing personal growth through individual analysis or group process, inmate rehabilitation is also pursued through vocational and educational training. While these two kinds of training sometimes differ in style and content, they can also overlap when, for example, education involves practical, job-related study.

The first prison treatment programs were in fact educational. A prison school was opened at the Walnut Street Jail in 1784. Elementary courses were offered in New York's prison system in 1801 and in Pennsylvania's in 1844. An actual school system was established in Detroit's House of Corrections in 1870, and Elmira Reformatory opened a vocational trade school in 1876. Today, most institutions provide some type of educational program. At some prisons, inmates

At some prisons, inmates can obtain a high school diploma or a GED certificate through equivalency exams. Here male inmates are studying for their GED at Alabama's Limestone Correctional Facility.

can obtain a high school diploma or a general educational development (GED) certificate through equivalency exams. Other institutions provide an actual classroom education, usually staffed by certified teachers employed full time at the prison or by part-time teachers who also teach full time at nearby public schools.

The number of hours devoted to educational programs and the quality and intensity of these efforts vary greatly. Some are full-time programs employing highly qualified and concerned educators, while others are part-time programs without any real goals or objectives. While worthwhile attempts are being made, prison education programs often suffer from inadequate funding and administration. The picture is not totally bleak, however. In some institutions, programs have been designed to circumvent the difficulties inherent in the prison structure. They encourage volunteers from the community and local schools to tutor willing and motivated inmates. Some prison administrators have arranged flexible schedules for inmate students and actively encourage their participation in these programs. In several states, statewide school districts serving prisons have been created. Forming such districts can make better-qualified staff available and provide the materials and resources necessary for meaningful educational programs.

Every state correctional system also has some job-related services for inmates. Some have elaborate training programs within the institution, while others have instituted prerelease and postrelease employment services. Inmates who hope to obtain parole need to participate in prison industry. Documenting a history of stable employment in prison is essential if parole agents are to convince prospective employers that the ex-offender is a good risk; postrelease employment is usually required for parole eligibility.[47]

A few of the more important work-related services are discussed in the following sections.

Basic Prison Industries. Prisoners are normally expected to work within the institution as part of their treatment program. Aside from saving money for the institution, prison work programs are supposed to help inmates develop good habits and skills. Most prominent among traditional prison industries are those designed to help maintain and run the institution and provide services for other public or state facilities, such as mental hospitals. These include

1. *Food services.* Inmates are expected to prepare and supply food for prisoners and staff. These duties include baking bread, preparing meat and vegetables, and cleaning and maintaining kitchen facilities.

2. *Maintenance.* The buildings and grounds of most prisons are cared for by the inmates. Electrical work, masonry, plumbing, and painting are all inmate activities. Of a less skilled nature are such duties as garbage collection, gardening, and cleaning.

3. *Laundry.* Most prisons have their own inmate-run laundries. Quite often, prison laundries will also furnish services to other state institutions.

4. *Agriculture.* In western and southern states, many prisons farm their own land. Dairy herds, crops, and poultry are all managed by inmates. The products are used in the prison and in other state institutions.

Vocational Training. Most institutions also provide vocational training programs. In New York, for example, more than 42 trade and technical courses are provided in organized training shops under qualified civilian instructors. Some of these courses not only benefit the inmate but also provide services for the institution. For example, New York has trained inmates to become dental laboratory technicians; this program provides dentures for inmates and saves the state money. Another New York program trains inmates to become optical technicians and has the added benefit of providing eyeglasses for inmates. Other New York correctional training programs include barber training, computer programming, auto mechanics, auto body work, and radio and television repair. The products of most of these programs save the taxpayers money, while the programs provide the inmates with practical experience. Many other states offer this type of vocational programming.

Despite the promising aspects of such programs, they have also been seriously criticized: inmates often have trouble finding skill-related, high-paying jobs on their release; equipment in prisons is often second-hand, obsolete, and hard to come by; some programs are thinly disguised excuses for prison upkeep and maintenance; and unions and other groups resent the intrusion of prison labor into their markets.

Work Release. To supplement programs stressing rehabilitation via in-house job training or education, more than 44 states have attempted to implement **work release** or **furlough** programs. These allow deserving inmates to leave the institution and hold regular jobs in the community.

Inmates enrolled in work release may live at the institutions at night while working in the community during the day. However, security problems (for example, contraband may be brought in) and the usual remoteness of prisons often make this arrangement difficult. More typical is the extended work release, where prisoners are allowed to remain in the community for significant periods of time. To help inmates adjust, some states operate community-based prerelease centers where inmates live while working. Some inmates may work at their previous jobs, while others seek new employment.

Like other programs, work release has its good and bad points. Inmates are sometimes reluctantly received in the community and find that certain areas of employment are closed to them. Citizens are often concerned about prisoners "stealing" jobs or working for lower than normal wages; consequently, such practices are prohibited by Federal Public Law 89-176, which controls the federal work release program.

On the other hand, inmates gain many benefits from work release, including the ability to maintain work-related skills, to maintain community ties, and to make an easier transition from prison to the outside world. For those who have learned a skill in the institution, work release offers an excellent opportunity to test out a new occupation. For others, the job may be a training situation in which new skills are acquired. A number of states have reported that few work release inmates absconded while in the community.

Helping Female Offenders. Critics have charged that educational and vocational programs are especially deficient in female institutions, which typically have offered only remedial-level education or occasional junior college classes. Female inmates were not being provided with the tools needed to succeed on the outside because the limited vocational training stressed what was considered traditional "women's work": cosmetology, secretarial work, and food services.

One survey by the American Correctional Association found that correctional authorities are now beginning to recognize the education and training shortfall in female institutions.[48] All but three states have instituted some sort of vocational training programs for women; the other three provide supplemental services for their few female inmates. While the traditional vocation of sewing is the most common industrial program, 16 states teach data processing, and female inmates are involved in such other industries as farming, printing, telemarketing, and furniture repair. In the survey, 36 states said they were planning to expand programming, while 14 indicated that their activities were influenced by litigation filed by female inmates charging that male inmates had more program opportunities than women did. Clearly, greater efforts are needed to improve the quality of work experiences for female inmates.

Private Prison Enterprise. While opposition from organized labor ended the profitability of commercial prison industries, a number of interesting efforts have been made to vary the type and productivity of prison labor.[49] The federal government helped put private industry into prisons when it approved the Free Venture program in 1976. Seven states, including Connecticut, South Carolina, and Minnesota, were given grants to implement private industries within prison walls. This successful program led to the Percy Amendment (1979), federal legislation that allowed prison-made goods to be sold across state lines if the projects complied with strict rules, such as making sure unions were consulted and preventing manufacturers from undercutting the existing wage structure.[50] The new law authorized a number of Prison Industry Enhancement pilot projects. These were certified as meeting the Percy Amendment operating rules and were therefore free to ship goods out of state; by 1987, 15 projects had been certified.

Today, private prison industries have used a number of models. One approach, the "state-use model," makes the correctional system a supplier of goods and services that serves state-run institutions. For example, La Pen, Inc., is a garment factory set up in a former gymnasium in the Nebraska State Penitentiary; it employs 80 men. In another approach, the "free enterprise model," private companies set up manufacturing units on prison grounds or purchase goods made by inmates in shops owned and operated by the corrections department. In the "corporate model," a semi-independent business is created on prison grounds whose profits go to the state government and inmate laborers.[51]

Despite widespread publicity, the partnership between private enterprise and the prison community has been limited to a few experimental programs. However, it is likely to grow in the future.

Postrelease Programs. A final element of job-related programming involves helping inmates obtain jobs before they are released and keep them once they are on the outside. A number of correctional departments have set up employment services designed to ease the transition between institution and community. Employment program staff assess inmates' backgrounds to determine their abilities, interests, goals, and capabilities. They also help them create job plans essential to receiving early release (parole) and successfully reintegrating into the community. Some programs maintain community correctional placements in sheltered environments that help inmates bridge the gap between institutions and the outside world. Services include job placement, skill development, family counseling, and legal and medical assistance.

Research studies generally agree that inmates who are able to maintain family ties have a better chance to succeed on the outside after they have been released.[52] A few correctional systems have developed programs that help inmates maintain their emotional stability by having closer ties with their families and living in an environment that is more "normal" than that provided in the typical correctional facility. For example, some women's prisons now allow inmates who give birth in prison to keep their child in a nursery in the institution for up to a year, followed by liberal visitation rights with the child. Others allow male and female inmates home visitation privileges if they show examplary behavior in the institution. Some programs provide direct support to families, such as by involving them in self-help groups, providing counseling, helping them obtain transportation to the prison, and finding them overnight lodging.

The **conjugal** (or family) **visit** enables prisoners to have completely private meetings with their spouse and family on a regular basis. The explicit purpose of the program is to grant inmates access to normal family and sexual outlets and thereby counteract the pains of imprisonment. Some institutions have even set up an on-grounds camping facility where inmates can stay overnight with their families.[53]

Maintaining Conventional Lifestyles

Those who favor family visitation argue that, if properly administered, it can provide a number of important benefits: reducing inmate frustration levels, strengthening family ties, and maintaining normal sexual patterns. Problems associated with conjugal visitation include

1. Such visits can serve only the minority of inmates who are married; there is a question of fairness.

2. Appropriate facilities are almost universally lacking.

3. Administrative problems abound: security, staff abuses of power, jealousy.

4. Administrative support is lacking.

5. Spouses may feel embarrassment at openly sexual visits.

6. Children may be born to parents who cannot support them.[54]

Coed Prisons

Since 1973, prisons housing both men and women have proliferated throughout the United States. About 35 institutions are now operating as **coed prisons** around the country.[55] While most are minimum-security institutions, coed prisons are also found at the medium- and maximum-security levels, and some institutions operate with a mix of security levels. Officials report that inmates commonly share food services, recreation, educational programs, and jobs.

The typical coed prison is a small, low-security institution, predominantly of one sex (either mostly male or mostly female), and populated by nonviolent, carefully screened offenders. In most instances, males and females live in physically separate housing—either in different buildings or in separate cottages—but they participate jointly in most institution activities, such as work, recreation, and vocational and educational programs.

The benefits of coed prisons include the ease and cost effectiveness of a joint operation, the more normal environment produced by heterosexual contact, the expansion of programs available to women because of joint participation, greater flexibility in staffing, alleviated overcrowding at male institutions, and the ability to house some inmates closer to home. Coed prisons are not without their drawbacks. The greatest problems listed by administrators are illicit relationships, supervisory and disciplinary problems, negative staff attitudes, developing similar and equal programs without joint participation, and security.

Inmate Self-Help

Recognizing that the probability of failure on the outside is acute, inmates have attempted to organize self-help groups to provide the psychological tools needed to prevent recidivism.[56] Membership in these programs is designed to improve inmates' self-esteem and help them cope with common problems, such as alcoholism, narcotics abuse, or depression.

Some groups are chapters of common national organizations, such as Alcoholics Anonymous. Other groups are organized along racial and ethnic lines. For example, there are chapters of the Chicanos Organizados Pintos Aztlan, the Afro-American Coalition, and the Native American Brotherhood in prisons stretching from California to Massachusetts. These groups try to establish a sense of brotherhood so members will work together for individual betterment. They hold literacy, language, and religious classes, and offer counseling, legal advice, and prerelease support. Ethnic groups seek ties with outside minority organizations, such as the National Association for the Advancement of Colored People (NAACP), Muslims, the Urban League, La Raza, and the American Indian Movement, as well as the religious and university communities.

A third type of self-help group helps inmates find the strength to make it on the outside. The best known are the Fortune Society, which claims 30,000 members, and the Seventh Step organization. These groups try to raise inmate self-esteem. Another group, the Self-Development Group (SDG), was founded in the 1960s by LSD advocate Timothy Leary. A number of groups have followed in

Inmates have attempted to organize self-help groups to provide the psychological tools needed to prevent recidivism. Here a group of female inmates at the Institute for Women in Frontera, California band together for support and to seek mercy from the governor. They are all incarcerated for killing men who they claim were abusive.

the footsteps of SDG, including Inward Bound, Church of the New Sing, Ring of Keys, Human Potential Seminars, Wake Up, and Discovery.

Self-help programs that embrace religious principles, do not engage in activities contrary to the corrections operation, and cultivate strong administrative and outside support are the ones most likely to flourish in modern prisons.

Can Rehabilitation Work?

Despite the variety and number of treatment programs in operation, questions remain about their effectiveness. In their oft-cited research, Robert Martinson and his associates (1975) found that a majority of treatment programs were failures.[57] Martinson found in a national study that with few exceptions, rehabilitative efforts seemed to have no appreciable effect on recidivism; his research produced a "nothing works" view of correctional treatment.

Martinson's work was followed by efforts showing that some high-risk offenders were more likely to commit crimes after they had been placed in treatment programs than before the onset of rehabilitation efforts.[58] A slew of reviews have claimed that correctional treatment efforts aimed at youthful offenders provide little evidence that rehabilitation can occur within correctional settings. Evidence is scant that treatment efforts, even those that include vocational, educational, and mental health services, can consistently lower recidivism rates.[59]

The so-called failure of correctional treatment has helped promote a conservative view of corrections in which prisons are considered places of incapacitation and punishment, not treatment centers. Current policies stress eliminating the nonserious offender from the correctional system while increasing the probability that serious, violent offenders will be incarcerated and serve longer sentences. This view supports the utility of mandatory and determinate sentences for serious offenders and the simultaneous use of intermediate sanctions, such as house arrest, restitution, and diversion, to limit the nonserious offender's involvement in the system.

While the concept of correctional rehabilitation is facing serious challenges, many experts still believe strongly in the rehabilitative ideal. Some believe that rehabilitation has just not been given a realistic chance because of inadequate budgets and programs.[60] Even where programs exist, there has been a low level of participation of inmates (both male and female) in work, vocational, mental

The No-Frills Movement

There is little question that some treatment does work and that the quest for offender rehabilitation should not be abandoned. Yet some correctional administrators and politicians believe that prisons should be places of punishment only and that all inmate privileges and treatment programs should be curtailed. Inmates in some states have suffered reduced visiting hours, removal of televisions and exercise gear, and substitution of cold sandwiches for hot meals. One county in Maryland plans to reintroduce chain gangs; instead of inmates being shackled to prevent their flight, they will be forced to wear "stun belts." After detonation, the belts give fleeing inmates an eight-second, 50,000-volt jolt of electricity, which renders them helpless for up to 10 minutes. Developed by Stun Tech Inc., more than 1,000 belts have been sold to law enforcement and correctional agencies. Amnesty International has asked Congress to ban the belts in part because they can be used for torture. Amnesty charges that the belts are "cruel, inhuman, and degrading."

Advocates of the no-frills or "penal harm" movement claim to be responding to the public's desire to get tough on crime. They are tired of hearing that some prison inmates get free education, watch cable TV, or get special educational programs. Some of the efforts to restrict inmates' rights include:

• The Alabama Department of Corrections (DOC) introduced no-frills chain gangs in each of the state's three prisons in 1994. Inmates in the gangs do not have telephones or visitation privileges, and recreation is limited to basketball on the weekends. Chain gang members include primarily parole violators and repeat offenders, especially offenders who are former gang members. After six months of good behavior, chain gang members return to the general population and are given standard inmate privileges.
• Throughout the 1990s, the Arizona DOC, supplementing the legislature's ban on weightlifting equipment, reduced the amount of property and clothing inmates may keep in their cells, the number of items for sale in the store, the number and types of movies and television programs they may watch, and the frequency of telephone calls.
• Effective January 1, 1996, the Kansas DOC introduced a formal incentive program in which incoming inmates have to earn a range of privileges, including television, handicrafts, use of outside funds, canteen expenditures, personal property, and visitation. Under a three-level system, new inmates who must spend their first 120 days (Incentive Level I) without disciplinary reports and participate in educational programs or work

assignments earn increased privileges (Incentive Level II). After another 120 days of similar behavior, additional privileges are made available (Incentive Level III). Inmates are reduced one level for misbehavior. Furloughs were the only privilege the DOC banned permanently for all inmates.
• Complementing the action of his governor, the commissioner of corrections in Wisconsin reduced the amount of personal property inmates may own, established limits on the amount of personal clothing and electronic equipment they may keep, and introduced monitoring of telephone calls.
• A number of sheriffs have eliminated privileges in their jails: seven sheriffs in Florida have eliminated television and weightlifting; seven jails in Los Angeles County have also eliminated weightlifting equipment; the Niagara County, New York, sheriff eliminated free coffee; and the sheriff of Maricopa County (Phoenix) eliminated "girlie" magazines, hot lunches, and most hot breakfasts, and coffee, and he reduced recreation time, television programming, visitation, and the number of items in the commissary.
• In 1995, the Federal Bureau of Prisons ordered—and federal legislation now requires—wardens to stop purchasing or repairing new televisions in individual cells.

While many politicians embrace the no-frills prison idea to appeal to their vengeful, conservative constituents, wardens and prison administrators are more wary of a policy that restricts inmate activities, increases boredom, and threatens their control over inmates. One approach is to limit privileges at first but return them as rewards for good behavior. Whether the no-frills approach is a political fad or a long-term correctional policy trend remains to be seen.

Critical Thinking Questions
1. Do you believe that inmates should be "harmed" by their prison experience in order to shock them into conformity? The penal harm movement is the antithesis of the rehabilitation ideal. By "harming" inmates and taking away privileges, are correctional administrators giving up on the prison as a place of reform?

SOURCES: Peter Finn, "No-Frills Prisons and Jails: A Movement in Flux," *Federal Probation* 60 (1996): 35–49; W. Wesley Johnson, Katherine Bennett, and Timothy Flanagan, "Getting Tough on Prisoners: Results from the National Corrections Executive Survey, 1995," *Crime and Delinquency* 43 (1997): 24–41; Peter Kilborn, "Revival of Chain Gangs Takes a Twist," *New York Times,* 11 March 1997, p. A18.

health, substance abuse, and parent counseling programs.[61] Other researchers have shown through careful analysis that while not all programs are successful for all inmates, many treatment programs are effective and that participants, especially younger clients, have a better chance of success on the outside than those who forgo treatment. If administered properly, correctional treatment programs have success rates in the magnitude of 20%–35%.[62] The characteristics associated with the most successful programs include

- Services are intensive, lasting only a few months.

- Programs are cognitive, aimed at helping inmates learn new skills to better cope with personality problems such as impulsivity.

- Program goals are reinforced in a firm, fair manner, making use of rewards rather than punishments.

- Therapists related to clients in a sensitive and positive way. Therapists are trained and supervised in an appropriate manner.

- Clients are insulated from disruptive interpersonal networks and placed in environments where prosocial activities predominate.

While institutional treatment is still the norm, there is a new movement within the prison system that focuses less on treatment and more on security and punishment. The "no-frills" approach is discussed in the accompanying Issues box.

Guarding the Institution

Control of a prison is a complex task. On the one hand, a tough, high-security environment may meet the goals of punishment and control but fail to reinforce positive behavior changes. On the other hand, too liberal an administrative stance can lower staff morale and place inmates in charge of the institution.

Caught up in the complexities of prison life is the guard staff. Over 120,000 correctional officers are working in the nation's state prison facilities, an increase of about 25% since 1986.[63] About 85% are male and 15% female, a ratio that has remained stable for a decade.

Most states require that candidates for correctional officer positions meet a minimum age requirement (usually 18 or 21) and have a high school education. Other common criteria are a "clean" criminal record, a driver's license, and being drug-free and in good physical condition. Most correctional officer candidates will have between one and six weeks of training. Surveys indicate that about two-thirds of all state correctional agencies have established independent training academies; however, as of 1991 correctional officers averaged only 116 hours of preservice training (compared to more than 800 for police officers).[64]

For many years, prison guards were viewed as ruthless people who enjoyed their positions of power over inmates, fought rehabilitation efforts, were racist, and had a "lock psychosis" developed from years of counting, numbering, and checking on inmates. This view has changed in recent years. Correctional officers are now viewed as public servants who are seeking the security and financial rewards of a civil service position.[65] Most are in favor of rehabilitation efforts and do not hold any particular animosity toward the inmates. The correctional officer has been characterized as a "people worker" who must be prepared to deal with the problems of inmates on a personal level and also a member of a complex bureaucracy who must be able to cope with its demands.

Corrections officers play a number of roles within the institution. They supervise cell houses, dining areas, shops, and other facilities, as well as perch up on the walls armed with rifles to oversee the yard and prevent escapes. Corrections officers also sit on disciplinary boards and escort inmates to hospitals and court appearances.

The greatest problem faced by prison guards is the duality of their role: maintainers of order and security and advocates of treatment and rehabilitation. Added to this basic dilemma is the changing inmate role. Where before corrections officers could count on inmate leaders to help them maintain order, they are now faced with a racially charged atmosphere in which violence is a way of life. Today, correctional work is filled with danger, tension, boredom, and little evidence that efforts to help inmates lead to success. And, unlike police officers, correctional workers apparently do not form a close-knit subculture with unique values and a sense of intergroup loyalty. Correctional officers experience alienation and isolation from the inmates, the administration, and each other. Interestingly, this sense of alienation seems greatest in younger officers; evidence exists that later in their careers, officers enjoy a revival of interest in their work and take great pride in providing human services to inmates.[66] It is not surprising that correctional officers perceive significant levels of stress related to such job factors as lack of safety, inadequate career opportunities, and work overload.[67]

Many state prison authorities have developed training programs to prepare guards for the difficulties of prison work. Guard unions have also commonly been formed to negotiate wages and working conditions with corrections departments.

Female Correctional Officers

The issue of female correctional officers in male institutions comes up repeatedly. Today, an estimated 5,000 women are assigned to all-male institutions.[68] The employment of women as guards in close contact with male inmates has spurred many questions of privacy and safety and a number of legal cases. In one important case, *Dothard v. Rawlinson* (1977), the Supreme Court upheld Alabama's refusal to hire female correctional officers on the grounds that it would put them in significant danger from the male inmates.[69] Despite such setbacks, women now work side by side with male guards in almost every state, performing the same duties. Research indicates that discipline has not suffered because of the inclusion of women in the guard force. Sexual assaults have been rare, and more negative attitudes have been expressed by the female guards' male peers than by inmates. Most commentators believe that the presence of female guards can have an important beneficial effect on the self-image of inmates and improve the guard-inmate working relationship.

Interestingly, little research has been conducted on male correctional officers in female prisons, although almost every institution housing female offenders employs male officers. What research there is indicates that male officers are generally well received, and while there is some evidence of sexual exploitation and privacy violations, female inmates generally believe that the presence of male correctional officers helps create a more natural environment and reduce tension. Both male and female inmates are concerned about opposite-sex correctional workers intruding on their privacy, such as being given assignments in which they may observe inmates dressing or bathing or in which they may come into physical contact, such as during searches or pat-downs.

Prison Rules and Discipline

Every penal institution—jail, prison, or reformatory—has a specific set of official rules that guide prisoners' lives and dictate what they can and cannot do. These rules are of great significance; a violation may result in a loss of good time, which can lengthen the inmate's stay in prison. Violation of prison rules may also result in harsh disciplinary measures, such as solitary confinement, suspension of privileges, or transfer to a more secure facility. Today, rules are more lenient than in the past. Conversation is no longer prohibited, and rigid, militarylike discipline is rare.

Any violation of prison rules may result in disciplinary action against the inmate. Usually, a disciplinary board will meet to hear cases referred by administrative staff. Typically, the board will consist of members of the custodial, treatment, and administrative staffs. Punishment, when deemed necessary, is meted out by these individuals, and it affects good time, privileges, and parole.

Which inmates are most likely to violate institutional rules? Research shows that violators tend to be younger, less intelligent predatory criminals with extensive prior records as adults and juveniles.[70]

Conflict, violence, and brutality are sad but ever-present facts of institutional life. Violence can involve individual conflict: inmate versus inmate, inmate versus staff, staff versus inmate. One common threat is sexual assault. Research has shown that prison rapes usually involve a victim viewed as weak and submissive and a group of aggressive rapists who can dominate the victim through their collective strength. Sexual harassment leads to fights, social isolation, fear, anxiety, and crisis. Nonsexual assaults may stem from an aggressor's desire to shake down the victim for money and personal favors, may be motivated by racial conflict, or may simply be used to establish power within the institution.

Violence can also involve large groups of inmates, such as the famous Attica riot in 1971, which claimed 39 lives, or the New Mexico state prison riot of February 1980, in which the death toll was 33. More than 300 prison riots have occurred since the first one in 1774, 90% of them since 1952.[71]

A number of factors can spark such damaging incidents. They include poor staff-inmate communications, destructive environmental conditions, faulty classification, and promised but undelivered reforms. The 1980 New Mexico State Penitentiary riot drew national attention to the problem of prison riots. The prison was designed for 800 but actually held 1,136 prisoners; conditions of overcrowding, squalor, poor food, and lack of medical treatment abounded. The state government, which had been called on to improve guard training, physical plant quality, and relief from overcrowding, was reluctant to spend the necessary money.

Although revulsion over the violent riots in New Mexico and the earlier riot in New York's Attica prison led to calls for prison reform, prison violence has continued unabated. About 75–100 inmates are killed by their peers each year in U.S. prisons, 6 or 7 staff members are murdered, and some 120 suicides are recorded.

The Causes of Prison Violence

What are the causes of prison violence?[72] While there is no single explanation for either collective or individual violence, a number of theories have been proposed. One position holds that inmates are often violence-prone individuals who have always used force to get their own way. In the crowded, dehumanizing world of the prison, it is not surprising that some inmates resort to force to exert their dominance over others.

A second view is that prisons convert people to violence by their inhuman conditions, including overcrowding, depersonalization, and the threat of sexual assault. Even in the most humane prisons, life is a constant put-down, and prison conditions are a threat to the inmates' sense of self-worth; violence is an expected consequence of these conditions.

Prison violence may also be caused by prison mismanagement, lack of strong security, and inadequate control by prison officials. Poor management may inhibit conflict management and set the stage for violence. Repressive administrations give inmates the feeling that nothing will ever change, that they have nothing to lose, and that violence is the only means for change.

Overcrowding caused by the rapid increases in the prison population has also been linked to prison violence. As the prison population continues to climb, unmatched by expanded capacity, prison violence may increase.

Violence may also result because prisons lack effective management styles that enable inmate grievances against either prison officials or other inmates to be handled fairly and equitably. Prisoners who complain about other inmates are viewed as "rats" or "snitches" and are marked for death by their enemies. Similarly, complaints or lawsuits filed against the prison administration may result in the inmate being placed in solitary confinement—"the hole." The frustration caused by living in a prison with a climate that promotes violence—that is, one that lacks physical security and adequate mechanisms for resolving complaints and where the "code of silence" protects violators—is believed to promote both collective and individual violence by inmates who might otherwise be controlled.

Managing Violence

Can prison violence be controlled, despite the fact that the inmate populations will not be declining significantly or become less aggressive and hostile? In his book *Governing Prisons,* John DiIulio suggests that reform of prison management can help alter the violent institutional climate.[73] After studying prisons in three states, DiIulio found that management could be classified into three types. The *consensual model,* practiced in California, is based on the notion that prison government rests on the consent of the governed, the inmates. This model fails to provide a coherent basis for dealing with violence because it allows inmates a say in the management process. In Michigan, the *responsibility model* is used. Here, inmates' rehabilitation is keyed to their participation in prison operations, and staff members are required to be facilitators in the process. The responsibility model has also failed because it offers weak controls on inmate behavior and produces disillusionment and alienation among the staff. DiIulio found that the *control model* used in the Texas prison system has more promise for reducing violence. The Texas system stresses clearly defined rules of behavior, inmate conformity with rules and regulations, and strong, independent top-down leadership.

DiIulio believes that the bureaucratic organization that works in large private corporations and government agencies can save prisons. In this approach, prison administrators act in a caring yet efficient manner without prejudice and bias, and experienced correctional leaders create and enforce clear and fair rules. While this system may seem logical, what is known about the operations of criminal justice agencies indicates that "informal" rules and behaviors often dominate at the expense of the formal system and that leaders may be more self-serving than selfless. The Texas prison system that DiIulio so admires was marked by overcrowding and brutality until subject to court-ordered reform. Even then, prison officials were reluctant to change and attempted to undermine reform efforts. While the control model may seem appealing to some experts, whether it can work in the "real world" remains to be seen.

Prisoners' Rights

Before the early 1960s, it was accepted that on conviction, an individual forfeited all rights not expressly granted by statutory law or correctional policy; inmates were "civilly dead." The Supreme Court held that convicted offenders should expect to be penalized for their misdeeds and that part of their punishment was the loss of freedoms free citizens take for granted.

History of Prisoners' Rights

One reason that inmates lacked rights was that state and federal courts were reluctant to intervene in the administration of prisons unless the circumstances of a case clearly indicated a serious breach of the Eighth Amendment's protection against cruel and unusual punishment. This judicial policy is referred to as the **hands-off doctrine.** The courts used three basic justifications for their neglect of prison conditions:

1. Correctional administration was a technical matter best left to experts rather than to courts ill-equipped to make appropriate evaluations.

2. Society as a whole was apathetic to what went on in prisons, and most individuals preferred not to associate with or know about the offender.

3. Prisoners' complaints involved privileges rather than rights. Prisoners were considered to have fewer constitutional rights than other members of society.[74]

As the 1960s drew to a close, the hands-off doctrine was eroded. Federal district courts began seriously considering prisoners' claims concerning conditions in the various state and federal institutions and used their power to intervene on behalf of the inmates. In some ways, this concern reflected the spirit of the times, which saw the onset of the civil rights movement, and subsequently was paralleled in such areas as student rights, public welfare, mental institutions, juvenile court systems, and military justice.

Beginning in the late 1960s, such activist groups as the NAACP Legal Defense Fund and the American Civil Liberties Union's National Prison Project began to search for appropriate legal vehicles to bring prisoners' complaints before state and federal courts. The most widely used device was the federal Civil Rights Act, 42 U.S.C. 1983:

> Every person who, under color of any statute, ordinance, regulation, custom, or usage of any State or Territory subjects, or causes to be subjected, any citizen of the United States or other person within the jurisdiction thereof to the deprivation of any rights, privileges, or immunities secured by the Constitution and laws shall be liable to the party injured in an action at law, suit in equity, or other proper proceeding for redress.

The legal argument went that as U.S. citizens, prison inmates could sue state officials if their civil rights were violated, such as, if they were the victims of racial or religious discrimination.

The Supreme Court first recognized the right of prisoners to sue for civil rights violations in cases involving religious freedom brought by the Black Muslims. This well-organized group had been frustrated by prison administrators who feared its growing power and desired to place limits on its recruitment activities. In the 1964 case of *Cooper v. Pate,* however, the Supreme Court ruled that inmates who were being denied the right to practice their religion were entitled to legal redress under 42 U.S.C. 1983.[75] Although *Cooper* applied to the narrow issue of religious freedom, it opened the door to providing other rights for inmates.

The subsequent prisoners' rights crusade, stretching from 1960 to 1980, paralleled the civil rights and women's movements. Battlelines were drawn between prison officials hoping to maintain their power and resenting interference by the courts and inmate groups and their sympathizers, who used state and federal courts as a forum for demanding better living conditions and personal rights. Each decision handed down by the courts was viewed as a victory for one side or the other; this battle continues today.

Through a slow process of legal review, the courts have granted inmates a number of **substantive rights** that have significantly influenced the entire correctional system. The most important of these rights are discussed in the following sections.

Substantive Rights of Inmates

Access to Courts, Legal Services, and Materials. Without the ability to seek judicial review of conditions causing discomfort or violating constitutional rights, the inmate must depend solely on the slow and often insensitive administrative mechanism of relief within the prison system. Therefore, the right of easy access to the courts gives inmates hope that their rights will be protected during incarceration. Courts have held that inmates are entitled to have legal materials available and be provided with assistance in drawing up and filing complaints. Inmates who help others, so-called **jailhouse lawyers,** cannot be interfered with or harassed by prison administrators. Federal courts have expanded this right to include virtually all inmates with various legal problems, as the following cases show:

1. *DeMallory v. Cullen* (1988). An untrained inmate paralegal is not a constitutionally acceptable alternative to law library access.[76]

2. *Lindquist v. Idaho State Board of Corrections* (1985). Seven inmate law clerks for a prison population of 950 were sufficient legal representation since they had a great deal of experience.[77]

3. *Smith v. Wade* (1983). An inmate who has been raped can have access to the state court to sue a guard for failing to protect the inmate from aggressive inmates.[78]

4. *Bounds v. Smith* (1977). State correctional systems are obligated to provide inmates with either adequate law libraries or the help of people trained in the law.[79]

Freedom of the Press and of Expression. Correctional administrators traditionally placed severe limitations on prisoners' speech and expression. For example, they have read and censored inmate mail and restricted their reading material. With the lifting of the hands-off doctrine, courts have consistently ruled that only when a compelling state interest exists can prisoners' First Amendment rights be modified; correctional authorities must justify the limiting of free speech by showing that granting it would threaten institutional security. The following list of cases related to prisoners' freedom of speech rights indicates current policy on the subject:

1. *Turner v. Safley* (1987). Prisoners do not have a right to receive mail from one another. Inmate-to-inmate mail can be banned if the reason is "related to legitimate penological interests."[80]

2. *Ramos v. Lamm* (1980). The institutional policy of refusing to deliver mail in a language other than English is unconstitutional.[81]

3. *Procunier v. Martinez* (1974). Censorship of a prisoner's mail is justified only when (a) there exists substantial government interest in maintaining the censorship to further prison security, order, and rehabilitation, and (b) the restrictions are not greater or more stringent than is demanded by security precautions.[82]

4. *Nolan v. Fitzpatrick* (1971). Prisoners may correspond with newspapers unless their letters discuss escape plans or contain contraband or otherwise objectionable material.[83]

Freedom of Religion. Freedom of religion is a fundamental right guaranteed by the First Amendment. In general, the courts have ruled that inmates have the right to assemble and pray in the religion of their choice but that religious symbols and practices that interfere with institutional security can be restricted. Administrators can draw the line if religious needs become cumbersome or impossible to carry out for reason of cost or security. Granting special privileges can also be denied on the grounds that they will cause other groups to make similar demands.

Some of the issues surrounding religious practices in prison are highlighted in the following cases:

1. *Mumin v. Phelps* (1988). If there is a legitimate penological interest, inmates can be denied special privileges to attend religious services.[84]

2. *O'Lone v. Estate of Shabazz* (1987). Prison officials can assign inmates work schedules that make it impossible for them to attend religious services as long as no reasonable alternative exists.[85]

3. *Rahman v. Stephenson* (1986). A prisoner's rights are not violated if the administration refuses to use the prisoner's religious name on official records.[86]

Medical Rights. In early prisons, inmates' right to medical treatment was restricted through the "exceptional circumstances doctrine." Using this policy, the courts would hear only those cases in which the circumstances totally disregarded human dignity, while denying hearings to less serious cases. The cases that were allowed access to the courts usually represented a situation of total denial of medical care.

To gain their medical rights, prisoners have resorted to class actions (that is, suits brought on behalf of all individuals affected by similar circumstances, in this case, poor medical attention). In the most significant case, *Newman v. Alabama* (1972), the entire Alabama prison system's medical facilities were declared inadequate.[87] The court cited the following factors as contributing to inadequate care: insufficient physician and nurse resources; reliance on untrained inmates for paramedical work; intentional failure in treating the sick and injured; and failure to conform to proper medical standards. The *Newman* case forced corrections departments to upgrade prison medical facilities.

It was not until 1976, in *Estelle v. Gamble,* that the Supreme Court clearly mandated an inmate's right to have medical care.[88] Gamble had hurt his back in a Texas prison and filed suit because he contested the type of treatment he had received and questioned the lack of interest prison guards had shown in his case. The Supreme Court said, "Deliberate indifference to serious medical needs of prisoners constitutes the 'unnecessary and wanton infliction of pain,' . . . proscribed by the Eighth Amendment."[89] Gamble was allowed to collect monetary damages for his injuries. The *Gamble* decision means that lower courts can decide, on a case-by-case basis, whether "deliberate indifference" to an inmate's medical needs occurred and to what damages the inmate is entitled.

Cruel and Unusual Punishment. The concept of **cruel and unusual punishment** is founded in the Eighth Amendment of the U.S. Constitution. The term itself has not been specifically defined by the Supreme Court, but the Court has held that treatment constitutes cruel and unusual punishment when it:

- Degrades the dignity of human beings[90]

- Is more severe (disproportional) than the offense for which it has been given[91]

- Shocks the general conscience and is fundamentally unfair[92]

- Is deliberately indifferent to a person's safety and well-being[93]

- Punishes people because of their status, such as race, religion, and mental state[94]

- Is in flagrant disregard of due process of law, such as punishment that is capriciously applied[95]

State and federal courts have placed strict limits on disciplinary methods that may be considered inhumane. Corporal punishment all but ended after the practice was condemned in *Jackson v. Bishop* (1968).[96] Although the solitary confinement of disruptive inmates continues, its prolonged use under barbaric conditions has been held to be in violation of the Eighth Amendment. Courts have found that inmates placed in solitary have the right to adequate personal hygiene, exercise, mattresses, ventilation, and rules specifying how they can earn their release.

Overall Prison Conditions. Prisoners have long had the right to the minimal conditions necessary for human survival, such as the necessary food, clothing, shelter, and medical care to sustain human life. A number of attempts have been made to articulate reasonable standards of prison care and make sure they are carried out. Courts have held that while people are sent to prison for punishment, it does not mean that prison should be a punishing experience.[97] Inmates are entitled to reasonable care, protection, and shelter. In the 1994 case of *Farmer v. Brennan,* the Court ruled that prison officials are legally liable if knowing that an inmate faces a serious risk of harm disregards that risk by failing to take measures to avoid or reduce it. Furthermore, the prison officials should be able to infer the risk from the evidence at hand; they need not be warned or told.[98]

While inmates retain the right to reasonable care, if there is a legitimate purpose for the use of government restrictions, they may be considered constitutional. For example, it might be possible to restrict reading material, allow strip searches, and prohibit inmates from receiving packages from the outside if the restrictions are legitimate security measures. If overcrowded conditions require it, inmates may be double-bunked in cells designed for a single inmate.[99]

Courts have also reviewed entire correctional systems to determine whether practices are unfair to inmates. In a critical case, *Estelle v. Ruiz,* the Texas Department of Corrections was ordered to provide new facilities to alleviate overcrowding; to abolish the practice of using inmate trustees; to lower the staff-to-inmate ratio; to improve treatment services, such as medical, mental health, and occupational rehabilitation programs; and to adhere to the principles of procedural due process in dealing with inmates.[100] A court-ordered master was appointed to oversee the changes and served from 1981 to 1990, when the state was deemed in compliance with the most critical of the court-ordered reforms.[101] A period of tension and violence followed the decision, which may be partially explained by the fact that the staff and administration felt that the court had undermined their authority. It took more than 18 years for the case to be settled.

It is likely that the overcrowding crisis will prompt additional litigation requesting overall prison relief. A number of correctional institutions are under court order to reduce their populations; in some jurisdictions, the entire correctional department is under court order to improve conditions and reduce the inmate population.[102]

Leaving Prison

At the expiration of their prison term, most inmates return to society and try to resume their life there. For some inmates, their reintegration into society comes by way of **parole,** the planned community release and supervision of incarcerated offenders before the expiration of their full prison sentences. In states where de-

Some inmates try to cut short their prison stay by escaping or absconding. Here a Los Angeles County sheriff handcuffs Manuel Olmedo, one of 14 inmates who escaped from an honor ranch in California in April 1996.

terminate sentencing statutes have eliminated discretionary parole, offenders are released after having served their determinate sentence, less time off for good behavior and other credits designed to reduce the term of incarceration. Their release may involve supervision in the community, and rule violations can result in return to prison for the balance of their unexpired sentence.

In a few instances, inmates are released after their sentence has been commuted by a board of pardons or directly by a governor or even the president of the United States. About 15% of prison inmates are released after serving their entire maximum sentence without any time excused or forgiven. And despite the efforts of correctional authorities, about 7,000 inmates escape every year from state and federal prisons (the number of escapes is actually declining, due in part to better officer training and more sophisticated security measures).[103]

Regardless of the method of their release, former inmates face the formidable task of having to readjust to society. This means regaining legal rights they may have lost on their conviction, reestablishing community and family ties, and finding employment. After being in prison, these goals are often difficult to achieve.

Most correctional administrations allow inmates to become eligible for parole after completing their minimum sentence less good time.[104] Parole is considered a way of completing a prison sentence in the community under the supervision of the correctional authorities. It is not the same as a pardon; paroled offenders can be legally recalled to serve the remainder of their sentence in an institution if the parole authorities deem the offenders' adjustment inadequate because they fail to obey the conditions of their release or commit another crime while on parole.

Parole

The decision to parole is determined by statutory requirement and usually occurs on completion of a minimum sentence less any good time or special release credits. In about 40% of all prison-release decisions, parole is granted by a parole board, a duly constituted body of men and women who review inmate cases and determine whether offenders have reached a rehabilitative level sufficient to deal with the outside world. The board also dictates what specific parole rules parolees must obey.

Once released into the community, the offender is supervised by a trained staff of parole officers who help the offender search for employment and monitor the parolee's behavior and activities to ensure that the conditions of parole are met.

Parolees are subject to strict rules, standardized and personalized, that guide their behavior and set limits on their activities. If these rules are violated, they can be returned to the institution to serve the remainder of their sentence; this is known as a **technical parole violation.** Parole can also be revoked by the offender committing a second offense while in the community. The offender may even be tried and sentenced for this subsequent crime.

Parole is generally viewed as a privilege granted to deserving inmates on the basis of their good behavior while in prison. Parole has two conflicting sides, however. On one hand, the paroled offender is allowed to serve part of the sentence in the community, an obvious benefit for the deserving offender. On the other hand, since parole is a "privilege and not a right," the parolee is viewed as a dangerous criminal who must be carefully watched and supervised. The conflict between the treatment and enforcement aspects of parole has not been reconciled by the criminal justice system, and the parole process still contains elements of both.

In recent years, the nation's parole system has come under increasing criticism from those who believe that it is inherently unfair to inmates and fails to protect the public. It is unfair to the inmate because the decision to release is based on the discretion of parole board members who are forced to make predictions about the inmate's future behavior, an uncertain activity at best. It fails to protect the public because predatory criminals released before the expiration of their sentence are free to once again attack innocent victims. The movement toward determinate and mandatory sentences has limited the availability of parole and restricted the discretion of parole boards.

Mandatory Parole Release. In addition to the 40% of inmates released at the discretion of correctional authorities, another 30% are mandatory parole releasees— inmates whose discharge was a requirement of determinate sentencing statutes or good-time reductions but whose release was supervised by parole authorities. Mandatory release begins when the unserved portion of the maximum prison term equals the inmate's earned good time (less time served in jail awaiting trial). In some states, determinate sentences can be reduced by more than half with a combination of statutory and earned good time. If the conditions of their release are violated, mandatory releasees can have their good time revoked and be returned to the institution to serve the remainder of their unexpired term.

The remaining 30% of inmates were released for a variety of reasons, including expiration of their term, commutation of their sentence, and court orders to relieve overcrowded prisons.

The movement to create mandatory and determinate sentencing statutes has significantly affected parole. The number of people leaving prison via discretionary parole has declined substantially in the past few years. While at one time more than 70% of releasees were paroled, that number has declined to 40%; conversely, mandatory releases have increased from about 6% in the late 1970s to 30% today. Almost all the mandatory parole releasees are in jurisdictions that rely heavily on determinate sentences, such as Illinois, Indiana, and Minnesota. The gap between the two forms of release has remained stable since 1985 because the rush to adopt determinate sentencing has also slowed.

The Parole Board. In those states that have maintained discretionary parole, the authority to release inmates is usually vested in the parole board. State parole boards have four primary functions:

1. To select and place prisoners on parole

2. To aid, supervise, and provide continuing control of parolees in the community

3. To determine when the parole function is completed and to discharge from parole

4. If violations of conditions occur, to determine whether parole should be revoked

Most parole authorities are independent agencies with their own staff and administration, while a few parole boards are part of the state department of corrections. Arguments for keeping the board within a corrections department usually include the improved communication and availability of more intimate knowledge about offenders.

Most boards are relatively small, usually numbering fewer than ten members. Their size, coupled with their large caseloads and the varied activities they are expected to perform, can prevent board members from becoming as well acquainted with the individual inmates as might be desired.

Parole Hearings. The actual (discretionary) parole decision is made at a parole grant hearing. At this hearing, the full board or a selected subcommittee reviews information, may meet with the offender, and then decides whether the parole applicant has a reasonable probability of succeeding outside prison. Each parole board has its own way of reviewing cases. In some, the full board meets with the applicant; in others, only a few members do that. In a number of jurisdictions, a single board member can conduct a personal investigation and submit the findings to the full board for a decision.

At the hearing, parole board members consider such information as police reports of the crime, the presentence investigation, psychological testing and scores developed by prison mental health professionals, and institutional reports of disciplinary actions, treatment, and adjustment. Letters may be solicited from the inmate's friends and family members. In some jurisdictions, victims may appear and make statements of the losses they suffered.

By speaking directly to the applicant, the board can also promote and emphasize the specific types of behavior and behavior changes it expects to see if the inmate is to eventually qualify for or effectively serve parole.

The inmate's specific rights at a parole grant hearing also vary from jurisdiction to jurisdiction. In about half of the parole-granting jurisdictions, inmates are permitted counsel or are allowed to present witnesses on their behalf; other jurisdictions do not permit these privileges. Because the federal courts have declared that the parole applicant is not entitled to any form of legal representation, the inmate may have to pay for legal services where this privilege is allowed. In almost all discretionary parole-granting jurisdictions, the reasons for the parole decision must be given in writing, while in about half of the jurisdictions, a verbatim record of the hearing is made.

Parole Rules. Before release into the community, a parolee is given a standard set of rules and conditions that must be obeyed and conformed to. As with probation, the offender who violates these rules may have parole revoked and be sent back to the institution to serve the remainder of the sentence.

Parole rules may curtail or prohibit certain types of behavior while encouraging or demanding others. Some rules tend to be so moralistic or technical that they severely inhibit the parolee's ability to adjust to society. By making life unnecessarily unpleasant without contributing to rehabilitation, such parole rules reflect the punitive side of community supervision. Rules such as these can prohibit marriage, ban the use of motor vehicles, or forbid the borrowing of money. Parolees must often check in and ask permission when leaving their residences, and they may find that the rules bar them from associating with friends with criminal records, which, in some cases, severely limits their social life.

The way in which parole rules are stated, the kinds of things they forbid or encourage, and their flexibility vary between jurisdictions. Some states expressly forbid a certain type of behavior, while others will require permission to engage in it.

Each item in the parole conditions must be obeyed lest the offender's parole be revoked for a technical violation. In addition, the parole board can impose specific conditions for a particular offender, such as demanding that the parolee receive psychiatric treatment.

Parole Supervision. Once released into the community, the offender normally comes under the control of a parole agent who enforces parole rules, helps the inmate gain employment, and meets regularly with the parolee for reasons of treatment and rehabilitation.

Supervision in probation and parole is quite similar in some respects. In both, supervision attempts to help clients attain meaningful relationships in the community and uses similar enforcement, counseling, and treatment skills to gain that end. However, some major differences exist.

First, parole officers deal with more difficult cases. The parolee has been institutionalized for an extended period of time; to be successful on parole, the former inmate must adjust to the community, which at first can seem a strange and often hostile environment. The parolee's family life has been disrupted, and the person may find it difficult to resume employment. The paroled offender may have already been classified by probation officers (in a presentence report) as dangerous or as a poor risk for community adjustment. Furthermore, a prison sentence probably does little to improve the offender's chances for rehabilitation.

To overcome these roadblocks to success, the parole officer may have to play a much greater role in directing and supervising clients' lives than the probation officer. Consequently, a significant number of parolees are sent back to prison for technical rule violations.

Intensive Supervision Parole. To aid supervision, some jurisdictions are implementing systems that classify offenders on the basis of their supervision needs. Typically, a point or **guideline system** (sometimes called a salient factor score) based on prior record and prison adjustment divides parolees into three groups: (1) those who require intensive surveillance, (2) those who require social service rather than surveillance, and (3) those who require limited supervision.

In some jurisdictions, parolees in need of closer surveillance are placed on **intensive supervision parole (ISP).** These programs use limited caseload sizes, treatment facilities, the matching of parolee and supervisor by personality, and shock parole (which involves immediate short-term incarcerations for parole violators to impress them with the seriousness of a violation).

Intensive supervision parole clients are supervised in smaller caseloads and are required to attend more office and home visits than routine parolees. ISP may also require frequent drug testing, a term in a community correctional center, and electronic monitoring in the home. More than 17,000 parolees are under intensive supervision, 1,400 of whom are monitored electronically by computer.[105]

While ISP seems like an ideal way of limiting already overcrowded prison populations, there is little evidence that ISP programs are effective; in fact, they may produce a higher violation rate than traditional parole supervision. Limiting caseload size allows parole officers to supervise their clients more closely and spot infractions more easily.[106]

Returning to Prison: The Effectiveness of Parole

Disagreement exists over the effectiveness of parole. It is popularly believed that recidivism rates are very high—approaching 70%. A federal study of 108,580 men and women released in 11 states in 1983 found that within six years, 63% had been rearrested for a felony or serious misdemeanor, 47% had been convicted of a new crime, and 41% had been sent back to prison.[107] The specter of recidivism is especially frustrating to the U.S. public: It is so difficult to apprehend and successfully prosecute chronic offenders that it seems foolish to grant them early release so they can prey on more victims. There seems to be a strong association between prior and future offending: The parolees most likely to fail on release are the ones who have failed in the past; chronic offenders are the ones most likely to reoffend (see Table 15.1). Other factors that seem to predict

Table 15.1
Rearrest Rates of State Prisoners Released in 1983, by Number of Prior Adult Arrests

SOURCE: Allen Beck and Bernard Shipley, *Recidivism of Prisoners Released in 1983* (Washington, D.C.: Bureau of Justice Statistics, 1989).

Number of Adult Arrests Prior to Release	Percent of Releases Who Were Arrested		
	Percent of All Releases	Within 3 years	Within 1 year
All released prisoners	100.0%	62.5%	39.3%
1	9.1	38.1	19.0
2	10.8	48.2	25.5
3	10.8	54.7	30.1
4	9.7	58.1	35.5
5	8.0	59.3	33.4
6	7.0	64.8	38.2
7–10	18.8	67.7	42.0
11–15	11.9	74.9	53.3
16 or more	14.0	82.2	61.5

Type of Violation	Percent of Technical Parole Violations*
Arrest for new offense	43.0%
Failure to report to parole officer/absconded	34.2
Left jurisdiction without permission	14.1
Positive test for drug use	10.2
Failure to report for drug testing/treatment	4.4
Failure to pay fines, restitution, or other financial obligation	2.9
Failure to secure or maintain employment	2.8
Maintained contact with other felons	2.5
Failure to report change of address	2.5
Weapons	2.5
Failure to report to other counseling	2.3
Alcohol or drug use	2.3
Failure to report for alcohol treatment	2.0
Other reasons	17.0

*Adds up to more than 100% because some inmates had more than one type of violation.

Table 15.2
Why Parolees Receive Technical Violations
SOURCE: Robyn L. Cohen, *Probation and Parole Violators in State Prison, 1991: Survey of State Prison Inmates, 1991* (Washington, D.C.: Bureau of Justice Statistics, 1995).

parole violations include family criminality and dysfunction, antisocial personality, criminal companions, substance abuse, and interpersonal conflict.[108]

A federal survey of parole violators serving time in the nation's prison system estimated that 156,000 people in prison are parole violators. Based on the offense that brought parolees back to prison, these offenders committed at least 6,800 murders, 5,500 rapes, 8,800 assaults, and 22,500 robberies while under supervision in the community an average of 13 months.

Of the parole violators in prison, 80% were in confinement following conviction for a new crime; the remaining 20% had been imprisoned for a technical violation. Over 40% of these technical violators, while not *convicted* of a new crime, had been arrested for a new crime while on parole supervision in the community. (An arrest for violating parole conditions was not counted as an arrest for a new crime.) Technical parole violators in prison who said they were not arrested for a new crime while on parole made up about 3% of the prison population.[109]

What did the technical parole violators do to warrant termination of their community release? As Table 15.2 indicates, the most common reasons for a technical violation were arrest for a new offense and failure to report to parole officers (presumably by absconding or leaving the jurisdiction).

Why do so many released inmates end up back behind prison walls? For one thing, the social, psychological, and economic reasons that led them to crime probably have not been eliminated by a stay in prison. Despite rehabilitation efforts, the typical ex-convict is still the same undereducated, unemployed, substance-abusing lower-class male he was when arrested. Being separated from friends and family, not sharing in conventional society, associating with dangerous people, and adapting to a volatile lifestyle probably has done little to improve offenders' personality or behavior. And when they return to society, it may be to the same destructive neighborhood and social groups that prompted their original law-violating behavior. Some ex-inmates may have to prove that the prison experience has not changed them: Taking drugs or being sexually aggressive may show friends that they have not lost their "heart."

Ex-inmates may find their home life torn and disrupted. Wives of inmates report that they must face the shame and stigmatization of having an incarcerated spouse while withstanding a barrage of calls from jealous husbands on the "inside" who try to monitor their behavior and control their lives. Family visits

Making It on the Outside

to the inmate become traumatic and strain interpersonal relationships because they often involve strip searches and other invasions of privacy.[110] Sensitive to these problems, some states have instituted support groups designed to help inmates' families adjust to their loneliness and despair.[111]

Ex-inmates may also find that going straight is an economic impossibility. Many employers are reluctant to hire people who have served time. Even if a criminal record does not automatically prohibit all chance of employment, why would an employer hire an "ex-con" when other applicants are available? If they lie about their prison experience and are later found out, ex-offenders will be dismissed for misrepresentation.

One reason that ex-inmates find it so difficult to make it on the outside is the legal restrictions they are forced to endure. These may include bars on certain kinds of employment, limits on obtaining licenses, and restrictions on their freedom of movement. One survey found that a significant number of states still restrict the activities of former felons.[112] Among the findings:

- Fourteen states permanently deny felons the right to vote; 18 suspend the right until after the correctional sentence has been completed.

- Nineteen states terminate parental rights.

- Twenty-nine states consider a felony conviction to be legal grounds for a divorce.

- Six states deny felons the opportunity for public employment.

- Thirty-one states disallow convicted felons the right to serve on juries.

- Twenty-five states prevent convicted felons from holding public office.

- Federal law prevents ex-convicts from owning guns. In addition, all states except Vermont employ additional legal measures to prevent felons from possessing firearms.

- Forty-six states now require that felons register with law enforcement agencies. This requirement is up sharply in recent years; in 1986 only 8 states required felons to register.

- Civil death, or the denial of all civil rights, is still practiced in four states.

In general, states have placed greater restrictions on former felons, part of the "get tough" movement. However, courts have considered individual requests by convicted felons to have their rights restored. It is common for courts to look at such issues as how recently the criminal offense took place and its relationship to the particular right before deciding whether to restore it.

A number of experts and national commissions have condemned the loss of rights of convicted offenders as a significant cause of recidivism. Consequently, courts have generally moved to eliminate the most restrictive elements of post-conviction restrictions.[113]

The prison experience is difficult not only for inmates but also for their families. The Family and Corrections Network is an organization dedicated to studying the effects of imprisonment on the family of the offender and what can be done to help

them. There are three papers on the net available from the FCN: (1) The Directory of Programs Serving Families of Adult Offenders was compiled as a guide to organizations in the United States and Canada that assist the families of offenders in coping; (2) the report on Families of Adult Prisoners is an attempt to look at the data concerning families with an incarcerated member; and (3) the FCN Proceedings is the transcript of a Family and Corrections Network conference held in Sacramento, California. These papers can be found at:

http://www.ifs.univie.ac.at/uncjin/ mosaic/famcorr.html

Violence is an ever-present threat in prisons. Stop Prisoner Rape is an organization committed to combating the rape of male and female prisoners and to helping survivors of jailhouse rape. Their webpage provides information, news, and updates; stories and advice from survivors; articles, lectures, and law; tips on what can be done to reduce prison sexual assaults; and comments and links. Among the articles contained in the site are "Rape Trauma Syndrome in Male Prisoners," "AIDS Advice for the Prisoner Rape Survivor," and "Practical Advice on Jailhouse Rape." The site is at:

http://www.igc.apc.org/spr/

Summary

On entering a prison, offenders must make tremendous adjustments to survive. Usual behavior patterns or lifestyles are radically changed. Opportunities for personal satisfaction are reduced. Passing through a number of adjustment stages or cycles, inmates learn to cope with the new environment.

Inmates also learn to obey the inmate social code, which dictates proper behavior and attitudes. If inmates break the code, they may be unfavorably labeled.

Inmates can avail themselves of a large number of treatment devices designed to help them readjust to the community once they are released. These include educational programs on the basic, high school, and even college levels, as well as vocational training programs. In addition, a number of treatment programs have offered inmates individualized and group psychological counseling. Work furloughs, conjugal visits, and coed prisons have also been employed.

Despite such measures, prisons remain forbidding structures that house desperate men and women. Violence is common in prisons. Women often turn their hatred inward and hurt themselves, while male inmates engage in collective and individual violence against others. The Attica and New Mexico riots are examples of the most serious collective prison violence.

In years past, society paid little attention to the incarcerated offender. The majority of inmates confined in jails and prisons were basically deprived of the rights guaranteed them under the Constitution. Today, however, the judicial system is actively involved in the administration of correctional institutions. Inmates can now take their grievances to courts and seek due process and equal protection under the law. The courts have recognized that persons confined in correctional institutions have rights—which include access to the courts and legal counsel, the exercise of religion, the rights to correspondence and visitation, and the right to adequate medical treatment.

Most inmates return to society before the completion of their prison sentence. The majority earn early release through time off for good behavior or other sentence-reducing mechanisms. In addition, about 40% of all inmates are paroled before the completion of their maximum term. Most state jurisdictions maintain an independent parole board whose members decide whether to grant parole. Their decision making is discretionary and is based on many factors, such as the perception of the needs of society, the correctional system, and the client. Once paroled, the client is subject to control by parole officers who ensure that the conditions set by the board (the parole rules) are maintained. Parole can be revoked if the offender violates the rules of parole or commits a new crime.

Inmates have a tough time adjusting on the outside, and the recidivism rate is disturbingly high. One reason is that many states restrict inmate rights and take away privileges granted to other citizens.

Key Terms

total institutions	prisonization	special-needs inmates
inmate subculture	make-believe family	work release
social code	less eligibility	furlough

conjugal visit
coed prisons
hands-off doctrine
substantive rights

jailhouse lawyers
cruel and unusual punishment
parole
technical parole violation

guideline system
intensive supervision parole (ISP)

Questions

1. What are the benefits and drawbacks of coed prisons? Of conjugal visits?

2. Should women be allowed to work as guards in male prisons? What about male guards in female prisons?

3. Should prison inmates be allowed a free college education while noncriminals are forced to pay tuition? Do you believe in less eligibility for prisoners?

4. Define parole, including its purposes and objectives. How does it differ from probation?

5. What is the role of the parole board?

6. Should a former prisoner have all the civil rights afforded the average citizen? Should people be further penalized after they have paid their debt to society?

Notes

1. Gresham Sykes, The *Society of Captives* (Princeton, N.J.: Princeton University Press, 1958).

2. David Eichenthal and James Jacobs, "Enforcing the Criminal Law in State Prisons," *Justice Quarterly* 8 (1991): 283–303.

3. David Anderson, *Crimes of Justice: Improving the Police, Courts, and Prison* (New York: Times Books, 1988).

4. Robert Johnson, *Hard Time: Understanding and Reforming the Prison* (Monterey, Calif.: Brooks/Cole, 1987), p. 115.

5. Kevin Wright, *The Great American Crime Myth* (Westport, Conn.: Greenwood Press, 1985), p. 167.

6. Sandra Gleason, "Hustling: The Inside Economy of a Prison," *Federal Probation* 42 (1978): 32–39.

7. Hans Toch, *Living in Prison* (New York: Free Press, 1977), pp. 179–205.

8. Ibid., p. 192.

9. Johnson, *Hard Time,* pp. 55–60.

10. Ibid., p. 70.

11. J. Stephan, *Prison Rule Violators* (Washington, D.C.: Bureau of Justice Statistics, 1989).

12. Leonore Simon, "Prison Behavior and Victim-Offender Relationships Among Violent Offenders," paper presented at the annual meeting of the American Society of Criminology, San Francisco, November 1991.

13. John Irwin, "Adaptation to Being Corrected: Corrections from the Convict's Perspective," in *Handbook of Criminology,* ed. Daniel Glazer (Chicago: Rand McNally, 1974), pp. 971–993.

14. Donald Clemmer, *The Prison Community* (New York: Holt, Rinehart, and Winston, 1958).

15. Sykes, *The Society of Captives,* pp. 1–36.

16. Gresham Sykes and Sheldon Messinger, "The Inmate Social Code," in *The Sociology of Punishment and Corrections,* ed. Norman Johnston et al. (New York: Wiley, 1970), pp. 401–408.

17. John Irwin and Donald Cressey, "Thieves, Convicts, and the Inmate Culture," *Social Problems* 10 (1962): 142–155.

18. James B. Jacobs, ed., *New Perspectives on Prisons and Imprisonment* (Ithaca, N.Y.: Cornell University Press, 1983); idem, "Street Gangs Behind Bars," *Social Problems* 21 (1974): 395–409; idem, "Race Relations and the Prison Subculture," in *Crime and Justice,* vol. 1, ed. Norval Morris and Michael Tonry (Chicago: University of Chicago Press, 1979), pp. 1–28.

19. Stanley Penn, "Prison Gangs Formed by Racial Groups Pose Big Problem in West," *Wall Street Journal,* 11 May 1983, p. A1.

20. Ibid.

21. Jacobs, *New Perspectives on Prisons and Imprisonment,* pp. 97–98.

22. Helen Eigenberg, "Homosexuality in Male Prisons: Demonstrating the Need for a Social Constructionist Approach," *Criminal Justice Review* 17 (1992): 219–223.

23. Nicole Hahn Rafter, *Partial Justice* (New Brunswick, N.J.: Transaction Books, 1990), pp. 181–182.

24. Darrell Gilliard and Allen Beck, *Prison and Jail Inmates at Midyear 1996* (Washington, D.C.: Bureau of Justice Statistics, 1977).

25. Meda Chesney-Lind, "Patriarchy, Prisons and Jails: A Critical Look at Trends in Women's Incarceration," paper presented at the International Feminist Conference on Women, Law and Social Control, Mont Gabriel, Quebec, July 1991.

26. Elaine DeCostanzo and Helen Scholes, "Women Behind Bars, Their Numbers Increase," *Corrections Today* 50 (1988): 104–106.

27. This section synthesizes the findings of a number of surveys of female inmates, including DeCostanzo and Scholes, "Women Behind Bars, Their Numbers Increase"; Ruth Glick and Virginia Neto, *National Study of Women's Correctional Programs* (Washington, D.C.: U.S. Government Printing Office, 1977); Ann Goetting and Roy Michael Howsen, "Women in Prison: A Profile," *Prison Journal* 63 (1983): 27–46; Meda Chesney-Lind and Noelie Rodrigues, "Women Under Lock and Key: A View from Inside," *Prison Journal* 63 (1983): 47–65; Contact, Inc., "Women Offenders," *Corrections Compendium* 7 (1982): 6–11.

28. Merry Morash, Robin Harr, and Lila Rucker, "A Comparison of Programming for Women and Men in U.S. Prisons in the 1980s," *Crime and Delinquency* 40 (1994): 197–221.

29. Data in this section come from Greenfeld and Minor-Harper, *Women in Prison* (Washington, D.C.: Bureau of Justice Statistics, 1991); other information comes from DeCostanzo and Scholes, "Women Behind Bars, Their Numbers Increase"; Goetting and Howsen, "Women in Prison: A Profile"; Chesney-Lind and Rodrigues, "Women Under Lock and Key: A View from Inside."

30. Greenfeld and Minor-Harper, *Women in Prison,* p. 6.

31. Candace Kruttschnitt and Sharon Krmpotich, "Aggressive Behavior Among Female Inmates: An Exploratory Study," *Justice Quarterly* 7 (1990): 370–389.

32. "Sex Abuse of Female Inmates Is Common, Rights Group Says," *Criminal Justice Newsletter* 16 December 1996, p. 2.

33. Edna Erez, "The Myth of the New Female Offender: Some Evidence from Attitudes Toward Law and Justice," *Journal of Criminal Justice* 16 (1988): 499–509.

34. Robert Ross and Hugh McKay, *Self-Mutilation* (Lexington, Mass.: Lexington Books, 1979).

35. Alice Propper, *Prison Homosexuality* (Lexington, Mass.: Lexington Books, 1981).

36. Charles Tarr, "Group Counseling," *Corrections Today* 48 (1986): 72–75.

37. Roger Crist, "Therapeutic Community Helps Change Inmates for the Better at Rincon," *Corrections Today* 53 (1991): 96–100.

38. Max Mobley, "Mental Health Services Inmates in Need," *Corrections Today* 48 (1986): 12–14; Edward Guy, Jerome Platt, Israel Swerling, and Samuel Bullock, "Mental Health Status of Prisoners in an Urban Jail," *Criminal Justice and Behavior* 12 (1985): 17–29.

39. Glenn Walters, Millard Mann, Melvin Miller, Leslie Hemphill, and Michael Chlumsky, "Emotional Disorder Among Offenders," *Criminal Justice and Behavior* 15 (1988): 433–453.

40. Jean Spruill and Jack May, "The Mentally Retarded Offender," *Criminal Justice and Behavior* 15 (1988): 484–491.

41. Ira Sommers and Deborah Baskin, "The Prescription of Psychiatric Medication in Prison: Psychiatric Versus Labeling Perspectives," *Justice Quarterly* 7 (1990): 739–755.

42. Judy Anderson and R. Daniel McGehee, "South Carolina Strives to Treat Elderly and Disabled Offenders," *Corrections Today* 53 (1991): 124–127.

43. American Bar Association, *The State of Criminal Justice* (Washington, D.C.: American Bar Association, 1996).

44. "Few Inmates Get Drug Treatment, But Most Need It, GAO Finds," *Criminal Justice Newsletter* 1 November 1991, p. 2.

45. ABT Associates, *1992 Update: HIV/AIDS in Correctional Facilities: Issues and Opinions* (Washington, D.C.: National Institute of Justice, 1993).

46. *Gates v. Deukmejian* (U.S.D.C., E.D. Cal.) CIVS 87-1636 (1990).

47. Howard Skolnik and John Slansky, "A First Step in Helping Inmates Get Good Jobs After Release," *Corrections Today* 53 (1991): 92.

48. Donna Duncan, "ACA Survey Examines Industry Programs for Women Offenders," *Corrections Today* 54 (1992): 114.

49. This section leans heavily on Barbara Auerbach, George Sexton, Franklin Farrow, and Robert Lawson, *Work in American Prisons, The Private Sector Gets Involved* (Washington, D.C.: National Institute of Justice, 1988).

50. Public Law 96-157, § 827, codified as 18 U.S.C. § 1761(c).

51. Diane Dwyer and Roger McNally, "Public Policy, Prison Industries, and Business: An Equitable Balance for the 1990s," *Federal Probation* 57 (1993): 30–35.

52. Barbara Bloom, "Families of Prisoners: A Valuable Resource," paper presented at the annual meeting of the Academy of Criminal Justice Sciences, St. Louis, March 1987.

53. Norma Stumbo and Sandra Little, "Campground Offers Relaxed Setting for Children's Visitation Program," *Corrections Today* 53 (1991): 136–144.

54. Donald Johns, "Alternatives to Conjugal Visits," *Federal Probation* 35 (1971): 48–50.

55. "Coed Prisons," *Corrections Compendium* 10 (1986): 7, 14–15.

56. This section leans heavily on Mark Hamm, "Current Perspectives on the Prisoner Self-Help Movement," *Federal Probation* 52 (1988): 49–56.

57. Douglas Lipton, Robert Martinson, and Judith Wilks, *The Effectiveness of Correctional Treatment: A Survey of Treatment Evaluation Studies* (New York: Praeger, 1975).

58. Charles Murray and Louis Cox, *Beyond Probation: Juvenile Corrections and the Chronic Delinquent* (Beverly Hills, Calif.: Sage, 1979).

59. Steven Lab and John Whitehead, "An Analysis of Juvenile Correctional Treatment," *Crime and Delinquency* 34 (1988): 60–83.

60. Ted Palmer, "The Effectiveness of Intervention: Recent Trends and Current Issues," *Crime and Delinquency* 37 (1991): 330–346.

61. Morash, Harr, and Rucker, "A Comparison of Programming for Women and Men in U.S. Prisons in the 1980s."

62. Paul Gendreau and Claire Goffin, "Principles of Effective Correctional Programming," *Forum on Correctional Research* 2 (1996): 38–41.

63. Emily Herrick, "Number of COs Up 25 Percent in Two Years," *Corrections Compendium* 13 (1988): 9–21.

64. Diane Carter, "The Status of Education and Training in Corrections," *Federal Probation* 55 (1991): 17–22.

65. Lucien X. Lombardo, *Guards Imprisoned* (New York: Elsevier, 1981); James Jacobs and Norma Crotty, "The Guard's World," in *New Perspectives on Prisons and Imprisonment,* ed. James Jacobs (Ithaca, N.Y.: Cornell University Press, 1983), pp. 133–141.

66. John Klofas and Hans Toch, "The Guard Subculture Myth," *Journal of Research in Crime and Delinquency* 19 (1982): 238–254.

67. Ruth Triplett and Janet Mullings, "Work-Related Stress and Coping Among Correctional Officers: Implications from the Organizational Literature," *Journal of Criminal Justice* 24 (1996): 291–308.

68. Peter Horne, "Female Correction Officers," *Federal Probation* 49 (1985): 46–55.

69. *Dothard v. Rawlinson,* 433 U.S. 321 (1977).

70. Leonore Simon, "Prison Behavior and the Victim-Offender Relationship Among Violent Offenders," *Justice Quarterly* 10 (1993): 489–506.

71. David Duffee, *Corrections, Practice and Policy* (New York: Random House, 1989), p. 305.

72. Randy Martin and Sherwood Zimmerman, "A Typology of the Causes of Prison Riots and an Analytical Extension to the 1986 West Virginia Riot," *Justice Quarterly* 7 (1990): 711–737.

73. John DiIulio, *Governing Prisons: A Comparative Study of Correctional Management* (New York: Free Press, 1987).

74. National Advisory Commission on Criminal Justice Standards and Goals, *Corrections* (Washington, D.C.: U.S. Government Printing Office, 1973), p. 18.

75. *Cooper v. Pate,* 378 U.S. 546 (1964).

76. *De Mallory v. Cullen,* 855 F.2d 442 (7th Cir. 1988).

77. *Lindquist v. Idaho State Board of Corrections,* 776 F.2d 851 (9th Cir. 1985).

78. *Smith v. Wade,* 103 S.Ct. 1625 (1983).

79. *Bounds v. Smith,* 430 U.S. 817 (1977).

80. *Turner v. Safley,* 107 S.Ct. 2254 (1987) at 2261.

81. *Ramos v. Lamm,* 639 F.2d 559 (10th Cir. 1980).

82. *Procunier v. Martinez,* 411 U.S. 396 (1974).

83. *Nolan v. Fitzpatrick,* 451 F.2d 545 (1st Cir. 1971); see also, *Washington Post Co. v. Kleindienst,* 494 F.2d 997 (D.C. Cir. 1974).

84. *Mumin v. Phelps,* 857 F.2d 1055 (5th Cir. 1988).

85. *O'Lone v. Estate of Shabazz,* 107 S.Ct. 2400 (1987).

86. *Rahman v. Stephenson,* 626 F.Supp. 886 (W.D. Tenn. 1986).

87. *Newman v. Alabama,* 92 S.Ct. 1079, 405 U.S. 319 (1972).

88. *Estelle v. Gamble,* 429 U.S. 97 (1976).

89. Ibid.

90. *Trop v. Dulles,* 356 U.S. 86, 78 S.Ct. 590 (1958); see also *Furman v. Georgia,* 408 U.S. 238, 92 S.Ct. 2726, 33 L.Ed.2d 346 (1972).

91. *Weems v. United States,* 217 U.S. 349, 30 S.Ct. 544, 54 L.Ed. 793 (1910).

92. *Lee v. Tahash,* 352 F.2d 970 (8th Cir. 1965).

93. *Estelle v. Gamble,* 429 U.S. 97 (1976).

94. *Robinson v. California,* 370 U.S. 660 (1962).

95. *Gregg v. Georgia,* 428 U.S. 153 (1976).

96. *Jackson v. Bishop,* 404 U.S. 571 (8th Cir. 1968).

97. *Bell v. Wolfish,* 99 S.Ct. 1873–1974 (1979); see "*Bell v. Wolfish:* The Rights of Pretrial Detainees," *New England Journal of Prison Law* 6 (1979): 134.

98. *Farmer v. Brennan,* 144 S.Ct 1970 (1994).

99. *Rhodes v. Chapman,* 452 U.S. 337 (1981); for further analysis of *Rhodes,* see Randall Pooler, "Prison Overcrowding and the Eighth Amendment: The *Rhodes* Not Taken," *New England Journal on Criminal and Civil Confinement* 8 (1983): 1–28.

100. *Estelle v. Ruiz,* 74-329 (E.D. Texas 1980).

101. "*Ruiz* Case in Texas Winds Down: Special Master to Close Office," *Criminal Justice Newsletter* 21 (1990): 1.

102. Geoffrey Alpert, Ben Crouch, and C. Ronald Huff, "Prison Reform by Judicial Decree: The Unintended Consequences of *Ruiz v. Estelle,*" *Justice System Journal* 9 (1984): 291–305.

103. *Prison Escape Survey* (Lincoln, Neb.: Corrections Compendium, 1991).

104. These sections make extensive use of Edward Rhine, William Smith, Ronald Jackson, Peggy Burke, and Roger Labelle, *Paroling Authorities, Recent History and Current Practice* (Laurel, Md.: American Correctional Association, 1991).

105. Ibid., p. 4.

106. Susan Turner and Joan Petersilia, "Focusing on High-Risk Parolees: An Experiment to Reduce Commitments to the Texas Department of Corrections," *Journal of Research in Crime and Delinquency* 29 (1992): 34–61.

107. Allen Beck and Bernard Shipley, *Recidivism of Prisoners Released in 1983* (Washington, D.C.: Bureau of Justice Statistics, 1989).

108. Paul Gendreau, Tracy Little, and Claire Goggin, "A Meta-Analysis of the Predictors of Adult Offender Recidivism: What Works?" *Criminology* 34 (1996): 575–607.

109. Robyn L. Cohen, *Probation and Parole Violators in State Prison, 1991: Survey of State Prison Inmates, 1991* (Washington, D.C.: Bureau of Justice Statistics, 1995).

110. Laura Fishman, *Women at the Wall: A Study of Prisoners' Wives Doing Time on the Outside* (New York: State University of New York Press, 1990).

111. Leslee Goodman Hornick, "Volunteer Program Helps Make Inmates' Families Feel Welcome," *Corrections Today* 53 (1991): 184–186.

112. Kathleen Olivares, Velmer Burton, and Francis Cullen, "The Collateral Consequences of a Felony Conviction: A National Study of State Legal Codes 10 Years Later," *Federal Probation* 60 (1996): 10–17.

113. See, for example, *Bush v. Reid,* 516 P.2d 1215 (Alaska 1973); *Thompson v. Bond,* 421 F.Supp. 878 (W.D. Mo. 1976); *Delorne v. Pierce Freightlines Co.,* 353 F.Supp. 258 (D.Or. 1973); *Beyer v. Werner,* 299 F.Supp. 967 (E.D. N.Y. 1969).

Glossary

absolute deterrent A legal control measure designed to totally eliminate a particular criminal act.

Academy of Criminal Justice Sciences The society that serves to further the development of the criminal justice profession and whose membership includes academics and practitioners involved in criminal justice.

access control A crime-prevention technique that stresses target hardening through security measures, such as alarm systems, that make it more difficult for criminals to attack a target.

accountability system A way of dealing with police corruption by making superiors responsible for the behavior of their subordinates.

actus reus An illegal act. The *actus reus* can be an affirmative act, such as taking money or shooting someone, or a failure to act, such as failing to take proper precautions while driving a car.

adjudication The determination of guilt or innocence; a judgment concerning criminal charges. The majority of offenders charged plead guilty; of the remainder, some cases are adjudicated by a judge and a jury, some are adjudicated by a judge without a jury, and others are dismissed.

adversary system The procedure used to determine truth in the adjudication of guilt or innocence in which the defense (advocate for the accused) is pitted against the prosecution (advocate for the state), with the judge acting as arbiter of the legal rules. Under the adversary system, the burden is on the state to prove the charges beyond a reasonable doubt. This system of having the two parties publicly debate has proved to be the most effective method of achieving the truth regarding a set of circumstances. (Under the accusatory, or inquisitorial, system, which is used in continental Europe, the charge is evidence of guilt that the accused must disprove; the judge takes an active part in the proceedings.)

aggressive preventive patrol A patrol technique designed to suppress crime before it occurs.

aging out The process in which individuals commit fewer crimes as they move beyond adolescence.

alien conspiracy theory The view that organized crime was imported by Europeans and that crime cartels restrict their membership to people of their own ethnic background.

alternative sanctions The group of punishments falling between probation and prison; "probation plus." Community-based sanctions, including house arrest and intensive supervision, serve as an alternative to incarceration.

American Society of Criminology The professional society of criminology devoted to enhancing the status of the discipline.

anger rape A rape incident motivated by the rapist's desire to release pent-up anger and rage.

anomie A condition produced by normlessness. Because of rapidly shifting moral values, a person has few guides to what is socially acceptable behavior.

appeal A review of lower-court proceedings by a higher court. There is no constitutional right to appeal. However, the right to appeal is established by statute in some states and by custom in others. All states set conditions as to the type of case or grounds for appeal, which appellate courts may review. Appellate courts do not retry the case under review. Rather, the transcript of the lower-court case is read by the judges, and the lawyers for the defendant and for the state argue about the merits of the appeal—that is, the legality of lower-court proceedings, rather than of the original testimony. Appeal is more a process for controlling police, court, and correctional practices than for rescuing innocent defendants. When appellate courts do reverse lower-court judgments, it is usually because of "prejudicial error" (deprivation of rights), and the case is remanded for retrial.

appellate courts Courts that reconsider a case that has already been tried in order to determine whether the measures used complied with accepted rules of criminal procedure and were in line with constitutional doctrines.

arbitrage The practice of buying large blocks of stock in companies that are believed to be the target of corporate buyouts or takeovers.

argot The unique language that influences the prison culture.

arraignment The step at which accused offenders are read the charges against them and are asked how they plead. In addition, the accused are advised of their rights. Possible pleas are guilty, not guilty, nolo contendere, and not guilty by reason of insanity.

arrest The taking of a person into the custody of the law, the legal purpose of which is to restrain the accused until he or she can be held accountable for the offense at court proceedings. The legal requirement for an arrest is probable cause. Arrests for investigation, suspicion, or harassment are improper and of doubtful legality. The police have the responsibility to use only the reasonable physical force necessary to make an arrest. The summons has been used as a substitute for arrest.

Aryan Brotherhood A white supremacist prison gang.

assembly-line justice The view that the justice process resembles an endless production line that handles most cases in a routine and perfunctory fashion.

atavistic traits According to Lombroso, the physical characteristics that distinguish born criminals from the general population and are throwbacks to animals or primitive people.

attainder The loss of all civil rights due to a conviction for a felony offense.

attorney general The senior U.S. prosecutor and cabinet member who heads the Justice Department.

Auburn system The prison system developed in New York during the 19th century that stressed congregate working conditions.

authoritarian A person whose personality revolves around blind obedience to authority.

bail The monetary amount for or condition of pretrial release, normally set by a judge at the initial appearance. The purpose of bail is to ensure the return of the accused at subsequent proceedings. If the accused is unable to make bail, he or she is detained in jail. The Eighth Amendment provides that excessive bail shall not be required.

bail bonding The business of providing bail to needy offenders, usually at an exorbitant rate of interest.

Bail Reform Act of 1984 Federal legislation that provides for both greater emphasis on release on recognizance for nondangerous offenders and preventive detention for those who present a menace to the community.

base penalty The modal sentence in a structured sentencing state, which can be enhanced or diminished to reflect aggravating or mitigating circumstances.

behaviorism The branch of psychology concerned with the study of observable behavior, rather than unconscious motives. It focuses on the relationship between particular stimuli and people's responses to them.

bill of indictment A document submitted to a grand jury by the prosecutor asking it to take action and indict a suspect.

Bill of Rights The first ten amendments to the U.S. Constitution.

blameworthiness The amount of culpability or guilt a person maintains for participating in a particular criminal offense.

blue curtain According to William Westly, the secretive, insulated police culture that isolates police officers from the rest of society.

booking The administrative record of an arrest listing the offender's name, address, physical description, date of birth, and employer; the time of arrest; the offense; and the name of the arresting officer. Photographing and fingerprinting of the offender are also part of booking.

boot camp A short-term militaristic correctional facility in which inmates undergo intensive physical conditioning and discipline.

bot Under Anglo-Saxon law, the restitution paid for killing someone in an open fight.

bourgeoisie In Marxist theory, the owners of the means of production; the capitalist ruling class.

broken windows A term used to describe the role of the police as maintainers of community order and safety.

brutalization effect The belief that capital punishment creates an atmosphere of brutality that enhances, rather than deters, the level of violence in society. The death penalty reinforces the view that violence is an appropriate response to provocations.

burglary Breaking into and entering a home or structure for the purposes of committing a felony.

capital punishment The use of the death penalty to punish transgressors.

career criminal A person who repeatedly violates the law and organizes his or her lifestyle around criminality.

Carriers **case** A 15th-century case that defined the law of theft and reformulated the concept of taking the possessions of another.

challenge for cause Removing a juror because he or she is biased or has prior knowledge about a case, or for other reasons that demonstrate the individual's inability to render a fair and impartial judgment in a case.

chancery court A court created in 15th-century England to oversee the lives of high-born minors who were orphaned or otherwise could not care for themselves.

charge In a criminal case, the specific crime the defendant is accused of committing.

Chicago Crime Commission A citizen action group set up in Chicago to investigate problems in the criminal justice system and explore avenues for positive change. The forerunner of many such groups around the country.

child abuse Any physical, emotional, or sexual trauma to a child for which no reasonable explanation, such as an accident, can be found. Child abuse can also be a function of neglecting to give proper care and attention to a young child.

Christopher Commission An investigatory group led by Warren Christopher that investigated the Los Angeles Police Department in the wake of the Rodney King beating.

chronic offender According to Wolfgang, a delinquent offender who is arrested five or more times before he or she is 18 and who stands a good chance of becoming an adult criminal; these offenders are responsible for more than half of all serious crimes.

civil death The custom of terminating the civil rights of convicted felons, such as forbidding them the right to vote or marry. No state uses civil death today.

civil law All law that is not criminal, including torts (personal wrongs), contract, property, maritime, and commercial law.

Civil Rights Division That part of the U.S. Justice Department that handles cases involving violations of civil rights guaranteed by the Constitution and federal law.

classical theory The theoretical perspective suggesting that (1) people have free will to choose criminal or conventional behaviors; (2) people choose to commit crime for reasons of greed or personal need; and (3) crime can be controlled only by the fear of criminal sanctions.

classification The procedure in which prisoners are categorized on the basis of their personal characteristics and criminal history and then assigned to an appropriate institution.

Code of Hammurabi The first written criminal code developed in Babylonia about 2000 B.C.

coeducational prison An institution that houses both male and female inmates who share work and recreational facilities.

cognitive theory The study of the perception of reality; the mental processes required to understand the world we live in.

cohort study A study utilizing a sample whose behavior is followed over a period of time.

common law Early English law, developed by judges, that incorporated Anglo-Saxon tribal custom, feudal rules and practices, and the everyday rules of behavior of local villages. Common law became the standardized law of the land in England and eventually formed the basis of the criminal law in the United States.

community policing A police strategy that emphasizes fear reduction, community organization, and order maintenance, rather than crime fighting.

community service restitution An alternative sanction that requires an offender to work in the community at such tasks as cleaning public parks or working with handicapped children in lieu of an incarceration sentence.

community treatment The attempt by correctional agencies to maintain convicted offenders in the community instead of a secure facility; it includes probation, parole, and residential programs.

compensation Financial aid awarded to the victims of crime to repay them for their loss and injuries.

complaint A sworn allegation made in writing to a court or judge that an individual is guilty of some designated (complained of) offense. This is often the first legal document filed regarding a criminal offense. The complaint can be "taken out" by the victim, the police officer, the district attorney, or another interested party. Although the complaint charges an offense, an indictment or information may be the formal charging document.

concurrent sentences Prison sentences for two or more criminal acts that are served simultaneously, or run together.

conduct norms Behaviors expected of social groups' members. If group norms conflict with those of the general culture, members of the group may find themselves described as outcasts or criminals.

conflict view The view that human behavior is shaped by interpersonal conflict and that those who maintain social power will use it to further their own needs.

conjugal visit A prison program that allows inmates to receive private visits from their spouses for the purpose of maintaining normal interpersonal relationships.

consecutive sentences Prison sentences for two or more criminal acts that are served one after the other or that follow one another.

consensus view of crime The belief that the majority of citizens in a society share common ideals and work toward a common good and that crimes are acts that are outlawed because they conflict with the rules of the majority and are harmful to society.

constable The peacekeeper in early English towns. The constable organized citizens to protect his territory and supervised the night watch.

constructive intent The finding of criminal liability for an unintentional act that is the result of negligence or recklessness.

constructive possession In the crime of larceny, willingly giving up temporary physical possession of property but retaining legal ownership.

continuance A judicial order to continue a case without a finding in order to gather more information, allow the defendant to begin a community-based treatment program, and so on.

contract system (attorney) Providing counsel to indigent offenders by having an attorney under contract to the county to handle all (or some) such cases.

contract system (convict) The system used earlier in the century by which inmates were leased out to private industry to work.

convict subculture The separate culture that exists in a prison, which has its own set of rewards and behaviors. The traditional convict culture is now being replaced by a violent gang culture.

conviction A judgment of guilt; a verdict by a jury, a plea by a defendant, or a judgment by a court that the accused is guilty as charged.

corporal punishment The use of physical chastisement, such as whipping or electroshock, to punish criminals.

corporate crime White-collar crime involving a legal violation by a corporate entity, such as price fixing, restraint of trade, or waste dumping.

corpus dilecti The body of the crime, made up of the *actus reus* and *mens rea*.

corrections The agencies of justice that take custody of offenders after their conviction and are entrusted with their treatment and control.

court administrator The individual who controls the operations of the courts system in a particular jurisdiction; he or she may be in charge of scheduling, juries, judicial assignment, and so on.

court of last resort A court that handles the final appeal on a matter. The U.S. Supreme Court is the official court of last resort for criminal matters.

courtroom work group The phrase used to denote that all parties in the adversary process work together in a cooperative effort to settle cases with the least amount of effort and conflict.

courts of limited jurisdiction Courts that handle misdemeanors and minor civil complaints.

crackdown Concentrating police resources on a particular problem area, such as street-level drug dealing, in order to eradicate or displace criminal activity.

crime A violation of societal rules of behavior as interpreted and expressed by a criminal legal code created by people holding social and political power. Individuals who violate these rules are subject to sanctions by state authority, social stigma, and loss of status.

crime control A model of criminal justice that emphasizes the control of dangerous offenders and the protection of society. Its advocates call for harsh punishments as a deterrent to crime, such as the death penalty.

crime fighter The police style that stresses dealing with hard crimes and arresting dangerous criminals.

Criminal Division The branch of the U.S. Justice Department that prosecutes federal criminal violations.

criminal justice process The decision-making points from initial investigation or arrest by police to the eventual release of the offender and his or her reentry into society; the various sequential criminal justice stages through which the offender passes.

criminal law The body of rules that define crimes, set their punishments out, and mandate the procedures in carrying out the criminal justice process.

criminal sanction The right of the state to punish people if they violate the rules set down in the criminal code; the punishment connected to commission of a specific crime.

criminology The scientific approach to the study of the nature, extent, cause, and control of criminal behavior.

cross-examination The process in which the defense and the prosecution interrogate witnesses during a trial.

cruel and unusual punishment Physical punishment or punishment that is far in excess of that given to people under similar circumstances and is therefore banned by the Eighth Amendment. The death penalty has so far not been considered cruel and unusual if it is administered in a fair and nondiscriminatory fashion.

cultural transmission The concept that conduct norms are passed down from one generation to the next so that they become stable within the boundaries of a culture. Cultural transmission guarantees that group lifestyle and behavior are stable and predictable.

culture conflict According to Sellin, a condition brought about when the rules and norms of an individual's subcultural affiliation conflict with the role demands of conventional society.

culture of poverty The view that people in lower-class society form a separate culture with its own values and norms that are in conflict with conventional society; the culture is self-maintaining and ongoing.

curtilage The fields attached to a house.

custodial convenience The principle of giving jailed inmates the minimum comforts required by law in order to contain the costs of incarceration.

cynicism The belief that most people's actions are motivated solely by personal needs and selfishness.

DARE Drug Abuse Resistance Education, a school-based antidrug program initiated by the Los Angeles Police Department and now adopted around the United States.

day fines Fines geared to the average daily income of the convicted offender in an effort to bring equity to the sentencing process.

day reporting centers Nonresidential community-based treatment programs.

deadly force The ability of the police to kill suspects if they resist arrest or present a danger to the officer or the community. The police cannot use deadly force against an unarmed fleeing felon.

decriminalization Reducing the penalty for a criminal act but not actually legalizing it.

defeminization The process by which policewomen become enculturated into the police profession at the expense of their feminine identity.

defendant The accused in criminal proceedings; he or she has the right to be present at each stage of the criminal justice process, except grand jury proceedings.

defense attorney The counsel for the defendant in a criminal trial who represents the individual from arrest to final appeal.

degenerate anomalies According to Lombroso, the primitive physical characteristics that make criminals animalistic and savage.

deinstitutionalization The movement to remove as many offenders as possible from secure confinement and treat them in the community.

demeanor The way in which a person outwardly manifests his or her personality.

demystify The process by which Marxists unmask the true purpose of the capitalist system's rules and laws.

desert-based sentences Sentences in which the length is based on the seriousness of the criminal act and not the personal characteristics of the defendant or the deterrent impact of the law. Punishment based on what people have done and not on what others may do or what they themselves may do in the future.

desistance The process in which crime rate declines with age; synonymous with the aging-out process.

detective The police agent assigned to investigate crimes, gather evidence, and identify the perpetrator.

detention Holding an offender in secure confinement before trial.

determinate sentences Fixed terms of incarceration, such as three years' imprisonment. Determinate sentences are felt by many to be too restrictive for rehabilitative purposes; the advantage is that offenders know how much time they have to serve—that is, when they will be released.

deterrence The act of preventing crime before it occurs by means of the threat of criminal sanctions.

deviance Behavior that departs from social norms.

discretion The use of personal decision making and choice in carrying out operations in the criminal justice system. For example, police discretion can involve the decision to make an arrest, while prosecutorial discretion can involve the decision to accept a plea bargain.

differential association According to Edwin Sutherland, the principle that criminal acts are related to a person's exposure to an excess amount of antisocial attitudes and values.

direct examination The questioning of one's own (prosecution or defense) witness during a trial.

directed verdict The right of a judge to direct a jury to acquit a defendant because the state has not proven the elements of the crime or otherwise has not established guilt according to law.

disposition For juvenile offenders, the equivalent of sentencing for adult offenders. The theory is that disposition is more rehabilitative than retributive. Possible dispositions may be to dismiss the case, release the youth to the custody of his or her parents, place the offender on probation, or send him or her to an institution or state correctional institution.

district attorney The county prosecutor charged with bringing offenders to justice and enforcing the laws of the state.

diversion A noncriminal alternative to trial usually featuring counseling, job training, and educational opportunities.

DNA profiling The identification of criminal suspects by matching DNA samples taken from their person with specimens found at crime scenes.

double bunking The practice of holding two or more inmates in a single cell because of prison overcrowding; upheld in *Rhodes v. Chapman*.

double marginality According to Alex, the social burden African American police officers carry by being both minority-group members and law enforcement officers.

drift According to Matza, the idea that youths move in and out of delinquency and that their lifestyles can embrace both conventional and deviant values.

drug courier profile A way of identifying drug runners based on their personal characteristics; police may stop and question individuals based on the way they fit the characteristics contained in the profile.

Drug Enforcement Administration (DEA) The federal agency that enforces federal drug control laws.

due process The basic constitutional principle based on the concept of the primacy of the individual and the complementary concept of limitation on governmental power; a safeguard against arbitrary and unfair state procedures in judicial or administrative proceedings. Embodied in the due process concept are the basic rights of a defendant in criminal proceedings and the requisites for a fair trial. These rights and requirements have been expanded by appellate court decisions and include (1) timely notice of a hearing or trial that informs the accused of the charges against him or her; (2) the opportunity to confront accusers and to present evidence on one's own behalf before an impartial jury or judge; (3) the presumption of innocence under which guilt must be proven by legally obtained evidence and the verdict must be supported by the evidence presented; (4) the right of an accused to be warned of constitutional rights at the earliest stage of the criminal process; (5) protection against self-incrimination; (6) assistance of counsel at every critical stage of the criminal process; and (7) the guarantee that an individual will not be tried more than once for the same offense (double jeopardy).

Durham rule A definition of insanity used in New Hampshire that required that the crime be excused if it was a product of a mental illness.

economic crime An act in violation of the criminal law that is designed to bring financial gain to the offender.

economism The policy of controlling white-collar crime through monetary incentives and sanctions.

electroencephalogram (EEG) A device that can record the electronic impulses given off by the brain, commonly called brain waves.

embezzlement A type of larceny that involves taking the possessions of another (fraudulent conversion) that have been placed in the thief's lawful possession for safekeeping, such as a bank teller misappropriating deposits or a stockbroker making off with a customer's account.

enterprise syndicate An organized crime group that profits from the sale of illegal goods and services, such as narcotics, pornography, and prostitution.

entrapment A criminal defense that maintains the police originated the criminal idea or initiated the criminal action.

equity The action or practice of awarding each his or her just due; sanctions based on equity seek to compensate individual victims and the general society for their losses due to crime.

ex post facto laws Laws that make criminal an act after it was committed or that retroactively increase the penalty for a crime. For example, an ex post facto law could change shoplifting from a misdemeanor to a felony and penalize people with a prison term even though they had been apprehended six months before; these laws are unconstitutional.

exceptional circumstances doctrine Under this policy, courts would hear only those cases brought by inmates in which the circumstances indicated a total disregard for human dignity, while denying hearings to less serious crimes. Cases allowed access to the courts would usually involve a situation of total denial of medical care.

exclusionary rule The principle that prohibits using evidence illegally obtained in a trial. Based on the Fourth Amendment "right of the people to be secure in their persons, houses, papers, and effects, against unreasonable searches and seizures," the rule is not a bar to prosecution, as legally obtained evidence may be available that may be used in a trial.

excuse A defense to a criminal charge in which the accused maintains he or she lacked the intent to commit the crime (*mens rea*).

expressive crime A crime that has no purpose except to accomplish the behavior at hand—such as shooting someone—as opposed to obtaining monetary gain.

false pretenses Illegally obtaining money, goods, or merchandise from another by fraud or misrepresentation.

Federal Bureau of Investigation (FBI) The arm of the U.S. Justice Department that investigates violations of federal law, gathers crime statistics, runs a comprehensive crime laboratory, and helps train local law enforcement officers.

felony A more serious offense that carries a penalty of incarceration in a state prison, usually for one year or more. Persons convicted of felony offenses lose such rights as the rights to vote, hold elective office, or maintain certain licenses.

fence A buyer and seller of stolen merchandise.

field training officer A senior police officer who trains recruits in the field, overseeing their on-the-job training.

fixed time rule A policy in which people must be tried within a stated period after their arrest; overruled by *Barker v. Wingo,* which created a balancing test.

flat or fixed sentencing A sentencing model that mandates that all people who are convicted of a specific offense and who are sent to prison must receive the same length of incarceration.

focal concerns According to Walter Miller, the value orientations of lower-class cultures whose features include the need for excitement, trouble, smartness, fate, and personal autonomy.

folkways Generally followed customs that do not have moral values attached to them, such as not interrupting people when they are speaking.

foot patrol Police patrols that take officers out of cars and put them on a walking beat in order to strengthen ties with the community.

forfeiture The seizure of personal property by the state as a civil or criminal penalty.

fraud The taking of the possessions of another through deception or cheating, such as selling a person a desk that is represented as an antique but is known to be a copy.

free venture Privately run industries in a prison setting in which the inmates work for wages and the goods are sold for profit.

functionalism The sociological perspective that suggests that each part of society makes a contribution to the maintenance of the whole. Functionalism stresses social cooperation and consensus of values and beliefs among a majority of society's members.

furlough A correctional policy that allows inmates to leave the institution for vocational or educational training, for employment, or to maintain family ties.

general deterrence A crime control policy that depends on the fear of criminal penalties. General deterrence measures, such as long prison sentences for violent crimes, are aimed at convincing the potential law violator that the pains associated with crime outweigh its benefits.

general intent Actions that on their face indicate a criminal purpose, such as breaking into a locked building or trespassing on someone's property.

gentrification A process of reclaiming and reconditioning deteriorated neighborhoods by refurbishing depressed real estate and then renting or selling the properties to upper-middle-class professionals.

good faith exception The principle of law holding that evidence may be used in a criminal trial even though the search warrant used to obtain it is technically faulty, if the police acted in good faith and to the best of their ability when they sought to obtain it from a judge.

good-time credit Time taken off a prison sentence in exchange for good behavior within the institution—for example, ten days per month. A device used to limit disciplinary problems within the prison.

grand jury A group (usually consisting of twenty-three citizens) chosen to hear testimony in secret and to issue formal criminal accusations (indictments). It also serves an investigatory function.

grass eaters A term used for police officers who accept payoffs when their everyday duties place them in a position to be solicited by the public.

greenmail The process by which an arbitrager buys large blocks of a company's stock and threatens to take over the company and replace the current management. To ward off the threat to their positions, members of management use company funds to repurchase the shares at a much higher price, creating huge profits for the corporate raiders.

guardian ad litem A court-appointed attorney who protects the interests of a child in cases involving the child's welfare.

habeas corpus *See* writ of habeas corpus

habitual criminal statutes Laws that require long-term or life sentences for offenders who have multiple felony convictions.

halfway house A community-based correctional facility that houses inmates before their outright release so they can become gradually acclimated to conventional society.

Hallcrest Report A government-sponsored national survey of the private security industry conducted by the Hallcrest Corporation.

hands-off doctrine The judicial policy of not interfering in the administrative affairs of a prison.

hearsay evidence Testimony that is not first-hand but relates information told by a second party.

hot spots of crime Places from which a significant portion of all police calls originate. These hot spots include taverns and housing projects.

house of correction A county correctional institution generally used for the incarceration of more serious misdemeanants, whose sentences are usually less than one year.

hue and cry A call for assistance in medieval England. The policy of self-help used in villages demanded that everyone respond if a citizen raised a hue and cry to get their aid.

hulks Mothballed ships that were used to house prisoners in 18th-century England.

hundred In medieval England, a group of 100 families that had the responsibility to maintain the order and try minor offenses.

hustle The underground prison economy.

importation model The view that the violent prison culture reflects the criminal culture of the outside world and is neither developed in nor unique to prisons.

incapacitation The policy of keeping dangerous criminals in confinement to eliminate the risk of their repeating their offense in society.

indentured servant Prior to the 18th century, a debtor or convicted offender who would work off his or her debt by being assigned a term of servitude to a master who purchased the services from the state.

indeterminate sentence A term of incarceration with a stated minimum and maximum length, such as a sentence to prison for a period of from three to ten years. The prisoner would be eligible for parole after the minimum sentence had been served. Based on the belief that sentences should fit the criminal, indeterminate sentences allow individualized sentences and provide for sentencing flexibility. Judges can set a high minimum to override the purpose of the indeterminate sentence.

index crimes The eight crimes that, because of their seriousness and frequency, the FBI reports the incidence of in the annual Uniform Crime Reports. Index crimes include murder, rape, assault, robbery, burglary, arson, larceny, and motor vehicle theft.

indictment A written accusation returned by a grand jury charging an individual with a specified crime after determination of probable cause; the prosecutor presents enough evidence (a prima facie case) to establish probable cause.

inevitable discovery A rule of law stating that evidence that almost assuredly would be independently discovered can be used in a court of law even though it was obtained in violation of legal rules and practices.

information Like the indictment, a formal charging document. The prosecuting attorney makes out the information and files it in court. Probable cause is determined at the preliminary hearing, which, unlike grand jury proceedings, is public and attended by the accused and his or her attorney.

initial appearance The stage in the justice process during which the suspect is brought before a magistrate for consideration of bail. The suspect must be taken for initial appearance within a "reasonable time" after arrest. For petty offenses, this step often serves as the final criminal proceeding, either by adjudication by a judge or the offering of a guilty plea.

inmate social code The informal set of rules that govern inmates.

inmate subculture The loosely defined culture that pervades prisons and has its own norms, rules, and language.

insanity A legal defense that maintains that a defendant was incapable of forming criminal intent because he or she suffered from a defect of reason or mental illness.

insider trading The illegal buying of stock in a company based on information provided by another who has a fiduciary interest in the company, such as an employee or an outside attorney or accountant hired by the firm. Federal laws and the rules of the Security and Exchange Commission require that all profits from such trading be returned and provide for both fines and a prison sentence.

instrumental Marxist theory The view that capitalist institutions, such as the criminal justice system, have as their main purpose the control of the poor in order to maintain the hegemony of the wealthy.

intensive probation supervision A type of intermediate sanction involving small probation caseloads and strict monitoring on a daily or weekly basis.

interactionist perspective The view that one's perception of reality is significantly influenced by one's interpretations of the reactions of others to similar events and stimuli.

interrogation The method of accumulating evidence in the form of information or confessions from suspects by police. This questioning has been restricted because of concern about the use of brutal and coercive methods and interest in protecting against self-incrimination.

investigation An inquiry concerning suspected criminal behavior for the purpose of identifying offenders or gathering further evidence to assist the prosecution of apprehended offenders.

jail A place to detain people awaiting trial, to serve as a lockup for drunks and disorderly individuals, and to confine convicted misdemeanants serving sentences of less than one year.

jailhouse lawyer An inmate trained in law or otherwise educated who helps other inmates prepare legal briefs and appeals.

just desert The philosophy of justice asserting that those who violate the rights of others deserve to be punished. The severity of punishment should be commensurate with the seriousness of the crime.

justice model A philosophy of corrections that stresses determinate sentences, abolition of parole, and the idea that prisons are places of punishment and not rehabilitation.

justification A defense to a criminal charge in which the accused maintains that his or her actions were justified by the circumstances and therefore he or she should not be held criminally liable.

juvenile delinquency Participation in illegal behavior by a minor who falls under a statutory age limit.

juvenile justice process Court proceedings for youths within the juvenile age group that differ from the adult criminal process. Under the paternal (parens patriae) philosophy, juvenile procedures are informal and nonadversary, invoked for the juvenile offender rather than against him or her; a petition instead of a complaint is filed; courts make findings of involvement or adjudication of delinquency instead of convictions; and juvenile offenders receive dispositions instead of sentences. Recent court decisions (*In re Kent* and *In re Gault*) have increased the adversary nature of juvenile court proceedings. How-

ever, the philosophy remains one of diminishing the stigma of delinquency and providing for the youth's well-being and rehabilitation, rather than seeking retribution.

Kansas City study An experimental program that evaluated the effectiveness of patrol. The Kansas City study found that the presence of patrol officers had little deterrent effect.

Knapp Commission A public body that led the investigation into police corruption in New York and uncovered a widespread network of payoffs and bribes.

labeling The process by which a person becomes fixed with a negative identity, such as "criminal" or "ex-con," and is forced to suffer the consequences of outcast status.

landmark decision A decision handed down by the Supreme Court that becomes the law of the land and serves as precedence for similar legal issues.

legalization The removal of all criminal penalties from a previously outlawed act.

life history A research method that uses the experiences of an individual as the unit of analysis, such as using the life experience of an individual gang member to understand the natural history of gang membership.

longitudinal cohort study Research that tracks the development of a group of subjects over time.

lower courts A generic term referring to those courts that have jurisdiction over misdemeanors and conduct preliminary investigations of felony charges.

make-believe families Peer units formed by women in prison to compensate for the loss of family and loved ones that contain mother and father figures.

***mala in se* crimes** Acts that are outlawed because they violate basic moral values, such as rape, murder, assault, and robbery.

***mala prohibitum* crimes** Acts that are outlawed by statute because they clash with current norms and public opinion, such as tax, traffic, and drug laws.

mandamus *See* writ of mandamus

mandatory sentence A statutory requirement that a certain penalty shall be set and carried out in all cases on conviction for a specified offense or series of offenses.

Manhattan Bail Project The innovative experiment in bail reform that introduced and successfully tested the concept of release on recognizance.

marital exemption The practice in some states of prohibiting the prosecution of husbands for the rape of their wives.

masculinity hypothesis The view that women who commit crimes have biological and psychological traits similar to those of men.

mass murder The killing of a large number of people in a single incident by an offender who typically does not seek concealment or escape.

matricide The murder of one's mother.

maxi-maxi prisons High-security prisons, based on the federal prison in Marion, Illinois, that house the most dangerous inmates in around-the-clock solitary confinement.

maximum security prisons Correctional institutions that house dangerous felons and maintain strict security measures, high walls, and limited contact with the outside world.

meat eaters A term used to describe police officers who actively solicit bribes and vigorously engage in corrupt practices.

medical model A view of corrections holding that convicted offenders are victims of their environment who need care and treatment to transform them into valuable members of society.

medium-security prisons Less secure institutions that house nonviolent offenders and provide more opportunities for contact with the outside world.

mens rea "Guilty mind." The mental element of a crime or the intent to commit a criminal act.

methadone A synthetic narcotic used as a substitute for heroin in drug-control efforts.

middle-class measuring rods According to Cohen, the standards by which teachers and other representatives of state authority evaluate lower-class youths. Because they cannot live up to middle-class standards, lower-class youths are bound for failure, which gives rise to frustration and anger at conventional society.

minimum-security prisons The least secure institutions that house white-collar and nonviolent offenders, maintain few security measures, and have liberal furlough and visitation policies.

Miranda warning The result of two U.S. Supreme Court decisions (*Escobedo v. Illinois* and *Miranda v. Arizona*) that require police officers to inform individuals under arrest that they have a constitutional right to remain silent, that their statements can later be used against them in court, that they can have an attorney present to help them, and that the state will pay for an attorney if they cannot afford to hire one. Although aimed at protecting an individual during in-custody interrogation, the warning must also be given when the investigation shifts from the investigatory to the accusatory state—that is, when suspicion begins to focus on an individual.

misdemeanor A minor crime usually punished by less than one year's imprisonment in a local institution, such as a county jail.

Missouri Plan A way of picking judges through nonpartisan elections as a means of ensuring judicial performance standards.

monetary restitution A sanction that requires that convicted offenders compensate crime victims by reimbursing them for out-of-pocket losses caused by the crime. Losses can include property damage, lost wages, and medical costs.

moonlighting The practice of police officers holding after-hours jobs in private security or other related professions.

moral entrepreneurs People who use their influence to shape the legal process in ways they see fit.

motion An oral or written request asking the court to make a specified finding, decision, or order.

murder transaction The concept that murder is usually a result of behavior interactions between the victim and the offender.

National Crime Survey The ongoing victimization study conducted jointly by the Justice Department and the U.S. Census Bureau that surveys victims about their experiences with law violation.

neighborhood policing A style of police management that emphasizes community-level crime-fighting programs and initiatives.

neurotics People who fear that their primitive id impulses will dominate their personality.

niche A way of adapting to the prison community that stresses finding one's place in the system (a niche), rather than fighting for one's individual rights.

no bill A decision by a grand jury not to indict a criminal suspect.

nolle prosequi The term used when a prosecutor decides to drop a case after a complaint has been formally made. Reasons for a nolle prosequi include evidence insufficiency, reluctance of witnesses to testify, police error, and office policy.

nolo contendere No contest. An admission of guilt in a criminal case with the condition that the finding cannot be used against the defendant in any subsequent civil cases.

nonintervention A justice philosophy that emphasizes the least intrusive treatment possible.

Among its central policies are decarceration, diversion, and decriminalization. In other words, less is better.

obscenity According to current legal theory, sexually explicit material that lacks a serious purpose and appeals solely to the prurient interest of the viewer. While nudity per se is not usually considered obscene, open sex behavior, masturbation, and exhibition of the genitals is banned in many communities.

official crime Criminal behavior that has been recorded by the police.

opportunist robber Someone who steals small amounts when a vulnerable target presents itself.

parole The early release of a prisoner from imprisonment subject to conditions set by a parole board. Depending on the jurisdiction, inmates must serve a certain proportion of their sentences before becoming eligible for parole. The conditions of parole may require the individual to report regularly to a parole officer, to refrain from criminal conduct, to maintain and support his or her family, to avoid contact with other convicted criminals, to abstain from using alcohol and drugs, to remain within the jurisdiction, and so on. Violations of the conditions of parole may result in revocation of parole, in which case the individual will be returned to prison. The concept behind parole is to allow the release of the offender to community supervision, where rehabilitation and readjustment will be facilitated.

parricide The killing of a close relative by a child.

partial deterrent A legal measure designed to restrict or control, rather than eliminate, an undesirable act.

particularity The requirement that a search warrant state precisely where the search is to take place and what items are to be seized.

paternalism An approach to government or organizations in which leaders are seen as father figures and others are treated as "children."

patriarchy A male-dominated system. The patriarchal family is one dominated by the father.

patricide The murder of a father.

Pennsylvania system The prison system developed during the 19th century that stressed total isolation and individual penitence as a means of reform.

peremptory challenge The dismissal of a potential juror by either the prosecution or the defense for unexplained, discretionary reasons.

persisters Those criminals who do not age out of crime; chronic delinquents who continue offending into their adulthood.

plain view The doctrine that evidence in plain view to police officers may be seized without a search warrant.

plea An answer to formal charges by an accused. Possible pleas are guilty, not guilty, nolo contendere, and not guilty by reason of insanity. A guilty plea is a confession of the offense as charged. A not guilty plea is a denial of the charge and places the burden on the prosecution to prove the elements of the offense.

plea bargaining The discussion between the defense counsel and the prosecution by which the accused agrees to plead guilty for certain considerations. The advantage to the defendant may be a reduction of the charges, a lenient sentence, or (in the case of multiple charges) dropped charges. The advantage to the prosecution is that a conviction is obtained without the time and expense of lengthy trial proceedings.

pledge system An early method of law enforcement that relied on self-help and mutual aid.

police discretion The ability of police officers to enforce the law selectively. Police officers in the field have great latitude to use their discretion in deciding whether to invoke their arrest powers.

police officer style The belief that the bulk of police officers can be classified into ideal personality types. Popular style types include supercops, who desire to enforce only serious crimes, such as robbery and rape; professionals, who use a broad definition of police work; service-oriented, who see their job as that of a helping profession; and avoiders, who do as little as possible. The actual existence of ideal police officer types has been much debated.

poor laws Seventeenth-century laws that bound out vagrants and abandoned children to masters as indentured servants.

population All people who share a particular personal characteristic, such as all high school students or all police officers.

positivism The approach to social science that uses the scientific method of the natural sciences and that suggests that human behavior is a product of social, biological, psychological, or economic forces.

power groups Criminal organizations that do not provide services or illegal goods but trade exclusively in violence and extortion.

power rape A rape motivated by the need for sexual conquest.

power syndicates Organized crime groups that use force and violence to extort money from legitimate businesses and other criminal groups engaged in illegal business enterprises.

praxis The application of theory in action; in Marxist criminology, applying theory to promote revolution.

preliminary hearings The step at which criminal charges initiated by an information are tested for probable cause; the prosecution presents enough evidence to establish probable cause—that is, a prima facie case. The hearing is public and may be attended by the accused and his or her attorney.

preponderance of the evidence The level of proof in civil cases; more than half the evidence supports the allegations of one side.

presentence report An investigation performed by a probation officer attached to a trial court after the conviction of a defendant. The report contains information about the defendant's background, education, previous employment, and family; his or her own statement concerning the offense; his or her prior criminal record; interviews with neighbors or acquaintances; and his or her mental and physical condition (i.e., information that would not be made record in the case of a guilty plea or that would be inadmissible as evidence at a trial but could be influential and important at the sentencing stage). After conviction, a judge sets a date for sentencing (usually ten days to two weeks from the date of conviction), during which time the presentence report is made. The report is required in felony cases in federal courts and in many states, is optional with the judge in some states, and in others is mandatory before convicted offenders can be placed on probation. In the case of juvenile offenders, the presentence report is also known as a social history report.

presumptive sentences Sentencing structures that provide an average sentence that should be served along with the option of extending or decreasing punishments because of aggravating or mitigating circumstances.

preventive detention The practice of holding dangerous suspects before trial without bail.

prison A state or federal correctional institution for incarceration of felony offenders for terms of one year or more.

pro bono The practice by private attorneys of taking without fee the cases of indigent offenders as a service to the profession and the community.

probability sample A randomly drawn sample in which each member of the population tapped has an equal chance of being selected.

probable cause The evidentiary criterion necessary to sustain an arrest or the issuance of an arrest or search warrant; less than absolute certainty or "beyond a reasonable doubt" but greater than mere suspicion or "hunch." Probable cause consists of a set of facts, information, circumstances, or conditions that would lead a reasonable person to believe that an offense was committed and that the accused committed that offense. An arrest made without probable cause may be susceptible to prosecution as an illegal arrest under "false imprisonment" statutes.

probation A sentence entailing the conditional release of a convicted offender into the community under the supervision of the court (in the form of a probation officer), subject to certain conditions for a specified time. The conditions are usually similar to those of parole. (Note: probation is a sentence, an alternative to incarceration; parole is administrative release from incarceration.) Violation of the conditions of probation may result in revocation of probation.

problem-oriented policing A style of police operations that stresses proactive problem solving, rather than reactive crime fighting.

procedural law The rules that define the operation of criminal proceedings. Procedural law describes the methods that must be followed in obtaining warrants, investigating offenses, effecting lawful arrests, using force, conducting trials, introducing evidence, sentencing convicted offenders, and reviewing cases by appellate courts (in general, legislatures have ignored postsentencing procedures). While the substantive law defines criminal offenses, procedural law delineates how the substantive offenses are to be enforced.

progressives Early 20th-century reformers who believed that state action could relieve human ills.

proof beyond a reasonable doubt The standard of proof needed to convict in a criminal case. The evidence offered in court does not have to amount to absolute certainty, but it should leave no reasonable doubt that the defendant committed the alleged crime.

property in service The 18th-century practice of selling control of inmates to shipmasters who would then transport them to colonies for sale as indentured servants.

proximity hypothesis The view that people become crime victims because they live or work in areas with large criminal populations.

psychopath A person whose personality is characterized by a lack of warmth and feeling, inappropriate behavior responses, and an inability to learn from experience. While some psychologists view psychopathy as a result of childhood trauma, others see it as a result of biological abnormality.

psychotics People whose id has broken free and now dominates their personality. Psychotics suffer from delusions and experience hallucinations and sudden mood shifts.

Racketeer Influenced and Corrupt Organizations Act (RICO) Federal legislation that enables prosecutors to bring additional criminal or civil charges against people whose multiple criminal acts constitute a conspiracy. RICO features monetary penalties that allow the government to confiscate all profits derived from criminal activities. Originally intended to be used against organized criminals, RICO also has been used against white-collar crime.

random sample A sample selected on the basis of chance so that each person in the population has an equal opportunity to be selected.

rationale choice The view that crime is a function of a decision-making process in which the potential offender weighs the potential costs and benefits of an illegal act.

reasonable competence The standard by which legal representation is judged: Did the defendant receive a reasonable level of legal aid?

reasonable doubt The possibility that the defendant did not commit the crime. A jury cannot find the defendant guilty if a reasonable doubt exists that he or she committed the crime.

recoupment Forcing indigents to repay the state for at least part of their legal costs.

reintegration The correctional philosophy that stresses reintroducing the inmate back into the community.

relative deprivation The condition that exists when people of wealth and poverty live in close proximity to one another. Some criminologists attribute crime rate differentials to relative deprivation.

release on recognizance A nonmonetary condition for the pretrial release of an accused individual; an alternative to monetary bail that is granted after the court determines that the accused has ties in the community, has no prior record of default, and is likely to appear at subsequent proceedings.

restitution A condition of probation in which the offender repays society or the victim of crime for the trouble the offender caused. Monetary restitution involves a direct payment to the victim as a form of compensation. Community-service restitution may be used in victimless crimes and involves work in the community in lieu of more severe criminal penalties.

routine activities The view that crime is a "normal" function of the routine activities of modern living. Offenses can be expected if there is a suitable target that is not protected by capable guardians.

sadistic rape A rape motivated by the offender's desire to torment and abuse the victim.

sample A limited number of persons selected for study from a population.

schizophrenia A type of psychosis often marked by bizarre behavior, hallucinations, loss of thought control, and inappropriate emotional responses. There are different types of schizophrenia: catatonic, which characteristically involves impairment of motor activity; paranoid, which is characterized by delusions of persecution; and hebephrenic, which is characterized by immature behavior and giddiness.

search and seizure The legal term, contained in the Fourth Amendment to the U.S. Constitution, that refers to the searching for and carrying away of evidence by police during a criminal investigation.

secondary deviance According to Lemert, accepting a deviant label as a personal identity.

selective incapacitation The policy of creating enhanced prison sentences for the small group of dangerous chronic offenders.

self-report study A research approach that requires subjects to reveal their own participation in delinquent or criminal acts.

sentence The criminal sanction imposed by the court on a convicted defendant, usually in the form of a fine, incarceration, or probation. Sentencing may be carried out by a judge, jury, or sentencing council (panel or judges), depending on the statutes of the jurisdiction.

sequester The insulation of jurors from the outside world so that their decision making cannot be influenced or affected by extralegal events.

serial murder The killing of a large number of people over time by an offender who seeks to escape detection.

sheriff The chief law enforcement officer in a county.

Sherman Report The national review of law enforcement education programs that found that a liberal arts–related curriculum is the most appropriate one for training police officers.

shield laws Laws designed to protect rape victims by prohibiting the defense attorney from inquiring about their previous sexual relationships.

shire reeve In early England, the senior law enforcement figure in a county, the forerunner of today's sheriff.

shock incarceration A short prison sentence served in boot camp–type facilities.

shock probation A sentence in which offenders serve a short prison term to impress them with the pains of imprisonment before they begin probation.

short-run hedonism According to Cohen, the desire of lower-class gang youths to engage in behavior that will give them immediate gratification and excitement but in the long run will be dysfunctional and negativistic.

social control The ability of society and its institutions to control, manage, restrain, or direct human behavior.

social disorganization A neighborhood or area marked by culture conflict, lack of cohesiveness, transient population, insufficient social organizations, and anomie.

special (specific) deterrence A crime control policy suggesting that punishment should be severe enough to convince convicted offenders never to repeat their criminal activity.

specific intent The intent to accomplish a specific purpose as an element of crime, such as breaking into someone's house for the express purpose of stealing jewels.

stare decisis To stand by decided cases. The legal principle by which the decision or holding in an earlier case becomes the standard by which subsequent similar cases are judged.

statutory law Laws created by legislative bodies to meet changing social conditions, public opinion, and custom.

sting An undercover police operation in which police pose as criminals to trap law violators.

stoopers Petty criminals who earn their living by retrieving winning tickets that are accidentally discarded by race track patrons.

stop and frisk The situation in which police officers who are suspicious of an individual run their hands lightly over the suspect's outer garments to determine whether the person is carrying a concealed weapon. Also called a "patdown" or "threshold inquiry," a stop and frisk is intended to stop short of any activity that could be considered a violation of Fourth Amendment rights.

strain The emotional turmoil and conflict caused when people believe they cannot achieve their desires and goals through legitimate means.

stratum formations According to the Schwendingers, adolescent social networks whose members have distinct dress, grooming, and linguistic behaviors.

street crime Illegal acts designed to prey on the public through theft, damage, and violence.

strict-liability crimes Illegal acts whose elements do not contain the need for intent or *mens rea;* usually acts that endanger the public welfare, such as illegal dumping of toxic wastes.

structural Marxist theory The view that the law and the justice system are designed to maintain the capitalist system and that members of both the owner and worker classes whose behavior threatens the stability of the system will be sanctioned.

subculture A group that is loosely part of the dominant culture but maintains a unique set of values, beliefs, and traditions.

subpoena A court order requiring the recipient to appear in court on an indicated time and date.

substantive criminal laws A body of specific rules that declare what conduct is criminal and prescribe the punishment to be imposed for such conduct.

summons An alternative to arrest usually used for petty or traffic offenses; a written order notifying an individual that he or she has been charged with an offense. A summons directs the person to appear in court to answer the charge. It is used primarily in instances of low risk, where the person will not be required to appear at a later date. The summons is advantageous to police officers in that they are freed from having to spend time on arrest and booking procedures; it is advantageous to the accused in that he or she is spared time in jail.

sureties During the Middle Ages, people who made themselves responsible for the behavior of offenders released in their care.

surplus value The Marxist view that the laboring classes produce wealth that far exceeds their wages and goes to the capitalist class as profits.

surrebuttal Introducing witnesses during a criminal trial in order to disprove damaging testimony by other witnesses.

suspended sentence A prison term that is delayed while the defendant undergoes a period of community treatment. If the treatment is successful, the prison sentence is terminated.

team policing An experimental police technique in which groups of officers are assigned to a particular area of the city on a 24-hour basis.

technical parole violation Revocation of parole because conditions set by correctional authorities have been violated.

technique of neutralization According to neutralization theory, the ability of delinquent youth to neutralize moral constraints so they may drift into criminal acts.

thanatos According to Freud, the instinctual drive toward aggression and violence.

threshold inquiry A term used to describe a stop and frisk.

tort The law of personal wrongs and damage. Tort-type actions include negligence, libel, slander, assault, and trespass.

totality of the circumstances A legal doctrine mandating that a decision maker consider all the issues and circumstances of a case before judging the outcome. For example, before concluding whether a suspect understood a *Miranda* warning, a judge must consider the totality of the circumstances under which the warning was given. The suspect's age, intelligence, and competency may influence his or her understanding and judgment.

transferred intent If an illegal yet unintended act results from the intent to commit a crime, that act is also considered illegal.

transitional neighborhood An area undergoing a shift in population and structure, usually from middle-class residential to lower-class mixed use.

Type I offenses Another term for index crimes.

Type II offenses All crimes other than index and minor traffic offenses. The FBI records annual arrest information for Type II offenses.

venire The group called for jury duty from which jury panels are selected.

vice squad Police officers assigned to enforce morally tinged laws, such as those on prostitution, gambling, and pornography.

victim-precipitated Describes a crime in which the victim's behavior was the spark that ignited the subsequent offense, as when the victim abused the offender verbally or physically.

victimization survey A crime measurement technique that surveys citizens to measure their experiences as victims of crime.

victimology The study of the victim's role in criminal transactions.

voir dire The process in which a potential jury panel is questioned by the prosecution and the defense in order to select jurors who are unbiased and objective.

waiver The act of voluntarily relinquishing a right or advantage; often used in the context of waiving one's right to counsel (e.g., *Miranda* warning) or waiving certain steps in the criminal justice process (e.g., the preliminary hearing). Essential to waiver is the voluntary consent of the individual.

warrant A written court order issued by a magistrate authorizing and directing that an individual be taken into custody to answer criminal charges.

watch system During the Middle Ages in England, men were organized in church parishes to guard at night against disturbances and breaches of the peace under the direction of the local constable.

watchman A style of policing that stresses reacting to calls for service, rather than aggressively pursuing crime.

wergild Under medieval law, the money paid by the offender to compensate the victim and the state for a criminal offense.

white-collar crime Illegal acts that capitalize on a person's place in the marketplace. White-collar crimes can involve theft, embezzlement, fraud, market manipulation, restraint of trade, and false advertising.

Wickersham Commission Created in 1931 by President Herbert Hoover to investigate the state of the nation's police forces. The commission found that police training was inadequate and that the average officer was incapable of effectively carrying out his duties.

widening the net The charge that programs designed to divert offenders from the justice system actually enmesh them further in the process by substituting more intrusive treatment programs for less intrusive punishment-oriented outcomes.

wite The portion of the wergild that went to the victim's family.

work furlough A prison treatment program that allows inmates to be released during the day to work in the community and returned to prison at night.

writ of certiorari An order of a superior court requesting that the record of an inferior court (or administrative body) be brought forward for review or inspection.

writ of habeas corpus A judicial order requesting that a person detaining another produce the body of the prisoner and give reasons for his or her capture and detention. Habeas corpus is a legal device used to request that a judicial body review the reasons for a person's confinement and the conditions of confinement. Habeas corpus is known as "the great writ."

writ of mandamus An order of a superior court commanding that a lower court, administrative body, or executive body perform a specific function. It is commonly used to restore rights and privileges lost to a defendant through illegal means.

Table of Cases

Name Index

Chaiken, Marcia, 283
Chamlin, Mitchell, 192, 360, 366
Champion, Dean, 365
Chappell, Duncan, 78
Charles, Michael, 225, 226
Chermak, Steven, 225
Chesney-Lind, Meda, 79, 436, 464
Chida, Craig V., 251
Chin, Ko-Lin, 138
Chitwood, Dale, 138
Chlumsky, Michael, 464
Clark, Cheri, 421
Clarke, Ronald, 79
Clear, Todd, 400, 428
Clede, Bill, 163
Clemmer, Donald, 434, 464
Cobb, Belton, 193
Cochran, John, 360, 366
Cocks, Jay, 401
Cohen, Fred, 108, 308
Cohen, Jacqueline, 78, 79
Cohen, Lawrence, 73, 78, 79
Cohen, Robyn, 38, 400, 461, 465
Cohn, Bob, 139
Cohn, Ellen, 192
Cohn, Steven, 366
Cole, George, 400
Cole, Phyllis, 401
Collins, Dean, 192
Conley, Darlene, 204, 225, 365
Connor, Gregory, 218, 226
Cook, Kimberly, 366
Cook, Philip, 79
Corbett, Ronald, 401
Cornish, Derek, 79
Corrado, Michael, 308
Cottey, Talbert, 139
Court, John, 139
Courtwright, David, 5, 38
Coutorie, Larry, 163
Cox, Louis, 118, 138, 465
Craig, Delores, 225
Crank, John, 193, 224
Cressey, Donald, 79, 464
Crist, Roger, 464
Crocker, Lawrence, 251
Cronin, Joseph, 251
Crotty, Norma, 465
Crouch, Ben, 465
Crutchfield, Robert, 366
Culbertson, Robert, 224
Cullen, Francis, 138, 162, 225, 283, 226,
    365, 401, 465
Cullen, John, 365
Cullen, Kevin, 227
Cuniff, Mark, 380, 400
Cunningham, William, 160, 163
Currie, Elliott, 116–117
Curry, G. David, 401
Cushman, Robert, 400
Cuvelier, Steven, 428

D
D'Alessandro, Mike, 193
D'Alessio, Stewart, 365

Daley, Robert, 221, 227
Daly, Kathleen, 79, 139, 365
Dann, Robert H., 367
Dannefer, Dale, 366
D'Asaro, B., 79
Dash, Leon, 428
Daum, James, 225
David, Robert, 365
Davidson, Laura, 225
Davis, James, 401
Davis, John, 163
Davis, Kenneth C., 283
Davis, Robert, 352
Davis, Samuel M., 108
Davoli, Edward, 428
Dawson, John, 366
Dawson, Robert, 108
Dean, Charles, 188, 192, 193, 226
DeCostanza, Elaine, 464
Del Carmen, Rolando, 214, 215, 400, 428
DeLone, Miriam, 204, 225, 353, 365
Dershowitz, Alan, 333
DeStefano, Anthony, 177
Devlin, Daniel, 162
Dieckman, Duane, 192
Diggs, David, 401
DiIulio, John, 396, 397, 428, 452, 465
Dix, George, 108
Dixon, Jo, 366
Doerner, William, 366
Doherty, William, 227
Doig, Jameson, 428
Donnerstein, Edward, 139
Doraz, Walter, 38
Dressler, J., 108
Duffee, David, 400, 428, 465
Duncan, Donna, 465
Dunford, Franklyn, 192, 309
Dunham, Roger, 193
Durham, Alexis, 356, 365, 366, 405, 428
Dwyer, Diane, 465

E
Early, Stephen, Jr., 108
Eaves, Lindon, 79
Eck, John, 193
Ehrlich, Isaac, 367
Eichenthal, David, 464
Eigenberg, Helen, 79, 225, 464
Eisenstein, James, 38
Ellingworth, Dan, 78
Elliott, Delbert, 192
Elliott, Frank, 333
Elrod, H. Preston, 366
Empey, LaMar, 78
Ennis, Philip, 78
Erez, Edna, 352, 464
Ericson, Maynard, 78
Ervin, Laurie, 400
Erwin, Billie, 401
Escovitz, Sari, 283
Eskridge, Chris, 308, 365, 401

F
Fagan, Jeffrey, 79, 138, 296, 365
Falcone, David, 150
Farmer, Richard, 226

Farnworth, E. Allen, 108
Farrell, Graham, 78
Farrington, David, 78
Farrow, Franklin, 428, 465
Faupel, Charles, 138
Feeley, Malcolm, 38, 254, 282, 309, 401
Feld, Barry, 428
Felsenthal, Edward, 251
Felson, Marcus, 73, 79
Ferguson, H. Bruce, 79
Ferraro, Kathleen, 192
Fiftal, Leanne, 428
Figlio, Robert, 70, 71
Finn, Peter, 138, 192, 400, 448
First, Brian, 308
Fisher, James, 401
Fisher, Stanley, 266, 283
Fishman, Laura, 465
Flanagan, Timothy, 283, 448
Fletcher, George, 305, 308
Flewelling, Robert, 138, 193
Fogel, David, 427
Fogelson, Robert, 163
Fogg, V., 401
Foote, Caleb, 308
Forer, Lois, 349
Forney, Mary Ann, 138
Foucault, Michel, 365, 407, 428
Fox, James A., 64, 79
Frank, James, 162, 192
Frank, Nancy, 308, 365
Frankfurter, Felix, 103
Frase, Richard, 365
Freedman, Alix, 138
Freedman, Monroe, 272, 283
Freels, Sally, 192
Freid, David, 400
Friday, Carolyn, 400
Friday, Paul, 401
Fridell, Lorie, 212, 226
Friedrichs, David, 138, 355, 366
Fyfe, James, 216, 219, 226, 251

G
Gaes, Gerald, 365
Galaway, Burt, 401
Gardner, Martin, 108
Gardner, Thomas, 108
Garner, Joel, 226
Garofalo, James, 193, 226
Garrett, Carol, 138
Garrison, Carole, 225
Garrow, David J., 109
Gartin, Patrick, 138, 192, 193
Gartner, Rosemary, 79
Gaskins, Carla, 283
Geerken, Michael, 78
Geis, Gilbert, 78
Gelb, Barbara, 227
Gellhorn, E., 108
Gendreau, Paul, 138, 365, 465
Georges-Abeyie, Daniel, 78
Gerard, Charles, 193
Gerber, Jurg, 389, 401
Gerlin, Andrea, 296, 308
Gershman, Bennett, 283
Gertz, Marc, 225

Y

Z

Subject Index

Hindelang Research Center (State University of New York at Albany), 35
Hispanics, in jail, 413
homicide, 45
See also murder
homicide rate, 46, 47, 48, 62
homosexuality, 134
in prison, 436
hormones, aggression and, 65
Horton, Willie, 411
hot spots of crime, 184
house arrest, 391
electronic monitoring for, 392–394
hue and cry, 142
hulks, 405
Human Rights Watch, 414
hundred, 142
hung jury, 328
hustling, in prison, 433

I

identification of suspects, 155, 156–157
ignorance of law, as criminal defense, 95
illegitimacy rates, crime and, 62
Immigration and Naturalization Service, 153
imprisonment. *See* prisons
impulsivity, criminality and, 71
in forma pauperis, 330
in-presence requirement, 21
incapacitation, 339
incarceration, 335
history of, 337–338
shock, 420–421
incarceration rate, 10, 423, 425
income
police discretion and, 203–204
victimization and, 59
indeterminate sentences, 342–343
index crimes, 44, 45, 53
indictment, 286, 297
indifference, deliberate, 215
indigent defendants, 273
bail and, 289, 296
cost of defending, 279–280
legal services for, 275, 277–280
information, 22, 286, 297
Ingles, Larry, 393
initial hearing, 286
inmates, 415, 418–419
drug abuse by, 419
educational/vocational programs for, 442–445
family visits to, 462
female, 436–440, 444, 446
jail, 411–413
male, 431–436
parole violators as, 461
prison life of, 432–436
processing of, 15–16
rights of, 452–456
self-help groups for, 446–447
social code of, 434–435
social programs for, 445–446
special-needs, 441–442
subculture of, 434–435
violence among, 451–452
innovative neighborhood-oriented policing (INOP), 182, 183

insanity defense, 90–92
Insanity Defense Reform Act, 92
insider trading, 98, 267
Institute for Law and Justice, 117
Institute for Social Research (ISR), 35, 55, 56
insurance fraud, 32
intake, 376
intelligence, crime and, 71
intensive probation supervision (IPS), 389–391
intensive supervision parole (ISP), 460
intent, 84, 89
interdiction strategies, 124
intermediate sanctions, 15, 369, 383–385
advantages of, 383, 385
future of, 397–398
pros and cons of, 396–397
target populations for, 385
internal affairs, 186, 222
Internal Revenue Service (IRS), 153
International Association of Chiefs of Police (IACP), 145, 191
International Association of Crime Analysts, 76
international crime trends, 48–49
interrogation
custodial, 242–244
field, 235
interviews, as source of crime data, 44
intimate violence, 5
intoxication, as criminal defense, 92
investigation
effectiveness of, 178–179
police, 20, 174–178
investigative techniques, legality of, 230, 232
involvement, 72
IPS (intensive probation supervision), 389–391
ISR (Institute for Social Research), 35, 55, 56
ISP (intensive supervision parole, 460
irresistible impulse test, 90–91

J

Jackson, Samuel L., 96
jail population, 295, 412, 413
jail time
as part of split sentencing, 389
jailhouse lawyers, 453
jails, 15
conditions in, 412, 414–415
early, 405
functions of, 411, 412
pretrial detention in, 295
Japan, crime in, 48
Jewell, Richard, 4
Joint Council on Law Enforcement and Private Security Associations, 160
judge-made law, 84
judges, 27, 35
discretion of, 23, 264
functions of, 263–264
plea bargaining and, 304
qualifications of, 264
selection of, 264–265
sentencing by, 328–329, 340–350
judicial reprieve, 370

judicial review, 86
judiciary, 263–264
jury, 254
death-qualified, 361–362
instructions to, 328
size of, 314
jury selection, 322, 324–325
jury trial, 22, 263, 310
right to, 312–314
steps in, 322–330
just desert, 120, 339
justice, 111–122
conflict perspective on, 120–121
crime control perspective on, 112–113
due process perspective on, 115–118
justice perspective on, 119–120
nonintervention perspective on, 118–119
rehabilitation perspective on, 113–115, 116
restorative, 121
See also criminal justice
Justice Department, 36, 43, 152–153
justice of the peace, 142, 258
justice perspective, 119–120, 122
Justice Technology Information Network (JUST-NET), 191
justification, as criminal defense, 93–97
Justinian, 82
juvenile court system, 92–93
juvenile crimes. *See* delinquency
juvenile justice system, 16–19
caseloads in, 255
compared to adult system, 18, 19
In re Gault and, 104
probation in, 372
size of, 19
juveniles
in adult jails, 412–413
in adult courts, 98
death penalty and, 361

K

Kansas City
gun experiment in, 172
study of police patrol techniques, 170
Kansas Department of Corrections, 448
Kelly, John, 291
Kevorkian, Jack, 97
Key Legislative Issues in Criminal Intermediate Sanctions, 398
Khashoggi, Adnan, 391
killed in line of duty, 217
King, Rodney, 140, 211, 214
Knapp Commission, 219–220, 221
Ku Klux Klan, 5

L

La Pen, Inc., 445
labeling theory, 118
landmark decisions, 260
larceny, 45
law
case, 85–86
civil, 81, 84–85
common, 82–84, 85, 336, 370

probation of, 370–383
repeat, 114
See also defendants; inmates
Office for Victims of Crime, 136
Office of Public and Congressional Affairs
    (FBI), 161
official crime statistics, 43, 44–45, 53–54
Oklahoma City bombing, 188
Olmedo, Manuel, 456
omission, crimes of, 88, 89
Omnibus Crime Control Act, 240
Omnibus Drug Law of 1988, 99
On Crime and Punishments (Beccaria), 7
open fields, search of, 239, 245
opening statements, 325–326
Operation ID, 181
Operation Pressure Point, 185
opportunity, criminal, 74
Orbach, Jerry, 287
order maintenance, 170
organized crime, 125
Organized Crime and Racketeering Unit,
    153
Osborne, Thomas Mott, 408, 409
overcrowding
    in correctional facilities, 295
    of jails, 254, 414–415
    of prisons, 14, 125, 385, 425–426,
        430–431

P

Panama, 123
parens patriae, 16
Parker, Bonnie, 6
Parkman, George, 327
parole, 16, 23, 343, 456–462
    abolishing, 120
    effectiveness of, 460–461
    rules of, 459
    violations of, 457, 460–461
parole board, 457, 458–459
parole hearings, 458–459
parole officers, 34, 459–460
parole supervision, 459–460
Part I crimes, 44, 45, 54
Part II crimes, 44
participant observation, 43–44
particularity, in search warrant, 232
patdown, 239
patrol function, of police, 169–174,
    181–182
PCR, 158
peacekeeping function, of police, 170
peacemaking, 73, 75, 121
Peel, Sir Robert, 142
peer pressure, 69
    police discretion and, 202
Pelican Bay State Prison, 416
penal institutions, 404
penitentiaries, 337
Penitentiary Act, 405
penitentiary house, 406
Penn, Sean, 359
Penn, William, 405
Pennsylvania, prison system in, 405–406,
    407–408
Pennsylvania system, 407–408
people's courts, 13

Percy Amendment, 445
peremptory challenge, 319, 324–325
Perry Mason, 313
personality
    crime and, 67
    impulsive, 71, 72
    of police officers, 197–198
personality profile, 376
personnel services, 186
Peru, 123, 124
Peterson, Brian, 2–4
Philadelphia, 405, 406
    police reforms in, 222
Pitt, Brad, 68
plain view, 238–239, 245
plea, 22, 299
    in felony cases, 286–287
    in misdemeanor cases, 286
plea bargaining, 22, 27, 284–285, 300–306
    bans on, 305
    decision-making process in, 301–302
    legal issues in, 300–301, 302
    pros and cons of, 300
    reform efforts in, 305–306
pledge system, 142
police
    arrest rates of, 167, 169
    confidence in, 141–142, 194
    decentralization of, 154–155, 182
    discretion of, 11, 21, 201–205, 220–221
    functions of, 11, 149
    history of, 142–146
    investigative function of, 174–179
    lawsuits against, 214–215
    metropolitan, 149–150
    patrol function of, 169–174
    private, 159–161
    productivity of, 188–190
    relationship with public, 180
    role of, 11, 12, 141, 167, 169, 179–180
    rural, 150
    state, 151–152
    violence and, 211–219
Police Administration (Wilson), 145
police administration boards, 144
police brutality, 211, 212–213
police chief, 165
police-community relations (PCR),
    180–181
police corruption, 144, 219–223
police departments, 31
    history of, 143
    policies of, 201–202
    budget supplementation by, 190
    community policing and, 182–183
    cooperative agreements between, 189
    cost of, 149
    organization of, 164–167
    promotion within, 166–167, 205
    size of, 149
    support functions in, 186–187
    use of civilian employees by, 190
    use of technology by, 155–159
Police Foundation, 36, 169, 170, 215
Police Information Network, 155
police officers
    careers as, 31
    chronic offenders among, 212

education of, 205
female, 207–210
minority, 206–207, 209–210, 216–217
minority female, 209–210
personality traits of, 197–198
profile of, 205–210
salaries of, 31
shooting of, 217
stress and, 210–211
police patrol, 169–174, 181–182
    activities of, 170
    effectiveness of, 170
    innovative programs in, 181–182
    proactive, 171–174
    purpose of, 169
police power, abuse of, 219, 221–222
police productivity, 188–190
police profession, 195, 197–201
police review boards, 222–223
police service districts, 190
police services
    consolidation of, 188–189
    privatization of, 160–161
police shootings, 213, 216–219
police subculture, 197, 209
policing
    changing concepts of, 179–180
    community, 180–184, 185–186
    new models of, 185–186
    problem-oriented, 184–185
    problems of, 210–223
    styles of, 198–201
*Politics and Plea Bargaining: Victims' Rights
    in California* (McCoy), 306
polymerase chain reaction (PCR), 158
poor, as crime victims, 59
poor laws, 337
Portland House, 395
postrelease adjustment, 23
poverty, crime and, 51, 67, 69
Powell, Benny, 116
precedent, 84, 260
predatory criminals, 5
preliminary hearing, 21, 22, 286, 297–298,
    299
preponderance of evidence, 85, 330, 331
presentence investigation, 375–376,
    377–378
presentence investigation report, 340
presentment, 297
President's Commission on Law
    Enforcement and the Administration
    of Justice, 8, 212, 306
press, freedom of, 318, 320
presumptive sentences, 344
pretextual stops, 242
pretrial detention, 295–296
pretrial diversion, 118, 306
pretrial identification process, 244, 246
pretrial motions, 263
pretrial procedures, 284–306
pretrial publicity, 318
pretrial release, 395
    debate over, 296
    types of, 288–289

RICO, 98–99, 386–387
Rifkin, Joel, 350
rights
    of defendants, 12, 103, 118, 312–322
    constitutional, 228–229
    individual, 103
    of juveniles, 17
    of prisoners, 409, 452–456
    of probationers, 381–382
    of suspects, 146, 242–244
rioting, 141, 146
riots, prison, 451
risk classification, of probationers, 378
robber barons, 5–6
robbery, 45
    sentences for, 344
    unsolved cases of, 179
robbery rate, 48
Robbins, Tim, 410
roll call training, 187
Roman law, 82
Rothenberg, Charles, 357
rotten pockets, 221
routine activities theory, 73–74, 75
rules, administrative, 86
ruling classes, 72
rural police agencies, 150
Rush, Benjamin, 405

S

Salerno, Anthony, 294
Salvi, John, 92
Sarandon, Susan, 276, 359
Sayles, John, 147
scandals, police, 219
schizophrenia, 66, 441
Schlup, Lloyd, 357
school, as crime site, 60
school failure, delinquency and, 70
Schultz, David, 92
search and seizure, 232–233, 245
    illegal, 246
search incident to a lawful arrest, 233, 245
search warrant, 232
    rules for, 230, 232–233, 239–240, 245
searches
    consent, 236–237
    warrantless, 233–240
season, crime rate and, 49
Second Amendment, 131
Secret Service, 154
secure corrections, 402
security, private, 159–161
selective enforcement, 170, 201, 220–221
selective incorporation, 102
self-control, criminality and, 72, 75
self-defense, 93–94
self-esteem, drug abuse and, 126
self-help groups, 446–447
self-incrimination, 101, 244, 245
self-mutilation, 439
self-protection, 131
self-report surveys, 42–43, 44, 54–57
    compatibility with other data sources,
        61–62
self-representation, right to, 316–317
Senate Judiciary Committee on Violence,
    48

sentences
    concurrent, 341
    consecutive, 341
    determinate, 120, 343–347, 458
    indeterminate, 342–343
    length of, 350–351
    mandatory, 113, 125, 347–350, 424
    maximum and minimum, 343
    probationary, 370–383
    split, 389
    suspended, 372
sentencing, 22–23, 328–329, 340–350
    disparity in, 120–121, 343, 345–346,
        348, 351–354
    extralegal factors in, 351–354
    factors in, 264, 340, 341
    federal guidelines for, 344–347
    future of, 354
    structured, 344, 347
    trends in, 350–354
sentencing guidelines, 344
Sentencing Matters (Tonry), 347
sequestration, 328
Seven, 68
sexual assault, 58, 83
sexual behavior, 134–135
sexual harassment, 209
Shawshank Redemption, The, 410
sheriff, 150
    colonial, 143
sheriff's department, 150–151
    jobs in, 32
shire reeve, 142, 150
shires, 142
shock incarceration, 389, 420–421
shock probation, 389
shootings, police, 213, 216–219
Simpson, O. J., 84–85, 140, 318, 324, 326
Singapore, 49
Singleton, Lawrence, 357
situational factors, in police discretion,
    202–203
Sixth Amendment, 14, 101, 273, 312,
    314–316, 317, 320
Sleepers, 371
slum areas, 67, 69
    crime and, 51
Smart, Pam, 257
Smith, Kermit, 359
Smith, Susan, 352
social agent, police officer as, 199
social class
    crime and, 51–52, 72–73
    sentencing and, 351
social code, of prison inmates, 434–435
social control, 133–136
    criminal justice as agency of, 8–9, 42
social control theory, 72, 75
social disorganization, 75
social engineering, 117
social learning theory, 66–67, 75
social problems, crime and, 62
social process theories, 69–72, 75
social structure theory, 67, 69, 75
socialization
    crime and, 70
    male, 73
sociopaths, 67

sodomy, 134
software piracy, 105
solitary confinement, 407, 409, 451, 455
source control, 123–124
Sourcebook of Criminal Justice Statistics, 35
Souter, David, 105
special-needs inmates, 441–442
special-needs populations, 169
specific deterrence, 339
speedy trial, right to, 317–318
Spencer, Timothy, 159
split sentences, 389
St. Petersburg, Florida, 159
staff counsel, 35
Stallone, Sylvester, 130
Standards Relating to a Speedy Trial
    (ABA), 317
stare decisis, 84
State of the Prisons (Howard), 337, 405
state courts, 254–258
state police, 32, 151–152
states, U.S. Constitution and, 102
status offenders, 16, 18
statutes, 85
    strict liability, 90
statutory rape, 93
stigmatization, 118
sting operations, 175–178
stop and frisk, 235, 245
Stop Prison Rate, 463
strain, 69, 75
stress, in law enforcement, 210–211
strict liability, 89–90
structured sentencing, 344
stun belts, 448
subculture
    lower-class, 69
    police, 197, 209
    of prison inmates, 434–435
substance abuse. *See* drug abuse
substantial capacity test, 91
substantive criminal law, 80
    reform of, 97–100
substantive due process, 86
substantive rights, of inmates, 453
sugar, violence and, 65
suicide
    among police officers, 211
    in jail, 414
    physician-assisted, 97
Sumners-Ashurst Act, 409
superior courts, 13, 258
Supreme Court, 260–262
    on automobile searches, 235–236, 237
    on children as witnesses, 312
    on competence of counsel, 281
    on confiscatory practices, 387
    on death penalty, 354, 360–361
    on double jeopardy, 95
    on due process, 118
    on electronic surveillance, 239–240
    on entrapment, 94, 176–178
    on exclusionary rule, 246–247
    on fair trial–free press issue, 320
    on Fourteenth Amendment, 102

Wells, Alice Stebbins, 207
Western frontier, 5
Western Penitentiary, 407
white-collar crime, 120, 267
white-collar criminals, 418
Wickersham Commission, 7
widening the net, 119, 306, 389, 394
Willis, Bruce, 168
Wines, Enoch, 408
wiretapping, 239–240

Wisconsin, 448
witness testimony, 326–327
witnesses, right to confront, 312
women's movement, 51
women
    as correctional officers, 450
    crime and, 73
    as crime victims, 58
    as criminals, 49, 50–51
    in jail, 413

    in police department, 207–210
    in prison, 419, 436–440, 444, 446
    sentencing of, 351
work release, 411, 444
workhouse, 337, 404
writ of certiorari, 260, 261
writ of habeas corpus, 329

Z
zero tolerance, 387

Photo Credits

Chapter 1

3: © David R. Frasier Photolibrary; **4:** The Record/Sipa Press; **6:** Brown Brothers; **11:** © Michael Newman/Photo Edit; **20:** © Gene Blevins/Daily News/Sygma; **30:** Touchstone/Shooting Star International.

Chapter 2

41: Scottish Daily Record/Sipa Press; **48:** Greg Davis, *Time* Magazine. © Time, Inc.; **57:** © Alon Reininger/Contact Press Images; **63:** © Andrew Lichentstein/Impact Visuals; **68:** Peter Sorel/New Line © 1995 New Line Cinema/The Kobal Collection; **69:** © Jonathan Elderfield/Gamma Liaison Network.

Chapter 3

81: © Frank Fournier/Contact Press Images; **83:** *A Wager of Battle.* From Le Coutume de Normandie. 1450–1470; **88:** Jussi Nurkari-Lehtikuva/Saba Press Photos; **96:** Warner Bros/Shooting Star; **97:** Richard Sheinwald/AP/Wide World Photos; **99:** Terry Ashe, *Time* Magazine, © Time, Inc.

Chapter 4

111: © Viviane Moos/Contact Press Images; **115:** © A. Ramey/Photo Edit; **119:** © Brian Palmer/Impact Visuals; **123:** © Andrew Holbrooke; **127:** © Gerry Gropp; **130:** Tri Star/Shooting Star.

Chapter 5

141: Kathy Willens/AP/Wide World Photos; **145:** Brown Brothers; **146:** Popperfoto/Archive Photos; **147:** Castle Rock Ent./Shooting Star; **154:** © Alex Quesada/Matrix; **158:** © Stephen Ferry/Gamma Liaison Network.

Chapter 6

165: Ralf-Finn Hestoft/Saba Press Photos, Inc.; **168:** 20th Century Fox/Shooting Star; **171:** (C) Douglas Burrows/Gamma-Liaison Network; **178:** *Miami Herald* © Bob Eighmie; **180:** © Bob Daemmrich/Stock, Boston; **187:** © Mark Richards; **188:** Paul Moseley/*Fort Worth Star Telegram*/Sipa Press.

Chapter 7

195: © David Walberg; **196:** Shooting Star; **199:** © Brian Palmer/Impact Visuals; **202:** © Tom Burton/Silver Image; **208:** © Ann States/Saba Press Photos; **213:** Reuters/Lee Celano/Archive Photos.

Chapter 8

229: © Jeff Share/Black Star; **230:** © *The Palm Beach Post,* photo by Lannis Waters; **231:** Warner Bros/The Kobal Collection; **236:** © Joe Rodriguez/Black Star; **241:** UPI/Corbis-Bettmann; **249:** © Roger E. Sandler/*Life* Magazine.

Chapter 9

253: © Owen T. B./Black Star; **257:** Reuters/Jim Bourg/Archive Photos; **265:** Photo by Therri Thuente, © 1997 *Los Angeles Daily News;* **276:** Warner Bros/Shooting Star; **277:** © Kenneth Jareche/Contact Press Images.

Chapter 10

285: Nick Ut/AP/Wide World Photos; **286:** © David R. Frazier Photolibrary; **287:** NBC photo by Jessica Borstein/The Kobal Collection; **291:** Ron Frehm-AP/ Wide World Photos; **298:** Tom Landers, Pool/AP/Wide World Photos; **303:** © Pat Carter/Gamma/Liaison Network.

Chapter 11

311: © John Neubauer/Photo Edit; **313:** Dan Golden/Shooting Star; **317:** © *Newsday,* photo by Dick Yarwood; **321:** © Todd Bigelow; **326:** Sygma; **329:** Henry A. Barrios/The Bakersfield Californian.

Chapter 12

335: Bob Daemmrich/Agence France Presse/Corbis-Bettmann; **342:** Phil Sheffield/*Tampa Tribune*/Silver Image; **350:** Mike Albans/AP/Wide World Photos; **352:** © J. Hedder-*The Herald*/Sgyma. **357:** William Campbell, *Time* Magazine, © Time, Inc.; **359:** Grammercy Pictures/Shooting Star.

Chapter 13

369: © A. Tannenbaum/Sygma; **371:** Warner Bros/Shooting Star; **377:** Bob Child/AP/Wide World Photos; **388:** © Mark Richards/Photo Edit; **393:** © Jack Kurtz/Impact Visuals; **394:** © Andrew Lichtenstein/Impact Visuals.

Chapter 14

403: van Gogh, Vincent: *Prisoner's Round* (detail), 1890, Pushkin Museum of Fine Arts, Moscow, Scala/Art Resource, NY; **410:** Castle Rock Ent./Shooting Star; **414:** © A. Ramey/Woodfin Camp & Associates; **420, 425:** © Eduardo Citrinblum.

Chapter 15

431: P. F. Bentley, *Time* Magazine, © Time, Inc. **432:** © Todd Buchanan; **438:** © A. Lichtenstein/Sygma; **439:** Yokam Kahana/Shooting Star; **442:** © Alon Reininger/Contact Press Images; **447:** Chris Martinez/AP/Wide World Photos; **456:** Michael Caulfield/AP/Wide World Photos.